services

marketing

a managerial approach

Rebekah Bennett

Liliana Bove

Susan Dann

Judy Drennan

Lorelle Frazer

Mark Gabbott

Railton Hill

Meredith Lawley

Sheelagh Matear

Chad Perry

Beverley Sparks

Jane Summers

Jillian Sweeney

Tony Ward

Lesley White

edited by Janet R. McColl-Kennedy

John Wiley & Sons Australia, Ltd

First published 2003 by
John Wiley & Sons Australia, Ltd
33 Park Road, Milton, Qld 4064

Offices also in Sydney and Melbourne

Typeset in 10/12.5 pt Caslon-Regular

© R. Bennett, L. Bove, S. Dann, J. Drennan, L. Frazer,
M. Gabbott, R. Hill, M. Lawley, S. Matear, C. Perry,
B. Sparks, J. Summers, J. Sweeney, T. Ward, L. White 2003

National Library of Australia
Cataloguing-in-Publication data

Services marketing: a managerial approach.

Bibliography.
Includes index.
For tertiary students.
ISBN 0 470 80068 2.

1. Service industries — Management — Textbooks. 2. Service
industries — Marketing — Textbooks. I. McColl-Kennedy, J. R.
II. Bennett, Rebekah.

658.8

Cover image: Leaves © 2002 Digital Vision/Nic Miller.
Internal design images: Leaves © 2002 Digital Vision/Nic Miller.

Printed in Singapore by
Seng Lee Press Pte Ltd

10 9 8 7 6 5 4 3 2 1

Contents

PART 2 Customer perceptions

PART 3 Marketing research

PART 4 Marketing strategies

Chapter 9
Relationship marketing and CRM

By Chad Perry, Sally Rao and Sarah Spencer-Matthews

Chapter 10
Communication in services marketing

By Rebekah Bennett

Chapter 11
Service product pricing

By Tony Ward

Case studies

Foreword

The services sector is expanding in every advanced economy in the world, thus making the understanding of services marketing increasingly important. This importance is further increased by the expanding role of service in the goods sector. More and more, businesses view the good as a commodity, and seek to differentiate based on the service part of the offering. Whether in the services sector or the goods sector, service has never been so important to business, and service has never been so central to marketing. The ideas and principles of services marketing are rapidly becoming the mainstream of marketing in the developed economies of the world.

Services Marketing: A Managerial Approach provides thorough coverage of the main issues in services today, including such current developments as e-services and CRM. Editor Janet McColl-Kennedy has done an impressive job of assembling the individually contributed chapters into a coherent and unified whole.

It is fitting that such a book be produced in Australia. Australia is one of the world's leading centres of services marketing teaching and research. Per capita, there are probably more services marketing academics in Australia than anywhere in the world, and that group is increasingly active in global research journals, helping push forward the leading edge of services marketing knowledge. Because all the authors are based in Australasia, the text speaks uniquely to the issues facing Australasian services marketing; for example, there is emphasis on the travel and tourism industries. Yet the text is not insular or provincial in its treatment of the major topics in services marketing. The coverage of the services marketing literature is current and global.

Very useful to the academic and student is the inclusion of 18 case studies, most of which are from Australia, New Zealand or South-East Asia. These case studies feature services marketing content, and have a geographic focus that should make them especially meaningful to Australasian students.

In summary, this is a well-written, skilfully edited book that provides a good summary of current knowledge in services marketing. Its emphasis on Australasian writers, cases and examples should make the book especially relevant to Australian and New Zealand students.

Roland T. Rust
David Bruce Smith Chair in Marketing
Robert H. Smith School of Business
University of Maryland, USA

Preface

Services marketing is a dynamic field of research, and there is growing interest in it from both the academic and the business worlds. Not only are the majority of employees working in the services sector, but service is also critical to the success of all businesses.

This book brings together leading research from internationally recognised scholars across Australia and New Zealand. The chapters have been written by a team of experts who have drawn from their research in their particular areas of speciality. As a result, the book has a very strong theoretical base.

The chapter authors are Dr Rebekah Bennett (University of Queensland), Liliana Bove (PhD (Qual.), La Trobe University), Tracey Dagger (PhD candidate, University of Western Australia), Associate Professor Susan Dann (Queensland University of Technology), Kirsten Dixon (of Deloitte Touche Tohmatsu), Dr Judy Drennan (University of Queensland), Associate Professor Lorelle Frazer (Griffith University), Professor Mark Gabbott (Monash University), Dr Railton Hill (Swinburne University of Technology), Dr Meredith Lawley (University of the Sunshine Coast), Associate Professor Sheelagh Matear (University of Otago), Professor Janet R. McColl-Kennedy (University of Queensland), Anthony J. McMullan (Director, Centre for Marketing Leadership), Derek Nind (Otago University), Professor Chad Perry (Southern Cross University), Sally Rao (PhD candidate, Griffith University), Professor Beverley Sparks (Griffith University Gold Coast), Sarah Spencer-Matthews (PhD candidate, University of Southern Queensland), Dr Jane Summers (University of Southern Queensland), Associate Professor Jillian Sweeney (University of Western Australia), Dr Carmen Tideswell (Griffith University Gold Coast), Dr Tony Ward (Central Queensland University), and Associate Professor Lesley White (Macquarie University).

There is also a strong focus on practical examples to clearly illustrate the theory. This includes vignettes within the chapters, and 18 original case studies located at the end of the book. The cases were developed by both academics and practitioners working in services marketing. These cases provide very practical applications of all the key services marketing concepts, and each case is related back to one or more chapters. The authors of the case studies are Paul Bradshaw, Janet Campbell, Cynthia Chong, Tracey Dagger, Professor Robert J. Donovan, Mark Francas, Associate Professor Lorelle Frazer, Professor Mark Gabbott, Kathy Gard, Anne-Marie Huartson Offer, Dr Meredith Lawley, Janelle McPhail, Genevieve Mezger, Steve Noakes, Carol Osborne, Donna Paterson, Professor Chad Perry, Nichola Robertson, David Rymer, Professor Beverley Sparks, Dr Jane Summers, Associate Professor Jillian Sweeney, Dr Carmen Tideswell, Dr Tony Ward, Farrah Yusof and Zoe Zhao.

This book has been written and structured especially for marketing students and managers. The contents are integrated, based on the conceptual model outlined in chapter 1, to help readers know where they are and where they are heading in their study of services marketing.

The authors have taken a holistic approach to services — that is, services marketing must be integrated with operations and human resource management. In addition, each chapter includes relevant international issues, to help readers better understand an increasingly global world.

Each chapter has a number of helpful pedagogical features, including learning objectives, chapter outlines, bullet-point summaries, highlighted key terms and definitions, a different font and shading for examples, Internet applications, review questions, application questions, practical vignettes and accompanying questions, and recommended reading lists.

Entire chapters are dedicated to in-depth exploration of significant concepts such as satisfaction, service quality, value, communication, and service recovery. In addition, a thorough marketing research chapter helps to introduce students to the unique characteristics of research in services marketing. We have also separated individual buyer behaviour and business-to-business services marketing in order to give due attention to these distinct contexts.

Furthermore, five specialist chapters are provided, covering e-services, tourism and hospitality, franchising, sport marketing, and public sector/government marketing. These chapters provide in-depth treatment of these emerging areas.

The book itself forms one part of a broader package that includes PowerPoint slides, case study solutions, a test bank for instructors and very practical recommendations for teaching. These have been prepared by Sharyn Rundle-Thiele.

I would like to acknowledge the reviewers, who provided insightful and helpful comments and suggestions. They included Robyn Stokes (Queensland University of Technology), Cathy Neal (Queensland University of Technology), Dr Len Coote (University of Queensland), Margo McOmish (James Cook University), and Dr Tony Ward (Central Queensland University).

Thanks to Professor Lester Johnson and Professor Susan Ellis, Mt Eliza Business School, for their constructive comments in the early stages of the project's development. Thank you also to Dr Jane Summers for her help on the culture section in chapter 2.

Thank you to my students and colleagues at the UQ Business School, especially Dr Gillian Sullivan Mort, Dr Jay Weerawardena, Dr Chris Hodkinson, Sharyn Rundle-Thiele, Margee Hume, Alastair Tombs, Doan Nguyen, Carl Sinclair, Margaret Johnston and Glenys Throssell, who have provided a sounding board for my ideas, and who have provided helpful feedback.

Thanks to Janine Spencer-Burford at Wiley for her enthusiasm and her faith in my ability to bring together an outstanding team of authors, and for coordinating their efforts. It has been a great pleasure working with the dedicated team at Wiley, and Cynthia Wardle deserves special mention for her meticulous attention to detail.

Finally, I would like to acknowledge the superb job that my research assistant Eric Manners has done in helping to bring the whole project together. Thank you all.

Professor Janet R. McColl-Kennedy
UQ Business School
University of Queensland
November, 2002

How to use this book

Important terms are highlighted in bold and defined in the margin, providing a running glossary throughout the text.

Within the text are concrete examples that relate to the issue being discussed; these are highlighted, allowing easy identification.

Services Marketing Action, Services Marketing on the Web, Ethical Issues, and International Issues vignettes appear throughout the text. They examine issues within the chapter in the context of contemporary organisations and real-life situations.

Learning objectives help the reader to identify the measurable student outcomes after reading each chapter.

The chapter outline provides a broad overview of the chapter content.

The 18 chapters of the book are divided into five parts, with part 5 dedicated to specialist topics, allowing services marketing theory to be applied to particular industries and environments.

One of the world's most successful companies is Berkshire Hathaway (www.berk-shirehathaway.com), which holds an annual gathering for shareholders that more resembles an evangelical rally than a corporate meeting. The shareholders start the meeting on Friday evening and continue until Sunday with dinners, meetings and festivities. The shareholders have a strong sense of community and many credit CEO Warren Buffet as the man behind their own financial independence.

Opinion leaders: individual or organisations whose opinions have a key influence on a consumer's purchasing process, products or services

Opinion leaders

Opinion leaders play an important role in services marketing. Given the increased emphasis on personal sources of information, opinion leaders who are known to the consumer can play either an advocate or adversarial role for an organisation. So too can opinion leaders who are not personally known to the consumer and who have no vested interest in the transaction. This can include industry leaders or associations such as the Australian Marketing Institute, the Law Society and the Australian Medical Association. If these opinion leaders endorse a product, this provides a great deal of credibility and reassurance to the consumer.

Services Marketing Action:
Sensis

Sensis is an Australian organisation that is a majority owned subsidiary of Telstra. While most Australians would not be familiar with the name of this organisation, they are very familiar with the services and products provided, including the Yellow Pages™ and the White Pages™. Sensis has two primary markets for the Yellow Pages products: the business customer who pays for advertising, and the consumer who uses the product.

The Yellow Pages directories generate close to A$1 billion each year from advertising revenue. With more than 80 per cent of the customer base defined as small business, it is important that Sensis has the support of opinion leaders who influence small business. This includes local chambers of commerce, government departments and industry associations such as the Motor Trades Association. In order to maintain goodwill with these groups, as well as provide resources for their advertisers, Sensis has embarked on a number of public relations campaigns to influence opinion leaders. These include the Yellow Pages Business Ideas Grants, and Yellow Pages Small Business Index.

The Yellow Pages Business Ideas Grants is a PR campaign that offers cash grants for people with a good idea that they would like to turn into a business. This campaign is publicised on The Small Business Show on Channel 9. This show presents information relevant to small business and acts as an opinion leader. Thus, when the show reports on the grants, this lends credibility and approval to Sensis, the company responsible for the grants. The Yellow Pages Small Business Index is quarterly research commissioned by Sensis to report on consumer and business confidence. The results of this report are widely reported in the media and used in government papers. The use of these figures by business opinion leaders, such as the media and government, again lends approval and credibility to Sensis.

es Marketing: A Managerial Approach

Chapter 1
Introduction to services

Janet R. McColl-Kennedy

LEARNING OBJECTIVES

After reading this chapter you should be able to:
- explain what services are
- discuss specific issues relevant to services
- outline the seven Ps of the services mix
- identify the managerial challenges that the characteristics of services create
- discuss the importance of the cooperation between marketing, operations and human resources to produce, deliver and manage quality services.

CHAPTER OUTLINE

The aim of this chapter is to provide an overview of services, pointing out that a holistic view incorporating marketing, human resources and operations is vital to delivering services, achieving appropriate levels of service quality and customer satisfaction, and building relationships with customers. There are a number of special issues relevant to services which make it particularly critical that all the key elements of an organisation — marketing, human resources and operations — work together to ensure that the service is appropriately produced, priced, promoted and delivered by the right people. A conceptual framework, which incorporates the key elements of services marketing and provides a focus for this book, is outlined.

Part 5
Specialisation

standards represent expectations as the most likely performance to occur (Parasuraman, Zeithaml & Berry 1988; Tse & Wilton 1988; Oliver 1981; Boulding et al. 1993). Miller (1977) notes that while the 'expected' and 'deserved' expectation standards can be separated conceptually, in practice differentiating between these two standards is often difficult.

- *Minimum tolerable standard:* the 'minimum tolerable' standard reflects the level of performance that is better than nothing, and represents the least acceptable level that performance 'must be' (Miller 1977).

Satisfaction researchers appear to agree that the baseline comparison for post-experience perceptions is what consumers 'would' expect. However, based on the expected performance construct, there is disagreement within the service quality literature about how to define what consumers 'should' expect: can it be defined in terms of ideal, deserved or some other standard of expectation? Regardless of these differences, expectations and perceptions are linked in both literatures through the disconfirmation paradigm.

These issues continue to be the subject of debate and research across many service industries. So while academics continue to explore various aspects of service quality, managers within service industries continue to benefit from the practical implications of much of this research.

Summary

LO1: Define service quality.
- Service quality is an elusive and abstract concept like an attitude.
- It is based on an evaluation of overall excellence and superiority.
- It requires a long-term global evaluation.
- It is related to but different from satisfaction.

LO2: Distinguish between service quality and satisfaction.
- Satisfaction requires experience, whereas service quality can be perceived without actually having to experience the service.

LO3: Understand the importance of service quality to the management of services.
- Service quality can have both positive and negative implications for managers depending on whether service quality is perceived to be high good or low poor.
- Positive outcomes of high service quality include insulating customers from competitors, creating competitive advantage, reducing failure costs, encouraging repeat performance, promoting loyalty, enhancing positive word of mouth, and lowering the cost of attracting new customers.
- Negative outcomes include loss of current customers, negative word of mouth and loss of repeat customers.

LO4: Describe various models of service quality.
- Various models of service quality have been developed in order to better understand what makes up service quality and how service quality works.
- The disconfirmation model forms the basis for many later models of service quality. Basically, the disconfirmation model highlights three possible outcomes from purchasing a service: we are dissatisfied (that is, the purchase did not meet our expectations), the purchase was as we expected, or we are satisfied (the purchase met our expectations) and we are delighted by the service (the purchase exceeded our expectations).

Chapter 4 Service quality 03

- The Nordic model was based on the disconfirmation model and considered quality to have two dimensions: the technical quality, or the outcome of the service process, and the functional quality, or how the service was delivered.
- The gaps model, again based on disconfirmation, looks at five gaps where expectations and actual performance can differ.
- SERVQUAL, closely related to the gaps model, specifically considers five dimensions: reliability, assurance, tangibles, responsiveness and empathy.
- Finally, the three-component models consider service quality in terms of the service product, service delivery and the service environment.

LO5: Be aware of current issues regarding service quality.
- Key issues currently being debated include the ordering of service quality and satisfaction, the measurement of quality and the role of expectations.

key terms

Assurance: the competence, courtesy and security a firm offers to consumers (p. 85)

Cognitive dissonance: the discomfort buyers may feel after purchase, for example, 'Did I get value for money?' (p. 75)

Credence qualities: service attributes that cannot be evaluated by consumers with any certainty even after they have experienced the service process (p. 75)

Customer satisfaction: 'the customer's fulfilment response; a judgement that a product or service feature, or the product or service itself, provided a pleasurable level of consumption-related fulfilment, including levels of under- or over-fulfilment' (Oliver 1997, p. 13) (p. 74)

Disconfirmation: state in which expectation levels are perceived to have been met, exceeded or not met in actual performance of the service (p. 79)

Empathy: the ability of a firm to provide individualised, caring service (p. 86)

Experience qualities: service attributes that can only be evaluated by consumers after the service production process (p. 75)

Functional quality: the components of the process used to arrive at the service outcome (p. 81)

Gaps model: a diagnostic model that helps identify the gaps between expectations and perceptions of management, employees and customers (p. 82)

Reliability: consistency and dependability in performing the service (p. 85)

Responsiveness: the timely manner in which a firm provides its services (p. 86)

Service delivery: the manner in which the firm chooses to deliver the service (p. 88)

Service environment: the internal culture of the organisation and the external or physical surroundings of the organisation (p. 88)

Service product: the consumer's overall perception of the service and any augmented services accompanying service delivery (p. 88)

Service quality: the result of an evaluation process in which the customer compares their perceptions of the service with their expectations (p. 74)

04 Services Marketing: A Managerial Approach

All key terms are listed and defined towards the end of the chapter.

Each chapter includes a summary that provides a useful study guide.

Review, application and vignette questions test the student's understanding of the material covered in the chapter.

LO3: Discuss the strategies that can be used to adjust supply to meet demand in cases of both high demand and low demand.
- Strategies for managing supply centre on creating flexibility within the elements of supply.
- The four major elements of supply are facilities, equipment, labour and time.
- Appropriate strategies will often combine various tactics concerning all elements of supply, and may vary according to the nature of the service.

LO4: Discuss the strategies that can be used to adjust demand to meet supply in cases of high demand and low demand.
- Strategies for managing demand focus on the elements of the marketing mix, notably product, price, promotion and place.
- Again, strategies may combine tactics from several areas as appropriate for the particular service.

key terms

Greater than maximum supply: higher demand than maximum available supply (p. 193)

Maximum supply: higher demand than optimal supply levels (p. 194)

Optimum supply: when demand and supply are well balanced (p. 194)

Less than optimum supply: lower demand than optimal supply levels (p. 194)

review questions

1. Why is it difficult for services to be inventoried?
2. Briefly explain why managers of services have to be able to manage supply and demand.
3. List and briefly describe the four elements of supply.
4. For each of the four element of supply, outline one tactic for managing supply when demand is too high and one tactic for managing supply when demand is too low.
5. For each element of the marketing mix, outline one tactic for coping with high demand and one tactic for coping with low demand.

application questions

1. For each of the following situations, identify what you consider to be their pattern of demand (daily, weekly, yearly) and, based on this pattern, recommend a combination of supply management and demand management strategies that could be adopted by management to optimise supply and demand:
   (a) a photocopying service located on a university campus
   (b) a theme park (like Movie World or Sea World) located at a coastal resort area
   (c) a tax accountant specialising in small businesses

Chapter 8 Managing supply and demand 207

A collection of case studies near the end of the book comprises a variety of typical and real-life examples. Each case study is followed by questions to help students apply theory from the corresponding chapters.

Case study 13

E-complaining: the world of online complaint sites[1]

By Nichola Robertson

Company background

Kiwi Insurance Services' call centre is located in Auckland, New Zealand. Kiwi Insurance is one of New Zealand's leading insurance companies in the motor vehicle and home insurance markets. More than 50 per cent of all Kiwi Insurance's interactions with its customers are channeled through its Auckland call centre. Indeed, call centres are nowadays at the forefront of many New Zealand businesses (Yousef 2001).

Contrary to the public perception that call centres do not offer a high grade of customer service, Kiwi Insurance's centre does a great job in meeting and exceeding its customers' expectations. Generally, the first personal contact a customer has with Kiwi Insurance is with the customer service representative who answers the phone. Good customer service often starts and ends with a pleasant telephone manner. The call centre provides the crucial, and often lasting, first impression of Kiwi Insurance.

All customer service representatives undertake six weeks of intensive training before starting work at the centre. Training programs are designed to teach representatives about the variety of insurance products offered by the company, the ins and outs of the business, and, most importantly, a range of customer service related skills designed to ensure caller satisfaction. Kiwi Insurance sees its call centre as an increasingly important part of its differentiation strategy — not to mention a tool both to acquire new customers and to retain existing ones.

The quarterly customer service meeting

It is Monday morning at Kiwi Insurance Services, and Jillian Smith, who heads the Customer Service Division at the call centre, is about to report to her customer service representatives on the past month's customer satisfaction ratings, and how well they have addressed their customers' complaints. She begins: 'Welcome, everyone. Our quarterly customer satisfaction survey results are now in, and you'll be happy to know it's been another great quarter. Overall, our customer satisfaction ratings were up a little on last quarter.' (Figure 13A outlines the customer satisfaction ratings for the first quarter, 2002.)

Jillian distributes a handout detailing the ratings and congratulates her representatives on a job well done. Satisfaction ratings are based on many specific elements that together make up the caller's service experience, and

---
[1] This is a fictional case based on research regarding consumer complaint behaviour and independent complaint sites. The call centre referred to in this case is based on the experiences of a composite of firms.

Case study 13 559

How to use this book xiii

Dr Rebekah Bennett

Rebekah Bennett, BCom, PhD, is a Lecturer in marketing at the University of Queensland, and is Deputy President of the Australian Marketing Institute (Qld). Her special areas of research are brand loyalty, services marketing and communication, and entrepreneurial women. She has worked in marketing management for the services-based Yellow Pages Australia, the Queensland State Government and SJP Financial Services Group. Rebekah has been published in leading specialist journals and has spoken at conferences of the American Marketing Association, British Academy of Management and the Australia and New Zealand Marketing Academy. Her paper on brand loyalty won the best paper award at the 2001 Market Research Society of Australia's national conference.

Liliana Bove

Liliana Bove, BAgrSc, BBus, PhD (Qual.), is a Lecturer in the School of Business at La Trobe University in Melbourne. Her teaching and research interests are in the areas of services marketing, customer loyalty and marketing research. Her doctoral thesis investigated the role of customer relationships with service personnel in customer loyalty to the firm. She has published in journals such as the *Journal of Business Research*, *International Journal of Service Industry Management*, *Australasian Journal of Market Research* and *International Quarterly Journal of Marketing*. Prior to commencing her academic career, she held various scientific, marketing and management roles over a 10-year period in the chemical, airline and health industries.

Tracey Dagger

Tracey Dagger is currently an Associate Lecturer in marketing at the University of the Sunshine Coast. One of her primary research interests is services marketing and, in particular, service quality research. Tracey also has a strong interest in the marketing of health care services and has worked as a senior researcher within the health care field. She is undertaking her PhD in marketing with specific emphasis on service quality issues in health care. As a small business owner, Tracey has first-hand experience in the application of services marketing concepts to the small business sector.

Associate Professor Susan Dann

Susan Dann, BA, MPubAdmin, PhD, FAMI, CPM, MAICD, is an Associate Professor in marketing at the Brisbane Graduate School of Business, QUT. She is the Queensland President of the Australian Marketing Institute, interim Chair of the National Board of the Australian Marketing Institute and a board member of the AFL Queensland Commission. She is a Fellow of the Australian Marketing Institute and a member of the Australian Institute of Company Directors. Susan's area of expertise is in marketing strategy and the non-traditional applications of marketing, particularly in the public and social sectors. Her most recent book, *Strategic Internet Marketing*, was published in 2001. Susan is a frequent speaker at national and international conferences on marketing issues and strategies.

Kirsten Dixon

Kirsten Dixon completed a Master of Commerce on customer preferences and industrial service design in the NZ–Asian shipping market at the University of Otago in 2000. She is now based in Melbourne, working as an analyst in the Assurance and Advisory division of Deloitte Touche Tohmatsu. Kirsten is currently completing a part-time conversion course at the University of Melbourne to meet ICAA requirements, and will then commence the Chartered Accountancy program in February 2003.

Dr Judy Drennan

Judy Drennan is a Lecturer in marketing at the UQ Business School, University of Queensland. She gained her PhD at Deakin University and her Master of Education degree at the University of Melbourne, and is undertaking research in the areas of m-marketing, Internet sponsorship and entrepreneurship. Her work has been published in the *Journal of Services Marketing*, *Journal of Database Marketing*, *International Journal of Innovation and Entrepreneurship* and *Small Enterprise Research*. She teaches in the areas of Internet marketing, marketing communications and marketing principles. She has a keen interest in online learning, and has been involved in the development and running of courses offered in electronic delivery mode.

Associate Professor Lorelle Frazer

Lorelle Frazer is an Associate Professor in the School of Marketing at Griffith University. She has been involved in franchising education and research for several years. She completed her PhD on the topic of franchise fee-setting practices in Australia. The *Franchising Australia* reports, which profile current franchising practices, were commissioned by the Franchise Council of Australia and were co-authored by Lorelle in 1998, 1999 and 2002. Her current research interests are concerned with the causes of franchisee failure, conflict in franchise organisations and franchising expansion strategies. Lorelle teaches franchising to undergraduate and postgraduate business students and to members of the franchising sector.

Professor Mark Gabbott

Mark Gabbott, BA, MSc, PhD, worked in government for six years in the area of consumer policy and protection. He has taught in the areas of electronic and direct marketing, services marketing, consumer behaviour and consumer policy. Mark is Professor of Electronic Marketing and Head of the Department of Marketing at Monash University. He has published three books on services marketing and his research has appeared in journals such as the *Journal of Business Research*, *Journal of Public Policy and Marketing* and *European Journal of Marketing*. He has acted as a consultant for both private and public sector clients, including the European Commission, IBM, Honda and the National Consumer Council in the UK.

Dr Railton Hill

Railton Hill holds separate qualifications in arts, marketing, media, librarianship and education, and has a PhD in marketing. He is a Senior Lecturer in marketing at Swinburne University of Technology, researching in the areas of services, marketing communications and social marketing. His work experience includes marketing, consulting and training for the Australian Institute of Management, Victoria; freelance media work; small business and independent consulting; and working as Client Service Manager at Deakin Australia. He has published in the *Australasian Journal of Market Research*, *New Zealand Journal of Business*, *Social Marketing Quarterly* and *Australian Financial Review*.

Dr Meredith Lawley

Meredith Lawley is a Senior Lecturer in marketing at the University of the Sunshine Coast. She has taught in several areas of marketing over the past 15 years, including marketing research, marketing management and e-marketing. She has considerable experience in writing study materials for both distance and online students, and has written a book on questionnaire design. One of her key research interests is services marketing, particularly the international marketing of services such as education. In this field she has completed several academic publications as well as consultancy projects for organisations such as IDP Education Australia. She has practical experience in services marketing, having undertaken key roles in the marketing of education internationally at two universities.

Associate Professor Sheelagh Matear

Sheelagh Matear is Associate Professor of Marketing at the University of Otago, New Zealand. She gained a PhD from Plymouth Polytechnic, UK, and has also worked in the Office of Economic Development at the University of Arizona. Her current research interests focus on competitive advantage, strategy and performance in service firms and inter-firm relationships and networks. Sheelagh teaches marketing on the Otago MBA, and postgraduate research methods in the Department of Marketing.

Professor Janet R. McColl-Kennedy

Janet R. McColl-Kennedy, BA, PhD, is Professor of Marketing at the UQ Business School, University of Queensland. She has over 70 research publications, including articles in *The Leadership Quarterly*, *Journal of Service Research*, *Journal of Business Research* and *Journal of Services Marketing*. Janet is a member of the editorial review board of *Australasian Marketing Journal*, and reviews for several international journals and conferences in marketing. She chaired the first two International Services Marketing Conferences, and is a Fellow of the Australian Marketing Institute. With over 20 years experience in teaching undergraduates, postgraduates and executives, she specialises in teaching marketing, services marketing and consumer behaviour. Janet won the University of Queensland School of Management Teaching Excellence Award in 2001.

Anthony J. McMullan

Tony holds a commerce degree and an MBA, with majors in marketing and human resource management. He is an Associate Fellow of the Australian Marketing Institute (AMI), a state councillor for the AMI and is Chairman of the AMI Government Marketing Special Interest Group for Queensland. He is also jointly responsible for the establishment of the Annual National Conference on Government Marketing. Tony is currently employed as Director of the Centre for Marketing Leadership, a private sector consulting and educational service provider in strategic marketing.

Derek Nind

Derek Nind is the Director of Executive Education in the School of Business at Otago University. He has worked in international marketing within the food and transport sectors, and works as a consultant providing expertise in logistics, marketing, strategic analysis and empirical research. His clients have included listed companies, SMEs and economic development organisations. Derek is involved in a number of research and consulting projects in the areas of service selection and service development. Two such projects focus on how Chinese shippers select shipping services between China and New Zealand, and how tertiary students choose a polytechnic in New Zealand.

Professor Chad Perry

Chad Perry has recently retired as Professor of Marketing and Management at the Graduate College of Management, Southern Cross University, Gold Coast. His research interests included relationship marketing and qualitative methods. He has written or co-written three textbooks, eight book chapters and more than 100 refereed journal articles and conference papers. He has presented management development workshops in Africa, Asia, Papua New Guinea, the United Kingdom and Australia, and worked on occasional management consulting projects in some of those countries.

Sally Rao

Sally Rao lectures in marketing at the School of Commerce, University of Adelaide. Her research interests include relationship marketing, Internet marketing and services marketing. Her PhD was about how the Internet affects business-to-business relationships. She has written journal articles about her research and presented several conference papers, one of which won the best paper award at an international conference.

Professor Beverley Sparks

Beverley Sparks, BA, GradDipBus, PhD, is a Professor with the School of Tourism and Hotel Management at Griffith University. Beverley is an active researcher in the area of services marketing and management, and has several publications in top quality journals. She is on the editorial board of two international journals: *International Journal of Contemporary Hospitality Management* and *Hospitality and Tourism Research Journal*. Beverley has been instrumental in the development of studies in the timeshare industry at Griffith University. She has received a range of grants for her research work and has presented her research nationally and internationally at many conferences.

Sarah Spencer-Matthews

Sarah Spencer-Matthews has been a marketing academic for over 10 years. She has worked at various universities in Brisbane and Melbourne and is presently lecturing at the University of Southern Queensland. Her research interests include customer relationships and customer service, and she has published in these areas as well as in the areas of advertising standards, organisational culture and database marketing. Sarah is currently finalising her PhD on customer contact management — how customers can receive tailored service wherever and whenever they interact with business. Her research is practical and has service implications for most organisations.

Dr Jane Summers

Jane Summers is Head of the Marketing Department at the Faculty of Business, University of Southern Queensland. She has spent many years as both a marketing practitioner and an academic. Her teaching and research interests are in the areas of consumer behaviour, e-marketing and sport marketing. Jane's recent academic and professional work focuses on the services industry and its unique issues and implications for marketing. Her specific interest in sport marketing has evolved due to the call from both practitioners and academics for more research in this area, particularly for a greater understanding of consumer behaviour and attitudes to sport consumption. Jane is currently researching the international applicability of some of these consumption-related issues.

Associate Professor Jillian Sweeney

Jillian Sweeney is an Associate Professor in marketing at the University of Western Australia. Before starting an academic career, she gained extensive experience in market research consultancies in London, Sydney and Perth, focusing on statistics and sampling, industrial research and consumer research. She was awarded a PhD in marketing in 1995. Her academic research focuses on quality, brand equity, perceived value and relationship marketing. Jill is also particularly interested in services marketing. She has published widely, including in the *Journal of Retailing*, *Journal of Services Marketing* and *Psychology and Marketing*. Jill coordinates and lectures in services marketing and marketing research, and supervises honours degree, master's degree and PhD students.

Dr Carmen Tideswell

Carmen Tideswell lectures in the School of Tourism and Hotel Management at Griffith University, Gold Coast. She was previously employed in the Centre for Tourism and Hotel Management Research from 1994 to 1998, during which time she worked on a number of research and consulting projects for industry and government organisations. Carmen's current research interests include consumer behaviour in tourism and hospitality services, tourism demand analysis, tourism forecasting, customer loyalty to hotels and tourism destinations, and other general issues in tourism and hospitality marketing.

Dr Tony Ward

Tony Ward, BTech, PhD, MEMA, MAMS, lectures in marketing and strategic management at the Faculty of Business and Law, Central Queensland University. He teaches mainly in the areas of international marketing and the marketing of service products. For the first 23 years of his working life, Tony was employed in the aerospace industry in Europe, spending 17 of those years marketing aerospace products worldwide. Tony's main interests are teaching and researching in relationship and services marketing, international marketing and the supervision of higher degree candidates. He heads the Research of Human Interactions in Marketing (RHIM) research group.

Associate Professor Lesley White

Lesley White, BPharm, MCom, MEd, PhD, is an Associate Professor at the Macquarie Graduate School of Management, Macquarie University, Sydney. Prior to commencing her academic career, Lesley spent 10 years in marketing management in a range of industries. Her current research interests focus on the areas of e-commerce and services marketing, particularly services quality and professional services.

Acknowledgements

The authors and publisher would like to thank the following copyright holders, organisations and individuals for permission to reproduce copyright material in this book.

Illustrative material:

• Front cover and internal design images © 2002 Digital Vision/ Nic Miller • Figure 1.2, G.L Shostack, vol. 41, p. 77; Figure 1.3, C. Lovelock, vol. 47, summer 1983; Figure 3.2, Anderson, Hakansson & Johanson, vol. 58, October 1994, p. 3; Figure 4.2, Parasuraman, Zeithaml & Berry, fall 1985, p. 44; Figure 4.4, Brady & Cronin, vol. 65, 2001, pp. 34–49; Figure 12.3, Meuter, Ostrom, Roundtree & Bitner, vol. 64, July 2000, p. 52, all reprinted with permission from *Journal of Marketing*, published by the American Marketing Association • Figure 2.1 from *Consumer Behavior*, 5th edn by Engel, Blackwell & Miniard, © 1986, reprinted with permission of South Western College Publishing — a division of Thomson Learning www.thomsonrights.com • Figures 2.6, 2.7, 2.8 from H. Schutte & D. Ciarlante, *Consumer Behaviour in Asia*, 1998, Macmillan Business, London, all reproduced with permission of Palgrave Macmillan Publishers • Figure 3.1 reprinted by permission of Professor Andrew C. Gross, from *Business Marketing* by Gross et al., Houghton Mifflin, 1993 • Figure 3.4 from *Business Marketing* by Ford et al., Houghton Mifflin, 1993, derived from P. J Robinson, C.W. Faris & Y. Wind, *Industrial Buying and Creative Marketing*, 1967 p. 14, reprinted with permission of D. Ford and original adapted with permission of Y. Wind. • Figure 3.5, adapted from Ferguson's model of B2B service purchasing from *Industrial Marketing Management*, vol. 8, 1979, p. 44, © 1979, reproduced with permission from Elsevier Science • Figure 4.1 adapted by permission of the Association for Consumer Research from Hill, D., *Satisfaction & Consumer Services in Advances in Consumer Research*, vol.13, 1986, Richard Lutz (ed), Michigan, p. 311 • Figure 4.3 from R. Rust & R. Oliver, *Service Quality: New Directions in Theory & Practice*, p. 11; Figure 5.10 from Patterson, Johnson & Spreng, 'Modeling the determinants of customer satisfaction for business-to-business professional services', *Journal of the Academy of Marketing Science*, vol. 25, no.1, pp. 4–17, Figure 13.3 from Stephens & Gwinner 'Why don't some people complain?', *Journal of the Academy of Marketing Science*, vol. 26, no. 3, p. 174, © 1998, all reprinted by permission of Sage Publications USA • Figures 5.1, 5.6, 5.7 © 1999 Photo-Disc, Inc. • Figure 5.2 from V. A. Zeithaml & M. J. Bitner, *Services Marketing: Integrating Customer Focus Across the Firm*, Irwin, McGraw-Hill, Boston, 2000, p. 75; Figure 5.8 from R. Oliver, *Satisfaction: A Behavioral Perspective on the Consumer*, McGraw-Hill, 1997, both reproduced with the permission of The McGraw-Hill Companies • Figure 5.3 from Patterson & Johnson 'Disconfirmation of expectations and the gap model of service quality: an integrated paradigm', *Journal of Consumer Satisfaction, Dissatisfaction & Complaining Behavior*, vol. 6, 1993, p. 90, reprinted with permission • Figure 5.9 from 'The structure & dynamics of expectations & customer satisfaction in channel member relationships in the Victorian fruit industry', ANZMAC conference paper 2000, by Railton Hill & Martin Nanere • Figure 6.2 from *Designing And Delivering Superior Customer Value*, 1st edn by Art Weinstein & William C. Johnson, © 1999 by CRC Press Inc; Figure 12.4 from 'Organization and customer', by Rikard Larsson & David E. Bowen, *Academy of Management Review*, © 1989 by Academy of Management, both reproduced with permission of Academy of Management via Copyright Clearance Center • Figure 6.6 ©

Virgin Blue, reproduced with permission • Figure 9.2 from *Customer Loyalty: How to Earn It, How to Keep It*, by Jill Griffin, 1995, reprinted by permission of John Wiley & Sons, Inc. • Figure 9.4 adapted with permission from 'Influences of service quality on relationship development and maintenance in the Australian financial services industry: an in-depth study' by John Teale, 1999 • Figure 10.8 from Sundaram & Webster, *Journal of Services Marketing*, vol. 14, no. 5, 2000, p. 380, reproduced by permission of Emerald • Figure 10.9 reproduced with permission of AMP Corporate Brand • Figure 10.10 reproduced with permission of Strategic Joint Partners Pty Ltd • Figure 10.11 © National Australia Bank, screen shot reproduced with permission • Figures 13.1, 13.2 /Centrelink © Commonwealth of Australia, reproduced by permission • Figure 13.4 from p. 9 of 'Cognitive appraisal and emotion in service recovery: a conceptual framework' by Doan T. Nguyen & Janet R. McColl-Kennedy, paper submitted to International Services Marketing Conference, 4, 5 July 2002 • Figure 14.1 © Nielsen/Netratings • Figure 14.2 reproduced with permission from NOIE, The National Office for the Information Economy, www.noie.gov.au • Figure 14.3, screen shot reproduced with the permission of John Fairfax Holdings Limited, all rights reserved; this image may not be published or redistributed in any form • Figure 14.4, screenshot reproduced with permission of realestate.com.au • Figure 14.5 © BizRate.com • Figure 14.6 reproduced by permission of the National Children's and Youth Law Centre • Figure 14.7 © Minter Ellison Lawyers • Figure 14.8 © eMedical • Figure 14.9 © 2000 eMarketer, Inc. www.eMarketer.com • Figure 15.1 © Tourism Queensland • Figure 16.7 © Greg Nathan 2002 • Figures 8A, 8B, 8C reproduced by permission of Kathy Gard & Genevieve Mezger, AMP • Figures 9A, 9B reproduced with permission of Q-RAPID • Figures 18A, 18B, photos by Anthony Edwards

Text:

• Table 2.2 from *Services Marketing* by D. L Kurtz & Kenneth E. Clow, © 1998, reprinted by permission of John Wiley & Sons, Inc • Tables 2.4, 2.5 from H. Schutte & D. Ciarlante, *Consumer Behaviour in Asia*, 1998, Macmillan Business London, reprinted by permission of Palgrave-Macmillan Publishers • Table 3.1 from *Business Marketing Management* by Bingham & Raffield © 1995 reprinted with permission of South-Western College Publishing, a division of Thomson Learning www.thomsonrights.com • Vignette p. 150, case study 1, pp. 499–503, © Anne-Marie Huartson Offer • Interview p. 151 reprinted with permission of PricewaterhouseCoopers • Vignette p. 253 © Jacqui Jones, Managing Director, WEBENZ, www.webenz.co.nz • Extract p. 333 reproduced with permission of Glenys Throssell • Extract p. 338/ Centrelink, © Commonwealth of Australia, reproduced by permission; Extract p. 381 from *Fact Sheet for Consumers #5: Shopping on the Internet*, Department of Communications, Information Technology & the Arts website, © Commonwealth of Australia, reproduced by permission • Vignette pp. 339–40 © Nichola Robertson • Extract pp. 351–2 reproduced with permission of Margaret Johnston • Vignette p. 359, reproduced with permission from NOIE, The National Office for the Information Economy www.noie.gov.au • Article pp. 449–51 by James Wakelin, *Cyber Journal of Sport Marketing* • Table 17.3 © Commercial Economic Advisory Service of Australia • Case study 5, pp. 525–8, adapted with permission from 'Optimising the service mix in local government' by Nicky Munro, Research Solutions, & Rob Avard, Cockburn Council, with John Green, Research for Today • Article pp. 533–4 Jennifer Foreshew, *The Australian*, 12 June 2001 • Case study 8, pp. 535–40, reproduced with permission of Kathy Gard and Genevieve Mezger, AMP • Case study 10, pp. 548–50, adapted with permission from Donovan, R. J., Paterson, D. & Francas, M. 'Targeting male perpetrators of intimate partner violence: Western Australia's 'Freedom from Fear' campaign', *Social Marketing Quarterly*, 1999, vol. 5, no. 3, pp. 127–44 • Case study 12, pp. 554–8, © Carol Osborne, Zoe Zhao and Farrah Yusof, reproduced by permission of the authors • Case study 14, pp. 565–7, © David Rymer • Case study 15, pp. 568–72, based on information kindly supplied by CRC for Sustainable Tourism, www.crctourism.com.au • Tables 16A, 16B © Just Cuts

Part 1

Understanding the basics

Chapter 1
Introduction to services

Janet R. McColl-Kennedy

LEARNING OBJECTIVES

After reading this chapter you should be able to:

- explain what services are
- discuss specific issues relevant to services
- outline the seven Ps of the services mix
- identify the managerial challenges that the characteristics of services create
- discuss the importance of the cooperation between marketing, operations and human resources to produce, deliver and manage quality services.

CHAPTER OUTLINE

The aim of this chapter is to provide an overview of services, pointing out that a holistic view incorporating marketing, human resources and operations is vital to delivering services, achieving appropriate levels of service quality and customer satisfaction, and building relationships with customers. There are a number of special issues relevant to services which make it particularly critical that all the key elements of an organisation — marketing, human resources and operations — work together to ensure that the service is appropriately produced, priced, promoted and delivered by the right people. A conceptual framework, which incorporates the key elements of services marketing and provides a focus for this book, is outlined.

Introduction

In today's global society, services are very much part of our everyday life. Using the Internet to purchase books and CDs, visiting a doctor, going to the hairdresser, collecting the dry cleaning, banking at an automatic teller machine (ATM) or staying at a ski resort are all examples of services.

Services can be defined in various ways. At the start of this chapter, it is important to recognise the distinction between services, hidden (support) services and customer service.

Services

Services: acts, performances and experiences

Services may be defined as acts, performances and experiences — that is, the production and delivery of a service. For example, a doctor gives you a check up by checking your blood pressure, observing your pulse rate, listening for your heartbeat and checking your reactions to sensory stimulation. A live band performs music that may make you feel good and generally entertain you. No physical good has been bought with either of these services. Rather the service 'product' in the case of the medical service is a series of acts, and in the case of the band, a performance has taken place, and there is an experience. In each case the customer takes nothing physical away — only memories. Sometimes in services, physical goods are provided as part of the service.

For example, a restaurant provides customers with a meal of their choice (product), and it is hopefully served to the customer's liking and presented by a friendly waiter (service).

International Issues:
Cultural differences in service expectations

Although services are available globally as a result of the World Wide Web, it is important to note that there are significant differences between the expectations of customers in different countries, due largely to their cultural differences. It is widely acknowledged that some cultures tend to be individualistic while others are essentially collectivist (Hofstede 1980; Kim 1994; Liu & McClure 2001). Individualistic societies value independence, self-sufficiency and emphasise 'I', whereas people from collectivist cultures value social norms that emphasise social harmony and focus on 'we' rather than 'I' (Hofstede 1980). Australia, New Zealand, Canada, the United States and Europe can be regarded as having individualistic cultures while Japan, Korea and China are examples of collectivist cultures.

Many studies have demonstrated cultural differences that have direct implications for services marketing. For example, Reisinger and Turner (1999) found significant differences in expectations among Japanese tourists coming to Australia, and argue that the decline in Japanese tourist arrivals to Australia is largely due to service expectations not being met due to cultural value differences. Specifically, Reisinger and Turner found that Japanese tourists valued courtesy, responsiveness, competence and interaction. The largest differences between Japanese and Australian consumers were found in their definitions of courtesy and responsiveness. This has significant implications for Australian service providers. Organisations may be unaware of what Japanese tourists expect service providers to do for them, and unaware of what service standards they require in order to be satisfied with the service.

Reisinger and Turner (1999) suggest that Australian service providers should position their services for the Japanese market by offering services tailored to Japanese preferences. Specifically, they argue that Australians should focus on 'delivering a significantly higher level of service quality and adopting the mentality of a Japanese tourist'. Emphasis should be on service punctuality, politeness, respect, accuracy, professional competence, an apologetic attitude, differential treatment based on age and respect for collectivist desires.

It is critical for organisations operating in different countries or throughout large regional areas to tailor their marketing efforts to the different cultural groups. Cultural differences between the service provider and the receiver can lead to problems in quality control, feedback and customer satisfaction (Katabe, Murray and Javalgi 1998).

Hidden (support) services

Hidden (support) services: *services an organisation offers to support, promote and/or facilitate its physical goods*

There are also 'hidden' (support) services (Grönroos 2000). These services are not the main focus of the respective organisation. These are the services organisations offer to support, promote and/or facilitate their physical goods. Such service activities could include such things as research and development, quality control, maintenance, leasing, customer training, invoicing and logistics.

Customer service

Customer service: *service provided directly to customers to support or facilitate a company's core products*

Customer service is the service provided directly to customers to support or facilitate a company's core products. This may be associated with either physical goods or services. Customer service typically includes taking the order, dealing with customer questions and complaints, and arranging repairs to goods.

This book will mainly focus on services as previously defined, but it will also include many examples of customer service, as good customer service is critical to relationship building. In addition, examples will be provided of hidden services that support the production and delivery of services.

Services as theatre

Servicescape: *the environment in which a service is produced and delivered*

Services have also been thought of as theatre (Grove, Fisk & John 2000). There is a stage at which the services are performed by actors (service providers). This is referred to as the **servicescape** — the environment in which a service is produced and delivered (Bitner 1992). There are actors — people who produce and deliver the service, and there is an audience — the customers who consume the performance. Yet there are limitations with this analogy. What about services in which the customers produce and deliver the service? An example for this could be self-serve restaurants, where the customers serve their own meals. This is more like street theatre where the audience is brought into the show and becomes part of the performance.

Service encounters

Service encounters: *interactions between customers and service providers, involving exchange, and varying in complexity and duration*

Dyadic: *involving two parties (in an interaction)*

Several terms have been used by services marketing researchers and practitioners to describe the interactions between service providers and customers. Yet most would agree that **service encounters** are **dyadic** (McColl-Kennedy

1998; Solomon et al. 1985), having a beginning and an end point (Berry 1983), and involving some exchange (Dwyer et al. 1987). Exchange may be regarded as having three components (Hume & McColl-Kennedy 1999). It involves two or more parties, a social network where the parties exchange, and an environment in which the exchange takes place (Dwyer et al. 1987). Singh (1991) argues that service encounters are made up of a number of incidents, some critical to delivery and customer satisfaction. These critical incidents can be defined as 'moments of truth' (Hume & McColl-Kennedy 1999). For instance, when going to visit a doctor, a moment of truth could be arriving at the doctor's surgery and being informed that the doctor has been called out on an emergency and that your appointment will be delayed by an hour or more. This is clearly a critical incident affecting the delivery of the service and satisfaction with the service.

Service encounters may take several forms, differing in terms of their duration and complexity (Bolton 1998; Singh 1991; Huffman & Houston 1993). They may be simple, one-off interactions between a customer and service provider (defined as a simple episode). An example is the purchase of fast food at a take-away store. Alternatively, they may be ongoing relationships with multiple interactions between the service provider and the customer (defined as simple continuous), with an ongoing revenue stream and an ongoing duration (Bolton 1998). Annual rates payments are one such example of a simple continuous encounter. A complex continuous service encounter is one where there is an ongoing revenue stream and an extended ongoing duration requirement to deliver the service (Hume, Sullivan Mort & McColl-Kennedy forthcoming). Ongoing management of an investment portfolio is an example of a complex continuous encounter. In contrast, a complex episodic encounter is one where there is a single revenue stream requiring customer and provider interaction in the delivery and the service (Bolton 1998). Complexity may occur because of high customer value and risk, the need for knowledge and expertise, and difficulties in evaluating the service. Examples of complex episodes are legal conveyancing and obstetric care (Hume, Sullivan Mort & McColl-Kennedy forthcoming). These four types of service encounters are shown graphically in figure 1.1.

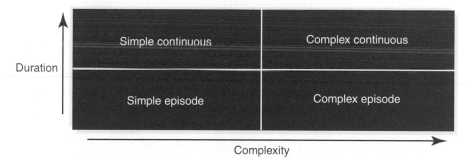

Figure 1.1: Typology for complexity and duration

What's so special about services?

The importance of services, particularly in the Western world, is well acknowledged, with the majority of employed persons being in the services sector. In the United States, approximately 80 per cent of those employed are in services (Zeithaml & Bitner 2000). This is also the case for New Zealand (Statistics

New Zealand 2000), and the percentage of employed persons who are in services in Australia is a little higher, at 82 per cent (ABS 2001).

However, these figures only account for those persons directly employed in the service sector, and do not include hidden service staff. Think about the people who are in the manufacturing and agriculture sectors who offer services such as selling equipment, merchandising and promoting primary industries. For instance, fertiliser companies and farm equipment companies may offer advice to customers regarding the products they produce, and in this way they are providing services. So the figures on persons directly employed in services tell us only part of the story.

There has been considerable debate, particularly during in the 1980s, about the differences between goods and services. Particular criticism, including from Enis and Roering (1981), has been directed at Berry's (1980) definitive article entitled 'Services marketing is different', which argued that services are different from physical goods in that services are:

1. intangible
2. heterogeneous
3. inseparable (i.e. they have simultaneous production and consumption)
4. perishable.

Although academics debate the details regarding the distinctions between services and physical goods marketing, it is important to note that the first person to clarify the differences between services and physical goods was a practitioner, Lynn Shostack. Shostack was vice president at Citibank at the time (Fisk, Brown & Bitner 1993) and made a significant impact through her provocative article 'Breaking free from product marketing' (Shostack 1977), in which she questioned the relevance of product marketing to services, particularly to banking services, where she was working.

It is possible to argue that some physical goods are closely associated with support services; that some physical goods cannot be easily stored (which is certainly the case for services); and that some goods have different uses and could be regarded as heterogeneous. However, there are a number of issues that tend to be associated with services, and these impact on their marketing. These issues are:

1. intangibility
2. inseparability
3. heterogeneity
4. the role of the customer in the production and delivery
5. perishability
6. ownership
7. evaluation difficulty.

Intangibility

Intangible: describes something that cannot be seen, touched or tasted

Unlike most physical goods, services are **intangible**. Services are acts, performances and experiences. They cannot be touched, tasted or taken home for a test drive! However, some services are associated with physical goods. (For example, consulting is regarded as an intangible service but it is usually accompanied by a physical report.) Likewise some physical goods are often produced and delivered to the customer with intangible support services. (For example, advice is given to a customer when a physical product such as a VCR is purchased.)

It is helpful to think about the tangibility of goods and services as being on a continuum, rather than thinking about physical goods in one category and services in another. At one end of the continuum there are highly intangible services such as consulting and teaching. At the other end there are highly tangible products like VCRs and cars. The concept of the tangibility continuum was put forward by Shostack in 1977 and is reproduced in figure 1.2. The following Services Marketing on the Web vignette extends this idea to show how a resort has tried to help potential customers better understand its service by focusing on tangible promotional elements.

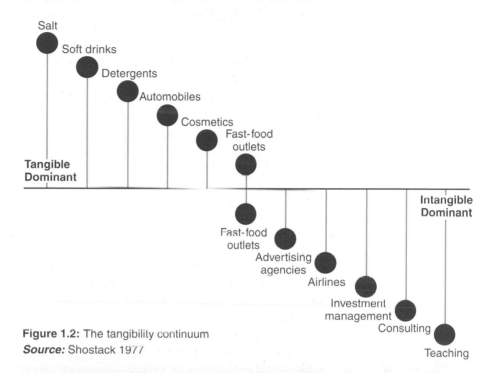

Figure 1.2: The tangibility continuum
Source: Shostack 1977

Services Marketing on the Web:
Using online tools to 'tangibilise' a service

Service organisations use tangible promotional materials such as hard-copy brochures, reports and videos to help 'tangibilise' a service. Tingirana, a five star resort at Noosa in Queensland just north of Brisbane, uses not only a brochure to promote itself but also a website — www.tingirana.com.au.

The Internet is accessible to a large number of people, particularly the type of customer Tingirana is trying to capture. The opening home page shows changing photographs of Noosa's beaches and shopping areas, and the resort's pool area. Five stars to symbolise Tingirana's five-star rating move down the page to reassure potential customers of the resort's reputation. Potential customers can read about the facilities at the resort, see a typical floor plan of two units, see the tariffs for different types of room and in different seasons. The virtual tour features 360-degree views from within an apartment and from the balcony. This way the viewer can imagine what it would be like to stay at the resort.

Tingirana reinforces the tangibility of the experience by allowing web users to download a brochure of the resort. The brochure shows very physical things associated with a holiday stay: the beach and wine glass signifying wining and dining and the 'good times'. The brochure shows people doing things to reinforce the pleasurable experience that potential guests can expect to enjoy. All these features serve to reassure a potential customer of the quality of the service provided at the resort.

Virtual tours are used widely in other tourism areas. For instance, potential customers can take a virtual tour of 'The Spit' at Southport at the Gold Coast by going to www.travelau.com.au/gold-coast or a tour of Denmark at www.vtour.dk/vtb/startkort.htm.

Virtual tours are also being employed by health professionals. Patients who are about to have an operation can visit a web site and see what is going to happen to their body during the operation. It is also possible to see what different parts of the body look like through web sites such as www.medtropolis.com/Vbody.asp and www.besthealth.com. Given that medical services are difficult to evaluate and understand because one cannot see inside one's own body, websites that illustrate the various body parts, and what to expect during and after surgery, can reduce much of the uncertainty and stress associated with medical procedures.

Inseparability

Unlike physical goods, it is often difficult to separate the service from the person who performs the service (the service provider). This means that the service provider plays a particularly important role. How the service provider interacts with the customer affects the customer's perceptions of the service and how satisfied the customer is, overall, with the service. It is difficult to separate the dentist from the work that they perform on the patient's mouth, or to separate the consultant from the consulting work they do for an organisation. If the dentist or consultant appears to be less than focused on the task, doesn't return phone calls and arrives late to appointments, then this is likely to affect the way their work is perceived by the consumer.

In contrast, it is easier to separate a physical good from the person who sold the item. Even if a person selling you the physical good (such as sound equipment, a bicycle or a car) is rude to the customer, this does not directly affect the performance of the sound equipment, bicycle or car.

Heterogeneity

Heterogeneity: difference or variability in a service

Given that different service providers perform services for their customers, it is difficult to achieve uniformity of service. **Heterogeneity** is the result of different people providing the same service in a slightly different way because no two people are identical. One restaurant waiter may give customers a very cheery welcome and follow up with efficient yet warm service, while another waiter from the same restaurant may pay less attention to the needs to the customer, be offhand in interactions with the customers, and be tardy in service. These differences in attitude and actions will typically result in very different customer perceptions of the quality of the restaurant's service and the customer's overall satisfaction level.

In contrast, physical goods such as VCRs and cars are checked meticulously for compliance with quality standards. If they do not comply exactly with the specifications, they are rejected. Certainly service providers can be trained to offer uniformity of service, but it is difficult to get people to conform precisely to service standards. Moreover, individual service providers may themselves vary in the way they deliver services on a weekly basis. For example, if a service provider is tired they may be less willing to be patient with a customer and may not give the necessary amount of time to the customer. However, at the beginning of a shift, they may be very happy to give the customer the amount of time the customer requires.

Perishability

Unlike physical goods, services cannot be stored. An airline seat cannot be stored after the plane has taken off. Similarly, a ticket for a particular show cannot be used after the show has taken place.

Likewise, services cannot be returned after they have been purchased. For instance, after a meal has been eaten, the meal cannot be returned in the way a product can be returned to the counter of a store.

We shall show in the service recovery chapter (chapter 13) that when customers believe the service is unsatisfactory, service providers can attempt to retain the customer by giving the customer a refund or discount, and/or apologising to them. The service itself, however, cannot be returned.

Role of the customer in the production and delivery

When customers go to a theme park or a restaurant, they are part of the service production and delivery (Berry 1980). For example, customers at a water park have to join in the various water sport activities to enjoy the experience. They cannot sit back and wait for the experience to be delivered as they may do with the purchase of an electrical product.

With services, other customers can directly affect the way services are perceived by the customer. For instance, if there are very boisterous customers present at the water park, other customers may feel threatened and unsafe. They may find the language offensive or get a headache from the noise, resulting in a less than satisfactory experience.

Ownership

Services cannot be owned. We buy tickets to a show but we do not buy the whole show. We stay at a hotel or resort but we do not take the hotel or resort home with us as we do physical goods. Although services cannot be owned, they certainly can be remembered. After we have been to a hotel, resort or show, we take away with us the memories of the service, such as how we were feeling during our stay at the hotel or resort and how we felt during the show.

Evaluation difficulty

Credence services: services that are difficult to evaluate even after use

We have seen that, due to the intangible nature of services, organisations use physical evidence such brochures, web sites, business cards and reports to promote themselves and allow the customer to evaluate their service. However, some services are more difficult to evaluate than others, even after use, and these are called **credence services**. These services are difficult to evaluate even after use and are regarded as being high in credence qualities (Zeithaml 1981).

An example of a credence service is medical surgery. How do you know if the surgeon has operated competently and the surgery has been a success if you don't have a degree in medicine? Likewise, how do you evaluate legal work?

Experiential services:
those that are easily
evaluated after use

Experiential services, on the other hand, are more easily evaluated after use. For example, after you have been to a theme park or a restaurant, you are in a very good position to evaluate the service. Credence and experiential services are further discussed in chapter 2.

Classification of services

Although it can be demonstrated that services differ from physical goods in a number of key ways, services should be not grouped together as one. It is important to recognise that there are different types of services and different ways of classifying services. Lovelock's (1983) seminal article suggests several different ways to divide services. One particularly useful way of classifying services is to identify whether the service is primarily aimed at people or things, and whether the service acts are tangible or intangible (Lovelock 1983).

As shown in figure 1.3, the four-way classification scheme identifies the following groups:

1. tangible action to people's bodies (people processing), including transportation, hairdressing, facials and surgery
2. tangible actions to goods, including air freight, lawn mowing, vet services and car repair
3. intangible actions to people, such as public broadcasting, sporting events and plays
4. intangible actions directed at things, such as insurance, consulting, engineering and architectural services.

	Who or what is the direct recipient of the service?	
	People	Things
What is the nature of the service act? Tangible actions	*Services directed at people's bodies* • Health care • Passenger transportation • Beauty salons • Exercise clinics • Restaurants • Haircutting	*Services directed at goods and other physical possessions* • Freight transportation • Industrial equipment repair and maintenance • Janitorial services • Laundry and dry cleaning • Landscaping/lawn care • Veterinary care
Intangible actions	*Services directed at people's minds* • Education • Broadcasting • Information services • Theatres • Museums	*Services directed at intangible assets* • Banking • Legal services • Accounting • Securities • Insurance

Figure 1.3: Lovelock's four-way classification scheme — people versus things/tangible versus intangible
Source: Lovelock 1983

Services marketing mix

The 'marketing mix' is the term used to describe all the things an organisation does to cater to the needs of the customer. Traditionally, the product-based marketing mix has been divided into four elements: product, price, place (distribution) and promotion. In the **services marketing mix**, the product is the service and we add three additional elements relevant to services: people, process and physical evidence, which are described in more detail in the following sections. Figure 1.4 illustrates the seven Ps of the services marketing mix.

Figure 1.4: The seven elements of the services marketing mix

People

The **people** who deliver a service to the customer are critical to the success of the service because, as we have already pointed out, it is very difficult to separate the service from the service provider. However, the service provider is not the only person important in services. Other people indirectly involved in the service production and delivery also play important roles. For instance, the person who assists the dentist in preparing the instruments for the procedures plays a role in the delivery of the dental service, as does the person who cleans up in the restaurant at the end of the evening. Indeed, people in services can be defined as all those who play a part in the production and delivery of the service. These people may be management, service providers, support personnel or even other customers.

Some organisations, such as Ritz Carlton, Singapore Airlines, McDonald's, TNT and Disney World, spend millions of dollars each year on developing their people and providing the necessary support, policies and processes required in order for them to deliver excellent services and excellent service. Singapore Airlines believes that to maintain their position as a leading global organisation they need to be committed to 'recruiting and nurturing bright, dynamic individuals' (Singapore Airlines 2002). McDonald's (2002) contends that its 'people promise is more than words', believing and practising:
1. respect and recognition
2. values and leadership behaviour
3. competitive pay and benefits
4. learning, development, and personal growth
5. resources to get the job done.

Process

The **process** is all the activities involved in producing and delivering the service. Some activities are seen directly by customers, for example the receptionist of a hotel taking the information to check the customer in, then the bell-boy taking the luggage to the room. These activities are referred to as **frontstage activities**. However, other activities that are unseen by the customer, such as kitchen staff preparing meals and laundry staff washing the sheets, are called **backstage activities**. Thus, a process may involve frontstage and backstage activities. More details on frontstage and backstage activities are provided in chapter 12.

Physical evidence

Have you ever wondered why hotel staff fold the toilet tissue in the bathroom when they have cleaned the room? It is not to be pretentious, but to show the customer that a service has taken place and that the room is now cleaned. This is **physical evidence** that a service has been performed. Physical evidence includes all physical representations of a service, such as business cards, reports, signage and equipment. Consultants provide reports to their clients and tax accountants give customers their tax return. The physical evidence helps a customer to assess a service when that service is performed out of the customer's sight. Physical evidence is extensively used in credence services, particularly in the form of reports, videos and simulations to show customers what will happen during the service. For example, patients about to undergo an operation may be given videos that show what will happen in the operation, thereby relieving their fears.

Physical evidence is also used by organisations to reinforce their positioning. For example, a high-priced, downtown accountant is likely to provide clients with a well-presented, bound report, while a less expensive accountant is likely to give clients an unbound, possibly stapled, report.

Managerial challenges for service organisations

The characteristics of services, outlined above, pose special challenges for management. Because services cannot be owned, stored or returned, estimating demand is particularly difficult. How do band venues, hotels, restaurants and airlines manage demand? As we will see in the chapters on managing demand (chapter 8) and pricing (chapter 11), demand is often managed through differential pricing. This is common with holiday apartment and hotel room rental rates. In the high season (when demand is high) prices are very high. Conversely, in the low season, prices are very attractive so as to avoid having empty rooms.

As other customers can directly affect how the service is delivered, as well as the overall satisfaction level, it is important for management to train customers in terms of what is expected of them in a service establishment and, if necessary, remove customers who behave in an offensive way. In five-star resorts and upmarket restaurants, for example, management, staff and other customers have expectations about how staff and customers should behave — even what they should wear. Sometimes signs are provided in the establishment, detailing the dress code. For example, it is common to see signs saying 'Shirts must be worn in the restaurant' and 'No thongs'.

Training staff to interact with customers appropriately, in order to reach uniform levels of service provision, is a very important function of management. Chapter 12, which deals with service delivery, elaborates on the importance of proper training in ensuring that services are of an appropriate standard for customers. Getting the right balance between imposing service standards (homogeneity versus heterogeneity) and still allowing the staff to be natural is a key challenge. Developing scripts and roleplaying, which will be discussed further in chapter 2, are essential to accomplish this balance.

A holistic approach — the service management trinity

To fully understand the complexity of producing and delivering services in today's world, it is important to grasp that marketing of services does not occur in a vacuum and that the successful production and delivery of services is not the responsibility of the marketing department alone. The successful production and delivery of services at the appropriate quality requires the cooperation of human resources, operations and marketing (Gummesson 1991). The mutual dependence of these key functions has been coined the **service management trinity**.

Service management trinity: the mutual interdependence of human resources, operations and marketing — a combination that will successfully produce and deliver services

Human resources

As we have seen above, it is difficult to separate 'marketing' and 'human resources' in services marketing, because without people many services could not be delivered. Employees play a central role in interactions with customers through individual encounters. They can directly influence how customers feel, and this in turn affects customer satisfaction and the nature of the customer's relationship with the organisation. It is clear that if customers are to experience high levels of satisfaction, then employees will need to provide good customer service through adding value and providing high levels of service quality.

Staff who work backstage, processing information and checking that components which make up the service are working well, play a vital role, even though they may never be seen by the customer. They may also be instrumental in putting together a plan to promote the service. Sometimes these people are referred to as part time marketers, because they are vital to the production and delivery of the service but they may not have a formal marketing title in the organisation.

Figure 1.5: Importance of human resources

As shown in figure 1.5, in order to be able to deliver value-added service in their various encounters with customers, service employees need to feel good about themselves and what they are doing. Management can significantly influence how employees feel. They can do this by showing staff that they are valued, and by training them to add value and to use their emotional intelligence when interacting with customers. Furthermore, staff who perform need to be rewarded for their efforts so that they continue to feel valued by the organisation.

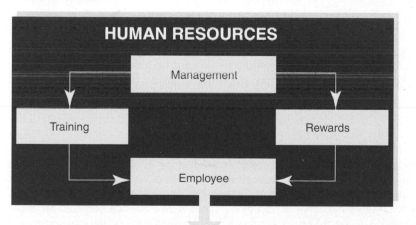

Often organisations give their staff training when they join the organisation, but management needs to continue to provide suitable training if their staff are to feel good about themselves and their work. The end result is customer satisfaction and a positive, ongoing relationship between the customer and the organisation.

Emotions

Emotions: feelings or affective responses

The **emotions** of both customers and employees are critical to the production and delivery of services. After considerable neglect, managers are beginning to acknowledge that emotions (feelings or affective responses) are part of everyday working life (Ashkanasy, Zerbe & Härtel 2002), and that the work environment — including environmental conditions, roles and job design — initiates emotions (Ashkanasy et al. 2002). Emotions have been studied by marketers largely in terms of consumer reactions to advertising and promotions (Richins 1997), or in terms of the use of products and services (Holbrook et al. 1984; Oliver 1994). More recently, researchers have investigated the role of emotions in service recovery; that is, how customers feel when things go wrong in the delivery of a service and during attempts to recover the customer after service failure (Nguyen & McColl-Kennedy forthcoming). This is discussed further in chapter 13.

Knowing how to respond to customers, including how to manage one's own emotions, is important, so organisations are increasingly providing training on emotional labour. **Emotional labour** takes place when service providers are required to display certain types of emotions, such as positive emotions (including being happy, smiling, and being attentive to customers) and negative emotions (including being stern faced). Funeral directors and debt collectors, for instance, are trained to display negative emotions. Rafaeli and Sutton (1989) demonstrated that service providers' displays of positive emotions were directly linked to positive customer emotions, and these in turn were linked to sales. Emotional labour is thought to be directly associated with service quality (Schneider & Bowen 1985). Recent research by Pugh (2001) has shown that there is a positive relationship between positive displays of emotion and service quality.

Emotional labour: the degree to which felt emotions are controlled so that socially desirable emotions are expressed

Operations

Operations need to function properly so that promises of the service match the delivery of the service. It is not enough just to have well-trained and well-motivated staff, and for management to fully support the staff. Systems must be in place to allow the delivery to be carried out. Think about what a theme park experience would be like if some of the rides were not working due to lack of maintenance. And how would a restaurant be able to satisfy customers if some of the main dishes were not available because essential food items had not been purchased? Other operational functions include such things as reservations, processing orders, paying invoices and carrying out backstage support activities. Some organisations spend thousands of dollars each year on maintenance of equipment and on the purchase of technology.

TNT believes its strength lies in providing excellence in operations in addition to high quality people (TNT 2002). Specifically, in terms of operations, TNT Logistics has developed a 'zero defect start-up policy' with key performance indicators that specifically measure customer expectations. Once a new service begins, TNT monitors the service using these performance indicators to ensure the service meets customer expectations.

Golden Rule Printing, a US printing firm, aims to provide the best possible service to its customers. In order to achieve this, it operates 24 hours a day and has invested in climate-controlled warehouse facilities to ensure that both the raw printing materials and the finished products are stored in the best possible way. The organisation also uses computer tracking so that shipments can be monitored and customers receive their orders as requested.

Services Marketing Action:
Sydney Harbour Bridge climb

Paul Cave's company takes people over the Sydney Harbour Bridge. It took nine years to make the dream happen. Mr Cave had to negotiate with 13 unions working on the bridge. But eventually, persistence paid off. Customers bring in about $150 per head. For what? An experience. The business has a turnover of $75 million and over 500 000 customers. The key to the success is the systems Mr Cave has in place. The entire operation is seamless, from 'the way staff handle the climbers to the wave after wave of climbers who traverse the bridge without incident' (Switzer 2001). Staff obviously play a key role in the delivery of this service. Staff need to help customers feel safe yet excited about the walk they are about to experience. With such a high volume of customers, it is important to have smooth operations and keep people moving across the bridge. This ensures that the next lot of people waiting to get onto the bridge will not be delayed.

Given that the bridge is high above the harbour and that windy conditions make the journey potentially dangerous, the organisation needs to have strict safety policies in place. Each customer must remove all items of jewellery and wear a jump suit. They are attached to a harness, which is attached to a metal bar on the bridge. In this way, customers can feel safe and they can also be kept moving. Before climbing the bridge, customers practise walking in the harness. Once at the top of the bridge, the tour guide takes a photograph of the group so they have a tangible reminder of their experience. The proof of success of the Harbour Bridge climb can be gauged not only in profits, but in the high levels of customer satisfaction that the company claims. It is reported that 97.8 per cent of customers say that they received value for money (Switzer 2001).

Marketing

Marketing is about satisfying customers with services that are promoted appropriately, delivered at the right time, in the right way and at the right price. Figure 1.6 shows the key components of marketing: buyer behaviour, customer perceptions, marketing strategies and marketing research.

As shown in figure 1.6, all the key components of marketing are linked, with marketing research being a key function. It is important to understand who the customers are and why they buy. It is also important to understand customer perceptions of service quality, value and satisfaction. With understanding through marketing research, organisations can better develop marketing strategies that are truly customer focused.

Figure 1.6: Key components of marketing

Framework for the book

Figure 1.7 shows how all three areas of human resources, operations and marketing fit together, and the complex interplay between the components. It also serves as a conceptual framework for the book.

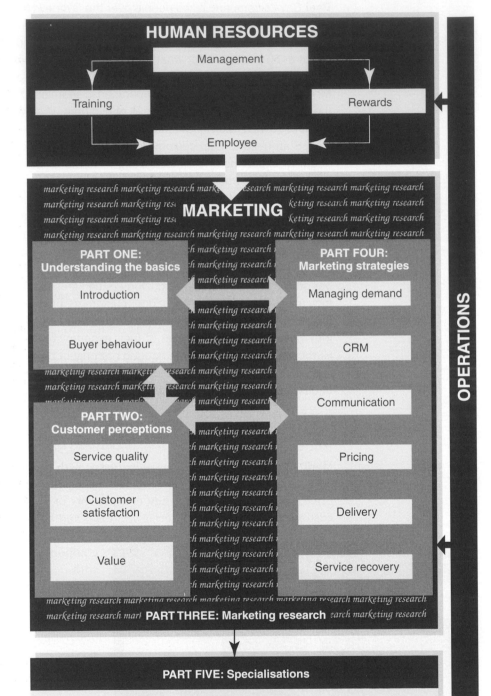

Figure 1.7: Conceptual framework for services marketing

Part 1 discusses the basics. It contains this chapter, which introduces services. Chapters 2 and 3 discuss the importance of buyer behaviour. Specifically, individual buyer behaviour is discussed in chapter 2, while business-to-business buyer behaviour is discussed in chapter 3.

In Part 2, customer perceptions are explored. Chapter 4 discusses service quality. Customer satisfaction is covered in chapter 5, and value is the focus of chapter 6.

Part 3 contains the chapter on services research, chapter 7. Marketing research should help inform the organisation as to which service products, which pricing strategy, which promotion, which distribution (place), which people and which types of physical evidence to provide and which processes to use.

Part 4 focuses on marketing strategies. Chapter 8 covers managing demand, a strategy that has been briefly outlined in this introductory chapter. Chapter 9 discusses customer relationship marketing (CRM). Customer relationship marketing clearly puts the customer at the centre of activities and involves the entire organisation, so that there is a seamless integration of the front and back offices. Essentially, CRM is a process of understanding the customer, and building and maintaining a relationship with the customer over time. The customer therefore feels close to the organisation, and so uses terms such as 'my bank', 'my dentist', 'my gym'. Technology can assist CRM, but does not on its own constitute CRM.

Communication of the services marketing mix to customers is critical, but so too is communication between customers and services providers, and between service providers within the organisation. Communication is discussed in chapter 10. Chapter 11 focuses on one of the seven Ps of services marketing — pricing.

Delivery can be considered part of the seven Ps of services marketing but can also be discussed as part of operations and human resources. It has a special place in services, owing to inseparability between the service provider and the service. It is therefore discussed separately in chapter 12.

Sometimes things go wrong in the delivery of services, and customers feel dissatisfied with the service. When this occurs they sometimes don't complain, but at other times they complain to their friends and associates and sometimes to the organisation itself. It is important to try and recover the customer who has been dissatisfied, and chapter 13 discusses ways in which this can be done.

Part 5 comprises five chapters which cover specialisations in services. The first of these is chapter 14, which contains e-services. Chapter 15 explores tourism and hospitality issues. Franchising is covered in chapter 16, sports services in chapter 17, and public sector and government marketing is discussed in the final chapter, chapter 18.

Summary

LO1: Explain what services are.
- Services are acts, performances and experiences.
- Services can also be thought of as theatre, where the servicescape is the environment in which the services are produced and delivered, the 'actors' are the people who produce and deliver the services, and the 'audience' are the customers who consume the service.
- The services this textbook focuses on are those services that are an organisation's main focus or 'product'. They are considered to be different to hidden services (which are support services that are not the main focus of

an organisation), and to customer service, (which is provided to support an organisation's core product).

LO2: Discuss specific issues relevant to services.

- Services are different from physical goods in that they can never be owned. They are intangible, heterogeneous, perishable and inseparable (simultaneously produced and consumed).
- Some services cannot be evaluated even after they have been consumed; these are regarded as credence services. Services that can be evaluated are called experiential services.

LO3: Outline the seven Ps of the services mix.

- The seven Ps of the services mix are service product, price, place, promotion, people, process and physical evidence.

LO4: Identify the managerial challenges that the characteristics of services create.

- Because services cannot be owned, stored or returned, estimating demand is particularly difficult.
- Because services are heterogenous, staff must be trained in order to reach uniform levels of service provision.
- As other customers can directly affect customer satisfaction, management should train customers in behavioural standards.

LO 5: Discuss the importance of the cooperation between marketing, operations and human resources to produce quality services.

- In order to successfully provide services to their customers, organisations must recognise the importance of ensuring that marketing, human resources and operations work together in a fully cooperative and integrative fashion.
- The successful marketing of a service is not the responsibility of the marketing department alone.
- Service employees play a critical role in terms of service delivery and satisfaction. They can add value to services and enhance customers' perception of value and of the organisation. Moreover, they will directly influence how customers feel and their satisfaction levels through each encounter they have with their customers.
- Operations also need to function properly so that promises match the delivery of the service.

 key terms

Backstage activities: all those that are part of the production and/or delivery of a service but that are not visible to the customer (p. 11)

Credence services: services that are difficult to evaluate even after use (p. 9)

Customer service: service provided directly to customers to support or facilitate a company's core products (p. 4)

Dyadic: involving two parties (in an interaction) (p. 4)

Emotional labour: the degree to which felt emotions are controlled so that socially desirable emotions are expressed (p. 14)

Emotions: feelings or affective responses (p. 14)

Experiential services: those that are easily evaluated after use (p. 10)

Frontstage activities: those that are visible to the customer (p. 11)

Heterogeneity: a difference or variability in a service (p. 8)

Hidden (support) services: services an organisation offers to support, promote and/or facilitate its physical goods (p. 4)

Intangible: describes something that cannot be seen, touched or tasted (p. 6)

People: all those who play a part in the production and delivery of the service (p. 11)

Physical evidence: all physical representations of the service, such as business cards, reports, signage and equipment (p. 12)

Process: all activities involved in producing and delivering the service (p. 11)

Service encounters: interactions between customers and service providers, involving exchange and varying in complexity and duration (p. 4)

Service management trinity: the mutual interdependence of marketing, human resources and operations — a combination that will successfully produce and deliver services (p. 13)

Services: acts, performances and experiences (p. 3)

Servicescape: the environment in which a service is produced and delivered (p. 4)

Services marketing mix: includes service product, price, place (distribution), promotion, people, process and physical evidence (p. 11)

 review questions

1. What makes services different from physical goods? Provide examples.
2. Why is integration of marketing, human resources and operations important to the success of the production and delivery of services? Give examples to illustrate.
3. What is meant by the term 'part-time marketers'? What role do they play in the delivery of services? Be specific.
4. Outline the seven Ps of services marketing. Using an example of your choice, show how each of these concepts is used in practice.
5. What are credence services? How are they different from experiential services? Provide specific examples of each to illustrate.

 application questions

1. Think about your favourite restaurant. To what extent could the concept of 'service as theatre' be applied?
2. With reference to a professional service that you have experienced, show how each of the seven Ps can be applied.
3. How useful are the classifications of services referred to in this chapter? Illustrate using three services that you have used in the last 12 months.
4. How useful is the Internet in helping to make credence services such as open heart surgery or neurosurgery easier to understand and evaluate? What else do you think these service providers could do? Be specific.

5. It is often said that it is people who make the difference in service organisations. Identify a service organisation that has, in your view, excellent people. What makes these people so special and effective as service providers? Compare this with another organisation that, in your view, has poor service providers.

vignette questions

1. Read the International Issues vignette on pages 3–4 and answer the following questions.
   (a) Do you think that Australian service providers should give different levels of service to different cultural groups?
   (b) Outline the way different cultural groups might give different assessments of service quality and satisfaction. Be specific.
2. Read the Services Marketing on the Web vignette on page 7 and answer the following questions.
   (a) Using the information in the website, how would you describe this resort? Which tangible elements helped convey this?
   (b) Which other services could benefit from using such tangible websites?
   (c) What other tangible things could the resort do or offer to compensate for customers never being able to 'own' the service?
   (d) Outline the benefits and disadvantages of medical procedures websites.
3. Read the Services Marketing Action vignette on page 15 and answer the following questions.
   (a) What sorts of people would be best for this type of job?
   (b) What sorts of training would these staff need?

recommended readings

The concept of service as theatre is discussed in the following article:
Grove, S. J., Fisk, R. P. & John, J. 2000, ' Services as theater: guidelines and implications', in Swartz, T. A. & Iacobucci, D. (eds), *Handbook of Services Marketing Management*, pp. 21–35, Sage, Thousand Oaks, CA.

For a full discussion of ways to classify services, see Lovelock's classic article:
Lovelock, C. 1983, 'Classifying services to gain strategic marketing insights', *Journal of Marketing*, vol. 47, pp. 9–20.

The following article is considered a classic paper on the distinguishing characteristics of services marketing:
Shostack, G. L. 1977, 'Breaking free from product marketing', *Journal of Marketing*, vol. 41, April, pp. 73–80.

references

Ashkanasy, N. M., Zerbe, W. J. & Härtel, E. J. (eds) 2002, *Managing Emotions in the Workplace*, M. E. Sharpe, Armonk, NY.
Berry, L. L. 1980, 'Services marketing is different', *Business*, vol. 30 (May–June), pp. 24–29.

Berry, L. L. 1983, 'Relationship marketing', in Berry, L. L., Shostack, G. L. & Upah, G. D. (eds), *Emerging Perspectives on Services Marketing*, American Marketing Association, Chicago, pp. 25–8.

Bitner, M. J. 1992, 'Servicescapes: the impact of physical surroundings on consumers and employees', *Journal of Marketing*, vol. 56, April, pp. 57–71.

Bolton, R. N. 1998, 'A dynamic model of the duration of the customer's relationship with a continuous service provider: the role of satisfaction', *Marketing Science*, vol. 17, no. 1, pp. 45–65.

Dwyer, F. R., Schurr, P. H. & Oh, S. 1987, *Moments of Truth: New Strategies for Today's Customer Driven Economy*, Harper & Row, New York.

Enis, B. M. & Roering, K. J. 1981, 'Services marketing: different products, similar strategy', in Donnelly, J. H. & George, W. R. (eds), *Marketing of Services*, American Marketing Association, Chicago, pp. 1–4.

Fisk, R. P., Brown, S. S. & Bitner, M. J. 1993, 'Tracking the evolution of the services marketing literature', *Journal of Retailing*, vol. 69, no. 1, pp. 61–103.

Grönroos, C. 2000, *Service Management and Marketing: A Customer Relationship Management Approach*, 2nd edn, John Wiley & Sons, New York.

Grove, S. J., Fisk, R. P. & John, J. 2000, 'Services as theater: guidelines and implications', in Swartz, T. A. & Iacobucci, D. (eds), *Handbook of Services Marketing and Management*, pp. 21–35, Sage, Thousand Oaks, CA.

Gummesson, E. 1991, 'Marketing — orientation revisited: the crucial role of the part-time marketer', *European Journal of Marketing*, vol. 25, no. 2, pp. 60–75.

Hofstede, G. H. 1980, *Culture's Consequences: International Differences in Work-Related Values*, Sage, Thousand Oaks, CA.

Holbrook, M. B., Chestnut, R. W., Oliva, T. A. & Greenleaf, E.A. 1984, 'Play as a consumption experience: the roles of emotions, performance and personality in the enjoyment of games' , *Journal of Consumer Research*, vol. 11, pp. 728–39.

Hume, M. & McColl-Kennedy, J. R. 1999, 'Episodic, extended and continuous service encounters: a theoretical framework', *Proceedings*, ANZMAC, December, Sydney.

Hume, M., Sullivan Mort, G. & McColl-Kennedy, J. R. forthcoming, 'Service encounters framework', working paper.

Kim, U. 1994, 'Individualism and collectivism: conceptual clarification and elaboration', in Kim, U., Triandis, H. C., Kagitcibasi, C., Choi, S. C. & Yoon, G. (eds), *Individualism and Collectivism: Theory, Method and Applications*, Sage, Thousand Oaks, CA, pp. 19–40.

Liu, R. R. & McClure, P. 2001, 'Recognising cross-cultural differences in consumer complaint behaviour and intentions: an empirical examination', *Journal of Consumer Marketing*, vol. 18, no. 1, pp. 54–74.

Lovelock, C. 1983, 'Classifying services to gain strategic marketing insights', *Journal of Marketing*, vol. 47, pp. 9–20.

McColl-Kennedy, J. R. 1998, 'Customer satisfaction, assessment, intentions and outcome behaviors of dyadic service encounters: a conceptual model', in Ford, J. & Honeycutt, E. Jr, (eds), *Developments in Marketing Science*, vol. 21, The Academy of Marketing Science, Coral Gables, FL, pp. 48–54.

McDonald's Corporation, accessed 30 May 2002, 'Why McDonald's has a people promise and a people vision', www.mcdonalds.com/corporate/promise/index.html.

Nguyen, D. T. & McColl-Kennedy, J.R. forthcoming, 'Customer cognitive appraisal and anger in service recovery context: a conceptual framework', *Australasian Marketing Journal*.

Oliver, R. L. 1984, 'Conceptual issues in the structural analysis of consumption emotions, satisfaction and quality', in *Advances in Consumer Research*, vol. 21, pp. 16–22.

Pugh, D. 2001, 'Service with a smile: emotional contagion in service encounters', *Academy of Management Journal*, vol. 44, pp. 1018–27.

Rafaeli, A. & Sutton, R. I. 1989, 'The expression of emotion in organizational life', *Research in Organizational Behavior*, vol. 11, pp. 1–42.

Reisinger, Y. & Turner, L. 1999, 'A cultural analysis of Japanese tourists: challenges for tourism marketers', *European Journal of Marketing*, vol. 33, no. 11/12, pp. 1203–27.

Richins, M. L. 1997, 'Measuring emotions in the consumption experience, *Journal of Consumer Research*, vol. 24, pp. 127–46.

Schneider , B. & Bowen, D. 1985, 'Employee and customer perceptions of service in banks: replication and extension', *Journal of Applied Psychology*, vol. 70, pp. 423–33.

Shostack, G. L. 1977, 'Breaking free from product marketing', *Journal of Marketing*, vol. 41, April, pp. 73–80.

Singapore Airlines, accessed 30 May 2002, 'Careers', www.singaporeair.com/saa/app/saa.

Singh, J. 1991, 'Understanding the structure of consumers' satisfaction evaluations of service delivery', *Journal of Academy of Marketing Science*, vol. 19, no. 3, pp. 223–244.

Solomon, M., Surprenant, C., Czepiel, J. & Gutman, E. 1985, 'A role theory perspective on dynamic interactions: the service encounter', *Journal of Marketing*, vol. 49, winter, pp. 99–111.

Statistics New Zealand 2000, *New Zealand Official Yearbook*, 102nd edn, David Bateman, Auckland.

Switzer, P. 2001, 'No bridge too far for this climber', *The Australian*, 26 April, p. 22.

TNT, accessed 2002, www.tnt.com.

Zeithaml, V. A. 1981, 'How customer evaluation processes differ between goods and services', in Donnelly, J. A. & George, W. R., *Marketing of Services*, American Marketing Association, pp. 181–90.

Zeithaml, V. A. & Bitner, M. J. 2000, *Services Marketing: Integrating Customer Focus Across the Firm*, 2nd edn, Irwin McGraw-Hill, Sydney.

Chapter 2
Buyer behaviour

Lesley White

LEARNING OBJECTIVES

After reading this chapter you should be able to:

- explain the impact of the characteristics of services on the purchase decision process
- outline the consumer's purchase decision process for services
- describe the factors that affect the pre-purchase phase, including perceived risk
- discuss the factors that are relevant to the consumer during the service encounter
- describe the relevance of the post-purchase phase of the decision process
- analyse the role of culture in consumer decision making and discuss how it is particularly important for services marketing.

CHAPTER OUTLINE

The chapter begins with a discussion of why, when it comes to services, consumer behaviour differs from the traditional models used for physical products. The consumer's purchase decision process is then addressed in three sections: pre-purchase, the service encounter and post-purchase. In the pre-purchase phase, both the internal and external factors affecting the purchase decision are considered, including the important issue of perceived risk. Following this, the service encounter is described, and the topics of role and script theory, the customer's emotions and mood and the impact of other customers are addressed. The post-purchase stage is then detailed, including the key issues of customer satisfaction, repeat purchase and loyalty. Finally, increasing globalisation of services and the emergence of a borderless business environment have resulted in cross-national and cross-cultural service provisions becoming more common. Therefore, culture and cultural impacts on consumer behaviour are examined in some detail.

Introduction

One person will visit only their well-known family dentist, another will choose a dental practitioner from the Yellow Pages and a third refuses to go near any dentist at all. Why?

The answer lies in the differing needs and wants of consumers, and this in turn is determined by their individual personalities and market experiences. The person who will not visit anyone but their family dentist may be a risk-averse person who dislikes making decisions and feels a high degree of stress about making the 'right choice'. Alternatively, they might be a brand-loyal consumer who is loath to change once they have found a product or service with which they are happy.

Understanding the motivations of different consumers and meeting their needs is central to any definition of marketing. In order to achieve this, companies must have a thorough knowledge of consumers and their behaviour.

So important is it to understand the customer that a lack of understanding of the customer is the first of the five gaps in Zeithaml, Berry and Parasuraman's (1988) conceptual model of service quality. While this model will be thoroughly examined in chapter 4, it is important to note that the basis of the model is a comparison of a customer's expectations and **perceptions**. If a customer's expectations are higher than their post-purchase perceptions, then the customer will be dissatisfied. However, if their perceptions meet or exceed their expectations, then the customer will be satisfied. Therefore, how well a firm understands its customers' needs will, in part, determine the customers' ultimate satisfaction with the service delivered.

While the models of **consumer behaviour** (such as the decision making, classical conditioning and learning models) which were developed for marketing physical goods are applicable to services, some modifications are necessary due to the well-established differences between services and goods: intangibility, variability, inseparability and perishability, as outlined in chapter 1.

The intangibility of services has the effect of making the consumer's evaluation of services more difficult, which therefore increases the levels of **risk** that the consumer perceives. The variability of services further exacerbates this perception of risk. Some consumers are risk-averse and will behave in a manner that minimises their risk exposure, for example by remaining with their current service provider even if dissatisfied. Others will seek significant amounts of information and advice before changing to a new service provider. Yet other consumers exhibit greater risk-taking behaviour and will seek new experiences readily.

The inseparability of services means that the consumer is part of the service delivery and a poor choice of service is therefore likely to have more immediate and significant implications than the choice of an unsatisfactory product. Indeed, the consumer can influence the outcome of the service encounter by their behaviour and actions during the encounter. In addition, the consumer's involvement in the service delivery may lead to different allocations of blame.

Finally, perishability may have implications for consumer behaviour in terms of the individual's response to the need for queuing or reservation systems. Some individuals queue patiently; others fume and even complain; some jump the queue. Consumer behaviour varies from individual to

Perception: the overall impression gained by the consumer after the service encounter

Consumer behaviour: the actions and mental processes that lead to and comprise the purchase and subsequent use of a product or service

Risk: exposure of the consumer to the chance of injury, loss, damage or other negative consequences resulting from the purchase decision

individual. The implications of each of these four characteristics of services and the ways in which companies can respond to them were addressed in detail in chapter 1.

Consumers evaluate products and services based on one or more of three properties or qualities: search, experience and credence properties (Zeithaml 1981). **Search qualities** are attributes that can be evaluated before a purchase, for example, by visual inspection, sampling or trial. Many physical goods are high in search properties, so they can be fully investigated and assessed before purchase and use. Clothes can be tried on, magazines can be skimmed and CDs can be listened to in the store. There are few post-purchase surprises here.

Experience qualities are attributes that must be experienced in order to be evaluated. Most services exhibit experience properties. For example, until you have had your washing machine repaired, or stayed in that five-star resort, you are not really in a position to judge the quality of the service. Owing to the four characteristics of services — intangibility, variability, inseparability and perishability — it is necessary to experience the service in order to assess it. This is particularly relevant for inexperienced consumers purchasing the service for the first time.

However, in some cases, even after experiencing the service, the consumer is still not able to judge the outcome. This category of services exhibits **credence qualities**, and includes most professional services. Here, consumers often do not have the ability to assess objectively the standard of the service performed. For example, even after consultation with a lawyer, how do you know whether you have been given the best advice? Could you have made more profit by using a different financial adviser? Did that tooth really need filling? In the following example, Ben and Teresa are faced with the issue of the credence quality of services and its resultant problems.

When Ben and Teresa were seeking an architectural firm to design their new home, they had little evidence on which to base their choice. Perhaps they could assess the companies' offices, the architects' personalities, the companies' reputations? Would the quoted fees help? They could try to visit houses previously designed by the companies in which they were interested. However, would this be proof that their house would be as well designed? And of course, once built, the house cannot be 'unbuilt'; they are aware that this is an irretrievable decision. With the relatively high cost involved, Ben and Teresa are very concerned, and see this as a high-risk decision because they are unsure of how to choose between the various companies. Many factors play a part in determining the success of a house design, and they are aware that there is no real way to be certain of the quality of this design until it is built. Even then, some would argue that the outcome of such a service is subjective, based on an individual's tastes and preferences.

In addition, Ben and Teresa are aware that they will have to provide a brief to the architect outlining their requirements. Even this worries them, because they have never attempted anything like this before. Maybe it will be partly their own fault if they are dissatisfied with the finished design. After finally choosing an architect, they are told that they will have to wait four months to start, because the company is so busy. Now they are really confused. Should they wait? Does this mean that the company is popular because they are exceptional architects or is it a sign of poor management skills? Could they really face having to go through the whole search process again?

Search qualities:
characteristics of the product or service that are physically evident rather than abstract

Experience qualities:
service attributes that can only be evaluated by consumers after the service production process

Credence qualities:
service attributes that cannot be evaluated by consumers with any certainty even after they have experienced the service process

The consumer's decision-making process

Various comprehensive models of consumer behaviour exist. Several that focus on consumer decision making are the Howard–Sheth model (Howard & Sheth 1969) and the Engel–Kollat–Blackwell (EKB) model — also known as the Engel–Blackwell–Miniard model (Engel, Blackwell & Miniard 1986). The latter model is shown in figure 2.1. The model comprises four interrelated sections: information input, information processing, the variables affecting the decision process and the decision process itself. The first three of these components are outside the scope of this text; however, the actual decision process is discussed below. As shown in figure 2.1, the decision process is described as a five-stage process comprising:

1. problem recognition
2. information search
3. evaluation of alternatives
4. purchase
5. outcomes (or post-purchase behaviour).

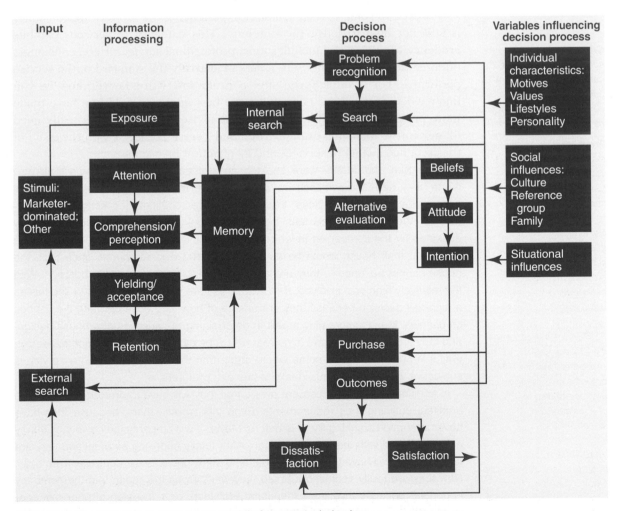

Figure 2.1: The Engel–Kollat–Blackwell model of consumer behaviour
Source: Engel, Blackwell & Miniard 1986

However, these traditional five steps are amalgamated into three steps for decisions regarding services (Fisk 1981). This is depicted in figure 2.2.

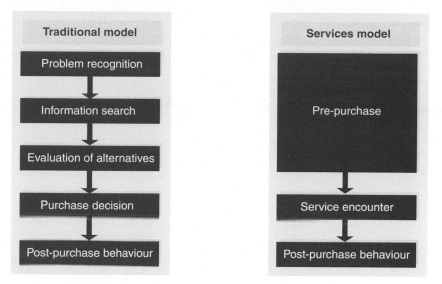

Figure 2.2: Customer's purchase decision process — comparison of the traditional five-stage model and the three-stage services model

Each of the three stages of the consumer decision process can be further broken down. These components are shown in table 2.1 and are discussed in the following section.

Table 2.1	Components of the consumer's purchase process for services	
1.	**Pre-purchase**	Realisation of need/want Search for information Evaluation of alternatives Choice of intended purchase
2.	**Service encounter**	Purchase of service Consumption of service
3.	**Post-purchase**	Post-purchase evaluation Repeat purchase Customer loyalty Positive or negative word of mouth Switching service providers

It must be noted that the extent to which a consumer will proceed through such a decision-making process will depend on the buying situation. Factors such as the level of **involvement** (high or low), the type of service and whether it is a first-time or a repeat purchase will all influence the effort and time that the consumer puts into each of the components. These points are addressed later in the chapter in the section concerning perceived risk. In addition, the process can be complicated with numerous loops and reiterations, possibly with the input of one or more influencers on the consumer.

Pre-purchase phase

The pre-purchase phase is the first of the three stages of the consumer's purchase decision process. It includes the realisation of the need or want (**problem recognition**), the **search** for relevant information, the evaluation of alternative service suppliers and the choice of the intended purchase.

Problem recognition: the awareness by the consumer that there is a difference between their actual and desired states

Search: the collection of data on the service of interest, either from personal recollections or conscious activities

Problem recognition (also known as need recognition) acts as the prompt that starts off the consumer's purchase decision process. For example, when Holly, a 19-year-old student, becomes the sole beneficiary of her great uncle's large fortune, she realises that she does not know how best to invest her inheritance and that she needs financial advice. There are two possible problem-recognition situations: actual state and desired state decisions. In an actual state decision, the individual recognises a problem with the current service provider. For example, a consumer may be so dissatisfied with the service level provided by his current bank that he decides to switch banks. In a desired state decision, the individual has a need or want for a new service. Holly's need for financial advice is an example of a desired state decision. The consumer then moves to the next stage of the purchase decision process: search.

Information search can be undertaken using either or both of two methods: recollection or active search. In using recollection, a consumer searches their memory of past experiences or information gathered previously, and may consider that this is enough data on which to base a decision. If not, the consumer will engage in active search activities, such as obtaining and reading advertisements and other promotional material, reading newspaper and magazine articles and speaking with sales representatives. Seeking advice from non-commercial sources such as friends, family or work colleagues is also common when seeking information regarding services. For example, Holly, being an impoverished university student, has previously had little interest in the financial services industry, and therefore has few memories from which to draw. Realising the importance of the decision, she spends significant periods of time reading the investment advice sections of various newspapers, ringing financial services advisers and discussing the options with older family members who already have investments. (A more detailed explanation of consumer search for services can be found in Murray (1991) and McColl-Kennedy and Fetter (1999, 2001).)

Having obtained what is considered to be sufficient information, the consumer moves to the next step, evaluation of alternatives. Here, the consumer considers an evoked set — that is, the options from which the selection will be made. In order to make the selection or choice of service provider, the consumer also uses a list of criteria against which each option will be judged. For example, the factors that Holly decides are important to her are: (1) the financial services firm must be well established and must have been in business for more than 10 years, thus demonstrating reliability and security; (2) the firm must be located in the CBD, since that would be convenient for her to visit; (3) it must employ friendly, helpful advisers; and (4) it must have a proven record of success in providing sound advice. Four firms seem to meet these criteria, and from these she makes her choice — the final step in this pre-purchase phase. A further example of this pre-purchase phase is given in the Services Marketing Action vignette which follows the next section, Internal Factors.

Different consumers will address this pre-purchase phase in different ways, depending on three factors. These are internal factors, external factors and the consumer's level of perceived risk. The components of each are outlined in table 2.2.

As well as leading to differences between consumers, these components may also lead to differing behaviour within one individual in different purchase situations.

Table 2.2	Determinants of the pre-purchase phase
Internal factors	Individual's wants and needs
	Past experience
	Expectations
	Involvement level
External factors	Company communication strategies
	Competitive strategies
	Word of mouth
	Social context
Perceived risk	Financial
	Functional
	Physical
	Psychological
	Sensory
	Social
	Temporal

Source: adapted from Kurtz & Clow 1998

Internal factors

Consumers are individuals and therefore have individual wants and needs. It is important that marketers understand these before trying to develop marketing strategies for the service. Consumers' wants and needs can be identified by formal or informal market research methodologies (see chapter 8).

Following previous experience with a service, the consumer will have learned what input was required of them, met the staff, experienced the service, gone through the post-purchase phase and, finally, made a judgement regarding their degree of satisfaction. Past experience with the service may also have led to some continuing commitment (for example, a mobile phone call plan or a gym membership) which has implications for future purchases.

Past experience will be one of the factors that determine a consumer's expectations of a service (see chapter 4 for a discussion of the gap model of services quality), which in turn is one of the key factors driving the level of the consumer's satisfaction.

The consumer's involvement level affects the mental and physical energy that the consumer puts into the pre-purchase phase. A high-involvement purchase such as choosing a financial institution for a home loan may require far greater thought and effort than that used for a low-involvement decision such as choosing a television repairer. It is important, however, to note that a decision that is high-involvement for one consumer may be considered low-involvement by another. For example, Joe is a real car enthusiast, and loves his Holden Special Vehicle Clubsport with passion; only the best mechanics are allowed near this car. Stephen, on the other hand, drives only to get from A to B, barely knows where the engine of his car is, and just drops it off at the closest garage for servicing. The choice of a mechanic is a low-involvement decision for Stephen, but definitely high-involvement for Joe.

Sally graduated with a Bachelor of Commerce eight years ago. She has worked as a sales representative and, for the last five years, as a product manager. Since she greatly enjoyed her studies and has ambitions to further her career, she has decided to return to university to undertake an MBA.

Advertisements for MBA programs appear regularly in the Higher Education section of the *Australian* newspaper. There is a confusing array of degrees: full time and part time, Australian and international, correspondence and attendance required. Sally is somewhat concerned by this range of options because she perceives her choice to be critical. All MBA degrees are relatively expensive and she is unsure of whether her employer will subsidise the course fees.

She is aware that standards of teaching, library facilities, subjects offered and the experience of other students vary between universities. Newspaper articles, university open days, brochures from the various universities as well as advice from friends, have provided her with a wealth of information (sometime conflicting) on various aspects of the courses. Since it would be difficult to change university mid-degree, she wants to ensure that she makes the right decision. She knows that the local universities vary widely in their appearance and aesthetics. Some are high-rise office towers, others have more appealing garden surroundings. Some facilities are very modern, others outdated. Her boss has strong views — the university where he studied for his MBA is certainly the best!

Sally is concerned about the travel time from work to the campus and then home again after the lectures, which finish late. All in all, Sally is beginning to think that making the right decision is more difficult than doing the degree!

External factors

Clearly, the consumer does not exist in a vacuum. External factors also play a role in determining the pre-purchase actions of the consumer. The marketing strategies of both the company and its competitors seek to influence the consumer's behaviour. These are discussed in detail in chapter 10. Word of mouth — that is, comments by other individuals such as friends and family — also plays a role in affecting a consumer's choice. The social context is also relevant. For example, the choice of restaurant for a romantic anniversary celebration for two will be very different from the fast-food restaurant where you take the kids after watching the local football team play.

Perceived risk

Perceived risk has long been identified as an important factor in consumer decision making (Guseman 1981; Kaplan et al. 1974). The extent of the perceived risk is generally determined by a combination of two factors. These are the expected consequences, such as danger, damage or importance, and the level of probability of such an outcome occurring. For example, a possibility that is most unlikely to occur but carries serious implications (such as losing your deposit if your travel agent declares bankruptcy) may be considered a greater risk than one

Characteristics of services

- Intangibility
- Inseparability
- Heterogeneity
- Perishability
- Role of customer (customisation)
- Ownership
- Evaluation difficulty

Consumer difficulty in evaluation

- Pre-purchase
- During consumption
- Post-purchase

Level of perceived risk

Other

- Level of involvement
- Experience of purchase
- Individual's risk threshold
- Situational factors
- Regulated safeguards

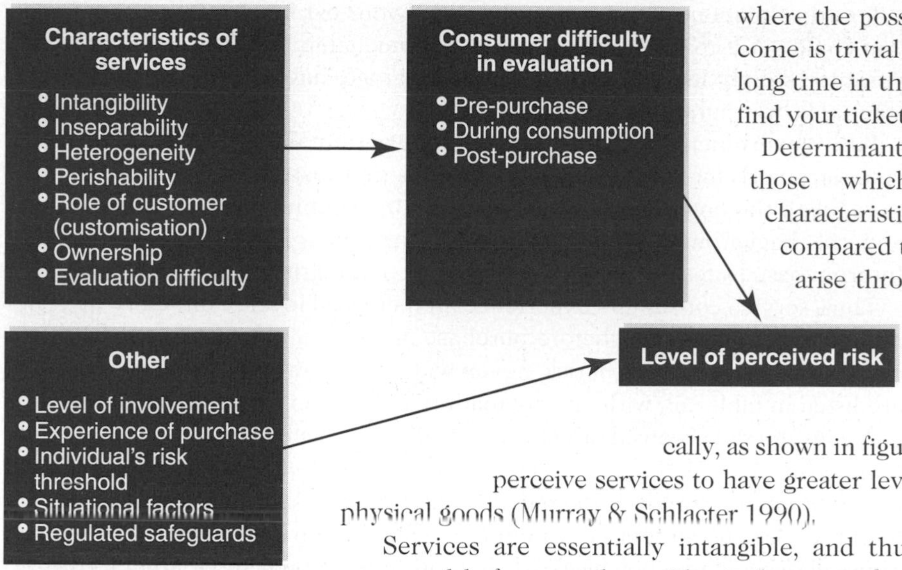

Figure 2.3:
Factors determining the consumer's level of perceived risk

Servicescape: the environment in which a service is produced and delivered

where the possibility is high but the outcome is trivial (such as having to wait a long time in the travel agency while they find your tickets and answer phone calls). Determinants of risk can be divided into those which are the result of characteristics specific to services (as compared to goods) and those which arise through other avenues. These determinants and their role in consumer decision making can be expressed diagrammatically, as shown in figure 2.3. Overall, consumers perceive services to have greater levels of associated risk than physical goods (Murray & Schlacter 1990).

Services are essentially intangible, and thus cannot be objectively assessed before purchase. Physical cues such as the appearance of the internal and external **servicescape** provide information for the potential consumer regarding the quality of the service. Services may vary widely in their level of quality, between and within service providers. Some services are customised to the requirements of the customer, and may be complex and beyond the knowledge base of the customer — for example most professional services such as architects, financial advisors, medical practitioners and lawyers. Guarantees and warranties, although used occasionally, are not widely used in the service area. (An example of an exception is Civic Video, which advertises a satisfaction guarantee — if you don't enjoy the movie then it's free.) A quick inspection of the Yellow Pages under Pest Controllers, for example, results in many pages of ads, but only a handful include a guarantee.

Each of these characteristics of services acts to determine the degree of difficulty that the consumer faces in evaluating service quality. This in turn determines the level of risk perceived by the consumer.

A range of miscellaneous factors also affect an individual's perception of risk. First, the consumer's level of involvement in the purchase is important. For example, Ben is an 18-year-old who doesn't care about his appearance and goes to the barber to have his hair cut only when it is falling over his eyes. On the other hand, Louis is very fashion-conscious, spends much of his pay on clothes and wants the latest styling when he visits his hairdresser. These young men have very different levels of involvement in their haircuts.

Second, prior experience in purchasing this type of service is also relevant in determining the perceived level of risk. Consider Sue, who has travelled widely, first with her parents and more recently for work and holidays, and who sees booking a trip as fairly routine. For someone who has never travelled overseas, however, the complexities and the range of possibilities available in international travel can be quite daunting.

Third, some individuals have a risk-taking attitude to life; they seek adventure holidays, going bungee jumping and sky diving. Others are risk-averse and have a lower risk threshold. As a generalisation, some cultures tend to exhibit risk avoidance behaviour (Schutte & Ciarlante 1998). For example, they may prefer to travel overseas in groups, often with a tour guide of their own nationality, rather than travel independently as is common in other cultures.

Fourth, situational factors are relevant. If your car breaks down near home, you could get it towed back to your usual mechanic, but if you are interstate you may simply leave it with the closest garage, having no knowledge of its standards or reputation.

Fifth, governments in some cases regulate certain industries in order to provide safeguards for consumers. For example, the Australian government seeks to regulate the on-shore gambling industry by examining percentage payouts and the background of the operators. However, gamblers using off-shore Internet-based sites have no such assurance of integrity.

Thus, service consumers experience an increased level of difficulty in evaluating competing services before purchase and consumption. As a result, they perceive increased levels of risk. Seven widely acknowledged categories of risk are listed in table 2.3, with an explanation and example of each.

A consumer's perceived risk is an amalgamation of all the possible types of risk outlined in table 2.3. However, not all seven categories will be of equal importance in any situation. Moreover, the relative importance of each will vary between different service encounters. For example, a bungee jump may be high in perceived physical risk and psychological risk, but low in functional and temporal risk.

Table 2.3	Categories of risk
Category of risk	**Explanation**
Financial	The consumer's monetary loss if the service fails, e.g. 'If the builder becomes bankrupt, will I lose my deposit?' Can also refer to unexpected costs, e.g. 'Will adding an extension to the house cost more than the original quote?'
Functional	Also known as performance risk, this refers to uncertainty as to whether the service will offer what was promised and/or expected, e.g. 'Will the travel insurance cover the lost items? Will the florist deliver the flowers as ordered?'
Physical	Possible damage or harm to the consumer or their possessions, e.g. 'Is my luggage safe in the hotel room?' 'Will I be safe while learning scuba diving?'
Psychological	Risk that the service will not fit the consumer's self-concept, e.g. 'Will I enjoy this concert?' 'Will I be as clever as the other students in the course?'
Sensory	Negative effects on sight, hearing, smell, touch or taste, e.g. 'Will I like the taste of a restaurant meal?' 'Will the dentist hurt me?'
Social	Closely related to psychological risk, but refers to the individual's concern regarding the opinions of others. e.g. 'Will my friends like my haircut?' 'Will my colleagues approve of the hotel I have chosen?'
Temporal	Concerns regarding wasted time or delays, e.g. 'Will I be able to check in in time for the flight departure?' 'Why did the service centre take four weeks to repair my video recorder?'

In this pre-purchase stage, consumers can take certain actions to reduce the perceived level of risk. The most widely used strategy is to search for further information. This can be obtained from family, friends or experts, from independent bodies such as consumer associations, from the Internet or even from the service companies under consideration.

Other options are to:

- seek guarantees or warranties (for example, some video stores offer a refund if you do not enjoy the movie hired)
- rely on price as a surrogate for quality (for example, if the law company is that expensive, then it must be good!)
- evaluate the reputation and image of the company (for example, Qantas has an excellent reputation for safety, while Singapore Airlines has an outstanding reputation for service)
- use an initial trial to evaluate the service (for example, first gym visit free)
- consider tangible cues as a guide to service quality (for example, the appearance and ambience of an insurance company's head office).

Companies should therefore be aware of these strategies used by consumers to decrease the perceived risk. Companies can enhance the probability of a consumer purchasing the service by facilitating these options, for example by introducing a guarantee or a trial offer, encouraging positive word of mouth, and using PR and advertising to enhance their reputation.

The service encounter

The service encounter or consumption stage of the purchase process for services follows the consumer's decision to purchase a specific service. The service encounter may be an exchange between the consumer and a member of the service firm's staff, for example Tom ordering flowers at a florist. Alternatively it may be an interaction between the consumer and a computer, telephone or other equipment, such as when Tom places an order for groceries through Coles Online or when he withdraws cash from an ATM. The service encounter may be a one-off interaction, such as the purchase of a vacuum cleaner from a department store. Alternatively, it may be a series of interrelated events such as being part of a 20-day Contiki tour through Europe, or a number of visits to an orthodontist for treatment over a four-year period.

The consumer's assessment of the level of service quality is determined during this phase of the purchase process. Their level of satisfaction depends on numerous factors (see figure 2.4), including the service environment (or servicescape), the appearance and actions of the employees and the backstage support services plus equipment and processes. Each of these points is discussed in detail in chapters 4 (Service Quality) and 5 (Satisfaction).

However, several other components of the service encounter can also affect the consumer's level of satisfaction. These include role and script theory, the customer's emotions and mood and the behaviour of other customers present.

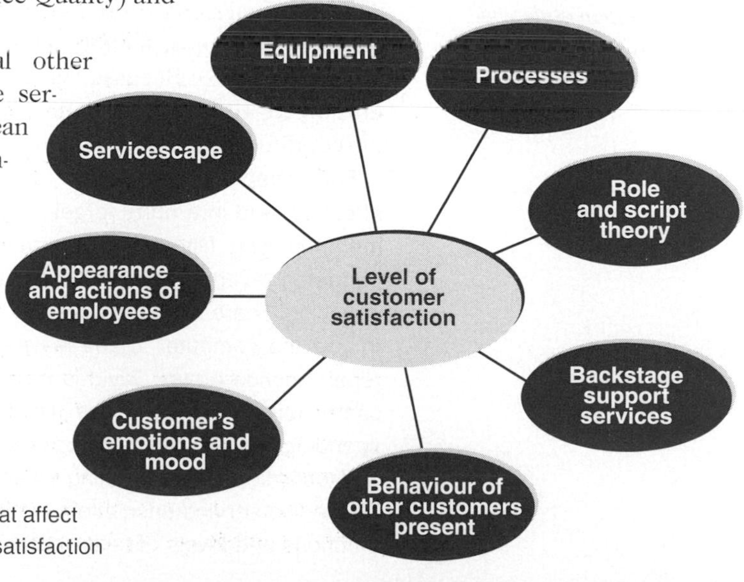

Figure 2.4: Factors that affect the level of customer satisfaction

Role and script theory

Role: *characterisations assumed by the buyer and seller that are based on the type of service encounter*

A service encounter can be seen as analogous to a dramatic performance, where actors play roles, wear costumes (uniforms) and follow predetermined scripts (Grove, Fisk, & Bitner 1992). Owing to the inseparability of services, the success of the service encounter in delivering a quality service depends in part on how well the actors perform their **roles** and follow the **script** (see chapter 1).

Script: *a learned sequence of buyer and seller behaviours that are expected for that service encounter*

For example, in a visit to a McDonald's restaurant, customers are expected to know where to queue, to quickly read the information signs regarding menu choice and prices, to know that they pay first and eat second, to place their rubbish in the bins provided and return the trays. This speeds up the delivery process and ensures that a relatively large number of customers are served quickly and cost efficiently. In addition, the staff have been trained to follow a script: 'And would you like fries with that?'

Many poor quality — even embarrassing — service encounters occur where one or more of the participants does not know their expected role or script. For example, a client visiting a lawyer or accountant for the first time may not know what is expected of them, how to act, and what information to provide. A clear objective for the company introducing a new service is to train the customers in their role and encourage them to learn what is required. For example, the introduction of Internet banking required the banks to encourage trials of this service through the use of promotional offers, and to provide explicit instructions and helplines for first-time customers.

The drama metaphor can be extended even further to include the audition (selection of staff), rehearsal (staff training), setting the stage (the physical environment or servicescape) and defining the on-stage and off-stage activities (for example, should the kitchen be visible to restaurant patrons?).

Scripts are of particular value in an organisation that has a large number of staff and where the firm's objective is service standardisation. Frontline bank and insurance company staff, telemarketers, customer service staff and retail assistants are often trained to respond in a certain way in a particular situation. This brings greater homogeneity to the service encounter, with the aim of increasing service quality. A valuable skill, however, is for the staff member not to appear to be reciting a memorised sequence of phrases.

Customers' emotions and moods

Affective state: *the emotions and mood of an individual at a particular time*

An individual's emotions and mood make up their **affective state**. A mood is a temporary state of feeling, while an emotion is more pervasive and intense (Gardner 1985). Because the consumer is an inseparable part of the service employed, their affective state will clearly play a role in determining their perception of the service quality.

For example, Diana has an important meeting first thing at work. She is uptight, stressed, and in a hurry to get to work. She is to present the latest sales figures to the Managing Director at 9 a.m. and the results are worrying, with lower than budgeted revenue and profits. On the way, however, she must drop in her car for servicing. There is a long queue to book in and the clerk doesn't seem to know how to use the computer. Diana leaves frustrated, angry and vowing never to use this repair service again. David is next in line after Diana, in the same queue with the same clerk. However, he has just started two weeks holiday and is looking forward to spending it by the beach doing very little. He passes the time daydreaming about the surf conditions and planning where to have lunch, blithely unaware of the delay. These two service encounters ought to be almost identical but they involve different emotions and levels of satisfaction.

Consumers who are in a positive mood are usually less argumentative, more obliging and more willing to be pleased (Gardner 1985). In addition, they are more likely to perceive that the service was in fact pleasant and satisfactory. Where possible, the service provider should attempt to encourage the consumer's positive mood by implementing such strategies as suitable music and colour schemes and helpful, friendly staff (Knowles et al. 1993).

A customer's perception of service quality can also be influenced by their perceived level of control during the service encounter (Hui & Bateson 1991). There are two types of control: behavioural and cognitive. **Behavioural control** allows the consumer to actually change the quality of the service. For example, self-service buffet restaurants remove the delays and frustrations that may occur in a restaurant where the waiter brings your meal. **Cognitive control** usually involves the service provider giving the customer updated information so that the customer knows the status of the service and the reason for any delays. For example, FedEx has sophisticated software that allows the customer to track the progress of a shipment. Thus the customer can adjust their expectations and feel part of the process, rather than feeling powerless.

Behavioural control: the individual's perception of their level of control of a situation, which is due to their own actions

Cognitive control: the individual's perception of their level of control of a situation, which is due to their knowledge, perception and beliefs

Behaviour of other customers

The presence, behaviour and compatibility of other customers has a major effect on the perceived level of customer satisfaction (Martin & Pranter 1989). While an almost empty plane can give you room to stretch out and sleep, an almost empty restaurant or theatre makes you wonder why it is unpopular, and the absence of other patrons negatively affects your experience. Conversely, a service location that is overcrowded or has a long queue of potential customers will cause some degree of dissatisfaction.

The behaviour of other customers, particularly in a prolonged service experience such as a holiday tour or hospital stay, can also affect the satisfaction levels of those around them. Have you ever had to put up with the person behind you in a lecture chatting on a mobile phone? A crying baby on a plane? A drunk football team in a restaurant? Service providers can enhance the satisfaction levels of customers by trying to bring together compatible customers. For example, a travel agent can explain to a retired couple that an Oz Experience camping tour may not be right for them; and there is a cinema in Sydney that shows midday 'mothers' movies, where parents are encouraged to bring babies and small children. Where possible, service providers should educate customers about appropriate standards of behaviour through the use of signs or verbal warnings and, in extreme cases, denial of service and removal of the offending customer (as nightclub bouncers do, for example).

The post-purchase phase

The last of the three phases in the consumer purchase process is the post-purchase phase, in which customers determine their level of satisfaction or dissatisfaction by comparing their perceptions with their expectations. A detailed description of this, the disconfirmation of expectations model, is given in chapter 4.

Satisfaction will lead to repeat purchase, loyalty to the company and positive word of mouth. Dissatisfaction may lead to switching behaviour (where possible) and negative word of mouth. Depending on the consumer's level of involvement regarding the service, this post-purchase behaviour may be almost subconscious (as it is when buying a train ticket) or structured and thoughtful (as it is when evaluating a 42-day trip of a lifetime through Europe with a tour operator).

Services on the web

Consumer behaviour on the Internet differs in a number of ways from traditional bricks and mortar consumer behaviour. These differences are summarised in figure 2.5.

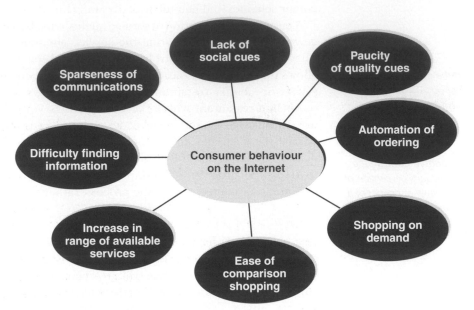

Since the usual interpersonal signs of body language and tone of voice are not present in Internet shopping, a more impersonal service encounter occurs. This can therefore remove the enjoyment that some consumers experience from shopping. Similarly, while the Internet is information rich, it is communication poor, which can prove frustrating and annoying for a consumer seeking to interact with a service provider over the Web. Accessibility may be an issue, with one study reporting that only 58 per cent of companies replied within five days to an emailed query (Zemke & Connellan 2001).

The very richness of information available on the Internet can make finding one specific piece of information difficult. Relatively few adults are formally trained in the use of the Internet and they may rely on browsing and amateur search strategies. Companies attempt to assist these consumers with lists of frequently asked questions and with search facilities incorporated in their site.

Since the only evidence of service quality pre-purchase is the website itself, consumers may perceive an increased risk, since many are aware that an impressive website does not necessarily mean a reputable company.

Moreover, decision making can be more difficult owing to the vast number of options available. Companies such as Amazon.com try to help consumers navigate through this huge range of choices by providing a top-10 list, making recommendations based on the consumer's previous choices and providing recommendations from other customers. Comparison shopping — either across websites or by using a specific comparison site — is relatively simple. Consumers are thus more likely to compare products and prices on the Internet.

The 24-hour convenience of the Internet directly affects consumer behaviour in that consumers can shop from home without having to travel to a retail centre, and can do so at any time of the day or night. The physical position of the store or outlet is therefore rendered irrelevant, removing one of the key traditional competitive advantages of a store: its physical location.

Since it is possible for a consumer to save their last order, automation of ordering is feasible. This allows a consumer to place the same or a modified version of the last order with minimal effort. While used widely in business-to-business marketing, it is also a feature promoted by retailers such as Coles Online and Greengrocer.com. The advantage of this for consumers is that it can greatly simplify the shopping process.

The vignette below provides an example of a service encounter using the Internet.

Services Marketing on the Web:
International couriers

International courier companies have taken to the Internet with alacrity, using this new technology to add value for customers. FedEx led the way with features such as:

- COSMOS — customer operations service master online system — an electronic network that contains critical information on the location of each shipment in the FedEx system
- Fedex Ship — free, downloadable software that allows customers to calculate rates, book a pick-up and complete all documentation on their computer.

Other major organisations such as DHL, Australia Post and TNT now have similar features.

While appealing to customers because of convenience and the additional value from extra information such as parcel tracking, overall customer satisfaction relies on criteria other than the sophistication of the website. Consider the following scenario.

Julie needed to send a small but valuable parcel to Austria, where it was required urgently by a customer. The international courier company's customer service representative answered the phone promptly and was helpful and friendly. He said that a customs clearance form was necessary and he would fax it through — the driver would do the rest. Delivery was promised in three to four days. The courier driver arrived at the promised pick-up time (Monday afternoon) but claimed that no customs form was necessary (no fax had arrived anyway). Julie was most impressed by the Internet tracking feature and emailed the consignment number to the customer in Austria so they could also track it across the world.

Later that night she logged on, following the simple instructions, and found that, rather than being well on its way, the parcel was sitting at Sydney North Base with a message to 'Please contact us'. She immediately rang and another helpful customer service representative told her that a customs form *was* necessary, so this was faxed that night and she was assured that the parcel would leave the next day (Tuesday). For all of Tuesday and well into Wednesday, the parcel was recorded as being at the departure facility with the message to contact the courier company still appearing. Another phone call elicited the information that the parcel had in fact left on the Tuesday but that 'the tracking centre is often not updated for a while'.

The parcel was in fact safely delivered within the four days originally promised but Julie felt that the delays in updating the tracking centre information had caused her additional anxiety and had not reassured her of the parcel's progress.

Culture

Although globalisation is undoubtedly affecting many countries and leading to worldwide homogenisation, clear distinctions are still obvious in the consumer behaviour of people from different cultures. Culture is a complex concept that includes the values, knowledge, beliefs, art, morals, laws, customs and habits of a group or a society. Thus, not all people from the one country have the same culture as many of the external manifestations of culture can differ from group to group.

Consumer behaviour is often the product of a particular culture. For example, people from Australia and New Zealand have the custom of eating three meals a day. Further, they may believe that eating cereal and toast is 'normal' as a breakfast meal. In contrast, the French like a cold croissant or roll and coffee, the Americans happily eat doughnuts, the Chinese eat rice, and Indians often eat curry for breakfast.

Culture is complex and can be difficult to fully describe. Schutte and Ciarlante (1998) have developed a useful model that divides culture into three levels: (1) behavioural practices, (2) values, beliefs, preferences and norms and (3) basic assumptions. These are shown in figure 2.6, with the differences between Asian and Western cultures shown.

Culture: the sum total of learned beliefs, values and customs that serve to regulate the consumer behaviour of members of a particular society

Figure 2.6:
Three levels of culture
Source:
Schutte & Ciarlante 1998

Behavioural practices

The behavioural practices of a culture are often obvious, being externally visible elements. As shown in figure 2.6, Western cultures, such as those found in Australia and New Zealand, attach great importance to rules, contracts, tasks, structure and planning. In contrast, Asian cultures tend to be more flexible, have less formal deals and contracts, place a great importance on relationships and networks and less emphasis on structure and rules.

These behavioural practices affect how consumers evaluate and use services. For example, people from Western cultures place great importance on seeking legal advice before entering into contractual agreements with others, while those from Eastern cultures rely more on the relationships and sense of honour implicit in the arrangement. Thus, a person seeking to start up a legal practice in an Eastern culture may have to think carefully about what services they will offer and how they will market them.

Values, beliefs, preferences and norms

Values, beliefs and norms are intrinsic to the person and culture being examined and are therefore more difficult to ascertain. Basic values are an important dimension of culture and provide guidelines on what is acceptable and unacceptable behaviour. These values will vary considerably across cultures. For example, in some cultures paying bribes and offering gifts is an acceptable way of doing business. In Australia, however, this is not acceptable and can be illegal. In some cultures, being polite to service staff is seen as the appropriate way to behave, whereas in other cultures service staff should be ignored. Even norms such as appropriate dress and manner of speech are culturally derived. In India, since cash is scarce, mobile phone users barter for their phone calls. Villagers use milk, wheat or sugar cane, which is then sold in the local market, to pay for phone bills. Two pounds of milk will pay for a call that costs twenty cents (Bajpai 2002). This is certainly a custom that would be difficult to replicate in Australia or New Zealand, and would be an important factor for telecommunications companies to consider if they were looking to expand their business to rural India.

Basic assumptions and cultural dimensions

Things that are important to and valued by a culture are also intangible and often taken for granted. The assumptions relating to time are particularly interesting and vary considerably even among western cultures. For example, issues of punctuality and politeness in relation to time can often get international travellers into trouble. Assumptions about time do not differ between only Eastern and Western cultures. Many Middle Eastern and Mediterranean cultures also have different and less restrictive perceptions of time and decision making.

Many US companies have failed in negotiations with other cultures because they have tried to impose deadlines and structured procedures into their negotiations. For some cultures, this makes them feel threatened and suspicious (Ricks 1993). For service firms, understanding assumptions and time values can be critical to satisfying customers from different cultures. For example, in an American restaurant patrons want fast, efficient service — not a lot of friendly discussion. On the other hand, many Mediterranean cultures people want time to think about their menu choices, to chat and to have a conversation with the service staff. It is easy to see how things could go wrong!

Another way of examining the underlying values, beliefs and assumptions of cultures is to consider Hofstede's (1984) four dimensions of culture. He proposed that the position of a culture along these four dimensions will determine what is culturally appropriate in a particular society (Lovelock et al. 2001). As Australia and New Zealand are Asia-Pacific nations, the cultural differences of our Asian neighbours can be particularly important. Hofstede's cultural dimensions as shown in table 2.4 can provide us with some valuable insights, and each will be discussed in more detail. It is important to understand that all Asian cultures are not identical, and that even within one Asian country there may exist several distinct subcultures. For example, although 95 per cent of Chinese are Han Chinese, there are nine sublanguages spoken and 23 dialects (Pecotich & Shultz 1998).

Table 2.4	Hofstede's underlying dimensions of cultural values		
Cultural dimension	**Basic issue**	**Contrasts across cultures**	**Examples**
1. Power distance	Does society value equality or inequality in interpersonal interactions?	*Low power distance* Power is relatively equally distributed.	West
		High power distance Hierarchy is strong and power is centralised at the top.	Asia
2. Uncertainty avoidance	What is the attitude towards risk in society?	*Low uncertainty avoidance* Calculated risk is seen as necessary in order to seize the opportunity.	Singapore Hong Kong Sweden USA
		High uncertainty avoidance Risk is regarded as threatening and to be avoided.	Portugal Japan France South Korea
3. Individualism/ collectivism	Do people rely on themselves or others (that is, the group)?	*Individualist* Self-reliance is valued, as is the need for the individual to satisfy their own needs within the group.	West
		Collectivistic Dependence is valued and society expects the individual to subordinate their own needs to those of the group.	Asia
4. Masculinity/femininity	To what extent and at whose expense should the weaker members of society be cared for?	*Feminine* Caring for others and nurturing roles and attitudes are favoured.	Scandinavia Thailand Netherlands
		Masculine Personal achievement and assertiveness are favoured.	Japan Switzerland Great Britain

Source: Schutte & Ciarlante 1998

Power distance

Power distance involves the degree to which a group values equality in interpersonal relationships. As table 2.4 shows, Western countries such as Australia, New Zealand, the United Kingdom and the United States tend to have low power distance and therefore are more egalitarian. Most Asian countries, however, tend to have high power distance and thus power tends to belong to only a few, while the masses are relatively powerless.

Interestingly, a study of power distance in eight countries, undertaken by Hofstede in 1984, showed that New Zealand had the lowest levels of power distance, and was therefore the most egalitarian country. It was followed by Australia, the United States, Japan, Taiwan, Thailand, Hong Kong and Singapore, in that order (Hofstede 1984).

In many Asian cultures, this high degree of power distance is also reflected in the importance of the family unit and a respect for the views of parents and grandparents. This is significant when it comes to the influences within the decision-making process. Multiple generations may live together. In Indonesia this practice is particularly common among urban Javanese and Chinese families. In China approximately 20 per cent of households consist of more than two generations (Pecotich & Shultz 1998).

For service marketers an understanding of the importance of equality is critical, particularly in the employment of service personnel. In some cultures, people from different ethnic backgrounds cannot mix, and people from particular social castes cannot do certain tasks or jobs. Moreover, some cultures have more complex ways of defining a person's 'rank' For example, an American manager of a large multinational company was sent to Malaysia to close an important deal. When introduced to his Malaysian counterpart, he learned that his Western name was Roger. The American then proceeded to call this person 'Rog', believing that he was of equal status and position. What he failed to understand was that this person was a member of the Malaysian nobility, and the use of his first name, particularly an abbreviated version of it, was so insulting and disrespectful that the deal was abandoned (Ricks 1993).

Likewise, the issue of 'maintaining face' is important in many cultures. Equally important is not causing others to lose face. Thus, Asians tend to avoid conflict, and do not like to to refuse any request. This issue is particularly evident in service encounters where the inseparability of the encounter means that the customer and the service provider are interacting.

Uncertainty avoidance

This dimension relates to the attitudes toward risk in a particular society. The majority of Asian cultures rate strongly on this dimension, indicating that risk is not welcome. This is reflected in the way these cultural groups are very brand conscious and brand loyal. Company image, branding and country of origin are considered important factors in their purchases, as they decrease the purchase risk. Western brand names are often seen as having higher status and being more prestigious products (Brooks 1994; Yan 1994). In addition, impulse shopping is less common than in Western consumer behaviour, with one study showing that only 8 per cent of Chinese consumers ever buy on impulse (Schutte & Ciarlante 1998). Further, this risk aversion is also seen in traditions such as feng shui (the belief that destiny can be affected by a building's alignment and design) and the belief that certain colours bring luck and good fortune.

Different perceptions of colour are very important when considering operating in different cultures. For example, white is a colour that is considered appropriate for weddings and symbolises purity in many Western cultures. However, in some Asian cultures white and pale blue are associated with death, and red is the colour of choice for weddings. Imagine the trouble a wedding organiser could get into if they didn't understand this!

Risk aversion is more common in many Asian cultures than risk-taking behaviour. In Western cultures, risk aversion occurs more in relation to monetary or financial risk, and this generally leads to complex decision making and problem solving (Lovelock et al. 2001). Asian consumers, however, tend to behave differently. Rather than triggering extended search, if a decision is seen as risky, it may completely prevent any decision making occurring at all. Thus, the traditional diagram showing the diffusion of innovation takes on a different shape when considering the Asian context (see figures 2.7 and 2.8).

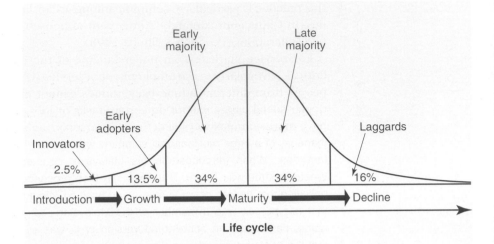

Figure 2.7: Traditional model of diffusion innovation
Source: (Schutte & Ciarlante 1998)

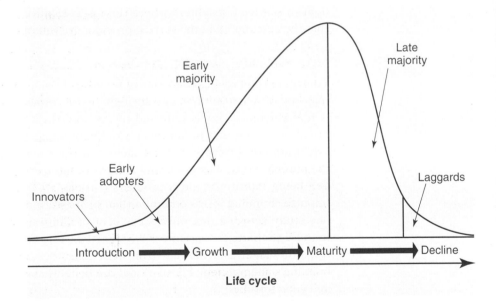

Figure 2.8: Asian model of diffusion of innovation
Source: Schutte & Ciarlante 1998

These diagrams show that in Asian cultures those who are the early majority (corresponding with the growth stage of the product lifecycle) form a far larger proportion than other stages. It seems that in Asian cultures, once an idea has caught on (past the early adopters) most people adopt and accept the concept, not wanting to be seen as different or as laggards. Thus the trick with introducing new services in an Asian culture would be to gain the trust and confidence of as many opinion leaders as possible. This could be done through free trials and by allowing people to experience the service (thus minimising risk) rather than by spending a lot of money on traditional advertising, as this would not reduce the risk or uncertainty.

Individualism and collectivism

This dimension examines the degree to which people of a particular culture rely on themselves or others in their society. As shown in table 2.4, Asian cultures have a strong collectivist orientation rather than an individual orientation. Individuals feel a strong need to belong to a group and to conform. The marketing implications of this may include the importance of reference groups and the existence of more distinct and well delineated market segments. Those from Taiwan, Singapore and Thailand are seen to have the lowest levels of individualism, while those from the United States and Australia are seen as having very high levels (Hofstede 1984).

The level of individualism or collectivism is also closely related to the concept of gift giving or reciprocity. In many countries gift giving protocol is complex, with the type, value and wrapping of gifts being important. Items purchased as a gift are high-involvement purchases (Pecotich & Shultz 1998). The care and appropriateness of the gift signal respect and appreciation of the person's role in the collective and it is a way of honouring their value.

Sometimes, however, the mere offer of a gift or token is seen as offensive. In the Middle East, for example, hosts are insulted if guests bring food or drink to their homes. In parts of Latin America, cutlery or handkerchiefs should be avoided as they imply the cutting off of a relationship, and when in China, never give clocks as the Chinese word for clock sounds like funeral. In many parts of Asia gifts are to be given privately to avoid embarrassment, but in the Middle East they should be publicly offered to avoid the impression of a bribe (Ricks 1993).

To avoid blunders in service marketing, there must be careful understanding of what must and must not be done, as well as what is appropriate and what is not.

Masculinity and femininity

The final dimension of Hofstede's cultural values relates to the degree of consideration given to those not masculine in the society. As shown in the diagram, those from Scandinavian countries and Thailand are very high in 'femininity' or caring for others, and they value nurturing roles. In contrast, many Western societies such as Australia, the United Kingdom and New Zealand rate more highly in terms of 'masculinity'. Japan is seen as one of the most masculine societies, where personal achievements and assertiveness are highly favoured. In highly masculine cultures, the methods of promotion and marketing need to be carefully considered, with images and role playing needing to accurately reflect the norms and decision roles. For example, it could be a mistake to show, in an advertisement, a Japanese woman making decisions about choice of school or banking services, as this would be contrary to the way such decisions are usually made in Japan.

Trompenaars' five value orientations

Another perspective of cultural values has been proposed by Trompenaars (1993) and, while these are very similar to Hofstede's classifications, the dimension of emotions is added. Trompenaars' five value orientations are shown in table 2.5.

Table 2.5	Trompenaars' five value orientations	
Value orientation		**Example**
Universalism versus particularism	Rules-based behaviour	Germanic countries
	Relationship-based behaviour	Asian countries
Individualism versus collectivism	Individual's rights are supreme	Western countries
	Group's rights are supreme	Asian countries
Neutral versus affective	Emotions subdued and expressed indirectly	Asian countries
	Emotions expressed freely and directly	Western countries
Diffuse versus specific	Focus is on the context of the situation	Asian countries
	Focus is on specific issues	Germanic countries
Achievement versus ascription	Status and respect achieved by 'doing'	Western countries
	Status and respect ascribed by 'being'	Asian countries

Source:
Schutte & Ciarlante 1998

This issue of emotions and their cultural dimensions is interesting in that it shows how different cultural groups handle their emotions differently. In Australia and New Zealand (and to a large extent in the United States) people are encouraged to show emotions openly and freely. They are taught to debate and to question the thoughts and opinions of others, and the entire schooling system encourages critical and analytical thinking. This creates difficulties for students from cultures where emotions and debate are not openly encouraged and where being outspoken is seen as disrespectful. Lecturers must therefore carefully design material to ensure that they do not marginalise different cultural groups with their assessment strategies and teaching styles.

International Issues:
French food is back in fashion

In the United States recently there has been a spate of openings of French restaurants right across the country. French food is seen as the 'ultimate comfort food' says Ruth Reichl, editor of *Gourmet* magazine, and since 11 September 2001, people are looking for things comfortable and familiar (Prewitt 2002). The American economy has suffered a downward trend since that fateful day, and people who used to dine out five times a week are now going out twice a week, and they want that experience to be luscious and pleasant. French food appears to fit the bill.

People's tastes, however, have changed. While the menu is still decidedly French, the food is simpler and lighter and portion sizes are substantial. French food gives diners great variety and provides infinite scope for the new breed of chef. One chef claims that 'French food is like rock music. No matter what style comes along — rap, hip-hop, punk, new wave — rock is always there'. The same is apparently true of French food (Prewitt 2002).

So it seems that people's tastes in food follow a similar vein to that of fashion. If you wait long enough, everything comes back into fashion.

Summary

LO1: Explain the impact of the characteristics of services on the purchase decision process.

- The four characteristics of services are intangibility, inseparability, heterogeneity and perishability.
- Intangibility means that the service cannot be judged prior to delivery, which increases the consumer's level of uncertainty and perceived risk.
- The inseparability of services results in the consumer commonly being present during the service delivery. This is likely to increase the level of involvement in the service.
- Variability also increases the consumer's level of perceived risk, since each service transaction is likely to be of a different perceived quality.
- Perishability affects consumer decision making to a lesser extent than the other three factors. However, the issues of over- and undersupply may affect decision making.

LO2: Outline the consumer's purchase decision process for services.

- The consumer's purchase process for services consists of three phases: the pre-purchase phase, the service encounter and the post-purchase phase.
- First, the pre-purchase phase includes the consumer's realisation of a need or want, the search for information, evaluation of alternatives and finally the choice of intended purchase.
- The second phase is the service encounter, consisting of the purchase and consumption of the service.
- Finally there is the post-purchase phase, where the consumer determines their level of satisfaction following the delivery of the service.

LO3: Describe the factors that affect the pre-purchase phase, including perceived risk.

The major influences in the pre-purchase phase are:

- internal factors, including an individual's wants and needs, past experience, expectations and involvement level
- external factors, including competitive options, social context, word of mouth recommendations and the firm's communication strategies
- perceived risk, including financial, functional, physical, psychological, sensory, social and temporal risk.

LO4: Discuss the factors that are relevant to the consumer during the service encounter.

- The servicescape is the location where the service encounter occurs.
- The appearance and actions of the employees directly affect the consumer due to the inseparability of services.
- Backstage support services, equipment, processes, and role and script theory determine the efficiency and quality of the service encounter.
- The customer's emotions and mood and the behaviour of other customers determine the perceived level of satisfaction or dissatisfaction due to the inseparability of services.

LO5: Describe the relevance of the post-purchase phase of the decision process.

- The post-purchase phase is important because it is in this stage that the consumer determines their level of satisfaction or dissatisfaction.
- This in turn will drive their future buying and word-of-mouth behaviours.

LO6: Analyse the role of culture in consumer decision making and discuss how it is particularly important for services marketing.

- Since culture is the sum of learned beliefs, values and customs, it is a critical determinant of consumer behaviour.
- While globalisation is to some extent smoothing the differences between cultures, significant differences remain.
- Aspects of Asian culture that create important differences in Asian consumer behaviour compared to Western consumer behaviour include a collectivist orientation, belief in the importance of the family unit, the importance of maintaining 'face', reciprocity, strong ties to traditional beliefs, and risk aversion.

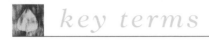 *key terms*

Affective state: the emotions and mood of an individual at a particular time (p. 34)

Behavioural control: the individual's perception of their level of control of a situation, which is due to their own actions (p. 35)

Cognitive control: the individual's perception of their level of control of a situation which is due to their knowledge, perception and beliefs (p. 35)

Consumer behaviour: the actions and mental processes that lead to and comprise the purchase and subsequent use of a product or service (p. 24)

Credence qualities: service attributes that cannot be evaluated by consumers with any certainty even after they have experienced the service process (p. 25)

Culture: the sum total of learned beliefs, values and customs that serve to regulate the consumer behaviour of members of a particular society (p. 38)

Experience qualities: characteristics of the product or service that are only evident after purchase and consumption (p. 25)

Involvement: the amount of time, effort, interest and emotion invested by a consumer in the purchase of the service (p. 27)

Perception: the overall impression gained by the consumer after the service encounter (p. 24)

Post-purchase phase: the stage in which the consumer evaluates the outcome of the service and determines their level of satisfaction or dissatisfaction (p. 27)

Pre-purchase phase: the stages through which a consumer progresses before the purchase and consumption of a service (p. 27)

Problem recognition: the awareness by the consumer that there is a difference between their actual and desired states (p. 28)

Risk: exposure of the consumer to the chance of injury, loss, damage or other negative consequences resulting from the purchase decision (p. 24)

Role: characterisations assumed by the buyer and seller that are based on the type of service encounter (p. 34)

Script: a learned sequence of buyer and seller behaviours that are expected for that service encounter (p. 34)

Search: the collection of data on the service of interest, either from personal recollections or conscious activities (p. 28)

Search qualities: characteristics of the product or service that are physically evident rather than abstract (p. 25)

Service encounter: the stage of the purchase process where interaction between the service provider and the customer results in delivery of the service (p. 27)

Servicescape: the environment in which a service is produced and delivered (p. 31)

 review questions

1. Describe the three phases of the consumer decision process for services.
2. The pre-purchase phase of the consumer decision process for services includes internal and external factors. Discuss the components of each of these.
3. Explain each of the factors that determine a consumer's level of perceived risk.
4. Define search, experience and credence attributes and give an example of each.
5. Discuss the importance of the servicescape in a service encounter.
6. Outline the two models that are useful in explaining the dimensions of culture.

application questions

1. Using the example of making an overseas hotel booking, describe the seven types of possible risk perceived by the customer. What could the hotel do to minimise each of the perceived risks?
2. Choose a recent service purchase that you have made, and describe each of the three stages of the consumer decision process that you experienced.
3. Find a service provider that sells its service through the Internet. Using figure 2.3, assess each of the factors that determines a consumer's level of perceived risk when purchasing through their website.
4. Interview three individuals, each from a different cultural background, and seek their views regarding the points raised in this chapter regarding the characteristics of different cultures.
5. Choose one service industry and divide the market into segments, providing examples of companies who have positioned themselves in each segment.

 vignette questions

1. Read the Services Marketing Action vignette on page 30.
   (a) What are the relevant factors in determining this pre-purchase phase of Sally's purchase decision?
   (b) What risks may Sally perceive regarding her decision? (There may be others as well as those described above.)
   (c) What could a university that is marketing an MBA do to reduce Sally's confusion and uncertainty?

2. Read the Services Marketing on the Web vignette on page 37.
   (a) Evaluate two of the websites listed in the vignette, summarising their features and any problems that you can identify.
   (b) What risks did Julie perceive and what factors determined her level of perceived risk?
3. Read the International Issues vignette on page 44.
   (a) How would an understanding of consumer behaviour have prepared restaurateurs for the popularity of French food?
   (b) What tools can marketers use to keep abreast of changing consumer tastes?
   (c) How can the return to comfort food and family values by Americans be explained using the information about culture in this chapter?

recommended readings

A summary of the key issues in consumer behaviour, in the context of the differences between goods and services, is given in:

Gabbott, M. & Hogg, G. 1994, 'Consumer behaviour and services: a review', *Journal of Marketing Management*, vol. 10, no. 4, pp. 311–24.

For a thorough discussion of all aspects of consumer behaviour pertaining to services, with an emphasis on academic references, see:

Gabbott, M. & Hogg, G. 1998, *Consumers and Services*, John Wiley & Sons, Chichester.

A general introduction to marketing, with an Asian focus, is provided in:

Kotler, P., Ang, S. H., Leong, S. M. & Tan, C. T. 1999, *Marketing Management: an Asian Perspective*, Prentice Hall, Singapore.

A thorough country-by-country analysis of the political, economic and social factors making up the marketing environment in East and South-East Asia is presented in:

Pecotich, A. & Shultz, C. J. 1998, *Marketing and Consumer Behaviour in East and South-East Asia*, McGraw-Hill, Sydney.

A comprehensive discussion of consumer behaviour in the Asian region, and the differences compared to Western consumer behaviour, is given in:

Schutte, H. & Ciarlante, D. 1998, *Consumer Behaviour in Asia*, Macmillan Business, London.

references

Bajpai, R. 2002, 'Bartering for mobile phone services', *Time*, vol. 145, issue 8, p. 56.

Brooks, J. R. 1994, 'Advertising: reaching China's billion consumers', *International Market News*, Hong Kong Trade Development Council, Hong Kong, pp. 4–12.

Engel, J. F., Blackwell, R. D. & Miniard, P. W. 1986, *Consumer Behaviour*, The Dryden Press, Fort Worth, TX.

Fisk, R. P. 1981, 'Toward a consumption/evaluation process model for services', in Donnelly, J. H. & George, W. R. (eds), *Marketing of Services*, AMA, Chicago, pp. 191–5.

Gardner, M. P. 1985, 'Mood states and consumer behaviour: a critical review', *Journal of Consumer Research*, vol. 12, pp. 281–300.

Grove, S. J., Fisk, R. P. & Bitner, M. J. 1992, 'Dramatizing the service experience: a managerial approach', in Swartz, T. A., Bowen, D. E. & Brown, S. W. (eds), *Advances in Services Marketing and Management: Research and Practice*, vol. 1, JAI Press Inc., Greenwich, CT, pp. 91–121.

Guseman, D. 1981, 'Risk perception and risk reduction in consumer services', in Donnelly, J. H. & George, W. R. (eds), *Marketing of Services*, AMA, Chicago, pp. 200–4.

Hofstede, G. 1984, *Culture's Consequences: International Differences in Work Related Values*, Sage, Thousand Oaks, CA.

Howard, J. A. & Sheth, J. N. 1969, *The Theory of Buyer Behaviour*, John Wiley & Sons, New York.

Hui, M. K. & Bateson, J. E. G. 1991, 'Perceived control and the effects of crowding and consumer choice on the service experience', *Journal of Consumer Research*, vol. 18, pp. 171–81.

Kaplan, L., Szybillo, G. J. & Jacoby, J. 1974, 'Components of perceived risk in product purchase: a cross validation', *Journal of Applied Psychology*, vol. 59, pp. 287–91.

Knowles, P. A., Grove, S. J. & Pickett, G. M. 1993, 'Mood and the service customer', *Journal of Services Marketing*, vol. 7, no. 4, pp. 41–52.

Kurtz, D. L. & Clow, K. E. 1998, *Services Marketing*, John Wiley & Sons, New York.

Lovelock, C., Patterson, P. & Walker, R. 2001, *Services Marketing: an Asia-Pacific Perspective*, 2nd edn, Prentice Hall, Sydney.

Martin, C. L. & Pranter, C. A. 1989, 'Compatibility management: customer to customer relationships in service environments', *Journal of Services Marketing*, vol. 3.

McColl-Kennedy, J. R. & Fetter, R. 1999, 'Dimensions of consumer search behaviour in services', *Journal of Services Marketing*, vol. 13, no. 3, pp. 242–63.

McColl-Kennedy, J. R. & Fetter, R. 2001, 'An empirical examination of the involvement to external search relationship in services marketing', *Journal of Services Marketing*, vol. 15, no. 2, pp. 82–98.

Murray, K. & Schlacter, J. 1990, 'The impact of goods versus services on consumers' assessments of perceived risk and variability', *Journal of the Academy of Marketing Science*, vol. 18, no. 1, pp. 51–65.

Murray, K. B. 1991, 'A test of services marketing theory: consumer information acquisition activities', *Journal of Marketing*, vol. 55, Jan., pp. 10–25.

Pecotich, A. & Shultz, C. J. 1998, *Marketing and Consumer Behaviour in East and South-East Asia*, McGraw-Hill, Sydney.

Prewitt, M. 2002, 'Ooh La La: French eateries put the saviour back in fare', *Nation's Restaurant News*, vol. 36, no. 16, pp. 1, 48.

Ricks, D. A. 1993, *Blunders in International Business*, Blackwell Business, Oxford.

Schutte, H. & Ciarlante, D. 1998, *Consumer Behaviour in Asia*, Macmillan Business, London.

Trompenaars, F. 1993, *Riding the Waves of Culture*, Economist Books, London, p. 29.

Yan, R. 1994, 'To reach China's consumers, adapt to Guo Qing', *Harvard Business Review*, September–October, pp. 66–74.

Zeithaml, V. A. 1981, 'How consumer evaluation processes differ between goods and services', in Donnelly, J. H. & George, W. R. (eds), *Marketing of Services*, AMA, Chicago, pp. 186–90.

Zeithaml, V. A., Berry, L. L. & Parasuraman, A. 1988, 'Communications and control processes in the delivery of service quality', *Journal of Marketing*, vol. 52, pp. 35–48.

Zemke, R. & Connellan, T. 2001, *E-service*, AMACOM, New York, p. 134.

Chapter 3
Business-to-business services

Sheelagh Matear, Derek Nind and Kirsten Dixon

LEARNING OBJECTIVES

After reading this chapter you should be able to:
- appreciate the nature of business markets
- understand how business markets differ from consumer markets
- understand the importance of relationships in business-to-business marketing
- understand the buying decision processes in businesses
- appreciate the factors that influence the business buying process
- understand the roles in a buying centre
- appreciate challenges facing managers of business-to-business services.

CHAPTER OUTLINE

This chapter considers services that are purchased by other firms or organisations. Business-to-business services marketing differs from marketing services to consumers in many ways. The chapter begins by recognising the importance and growth of the B2B service sector and introduces buying and selling business organisations. The chapter then examines the differences between business and consumer markets and introduces the 'markets as networks' approach.

A fundamental notion in business-to-business marketing is that purchases do not take place in isolation. Environmental and network factors will affect the purchase decision, as will factors inside the organisation, including the individuals involved in the purchase decisions. This chapter also examines how relationships develop between buyer and seller organisations and what the general steps are in the purchase decision process. The chapter concludes by examining some of the challenges facing managers of business-to-business services.

Introduction

Many services are purchased by businesses and other organisational buyers such as universities, charities and government. The marketing activities that accompany these purchases may be referred to as industrial marketing or business-to-business services marketing. This chapter will use the terminology **business-to-business** or **B2B services marketing** as this better captures the nature of the exchange. It is important to note, however, that many types of organisation — not just for-profit businesses — purchase business-to-business services. This chapter will refer to for-profit businesses as well as organisations with other objectives.

Business-to-business or *B2B services marketing:* services marketing that is concerned with the exchange of services between organisations, not between individual consumers

Organisations purchase services such as transport for goods, legal services, equipment maintenance and rental, and market research. These activities make B2B services one of the fastest growing sectors of the service economy (Gross et al. 1993; Fitzsimmons, Noh & Thies 1998).

Figure 3.1 provides a simplified view of the major types of organisation in B2B markets and the range of services exchanged by these organisations. B2B organisations may be both service providers (sellers) and service users (buyers) at the same time. For instance, a management consulting firm may hire temporary staff for a data entry project from an organisation that finds work experience opportunities for people returning to work after injury. The same management consulting firm will in turn be commissioned to report on the service quality of a government-operated transport service.

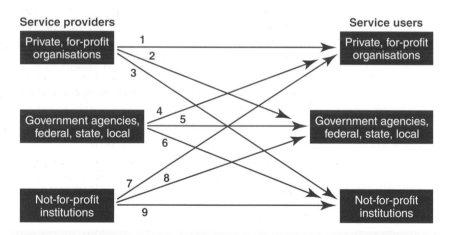

Line 1: A shipping company transports products from Australia to the USA.

Line 2: A private firm provides a prison security service to government.

Line 3: An accounting firm audits a sports club's accounts.

Line 4: A government agency organises an overseas market mission.

Line 5: The IRD provides training for local council payroll departments.

Line 6: A local council hires a venue to a sports club.

Line 7: A back to work organisation provides temporary staff.

Line 8: A university professor serves on a royal commission.

Line 9: A chamber of commerce provides Internet training for a charity.

Figure 3.1: Simplified view of major types of organisations and services in B2B markets
Source: adapted from Gross et al. 1993

How business markets differ

Organisational buying differs from consumer buying in several ways, and service providers need to understand these differences to market their services effectively to industrial buyers. There are likely to be more people involved in the decision to purchase a business service. The purchase decision is more likely to follow a formal or semi-formal process, particularly the first time an organisation purchases a service. In addition, much organisational purchasing takes place within existing relationships, and relationships shape much of the purchasing and other decisions of B2B organisations. Within relationships, organisational buying is characterised by high levels of interaction, customisation and inter-firm learning.

Derived demand:
demand that is derived from the demand for other products and services

A fundamental difference that distinguishes B2B services marketing from business-to-consumer (B2C) services marketing is that B2B services have **derived demand**. For example, the demand for container handling services at a port is derived from the demand for containers that transport goods to other markets, which in turn is derived from the demand for the contents of the container. Each of the drivers from which the demand is derived needs to be understood in order to forecast the demand for a B2B service. Thus, managers of B2B services have to understand not only the needs of their customers, but also the needs of their customers' customers, as these affect their forecasts, service design and delivery.

Table 3.1 outlines key differences between B2B and consumer markets. The size of the buyers, the sales volume, number of buyers, and purchase volume all create dynamics that increase the risk and importance of interactions and decisions. Large customers require individual, tailored solutions. The diversity of business customers and high levels of customisation required mean that B2B firms are becoming selective about which customers to serve, and are focusing on creating value for specific customers or groups of customers (Sharma et al. 2001). Moreover, high levels of customisation and complex organisational needs may lead to B2B services being more technological (Fitzsimmons et al. 1998). The personal and organisational risks of a company's decisions are generally much greater than those faced by consumers (Moriarty 1983).

Table 3.1	Differences between business and consumer markets	
Characteristic	**Business market**	**Consumer market**
Purchase volume	Varies widely	Smaller
Number of buyers	Fewer	Many
Size of individual buyers	Varies widely	Smaller
Buyer–seller relationships	Closer	More impersonal
Buyer–seller dynamic	Interactive	Action–reaction
Nature of buying	More professional	More personal
Nature of buying influence	Multiple	Fewer
Type of negotiations	More complex	Simpler
Use of reciprocity	Yes	No
Primary promotional method	Personal selling	Advertising

Source: adapted from Bingham & Raffield 1995, p. 7

The size of buying and selling organisations varies widely, from multi-national organisations employing tens of thousands of people to owner-operated single person enterprises. Often the buying firm is much larger than the service provider, as is the case when a local market research firm conducts focus groups for a multinational.

Table 3.1 outlines important differences between business and consumer markets but it does not provide a sense of the interdependence that exists between firms in business markets (Ford et al. 1998, p.1). This interdependence can be seen more clearly by looking at business markets from an interaction perspective, rather than considering service providers and users separately.

The interaction approach

The interaction approach suggests that business buying cannot be understood by looking at single purchase decisions or occasions. Most business purchases simply do not happen as one-off interactions and cannot be fully understood if treated in this way. **Business purchasing** is an interactive process where buyers and sellers are actively engaged with one another. It is not a case of a seller designing a service that a buyer may decide to purchase. Both buyers and sellers interact to design, produce and consume the service. These interactions take place within the context of a **relationship**. The process is ongoing, as the interactions that occur within a relationship contribute to the development of the relationship. The members of the organisation involved in the relationship have a memory of previous inter-actions within this relationship and others, and these past experiences influence their behaviour (Turnbull, Ford & Cunningham 1996).

Not all interactions will directly relate to the purchase of the service; some may be more social or personal in nature. Alternatively, interactions could be more technological in nature. For example, a company on the east coast of Australia may send data at the end of the day to an organisation in Perth for processing. The range of different interactions gives rise to multiple links between buyers and sellers in B2B relationships.

Relationships

Developing and managing relationships is critically important for B2B service firms. David Ford (1980, 1997) suggests that relationships develop through a series of stages, during which changes occur in experience, uncertainty, distance, commitment and the adaptations made by both buyer and seller in order to work together. He stresses, however, that not all relationships will develop through this sequence of stages.

The first stage of a relationship is the pre-relationship stage that occurs when a new service supplier is sought. There is no engagement between buyer and seller in the pre-relationship stage but the buyer and seller evaluate one another. The second or early stage of the relationship involves the buyer and seller interacting to develop the requirements or specifications for the service. It is difficult for services to be pilot-tested, as this may mean the development of entire systems, and the early stage of the relationship carries a high risk for both buyers and sellers, owing to uncertainty and a lack of information. Service provision occurs in the development stage, and the distance between the parties diminishes as they work together in producing and consuming the service. The experience of working together helps reduce the uncertainty in dealing with a new supplier, and buyers and sellers may show their commitment to developing the relationship by adapting to meet the needs of the other.

Business purchasing: the process of deciding and specifying what to buy, from which source and how much, as well as implementing these decisions, paying, and monitoring performance

Relationship: a mutual orientation of two parties, with a sense that this will develop and persist over a period of time and that both parties need to invest in the relationship

The development and adaptation process may occur quickly or over a long period of time until the long-term stage characterised by mutual dependence and standardised procedures (which may form barriers to exit) is reached. The final stage of the relationship is reached in stable markets over a long period of time. Here the relationship between the buyer and seller has become institutionalised and the business is conducted according to industry codes of practice (Ford 1997).

Thinking about the development of a personal relationship may help you understand how business-to-business relationships develop. For example, if you join a new gym you may need to find a new personal trainer. Initially there may be no contact between you and personal trainers at the new gym but you might watch how they work with other clients and they might assess your efforts in the gym. The relationship could then move into an early stage by discussing your requirements (or specifications) with the trainer. The specifications could include training for a half-marathon or reaching a target weight. The trainer may also have requirements in terms of frequency of gym visits (commitment) and other activity outside the gym sessions (investment and adaptations). There is a higher level of risk associated with the relationship at this stage as it is difficult to assess how you and the trainer will work together (uncertainty). By spending time (investing resources) developing specifications with this trainer, you are reducing the time available to consider other trainers. However, if you can agree on specifications, the relationship moves into a development stage; you begin to work with the trainer and service provision occurs. As the relationship continues, you and your trainer get to know each other better and understand each other's requirements better and uncertainty reduces. Both partners may show their commitment to the relationship by making adaptations and other investments in the relationship, such as meeting half an hour earlier in the morning or doing some research into suitable diets. The relationship may develop quickly, or you may take a long time to develop ways of working together, or the relationship may never develop satisfactorily. If the relationship does continue and moves into a long-term stage, it may last for several years and you and your trainer may develop a mutual dependence. The dependence from the trainer's perspective is likely to be more than monetary: you may be someone who they can use to trial new training regimes or diets or your success may attract other clients to the trainer. The time and effort that you have invested in working with this trainer would make it difficult to switch to another, as you would have to develop ways of working with someone else. Both you and the trainer would have to overcome these barriers to exit the relationship.

Not all relationships progress through every stage. Moreover, the progression is not always forward. Long-term relationships are likely to have passed through several stages of development and stability. Other relationships may never progress beyond the pre-development stage, and relationships can be terminated at any stage. However, the longer a relationship has existed and the more complex it is, the more difficult it is to terminate, as relationship termination can incur significant direct and indirect costs — and trauma.

An organisation will have many different types of relationship, ranging from long-term, close ones to more distant relationships. The relationships may also include collaborative, cooperative relationships, in which both organisations trust each other and are committed to maintaining the relationship. There are many different elements that make up relationships. Terms commonly used to describe and analyse relations include commitment, trust, cooperation, mutual goals, interdependence, power balance, performance satisfaction, comparison level of the alternatives, adaptations, non-retrievable investments, shared technology, and structural and social bonds (Wilson 1995).

Bluff is the southernmost port in New Zealand but its hinterland is a major exporter of products such as timber, meat and wool. In 1999, markets for these products were increasing in North Asia but no shipping line provided a service between Bluff and North Asia. South Port, the company that operates the port, decided to try to develop a relationship with New Zealand Orient line (NZOL), an independent shipping company serving North Asia. Before approaching NZOL, South Port commissioned research from a university to examine the market potential for such a service. The results suggested that South Port would have sufficient export cargo destined for North Asia to justify a port call. South Port took the results of the study to NZOL and then worked closely with NZOL and the exporters in the region to convince them to use an NZOL service calling at Bluff to supply their export markets. South Port also worked with other groups such as stevedores and inland transport operators to develop a port service that would suit NZOL. This was a different way of operating for South Port who, in common with many ports, had traditionally had an 'arm's-length' relationship with shipping companies. From NZOL's perspective, they have also changed the way they operate and now call at Bluff twice a month.

Markets as networks

Network: the group formed from relationships between organisations

The relationships that organisations have with other organisations form a **network**. B2B marketing (and other) decisions are taken within the context of this network. Figure 3.2 shows a simplified network between two firms. The focal relationship is the one that the buyer and seller are currently paying attention to, although this does not necessarily mean that it is the most important relationship for either company.

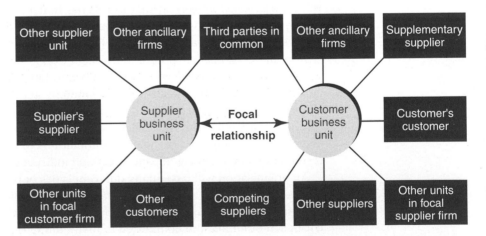

Figure 3.2: A simplified network
Source: Anderson, Hakansson & Johanson 1994, p.3

Figure 3.2 illustrates that other relationships affect the focal relationship. For instance, in the case of an aircraft cleaning contract, the buyer may also use another company to clean a proportion of planes, either at certain times of the day or in particular airports, so the relationship with the supplementary supplier also needs to be considered. Should the supplementary supplier also be offered an extension to their contract or should the volume of service supplied by the supplementary supplier be increased, this will affect the relationship between the main supplier and the buyer. The customer's customers (airline passengers) will also affect the focal relationship. If passengers are dissatisfied with the cleanliness of the plane, this will affect the focal relationship. Similarly, if the service provider also provides cleaning services to other airlines or other businesses then these relationships will affect their ability to invest in the focal relationship.

Understanding the network position of an organisation is important for managers, as network relationships can facilitate organisational learning through technology transfer and through working with other organisations in project marketing efforts, competitive strategy and internationalisation.

International Issues:
Airways Corporation, New Zealand

Despite the shock to global air travel caused by the September 11 terrorist attacks in the United States, air traffic congestion continues to pose a major challenge for aviation authorities. In the late 1990s, Airways Corporation considered that, by 2010, there would be a small number of alliances that would provide air traffic management systems worldwide. Airways therefore established the strategic goal of being a key player in one of these alliances, and in 1999 announced a 10-year partnership with Lockheed Martin Air Traffic Management. Airways, together with Lockheed Martin and Australian software development company Adacel, were successful in gaining a US$200 million contract to provide air traffic control technology and skills to cover United States oceanic airspace. This contract utilises Airways' satellite-based Oceanic Control System to provide a 'seamless air traffic management system' for three major air traffic regions. The system increases air route capacity by allowing planes to fly closer together and on preferred tracks. Passengers benefit through shorter flight times and airlines through lower fuel costs. Ultimately, Airways hope to develop a single air traffic management system across the entire north and south Pacific.

However, network membership does not guarantee success, as Airways, together with Lockheed Martin and other partners, were shortlisted for but not awarded the contract for the 46 per cent of the UK's air traffic management system being privatised. Nevertheless, Airways has gained valuable experience, which will serve it well in responding to future opportunities.

Sources: Airways Corporation 2001; Riordan 2001

Influences on B2B buying

This chapter has stressed that B2B buying decisions do not occur in isolation. The external environment, the memory of past decisions, future goals, the personnel involved, resources, and other organisational factors influence every decision. The multiplicity of influences on buying decisions can be grouped into different levels of influence (Gross et al. 1993):
- *Environmental factors:* physical, economic, technological, legal, political, cultural
- *Network factors relationships:* embeddedness, activities

- *Organisational factors:* technology, objectives, goals, tasks, actors, structure
- *Buying centre factors:* roles, resources
- *Individual factors:* status, politics, ethics.

Environmental factors

Environmental influences are those that influence the buying process by providing information as well as constraints. These factors are normally out of the control of the marketer, but they do have a major influence on why and how different organisations behave (Webster & Wind 1972). Environmental factors include the economic, political and technological environments. Of course, the major technological factor that is changing the way B2B firms create value for their customers and compete is the Internet.

The Internet has had a considerable impact on consumer markets but the impact on B2B markets is much greater, with the volume of B2B Internet transactions estimated to be five times greater than B2C transactions. It is expected to reach US$800 billion in 2003 (Sharma 2002). The Internet is fundamentally changing B2B marketing, and is expected to become the dominant marketing and delivery mechanism for B2B services (Sharma et al. 2001). Sharma et al. (2001) suggest that the Internet creates value for B2B customers, with an emphasis on one-to-one marketing allowing customers to seek, and suppliers to respond to, unique and specific needs.

Services Marketing on the Web:
Animation Research Limited

Animation Research Limited is a company based in Dunedin, New Zealand, that provides computer graphics services to television and other media companies, including advertising agencies. In 1992 ARL developed a computer graphics package that allowed real-time graphics to be incorporated into a live sports television broadcast (www.virtualspectator.com). The software allowed commentators to explain the tactics and ploys in yacht match racing to a much wider audience (not just yachting enthusiasts) and made it attractive for prime-time sports news reporting. The software revolutionised television coverage of the America's Cup. Since then, the company has developed 3D animation graphics for the Whitbread Round the World race, the flyover 3D graphics that are shown on live-to-air golf coverage and graphics for motor racing. Additionally, ARL has developed computer-generated animation of historical sites for major television documentaries, including a virtual model of Mt Everest. ARL uses its website as a promotional tool to showcase past projects to prospective clients; as a service delivery system; and as a development tool that allows clients to view progress and provide input into current projects.

Sources: Animation Research Ltd 2002; Virtual Spectator International Ltd 2002

Networks and relationships

As discussed above, the duration and scope of relationships varies widely. Relationships may be short-term and focus only on economic aspects or may exist over decades (as do relationships between airports and airlines) and include technological, social and economic aspects. The quality of relationships also varies widely, from poor relationships that are tolerated because of cost advantages or the lack of a suitable alternative provider, to excellent relationships in which both buyer and seller benefit and want to see the relationship continue.

Development and maintenance of relationships requires firm resources. If resources are limited, organisations may have to decide to develop one relationship instead of another. Similarly, organisations may not wish to or may be unable to develop new relationships because of the presence of existing relationships. For example, a company may not use an advertising agency if the agency already has a relationship with a major competitor.

Organisational factors

Organisational influences are the organisation's resources, culture, goals and objectives. These influences determine how the organisation will behave and how the individuals within the organisation will act when purchasing. Some organisations have very controlled, strict procedures, with heavy penalties when any employee operates outside these rules. For example, government agencies and state-owned enterprises often have strict procedures that must be followed for purchasing products and services.

Other organisations have few rules and procedures, so the employees have more freedom, which affects the buying process. Webster and Wind (1972) state that organisational influences comprise the organisational technology, organisational structure, organisational goals and tasks, and the organisational actors. These influences will determine how the buying centre will operate.

Buying centres

Business purchasing is often a multi-person and multi-role function within the organisation. The group or team of personnel involved with the purchase is known as a **buying centre** (Spekman & Stern 1979) or buying team (Anderson & Narus 1999). The roles within the buying centre (see figure 3.3) are described as user, buyers, influencers, deciders and gatekeepers.

Buying centre: all those involved in a purchase decision

Users are those members of the organisation who use the purchased services. Buyers are those with formal responsibility and authority for contracting with suppliers. Influencers are members of the organisation who influence the decision process directly or indirectly by providing information and criteria for evaluating alternative buying actions. The deciders are those with authority to choose among alternative buying actions, and gatekeepers control the flow of information into the buying centre (Webster & Wind 1972).

Each of the roles may be filled by employees from different functional areas and levels within the organisation. Alternatively, the same individual could perform more than one role. Key tasks in marketing B2B services are to identify who fills each role within the purchasing organisation and to understand the interrelationships between the different members of the buying centre. Understandably, this is not easy to do from outside the organisation, and it may be difficult to identify key members. Additionally, members of the buying centre could be drawn from outside the purchasing company. The roles in the buying centre, interactions between members of the group and members outside the group, and the function of the group itself will influence the purchase decision.

User

Buyer

Influencer

Gatekeeper

Decider

Figure 3.3: Roles within the buying centre

Services Marketing Action:
Who's in the buying centre?

Universities are significant purchasers of data and computer software. However, Angus, a sales representative for a company selling census information in a software mapping package, found it difficult to achieve any sales at a particular university, despite the interest shown in the software and other data products that he demonstrated to university departments. Angus arranged demonstrations through a department's technical officer, although he discovered that not all departments had someone in this role. The lecturers were usually enthusiastic about the software and data, although it was often difficult to find a demonstration time that suited many people. Despite this positive reaction, no sales were made. Angus followed up with the technical officer who told him that none of the lecturers had decided to buy the software and data. Also, as the technical officer, he tended to recommend the purchase of systems and software that would be used by the whole department rather than more specialist software that might only be used by a couple of lecturers. Angus then followed up with one of the lecturers who had been at his presentation. This lecturer told him that although it looked like a very useful package, she couldn't actually write out a purchase order but would have to request this through the department administrator. However, before this could happen, the purchase would have to be approved by the head of department. Angus wondered how he should approach future sales in the university and how he could find out who would use the products and who was actually able to purchase them.

Individual factors

It is important to remember that buying centres are composed of individuals. Individual personalities, perceived role, role stress, motivation and learning are the individual-level factors that may influence the purchasing decisions. Individuals may be motivated differently by reward systems, and decision makers may respond differently to buying decisions depending on the career opportunities afforded by that decision (Tanner 1999).

Models of buying behaviour

Buy-phase model:
commonly followed steps in the purchasing process — identification of need, establishment of specification, identification and subsequent evaluation of alternatives, selection of suppliers, and performance feedback

Many organisations follow a structured process in selecting services. The processes followed by organisations vary widely. The **buy-phase model** outlines commonly followed steps in the purchase process. This model takes the perspective of a purchasing organisation, and was developed before much of the work was done on how buyers and sellers form a relationship. Tanner (1999) suggests that the recent emphasis on understanding B2B relationships may have resulted in neglecting the value of traditional approaches, when they still have much to offer.

The buy-phase process model of buying decisions is a model that can be viewed from both traditional and interactive perspectives. It is a useful framework from which to examine the purchase process, as interactions between purchasing organisations and service suppliers can occur at different stages of the buying process and will continue after the purchase has been completed.

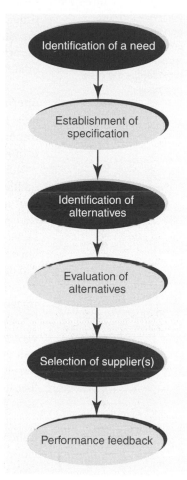

Figure 3.4: The buying decision (buy-phase) model
Source: Gross et al. 1993, p. 86, adapted from Robinson, Wind & Farris 1967

Steps in the buying process

The buying process begins with the identification of the need for the service. Some service needs, such as routine maintenance or transport services to meet a delivery schedule, may be forecast with reasonable accuracy. Others, such as the need for a lawyer, may occur unexpectedly and infrequently. This is similar to the pre-relationship stage in the relationship development model.

Specifications: a detailed description of the requirements of the service

Having established the need for a B2B service, the next stage is to develop **specifications** for the service. The intangible nature of services can make this step difficult. In the case of highly technical, specialised services, the service providers may have a better understanding of the service than its customers. Service blueprinting or flowcharting (Lovelock et al. 1999) can help in the development of specifications. Service providers may be involved in developing specifications, particularly existing service providers. This is likely to be a desirable position for the existing service provider but presents difficulties for new providers. The specification may be developed into a request for proposals or request for quotations (RFP/RFQ).

The next step is to identify alternative providers. As business buyers are actively seeking providers, they may approach providers and encourage them to respond to the RFP. Alternatively, buyers may consider whether to perform the service themselves, rather than using an external service provider (Grönroos 1979). The benefits of **outsourcing** service requirements are that the buying organisation can focus on its own core competencies and, at the same time, take advantage of the specialisation developed by the external service provider. Increasingly companies are choosing to outsource non-core requirements, which has contributed to the growth in B2B service firms (Fitzsimmons et al. 1998).

Outsourcing: an arrangement in which one company provides services for another company that could, or would normally, be provided by the client company

In responding to an RFP, a service provider must get customers to view its offering favourably. It can do this by developing a service design that incorporates the attributes (tangible and intangible) that customers consider most important. The identification of customers' key buying criteria is therefore of utmost importance in B2B service markets.

Reliability is one of the most important attributes of B2B services. Service quality and customer service are also very important. Price, too, is an important attribute, as it is a tangible indication of value (Zeithaml 1988). Despite this, price is rarely considered in isolation in a B2B situation. The ability of the service to meet customer needs is likely to be paramount. The service brand, corporate reputation and image are also important selection factors, although it can be difficult to distinguish between these elements in B2B service firms. The service brand is often synonymous with the corporate reputation or image.

Customers are more likely to use intangible cues rather than tangible elements to evaluate and select a service provider when the perceived level of risk is high, or when the customer cannot trial or evaluate the service before purchase (Bharadwaj et al. 1993; Flipo 1991). For example, customers of industrial trucking companies may base their selection of company on intangible cues such as the drivers' courtesy and professionalism (Richardson 1994).

The importance of these attributes varies across markets and segments, indicating that each market is unique in the way its member firms can create value for customers. The range of attributes found to be important in the selection of freight transport services, for example, is listed below (Dixon 2001).

- Freight charges
- On-time delivery and pick-up
- Reputation for reliability
- Transit time
- Directness of routes
- Frequency
- Geographic coverage
- Flexibility
- Capacity
- Suitability for goods
- Professionalism
- Communication
- Responsiveness
- Willingness to improve
- Speed of claims settlement
- Safe delivery
- Real-time tracking
- Technological sophistication
- Error-free billing
- Customer service
- Treatment of loss or damage

Once the alternatives have been evaluated, the service provider is selected and the service provided and consumed. Finally, the service provider is evaluated. Each of these steps requires interaction between buyer and seller and contributes to the development of the relationship.

As with many models of this type, the buy-phase model provides a generic description of the buying process. Not all organisations follow all steps of the model in every buying situation and the task of the B2B service provider is to understand the process its customers use and to appreciate where its efforts can be most effectively directed. Factors such as risk and the type of purchase decision will influence the number of steps followed and the degree of emphasis placed on different stages of the process.

Purchase types

Buying decisions can be broadly divided into three groups of purchase types or 'buy-classes': new task, modified rebuy and rebuy. New task situations are not as common as other buying situations and the purchase decision is more complex. As a result, the buying centre is usually large and the situation is perceived to have higher risk than a straight rebuy or modified rebuy. The risk and newness means the buyer usually looks for a larger number of alternatives. The straight rebuy is a common purchase situation. If the purchase is routine, then the buying centre is small and no alternative suppliers are considered. A modified rebuy has some features of both a straight new-buy and a straight rebuy. There is some familiarity with the service but the changes required create the uncertainty associated with a new-buy, as the outcome is unknown. Therefore the buying centre is larger than for a straight rebuy and once the specification is determined, a limited number of alternatives are likely to be considered.

The type of purchase also influences the buying decision process. In a straight rebuy situation, the customer will probably select a supplier after identifying a need, without having to establish new specifications or evaluate alternative suppliers, as long as the performance of the current supplier is satisfactory. In contrast, a new-buy situation will probably involve all steps in the buy-phase model, with extensive evaluation of suppliers.

Consequences of risk

Risk: *exposure of the consumer to the chance of injury, loss, damage or other negative consequences resulting from the purchase decision*

The level of perceived **risk**, defined by Sheth as the 'magnitude of the adverse consequences felt by decision-makers if they make a wrong choice, and the uncertainty in a buying situation' (1973), also affects the purchase process. Johnston and Lewin (1996) suggest eight consequences of increased risk: (1) the buying centre will become larger and more complex; (2) participants in the purchase decision-making process will have higher education and more expertise; (3) sellers of proven products and solutions will be favoured; (4) information searches will be active, and a wide variety of information sources will be used to guide and support decisions; (5) conflict between buyer centre members will increase because of the increased numbers and importance; (6) the decision rules for a purchase are firm specific, so for new buys there are often no decision rules, and risk is therefore much higher; (7) role stress will increase if the size and complexity of the purchase are high and if the purchase is highly visible and the outcome uncertain; (8) inter-firm relationships and communication networks become increasingly important in higher risk purchase situations.

Buyers are generally not rewarded for taking risks. When risk is increased, the status quo becomes the customer's preferred choice — assuming the status quo is satisfactory (Jackson, Neidell & Lunsford 1995). This is especially true when a new service supplier is being considered.

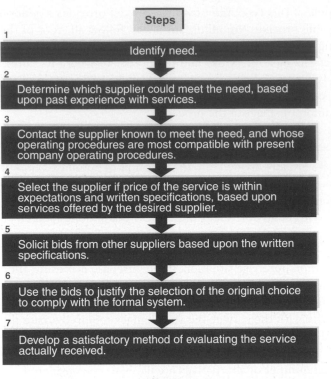

	Steps
1	Identify need.
2	Determine which supplier could meet the need, based upon past experience with services.
3	Contact the supplier known to meet the need, and whose operating procedures are most compatible with present company operating procedures.
4	Select the supplier if price of the service is within expectations and written specifications, based upon services offered by the desired supplier.
5	Solicit bids from other suppliers based upon the written specifications.
6	Use the bids to justify the selection of the original choice to comply with the formal system.
7	Develop a satisfactory method of evaluating the service actually received.

An alternative model of B2B service purchasing

An alternative model of B2B service purchasing (figure 3.5) takes more account of the context of buyers and sellers and the influence of service characteristics. Ferguson's (1979) model highlights the effects of intangibility and the resulting risk, which encourages the use of suppliers who are known to have operating systems compatible with the company's operating procedures. The model is based on findings from the warehousing industry, where the ability to evaluate the performance of different companies might be difficult. Therefore, prior experience and word of mouth within the purchasing organisation becomes important.

Figure 3.5: Ferguson's model of B2B service purchasing
Source: Ferguson 1979

Ethical Issues:
A development opportunity?

Sean had recently joined a software company that specialised in developing database management systems. He wanted to respond to a request from an old flatmate who now worked for a government agency to help develop specifications for an upcoming database project. Sean's manager wasn't very supportive of the idea as his experience of government agencies was that they were very price driven in their choice of supplier, whereas their company provided high quality solutions rather than lowest price. However, Sean argued that in working with the agency to develop specifications, their company would have a good chance of bidding successfully for the contract when it was announced and it would be a good opportunity to trial a new flowcharting method for developing specifications. Sean worked closely with the agency for two months and felt he had developed a good understanding of the needs of the agency. Moreover, the flowcharting method had helped to develop specifications that would ensure the agency got the database system it really needed. He also felt that he had been objective and hadn't allowed himself to be too biased towards the strengths of his company in developing the specifications. The request for proposals was announced and interested companies were sent a copy of the specifications to respond to. However, Sean's company wasn't even shortlisted. Sean felt that, although he hadn't expected the contract to go automatically his company, he should have been given more of a chance considering all the work that he had put into developing the specifications.

Managerial challenges

The combination of characteristics of services and a B2B marketing environment give rise to challenges for managers of B2B services. Two challenges that deserve particular attention are managing relationships and designing service offerings that create competitive advantage for the company.

Managing relationships

A key managerial task is to manage the portfolio of relationships. Most relationships are likely to have both positive and negative components. Relationships require investment and, if functioning well, can be assets for both buyers and sellers. However, poorly performing relationships can be liabilities for organisations. Organisations are likely to have a range of relationships, but the relationships that exist today may not be the right relationships to ensure success or even survival in the future. An organisation's portfolio of relationships is a key component of its strategy and strategic decision making.

Designing service offerings for competitive advantage

Managers also need to consider how their services will gain competitive advantage for the company. Competitive advantage will result from services that have attributes that are desired by customers. Therefore, service offerings need to be carefully designed before being offered to a customer (Grönroos 1990). For a service to be preferred by customers, it must either be of lower relative cost or superior value (Day & Wensley 1988). In designing customer-oriented services, it is important for managers to understand which attributes are most valued by customers and which cannot easily be replicated by competitors. Attributes such as service quality, customer service and reputation are less easily replicated by competitors and therefore have the potential to deliver competitive advantage.

Because the intangible nature of B2B services makes them difficult to assess, customers may also use tangible cues to help assess the service. These tangible clues could include the cleanliness of uniforms of personnel or the state of repair of equipment. Other opportunities to 'tangibilise' the service are afforded by communicating the outcome of the service delivery process to the customer. The most common tools used are bills, invoices, reports and presentations (Flipo 1991).

In addition to understanding the elements that are important in service design, managers also need to consider the trade-offs that customers are prepared to make between attributes. For example, research into service design for a shipping company found that customers were prepared to trade off a lower freight rate for the inclusion of key ports in the schedule.

Summary

LO1: Appreciate the nature of business markets.
* Business markets are composed of private for-profit, government and not-for-profit organisations.
* Organisations may be both buyers and sellers of B2B services.
* Business markets are characterised by high levels of interaction between buyers and sellers.

LO2: Understand how business markets differ.
* Demand for B2B services is derived from the demand for other products and services.

- B2B services are likely to be highly customised.
- Personal and organisational risks are generally much higher than for consumer decision making.
- B2B service provision is not a one-off interaction but is characterised by ongoing interactions between service provider and user.

LO3: Understand the importance of relationships in B2B marketing.

- Organisational buying takes place in relationships and contributes to the development of relationships.
- Relationships develop through interactions.
- Relationships develop through a series of stages.
- The relationships that exist between an organisation, its customers and suppliers form the network context for the organisation.

LO4: Understand the buying decision process.

- B2B buying decisions are likely to progress through a formalised sequence of steps.
- Interaction between provider and users can occur at each of the steps.

LO5: Appreciate the factors that influence the buying process.

- These factors can be grouped into environmental, network, organisational, buying centre and individual factors.
- There may be interrelationships between different groups of factors.

LO6: Understand the roles in a buying centre.

- User, decider, influencer, buyer and gatekeeper roles can be identified within buying centres.
- More than one individual can play these roles.
- An individual can play multiple roles.

LO7: Appreciate the challenges facing managers of B2B services.

- Managers need to manage a portfolio of relationships.
- Service design is an important element of competitive advantage.

key terms

Business purchasing: the process of deciding and specifying what to buy, from which source and how much, as well as implementing these decisions, and paying and monitoring performance (p. 54)

Business-to-business or B2B services marketing: service marketing that is concerned with the exchange of goods and services between organisations, not between individual consumers (p. 52)

Buying centre: all those involved in a purchase decision (p. 59)

Buy-phase model: commonly followed steps in the purchasing process — identification of need, establishment of specification, identification and subsequent evaluation of alternatives, selection of suppliers, and performance feedback (p. 61)

Derived demand: demand that is derived from the demand for other products and services (p. 53)

Network: the group formed from relationships between organisations (p. 56)

Outsourcing: an arrangement in which one company provides services for another company that could, or would normally be provided by the client company (p. 62)

Relationship: a mutual orientation of two parties, with a sense that this will develop and persist over a period of time and that both parties need to invest in the relationship (p. 54)

Risk: exposure of the consumer to the chance of injury, loss, damage or other negative consequences resulting from the purchase decision (p. 53)

Specifications: a detailed description of the requirements of the service (p. 61)

review questions

1. How do B2B markets differ from consumer markets?
2. How is B2B purchasing likely to differ from consumer purchasing?
3. How are interactions, relationships and networks related to one another?
4. Outline the steps that an organisation might follow in purchasing B2B services.
5. What roles could one expect to find in a buying centre?
6. How does Ferguson's model of B2B purchasing differ from the buy-phase model?
7. What impact could risk be expected to have on the buying centre?
8. How do the characteristics of services influence B2B services marketing?

application questions

1. Think of examples of services that may be purchased by organisations. Who would you expect to be part of the buying centre and what buying process would you expect to be used?
2. Think about the development of different personal relationships. What stages can you identify in the development of the relationship? To what extent are they similar to the stages that B2B relationships are considered to go through?
3. Think of a relationship between a B2B service provider and user. Try to identify other members of the network and their influence on this focal relationship.
4. Develop specifications for a night-time security service for a university campus.
5. Identify examples of new-buy, modified rebuy and rebuy purchases of B2B services, and examine the steps in the buying process for each.
6. Suggest attributes that are likely to be important in the selection of a bank by a small business. Are the same attributes likely to be important for a large company? What differences would you expect and why?

vignette questions

1. Read the Services Marketing Action vignette on South Port and New Zealand Orient Line on page 56 and answer the following questions.
   (a) Map the network likely to influence the focal relationship between South Port and NZOL.
   (b) Which relationships are most important for South Port and NZOL to manage?

2. Read the International Issues vignette on page 57. What strengths do Airways Corporation and Lockheed Martin Air Traffic Management bring to their partnership, respectively?
3. Read the Services Marketing on the Web vignette on page 58. How has the Internet influenced Animation Research Ltd?
4. Read the Services Marketing Action vignette on buying centres on page 60. How would you suggest that Angus approaches universities in future?
5. Read the Ethical Issues vignette on page 64.
   (a) What ethical issues can you identify in Sean's experience with the government agency?
   (b) How should both Sean and the agency approach these issues in the future?

 ## *recommended readings*

This chapter has provided a very brief introduction to B2B marketing. However, there are many B2B marketing texts that provide more information. Two recommended B2B texts are:

Bingham, F. G. & Raffield B. T. 1995, *Business Marketing Management*, South-Western College Publishing, Cincinatti, OH.
Gross, A. C., Banting, P. M., Meredith, L. N. & Ford, I. D. 1993, *Business Marketing*, Houghton Mifflin, Boston.

The importance of networks, relationships and interactions as a way of understanding B2B marketing has also been discussed in this chapter. Further background about the development of this approach and how it can be applied may be found in:

Ford, I. D. (ed.) 1997, *Understanding Business Markets*, 2nd edn, The Dryden Press, London.

For students who want to learn more about business buying behaviour, detailed models are provided by:

Johnston, W. J. & Lewin, J. E. 1996, 'Organisational buying behaviour: towards an integrative framework', *Journal of Business Research*, vol. 35, pp. 1–15.
Webster, F. E & Wind, Y. 1972, 'A general model for understanding organisational buying behavior', *Journal of Marketing*, vol. 36, April.

Finally, a recent examination of the particular characteristics and marketing challenges of B2B services is provided by:

Fitsimmons, J. A., Noh, J. & Theis, E. 1998, 'Purchasing business services', *Journal of Business and Industrial Marketing*, vol. 13, no. 3/4, pp. 370–80.

references

Anderson, J. C., Hakansson, H. & Johanson, J. 1994, 'Dyadic business relationships within a network context', *Journal of Marketing*, vol. 58, October, pp. 1–15.
Anderson, J. C. & Narus, J. A. 1999, *Business Market Management: Understanding, Creating, and Delivering Value*, Prentice Hall, Upper Saddle River, NJ.

Airways Corporation 2001, *Annual Report 2001*, www.airways.co.nz.

Animation Research Ltd 2002, viewed 18 May 2002, www.arl.co.nz.

Bharadwaj, S. G., Varadarajan, P. R. & Fahy, J. 1993, 'Sustainable competitive advantage in service industries, a conceptual model and research proposition', *Journal of Marketing*, vol. 57, October, pp. 83–99.

Bingham, F. G. & Barney, T. R. 1995, *Business Marketing Management*, South-Western College Publishing, Cincinatti, OH.

Day, G. S. & Wensley, R. 1988, 'Assessing advantage: a framework for diagnosing competitive superiority', *Journal of Marketing*, vol. 52, April pp. 1–20.

Dixon, K. L. 2001, 'Customer preferences and service design in the New Zealand — North Asian industrial shipping market', MCom thesis, University of Otago.

Ferguson, W. 1979, 'An evaluation of the BUYGRID analytic framework', *Industrial Marketing Management*, vol. 8, pp. 40–4.

Fitzsimmons, J. A., Noh, J. & Theis, E. 1998, 'Purchasing business services', *Journal of Business and Industrial Marketing*, vol. 13, no. 4/5, pp. 370–80.

Flipo, J. P. 1991, 'On the strategic implications of tangible elements in the marketing of industrial services', in Brown, S. W., Gummesson, E., Evardsson, B. & Gustavsson, B. (eds), *Service Quality: Multidisciplinary and Multinational Perspectives*, Lexington Books, New York.

Ford, D., Gadde, L., Hakansson, H., Lundgren, A., Snehota, I., Turnbull, P. & Wilson, D. 1998, *Managing Business Relationships*, John Wiley & Sons, New York.

Ford, I. D. 1980, 'The development of buyer–seller relationships in industrial markets', *European Journal of Marketing*, vol. 14, no. 5/6, pp. 339–54.

Ford, I. D. (ed.) 1997, *Understanding Business Markets*, 2nd edn, The Dryden Press, London.

Grönroos, C. 1979, 'An applied theory for marketing industrial services', *Industrial Marketing Management*, vol. 8, pp. 45–50.

Grönroos, C. 1990, *Service Management and Marketing: Managing the Moments of Truth in Service Competition*, Lexington Books, New York.

Gross, A. C., Banting, P. M., Meredith, L. N. & Ford, I. D. 1993, *Business Marketing*, Houghton Mifflin, Boston.

Johnston, W. J. & Lewin, J. E. 1996, 'Organisational buying behaviour: towards an integrative framework', *Journal of Business Research*, vol. 35, pp. 1–15.

Lovelock, C., Vandermerwe, S. & Lewis, B. 1999, *Service Marketing: A European Perspective*, Prentice Hall Europe.

Moriarty, R. T. 1983, *Industrial Buying Behaviour: Concepts, Issues and Applications*, Lexington Books, Lexington, MA.

Richardson, H. L. 1994, 'Intangibles: new role in carrier selection', *Transportation and Distribution*, vol. 35, no. 4, p. 41.

Riordan, D. 2001, 'Bid for foreign airways work no flight of fancy', *New Zealand Herald*, 5 June.

Robinson, P. J., Faris, C. W. & Wind, Y. 1967, *Industrial Buying and Creative Marketing*, Allyn & Bacon, Boston, p. 14.

Sharma, A. 2002, 'Trends in Internet-based business-to-business marketing', *Industrial Marketing Management*, vol. 31, pp. 77–84.

Sharma, A. , Krishnan, R. & Grewal, D. 2001, 'Value creation in markets: a critical area of focus for business-to-business markets', *Industrial Marketing Management*, vol. 30, pp. 391–402.

Sheth, J. N. 1973, 'A model of industrial buyer behavior', *Journal of Marketing*, vol. 37, October, pp. 50–6.

Spekman, R. E. & Stern, L. W. 1979, 'Environmental uncertainty and buying group structure: an empirical investigation', *Journal of Marketing*, vol. 43, spring, pp. 54–64

Tanner, J. F. 1999, 'Organisational buying theories: a bridge to relationships theory', *Industrial Marketing Management*, vol. 28, pp. 245–55.

Turnbull, P., Ford, D. & Cunningham, M. 1996, 'Interaction, relationships and networks in industrial markets: an evolving perspective', *Journal of Business and Industrial Marketing*, vol. 11 no. 3/4, pp. 44–62.

Virtual Spectator International Ltd, accessed 20 May 2002, www.virtualspectator.com.

Webster, F. E. & Wind, Y. 1972 'A general model for understanding organisational buying behavior', *Journal of Marketing*, vol. 36, April, pp. 12–19.

Wilson, D. T. 1995, 'An integrated model of buyer–seller relationships', *Journal of the Academy of Marketing Science*, vol. 4, no. 23, pp. 335–45.

Zeithaml V. A. 1988, 'Consumer perceptions of price, quality and value: a means-end model and synthesis of evidence', *Journal of Marketing*, vol. 52, no. 3, pp. 2–22.

Part 2

Customer perceptions

Chapter 4
Service quality

Tracey Dagger and Meredith Lawley

LEARNING OBJECTIVES

After reading this chapter you should be able to:

- define service quality
- distinguish between service quality and satisfaction
- understand the importance of service quality to the management of services
- describe various models of service quality
- be aware of current issues regarding service quality.

CHAPTER OUTLINE

Service quality is of increasing importance in the management of services, as it is clearly linked to profitability. Basically, customers are prepared to pay a premium for quality and are more likely to repeat the purchase and to relay positive perceptions of an organisation to other customers when quality is high. Hence, the purpose of this chapter is to introduce and explore the concept of service quality.

This chapter has four major sections. The first section defines service quality and clearly distinguishes between service quality and satisfaction. Next, the importance of service quality to the management of services is discussed, followed by a description of five models of service quality. The chapter finishes by reviewing some current issues and debates in the field of service quality, including issues of measurement and the link between service quality and satisfaction.

Introduction

What is service quality? When people think about a Hilton Hotel or a Sheraton Hotel, they imagine five-star luxury, large rooms, a spacious lobby and high standards of service. When people think about a Travelodge or a Novotel they think three to four star — comfortable but not luxurious, rooms not quite as large, not as many additional services. Note too, that people can have clear expectations of service quality without necessarily ever having stayed at these hotels. Similarly, a variety of attributes can contribute to service quality, including physical aspects such as quality of furnishings, and interpersonal aspects such as attitudes of staff.

Why is service quality important? Again, think of the manager of a Hilton Hotel — think about why they would want to maintain high levels of service quality. If the service quality is not what guests expect, they are unlikely to come back. Moreover, those guests are likely to tell their friends and associates. Very soon, either the business will suffer or the manager will be out of a job.

The purpose of this chapter is to explore the concept of service quality and its importance to businesses. Service quality is very closely linked to satisfaction. While interest in satisfaction predated the current interest in service quality, service quality has emerged as a field of equal, if not greater, interest to academics and practitioners. However, satisfaction is still the subject of considerable research; therefore it is discussed in detail in the following chapter.

This chapter begins by clearly distinguishing between service quality and satisfaction before going on to establish the importance of service quality. Next, some common models of service quality are described and the practical implications of these models for managers are examined. The chapter finishes with a review of current issues in service quality.

What is service quality?

We previously considered the service quality of various hotels — now let's go back one step. What do you think of when 'quality' is mentioned: how good something is? the level of excellence of certain features? When we talk about the quality of a physical product like a shirt, we would probably look at the quality of the material, how good the workmanship is, the stitching, the styling and so on. But what do we think of when determining how good a service is? Again, think about service quality in a hotel. It is not as straightforward as the physical product example, as several different aspects of the hotel experience contribute to overall service quality.

Researchers often describe service quality as an elusive and abstract concept, similar in nature to an attitude, as it represents a general, overall appraisal of a product or service (Bitner 1990; Parasuraman, Zeithaml & Berry 1985).

Quality perceptions can occur at several levels in an organisation. Consumers may think about the quality of the interaction, the core service or the organisation as a whole. Note in the following International Issues vignette how Raffles combines the different aspects of the hotel experience, including staff training, to ensure the ultimate in service quality.

International Issues:
Raffles Singapore — international service quality

Raffles International operates and manages 17 hotels and resorts in 10 countries within the Asia-Pacific region, Europe and North America, using two brand names — Raffles and Merchant Court. The flagship of the Raffles brand is Raffles in Singapore. The name Raffles conjures up images of the ultimate in service quality. This is reflected in the credo of Raffles: 'A successful hotel is something beyond its location, its décor or its amenities. A successful hotel is a place where you are treated so well that you want to come back . . . We take pride in going the extra mile to create that little bit of magic, which separates landmarks from mere hotels and resorts' (Raffles International 2001).

But what makes up the 'going the extra mile' that gives Raffles its reputation for outstanding service? A few anecdotes from Raffles Singapore may give some insight. Raffles receptionists are trained to notice, when a guest is checking in, whether the guest is left- or right-handed. If the guest is left-handed, they are assigned a room set up for a left-handed person, that is, with telephone and desk set up appropriately. If a 'left-handed' room is not available, a staff member is sent to rearrange a room. In addition, frontline staff are trained to meet the specific needs of guests of various nationalities. For example, staff will make eye contact with American guests but will not make eye contact with Japanese guests. Americans think you are rude if you talk to them without looking them in the eye, while the Japanese think you are rude when you do.

Raffles International maintains this standard of service quality throughout all their properties worldwide.

Service quality: the result of an evaluation process in which the customer compares their perceptions of the service with their expectations

Customer satisfaction: 'the customer's fulfilment response; a judgement that a product or service feature, or the product or service itself, provided a pleasurable level of consumption-related fulfilment, including levels of under- or over-fulfilment' (Oliver 1997, p. 13)

Service quality can be defined as a consumer's judgement or perception of an entity's overall excellence or superiority, often as a result of comparing expectations with perceived performance (Parasuraman, Zeithaml & Berry 1988). Note that in this definition we are talking about judgements and perceptions that, unlike **customer satisfaction**, are not experience dependent; that is, we have a perception of the quality of a restaurant (based on our expectations) without necessarily having eaten there. In contrast, we cannot decide if we are satisfied until after we have had a meal at the restaurant. This definition highlights the role of expectations in service quality evaluation and also highlights the comparison process through which consumers compare expectations with performance.

The origin of service quality theory can be found in the early product quality and customer satisfaction literature. Shostack's (1977) seminal article 'Breaking free from product marketing' marked the beginning of a move away from the adoption of product-oriented strategies by service firms. The quality of services is more difficult for consumers to evaluate than that of physical products, primarily because of the intangibility, inseparability and variability of services. Perishability is not covered here, as it does not have a major impact on service quality beyond its interrelationship with intangibility, inseparability and variability, which are discussed next. Each of these characteristics greatly affects the way in which service quality is evaluated by consumers and managed by marketers.

Intangibility

The intangible nature of services results in the inability of consumers to make a full assessment of the quality of a service before purchase. The quality of physical products can be determined before purchase, as consumers can usually test, sample, touch, smell and feel a product before making a purchase decision. Take the example of a new computer. We can readily compare a number of brands within the one retail outlet, we can touch, experiment with, and easily see the differences between competing brands before making our purchase decision. Services however, are very different. As services are inherently intangible, consumers cannot easily determine the quality of the service before purchase. In addition, competing service providers are generally geographically dispersed. More importantly, services cannot often be sampled or experimented with before they are actually purchased. This results in consumers experiencing higher levels of perceived risk, be it functional, financial, temporal, psychological, sensory or social risk.

Services, by nature, are either high in **experience qualities** or **credence qualities**. For services high in experience qualities, the consumer can only determine the quality of the service once it has actually been experienced, or once the consumer has spent considerable time, effort and money evaluating and making a purchase decision. For services high in credence qualities, even after consumers have purchased a service, they have difficulty determining the quality of their purchase and making a post-purchase evaluation of their buying decision. For example, when negotiating a home loan you do not know whether you have received excellent service quality even after finalising the loan because the service is highly individualised and difficult to compare with other financial offerings. While consumers are more likely to experience anxiety when purchasing services exhibiting credence qualities rather than experience qualities, consumers will still be much more likely to experience some post-purchase anxiety when purchasing a service (because of its unique characteristics) than when purchasing a tangible good.

Services marketers must be aware that it is often difficult, if not impossible, for consumers to determine the quality of services before, during and even after the service has been performed. Therefore, marketers must develop strategies aimed at tangibilising the intangible, standardising production and consumption (as much as possible), and reducing the perceived risk and cognitive dissonance often associated with the purchase of services. This can be done through the introduction of warranties, money-back guarantees, and so on. Nevertheless, comparing service products is still very difficult for consumers.

Compare, for example, the purchase of accountancy services with the purchase of a computer. In the case of a computer, you can see, touch and sample the product, its functions and output before purchase, so you can assess the level of quality before actually purchasing the computer. The fact that physical goods are generally high in search qualities means that consumers can assess their colour, style, shape, functionality, price and performance, and make a judgement on the quality of the good before purchase and consumption. In the case of the computer, assessing the quality before purchase and consumption lowers the perceived risks (function, financial, temporal, psychological, sensory) associated with purchasing a physical good and reduces any **cognitive dissonance** in the post-purchase phase of the

Experience qualities:
service attributes that can only be evaluated by consumers after the service production process

Credence qualities:
service attributes that cannot be evaluated by consumers with any certainty, even after they have experienced the service process

Cognitive dissonance:
the discomfort buyers may feel after purchase, for example, 'Did I get value for money?'

buying decision process. In contrast, you cannot feel, touch or sample the accountant's consultation or advice before partaking in, purchasing and consuming the service. Moreover, you may find it very difficult to compare the financial advice of different accountants and even more difficult to judge the quality of the advice because of these factors. Put simply, you cannot go to the accountant to sample or try out the advice, as you would the computer, and then decide if you want to purchase the service.

Similarly, you cannot sample a haircut to make sure you are getting the best quality available before you actually become involved in the service process and have your hair cut. Therefore, post-purchase anxiety and perceived risk are often high when purchasing services. The role of marketers is in realising that the more intangible a service, the fewer visible cues consumers have on which to base their quality perceptions, and the more marketing is required to 'tangibilise' the intangible. This may involve augmented services such as warranties, guarantees and after-sales service as well as the provision of tangible cues such as logos, brand names, staff uniforms and so on.

Inseparability

As services are inseparable, production and consumption take place simultaneously. This suggests that consumers' involvement in the production process will affect the performance and quality of the service encounter. As consumers are often both co-producers and co-consumers of services, the quality of the service becomes dependent on the quality of the interaction between the service provider and customer. Within health care, for example, the patient's role — from diagnosis to administering treatment in the absence of the provider — may ultimately determine the success or failure of the health care process in reaching a desirable outcome. Thus, the active and collaborative role patients play in the success of treatment outcomes, including physical and psychological functioning, reflects the complex nature of the relationship between health care service providers and consumers. Within this setting, the interaction between the doctor and patient as well as any tangible cues, such as the waiting room and the receptionist, act as surrogate indicators of quality upon which health care patients base their quality assessments. Consumers often rely on this interpersonal process as an indicator of quality when evaluating services products.

Variability

Simultaneous consumption and production, the involvement of other customers, the use of service personnel as distribution channels and a host of environmental influences may result in variability of service quality and performance between encounters. Service variability makes it difficult to apply quality standards in order to ensure an identical output each time the service is performed. The involvement of individual customers with differing cognitive and emotional orientations in the production of a service makes controlling the service outcome difficult. Positive and negative service perceptions and evaluations are greatly influenced by customer and provider orientations. Similarly, the appearance, manner, actions and personality of contact personnel can dramatically affect customers' overall service perceptions and can lead to differentiation at the service level. Hence, consumers may rely on the interpersonal process or the relationships they perceive with service personnel as key indicators of quality when evaluating service products. Note in the Services Marketing on the Web vignette how Dell computers are using the Internet to reduce reliance on contact personnel and so reduce variability.

In summary, this section has provided a definition of service quality and explored the reasons why service quality is more difficult to evaluate than the quality of physical products. On this basis, the reasons for the importance of service quality to the management of services will be explored next.

Services Marketing on the Web: Dell Computers — service online

From their beginning in 1984, Dell Computers pioneered the direct selling of computing products and services, with the move to full e-commerce in 1996. Dell allows you to customise your computer and order it online. What's more, once it is ordered you can track the progress of your order online through the Dell site. About half of Dell's technical support is also done over the Internet. This innovative approach to channel management has been carried through to Dell's approach to customer service. Customers in the Asia-Pacific region can order and receive their computer within seven to 10 working days. Further, warranty and service guarantees are clearly detailed on the Dell site at www.dell.com, including 24-hour access to phone support, lifetime technical online support and next-day troubleshooting support.

Dell not only makes these claims, but also has the awards to support them, including awards from *PC World* for reliability and service, based on customer surveys and feedback. The outcome of all this: Dell has a reputation for service quality that is the envy of many companies doing business on the Internet.

Importance of service quality to the management of services

Service quality is of increasing importance to organisations as improvements in service quality have been linked to increased profit margins; repeat purchase behaviour; a willingness on the part of consumers to pay price premiums; lower administrative, billing and account maintenance costs; and increased positive word-of-mouth recommendations from customers (Halstead, Casavant & Nixon 1998; Zeithaml 2000). Financial indicators such as market value, overall corporate performance and market share (Rust & Zahorik 1993) have also been linked to service quality improvements.

Given that the improvement of service quality is an investment in the long-term survival and growth of organisations operating within competitive markets (Parasuraman, Zeithaml & Berry 1991), success within service sectors will depend on the ability of organisations to generate high levels of perceived service quality. Let's look at the health care sector as an example.

The key benefits associated with improving service quality within the health care sector may include the following:

- *Insulating customers for competitors*. Consumers are more likely to continue to patronise a firm that has excellent service quality, even when competitors' offerings are attractive to consumers. Within the health care industry, research has found that positive service quality perceptions resulted in consumers being more willing to pay price premiums for the services they received and having a greater intention to use the service again (Bowers, Swan & Koehler 1994; Taylor & Baker 1994).

- *Creating competitive advantage.* High service-quality perceptions can provide an organisation with a competitive advantage that may be difficult for competing firms to replicate. (For example, consider the case of Raffles Hotels as described in the previous International Issues vignette.)

- *Encouraging repeat purchasing.* Service quality levels have been linked to repeat purchasing behaviour on the part of consumers. Research has indicated that it costs three to five times more to replace a lost customer than to retain a repeat customer (Horovitz 2000; Fisk, Grove & John 2000). Within health care, researchers have found that higher levels of service quality are associated with greater intentions to use the service again (Bowers, Swan & Koehler 1994; Taylor & Baker 1994) and a decrease in the likelihood that health care consumers will switch institutions or discontinue treatment (Headley & Miller 1993).

- *Promoting loyalty.* High levels of service quality facilitate customer loyalty. Within the health care industry, research has shown that positive service quality perceptions are associated with the choice of provider, with decreases in patient turnover and malpractice law suits (Marshall, Hays & Mazel 1996) and with greater intentions to use the service again (Woodside, Frey & Daly 1989; Taylor & Baker 1994).

- *Enhancing positive word of mouth.* Positive service quality perceptions have been linked to the likelihood of consumers spreading positive word-of-mouth advertising about the service firm. Within the health care sector, patients with positive perceptions of the quality of service they received were more likely to spread positive word-of-mouth communications to other consumers.

- *Lowering the costs of attracting new customers.* The benefits of fostering positive service quality perceptions — that is, positive word-of-mouth communications, loyalty and repeat purchase behaviour — results in lower costs for attracting new customers (Horovitz 2000; Fisk, Grove & John 2000). Within the health care industry, lower operating costs have been associated with positive service quality perceptions as a result of increased repeat purchase behaviour and consumer loyalty (Rust & Zahorik 1993).

- *Facilitating a positive service outcome.* If consumers perceive the quality of the service they are receiving to be of a high standard, they are more likely to put extra effort into the co-production of the service. Often this will result in service outcomes that are more positive for the consumer and organisation. For example, positive service quality perceptions within the health care sector have been linked to decreases in the discontinuation of treatment, increased efficiency in patient involvement in the co-production of the health care program and, most importantly, better health outcomes (O'Connor, Trinh & Shewchuk 2000).

For all the previously mentioned reasons, service quality should be of concern to all managers. But what strategies can management adopt to improve and maintain levels of service quality? The next section will address this question by presenting several models of service quality and examining the implications of these models for improving and managing service quality.

Models of service quality

Various researchers have developed models of service quality. Five of the key models include, in chronological order: the disconfirmation of expectations model (Oliver 1977, 1980, 1981); the Nordic model developed by Grönroos (1984); the SERVQUAL/Gaps model developed by Parasuraman, Zeithaml and Berry (1985, 1988, 1991); and the three-component model developed by Rust and Oliver (1994). More recently, researchers (Dabholkar, Thorpe & Rentz 1996; Brady & Cronin 2001) have focused on integrating the perspectives of these four service quality models in an effort to extend current thought in service quality. It is important that we explore each of these models so that we can see how service quality as a construct has developed over time. We begin with the **disconfirmation** of expectations model, which is the cornerstone of service quality research.

Disconfirmation: state in which expectation levels are perceived to have been met, exceeded or not met in actual performance of the service

Disconfirmation of expectations model

As noted earlier, the theoretical underpinnings of service quality are based on early product and satisfaction research (Oliver 1977; Olshavsky & Miller 1972). Much of the early service quality theory draws from research into how disconfirmed expectations affect product perceptions. That is, if our expectations are not met we change our perception and attitude toward a product. Thus, many early models of service quality (e.g. Grönroos 1982, 1984; Parasuraman, Zeithaml & Berry 1988) are based on the disconfirmation model used in the physical goods literature (Oliver 1977).

The disconfirmation of expectations model shown in figure 4.1 proposes that there are three determinants of customer (dis)satisfaction: expectations, perceptions and (dis)confirmation. Using adaptation level theory as a basis, Oliver (1980) claims that customers form expectations before the purchase of a product or service, with expectations acting as a standard or frame of reference against which service performance is judged.

For example, before we go to the movies or attend the theatre, we have an idea of what the experience will be, of whether will enjoy the movie, laugh if it is a comedy, cry if it is a tearjerker, and so on. We then judge the movie experience against these expectations. One teenage male friend was very disappointed after going to see the movie *Pearl Harbor* — he expected a war movie with lots of action and, as anyone who has seen the movie would know, *Pearl Harbor* is not really a war movie but a love story. Indeed he was so disappointed he did not even stay to see the complete movie but walked out part way through. However, another teenage female friend expected a love story, and enjoyed the film so much she went to see it again.

Within this model, expectations form a baseline for consumers' satisfaction levels. The higher the expectation in relation to actual performance, the greater the degree of disconfirmation and the lower the level of satisfaction to be achieved. Conversely, the lower the expectation in comparison to actual performance, the smaller the degree of disconfirmation and the higher the level of satisfaction (Tse & Wilton 1988).

Conceptually there are three possible outcomes of this model (see figure 4.1). If service performance exceeds pre-purchase expectations, positive disconfirmation results, and consumers are likely to demonstrate a high level of satisfaction; in other words, they are pleasantly surprised. For example, if you put your car in for a regular service and find when you pick it up, that it has been washed at no extra cost, you will be very pleased. Remember, also, the example of the teenager enjoying the movie *Pearl Harbor* — she was so satisfied she repeated the experience within a matter of days.

The second possible outcome occurs when a service experience simply meets consumer expectations: confirmation results and the consumer is merely satisfied. For example when eating at a McDonald's restaurant, consumers know what to expect in relation to service quality.

Finally, if the service experience does not meet or is below consumers' expectations, negative disconfirmation results, and consumers are dissatisfied. This occurred in the 2001 maintenance problems of Ansett Airlines, when several planes were not allowed to fly in a peak period, resulting in cancellation of many flights and long delays with others. As the delays and cancellations were unexpected, consumers expressed extreme dissatisfaction. Again, recall the example of the male teenager who walked out of *Pearl Harbor*, as it was not what he expected.

The model also implies that if customer expectations for a service are relatively low, then they may be satisfied with a service experience even if the performance is poor. For example, if a restaurant has a reputation for inexpensive meals, customers will probably expect to wait or queue for a table and may not expect a high degree of personal service.

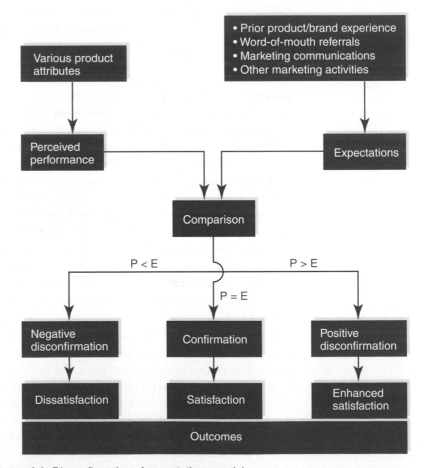

Figure 4.1: Disconfirmation of expectations model
Source: Patterson 1993, adapted from Hill

Although originally developed to explain the formation of consumer satisfaction judgements, the disconfirmation of expectations model has also been used to explain service quality perceptions, and has influenced subsequent service quality models (such as those of Grönroos 1982; Parasuraman, Zeithaml & Berry 1985, 1988). These models will be discussed in turn.

The Nordic model of service quality

As one of the first models of service quality that adopted the disconfirmation of expectations paradigm, Grönroos's (1984) model represents the service experience on the basis of functional and technical elements. The concept of **technical quality** refers to what the consumer receives from the service, or the outcome of the service process — for example the actual haircut from a hairdresser or legal advice from a solicitor. The **functional quality** of the service refers to the way the service is delivered as reflected through the consumer's perception of interactions that occur during the service encounter. This might include, for example, the friendliness of the hairdresser, the amount of attention given to the customer and so on.

Technical quality: the outcome of the service

Functional quality: the components of the process used to arrive at the service outcome

Based on early satisfaction literature, Grönroos's model of perceived service quality reflects the effect of the disconfirmation of expectations model on the development of service quality models. Within this model, Grönroos contends that, in forming service quality perceptions, consumers compare the expected level of service and the actual service performance they receive.

The key implication of this model for managers is the clear distinction drawn between the service itself and how it is delivered. This model emphasises that companies must be very careful in what they promise to consumers. The attributes and benefits popularised by companies through traditional marketing activities, such as advertising and promotion, must be realistic when compared to the service that customers eventually receive. If organisations promise a level of service that is higher than what they can actually deliver, customers will be dissatisfied and unhappy with the service they receive.

The model also implies that the interaction between the buyer and seller in a service setting is as important as the technical quality of the service. The technical quality dimension results from the know-how of the firm and includes good technical solutions, the technical abilities of employees, and so on. While it is important to have high technical quality in the service outcome (a customer receiving a good haircut, for example) it is not enough in itself. Firms also need to ensure that they provide good functional quality. Thus, the contact staff in an organisation are important when consumers are forming their overall service quality perceptions. The accessibility of the firm's services, the customer orientation of self-service systems, and the firm's ability to maintain contact with its customers are vital in generating positive service quality perceptions.

Technical and functional quality dimensions are interrelated. For some services, these two quality aspects can compensate for each other. For example, if the teller at the bank is not really friendly but is very efficient and completes your transaction quickly and accurately, you may still be satisfied, despite the teller's poor interpersonal (functional) manner. Similarly, a friendly manner may compensate for unsatisfactory technical quality. As technical quality relates to the core product, this is hard to achieve.

Gaps model: *a diagnostic model that helps identify the gaps between expectations and perceptions of management, employees and customers*

SERVQUAL: *a 44-item instrument used to measure customer expectations and perceptions according to five service quality dimensions: responsiveness, tangible aspects, assurance,*

The basis of much of the current thought in service quality research stems from the work of Parasuraman, Zeithaml and Berry (1985, 1988, 1991, 1994), who developed two of the most widely used models of service quality: the **gaps model** and **SERVQUAL**. Based on the disconfirmation model, these models view service quality as the gap between the expected level of service and the customer's perceptions of the actual service received. To illustrate, imagine a friend tells you about an exceptional restaurant: great service, cosy atmosphere, delicious food. Dining at the restaurant, you find the atmosphere noisy, you wait a long time for service and you think the food is average. Your expectations have not been met. Performance is below what you expected. Your service quality perception is low. Essentially, the greater the gap between expectations and performance, the lower the level of perceived service quality.

The gaps model (see figure 4.2) serves as a useful diagnostic tool for evaluating why service quality is failing, and comprises two primary sections. The first section, comprising four gaps that are aimed at management, reflects potential service failure as a result of management's actions. These gaps provide a framework for management to understand the causes of service quality failure. The second section, or fifth gap, occurs at the consumer level. This gap suggests that the difference between expected and perceived levels of service form consumers' overall perception of service quality. It is this gap that is the central focus of the gaps model. It is also this gap that SERVQUAL measures. The customer gap (or fifth gap) identifies service performance problems but does not determine the causes of these problems; it is the four provider gaps that help management identify where service quality has failed. Service firms need to close the gap between customer expectations and perceptions of the

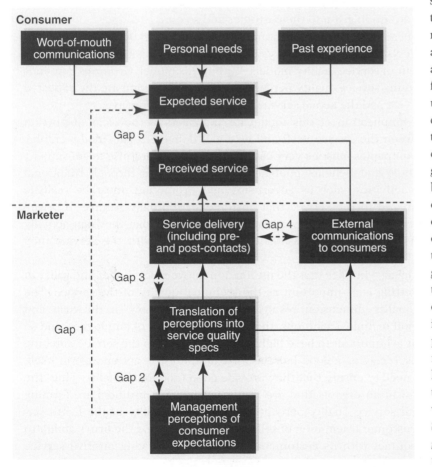

Figure 4.2: Gaps model of service quality
Source: Parasuraman, Zeithaml & Berry 1985

actual service received if they want to satisfy their customers and build long-term relationships. To do this, the model suggests that the four provider gaps need to be closed.

The five gaps are:

- *Provider gap 1* — management does not understand what the customer expects. This results in service design and delivery that does not match the expectations of consumers.

- *Provider gap 2* — management fails to design service standards that meet customer expectations.
- *Provider gap 3* — the service delivery fails to meet service standards. The people, processes and systems fail to deliver the service to the necessary standards.
- *Provider gap 4* — the promises made by the organisation in external marketing communications do not match actual service delivery. That is, the organisation promised what it could not deliver.
- *The customer, gap 5* — where the customer's perception of the service experience does not match their expectations of the service performance and outcome.

In summary, the gaps model emphasises that managers must understand what customers expect from the service experience. They must also understand the barriers that prevent the firm meeting the needs of its customers.

The managerial implications of the gaps model are summarised in table 4.1. As indicated in this table, a variety of strategies and tactics are available to address each of the identified gaps.

Table 4.1   The gaps model — managerial implications

Gap	Explanation	Reasons for occurrence	Strategy/tactics
1	Customers' expectations versus management's perceptions of customers' expectations	Failure of management to understand consumers' expectations of service provision	• Determine what customers' expectations are through research • Improve communication • Flatten hierarchical structure to open up communication between management and consumers • Foster upward communication
2	Management's perceptions of expectations versus translation of perspectives into service quality specifications	Management myopia, market conditions, resource allocations, management skill and expertise	• Establish the right service quality standards • Have staff and managers committed to quality • Make service improvement a part of business • Provide training • Determine and overcome service quality barriers • Standardise tasks to reduce service variability • Implement service quality goals • Measure performance • Gain service quality feedback • Reward service quality • Assess feasibility of customer expectations • Conduct research • Outsource needed skills and competencies
3	Difference between service quality specifications and the the delivery of those specifications to the consumer	Low employee awareness of specifications Low skill levels in implementing specifications Employees' unwillingness to implement specifications	• Ensure that service performance meets standards • Determine how employee jobs contribute to service quality • Reduce role conflict and ambiguity • Ensure employee job fit • Training • Recruit best people • Rewards • Empower employees/managers • Teamwork

(continued)

Table 4.1   (*continued*)

Gap	Explanation	Reasons for occurrence	Strategy/tactics
4	Difference between service delivered and external communications	Poor communication Over-promising	• Ensure that delivery matches promises • Ensure advertising promises reflect service quality priorities • Make service consistent • Manage expectations (what is/isn't possible) • Explain/rectify problems with service delivery • Create horizontal communication • Avoid over-promising
5	Difference between what consumers expect and what they receive	Consumers' expectations do not match the level of service provided	• Gaps 1–4 must be closed if the gap between customers' expectations and their perceptions of the actual service provided is to be closed

Derived from Parasuraman, Zeithaml & Berry 1988; McGuire 1999; Zeithaml & Bitner 2000

The SERVQUAL instrument is also based on the disconfirmation model (assessing the gap between customers' expected level of service and their perceptions of the actual service received (gap 5 in the gaps model)). SERVQUAL consists of five key dimensions, upon which consumers evaluate service performance. These are reliability, assurance, tangibles, responsiveness and empathy, as summarised in table 4.2. Designed as a generic model to measure service quality, the SERVQUAL instrument has been applied across many service industries including local government, libraries, banks, financial institutions, and hospitals.

Table 4.2   SERVQUAL — service quality dimensions

Dimension	Description	Example — airline
Reliability	Ability to deliver the promised service dependably and accurately	Flights are kept on schedule Arrivals and departures occur on time
Assurance	Knowledge and courtesy of employees who are able to inspire trust and confidence	Safety record is good Brand name is trusted and respected Staff are experienced
Tangibles	Physical facilities, equipment and appearance of personnel	Aeroplane, ticketing information, uniforms, baggage retrieval, check-in counters, arrivals and departures lounge
Responsiveness	Service provider's willingness to help customers and provide prompt service	System is efficient and timely Employees are responsive to needs
Empathy	Giving individual attention to customers; understanding and caring for the customer	Employees understand consumers needs, listen to concerns, are patient, and anticipate needs

Source: Parasuraman, Zeithaml & Berry 1985

While these five dimensions are important in service quality evaluation, they may not all be important in every service setting. Take, for example, the services provided by the ATM at your local bank. While tangibles and reliability are very important service quality dimensions for this service setting, empathy will not be important, because the customer interacts with a machine rather than with one of the banks employees.

The five dimensions of the SERVQUAL instrument are briefly summarised below.

Reliability

Reliability: consistency and dependability in performing the service

Reliability refers to the firm's ability to deliver a promised service dependably and accurately (Parasuraman, Zeithaml & Berry 1985). An example of this is a taxi driver arriving promptly and taking you to your destination safely and efficiently. Reliability is essential to the success of service firms. Consumers are unlikely to do business with firms that have a reputation for unreliable service or for not keeping their promises about service delivery. Consumers are most likely to be loyal to firms that continually deliver their promises. Useful strategies for ensuring reliability of the core service include:

- understanding customer needs and wants through market research
- developing systems and procedures that standardise service production to ensure that the core service is delivered as reliably and consistently as possible
- making sure that the promises made in marketing communications are realistic and achievable
- managing customer expectations of the reliability of the service.

Assurance

Assurance: the competence, courtesy and security a firm offers its consumers

Assurance refers to the knowledge and courtesy of employees and their ability to inspire trust and confidence (Parasuraman, Zeithaml & Berry 1985). For example, an accountant is knowledgeable, skilled, qualified and has a good reputation. Assurance is particularly important in services that are high in perceived risk and customer involvement. For services high in credence qualities, such as legal advice, where quality is difficult for the consumer to evaluate even after purchase and consumption, assurance is an important dimension on which customers base their service quality perceptions. Strategies useful for assuring customers and reducing the perceived risk associated with the purchase and consumption of services include:

- creating trust and confidence through the knowledge and skills of contact personnel
- creating continuity of service staff
- creating an organisation-wide image that reflects the core values of the organisation
- building a strong corporate brand image
- using cues such as employee dress, appearance of the interior and exterior of the firm, employee attitudes, visible qualifications and credentials, and pleasant surroundings to reassure the customer.

Tangibles

Tangibles: the tangible elements of a service that create a physical presence

Tangibles are the physical facilities, equipment and the appearance of staff (Parasuraman, Zeithaml & Berry 1985). For example, a hairdressing salon should be neat and tidy, employees appropriately dressed, and so on. Tangibles create a physical presence that affects customers' sensory perceptions. Customers often have to use physical evidence to evaluate the quality of a service, particularly when they are inexperienced with the service process or unsure of its outcome. Tangible cues are readily available to consumers in most service settings and can make an intangible service seem more tangible. Thus, tangible elements in the service process act as surrogate indicators of quality and are often used in conjunction with other dimensions to create the overall quality perception of the organisation. The more 'pure' a service is, or the higher it is in credence qualities, the more important tangible cues become in aiding customers in their service quality evaluations. Strategies relevant to managing the intangibility of services include:

- considering the impact of the servicescape, including buildings, interior, exterior, furniture, equipment, colours
- giving customers tangible items as a record of the service transaction, for example brochures, business cards, receipts and documents.

Responsiveness

Responsiveness: the timely manner in which a firm provides its services

Responsiveness refers to the service provider's willingness to help customers and provide prompt service (Parasuraman, Zeithaml & Berry 1985). In a dental surgery, for example, the dentist should be accessible, there should be no waiting and staff should be willing to listen.

Responsiveness concerns how quickly and appropriately customers' concerns, questions, requirements and complaints are dealt with. Service providers communicate responsiveness through the length of time they require customers to wait for assistance or for a response to their problems. Consumers often judge service quality by a firm's responsiveness. A telephone answering service that makes customers wait for half an hour before someone responds is unlikely to receive a high service-quality rating from customers. Strategies aimed at increasing responsiveness include:

- individualising or customising the service as much as possible
- determining how the service process and outcome are viewed by the customer
- implementing standard procedures to maximise responsiveness to service situations that may occur reasonably regularly
- training staff well, so that they can respond when necessary
- developing procedures manuals to help staff respond to customer questions, complaints and requests
- ensuring that customers do not have to wait too long for assistance or to receive the service.

Empathy

Empathy: the ability of a firm to provide individualised, caring service

Empathy is demonstrated by giving caring, individualised attention to customers (Parasuraman, Zeithaml & Berry 1985). For example, employees should understand consumers' needs, listen to their concerns and be patient. Service firms need to ensure that customers feel they are important and that the service being provided is tailored to their needs. It is difficult for service firms to develop long-term customer relationships if their customers do not feel that the company understands and is trying to meet their needs and wants. Similarly, customers will not feel that a company's service quality is high if they do not believe staff and the organisation have acted empathically towards them. Strategies that can be used by service firms to show empathy include:

- tailoring service offerings to individual customers as much as possible
- making customers feel important by developing long-term relationships — so long as the service situation suits relationship building and the customer wants to maintain a relationship with the service provider

- making customers feel important by responding to their needs and understanding their concerns
- training staff to be empathetic towards the needs of customers
- training staff to know customers by name and by their service needs.

Criticism of the SERVQUAL model

Despite the widespread popularity of the SERVQUAL instrument (as evidenced in the following Services Marketing Action vignette), the conceptual foundation and practical application of SERVQUAL have been the centre of criticism (Babakus & Boller 1992; McAlexander, Kaldenberg & Koenig 1994). SERVQUAL has been criticised on the following points.

- The model's dimensions (e.g. Babakus & Boller 1992; Carman 1990; McAlexander, Kaldenberg & Koenig 1994). Reviewing eighteen studies where SERVQUAL was applied to a variety of industries, Asubonteng, McCleary and Swan (1996) concluded that the findings of most studies differed from Parasuraman, Zeithaml and Berry's initial study in terms of the instrument's five dimensions: reliability, assurance, tangibles, responsiveness and empathy. For example, three factors were extracted in Bouman and van der Wiele's (1992) research into automotive servicing. In the retail clothing sector, Gagliano and Heathcote (1994) recognised four factors, and one factor was identified in Babakus, Pedrick and Inhofe's (1993b) utility company study. Therefore it is questionable whether the SERVQUAL model applies to industries other than that in which the model was developed (Dabholkar, Thorpe & Rentz 1996).
- The appropriateness of measuring service quality using the disconfirmation model (Babakus & Boller 1992). It is suggested that measuring expectations provides no additional information beyond what is obtained from measuring performance alone. Measuring the gap or difference between expectations and perceptions seems to add little to the evaluation of service quality.

The problematic nature of SERVQUAL brings into question its applicability and validity in many service settings (Asubonteng, McCleary & Swan 1996; Shemwell & Yavas 1999). Thus, although the SERVQUAL model is one of the most significant contributions to service quality research to date, it has been criticised for its limitations.

Services Marketing Action:
Award winning service quality

The year is 1997. A resident rings the local council with queries about registering a dog, library hours and rates. After three attempts she gets through to the library staff who give her the information about opening hours. However, when she asks about dogs, the library staff can't help and tell her to ring another division — they think it might be the health division. To find out about rates requires yet another phone call. This one rings out — apparently everyone is at lunch. Finally, after several attempts, the resident gives up on the dog registration query and decides she will run the risk of having an unregistered dog! No wonder public opinion about council service is low.

Fast-forward to 2001. The call centre of Maroochy Shire Council has just won the Australian Customer Service Association (ACSA) 2000 Queensland Award. Customers can now make one phone call to Maroochy Shire for all queries, and it is guaranteed that 80 per cent of their questions will be answered without their having to be transferred to another officer. Furthermore, customers know that over 80 per cent of calls will be answered within 25 seconds of calling and any voicemail messages will be answered within 20 minutes of leaving the message.

How did they effect this dramatic change? Basically, by adopting best practice in service quality. When the call centre was first established in 1998, a wide search of best practice in other organisations was made. The results of this search were implemented, and service quality began to be continuously monitored and improved. Not only does the call centre regularly survey its external customers, it also surveys its internal clients (other divisions of council), using SERVQUAL to benchmark progress and set further goals. By taking service quality seriously, Maroochy Shire has significantly improved its image with consumers . . . and dog registrations have almost tripled! What award are they aiming for next?

The three-component model

Three-component model: *model that brings together the three service quality components: service product, service delivery and service environment*

With the decreasing popularity of the SERVQUAL model, there was renewed interest in the technical and functional quality dimensions developed by Grönroos (1982, 1984) in the Nordic model. This resulted in Rust and Oliver (1994) presenting a **three-component model** of service quality. Their model includes factors relating to the **service product**, **service delivery** and **service environment**, as shown in figure 4.3.

Service product: *the consumer's overall perception of the service and any augmented services accompanying service delivery*

Service delivery: *the interaction between customer and firm necessary to deliver the service*

Service environment: *the internal culture of the organisation and the external or physical surroundings of the organisation*

Figure 4.3:
The three-component model of service quality
Source:
Rust & Oliver 1994, p. 11

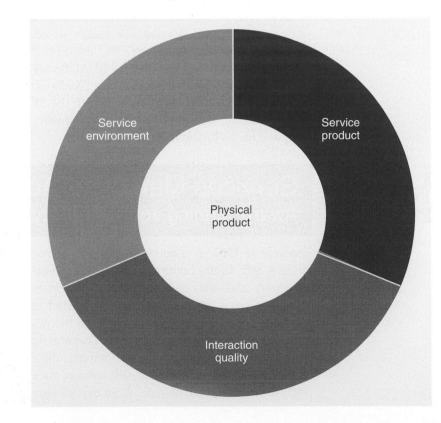

The service product is the consumer's overall perception of the service offering and outcome, including any additional services that accompany its delivery. The customer's assessment of the service product results from an evaluation of what the customer gets from the service provider as opposed to how it is received.

The service delivery is the interaction between consumers and the organisation within the service setting. Because services are intangible, variable and inseparable, the communication between provider and customer shapes the way the customer perceives the service delivery. Service delivery refers to the process of consuming the service. It involves all events and performances taking place during the delivery of the service.

The service environment is the internal and external environment. Literature on the internal environment focuses on the organisational culture and philosophy of management. The external environment, termed the 'servicescape' by Bitner (1992) reflects the setting in which the service is delivered. Ambience, space and function, and symbolic elements combine to form the whole external environment.

Other researchers also support conceptualising service quality based on a technical (outcome dimension), a functional (interpersonal dimension), and a physical environment dimension (e.g. McDougall & Levesque 1994; McAlexander, Kaldenberg & Koenig 1994; Brady & Cronin 2001).

The implication of this model is that organisations can target three main elements of service quality to improve overall service quality perceptions. The model helps us to better understand how service quality works and suggests the elements on which managers should base service quality research. Management would need to develop surveys that reflect these three dimensions, in their specific industries, to properly assess consumers' service quality perceptions.

An integrated model of service quality

Furthering the discussion of service quality measurement into the twenty first century, Brady and Cronin (2001) present a model that integrates the many dimensions of service quality. The model also shows that service quality may be made up of three different tiers of dimensions. That is, the model is hierarchial.

- *Tier one:* this level reflects the customers' overall perceptions of service quality.
- *Tier two:* this level reflects the primary dimensions that consumers use to evaluate service quality.
- *Tier three:* this level identifies the sub-dimensions and individual items that make up the primary dimensions in the model.

In recognising that service quality may occur at three different levels, this model moves beyond the models already presented in this chapter to provide a more detailed and comprehensive look at the dimensions consumers use when evaluating service quality.

This model assists managers in understanding how consumers assess service quality, as it allows management to view service quality at different levels. This enables management to concentrate resources on improving those aspects of service quality where problems are arising. Moreover, because of its three-tiered structure, the model goes further in capturing consumers' evaluations of service quality and in giving management a more detailed and accurate picture of consumers' service quality perceptions. For example, if a manager wants to be able to determine consumers' overall perceptions of service quality, they can use the overall service quality dimension (first tier). If the manager only wants to know how well the organisation is delivering quality on each of the service quality dimensions measured in the model, the primary dimensions can be used (tier two).

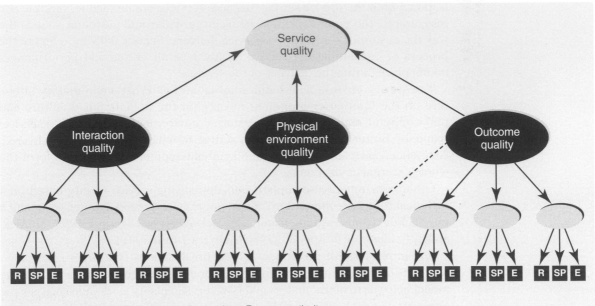

Note: R = a reliability item, SP = a responsiveness item, E = an empathy item.
The broken line indicates that the path was added as part of model respecification.

Figure 4.4: Hierarchical model of service quality
Source: Brady & Cronin 2001, p. 38

Finally, if management wants a comprehensive analysis of service quality, the complete model can be used to determine consumers' overall service quality evaluations and to identify specific areas that are in need of attention by management (tiers one, two and three). This enables management to devote resources either to improving overall service quality or to improving specific areas of the service process on which the company is not performing well.

In summary, the various models of service quality serve as useful tools for management, as they provide a framework for managers to evaluate various aspects of their performance and develop strategies to improve service quality. The development of service quality models continues to be an area of intense research today. Reviewing current research suggests that most models appear to be modified versions of either the American five-factor SERVQUAL model (Parasuraman, Zeithaml & Berry 1985, 1988) or the two-factor Nordic model presented by Grönroos (1982). While no single model has been conclusively proven to be better than any of the other models, each makes a contribution and can give valuable insight to the implementation and management of service quality.

Current issues in service quality

Conceptualising and measuring service quality is one of the most controversial and debated topics in services marketing literature. Some current key issues include the following:

• Causality — does satisfaction lead to quality or does quality lead to satisfaction?

- Relationships — what is the relationship between service quality, customer satisfaction and behavioural intent?
- Is the disconfirmation of expectations model appropriate as a basis for service quality models?
- Should researchers use performance-only measures or expectation minus performance measures (E − P) when assessing service quality?
- How are expectations currently being used in service quality and customer satisfaction research?

Causality: satisfaction and service quality

While it is generally agreed that satisfaction and service quality are related yet distinct constructs, agreement on the causality between these constructs cannot be found within the literature (Rust & Oliver 1994). Although the relationship between satisfaction and quality is considered equivocal, three distinct perspectives have arisen from the literature:

- Satisfaction is antecedent to perceived service quality. That is, customer satisfaction leads to perceptions of service quality (Bitner & Hubbert 1994; Bolton & Drew 1991).
- Service quality is antecedent to satisfaction. That is, service quality perceptions lead to customers' satisfaction evaluations (Cronin & Taylor 1992; Anderson & Sullivan 1993; de Ruyter, Bloemer & Peeters 1997).
- Service quality and customer satisfaction are both considered antecedent to each other. That is, service quality leads to customer satisfaction, and customer satisfaction leads to service quality. A non-recursive relationship exists between service quality and satisfaction (Dabholkar 1995; McAlexander, Kaldenberg & Koenig 1994; Cronin & Taylor 1994).

Reviewing the service quality literature indicates that the weight of empirical evidence supports the idea that conceptualising service quality is antecedent to satisfaction. However, the causal ordering of these constructs may depend on factors such as the nature of the service (high/low involvement) and the personality of the consumer.

Causality: relationship between service quality, customer satisfaction and behavioural intent

As a consequence of the ambiguous relationship between service quality and satisfaction, the relationship between these constructs and behavioural intent remains unclear. These differing perspectives are evident in the literature:

- The first perspective conceptualises satisfaction as directly determining consumer behaviour. In contrast, service quality is viewed as indirectly influencing behavioural intent through its effect on satisfaction (Anderson, Fornell & Lehmann 1994; Anderson & Fornell 1994; Cronin & Taylor 1992; Gotlieb, Grewal & Brown 1994; Brady & Robertson 2000).
- The second perspective sees service quality as directly influencing behavioural intentions, while satisfaction indirectly influences intentions through its effect on service quality perceptions (Boulding, Kalra, Staelin & Zeithaml 1993; Zeithaml, Berry & Parasuraman 1996).
- The third perspective conceptualises both satisfaction and service quality as directly determining behavioural intention (McAlexander, Kaldenberg & Koenig 1994; Rust & Oliver 1994; Taylor & Cronin 1994).

Disconfirmation of expectations paradigm

Raising concerns about the efficacy of using the disconfirmation model as a basis for service quality evaluation, Carman (1990) and Babakus and Boller (1992) questioned the empirical usefulness of the expectations items. Instead, they favoured direct measures of perceived service quality. Adding to this, Cronin and Taylor (1992) argued that conceptualising service quality on the basis of the disconfirmation of expectations model, which is intended as a measure of satisfaction, not service quality, could result in misleading information.

Performance-only measures

SERVPERF: an instrument used to measure customer perceptions of service quality

In response to the criticisms of the SERVQUAL scale and its use of the disconfirmation model, Cronin and Taylor (1992, 1994) developed a perceptions-only service quality scale: **SERVPERF**. Using the SERVPERF model, Cronin and Taylor (1992, 1994) provide evidence that performance-only measures are superior to expectations and performance measures, as derived from the disconfirmation model. Recent research cites strong empirical evidence that service quality should be measured using performance-based measures (Babakus & Boller 1992; Cronin & Taylor 1994) rather than the disconfirmation of expectations concept frequently cited in the literature.

Expectation levels

Expectations, as operationalised within the disconfirmation of expectations paradigm, are pre-consumption beliefs about service performance that act as a dynamic standard (Miller 1977) of reference against which service delivery can be judged (Oliver 1980; Parasuraman, Zeithaml & Berry 1994). Although expectations and perceptions are linked via the disconfirmation of expectations paradigm in both the service quality and satisfaction literatures (Cadotte, Woodruff & Jenkins 1987; Oliver 1980; Tse & Wilton 1988), the level at which expectations are operationalised differs between these literatures. Debate therefore surrounds the most appropriate way to measure expectations in service quality and satisfaction research. Moreover, service quality and satisfaction researchers are questioning the importance of the role played by expectations in both literatures, as indicated in the previous section.

Within service quality literature there are four generally adopted levels of expectations: ideal, deserved, predictive and minimum tolerable.

- *Ideal expectations:* based on models of consumer preference (Tse & Wilton 1988) the ideal product-performance expectation represents an optimal or ideal level of performance (Miller 1977) — a level at which the consumer wanted the product to perform in order to be completely satisfied.
- *Deserved expectations:* the 'deserved' expectation standard reflects what performance 'should be' or 'ought to be' given the costs and benefits associated with a particular outcome (Miller 1977; Tse & Wilton 1988). Service quality researchers view deserved expectations as a normative standard of what consumers should expect to receive from a service encounter (Boulding et al. 1993).
- *Expected or predictive expectations:* the 'expected' standard, as a calculation of probability, is based on average performance and reflects what performance 'will be' (Miller 1977). Based on expectancy theory, predictive

standards represent expectations as the most likely performance to occur (Parasuraman, Zeithaml & Berry 1988; Tse & Wilton 1988; Oliver 1981; Boulding et al. 1993). Miller (1977) notes that while the 'expected' and 'deserved' expectation standards can be separated conceptually, in practice differentiating between these two standards is often difficult.

- *Minimum tolerable standard:* the 'minimum tolerable' standard reflects the level of performance that is better than nothing, and represents the least acceptable level that performance 'must be' (Miller 1977).

Satisfaction researchers appear to agree that the baseline comparison for post-experience perceptions is what consumers 'would' expect. However, based on the expected performance construct, there is disagreement within the service quality literature about how to define what consumers 'should' expect; can it be defined in terms of ideal, deserved or some other standard of expectation? Regardless of these differences, expectations and perceptions are linked in both literatures through the disconfirmation paradigm.

These issues continue to be the subject of debate and research across many service industries. So while academics continue to explore various aspects of service quality, managers within service industries continue to benefit from the practical implications of much of this research.

Summary

LO1: Define service quality.
- Service quality is an elusive and abstract concept like an attitude.
- It is based on an evaluation of overall excellence and superiority.
- It requires a long-term global evaluation.
- It is related to but different from satisfaction.

LO2: Distinguish between service quality and satisfaction.
- Satisfaction requires experience, whereas service quality can be perceived without actually having to experience the service.

LO3: Understand the importance of service quality to the management of services.
- Service quality can have both positive and negative implications for managers depending on whether service quality is perceived to be high/good or low/poor.
- Positive outcomes of high service quality include insulating customers from competitors, creating competitive advantage, reducing failure costs, encouraging repeat performance, promoting loyalty, enhancing positive word of mouth, and lowering the cost of attracting new customers.
- Negative outcomes include loss of current customers, negative word of mouth and loss of repeat customers.

LO4: Describe various models of service quality.
- Various models of service quality have been developed in order to better understand what makes up service quality and how service quality works.
- The disconfirmation model forms the basis for many later models of service quality. Basically, the disconfirmation model highlights three possible outcomes from purchasing a service: we are dissatisfied (that is, the purchase did not meet our expectations), the purchase was as we expected, or we are satisfied (the purchase met our expectations) and we are delighted by the service (the purchase exceeded our expectations).

- The Nordic model was based on the disconfirmation model and considered quality to have two dimensions: the technical quality, or the outcome of the service process, and the functional quality, or how the service was delivered.
- The gaps model, again based on disconfirmation, looks at five gaps where expectations and actual performance can differ.
- SERVQUAL, closely related to the gaps model, specifically considers five dimensions: reliability, assurance, tangibles, responsiveness and empathy.
- Finally, the three-component models consider service quality in terms of the service product, service delivery and the service environment.

LO5: Be aware of current issues regarding service quality.

- Key issues currently being debated include the ordering of service quality and satisfaction, the measurement of quality and the role of expectations.

key terms

Assurance: the competence, courtesy and security a firm offers to consumers (p. 85)

Cognitive dissonance: the discomfort buyers may feel after purchase, for example, 'Did I get value for money?' (p. 75)

Credence qualities: service attributes that cannot be evaluated by consumers with any certainty even after they have experienced the service process (p. 75)

Customer satisfaction: 'the customer's fulfilment response; a judgement that a product or service feature, or the product or service itself, provided a pleasurable level of consumption-related fulfilment, including levels of under- or over-fulfilment' (Oliver 1997, p. 13) (p. 74)

Disconfirmation: state in which expectation levels are perceived to have been met, exceeded or not met in actual performance of the service (p. 79)

Empathy: the ability of a firm to provide individualised, caring service (p. 86)

Experience qualities: service attributes that can only be evaluated by consumers after the service production process (p. 75)

Functional quality: the components of the process used to arrive at the service outcome (p. 81)

Gaps model: a diagnostic model that helps identify the gaps between expectations and perceptions of management, employees and customers (p. 82)

Reliability: consistency and dependability in performing the service (p. 85)

Responsiveness: the timely manner in which a firm provides its services (p. 86)

Service delivery: the interaction between customer and firm necessary to deliver the service (p. 88)

Service environment: the internal culture of the organisation and the external or physical surroundings of the organisation (p. 88)

Service product: the consumer's overall perception of the service and any augmented services accompanying service delivery (p. 88)

Service quality: the result of an evaluation process in which the customer compares their perceptions of the service with their expectations (p. 74)

SERVPERF: an instrument used to measure customer perceptions of service quality (p. 92)

SERVQUAL: a 44-item instrument used to measure customer expectations and perceptions according to five service quality dimensions — responsiveness, tangibles, assurance, empathy and reliability (p. 82)

Tangibles: the tangible elements of a service that create a physical presence (p. 85)

Technical quality: the outcome of the service (p. 81)

Three-component model: model that brings together the three service quality components: service product, service delivery and service environment (p. 88)

 review questions

1. Using examples, clearly differentiate between service quality and satisfaction.
2. List and briefly describe five reasons why service quality is important to the management of services.
3. What are the five gaps in the gaps model? Give two examples of possible strategies management can use to minimise each of these gaps.
4. Briefly summarise the five key components of the SERVQUAL model.
5. What are the two components of Grönroos's Nordic model of service quality? Give a specific example of each.
6. List and briefly describe the three components in Rust and Oliver's model of service quality.
7. List and briefly describe two current issues in the area of service quality.

 application questions

1. Identify three local restaurants of different standards — perhaps a fast-food restaurant, a family restaurant and an upmarket, exclusive restaurant.
   (a) List your expectations of the service quality for each restaurant.
   (b) Compare your lists. What are the criteria you used? How did your expectations of each restaurant differ, based on these criteria?
   (c) Now go back to the SERVQUAL model. Which attributes from this model did your list cover?
   (d) Consider the Grönroos model and the three component model. How does your list of expectations fit with these models?
   (e) Which of these models do you think would be of most use to each of the three restaurant managers? Why?
2. Think of a situation in which you were disappointed in the service quality delivered — it could be your local library, bank or hairdresser.
   (a) Apply the gaps model to this situation. Where was the major gap that resulted in your dissatisfaction?
   (b) What strategies could management implement to address this gap?
3. This chapter presented several models of service quality. Briefly summarise what you see as the advantages and disadvantages of each model. As a manager, which model would you prefer to use and why?
4. Services are not homogenous. That is, different service industries require different service strategies. Thinking of three different industries — for

example tertiary education, party hire and fast food — what different service-quality strategies would be most applicable in each industry and why?

5. One of the current debates about service quality looks at how and when service quality should be measured. What are your views and why? Support your arguments with examples.

 vignette questions

1. Read the International Issues vignette on page 74. This vignette of Raffles highlighted the importance of considering different cultural backgrounds to ensure outstanding service quality. In addition to staff training, in what other ways could Raffles cater for the differing needs of international guests?

2. Read the Services Marketing on the Web vignette on page 77.
   (a) Go to the Dell computers site and look at the service related areas. Find two other sites of companies supplying computer software and/or hardware and compare and contrast their online service provision.
   (b) Try the same exercise with two banks providing online service. Which site did you prefer? Why? Which bank seemed to provide better service? Why?

3. Read the Services Marketing Action vignette on pages 87–8.
   (a) What problems do you think a local government authority like Maroochy Shire would have in implementing service quality standards. How would you suggest they deal with these issues?
   (b) Service quality has been proven to be important to private sector organisations. Why should it also be important to government authorities like Maroochy Shire?
   (c) Maroochy Shire have adopted SERVQUAL as an instrument to assist them in measuring service quality, for both internal and external customers. Do you think this model is appropriate or would another model be equally useful? Justify.

 recommended readings

For a critical review of the SERVQUAL instrument and its effectiveness in assessing service quality, see:

Asubonteng, P., McCleary, C. & Swan, J. 1996, 'SERVQUAL revisited: a critical review of service quality', *The Journal of Services Marketing*, vol. 10, no. 6, pp. 62–81.

A review of service quality models, and the conceptualisation of perceived service quality as being multidimensional and hierarchical, is given in:

Brady, M. & Cronin, J. 2001, 'Some new thoughts on conceptualising perceived service quality: a hierarchical approach', *Journal of Marketing*, vol. 65, no. 2, pp. 34–49.

For a critical review of SERVQUAL as an instrument used to assess service quality, see:

Buttle, F. 1996, 'SERVQUAL: review, critique, research agenda', *European Journal of Marketing*, vol. 30, no. 1, pp. 8–32.

The following article gives a hierarchical model of service quality to improve current measures that do not adequately capture customers' perceptions:

Dabholkar, P., Thorpe, D. & Rentz, J. 1996, 'A measure of service quality for retail stores: scale development and validation', *Journal of the Academy of Marketing Science*, vol. 24, no. 1, pp. 3–16.

For a review of the divergent literatures on service quality and satisfaction, see:

de Ruyter, K., Bloemer, J. & Peeters, P. 1997, 'Merging service quality and service satisfaction: an empirical test of an integrative model', *Journal of Economic Psychology*, vol. 18, pp. 387–406.

The following is an article outlining the early development of a service quality model which has been the foundation of service quality research to the present day:

Grönroos, C. 1984, 'A service quality model and its marketing implications', *European Journal of Marketing*, vol. 18, pp. 36–44.

A seminal article describing the initial development of the gaps model and the determinants of service quality:

Parasuraman, A., Zeithaml, V. & Berry, L. 1985, 'A conceptual model of service quality and its implications for future research', *Journal of Marketing*, vol. 49, fall, pp. 41–50.

This article presents the development of the SERVQUAL model and its implications for future research:

Parasuraman, A., Zeithaml, V. & Berry, L. 1988, 'SERVQUAL: a multiple-item scale for measuring consumers' perceptions of service quality', *Journal of Retailing*, vol. 64, no. 1, pp. 22–37.

This is a text chapter that outlines early thinking on the development of service quality models:

Rust, R. & Oliver, R. 1994, 'Service quality: insights and managerial implications from the frontier', in Rust, R. T. & Oliver, R. L. (eds), *Service Quality: New Directions in Theory and Practice*, Sage Publications, Thousand Oaks, CA.

 references

Anderson, E. & Fornell, C. 1994, 'A customer satisfaction research prospectus', in Rust, R. T. & Oliver, R. L. (eds), *Service Quality: New Directions in Theory and Practice*, Sage Publications, Thousand Oaks, CA, pp. 241–68.

Anderson, E., Fornell, C. & Lehmann, D. 1994, 'Customer satisfaction, market share and profitability; findings from Sweden', *Journal of Marketing Research*, vol. 10, February, pp. 38–44.

Anderson, E. & Sullivan, M. 1993, 'The antecedents and consequences of customer satisfaction', *Marketing Science*, vol. 12, pp. 125–43

Asubonteng, P., McCleary, C. & Swan, J. 1996, 'SERVQUAL revisited: a critical review of service quality', *The Journal of Services Marketing*, vol. 10, no. 6, pp. 62–81.

Babakus, E. & Boller, G. 1992, 'An empirical assessment of the SERVQUAL scale', *Journal of Business Research*, vol. 24, pp. 253–68.

Bitner, M. 1990, 'Evaluating service encounters: the effects of physical surrounding and employee responses', *Journal of Marketing*, vol. 54, no. 2, pp. 69–81.

Bitner, M. 1992, 'Servicescapes: the impact of physical surroundings on customers and employees', *Journal of Marketing*, vol. 56, pp. 57–71.

Bitner, M. & Hubbert, A. 1994, 'Encounter satisfaction versus overall satisfaction versus quality', in Rust, R. & Oliver, R. (eds), *Service Quality: New Directions in Theory and Practice*, Sage Publications, Thousand Oaks, CA.

Bolton, R. & Drew, J. 1991, 'A longitudinal analysis of the impact of service changes on customer attitudes', *Journal of Marketing*, vol. 55, pp. 1–9.

Boulding, W., Kalra, A., Staelin, R. & Zeithaml V. 1993, 'A dynamic process model of service quality: from expectations to behavioural intentions', *Journal of Marketing Research*, vol. 30, pp. 7–27.

Bowers, M., Swan, J. & Koehler, W. 1994, 'What attributes determine quality and satisfaction with health', *Health Care Management Review*, vol. 19, no. 4, pp. 49–56.

Brady, M. & Cronin, J. 2001, 'Some new thoughts on conceptualising perceived service quality: a hierarchical approach', *Journal of Marketing*, vol. 65, no. 2, pp. 34–49.

Brady, M. K. & Robertson, C. J. 2001, 'Searching for a consensus on the antecedant role of service quality and satisfaction: an exploratory cross-national study', *Journal of Business Research*, vol. 41, pp. 53–60.

Buttle, F. 1996, 'SERVQUAL: review, critique, research agenda', *European Journal of Marketing*, vol. 30, no. 1, pp. 8–32.

Cadotte, E., Woodruff, R. & Jenkins, W. 1987, 'Expectations and norms in models of consumer satisfaction', *Journal of Marketing Research*, vol. 58, pp. 53–66.

Carman J. M. 1990, 'Consumer perceptions of service quality: an assessment of the SERVQUAL dimensions', *Journal of Retailing*, vol. 66, pp. 33–55.

Cronin, J. & Taylor, S. 1992, 'Measuring service quality: a re-examination and extension', *Journal of Marketing*, vol. 56, pp. 55–68.

Dabholkar, P. 1995, 'The convergence of customer satisfaction and service quality evaluations with increasing customer patronage', *Journal of Consumer Satisfaction, Dissatisfaction and Complaining Behavior*, vol. 8, pp. 31–43.

Dabholkar, P., Thorpe, D. & Rentz, J. 1996, 'A measure of service quality for retail stores: scale development and validation', *Journal of the Academy of Marketing Science*, vol. 24, no. 1, pp. 3–16.

de Ruyter, K., Bloemer, J. & Peeters, P. 1997, 'Merging service quality and service satisfaction: an empirical test of an integrative model', *Journal of Economic Psychology*, vol. 18, pp. 387–406.

Fisk, R., Grove, S. & John, J. 2000, *Interactive Services Marketing*, Houghton Mifflin, Boston, MA.

Gotlieb, J. B., Grewal, D. & Brown, S. W. 1994, 'Consumer satisfaction and perceived quality: complementary or divergent constructs?', *Journal of Applied Psychology*, vol. 79, no. 6, pp. 875–85.

Grönroos, C. 1982, *Strategic Management and Marketing in the Service Sector*, Swedish School of Economics and Business Administration, Helsingfors.

Grönroos, C. 1984, 'A service quality model and its marketing implications', *European Journal of Marketing*, vol. 18, pp. 36–44.

Halstead, D., Casavant, R. & Nixon, J. 1998, 'The customer satisfaction dilemma facing managed care organisations', *Health Care Strategic Management*, vol. 16, no. 6, pp. 18–20.

Headley, D. & Miller, S. 1993, 'Measuring service quality and its relationship to future consumer behaviour', *Marketing Health Services*, vol. 13, no. 4, pp. 32–42.

Hill, D. J. 1986, 'Satisfaction and consumer services', *Advances in Consumer Research*, vol. 13, Association for Consumer Research, Michigan, p. 311.

Howard, J. & Sheth, J. 1969, *The Theory of Buyer Behavior*, John Wiley & Sons, New York.

Horovitz, J. 2000, *Seven Secrets of Service Strategy*, Pearson Education, London.

Marshall, G., Hays, R. & Mazel, R. 1996, 'Health status and satisfaction with health care: results from the medical outcomes study', *Journal of Consulting and Clinical Psychology*, vol. 64, no. 2, pp. 380–90.

Mazis, M., Ahtola, O. & Klippel E. 1975, 'A comparison of four multi-attribute models in the prediction of consumer attitudes', *Journal of Consumer Research*, vol. 2, pp. 38–52.

McAlexander, J., Kaldenburg, D. & Koenig, H. 1994, 'Service quality measurement', *Marketing Health Services*, vol. 14, no. 3, pp. 34–44.

McDougall, G. & Levesque, T. 1994, 'A revised view of service quality dimensions: an empirical investigation', *Journal of Professional Service Marketing*, vol. 11, pp. 189–209.

McGuire, L. 1999, *Australian Services Marketing and Management*, Macmillan Education Australia, Melbourne.

Miller, J. 1977, 'Studying satisfaction, modifying models, eliciting expectations, posing problems and making meaningful measurements', in Hunt, H. K. (ed.), *Conceptualisation and Measurement of Consumer Satisfaction and Dissatisfaction*, Marketing Science Institute, Cambridge, MA, pp. 72–91.

O'Connor, S., Trinh, H. & Shewchuk, C. 2000, 'Perceptual gaps in understanding patient expectations for health care service quality', *Health Care Management Review*, vol. 25, no. 2, pp. 7–23.

Oliver, R. 1977, 'Effect of expectation and disconfirmation on post-expense product evaluations: an alternative interpretation', *Journal of Applied Psychology*, vol. 62, pp. 25–48.

Oliver, R. 1980, 'A cognitive model of the antecedents and consequences of satisfaction decisions', *Journal of Marketing Research*, vol. 17, pp. 460–9.

Oliver, R. 1981, 'Measurement and evaluation of satisfaction processes in retail settings', *Journal of Retailing*, vol. 57, pp. 25–48.

Olshavsky, R. & Miller, J. 1972, 'Consumer expectations, product performance and perceived product quality', *Journal of Marketing Research*, vol. 9, pp. 19–21.

Parasuraman, A., Zeithaml, V. & Berry, L. 1985, 'A conceptual model of service quality and its implications for future research', *Journal of Marketing*, vol. 49, fall, pp. 41–50.

Parasuraman, A., Zeithaml, V. & Berry, L. 1988, 'SERVQUAL: a multiple-item scale for measuring consumers' perceptions of service quality', *Journal of Retailing*, vol. 64, no. 1, pp. 22–37.

Parasuraman, A., Zeithaml, V. & Berry, L. 1991, 'Refinement and reassessment of the SERVQUAL scale', *Journal of Retailing*, vol. 64, pp. 12–40.

Parasuraman, A., Zeithaml, V. & Berry, L. 1994, 'Reassessment of expectations as a comparison standard in measuring service quality: implications for further research', *Journal of Marketing*, vol. 58, no. 1, pp. 111–32.

Patterson, P. 1993 'Expectations and product performance as determinants of satisfaction for a high-involvement purchase', *Psychology and Marketing*, vol. 10, no. 5, September/October, pp. 449–62.

Raffles International, accessed 14 September 2001, home page, www.raffles.com/raffles.htm.

Rust, R. & Oliver, R. 1994, 'Service quality: insights and managerial implications from the frontier', in Rust, R. & Oliver, R. (eds), *Service Quality: New Directions in Theory and Practice*, Sage Publications, Thousand Oaks, CA.

Rust, R. & Zahorik, A. 1993, 'Customer satisfaction, customer retention, and market share', *Journal of Retailing*, vol. 69, no. 2, pp. 193–215.

Shemwell, D. & Yavas, U. 1999, 'Measuring service quality in hospitals: scale development and managerial applications', *Journal of Marketing Theory and Practice*, vol. 7, no. 3, pp. 65–75.

Shostack, L. 1977, 'Breaking free from product marketing', *Journal of Marketing*, supplementary, pp. 73–80.

Taylor, S. & Baker, J. 1994, 'An assessment of the relationship between service quality and customer satisfaction in the formation of consumers' purchase intentions', *Journal of Retailing*, vol. 70, no. 2, pp. 163–78.

Taylor, S. & Cronin, J. 1994, 'Modelling patient satisfaction and service quality', *Journal of Health Care Marketing*, vol. 14, no. 1, pp. 33–44.

Tse, K. & Wilton, P. 1988, 'Models of customer satisfaction formation: an extension', *Journal of Marketing Research*, vol. 15, pp. 204–12.

Woodside, A., Frey, L. & Daly, R. 1989, 'Linking service quality, customer satisfaction and behavioural intention', *Journal of Health Care Marketing*, vol. 9, no. 4, pp. 5–17.

Zeithaml, V. 2000, 'Service quality, profitability, and the economic worth of customers: what we know and what we need to learn', *Academy of Marketing Science*, vol. 28, no. 1, pp. 67–85.

Zeithaml, V., Berry, L. & Parasuraman, A. 1996, 'The behavioural consequences of service quality', *Journal of Marketing*, vol. 60, pp. 31–46.

Zeithaml, V. and Bitner, M. 2000, *Services Marketing: Integrating Customer Focus Across the Firm*, McGraw-Hill, Boston.

Chapter 5
Satisfaction

Railton Hill

LEARNING OBJECTIVES

After reading this chapter you should be able to:

- explain what customer satisfaction/dissatisfaction (CSD) is
- identify key differences and similarities between service satisfaction and service quality
- understand some mechanisms that operate in the formation of customer satisfaction
- outline the relation between customer satisfaction and other pre- and post-consumption constructs such as equity, attribution, customer loyalty and repurchase
- measure customer satisfaction/dissatisfaction and use customer research to understand the dynamics of CSD formation
- understand the purpose and methodology behind national CSD indices
- be aware of recent research findings and trends in the management of customer satisfaction with services.

CHAPTER OUTLINE

The aim of this chapter is to develop an understanding of the service satisfaction response, within the context of a range of related pre- and post-consumption constructs and phenomena. The chapter begins by considering what we know about the nature of satisfaction, and the dynamics of satisfaction formation in service industries. The controversial relationship between satisfaction and service quality is canvassed. Links between satisfaction and other important aspects of service consumption experience, both pre- and post-consumption, are explored. National customer satisfaction indices and some recent trends in service satisfaction research are examined.

Introduction

As marketers, we know intuitively that we want satisfied customers. The notion of 'mutually satisfying exchange', whether in a one-off transaction or as part of an ongoing marketing relationship, is at the core of the marketing concept (Bagozzi 1975). Marketing exists to 'satisfy' consumers needs and wants. Indeed, satisfaction is probably the single most heavily researched aspect of marketing. Nevertheless, the nature of satisfaction and dissatisfaction, the mechanisms for their formation, and their relation to other important marketing concepts such as service quality remain controversial. So what do we know with a degree of confidence about satisfaction and dissatisfaction? What practical impact does this knowledge have on our activities as service marketers?

What is satisfaction?

Oliver (1997, chapter one) summarised the variety of interpretations of the construct of satisfaction/dissatisfaction, before settling on a definition of **customer satisfaction** as '. . . the consumer's fulfilment response . . . a judgement that a product or service feature, or the product or service itself, provided (or is providing) a pleasurable level of consumption-related fulfilment, including levels of under- or over fulfilment, (Oliver 1997, p. 13). As explained below, this human response seems to involve both cognitive (thinking) and emotional (feeling) elements. Recent research suggests that, with regard to services, it may also embrace dimensions of response to both outcome and process, rather similar to the distinction often made between 'functional' and 'technical' aspects of service quality (Grönroos 1990) (see also chapter 4). Discussion of the issue of whether dissatisfaction is distinct in nature from satisfaction, or whether they are aspects of a single response mechanism, also continues among researchers.

Customer satisfaction: *'the customer's fulfilment response; a judgement that a product or service feature, or the product or service itself, provided a pleasurable level of consumption-related fulfilment, including levels of under- or over-fulfilment' (Oliver 1997, p. 13)*

Affect, cognition and satisfaction

Is satisfaction an emotion? It seems obvious that the experience of both satisfaction and dissatisfaction often involves an aspect of emotion. Yet early researchers treated satisfaction largely as a process of **cognition** (thinking), focused on rational evaluations. Emotions have been the subject of decades of research by psychologists, who have devised a number of descriptive schemes that attempt to classify and explain the nature of emotions or **affect** (feeling). These typically attempted to classify emotions according to their degree of 'pleasantness/unpleasantness' (positivity/negativity) and 'arousal' or 'engagement' (Reisenzein 1994; Russell 1979). Research using such schemes places satisfaction somewhere between 'elation' or 'excitement' and 'pleased' or 'enjoyment', treating it as a positive emotion with a fairly strong degree of arousal or engagement. Similarly, dissatisfaction in such schemes tends to have a lesser degree of arousal than negative emotions such as disgust, contempt or sadness (Havlena, Holbrook & Lehmann 1989; Watson & Tellegen 1985).

It seems that a mix of emotion and cognitive appraisals exists in the satisfaction response. Some consumers may place greater emphasis on the affective, while others place more emphasis on cognitive components. For example, the

Cognition: *thinking or reasoning*

Affect: *feeling or emotion*

satisfaction experienced with a swim or massage may be more emotional in nature than the intellectual satisfaction experienced as a result of listening to a complex educational lecture, which requires more cognition. Clearly, we have moved a long way from our early understanding of satisfaction as simply the summation of performance ratings (cognitive assessment).

Bagozzi et al. (1999, p. 201) lists frustration, anger, disappointment, alienation, disgust, anxiety, alarm, guilt, shame, joy, happiness, hope, pride and other as emotions which may result from consumer purchases under varying conditions. However, while other emotions may be important, we need to remember that consumer satisfaction/dissatisfaction (CSD) is more than emotion. It has a cognitive, evaluative component. It is also the construct most closely

Figure 5.1:
Consumer satisfaction/ dissatisfaction is affected not only by emotions but also by cognitive evaluation.

linked in the literature to post-consumption behaviours such as repurchase intentions and word of mouth (WOM).

Satisfaction and service quality: similar but distinct

Two related but distinct approaches to the issue of consumer evaluation of services have dominated the literature. The CSD stream, using the 'disconfirmation of expectations' model, is the older of the two streams. Although its history is long, it has only relatively recently been applied to services, and only very recently within specific categories of services such as professional services. The service quality (SQ) school, with the now heavily researched SERVQUAL and the more recently developed SERVPERF models, evolved specifically within services marketing. Both utilise an element of disconfirmation of expectations.

Many writers have considered how SQ and CSD may be distinguished from each other and, in some cases, reconciled (Dabholkar 1993; Iacobucci, Grayson & Ostrom 1994; Merrilees 1995; Oliver 1993b; Patterson & Johnson 1993; Woodside, Frey & Daly 1989). CSD and SQ are currently seen as similar, linked concepts, which are nevertheless distinct.

Oliver (1993b) suggested four key differences. Probably the most critical characteristic distinguishing CSD from SQ is that CSD is experience dependent. It is a response to a specific service experience. Whether the service involved is a personal one such as a haircut or the sale of one's home, or a business-to-business service such as auditing or advertising services, it must be personally experienced if satisfaction or dissatisfaction is to result. Service quality, on the other hand, can be assessed prior to actual experience, on the basis of reputation, brand, word of mouth and previous experience within the service category. Selecting an educational institution provides an example of a situation where we may have a definite perception of quality, obtained through the comments of others and through sources such as entry score requirements. However, in most cases we initially have no direct experience of the services offered by an institution, and cannot experience satisfaction.

Consensus is growing that the predominantly cognitive basis of quality evaluations (Dabholkar 1993; Iacobucci et al. 1994) is a key point of difference from CSD. As discussed previously, research suggests that satisfaction is both cognitive and affective in nature (Oliver 1993a, 1994). In a 1994 study, Oliver found that quality was predicted by a cognitive evaluation of performance alone. Responses observed during a recent study of advertisers concerning agency creative services (Hill 2000) included statements such as these:

Respondent: (If the agency still don't have it right) ... normally we'll get a bit testy at this stage and start pushing what we want to see.
Interviewer: What does 'testy' mean?
Respondent: We've got a philosophy ... shared with the agency ... We are the marketing arm of the company, and [they] are the advertising experts. We set the strategy and then [they] design the advertising to meet the strategy. We will enjoy debating, but ... then [they] are going to heel ... because we're paying the money and taking the risk, and [they] going to do what we want [them] to.

The intensity of such comments certainly confirms an emotional dimension to the experience of these services. Further, even the creative services of an agency known for its high level of quality may result in both satisfying and less satisfying experiences. This highlights a further widely held difference between CSD and SQ — that of short or long-term temporal focus. Although Oliver acknowledges several possible interrelationships between the two constructs (1993, p. 76), it is likely that satisfaction is experienced more in association with specific service encounters, while quality is commonly experienced as an overall aspect of a service over a longer timeframe (Patterson & Johnson 1993).

The satisfaction gained from using an advertising agency renowned for quality creative work may be undermined by short-term factors, which can be beyond the control of the service provider. For example, individual creative ideas may be undermined by the prior release of a similar campaign by a competitor. A campaign that uses a celebrity endorser may be rendered dissatisfying by the arrest of the celebrity on criminal charges. It is also possible, under certain circumstances, to be highly satisfied with a service of less than excellent quality.

Expectations: standards for comparison, based on excellence, prediction or normative belief

In evaluating quality, the yardstick ('referent') for **expectations** will involve some kind of ideal of excellence. Satisfaction, however, may involve expectations based on predictive (what is actually predicted), normative (what should be received) and other possible yardsticks (Iacobucci et al. 1994).

Research has also yielded a number of other conceptual antecedents known to precede satisfaction evaluations, such as equity, attribution, affect, dissonance and regret. A discussion of some of these constructs follows. However, at this point it is simply noted that such things as perceptions of equity and attribution have been theoretically linked to the formation of satisfaction, and are not merely cues to its presence. The conceptual antecedents of quality have generally been limited to external cues such as price, reputation and various communication sources, which are not necessarily linked in a causal manner.

As noted, a number of writers have attempted to reconcile CSD and SQ, taking into account the apparent differences discussed above. Zeithaml and Bitner (2000, p. 75) take the view that SQ is an antecedent of CSD (see figure 5.2). It is entirely possible to have a view of the quality of a service before actually receiving it, based on brand perceptions, word of mouth and marketer communications. This SQ perception can be viewed as one input to consumer expectations, which may be confirmed or may be positively or negatively **disconfirmed**. In this way, SQ can be seen as a component part that contributes to a broader evaluation of CSD. CSD will affect not only quality related perceptions, but also pricing perceptions.

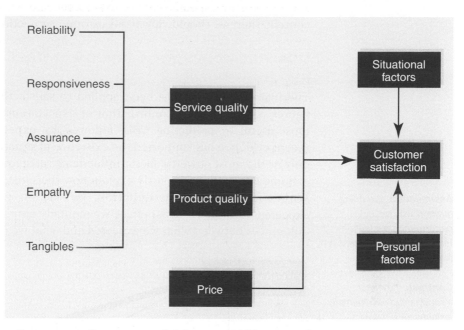

Figure 5.2: SQ as an antecedent of CSD
Source: Zeithaml & Bitner 2000

In contrast, Patterson and Johnson (1993) argue that, over time, successive individually satisfying or dissatisfying service encounters feed into and modify our perception of overall service quality (see figure 5.3). In this way a range of views of the relationship between SQ and CSD can be reconciled.

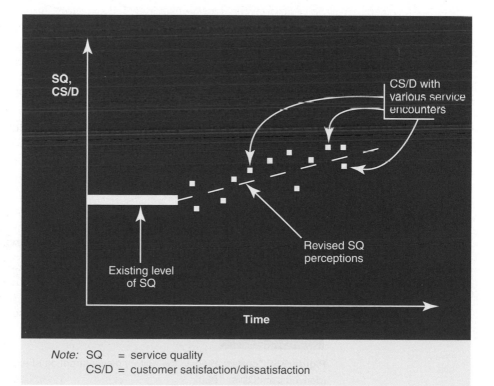

Figure 5.3: SQ as a consequence of CSD
Source: Patterson & Johnson 1993

Note: SQ = service quality
CS/D = customer satisfaction/dissatisfaction

In summary, service marketers should consider whether the evaluation they seek is experience dependent or is assessable from branding, reputation and other secondary clues — primarily cognitive, or both cognitive and affective in nature — and whether it has a limited or a global temporal focus. If the evaluation relates to a specific service experience and entails significant emotional content, then we should view it as customer satifaction.

Dualistic conceptualisations in the CSD and SQ literatures

The main model that has been applied to satisfaction research is shown in figures 5.4 and 5.5. Disconfirmation of expectations has been the construct most useful in predicting CSD, followed by expectations. However, some recent evidence has supported the existence of situations where 'performance only' is the most powerful factor influencing satisfaction.

Some effects seem to partly explain how the satisfaction response is evoked With effects such as **assimilation**, satisfaction tends towards what was expected; with the **contrast** effect, we mentally emphasise positive or negative differences between what we expected and what we perceived we were given.

Assimilation: the effect through which performance evaluation tends towards what was expected

Contrast: the effect through which we mentally emphasise positive or negative differences between what we expected and what we perceived we were given

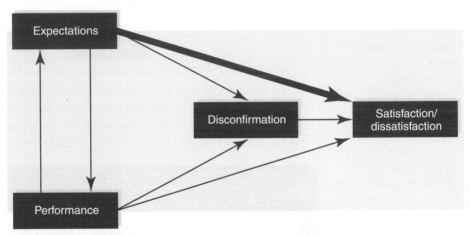

Figure 5.4: Assimilation effect in the unitary disconfirmation of expectations model (derived from Oliver 1980)

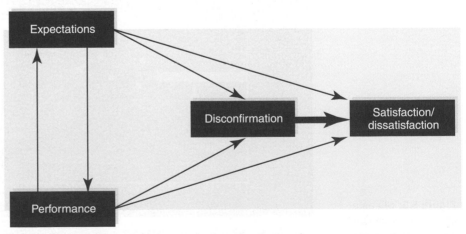

Figure 5.5: Contrast effect in the unitary disconfirmation of expectations model (derived from Oliver 1980)

Yet many researchers do not regard the traditional unitary expectancy disconfirmation model as an adequate explanation of the mechanism behind the formation of satisfaction. Many alternative conceptualisations have been proposed. Table 5.1 offers a summary of some **dualistic** interpretations that have been applied over many years to expectations, disconfirmation or satisfaction itself by researchers seeking a clearer picture of the dynamics of satisfaction formation.

Dualistic: (in expectations, performance etc.) exhibiting dimensions of process and outcome

Table 5.1	A short history of dualism in the satisfaction and quality literatures		
Authors	**Date**	**Dimensions**	**Context of study**
Swan & Combs	1976	Instrumental (dissatisfier) and expressive (satisfier)	Clothing
Eiglier & Langeard	1977	Core and peripheral	Various
Berry, Zeithaml & Parasuraman	1985	Outcome and process	Various
Zeithaml et al.	1988	Intrinsic and extrinsic	Various
Schulz & Dickinson	1988	Process and outcome	Small Claims Tribunal
Parasuraman et al.	1988	Process and outcome	Various
Zemke & Schaaf	1989	Core and peripheral	Hospital services
Brown & Swartz	1989	Core and peripheral	Dyadic relationships
Grönroos	1990	Technical and functional	Various
Lovelock	1992	Core and supplementary services ('flower of service')	Various
Lai & Widdows	1993	Process and outcome	Consumer electronics repairs (involvement study)
Halstead, Hartman & Schmidt	1994	Intellectual environment and employment preparation	Higher education
Spreng, Harrell & Mackoy	1995	Four elements of the service: packing, timeliness, etc.	Household goods removals
Walker	1995	Core and peripheral plus multiple stages	Various search, experience and credence services
Jayanti	1995	Affect and cognition	Health services
Powpaka	1996	Outcome and process	Banking
Spreng, MacKenzie & Olshavsky	1996	Attribute and information satisfaction	Camcorders
Hill	2000	Outcome and process	Advertising creative services

Process dimension: *a dimension of constructs such as expectations, performance and disconfirmation that reflects the processes of service delivery*

Outcome dimension: *a dimension of constructs such as expectations, performance and disconfirmation that reflects the outcomes of service delivery*

Considerable attention has been given to the process and outcome dimensions of satisfaction. The **process dimension** is a dimension of constructs such as expectations, performance and disconfirmation, and it reflects the processes of service delivery. The **outcome dimension** is a dimension of those same constructs, but it reflects the outcomes of service delivery.

The inclusion of both process and outcome dimensions within the attributes of the service and within subsequent consumer evaluations helps to tie together much previous knowledge available through the literature. For example, the findings on the role of affect may be substantially captured by inclusion of the process dimension. What did the customer feel during the service process? What did the customer get at the conclusion of the service (outcome dimension)?

Each of the above dualistic studies represents an attempt to better understand the process of customer satisfaction/dissatisfaction. It is clear that no universal set of dynamics applies across all categories and situations. Rather, researchers and managers need to explore the particular dynamics acting on satisfaction within their specific business context, in the same way that they need to initially uncover the particular structure of expectations evident within their own customers.

Satisfaction formation

The disconfirmation paradigm has been researched extensively with regard to consumer goods and services (Bolton 1991; Brown & Swartz 1989; Tse, 1988; Oliver 1980). It was only recently applied to business-to-business services (Nowak & Washburn 1998; Patterson, Johnson & Spreng 1997; Patterson 2000).

Research has found that the traditional disconfirmation model can be applied in highly distinctive service areas such as management consulting and even in an 'applied creative' service such as the generation of creative ideas in response to a brief from an advertiser. However, as mentioned above, recent research also suggests that a better understanding of the dynamics of satisfaction/dissatisfaction formation may require the incorporation of new outcome- and process-based views of expectations, performance and disconfirmation.

Studies illustrate the considerable variation to be found in the way expectations, perceived performance, and disconfirmation (positive or negative) may interact to form satisfaction and dissatisfaction. For example, expectations have been found to be strong in conditions where the consumer is not able to judge performance; where it may be impractical to measure performance; or where consumers may actually be unwilling to measure performance (Oliver 1997, p. 114; Olshavsky & Miller 1972). The services of a surgeon could provide an example of such a service. These services are high in credence qualities (being difficult to assess until much later) and are very difficult for the lay-person to assess.

Disconfirmation is more dominant in determining satisfaction levels in situations where consumers are highly involved; where performance clearly and unambiguously refutes expectations; and where there is a significant delay between expectations and performance. Under these conditions, a contrast effect is likely. An investment service, for example, could fit this description. However, customer satisfaction research testing these dynamics in service settings is still quite rare.

We need more research testing these dynamics in a wide range of services of different types to fill out our picture of the specific dynamics at play. An examination of the many studies that explore this model shows that consumer satisfaction may be influenced by any one or more of the model's components. Hence it is recommended that managers explore with consumers the dynamics that apply within the particular product category and buying situation. These will vary. The better they are understood, the better will be management of the customer's experience.

Figure 5.6: Management of the customer's experience requires understanding of the dynamics of the particular service product and buying situation.

Satisfaction and other pre-consumption constructs

A range of situational and individual factors have been found to affect the satisfaction/dissatisfaction judgements of consumers. We will not attempt to examine all of these here, but will introduce two for consideration: **equity** and **attribution**.

Equity: consumer perceptions of fairness, equality

Attribution: consumer allocation of responsibility for perceived positive or negative performance levels

Equity

Australians and New Zealanders have long been considered to exhibit a strong sense of fairness or unfairness. It is an oft-quoted element of our national culture, linked to our alleged egalitarianism, and evidenced in measures of social distance in the workplace, for example. When it comes to consumer judgements of fairness, we need to think beyond the obvious dimensions of equity in pricing ('Is it fair to charge $3.95 for a can of soft drink at the footy?') to aspects such as the effort put in, shopping effort, honesty in marketing, and the like. There is significant psychological literature on equity in general, which writers such as Martins and Monroe (1994) and Oliver (1997) have applied and extended in relation to marketing transactions. (Fairness theory is discussed further in chapter 13.)

Consider the importance of consumer effort in the delivery of services in which the consumer plays a major role in self-delivery: for example, EFTPOS, and professional services that require a detailed brief from the consumer and that involve an extended interactive process (as many business-to-business services do). The equity of effort in these cases may be seen as a major issue in determining our satisfaction. Of course, equity becomes a key issue when service failure occurs (Goodwin & Ross 1990). Chapter 13 discusses this important influence on the customer's satisfaction with the service recovery process.

Figure 5.7:
ATMs require the consumer to play a major role in self-delivery.

Attribution

Similarly, the issue of relative effort raises the issue of attribution for performance, disconfirmation and satisfaction/dissatisfaction experienced. In many services the consumer is effectively an active member of the service delivery team. Consider the cases of providing extensive documentation to an accountant for preparation of a tax return; the briefing of a management consultant; and the highly interactive delivery process that occurs between client and an advertising agency. In each case, a great result could easily be attributed to any of several stakeholders/participants. Such judgements are thought to affect satisfaction levels in a variety of ways. Again, marketing researchers started by following conceptual trails blazed by psychologists (Curren & Folkes 1987; Harvey & Weary 1984; Kelly & Michela 1980). Attribution has received limited research attention in recent years (Machleit & Mantel 2001; Weiner 2000). Attribution is discussed also in chapter 13.

After satisfaction: long- and short-term consequences

Research suggests that consumers actually *do* very little as a result of either successful or unsuccessful consumption. Particularly satisfying consumption may generate compliments of some sort, while particularly dissatisfying consumption may generate complaining behaviour. Complaining behaviour has been studied more than complimenting behaviour. We know that a high proportion (estimates range from 24 to 60 per cent) of dissatisfied customers do not identify themselves to management. This is clearly a major problem in that it hinders marketers in their efforts to improve their services and influence the future satisfaction levels of their customers. Complaining behaviour has been found to be highest for durables and lowest for services (Oliver p. 361).

What factors influence the decision to complain or not complain? Oliver summarises both economic and behavioural influences on this decision. The economic decision considers perceived costs, benefits and an assessment of the probability of success. For example, perceived benefits could include getting one's money back, replacement, additional reimbursement, having the problem corrected, obtaining an apology and experiencing a sense of emotional catharsis or release as a result of 'having your say' (see table 5.2). Behavioural factors are summarised by their influence or effect on either the ability to respond or the motivation to respond. For example, an aggrieved consumer's knowledge of communication channels, access to those channels and level of communications skills influences their ability to complain (see table 5.3). Complaint behaviour is further discussed in chapter 13.

Table 5.2 Economic factors in the decision to complain

Perceived costs	Perceived benefits	Probability of success
Monetary loss	Money back	Firm's reputation
Ancillary loss	Replacement	Threat to business
Time	Extra reimbursement	Perceived efficacy
Effort	Correct the problem	
Product importance	Apology	
	Catharsis	

Table 5.3 Behavioural factors in the decision to complain

Ability	Motivation
Knowledge of channels	Cultural norms
Access to channels	Formal institutions
Communication skills	Complaining identity
	Willingness to confront
	Threat of intimidation

Facilitation of consumer feedback is attempted by a range of techniques that attempt to overcome the various barriers identified in tables 5.2 and 5.3. These include offering cost-free phone calls, post-free feedback cards, call-back (the 'courtesy call') and generally fostering a company culture that is open and encouraging towards complaints. Appropriate mechanisms must be developed as well in order to get effective positive responses into action once complaints are received. Not only should the problem be solved promptly and effectively, but communication with the consumer should also be personalised and display professionalism and customer focus.

Unsurprisingly, the complaint process itself is subject to satisfaction and dissatisfaction. Figure 5.8 summarises post-satisfaction processes that may result in considerable secondary satisfaction/dissatisfaction. In turn, consumer satisfaction or dissatisfaction with the results of complaining (or even of complimenting) behaviour may affect longer term post-consumption behaviour such as word of mouth and customer loyalty. Complaining behaviour and service recovery are examined in more detail in chapter 13.

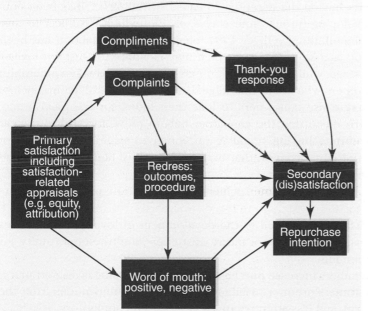

Figure 5.8:
Post-satisfaction process
Source: Oliver 1997

Complaining, word-of-mouth and recommendation behaviour all have validated measurement scales available in the literature. Some are included below in the section 'Measuring customer satisfaction/dissatisfaction'.

Linking satisfaction to loyalty and profitability

The bottom line for any discussion of customer satisfaction has to be 'Does it lead to customer loyalty and to profitability?'. A caveat must be placed before examining this question: it cannot be assumed that customer loyalty will always be linked to profitability. To the frustration of many small customers of banking organisations, such institutions have recently made this important discovery. This raises important social and ethical issues concerning the obligations of large organisations to provide basic services to all members of communities, perhaps subsidised by more profitable business within other segments. Nevertheless, there are limits to the extent to which any commercially oriented organisation can provide services to customers who are loyal but whose service needs cost more than the revenue generated from that business.

US researchers have provided empirical evidence of the limitations of the generally well-supported loyalty–profitability relationship, notably in a large-scale study of the retail banking industry (Hallowell 1996). Within this limitation, the satisfaction–profitability relationship is generally well supported. Hallowell's study found that as much as 37 per cent of the variance observed in loyalty levels of customers with different banking divisions was accounted for by satisfaction levels, while a number of other variables (such as recency of contact and household income) held constant.

Customer loyalty:
'a deeply held commitment to rebuy a preferred service consistently in the future, despite situational influences and marketing efforts having the potential to cause switching' (Oliver 1997)

The concept and manifestation of loyalty is not as simple as it may first appear. **Customer loyalty**, 'a deeply held commitment to rebuy … a preferred service consistently in the future, despite situational influences and marketing efforts having the potential to cause switching …', has been conceived of as developing through four stages, each of which is subject to 'sustainers' and 'vulnerabilities' (Oliver 1997, chapter 14). Satisfaction has been found to function as a key sustainer, which may facilitate (or sustain) loyalty at the affective stage, while dissatisfaction may threaten (or make vulnerable) loyalty for customers who are at this stage. Dissatisfaction, dislike or a lack of involvement may cause consumers to lose their liking for the focal brand. This may in turn mean that the consumer fails to move forward to a clear intention to continue buying brand X (a 'conative' stage), and may even undermine the initial perception that brand X has more benefits than others in its class (cognitive loyalty).

There are at least four ways in which the satisfaction–profit link occurs (Anderson 1998):

- Because satisfaction is linked to the development of loyalty, it influences retention, ensuring a supply of future customers, and the opportunity for corporate planning.
- Satisfied customers increase purchasing where purchasing is discretionary.
- Satisfied customers are more vigilant in noting communications from the 'satisfying' firm, and less attentive to messages from competitors.
- Satisfied customers also tolerate lower price elasticity.

A clear overall link exists between satisfaction and profitability, despite the necessary caveats mentioned concerning the possibility of some 'satisfied' customers proving to be unprofitable. Hence the maximisation of customer satisfaction is not just something that is 'nice to have'; it is definitely good business.

Customer 'delight'

You may have had the experience of being pleasantly surprised — even delighted — by the receipt of some unexpectedly outstanding service. A customer experienced this on a recent cold Sunday evening. At around 10.30 p.m., while waiting for a prescription to be filled in an 'after-hours' pharmacy, he was directed to a specially set up waiting area, complete with comfortable lounge, television and free coffee. He was sorry when it was time to collect the prescription. Two days later, a letter arrived thanking him for his custom, and enclosing a $5 voucher that could be spent at the store during his next visit.

Such service goes against the commonly perceived trend of declining service levels caused by businesses attempting to achieve more with less. The unexpected service strongly differentiates this pharmacy from others in the area. However, does the loss of floor space and the additional costs of furniture, a television and coffee result in net gain in revenue? Also, if other nearby pharmacies replicated this service, would this not only cancel out the advantage, but also saddle all the pharmacies with an additional cost, without any commensurate advantage?

This phenomenon has received some recent research attention. Rust and Oliver (2000) surveyed the available literature and concluded that although delighting the customer 'heightens repurchase expectations and makes satisfying the customer more difficult in the future ... the (nondelighting) competition is hurt worse through customer attrition to the delighting firm' (Rust & Oliver 2000, p. 86). Not surprisingly, delight creates dissatisfaction among the customers of competitor firms, as those customers observe vicariously or as they receive word-of-mouth information. Over time, profit should flow to the delighting firm through additional loyalty from existing customers, as well through the defection of customers from competitors. The extent to which this occurs will be influenced by the extent to which customers are loyal to competitor companies, and by the cost of the additional service.

Customer delight: 'a profoundly positive emotional state generally resulting from having one's expectations exceeded to a surprising degree' (Rust & Oliver 2000)

Rust and Oliver have actually developed a mathematical model of **customer delight** This is complex, but the assumptions it uses are simple. Taken together, they summarise much of what we know — or at least feel confident about — regarding customer delight. Rust and Oliver include two non-research-based assumptions in their model to ensure that it deals with the simplest case possible. Specifically, they assume that the market is a duopoly and that the competitor cannot duplicate the delighting service. Here are the research-based assumptions:

- *Assumption 1.* Satisfaction is driven by disconfirmation.
- *Assumption 2.* Expectations are updated based on the quality perceived on particular transactions.
- *Assumption 3.* A negative disconfirmation will result in a greater change of behaviour than would be observed from a positive disconfirmation of equal magnitude.
- *Assumption 4.* An increase in behavioural indicators (e.g. retention, word of mouth) is associated with increased profits.
- *Assumption 5.* A decrease in the competition's behaviour indicators is associated with increased profits.
- *Assumption 6.* Total net discounted profits are a combination of current profits and future profits.
- *Assumption 7.* Improving service quality costs money.
- *Assumption 8.* The market expectation equals the expectation for the firm with the highest expectation level.
- *Assumption 9.* Quality expenditures have diminishing returns.

The model based on these assumptions gives a tentative answer to the question 'does delighting the customer pay?'. Delight is a useful strategy if:

- satisfaction has a strong influence on behaviour (i.e. it generates repurchase, word of mouth, etc.)
- future profits receive significant weight
- the satisfaction of competitor customers has a strong impact on retention and other behaviours
- the firm is able to capitalise on the dissatisfied customers of competitors, by converting them into its own customers.

The reality is that it remains difficult to calculate the cost–benefit equation needed for rigorous prediction of the effects of delighting your customers. This is especially true in real commercial situations of multiple competitors and rapid copying of service innovations. The best advice is probably to develop satisfaction-enhancing innovations that are not easily imitated, and to venture carefully in 'raising the bar'.

Measuring customer satisfaction/dissatisfaction

Efforts to measure customer satisfaction range from brief customer feedback cards left for customers during a hotel stay (which are not always noticed) to extensive pre- and post-consumption surveys that use sophisticated sampling techniques and detailed statistical analysis (McColl-Kennedy & Schneider 2000; Vavra 1997). If we accept the centrality of customers' satisfaction/dissatisfaction to the building of long-term profitability, then we need to find efficient and effective ways of measuring satisfaction responses.

As discussed, customer expectations appear to play a key role in both the service quality (SQ) and customer satisfaction/dissatisfaction (CSD) approaches to service evaluation (Oliver 1980, 1993b; Parasuraman, Berry & Zeithaml 1991a, 1991b; Parasuraman, Zeithaml & Berry 1985, 1993). In both approaches expectations are seen to offer standards against which later experiences are evaluated. In exploring expectations and performance of a service product, it is necessary to first outline the salient attributes, features or dimensions of the service from the client point of view. Before expectations or performance of a service can be evaluated, it is necessary to ask 'expectations or performance of what?'.

The following list summarises a process for measuring customer service expectations and subsequent evaluations:

1. Conduct focus groups and/or in-depth interviews with actual customers, focusing on customer expectations. What range of service attributes, features or dimensions are consumers expecting?
2. Analyse the information gathered. What are the commonalities? What themes come through about the structure of consumer expectations?
3. Devise some questions that elicit scaled information about the level of expectations for each of the salient elements.
4. Devise a brief questionnaire incorporating these measures.
5. Pilot the questionnaire. Does it capture the things you intended to capture in terms of measuring the various components of customer expectations?
6. Translate the measures devised and tested into measures of performance.
7. Add appropriate measures of disconfirmation (positive or negative) and customer satisfaction/dissatisfaction.

8. The measures of performance, disconfirmation and CSD should be formed into a second short questionnaire.
9. Administer the two questionnaires: the first one on pre-consumption and the second on post-consumption.
10. Analyse the findings in terms of levels of perceived performance, disconfirmation from expectations and overall CSD. This provides crucial information for management to act upon in enhancing the customer experience.
11. Repeat this process regularly as part of an effective, continuing program of customer research.

It is clearly desirable to undertake two separate questionnaires pre- and post-consumption, as any other method actually measures consumer's ability to recall expectations they had at a previous time. Nevertheless, if steps 1 to 10 are carried out well and periodically, it may be possible to obtain useful information in a 'one shot' questionnaire tapping measures of performance and satisfaction. The danger, however, is that you may miss changes in the structure of consumer expectations, a potentially fatal mistake in the competitive business world.

Figure 5.9 describes a proposed measurement model of fruit-grower expectations of the packing services they use. This summarises the findings of individual and focus-group interviews with growers.

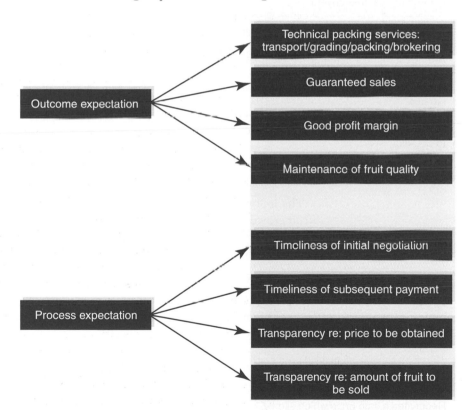

Figure 5.9:
Measurement models — outcome and process dimensions of fruit grower expectations
Source: adapted from Nanere & Hill 2001

Question 1, on the following page, is from a questionnaire on grower expectations of fruit-packing services, based on the measurement model in figure 5.9. The structure of expectations revealed here was obtained from an earlier series of interviews with fruit growers, which probed for critical aspects of their expectations of fruit-packing services. This initial questionnaire was administered when growers were selecting a fruit-packing service, before the actual delivery of the service. Because data on performance perceptions, disconfirmation and satisfaction/dissatisfaction is collected later, when services are actually delivered, this longitudinal design does not rely on the respondent's memory of their expectations some months earlier. Note that the words in square brackets do not appear on the actual questionnaire.

Q1. [Measures expectations] Please read the following statements and indicate, by circling ONE (1) number only, the extent of your agreement or disagreement with each.

You expect the packing service will:	Strongly disagree						Strongly agree
Provide technical packing services such as transport, grading and packing	1	2	3	4	5	6	7
Broker guaranteed sales	1	2	3	4	5	6	7
Negotiate a sale price which allows a good profit margin for me	1	2	3	4	5	6	7
Maintain the quality of my fruit through to final delivery of my fruit to eventual buyers	1	2	3	4	5	6	7
Engage in a timely initial negotiation with me	1	2	3	4	5	6	7
Arrange for timely final payment to me for sale of my fruit	1	2	3	4	5	6	7
Ensure transparency regarding the price to be obtained on sale	1	2	3	4	5	6	7
Ensure transparency regarding the amount of fruit to be sold	1	2	3	4	5	6	7

The following questions are from a subsequent questionnaire on consumer (fruit-grower) evaluations of performance, disconfirmation, satisfaction and estimates of future rebuying and word-of-mouth behaviour. This questionnaire would be administered at the time of receipt of the actual services.

Q2. [Measures performance perceptions] Based on your most recent experience, please indicate your opinion of the performance of the packing service you used. Please circle one number on each item listed. Your packer:

Broker guaranteed sales	1 2 3 4 5 6 7	Broker did not guarantee sales
Negotiated a sale price which allows a good profit margin for me	1 2 3 4 5 6 7	Did not negotiate a sale price which allowed me a good profit margin
Maintained the quality of my fruit through to final delivery of my fruit to eventual buyers	1 2 3 4 5 6 7	Allowed my fruit quality to be degraded or spoiled before final delivery to eventual buyers

(continued)

Q2. (*continued*)

Engaged in a timely initial negotiation with me	1	2	3	4	5	6	7	Delayed initial negotiations or approached me too early
Arranged for timely final payment to me for sale of my fruit	1	2	3	4	5	6	7	Failed to arrange a timely final payment for me for the sale of my fruit
Ensured transparency regarding the price to be obtained on sale	1	2	3	4	5	6	7	Did not allow me to have a clear idea of the price to be obtained on sale
Ensured transparency regarding the amount of fruit to be sold	1	2	3	4	5	6	7	Did not allow me to have a clear idea of the amount of fruit to be sold

Q3. [Measures overall disconfirmation] Please consider the overall packing service provided. How close did it come to what you had expected?

Much worse than expected?			About as expected?		Much better than expected?	
1	2	3	4	5	6	7

Q4. [Measures overall disconfirmation, reverse scored from question 3 as a validity check on these items] Thinking about the benefits of the packing work to you, the grower, would you say they were:

Much worse than expected?			About as expected?		Much better than expected?	
1	2	3	4	5	6	7

Q5. [Measures overall disconfirmation] Concerning any problems you had with the packer during the course of the assignment, would you say they were:

Much worse than expected?			About as expected?		Much better than expected?	
1	2	3	4	5	6	7

Q6. [Measures process disconfirmation] Think about your expectations of the process which occurred between the time that you approached the packer with this assignment and when you actually received the creative ideas. How close did that process come to what you had expected?

Much worse than expected?			About as expected?		Much better than expected?	
1	2	3	4	5	6	7

Q7. [Measures outcome disconfirmation] Consider your personal expectations of the actual packing services you ultimately received. How close did the work received come to what you had expected?

Much worse than expected?			About as expected?		Much better than expected?	
1	2	3	4	5	6	7

Q8. [Measures disconfirmation at the level of elements of individual expectations] I would like to know how well the packing service performed on various aspects of this specific packing assignment. How close did it come to what you had expected when you arranged the work? Choose one number to circle: if they performed *much worse* than you expected, then circle 1; if their performance was much better than you expected, circle 7, and so on. If their performance was much as you expected then circle 4.

The packing service:	Much worse than expected?			About as expected?		Much better than expected?	
Brokered guaranteed sales	1	2	3	4	5	6	7
Negotiated a sale price which allows a good profit margin for me	1	2	3	4	5	6	7
Maintained the quality of my fruit through to final delivery of my fruit to eventual buyers	1	2	3	4	5	6	7
Engaged in a timely initial negotiation with me	1	2	3	4	5	6	7
Arranged for timely final payment to me for sale of my fruit	1	2	3	4	5	6	7
Ensured transparency regarding the price to be obtained on sale	1	2	3	4	5	6	7
Ensured transparency regarding the amount of fruit to be sold	1	2	3	4	5	6	7

Q9. [Measures satisfaction] Please read each statement and indicate the extent to which you agree or disagree. Circle one number corresponding to each statement.

	Strongly disagree						Strongly agree
Overall, you are very satisfied with the packing services you received on this specific occasion.	1	2	3	4	5	6	7
Overall, if you had to do it all over again, you would not choose the same packer.	1	2	3	4	5	6	7

Q10. [Measures satisfaction/dissatisfaction] Taking everything into consideration, how do you feel about the packing services you have received during the course of the assignment? Please circle one number for each item.

Very dissatisfied	1 2 3 4 5 6 7	Very satisfied
Very pleased	1 2 3 4 5 6 7	Very displeased
Completely disgusted	1 2 3 4 5 6 7	Completely contented
Packer did a very poor job	1 2 3 4 5 6 7	Packer did a very good job

Q11. [Measures word-of-mouth intention] Would you recommend this packer to another grower?

Definitely would not recommend	1 2 3 4 5 6 7	Definitely would recommend

Q12. [Measures repurchase intention] If your organisation required the services of a packer in the near future, would you use the same packer? Please circle one number for each item.

Unlikely	1 2 3 4 5 6 7	Likely

Very probable	1 2 3 4 5 6 7	Not probable

Modelling satisfaction

Correlation matrix: a matrix that arrays all variables measured across and downwards, so that we can see at a glance the level of correlation between any two variables

Convergent validity: a characteristic of measures (such as items in a questionnaire) which allows us to determine whether a construct measured as being the same or similar to another is actually the same or similar to real world phenomena which are alike

Discriminant validity: a characteristic of measures (such as items in a questionnaire) which allows us to determine whether constructs measured as being different do reflect differences in the actual phenomena measured

Frequency distribution: a tabular or graphical summary of the frequency of all possible responses

Descriptive statistics: statistics that summarise response data in a descriptive way, summarising such characteristics as central tendency and spread

Using well-constructed questionnaires, it is possible to model not only individual constructs such as expectations, performance, disconfirmation and satisfaction, but also the dynamics between them. The first step is to assess the reliability individual construct measurement using statistical tools such as the Cronbach alpha statistic. Examination of the **correlation matrix** will provide an initial test of the direction of expected associations, such as whether disconfirmation is associated with CSD. We can look for evidence of **convergent** and **discriminant validity** by this means.

If we are satisfied with the reliability of our constructs, we are in a position to go ahead and use a **frequency distribution** and **descriptive statistics**, which are available through statistical packages (e.g. SPSS) or via a spreadsheet. These can assess how satisfied or unsatisfied consumers are with our service.

Over time, repeated use of our questionnaires will allow tracking of changes in satisfaction levels. Of course, simply knowing the structure of our customers' expectations from the earlier work is itself a great start to the development of services that satisfy.

However, customer satisfaction research at the level described here, with careful delineation of the structure of expectations, where reliable and valid measurement of all variables occurs within a well-established theoretical model, allows actual understanding of the dynamics of CSD formation and of subsequent consequences within our particular business context. For example, how dangerous is any overpromising? Understanding the strength of any contrast effects (driven by disconfirmation) will answer this question. How critical is the avoidance of any service delivery failure or what potential benefits may accrue to satisfaction from actually over-delivering (i.e. achieving positive disconfirmation)?

Patterson et al. (1997; Patterson 2000) employed a longitudinal design in the measurement of satisfaction/dissatisfaction with management consulting services. Subsequent measurement of service performance, disconfirmation and satisfaction allowed these authors to model the dynamics of satisfaction formation in this professional, business-to-business service category. As noted in figure 5.10, Patterson found considerable personal and situational effects as illustrated in his model. However, the model reveals a strong and positive

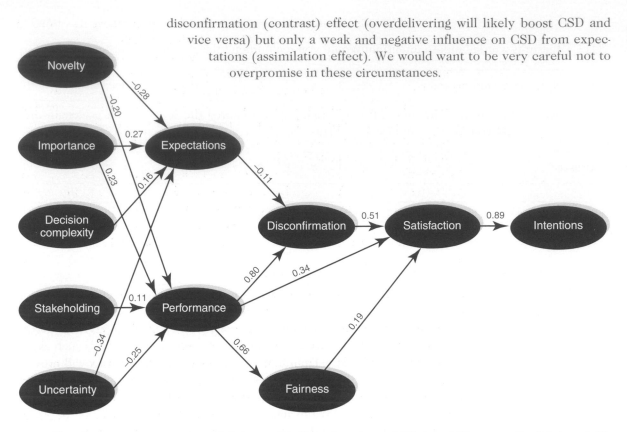

disconfirmation (contrast) effect (overdelivering will likely boost CSD and vice versa) but only a weak and negative influence on CSD from expectations (assimilation effect). We would want to be very careful not to overpromise in these circumstances.

Note: χ^2 = 222.52; *df* = 155; goodness-of-fit index = 0.85; adjusted goodness-of-fit index = 0.80; comparative fit index = 0.97. The higher the number on the arrow, the stronger the relationship found.

Figure 5.10: Structural equation model: satisfaction formation and consequences with management consulting services
Source: Patterson, Johnson & Spreng 1997, p. 13

Hill (2000) took such modelling a stage further in his studies of advertiser satisfaction with agency creative work. As discussed above, he split expectations, performance and disconfirmation into 'outcome' and 'process' dimensions, providing a much clearer picture of the dynamics of these dimensions.

Customer satisfaction indices

Given the importance of customer satisfaction to business, it is not surprising that in Sweden and, subsequently, in the United States (Fornell 1996), as well as in a number of other countries (Meyer & Dornach 1997; Bruhn & Grund 2000; Dermanov & Eklof (1997); Johnson et al. 2001), attempts have been made to generalise about customer satisfaction other than within the individual transactions or ongoing relationships, as is the main focus in this chapter. In fact, econometric techniques have been applied in attempts to measure customer satisfaction at the level of firms, industries, economic sectors and even national economies.

For example, the American Customer Satisfaction Index gathers data from 200 firms, within 40 industries, and across seven major consumer sectors of the United States economy. Indices of customer satisfaction are developed at each of these levels, offering managers the prospect of useful benchmarking.

Here levels of satisfaction can be compared, with best practices identified in the companies, industries or sectors with the highest ratings.

Tantalising as this prospect is, such indices should be viewed within context. While a number of antecedents of satisfaction are measured at the firm level ('perceived quality', 'perceived value' and 'customer expectations') no measure of disconfirmation is taken. More importantly, all measures are taken at a single time. As discussed, the most meaningful measures of expectations should be taken before consumption, with other measures such as satisfaction being measured after consumption.

Such models may yet provide strategic guidance for companies and even industries or sectors for the enhancement of satisfaction. In the United States it has been found that in the years since its introduction in 1994, in aggregate across sectors, customer satisfaction is actually declining. Further, according to the index, this is largely the result of increasing dissatisfaction with services rather than with goods.

The US index findings also suggest that:

1. customisation is more important than reliability as a determinant of customer satisfaction
2. customer expectations play a larger role in sectors in which variance in production and consumption is relatively low; and
3. customer satisfaction is more quality driven than value or price driven.

In Australia a number of indexes are underway, but to date no truly national multi-sectoral index exists. However, an index emerging as a joint Victoria University, industry and government collaboration, aimed initially at the agribusiness and food sectors (Bhaskaran 2001) holds potential.

Other recent findings and trends in satisfaction research

Recent research has complicated our picture of the role of satisfaction in relation to customer post-purchase behaviour. Grayson and Amber (1999) published a study revealing 'the dark side of long-term relationships in marketing services'. While high levels of satisfaction have been linked to repurchase and loyalty, loyalty itself, as manifested by long-term business relationships, can have a negative effect on service use, dampening the impact of trust, and presumably of customer satisfaction. Long-term satisfaction may not indefinitely sustain the use of business services. There may be a business equivalent of the infamous 'seven year itch'.

Even more alarming is a report from Chezy and Simonson (2001). They found that when customers expect to evaluate services such as telephone software support, museums or supermarket shopping, they evaluate both quality and satisfaction less favourably. In this study, customers were less likely to repurchase and to recommend the service if they expected to evaluate them.

These results require both replication and further explanation. However, they should cause marketers to consider carefully their customer feedback measurement methods. These findings suggest managers should avoid placing too much emphasis on the fact that customers will be asked to perform evaluations, or at least should take a negative bias into account in assessing the evaluations they obtain.

Another rapidly expanding area of research is the impact on satisfaction of the slowly diffusing e-store concept and other forms of doing business electronically. The amount of e-business as a proportion of all business is still very small, so service marketers who wish to move in this direction need to come to terms with some apparent contradictions. For example, the two-way, constant information flow made possible by the Internet has long been touted as a revolution for consumers, who at last can redress the balance of knowledge with suppliers. However, researchers are discovering that consumers may not actually be impressed by server capacity, bandwidth, extremely creative interactive web pages and the like. Marketers can fall for the classic 'technology fallacy': the danger of thinking that infrastructure and applications are more important than actions such as regular updates of sites in line with consumer needs (Liebmann, 1999).

Services Marketing on the Web:
Online? Not so fast

Despite considerable hype about online service delivery, the actual electronic diffusion of services delivery and the use of e-marketing as a service are actually quite slow. Research from Neilson NetRatings, an organisation that monitors Australian online activity, indicates that although the total proportion of Australian sales made via the Internet increased by 14 per cent over a 12-month period to early 2002, the proportion of all sales made via the Internet was still only three per cent. Of this, only one service category appears as a 'favourite purchase' — that of airline ticket bookings.

Apparently these purchases were made by about 430 000 Australians. If we compare this figure to the three million Australians who regularly visit Internet retailers to 'window shop' but who don't actually purchase, it becomes clear that the retailing of goods and services via electronic means (e-marketing) is only at the introduction phase of its product life-cycle. To build the use of this service, marketers need information on the satisfaction or dissatisfaction experienced by consumers of e-marketing services. They also need to know more about the expectations of those who are yet to take the e-plunge.

Lassk (2000) found that the three top reasons why non e-store users have not accepted online buying were 'inconvenient location', 'high prices' and 'loyalty to other retailers'. Such things have everything to do with marketing communications to get across site location, and fundamental issues of pricing and relationships with the marketer. They have nothing to do with technology.

Another strong trend in service delivery is self-delivery — the involvement of customers in delivery of their own services. This trend also has implications for satisfaction. One obvious way this could manifest is via the attribution and equity evaluations discussed earlier. If I am having trouble using a bank's online services, is this my fault or the bank's? We have been trained to self-enter payment details via the telephone, or via EFTPOS. At what point in self-service is the perception of equity in the service delivery upset, and we say 'Enough is enough. I expect you, the service provider to do that!' ?

Research suggests that the process of self-delivery does affect satisfaction. Kelley, Donnelly and Skinner (1990, p. 322) suggest that customers require strong congruity between the roles they expect to play and actually play during service delivery, for the attainment of high satisfaction levels in services where their input is important. One implication of this is the importance of the socialisation/training process that customers undergo. This need for congruity of expected and actual customer roles also suggests the importance of careful segmentation of customers, who may vary on their skill levels and preferences for amount and type of customer involvement, with or without any amount of socialisation.

The relatively recent concept of internal customer service is starting to mature. Measures are now available to assess the degree to which employees in internal teams can accurately predict how effective they are as perceived by their internal customers (Gilbert 2000). Such research opens up interesting new lines of inquiry linking internal aspects of marketing, external customer responses and profitability.

Recent research has suggested that it may be unwise to assume mono-cultural satisfaction responses to service offerings. For example, Choi and Chu (2000) found definite differences in the drivers of satisfaction for Asian and Western tourists visiting Hong Kong. They found that Asians were driven more by value, whereas Westerners were more influenced by room quality. Winstead (1999) undertook empirical research with students in the United States and Japan. Her work suggests that formality is more important in status-conscious societies than in egalitarian ones, while personalisation is more important in individualistic countries than in collectivist ones. This has implications for services marketers within multi-racial Australia, as well as for exporters of services.

Customer satisfaction is clearly a moving target. It is obvious that customer wants (the expression of underlying 'needs') evolve and change over time. Much of the satisfaction measurement effort discussed earlier is designed to keep close track of this change in order to ensure the continuing success of marketers in providing satisfying services. This challenge is multiplied, however, when the increasing impact of service internationalisation (Samiee 1999) and of rapid technology change in service delivery (Fisk 1999; Wymbs 2000) is taken into account.

Services are an increasingly important component of international trade. For example, Australia is a major provider of international education services for international students within Australia and via a range of joint initiatives in other countries, especially in Asia. As suggested above, it cannot be assumed that courses which satisfy Australian students will automatically satisfy international students. Educational services also illustrate the increasing impact of technology. A range of technology-enhanced learning methods are increasingly being used in the delivery of educational services. While the benefits of 24-hour access to on-line tutorial materials and the like seem obvious, the impacts of such technology on user satisfaction are currently under-researched. Better understanding of the satisfaction implications of our current rush to technology-enabled education, whether local or international, is needed urgently. The importance of such research becomes plain when we realise that Internet and related technologies are spreading through all service categories, not just education. Customer satisfaction is indeed a moving target — more so than ever before.

Summary

LO1: Explain what customer satisfaction/dissatisfaction is.

- Customer satisfaction is a post-consumption fulfilment response exhibiting both cognitive and affective dimensions. It also incorporates elements of over-or under-fulfilment.

- The question of whether satisfaction is an emotion is not resolved, but affect appears to be linked to satisfaction as both an antecedent and a consequence.

LO2: Identify key differences and similarities between service satisfaction and service quality.

- Satisfaction and service quality perceptions are generally acknowledged to be similar but distinct consumer evaluations. Specific CSD is experience dependent, while SQ evaluations may be present pre-consumption. CSD is a response to a specific service experience, while SQ appears to represent a more global, overall evaluation.

- SQ appears to result from a smaller number of antecendent conditions (for example, the SERVQUAL dimensions of empathy etc.). CSD encompasses both cognitive and affective components, while SQ appears to be predominantly cognitive in nature.

- CSD has been found to be linked to a variety of pre- and post-consumption variables, such as personal and situational variables, equity, attribution, loyalty, word of mouth and profitability.

- SQ is much less firmly linked to such variables in theoretical terms. The actual relationship between CSD and SQ is not resolved, with evidence available that SQ functions as an antecendent of CSD evaluations, while other evidence points to SQ as a cumulative consequence of successive experiences of satisfaction/dissatisfaction.

LO3: Understand some mechanisms that operate in the formation of customer satisfaction.

- The traditional disconfirmation model, developed in the context of goods marketing, but now receiving support in service categories, emphasises processes of assimilation between expectations and CSD (we tend to get what we expect) and contrast effects between disconfirmation (positive and negative) and CSD. Recent research has extended this model in business-to-business professional services to include dimensions of outcome and process, a clearer view of satisafaction formation. Further research is needed to establish the role of affect and cognition in these processes.

- It is important to acknowledge the wide range of dynamics that can occur in the formation of customer satisfaction. These may be complicated further by a range of personal and situational variables, and factors such as product involvement, and perceptions of equity and attribution.

LO4: Outline the relation between customer satisfaction and other pre- and post-consumption constructs such as equity, attribution, customer loyalty and repurchase.

- Research supports definite positive links between CSD and subsequent repurchase, loyalty and, with some reservations, profitability.

- Given the variety of dynamics that are emerging in satisfaction formation, it would be surprising if a variety of dynamics were not found in post-consumption relationships.

LO5: Measure customer satisfaction/dissatisfaction and use customer research to understand the dynamics of CSD formation.

A process was outlined for the measurement of CSD. It involved:

- initial work to delineate the nature of service expectations that consumers hold
- measurement of such expectations pre-consumption
- subsequent post-consumption measurement of performance
- disconfirmation and satisfaction perceptions.

LO6: Understand the purpose and methodology behind national CSD indices.

- While indexes such as the American CSI provide some guidance concerning, for example, broad differences between satisfaction levels in goods compared with services (services are significantly less satisfyingly delivered) and overall trends (such as an alarming trend in decreasing overall satisfaction levels), they require much refinement.
- Sectoral indices covering particular categories of services may be more directly usable for benchmarking purposes.

LO7: Be aware of recent research findings and trends in the management of customer satisfaction with services.

This section outlined a number of trends requiring the attention of both practitioners and researchers. These included:

- 'dark side' and satisfaction measurement effects that could undermine satisfaction and loyalty in long-term business relationships
- mixed effects of technological innovation on customer satisfaction
- the trend towards self-delivery of services and the attribution consequences that could affect satisfaction of consumers
- the dangers of monocultural approaches to service satisfaction, illustrated in relation to multi-racial Australia and the export of services from Australia to foreign markets.

All of these trends illustrate why service satisfaction is very much a 'moving target'.

 key terms

Affect: feeling or emotion (p. 102)

Assimilation: the effect through which performance evaluation tends towards what was expected (p. 106)

Attribution: consumer allocation of responsibility for perceived positive or negative performance levels (p. 109)

Cognition: thinking or reasoning (p. 102)

Contrast: the effect through which we mentally emphasise positive or negative differences between what we expected and what we perceived we were given (p. 106)

Convergent validity: a characteristic of measures (such as items in a questionnaire) which allows us to determine whether a construct measured as being the same or similar to another is actually the same or similar to real world phenomena which are alike (p. 119)

Correlation matrix: a matrix that arrays all variables measured across and downwards, so that we can see at a glance the level of correlation between any two variables (p. 119)

Customer delight: 'a profoundly positive emotional state generally resulting from having one's expectations exceeded to a surprising degree' (Rust and Oliver 2000) (p. 113)

Customer loyalty: 'a deeply held commitment to rebuy a preferred service consistently in the future, despite situational influences and marketing efforts having the potential to cause switching' (Oliver 1997) (p. 112)

Customer satisfaction: 'the customer's fulfilment response; a judgement that a product or service feature, or the product or service itself, provided a pleasurable level of consumption-related fulfilment, including levels of under- or over-fulfilment' (Oliver 1997, p. 13) (p. 102)

Descriptive statistics: Statistics that summarise response data in a descriptive way, summarising such characteristics as central tendency and spread (p. 119)

Disconfirmation: state in which expectation levels are perceived to have been met, exceeded or not met in actual performance of the service (p. 105)

Discriminant validity: a characteristic of measures (such as items in a questionnaire) which allows us to determine whether constructs measured as being different do reflect actual differences in the actual phenomena measured (p. 119)

Dualistic: (in expectations, performance etc.) exhibiting dimensions of process and outcome (p. 107)

Equity: consumer perceptions of fairness, equality (p. 109)

Expectations: standards for comparison, based on excellence, prediction or normative belief (p. 104)

Frequency distribution: a tabular or graphical summary of the frequency of all possible responses (p. 119)

Outcome dimension: a dimension of constructs such as expectations, performance and disconfirmation reflecting the outcome/s of service delivery (p. 108)

Process dimension: a dimension of constructs such as expectations, performance and disconfirmation reflecting the process/es of service delivery (p. 108)

 review questions

1. What is customer satisfaction?
2. This chapter suggested four key differences between service satisfaction and service quality. What were they? Can you think of service products that are exceptions to each of these? For example, consider services where satisfaction is not experience dependent, or where quality perception is experience dependent.
3. Explain why the apparently simple concept of expectations may be surprisingly difficult to interpret.
4. Why is understanding the structure of customer expectations the first step towards measuring customer satisfaction? From your own experience and that of your friends, undertake this initial step with regard to tertiary education services.
5. What safeguards are (a) necessary and (b) available to service marketers who contemplate increased consumer involvement in delivery of their services?

6. How useful would an Australian Customer Satisfaction Index (modelled on the US CSI) be to individual service managers in Australia?

7. Imagine you are an Australian service marketer wishing to export your health care related services to Hong Kong, Singapore and other major urban centres in Asia. How will you go about ensuring the satisfaction of your prospective clients?

8. Explain what is meant by the terms 'assimilation' and 'contrast'. What are the conditions under which each of these is likely to dominate?

application questions

1. Describe one or more services where the satisfaction experienced seems to be largely cognitive. Then select one or more services where the satisfaction experienced seems to be largely emotional in character.

2. With reference to each of the services you selected in question 1), to what extent do you think satisfaction is linked to the delivery process experienced, as compared to the outcome of the service? In your experience, is there an overlap between emotionally dominant satisfaction and a predominance of process influences on satisfaction? Similarly, is there overlap, in your experience, between cognitive dominance in the satisfaction experience and outcome influences?

3. To what extent is the 'outcome/process' distinction in the determinants of satisfaction specific to particular types of services? Can you think of some services where such a distinction is not meaningful?

4. A 'cultural climate' audit in a large industrial organisation reveals that many employees cannot identify any time during the past three years when they have been specifically and personally thanked for their work. Morale, not surprisingly, is low. A marketing executive comments: 'Well, I can't see what that has to do with my department'. Do you agree, in light of the concept of 'internal marketing'?

5. With regard to the educational services you are currently experiencing, do you think that processes of assimilation (where expectations dominate as a determinant of satisfaction levels) or contrast (where disconfirmation, positive or negative, exerts a strong influence on our evaluations of the service) are more evident in the satisfaction/dissatisfaction responses of you and your friends?

6. Consider any differences that may occur in retail consumer services as compared with business-to-business services regarding the likely impact of pre-consumption constructs such as equity, stakeholding, importance and difficulty. Consider also any such differences between retail and business-to-business services concerning the operation of post-consumption constructs such as attribution and loyalty.

7. What is your perception of the impact of new technology on the delivery of education services? If you are not a first-year student, have such services changed in your experience over the course of your university studies? What are the pluses and the minuses of any such changes? Overall, would you say that new technology is enhancing or eroding your satisfaction with the educational services you receive?

vignette questions

Read the Services Marketing on the Web vignette on page 122.
1. Calculate how long it will take for, say, 25 per cent of all purchases to occur on the Internet at the rate of increase described in the vignette.
2. What light is shed by the findings of Liebman (1999) and Lassk (2000) respectively (see page 122) on the rate of diffusion of e-marketing services?
3. Comment on the findings of Kelley, Donnelly and Skinner (1990) (see page 123) in relation to the fact that customer satisfaction can be affected by self-delivery, as occurs in e-buying.

recommended readings

A popularly written but useful consideration of internal customer service, including satisfaction measurement is:
Albrecht, K. 1990, *Service Within,* Irwin, Illinois:.

The most comprehensive and rigorous overview of customer satisfaction research currently available can be found in:
Oliver, R. L. 1997, *Satisfaction: A Behavioral Perspective on the Consumer,* McGraw-Hill International, New York.

The following articles extend consideration of topics introduced in this chapter. In a few instances they are already referenced, but have been singled out as worthy of extended study. The themes they extend are fairly obvious from the titles. They include:
- customer satisfaction measurement: comparison standards and measurement scales issues
- the continuing dialogue between CSD and SQ — can they be reconciled?
- affect and cognition in satisfaction processes, and other work refining our knowledge of the nature of satisfaction itself and consequences such as WOM
- customer involvement as a factor in satisfaction
- an example (Hill & Phelan 1999) of research seeking to delineate expectations on two sides of a professional service exchange (the case of advertisers and their agency).

Babin, B. & Griffin, M. 1998, 'The nature of satisfaction: an updated examination and analysis', *Journal of Business Research*, vol. 41, pp. 127–36.
Bitner, M. J., Faranda, W. T., Hubbert, A. R. & Zeithaml, V. A. 1997, 'Customer contributions and roles in service delivery', *International Journal of Service Industry Management*, vol. 8 no. 3, pp. 193–205.
Chiou, J. 1999, 'A contingency framework of satisfaction formation', *Journal of Consumer Satisfaction, Dissatisfaction and Complaining Behavior*, vol. 12, pp. 81–9.
de Ruyter, K., Bloemer, J. & Peeters, P. 1997, 'Merging service quality and service satisfaction: an empirical test of an integrative model', *Journal of Economic Psychology*, vol. 18, pp. 387–406.

Dube. L. & Morgan, M. S. 1998, 'Capturing the dynamics of in-process consumption emotions and satisfaction in extended service transactions', *International Journal of Research in Marketing*, vol. 15, pp. 309–20.

Hausknecht, D. R. 1990, 'Measurement scales in consumer satisfaction/dissatisfaction', *Journal of Consumer Satisfaction, Dissatisfaction and Complaining Behavior*, vol. 3, pp.1–11.

Hill, R. & Phelan, S. 1999, 'Expectations of excellence in creative product: the views of senior creatives and advertising clients contrasted', *Australasian Journal of Market Research*, vol. 7, no. 1, pp. 33–47.

Iacobucci, D., Grayson, K. A. & Ostrom, A. L. 1994, 'The calculus of service quality and customer satisfaction: theoretical and empirical differentiation and integration', in Swartz, T. A., Bowen, D. E. & Brown, S. W. (eds), *Advances in Services Marketing and Management*, vol. 3, pp. 1–67, JAI Press, Greenwich, CT.

Jayanti, R. K. 1995, 'The relative influence of affective and cognitive factors in determining service encounter satisfaction', *Journal of Consumer Satisfaction, Dissatisfaction and Complaining Behavior*, vol. 8, pp. 147–54.

Mittal, V., Ross, W. T. J. & Baldasare, P. M. 1998, 'The assymetric impact of negative and positive attribute — level performance on overall satisfaction and repurchase intentions', *Journal of the American Marketing Association*, vol. 62, no. 1.

Park, J. W. & Choi, J. 1998, 'Comparison standards in consumer satisfaction formation: involvement and product experience as potential moderators', *Journal of Consumer Satisfaction, Dissatisfaction and Complaining Behaviour*, vol. 11, pp. 28–39.

Soderlund, M. 1998, 'Customer satisfaction and its consequences on customer behaviour revisited: the impact of different levels of satisfaction on word-of-mouth, feedback to the supplier and loyalty', *International Journal of Service Industry Management*, vol. 9, no. 2, pp. 169–88.

Walker, J. L. 1995, 'Service encounter satisfaction: conceptualized', *Journal of Services Marketing*, vol. 9, no. 1, pp. 5–23.

Woodruff, R. B., Clemons, D. S., Schumann, D. W., Gardial, S. F. & Burns, M. J. 1991, 'The standards issue in CS/D research: a historical perspective', *Journal of Consumer Satisfaction, Dissatisfaction and Complaining Behavior*, vol. 4, pp. 103–9.

 references

Anderson, E. W. 1998, 'Customer satisfaction and word of mouth,' *Journal of Service Research*, vol. 1, no. 1, pp. 5–17.

Bagozzi, R. P. 1975, 'Marketing as exchange', *Journal of Marketing*, vol. 39, October, pp. 32–9.

Bagozzi, R. P., Gopinath, M. & Nyer, P. U. 1999, 'The role of emotions in marketing', *Journal of the Academy of Marketing Science*, vol. 27, no. 2, pp. 184–206.

Berry, L., Zeithaml, V. & Parasuraman, A. 1985, 'Quality counts in services, too', *Business Horizons*, vol. 28, pp. 44–52.

Bhaskaran, S. 2001, 'Applying a national index of customer satisfaction for improved strategic marketing in the agribusiness sector', paper presented at the IAMA 2001 Agribusiness Forum and Symposium, Sydney, Australia.

Bolton, R. N. & Drew, J. H. 1991, 'A multistage model of customers' assessments of service quality and value', *Journal of Consumer Research*, vol. 17, no. 4, pp. 375–84.

Brown, S. W. & Swartz, T. A. 1989, 'A gap analysis of professional service quality', *Journal of Marketing*, vol. 53, April, pp. 92–8.

Bruhn, M. & Grund, M. 2000, 'Theory, development and implementation of national customer satisfaction indices: the Swiss Index of Customer Satisfaction (SWICS)', *Total Quality Management*, vol. 11, no. 7, pp. 1017–28.

Chezy, O. & Simonson, I. 2001, 'In search of negative customer feedback: the effect of expecting to evaluate on satisfaction evaluations', *Journal of Marketing Research*, vol. 28, May, pp. 170–82.

Choi, T. Y. & Chu, R. 2000, 'Levels of satisfaction among Asian and Western travellers', *The International Journal of Quality and Reliability Management*, vol. 17 no. 2, pp. 116–31.

Curren, M. T. & Folkes, V. S. 1987, 'Attributional influences on consumers' desires to communicate about products', *Psychology and Marketing*, vol. 4, spring, pp. 31–45.

Dabholkar, P. A. 1993, 'Customer satisfaction and service quality: two constructs or one?', in Cravens, D. & Dickson, P. R. (eds), *Enhancing Knowledge Development in Marketing*, vol. 4, Chicago: American Marketing Association, pp. 10–18.

Dermanov, V. & Eklof, J. 1997, 'Using an aggregate customer satisfaction index: challenges and problems of comparison with special reference to Russia', *Total Quality Management*, vol. 12, nos 7 & 8, pp. 1054–63.

Eiglier, P. & Langeard, E. 1977, 'Services as systems: marketing implications', *Marketing Consumer Services: New Insights, Marketing Science Institute*, Cambridge, MA, pp. 83–103.

Fisk, R. P. 1999, 'Wiring and growing the technology of international services marketing', *Journal of Services Marketing*, vol. 13, nos 4 & 5, pp. 311–18.

Fornell, C., Johnson, M. D., Anderson, E. W., Cha, J. & Bryant, B. E. 1996, 'The American customer satisfaction index: nature, purpose and findings', *Journal of Marketing*, October, pp. 7–18.

Gilbert, R. 2000, 'Measuring internal customer satisfaction', *Managing Service Quality*, vol. 10, no. 3, pp. 178–86.

Goodwin, C. & Ross, I. 1990, 'Consumer evaluations of responses to complaints: what's fair and why', *Journal of Services Marketing*, vol. 4, summer, pp. 53–61.

Grayson, K. & Amber, T. 1999, 'The dark side of long-term relationships in marketing services', *Journal of Marketing Research*, vol. 36, no. 1, pp. 132–41.

Grönroos, C. 1990, 'Relationship approach to marketing in service contexts: the marketing and organizational behavior interface', *Journal of Business Research*, vol. 20, no. 1, pp. 3–12.

Hallowell, R. 1996, 'The relationships of customer satisfaction, customer loyalty, and profitability: an empirical study', *International Journal of Service Industry Management*, vol. 7, no. 4, pp. 27–42.

Halstead, D. Hartman, D. & Schmidt, S. 1994, 'Multisource effects on the satisfaction formation process', *Journal of the Academy of Marketing Science*, vol. 22, spring, pp. 114–29.

Harvey, J. H. & Weary, G. 1984, 'Current issues in attribution theory and research', *Annual Review of Psychology*, vol. 35, pp. 427–59.

Havlena, W. J., Holbrook, M. B. & Lehmann, D. R. 1989, 'Assessing the validity of emotional typologies', *Psychology and Marketing*, vol. 6, summer, pp. 97–112.

Hill, R. 2000, 'Modelling advertiser satisfaction with agency creative product: an empirical study of the disconfirmation of expectations model in an applied creative, business to business, professional service', PhD thesis, La Trobe University, Melbourne.

Iacobucci, D., Grayson, K. A. & Ostrom, A. L. 1994, 'The calculus of service quality and customer satisfaction: theoretical and empirical differentiation and integration', in Swartz, T. A., Bowen, D. E. & Brown, S. W. (eds), *Advances in Services Marketing and Management*, JAI Press, Greenwich, CT, vol. 3, pp. 1–67.

Jayanti, R. K. 1995, 'The relative influence of affective and cognitive factors in determining service encounter satisfaction', *Journal of Consumer Satisfaction, Dissatisfaction and Complaining Behavior*, vol. 8, pp. 147–54.

Johnson, M., Gustafsson, A., Andreassen, W., Lervik, L. & Cha, J. 2001, 'The evolution and future of national customer satisfaction index models', *Journal of Economic Psychology*, vol. 22, no. 2, pp. 217–45.

Kelley, S. W., Donnelly, J. H. J. & Skinner, S. J. 1990, 'Customer participation in service production and delivery', *Journal of Retailing*, vol. 66, no. 3, pp. 315–35.

Kelly, H. H. & Michela, J. L. 1980, 'Attribution theory and research', *Annual Review of Psychology*, vol. 31, 457–501.

Lai, M. & Widdows, R. 1993, 'Determinants of consumers' satisfaction with service: a preliminary study', *Journal of Consumer Satisfaction, Dissatisfaction and Complaining Behavior*, vol. 6, pp. 166–74.

Lassk, F. G. 2000, 'Investigating aspects of customer satisfaction at the e-store: the e-store product mix and image', *Journal of Professional Services Marketing*, vol. 21, no. 2, pp. 15–26.

Liebmann, L. 1999, 'How to fail at e-business without really trying', *Communication News*, vol. 36, no. 7, p. 94.

Lovelock, C. H. 1992, 'Cultivating the flower of service: new ways of looking at core and supplementary services', in Eiglier, P. & Langeard, E. (eds), *Marketing, Operations, and Human Resources: Insights into Services*, IAE, Universite d'Aix-Marseille III, Aix-en-Provence, France, pp. 296–316.

Machleit, K. & Mantel, S. P. 2001, 'Emotional response and shopping satisfaction: moderating effects of shopper attributions', *Journal of Business Research*, vol. 54, no. 2, pp. 97–106.

Martins, M. & Monroe, K. 1994, 'Perceived price fairness: a new look at an old concept', in Allen, C. T. & Roedder, J. (eds), *Advances in Consumer Research*, vol. 21, Provo, UT, pp. 75–8.

McColl-Kennedy, J. & Schneider, U. 2000, 'Measuring customer satisfaction: why, what and how', *Total Quality Management*, vol. 11, no. 7, pp. 883–98.

Merrilees, B. 1995, 'What drives customer satisfaction? Linking process performance, critical incidents, service quality and customer satisfaction', *Australasian Journal of Market Research*, vol. 3, no. 2.

Meyer, A. & Dornach, F. 1997, 'The German customer satisfaction barometer, 1997', *Yearbook of Customer Satisfaction in Germany*, German Marketing Association/Deutsche Post AG.

Nanere, M. G. & Hill, R. 2001, 'The structure and dynamics of expectations and customer satisfaction in channel member relationships in the Victorian fruit industry', Proceedings of 2001 conference of the Australian and New Zealand Academy of Marketing, Auckland.

Nowak, L. & Washburn, J. 1998, 'Antecedents to client satisfaction in business services', *Journal of Services Marketing*, vol. 12, no. 6, pp. 441–52.

Oliver, R. L. 1980, 'A cognitive model of the antecedents and consequences of satisfaction decisions', *Journal of Marketing Research*, vol. 17, November, pp. 460–9.

Oliver, R. L. 1992, 'An investigation of the attribute basis of emotion and related affects in consumption: some suggestions for a stage-specific satisfaction framework', in Sherry, J. F. (Jr) & Sternthal, B. (eds), *Advances in Consumer Research*, vol. 19, Association for Consumer Research, Provo, UT, pp. 237–44.

Oliver, R. L. 1993a, 'Cognitive, affective, and attribute bases of the satisfaction response', *Journal of Consumer Research*, vol. 20, December, pp. 418–30.

Oliver, R. L. 1993b, 'A conceptual model of service quality and service satisfaction: compatible goals, different concepts', in Swartz, T. A., Bowen, D. E. & Brown, S. W. (eds), *Advances in Services Marketing and Management*, vol. 2, JAI Press, Greenwich CT, pp. 65–85.

Oliver, R. L. 1994, 'Conceptual issues in the structural analysis of consumption emotion, satisfaction and quality', in Allen, C. T. & John, D. R. (eds), *Advances in Consumer Research, Association for Consumer Research*, Provo, UT, pp. 16–22.

Oliver, R. L. 1997, *Satisfaction: A Behavioral Perspective on the Consumer*, McGraw-Hill International, New York.

Olshavsky, R. & Miller, J. A. 1972, 'Consumer expectations, product performance, and perceived product quality', *Journal of Marketing Research*, vol. 9, February, pp. 19–21.

Parasuraman, A., Berry, L. L. & Zeithaml, V. A. 1991a, 'Refinement and reassessment of the SERVQUAL scale', *Journal of Retailing*, vol. 67, no. 4, pp. 420–50.

Parasuraman, A., Berry, L. L. & Zeithaml, V. A. 1991b, 'Understanding, measuring, and improving service quality: findings from a multiphase research program', in Brown, S. W., Gummesson, E., Edvardsson, B. & Gustavsson, B. (eds), *Service Quality: Multidisciplinary and Multinational Perspectives*, Lexington Books, pp. 253–68.

Parasuraman, A., Zeithaml, V. A. & Berry, L. L. 1985, 'A conceptual model of service quality and its implications for future research', *Journal of Marketing*, vol. 49, fall, pp. 41–50.

Parasuraman, A., Zeithaml, V. A. & Berry, L. L. 1988, 'SERVQUAL: a multiple-item scale for measuring customer perceptions of service quality', *Journal of Retailing*, vol. 64, spring, pp. 12–40.

Parasuraman, A., Zeithaml, V. A. & Berry, L. L. 1993, 'More on improving service quality measurement', *Journal of Retailing*, vol. 69, no. 1, pp. 140–7.

Patterson, P. G. 2000, 'A contingency approach to modeling satisfaction with management consulting services', *Journal of Service Research*, vol. 3, no. 2, pp. 138–53.

Patterson, P. G. & Johnson, L. W. 1993, 'Disconfirmation of expectations and the gap model of service quality: an integrated paradigm', *Journal of Consumer Satisfaction, Dissatisfaction and Complaining Behavior*, vol. 6, pp. 90–9.

Patterson, P. G., Johnson, L. W. & Spreng, R. A. 1997, 'Modeling the determinants of customer satisfaction for business-to-business professional services', *Journal of the Academy of Marketing Science*, vol. 25, no. 1, pp. 4–17.

Powpaka, S. 1996, 'The role of outcome quality as a determinant of overall service quality in different categories of service industries: an empirical investigation', *The Journal of Services Marketing*, vol. 10, no. 2, pp. 5–25.

Reisenzein, R. 1994, 'Pleasure-arousal theory and intensity of emotions', *Journal of Personality and Social Psychology*, vol. 67, September, pp. 525–39.

Richins, M. L. & Bloch, P. H. 1988, 'Post-purchase product satisfaction: incorporating the effects of involvement and time', *Journal of Business Research*, vol. 23, September, pp. 145–58.

Russell, J. 1979, 'Affective space is bipolar', *Journal of Personality and Social Psychology*, vol. 37, March, pp. 345–56.

Rust, R. T. & Oliver, R. L. 2000, 'Should we delight the customer?', *Journal of the Academy of Marketing Science*, vol. 28, no. 1, pp. 86–94.

Samiee, S. 1999, 'The internationalization of services: trends, obstacles and issues', *Journal of Services Marketing*, vol. 13, nos 4 & 5, pp. 319–28.

Schutz, H. G., & Dickinson, R. 1988, 'Small claims court litigant satisfaction: it's how they play the game that counts', *Journal of Consumer Satisfaction, Dissatisfaction and Complaining Behavior*, vol. 1, pp. 60–8.

Spreng, R. A., Harrell, G. D., & Mackoy, R. D. 1995', 'Service recovery: impact on satisfaction and intentions', *Journal of Services Marketing*, vol. 9 no. 1, pp. 15–23.

Spreng, R. A., MacKenzie, S. B., & Olshavsky, R. W. 1996, 'A reexamination of the determinants of consumer satisfaction', *Journal of Marketing*, vol. 60 July, pp. 15–32.

Swan, J. E. & Combs, L. J. 1976, 'Product performance and consumer satisfaction: a new concept', *Journal of Marketing*, vol. 40, April, pp. 25–33.

Tse, D. K. & Wilton, P. C. 1988, 'Models of consumer satisfaction formation: an extension', *Journal of Marketing Research*, vol. 25, May, pp. 204–212.

Vavra, T., G. 1997, *Improving Your Measurement of Customer Satisfaction: a Guide to Creating, Conducting, Analyzing and Reporting Customer Satisfaction Measurment Programs*, ASQC Quality Press, Milwaukee, WI.

Walker, J. L. 1995, 'Service encounter satisfaction: conceptualized,' *Journal of Services Marketing*, vol. 9, no.1, pp. 5–23.

Watson, D., & Tellegen, A. 1985, 'Toward a consensual structure of mood', *Psychological Bulletin*, vol. 98, September, pp. 219–35.

Weiner, B. 2000,' Attributional thoughts about consumer behaviour', *Journal of Consumer Research*, vol. 27, no. 3, pp. 382–7.

Westbrook, R. A. 1987, 'Product/consumption-based affective responses and postpurchase processes', *Journal of Marketing Research*, vol. 24, August, pp. 258–70.

Winstead, K. F. 1999, 'Evaluating service encounters: a cross-cultural and cross-industry exploration', *Journal of Marketing Theory and Practice*, vol. 7, no. 2, pp. 106–23.

Woodside, A. G., Frey, L. L. & Daly, R. T. 1989, 'Linking service quality, customer satisfaction, and behavioral intention', *Journal of Health Care Marketing*, vol. 9, no. 4, pp. 5–17.

Wymbs, C. 2000, 'How e-commerce is transforming and internationalizing service industries', *Journal of Services Marketing*, vol. 14 no. 6, pp. 463–78.

Zeithaml, V. A., Berry, L. L. & Parasuraman, A. 1988, 'Communication and control processes in the delivery of service quality', *Journal of Marketing*, vol. 52, April, pp. 35–48.

Zeithaml, V. V. & Bitner, M. O. J. 2000, *Services Marketing: Integrating Customer Focus Across the Firm*, McGraw-Hill/Irwin, Burr Ridge, IL.

Zemke, R. & Schaaf, D. 1989, *The Service Edge: 101 Companies That Profit from Customer Care*, NAL Books, New York.

Chapter 6
Customer-perceived value

Jillian Sweeney

LEARNING OBJECTIVES

After reading this chapter you should be able to:

- define customer-perceived value
- describe why value perceptions are so important
- identify how customer value is derived and what it leads to
- develop a measure of customer value
- describe how we can create value and add value
- list managerial and marketing applications of value.

CHAPTER OUTLINE

This chapter introduces you to the important marketing concept of consumer-perceived value. First, the background to the term 'value' is described, then consumer-perceived value is defined. In addition, the difference between value and other related marketing concepts, such as satisfaction and service quality, is made clear. Various models are used to describe where value fits in the marketing equation and why it is important.

Discussing value is one thing; measuring it to manage it is another. Hence, the section on operationalising or measuring customer-perceived value is very important. The chapter finishes with a discussion of the managerial uses of the value concept — for example how to add value.

Introduction

While service quality and satisfaction are widely discussed in almost all services marketing textbooks and have been the focus of numerous academic journal articles over the last 30 years, the importance of customer-perceived value has only recently been recognised. There is practically no discussion of perceived value in marketing before 1985. Since then, however, it has soared in importance, rivalling satisfaction for management attention (Rust & Oliver 1994).

Value is of major concern to consumers and marketers. It is the strategic imperative of this decade, and has arguably attracted more attention than customer satisfaction. Many leading companies feel that the creation of outstanding consumer value is critical in achieving sustainable financial and market success. Hence, the creation of customer value must be the core driving factor in business today. Organisations face an increasingly changing environment that is both complex and turbulent. Customers also are changing; they are becoming more demanding and more knowledgeable. In the midst of this turmoil, successful organisations are increasingly looking for the winning formula. Some organisations have employed complex strategies; many successful organisations, on the other hand, have used simpler strategies with a strong vision. McDonald's, for example, specifically includes the delivery of value in its vision statement. McDonald's vision is 'to be the world's best quick service restaurant experience. Being the best means providing outstanding quality, service, cleanliness and value, so that we make every customer in every restaurant smile' (McDonald's 2002). In contrast, the Ikea business idea is 'to offer a wide range of home furnishings [with] good design and function at prices so low that as many people as possible will be able to afford them. And still have money left!' (Ikea 2002).

The importance of value is underlined by the following researchers.

> The only thing that matters in the new world of quality is delivering customer value: doing things well to win and keep the customer's business. (Albrecht 1992, p. 7)

> Although necessary to compete in today's industries, quality may no longer provide a clear source of competitive advantage . . . the next major management transformation likely will come as organisations turn more of their attention outward to markets and customers. Consistent with this prediction, there are no shortages of calls for organisations to reorient strategy toward superior customer value delivery. (Woodruff 1997, pp. 139–40)

> As marketers we should be committed to the proposition that the creation of customer value must be the reason for the firm's existence and certainty for success. (Slater 1997, p. 166)

> The creation of outstanding consumer value is the only secure route to achieving sustainable financial and market success. (Sweeney, Soutar & Johnson 1999, p. 75)

> Value is the cornerstone of business market management because of the predominant role that functionality or performance plays in business markets. (Anderson & Narus 1999)

Note that value is not only important in consumer markets, but also in business markets, as Anderson and Narus point out.

International Issues:
Postal organisations gear up for customer value

Postal organisations have, in the past, tended to view themselves as utilities with minimal customer focus. Traditionally, money has been spent on physical infrastructure, such as sorting equipment, and on expanding networks — all at a vast cost. Speaking at the twenty-second Congress of the Universal Postal Union in China, Chris Brennan, a managing partner at Andersen Consulting, said, 'Postal organisations must recognise that they are not public utilities but rather are, or must become, profitable providers of value-added services'. The key to customer value is through value-added services that attract customers to select a country's postal services over private-sector alternatives.

Recognising China's drive to become more productive and efficient and to offer better services, Brennan emphasised the importance of being competitive in light of the rise of e-commerce and non-traditional delivery companies. Electronic commerce plays a significant role in offering higher value services to customers. For example, Deutsche Post and the United States Postal Service have both introduced online shopping, electronic bill-paying, and helping organisations with marketing, sales and supply-chain management. However, postal executives should not use e-commerce for technology's sake. Rather, they should look to see how they may use e-commerce to operate more efficiently and more effectively and hence offer better value to the customer. This is the imperative to meet the challenges of the third millennium.

Source: adapted from *China Daily* 1999

The concept of value

The word 'value' is used by everyone. The terms customer value, shareholder value, added value, creating value, valuable, value for money, personal values and value analysis are common terms. The word 'evaluation' is also in everyday language. For example, university lecturers evaluate your work, and you might receive a project evaluation sheet. In turn, a lecturer may ask you to evaluate their teaching or the unit. What do you do when you have the chance to evaluate a unit? You consider how well the unit works for you. You assess its value to you, and this value is how you perceive it. This issue is explored in greater detail later in this chapter.

Defining customer-perceived value

As we discussed earlier, customer-perceived value is something that is personal. The discussion of value in other contexts, such as economics and industrial management, fails to address the personal component. So let us explore what value means from a more personal viewpoint.

Most simple definitions of value concern some aspect of quality compared to price. Indeed, the most common definition of value in the marketing literature is the ratio or trade-off of quality to price (e.g. Monroe 1990). In this case value can be increased through increasing quality while keeping the price the same;

or through decreasing price while keeping quality the same. We may think of value for money as a simple trade-off of quality to price — how good was it and how much did it cost. However, Zeithaml (1988) examined value through qualitative research revealing four consumer definitions of value:

- value is low price
- value is whatever the consumer wants in a product
- value is the quality the consumer gets for the price paid
- value is what the consumer gets for what they give.

In the first definition value is price and this would appeal to people who are most concerned about cost. People who prefer the second definition are more concerned about the benefits; that is, what they receive from the product. The third definition represents people who think of value as the simple quality–price trade-off, while the fourth definition represents people who look for a more complex bundle of benefits and costs. This fourth definition describes a process of comparing all **get components** (i.e. what the customer gets) with all **give components** (i.e. what the customer gives up). If you were to choose a financial planner, you would probably consider a range of investment strategies, the style of the organisation (e.g. deals with government employees or 'would be' entrepeneurs) and the cost of setting up a financial portfolio. However, there may be other benefits such as how knowledgeable the planner is, and how you feel about the way you are treated by the organisation. These are examples of 'get' components other than quality. On the other hand, you may have spent quite a bit of time shopping around for a financial planner and you may be concerned about whether you should be choosing a financial planner at all rather than 'doing it yourself'. These are examples of 'give' components or costs beyond the price. Hence, defining value in terms of quality and price is clearly limiting.

In the four definitions described above, the fourth definition is the broadest; that is, all three previous definitions are sub-cases of the fourth. We will therefore adopt this broader definition of value for the chapter and formally define **perceived value** as the consumer's overall assessment of the utility of a service based upon perceptions of what is received and what is given (Zeithaml 1988). The important aspect to note in defining value is that it is the customer who defines what they perceive as value. We will return to the detail of how value has been measured in the section 'measuring customer-perceived value'.

Get components: *what the customer perceives they have received when using a service*

Give components: *what the customer perceives they have given up when using a service*

Perceived value: *'the consumer's overall assessment of the utility of a service based upon perceptions of what is received and what is given'* (Zeithaml 1988)

Services Marketing Action:
Let the customers decide on what is value

1. A new independent school in Perth, Western Australia, conducted research among parents with children studying at the school. In explaining their reasons for sending their child to a Christian school, parents reported the more obvious benefits of academic standards, discipline, the strong reputation of the principal, the fostering individual growth and teaching of religion. However, one of the key factors related to the parents rather than the student. Parents reported that sending their child to an independent school positively influenced their (parents') self-concept: 'professional people send their children to private schools'.

2. In Asia, it seems that the press is full of firms congratulating themselves on getting the ISO (International Standards Organisation) 9000 certificate, says Dr Peter Wilton, academic director of business studies at the University of California, Haas School of Business. Dr Wilton explains that quality is merely the minimum required to be in business. Offering quality cannot be used to differentiate a firm — some other advantage is needed. In Dr Wilton's view the corporate focus is shifting to a flexible delivery of customer value solutions. In implementing quality, most firms violate the number one principle of quality theory, which is that the customer decides on what is quality. 'If you ask 1000 people what quality is, I guarantee that you'll have a minimum of 200 answers.' In catering to this diversity, firms should modify what they are doing. Most firms cannot be that flexible, and so turn inwards to internal performance indicators to simplify matters. Today, however, it is important to be obsessively customer focused and deliver value based on customer needs.

3. The Hyatt Regency Hotel in Perth, which caters for business travellers and leisure travellers, has a contract with Qantas Airlines for accommodation of flight crew. This specific market is attractive to the Hyatt because Perth, being such an isolated city, is a required stopover for almost all airline crew. Since incoming and outgoing flights are likely to be at unusual hours, with perhaps a 12-hour stopover or longer, the crew often need to sleep during the day. One of the most important requirements of this group (and a requirement of the Flight Attendants Association of Australia) is therefore that rooms are very quiet, and have curtains that block out the light. Thus, this group has specific requirements over and above the usual requirements of business or leisure travellers.

Where customer-perceived value fits in

Now that the meaning of perceived value has been discussed and its importance demonstrated, the discussion turns to identifying where value fits in the chain of customer perceptions, especially compared with service quality and satisfaction.

Customer value development

We defined value earlier as a comparison of what the customer gets compared with what they give up, which, in its simplest form, was a ratio of quality and price. However, there are other 'get' components beyond service quality and other give components besides price, so the trade-off of quality and price has been criticised as being too simplistic (Sweeney & Soutar 2001). For example, in a supermarket context, value can be described as the sum total of the shopping experience, including quality, service, variety, ambience, comfort, cleanliness and dependability (Schechter 1984; Bishop Jr. 1984; Doyle 1984). Value, therefore, can be experiential as well as financial. A full discussion of other components can be found in the section on measurement.

For the purposes of discussing the customer value development model (figure 6.1), we will presume that service quality, perceived value and satisfaction relate to a specific service incident. The first steps of the model comprise a perception of pre-purchase and post-purchase value, based on a comparison of get and give components. It is likely that factors which contribute to pre-purchase and post-purchase value differ. One of the key differences between these stages is that customers form perceptions of value in the pre-purchase stage, based on expectations of service quality. These expectations are largely based on past experience, media and personal communication. However, following purchase, the customer forms perceptions that are largely based on the experience of the service encounter. Price perceptions may also differ before and after the service is consumed. Price is notoriously difficult to estimate before initial use of the service, especially if the customer is not an experienced user. For example, how many people know what a visit to an optometrist costs? Other factors, unanticipated or unknown before the service experience, may also influence post-purchase value perceptions. These include experiential factors such as courtesy and responsiveness. In reverse, some factors that are important before the purchase decision, such as parking and the costs and hassle of using the service, may no longer be relevant in post-purchase evaluation. Ultimately, perceived value after the service experience leads to an evaluation of satisfaction with the service. Satisfaction is a summary state — an overall evaluation — and is a super-ordinate construct to value. Customer satisfaction depends on the service organisation's capacity to create customer value. Satisfaction in turn leads to affective and cognitive behavioural intentions, including commitment to the organisation, loyalty and engaging in positive word of mouth.

The Executive Director of the Hong Kong and Shanghai Banking Corporation, Christopher Langley, emphasises the importance in delivering value to increase loyalty: 'We know that customers who come to HSBC do not only look for efficient services. They also expect sincere, courteous and professional service. When we deliver value that customers enjoy, they will come back and bring us more business' (Pawlyna 1999). These positive outcomes (loyalty, word of mouth etc.) improve business performance, generate profits, and lead to other benefits such as improved organisational culture, better employee morale, and greater effectiveness and efficiency gained through knowledgeable customers who understand the service process.

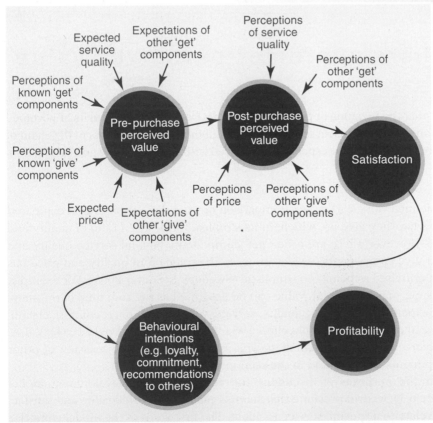

Figure 6.1: Customer value development model

It is important to determine the value drivers for a service. As implied in the previous paragraph, it would be a mistake to assume that factors which customers value in making a choice to use the service (perceptions of known factors and expectations of unknown factors) are also used in evaluating the service after use, when perceptions of possibly different factors are used. Although developing a strategy for creating value perceptions based on pre-selection criteria clearly targets the new customer, creating value based on post-use perceptions leads to a satisfied customer, retains the customer and enhances word-of-mouth opportunities. Some of the factors contributing to pre- and post-purchase value when choosing a university course are suggested below.

Pre-selection (choice)	Post-use
Reputation	Knowledge gained
Quality of staff	Quality of staff
Cost	Cost
Location/distance from home	Other students (motivation, friendships, quality of students)
Availability of desired degree (e.g. Master of Electronic Commerce)	Library/Internet and computer access
Length of course/time	Length of course/time
Where friends going	Industry links
Social clubs/social life	Social clubs/social life

Following figure 6.1, students typically consider the appropriateness of the course, where their friends are going and the reputation of the university (perceptions of known 'get' factors). They are also likely to consider the cost and how far they have to travel (perceptions of known 'give' factors), and they will have expectations of other factors such as quality of the staff (expected service quality). Following use, however, the students can evaluate almost all aspects of the service, so their evaluations are based totally on perceptions.

Note that as in the example above, many of the factors used to evaluate the service before selection are no longer important in post-use evaluation. Other factors are likely to be relevant in the post use stage, such as what the student learns, industry contacts and how other students contribute to their learning and enjoyment of the course.

Note that some factors, such as the cost and the length of the course, the quality of the staff and the social life, are likely to be relevant to both stages of value assessment.

Customer value funnel

The creation of customer value within an organisation must also be viewed within a macro context. Organisations exist within an industry, which itself is based within a macroenvironment. This can be displayed through the value funnel shown in figure 6.2 (Weinstein & Johnson 1999). In essence, the industry operates within a wider environment, which can be described in terms of societal, demographic, economic, natural, political/legal and technological characteristics. The technological environment will, for example, be particularly important for Internet service providers, while eco-based tourism operators will be more dependent on the natural environmental issues within the wider community. Individual organisations operate within an industry, which itself can be described in terms of collaboration, competition, suppliers and regulators. Organisations are described in terms of their stakeholders, business culture, organisational structure, strategies and people. It is the organisation that delivers value to customers. In this model, the value drivers are what society values; what suppliers, partners, competitors and regulators value; what owners and employees value; and what customers value. Ultimately, a higher customer-perceived value increases business performance outcomes. In turn, these outcomes affect the organisation's strategy, tactics and values for the future. The broken lines refer to the dependency of one level on the level below; for example, there would be no organisation without customers, and organisations are critical for a market to exist. The feedback loop, from business performance to the organisation and from the organisation to the microenvironments and macroenvironments above, suggests that use of market intelligence is ongoing and integrated. This is necessary for firms operating within the dynamic and rapidly changing world we live in.

The essence of this model is that delivering value to customers is maximised when the organisational values are in harmony with the wider community.

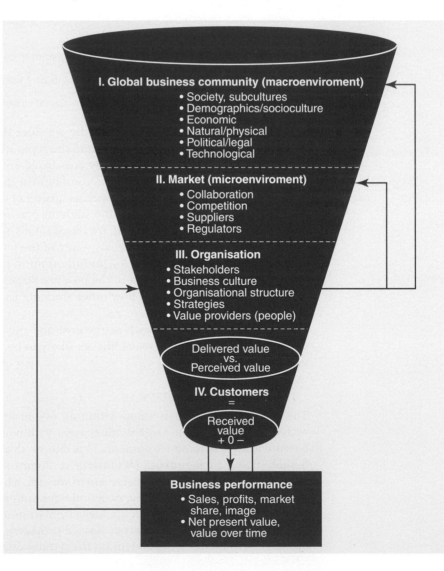

Figure 6.2: The value funnel
Source: Weinstein & Johnson 1999

Measuring customer-perceived value

Offering customer value is an imperative in business today. However, merely discussing value is not enough; it needs to be managed. Consequently, managers need a firm understanding of how it can be measured, so that they can implement strategies according to customer value perceptions. This section discusses two levels at which customer value can be measured.

Levels at which customer-perceived value can be measured

As stated in the definition section, customer-perceived value is based on the consumer's overall assessment of what is received and what is given. Given the complexity of the value construct, we propose to examine value and its measurement according to two of the three levels of value defined by Woodruff (1997) and illustrated in figure 6.3.

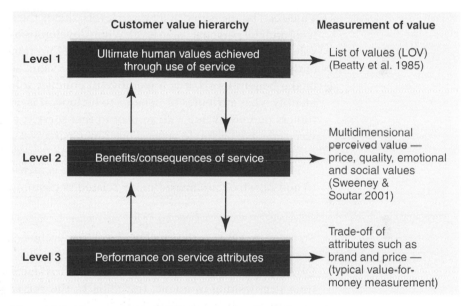

Figure 6.3: Measurement of CPV across value hierarchy levels

This model proposes that customers view value in three related ways. First (level 3) customers think of services as a bundle of attributes, such as price and quality. This leads to certain benefits or consequences, such as emotional consequences, which are more strongly linked to the achievement of a customer's goals than the attributes themselves. The benefits in turn lead to the ultimate set of personal values that consumers want to attain, for example self-fulfilment and security. Clearly these levels interrelate. For example, a restaurant customer may trade off the quality of the food and the service against the price in order to establish a perception of the value for money. At a consequences level, the customer has a deeper understanding of the service, which includes the emotional pay-off (pleasure derived from the experience) and the social pay-off (Will visiting this restaurant enhance my social self-concept?). Finally, at the ultimate human values level, the customer achieves an end-state such as the development of warm relationships with others or fun and enjoy-ment of life. This rationale is based on the means-end-chain model, which seeks to explain how a product or service selection facilitates the achievement of desired end-states (Gutman 1982).

An act of consumption must occur for the desired consequences and the human values to be achieved. This is represented by the upward arrows in figure 6.3. However, to make a service choice, the customer has to learn which services have the attributes that produce the desired consequences. 'Products and/or attributes are valued to the extent that they are instrumental in pro-viding valued consequences' (Clemons & Woodruff 1992, p. 417). Hence, con-sumers are guided by their ultimate desires and the importance of the various human values. This implies an importance ordering of benefits, which in turn implies an importance ordering of the attributes to look for in a service. This process is represented by the downward arrows in figure 6.3. The means-end-chain model helps marketers focus on the basic goals of consumers while keeping in sight the way these goals influence choices in specific situations.

Methods of measuring customer-perceived value

Value can be measured at all three levels, that is the attribute level, the benefit level and the personal value level. When developing a questionnaire to measure value, you need to consider the length of the questionnaire and the complexity of the questions. When measuring perceived value at either the attribute level or the benefit levels, it is imperative to conduct some qualitative research to identify what attributes or benefits to include. It is critical to identify how cus-tomers perceive value with respect to that service, since this will vary by ser-vice type. For example, what a customer perceives as value in a professional service will differ from what they see as value in a restaurant or a bank.

The following sections describe how value is measured at the first two levels (3 and 2), which are most directly related to customer-perceived value.

Attribute level measurement

To measure value at the attribute level, researchers should ask respondents to rate the service on characteristics of service quality, for example using SERV-QUAL (Parasuraman et al. 1988), as well as cost factors such as dollar cost and time (e.g. waiting in queue, travelling to the service outlet). These may be measured as shown in figure 6.4.

Please indicate your perception of the service at ABC.				
	Low			High
Courtesy of employees	1	2	3	4	5
Willingness of employees to help you	1	2	3	4	5
Cost of the service compared to similar services	1	2	3	4	5

Figure 6.4: Example of how service quality attributes can be measured

Value can be established through a comparison of the perceptions of what customers receive, compared with their costs. A variety of attributes beyond service quality and price can be considered. Such aspects may relate, on the get side, to the physical environment, the website, contact with other customers, and relationship marketing initiatives such as newsletters; and on the give side to the amount of time taken up and the hassle factor to reach the service provider. A simple comparison of the average of all get attributes compared with average of all give attributes could be used to summarise value. Nonetheless, as in Zeithaml's original definitions, value quality and price factors are weighted differently by different people. Therefore, it would also be useful to measure the importance of these components to each person.

The calculation of perceived value, taking into account perceived give and get components and their relative importances, would therefore be:

$$\frac{(\text{Get } 1 \times \text{Imp of Get } 1) + (\text{Get } 2 \times \text{Imp of Get } 2)\ldots}{(\text{Give } 1 \times \text{Imp of Give } 1) + (\text{Give } 2 \times \text{Imp of Give } 2)\ldots}$$

where:

Get 1, Get 2 etc. are the perceptions of the 'get' characteristics which add to value.

Imp of get 1, Imp of Get 2 etc. are the importance weights placed on Get 1, Get 2 etc.

Give 1 and Give 2 are the perceptions of the 'give' characteristics which reduce value.

Imp of give 1, Imp of Give 2 etc. are the importance weights placed on Give 1, Give 2 etc.

The advantage of this attribute approach to measuring perceived value is that it is easy for the customer to evaluate. The disadvantages are:

- that it operates at a cognitive level only, and does not incorporate some of the more complex thought structures of consumers
- that it may lead to a long questionnaire if many individual attributes are considered
- that there is a need to develop a list of attributes for each service.

The disadvantages in this approach therefore outweigh the advantages. A better way to measure value is described in the following section.

Benefit/consequence level measurement

This level of measuring value provides a far richer understanding of the value of a service than measurement of attributes can offer, since underlying motives for using a service are addressed. Many authors have suggested different components of value at this level, particularly with respect to the 'get' components.

A scale developed at the consequences level by Sweeney and Soutar (2001) in the context of durable goods has been adapted to a service context by Chua (2002). The dimensions of interest developed by Sweeney and Soutar are:

- emotional value — the utility derived from the feelings or affective states that a product generates
- social value (enhancement of social self-concept) — the utility derived from the product's ability to enhance social self-concept
- functional value (price/value for money) — the utility derived from the product due to the reduction of its perceived short-term and longer term costs
- functional value (performance/quality) — the utility derived from the perceived quality and expected performance of the product.

Qualitative research in the context of short recreational courses (e.g. guitar, kick boxing, yoga, leadlight, dance) suggested, in addition to the above dimensions of functional value, social value and emotional value, that other customers also add value to the recreation course. This is consistent with the 'Servuction' model of service, which highlights the key role played by other customers in services (Langeard et al. 1981). This is particularly relevant in some services where the presence of other customers is critical to the enjoyment, and even the occurrence, of the service (e.g. theatres, restaurants, airlines, courses).

The items below, used to evaluate the value of a recreational course, can be measured on a Likert (disagree/agree) scale.[1]

Perceived value — scale items (recreational centre courses)

Functional value (quality)
1. The course was well coordinated.
2. The course was run with consistent quality.
3. The course had an acceptable standard of quality.
4. The course was well structured.

Social value
5. Attending this course made a good impression on other people.
6. Doing the course helped me feel acceptable to others (e.g. friends, family).
7. Doing the course improved the way I was perceived by others.

Emotional value
8. Attending the course gave me pleasure.
9. I wanted to continue attending this course.
10. The course gave me enjoyment.
11. Attending the course made me feel good.

Social interaction value
12. Doing this course gave me the opportunity to meet interesting people.
13. The course allowed me to share my interest with others.
14. Through the course I found a sense of group belonging.
15. The course gave me an opportunity to socialise with others.

Functional value (price)
16. The course was reasonably priced.
17. It was a good course for the price.
18. The course offered value for money.

Note that the quality dimension and the social interaction dimension are almost unique to this particular service, while emotional value, social value and functional (price) value are essentially generic. You may need to amend this scale when using it in other contexts. For example, social interaction value may not be appropriate in some services.

The relative importance of these dimensions in predicting outcomes such as satisfaction and loyalty are illustrated in table 6.1. The table shows the results of regressing the outcomes on the five dimensions of value. Looking at the table you can see that different value dimensions have a different effect on different outcomes. While the functional quality aspect had a key role in satisfaction evaluation, it did not have a significant influence on intentions to return to the recreation centre, or to give positive word of mouth. Rather, emotional value influenced intentions to return, while the value of social aspects, including social interaction and the enhancement of the social self-concept, increased the chances of word of mouth. Regarding satisfaction with the people aspects of the service, the instructor and the course were found to be associated with emotional value, while satisfaction with the centre was associated with quality and

---

[1]These results are based on a study by Chua (2002) of 236 participants of short courses at five recreation centres in Perth, Western Australia, in 2000. Participants were interviewed six weeks into their 10-week course.

price aspects. The rationale for these differences is intriguing. The most important point is that value components beyond quality and price influence attitudinal and behavioural outcomes. This is particularly true for emotional value. Clearly the manager of a recreation centre would benefit knowing that (a) customers evaluated the recreation centre on the traditional quality and price factors (b) emotional value was key to satisfaction with the instructor, the course and the customer's intentions to return for another course and that (c) social aspects were important in generating word-of-mouth advertising.

Table 6.1 **Relative importance of the five-value dimensions in predicting attitudes and behaviour: results of stepwise regression**

Outcome	Dimension	[a]Standardised slope coefficient	[b]Adjusted R^2
Satisfaction with instructor	Functional — quality	0.56**	0.16
	Emotional	0.32**	
	Functional — price	–	
	Social — enhancement of social self-concept	–	
	Social interaction	–	
Satisfaction with recreation centre	Functional — quality	0.22**	0.40
	Emotional	–	
	Functional — price	0.20**	
	Social — enhancement of social self-concept	–	
	Social interaction	–	
Satisfaction with course	Functional — quality	0.30**	0.87
	Emotional	0.55**	
	Functional — price	0.11**	
	Social — enhancement of social self-concept	0.06**	
	Social interaction	–	
Intention to recommend	Functional — quality	–	0.23
	Emotional	–	
	Functional — price	–	
	Social — enhancement of social self-concept	0.30**	
	Social interaction	0.25**	
Intentions to return to this recreation centre for another course	Functional — quality	–	0.08
	Emotional	0.28**	
	Functional — price	–	
	Social — enhancement of social self-concept	–	
	Social interaction	–	

Key

a: Standardised slope coefficient varies between –1 and +1 and reflects the extent of the effect of the dimension on the outcome.

b: R^2 varies between 0 and 1 and indicates the variance explained in the outcome variable, by the significant dimensions. The higher the R^2, the greater the combined effect of the dimensions on the outcome variable and also the more managerially useful the equation.

** $p<0.05$. That is, the relationship between variables is significant. Blanks mean that the relationship was not significant.

Examples of other types of value that may be relevant in different contexts are:

- epistemic or novelty value — defined as the utility derived from an alternative as a result of its ability to arouse curiosity and/or satisfy a desire for knowledge (Sheth, Newman & Gross 1991)
- rarity value — the lack of or limited availability of a service also makes it more desirable. For example, tours to Antarctica are infrequent and limited in number. This is consistent with commodity theory, which states 'any commodity will be valued to the extent that it is unavailable' (Brock 1968, p. 246).
- relationship value — the utility derived from having an ongoing relationship with a service provider (e.g. knowing what to expect in the process).

Note that types of value vary across different services and some aspects of value are likely to be more important for some services than others. Thus the **value package** is likely to differ across services. The value package associated with a credit card service is likely to differ from the value package associated with an investment service even though both may be offered by the same bank.

Value package: all aspects that contribute to the perceived value of a service

Likewise, different segments may define value differently. This same point was made with regard to attributes in the section Attribute Level Measurement. Customers may weight the benefits differently. Cash-strapped families with young children will see value differently from empty-nesters with less time and a greater disposable income. To assume that value is the same across groups is incorrect. So, segmenting on value perceptions is of tremendous use to marketers. This is discussed further in the section Segmenting the Market Based on Value.

The advantages of this consequence approach to measuring perceived value are that:

- consequences are fewer in number than attributes (Clemons & Woodruff 1992)
- it is more managerially useful than dealing with specific attributes
- it represents consumer end values (i.e. personal values) more closely than attributes, so it is likely to have a stronger impact on evaluation of services (Clemons & Woodruff 1992)
- measures are more generic than service attributes, so comparison across services or service products is easier. That is, the content of the scale based on benefits will change less across services than will a scale based on attributes.

The disadvantages are that:

- it may lose some detail that would be included in attributes
- it may be necessary to enhance the list of get and give components for each service.

Overall, the second approach to measuring value is recommended. This capitalises on the advantage of enabling managers to identify critical benefits. Associated attributes that convey these benefits can be derived and used in the service design and promotion of the service. For example, if emotional value is important in a restaurant or retail outlet, then music, other atmospherics such as smell and perhaps cultural aspects (important in, say, a restaurant with Asian origins) could be used in promotion.

Managerial and marketing applications of value

So what can managers do with value? As mentioned in the previous section, it is not enough to know that value is important or to discuss it. It needs to be used in development of organisational strategy. You now know how to measure it; this section identifies how it can be used. Four approaches are discussed: positioning on value, adding value, evaluating the lifetime value of a customer and segmenting on value.

Positioning on value

Positioning is used by an organisation to differentiate itself from competitors. A service organisation should first identify itself in terms of value components that are important to customers. This may be quality, price, emotional value, offering service guarantees, reliability and so forth. If the important dimensions are quality and price, an organisation can position itself as 'expensive value', for example by offering high quality at a high price (number one in figure 6.5), 'discount value' by offering lower quality at a lower price (number two in figure 6.5) and 'best value', where the service is high quality at a moderate price (number four in figure 6.5). Note that 'poor value', in which the quality is relatively low compared to the price paid (number three in figure 6.5), is unlikely to be a positioning strategy of a service firm in the long term.

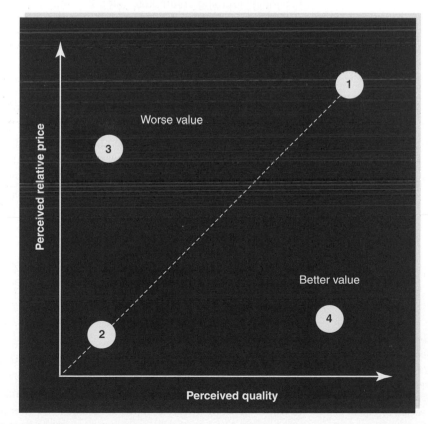

Figure 6.5: The value matrix

Examples of organisations positioning on value are Budget with 'Drives your Dollar Further', and Virgin Blue with 'Keeping the Air Fair'. (Table 6.2, page 155, lists further examples.)

Services Marketing on the Web:
Value achieved through a global network

by Anne-Marie Huartson Offer

Accounting firm SMEs [small-to-medium enterprises] face industry fragmentation and increased competition. Through championing debate about changes in the profession, RAN ONE has been positioned as a solution provider, and is the world's largest network of independent accounting firms operating in the Americas, Europe and the Asia-Pacific region. RAN ONE teaches members how to deliver services to their clients in a sustainable, profitable way. Creating a differentiated, more valuable accounting practice is a promoted benefit of implementing the RAN ONE tools and systems.

RAN ONE provides benefits to members through training programs, practice consulting services, methodologies and a support network. Active membership offers firms the opportunity to evolve from a traditional taxation and compliance service delivery to a value-added, business development consultancy for clients. A comprehensive set of 'solutions' are available online at www.ranone.com, including learning materials, step-by-step implementation guidelines, procedures templates, industry reviews, network branding collateral and software applications. The RAN ONE member-only web area is also a knowledge management tool for new resources and provides online member networking and referral opportunities.

Through network membership, RAN ONE accountants can benefit from the combined experience and knowledge of the member base, and leverage the branding power of this global alliance. At the same time, these firms can deliver personalised services as independent SME practices. As such, the ability to access 'worldwide best practice' systems and resources from any location, cost-effectively, may offer members a competitive advantage in their local market. According to a RAN ONE member, 'Firms have to think about what differentiates their firm from the Big Five firms . . . team culture, stronger client relationships, flexible working hours or bonuses or the opportunity to engage in interesting work such as business consulting. Firms can look at the benefits of joining a structured network such as RAN ONE. These include opportunities for international exchanges and training and development'.

Creating/adding value

Added value: offering benefits, beyond those offered by both the core service and essential facilitating services, that are valued by one or more customer segments

The term **added value** is most commonly used in practitioner literature but features hardly at all in academic literature. Often it is a loose concept, and means anything from delivering value to performing above expectations, or 'delighting' the customer. In 'adding value' we mean offering benefits, beyond those offered by both the core service and essential facilitating services, that are valued by one or more customer segments. We will discuss several approaches to creating and adding value:

- understanding dimensions or attributes valued by customers
- facilitating and support services
- brand names
- including customers in the service delivery process (participation).

Profile: How a financial services firm adds value

Interview with Alan Good, Managing Partner, PricewaterhouseCoopers, 12 October 2001

Do you specifically try to add value? How?

It is a term that is often used. We tell our staff that part of their job is that they should look for opportunities with the client to add value... We also tell the staff that they have got to get to understand the industry and what drives the client. We market by industry — I am in the energy and mining industry consultancy area. We want our staff to understand the mining industry for example. They may go on a week-long course to Kalgoorlie, and we get geologists, merchant bankers, miners, mining engineers and

so on to speak to them. We hope that they then apply that knowledge to industry. They may pick up, for example, something that is not right according to their professional expertise; they can highlight where there is a potential issue to clients in the industry.

Recently we were doing a lot of work in the GST area. We were getting our non-tax staff to understand some of the problem areas with the tax. If they identified a potential problem when out with clients we would get our specialists out there. This is where we can add value to the client. A lot of

clients do not understand GST and it can become a big problem very quickly if they are not doing it properly. The key is to spot opportunities.

We may also offer fees on a success basis. Perhaps we may go to a client in a particular area entitled to a tax rebate, and we may say 'You have been claiming XYZ in the last five years, and we think you could have claimed more. If we deal with it and get more can we claim 10 per cent?'. Then our fee is purely on the success of the outcome. We may also do it on a cost reduction job [and] take a percentage.

Creating value through understanding attributes valued by customers

How can a service organisation create value? Essentially value is created by knowing what customers value. Supposing that we knew that emotional value is important, say, when choosing a dine-in restaurant, or that functional value (quality) is important when choosing a take-away pizza restaurant; this information would enable the service provider to focus on the appropriate benefit and associated attributes. Some specific ways to go about adding value are described in the sections Facilitating and Support Services through to Including Customers in the Service Delivery Process, below.

Facilitating and support services

One of the ways to add value is to differentiate between minimum requirements and determining services or benefits. The former includes aspects that a customer perceives as essential to the service. These relate to the core service — the reason for being in business (Shostack 1977). Take the example of an airline. The minimum requirement is safe, comfortable transport that runs on time. In addition, however, other benefits are now expected. The first Frequent Flyer program was originally set up by American Airlines to increase customer loyalty among the top three per cent of customers: business travellers. However, due to the popularity of the program, competitors set up their own programs and, once underway, the programs were impossible to stop or restrict. Now all of us expect to gain frequent flyer points for flying. Frequent flyer points, while originally adding value and being a determining feature, are now a minimum requirement. Many customers will not even consider choosing a service without these benefits attached. Offering added value must therefore come through determining features — the aspects that make a difference beyond the core service. These are often associated with the offering of supplementary services. There are two types of supplementary services that we can focus on as a source of added value:

Supplementary facilitating services (and goods): services and goods that make it possible for the customers to use the core service

Supplementary upporting services (and goods): additional services beyond the core and facilitating services

- **Supplementary facilitating services (and goods)** are those that make it possible for the customers to use the core service (for example the reception service at a hotel, check-in at airport, card at ATM).
- **Supplementary supporting services (and goods)** are additional services beyond the core and facilitating services (for example hotel restaurants, dry cleaning services in hotels, the wide choice of in-flight entertainment on Singapore Airlines).

Clearly, supporting services add value. They are beyond what is expected and yet for some customers (not all), they provide important benefits. Facilitating services, however, can also be used to add value. In our busy, complex world, where customers demand faster, better service, improved service delivery can create additional value. For example, value can be added through information, including the process of making information easier to access and faster to find, or through helping customers identify the important information.

Federal Express, for example, enables customers to track the progress of their own packages in transit, through an automated FedEx shipping system. As well as tracking parcels, customers are able to reduce paperwork and streamline billing through this system, thereby increasing the value of the service to customers.

Not all customers may perceive added value. Perhaps some people cannot use the supplementary aspect of the service, or the service is poorly performed. If the supplementary services are not perceived positively, they can detract from the value of the core service and the total perceived value is thus is reduced.

Virgin Blue's advertising points out that other airlines offer supplementary services that may be irrelevant to some customers, and that this can add to the price of the ticket (see figure 6.6). By making supplementary services such as meals optional, they enhance the value of their own service to a wider range of potential customers.

Hence the supplementary services, particularly supporting services, need to be carefully chosen to suit the target market and they should be performed well. The example of frequent flyer points demonstrates this. The core service of transport may be reduced in value if frequent flyer points are not made available when they are available on competitor airlines. Another example is a bank, which may offer efficient, friendly service but the core service may be jeopardised if the lending and risk management policies are inadequate (Francis 1991).

LOW FARE AIR TRAVEL. HERE'S OUR BLUE PRINT.

TRUE BLUE VALUE.

For too long, affordable flying has been a blue sky dream in Australia. But, since we launched over a year ago, we've brought low cost air travel to more than 2 million Australians. So now, you're free to fly when before you either took the slow route by road or rail, paid through the nose for the privilege, or simply stayed at home.

Virgin **Blue**, Australia's low-fare airline, is based on the idea that people would fly a lot more, if it cost a lot less. We are here to make air travel the most simple, convenient and inexpensive way to get around Australia.

LOOK, UP IN THE SKY.

It's true, we look different. Our planes are red. (That is why we liked the name blue.) Our logo includes a blue stroke representing the nose of our planes, as well as a boomerang - because we're always happy to bring you home. Our people will look anything but airline-like. In fact, you won't find a scarf within cooee of our uniform!

KEEPING THE AIR FAIR™

We are different inside out. Looks aside, it's our philosophy that sets us apart. Summed up in our slogan 'Keeping the Air Fair', Virgin **Blue** is committed to changing the Australian airline industry. We just want more people to fly. And fly for less. It is time, don't you think?

YOU'RE JUST BUYING THE FLYING.

Virgin **Blue** took an innovative look at lowering airfares. If your focus is getting to your destination on time and on budget, who needs all the extras? Without the add-ons, we can lower operating costs dramatically and pass the savings on to you, while focusing on what matters most - quality service, consistently. In fact, you won't find a crew more committed to your well being, on and off the ground.

WHERE THE MONEY SHOULD GO.

We'll never compromise on what's essential: the most experienced pilots in Australia, qualified ground personnel and maintenance that's nothing short of top-notch.

WHAT YOU WON'T FIND IN OUR LOW FARES.

• **THE COST OF THE TICKETS**. It costs money to print, process and mail tickets. What you'll get instead is a booking number when you make a reservation with us. Simply quote this number at airport check-in, and present your photo i.d. to collect your boarding pass.

• **THE COST OF AIRLINE LOUNGES AND FREQUENT FLYER PROGRAMS**. Expensive add-ons like airline lounges are hardly essential for domestic travel. And when you finally chalk up enough points for free flights on frequent flyer programs, you can never fly when you want to. At Virgin **Blue** we focus on giving you true service. Like on time performance and a dynamic, customer focused crew.

WE FOCUS ON WHAT MATTERS MOST.

• **THE COST OF "FREE" MEALS**. Everyone jokes about it, but the biggest joke with airline food is that you're paying for your "free" meal in the cost of your ticket. At Virgin **Blue**, we respect your right to choose what you pay for, so we offer you a menu including snacks and beverages for you to purchase on board.

• **THE COST OF RUNNING MANY TYPES OF PLANES**. While the big airlines spend money training staff to fly and maintain many types of aircraft, we concentrate on just one - modern Boeing 737 jets.

Our pilots, flight attendants and engineers are experts in our aircraft – which means operations and maintenance remain efficient and focused. Our fleet is the youngest and most technologically advanced flying in the Australian skies.

LOW FARES, MORE FLEXIBILITY.

Historically, a discount fare meant painfully long advanced bookings or a mandatory Saturday night stay. Who can be restricted by schedules like that? With Virgin **Blue**, you can book one way, at the last minute, hassle-free, and receive flexibility as well as a great low fare. Sounds fair?

BOOK ONLINE AND SAVE.

Our online booking service at virgin**blue**.com.au is not only easy to use but also saves time and money. You can book 24 hours a day and receive our net discounts.

WE'VE TAKEN OFF.

From December 9 we're adding Perth – Adelaide and Perth – Melbourne to our expanding route network. As we continue to grow, Virgin **Blue** will offer a greater choice of low fare flights so you can fly for less more often.

Book online 24 hours a day, phone 13 6789 or your travel agent. virginblue.com.au
KEEPING THE AIR FAIR™

*Fare is exclusive of government taxes and airport related charges, and is subject to availability. Everyday low fares will be available from $199 one way, and fully flexible fares to Adelaide from $439 and to Melbourne from $469 one way.

cummins © VA 838

Figure 6.6: Virgin Blue advertisement

How value can be added through facilitating or support services is illustrated in the further examples below.

- IBM is well known as being in the business of selling computers. However, it has recently redefined its role as supporting PC users in all their requirements. The website developed for PC users offers additional support services: free downloads such as extra BIOS to enable compatibility with the latest software; warranty information for your computer (such as when expires), tips on a variety of topics ranging from hard drives to problem determination checklists; and alerts about viruses. See www.pc.ibm.com/support

- Hooked on Flowers offers flowers for a variety of occasions. A variety of arrangements and prices are available and flowers can be delivered to any address in the metropolitan area of Perth. They also offer hints on flower care and suggest messages for various occasions (such as 'Sending you a floral hug' and 'Tucked inside these flowers are thoughts from afar'). See www.hookedonflowers.com.au

- Optus Direct offers a range of products including mobile phone packages, SIM cards, and accessories. Horoscopes, sports reports, ring tones, stock quotes, jokes and customised news can be relayed to your telephone via SMS messages. Email alerts are also available, for all or selected message sources. Email alerts also enable friends or family without a mobile phone to send short messages to your mobile via an email account, and vice versa. WAP capable mobile phones can also access Internet-based information. See www.info2you.com.au/

- Singapore Airlines prides itself on service, but offers additional services to add value for its customers. It is particularly renowned for its unique Krisworld in-flight entertainment. A choice of entertainment is offered to each passenger through personal screens. Entertainment includes interactive games, a choice of at least 15 latest-release movies, hit television shows and interesting features. The entertainment also includes exercises that passengers can do while seated to maintain their health and stay relaxed. The airline also offers additional ground services to its most valuable frequent flyer members and to first-class and business-class travellers. Examples are the Silver Kris lounge facilities, available at many locations around the world, free rental of a mobile phone for a week when visiting Singapore, personalised assistance on arrival at Changi Airport, including unloading baggage and checking in on the passenger's behalf. Passengers are also able to register for a global SMS alert service, which automatically notifies them of changes in flight arrival or departure times. The message can be channelled through an SMS on a mobile phone, through email or through a pager. See www.singaporeair.com/saa/app/saa

Brand names

Adding value through a brand name is similar to the concept of creating customer-based brand equity, which is defined as 'the differential effect of brand knowledge on the consumer response to the marketing of the brand' (Keller 1993, p. 2). It has also been described as 'the added value with which a given brand endows a product' (Farquhar 1990, p. RC7). Value added through a brand name occurs when the customer is familiar with the brand, is positive towards the brand and sees that the brand adds some extra information beyond that of the product as a commodity. Therefore the brand can play a significant role in adding value. The brand essentially adds value for the customer by making the decision processes simpler and more efficient. Since the consumer is faced with many forms of information, shortcuts (such as purchasing brands that have proved satisfactory in the past) are often used (Doyle 1990).

The brand is equally important, if not more so, in the service context than the goods context. For one thing, services are highly intangible compared to goods (e.g. Zeithaml & Bitner 2000): services cannot be seen, touched, tasted or smelt. Further, they are often more complex; that is, they may comprise a different bundle of attributes for each buyer, and are also more difficult to grasp mentally, leading to consumer comprehension difficulties (Bateson 1979). Hence, there are clear opportunities to add value to a service through a brand name.

Services are also known for their perceived risk compared to goods, the risk arising not only before the purchase (e.g. Murray 1991) but continuing after the service. The after-service risk occurs because of a degree of uncertainty following purchase. This is evoked by a difficulty in comparing alternative services, and the fact that a portion of the service itself (the process or functional service component), although already experienced, remains intangible. Both the intangibility of the service and the resulting perceived risk may be reduced through branding. Developing a service brand helps managers define the actions that will make the service more attractive, tangible, distinctive, measurable and guaranteed (Dobree & Page 1990).

Aaker (1996, p. 7) proposes that 'brand equity is a set of assets and liabilities linked to a brand's name and symbol that add to (or subtract from) the value provided by a product or service to a firm and/or to that firm's customers'. The four categories of assets and liabilities on which brand equity is based are:
1. brand loyalty
2. name awareness
3. perceived quality/leadership
4. brand associations/differentiation other than perceived quality.

We can therefore increase the value of a service through the brand name by focusing on, for example, creating positive brand differentiation or brand associations. Examples of strong brand names and brand differentiation are listed in table 6.2.

Table 6.2	Examples of positioning statements
Organisation	**Positioning statement**
RAC	We're there for you
Holiday Inn	More is better
Qantas	Spirit of Australia
Optus	The power of 'yes'
AAPT	The total communications solution
Budget Rent a Car	Budget drives your dollar further
Alinta Gas	The natural choice
Singapore Airlines	A great way to fly
Commonwealth Bank	Make it happen
Virgin Blue	Keeping the air fair

Another example of value created through the brand is McDonald's, one of the most powerful brands in the world. McDonald's aims to offer the world's best quick-service restaurant experience through outstanding quality, service, cleanliness and value. McDonald's is clear about this position; there is no ambiguity. The meals are simple and limited in variety, which ensures that these promises are kept. The marketing mix aspects, such as pricing, premises, process of ordering, and promotion, each reflect this position and hence are consistent. The result is therefore a credible brand name, and McDonald's is perceived as truthful and dependable.

Including customers in the service delivery process (participation)

A distinctive feature of services is the role played by the customer in the service process. (This is discussed more fully in chapter 12.) Customers define their own service by communicating their needs, but customers also produce, at least partially, their own service (Mills & Morris 1986; Kelley, Donnelly & Skinner 1990). To varying degrees, customers are 'included' in the production process of service industries in the sense that they provide both information and labour in producing the service. They also provide the physical focus of the service, which may be themselves for example, in the case of health clubs, education, hairdressers and dental care; or it may be their possessions in the case of banks, auto care and legal services. Customers therefore have both consumption and production roles. The creation of the service depends partly on the participation and cooperation of the customer (Andreason 1983; Lovelock & Young 1979). Services that have any element of self-service (ATMs, for example) require considerable self-discipline and autonomous action from customers in the service production (Eiglier & Langeard 1977). Indeed, the role of the customer is often described as that of a 'partial employee'. Attribution theory suggests that customers diagnose the causes of the positive or negative evaluation before the final evaluation takes place and that, depending on the nature of the causes, they may modify their evaluations and subsequent behaviours. If customers have been involved in the service production, then they may take a better view of the outcomes, since they hold themselves partly responsible for the service process. Customers therefore contribute to perceptions of a service's value that they have helped to create. Thus, when 'handled' appropriately by the service organisation, a customer can make a major contribution to a valued outcome.

Not all customers, however, want to play an active role. Some want to be dependent and prefer the employee to take the active role (Guiry 1992). Examples of this are some older people who trust that the doctor knows best and want to be 'told' what to do; students who dislike contributing to tutorials and hope that the tutor will give them the model answer; and, when using complex services such as lawyers, customers who wish to devolve responsibility to the expert.

Customer value can therefore be increased either by careful involvement of appropriate customers in the service production, or by offering the possibility of a dependence role (minimal involvement of the customer in the service provision). In the latter case, the organisation would provide more in the way of service to the customer. Some organisations have addressed this through charging extra for additional services. For example, Microsoft offers technical support at different levels according to the needs of the customer. They offer personal support for beginners and home users of Microsoft software, and professional support for experts and businesses. These are costed on a per incident basis. Businesses can, however, opt for the premium support level, in which problems of all kinds are addressed as a priority by Microsoft (see www.microsoft.com/australia/support/options.htm).

Further examples of online services in which customers can contribute to the service are given below.

- Bangkok Airways has a 'one stop shop' information and reservation source for travellers within the Thailand, Cambodia and Singapore region. Customers take on the role of partial employee by deciding on destinations and flights and making their own booking. See www.Bangkokair.com
- Federal Express is an overnight courier system, which originated in the United States and operates in a variety of countries including Australia and New Zealand. Customers contribute to service and to value by using FedEx's automated shipping system, POWERSHIP. The system reduces paperwork and enables customers to track the progress of their own parcels. See www.fedex.com
- ANZ E-Trade allows you to search the market by using indicators such as market movers and stock filters. For example, you can chart a particular stock against other stocks and indices. You can also get stock advice, buy and sell stock, review your portfolio and set up a personal stock watchlist to track stocks of particular interest. See www.anz.com/wealth/etrade

Ethical Issues:
Adapting the retail environment

Retailers are fascinated by factors that influence shopping behaviour. Factors such as music, colour, smell, furnishings, lighting and space are designed with the customer in mind. Music is often tailored to the time of day, for example it can be soothing in the morning when older customers are shopping and with rhythm and a strong beat for the teens later in the day after school finishes. Colour is often used to send messages. According to Australian retailing consultant Annie Harper, who has advised leading retailers such as David Jones, Myer and Sportscraft, pastels symbolise cocooning and peace. 'Soft pastel colours make us feel peaceful: it's got a lot to do with nurseries when we were children — we keep that in our memory bank.' (Bita 2001) Thus retailers are creating perceptions of value by ensuring that the customer experience is positive. They are catering to their target markets, as the saying goes. Or are they?

While pastels mean peace and serenity, red means speed and hence can be effectively used to speed shoppers or diners up. Harper says that casinos traditionally use dim lighting to eliminate the concept of time and keep people playing longer. Eventually, this was changed as customers have complained that the dimness is depressing (Bita 2001).

When combining these elements, such as soft lighting, pastel colours, classical music and merchandise laid out to encourage you to pick it up, the combined effect can send a powerful value signal to customers.

We therefore have a conflict. Are retailers manipulating individuals to increase perceived value of the shopping trip, thus improving their own outcomes such as sales and profitability? Or are they merely catering to customer needs and even broader community needs? The dilemma is summarised by a Sydney shopping centre manager: 'We try to make the shopping centre an attractive place to visit. We also know that a lot of people, especially young women, like to shop with their boyfriend or mum or in a group of friends. We encourage them to stay and enjoy themselves. It's about trying to show that we care but it's also about sales'.

Derived from Bita 2001, Aubert-Gamet & Cova 1999

Lifetime value of a customer

Lifetime value: what customers are worth over a lifetime of their custom

Customer **lifetime value** is discussed a great deal today by marketers. It refers to what customers are worth over a lifetime of their custom. Lifetime value (LV) is closely linked to customer retention, and a small difference in customer retention can have a high impact on profitability. It has been said that 20 per cent of customers provide 80 per cent of profits to a firm, and a five per cent reduction in customer defections can improve a business's long-term profits by 25 to 85 per cent (Reichheld & Sasser 1990). To improve retention, an organisation needs to look at the basic building blocks — individual customers. So the calculation of customer lifetime value is an important consideration for managers. Wise organisations segment their customer market and 'let unprofitable customers go'. However, managers need to look beyond the profit a customer contributes today to the longer term view of the potential profitability of a customer.

So what lifetime value does each customer contribute to the organisation? Internet analysts believe that this question may hold the key to determining the fundamental market value of amazon.com and other multibillion-dollar market-cap Internet stocks. 'The lifetime value of the customer is absolutely the most important metric' according to Lise Buyer, a former analyst for Credit Suisse First Boston (Veverka 2000). Amazon founder and chief executive Jeff Bazos strongly believes in the customer focus of Amazon, and states that 'If you look at the fundamentals of this business [you can see] the kind of value you can drive per customer through the economic model' (Veverka 2000). Jamie Kiggen, an analyst with Donaldson, Lufkin and Jenrette, is enthusiastic about modelling customer value. Following a lifetime of involvement in the intricate detail of response rates, customer lifespan, revenue-per-customer, direct marketing costs and conversion costs, he emphasises three inputs to customer LV: the customer acquisition costs, the revenues generated over the lifetime of the customer and the steady-state margin per customer. Kiggen then put these into a classical dividend discount model to determine the worth of a customer (Veverka 2000). Kiggen's approach has attracted criticism recently, following the severe underperformance of amazon.com based on his model. Other analysts highlight that Kiggen ignored the attrition rate; that is, he assumed that Amazon customers never leave (Veverka 2000). MBNA, a US credit card issuer, along with many other loyalty-oriented organisations, has a simple strategy: getting the right customers and keeping them. MBNA have identified that the organisation has to spend $51 to acquire a customer. The contribution of a customer then rose from $30 in the first year to $55 in the fifth year and $67 in the tenth year. However, retaining a customer is a challenge. A typical customer in a highly developed economy is loyal for just five years. Employees are loyal for just three years and shareholders for just one year (Gopalakrishnan 1996). '...Companies that grasp the virtue of loyalty-based management will step into a virtuous circle of economic growth, identify and target the right customers, deliver superior value to target customers, improve retention of the right customers and thus generate superior economics.' (Gopalakrishnan 1996, p. 27).

Banks are an interesting example of an organisation that considers the LV of customers. They encourage tertiary students to become customers in anticipation of their significantly above average wealth following a degree. In contrast, some organisations have a clear policy of disengaging unprofitable customers. For example, some years ago Telstra suggested to less profitable customers that they move to Optus, who positioned themselves on a lower price.

Assessing CLV managers need to consider:

- the expected length of time that a customer will spend with the firm
- the expected expenditure of the customer and the extent that this increases over time
- the costs of acquiring the customer
- the positive and negative word of mouth that the customer will spread, potentially leading to new customers, remembering that a dissatisfied customer will tell ten others about the experience
- the indirect cost savings acquired by not having to identify and attract new customers. It is well known that the cost of acquiring a new customer from the reasonably static pool of potential customers is far greater (six times) than maintaining a current customer.
- the indirect cost savings acquired by the fact that the established customer knows the procedures and culture of the organisation and hence does not have to be 'educated' about procedures and reasonable expectations.

Some more sophisticated organisations have customer profitability models to calculate exactly this. However, it is more common in a supply-chain context where the profitability index refers to a business customer. The analysis in all settings is complex, owing to the unknowns, especially the length of time a customer will remain with the organisation. This depends on a multitude of factors, not least of which is the organisation's strategies and its competitors' strategies over a long period of time. Nevertheless, calculations of LV can be sobering and are worthwhile in demonstrating the importance of customer retention.

Segmenting the market based on value

The customer value 'package' consists of various factors including price, product quality, service quality, brand image and other factors. However, if we recall the formula for value measurement at the attribute level and the benefit level, it is clear that different components will be valuable in different ways to different people. This is evident in the definitions of value as given by Zeithaml (1988) and discussed in the section Defining Customer-Perceived Value. Thus the market can be segmented into groups that value a service differently. For example, some students may perceive a higher emotional value attached to a restaurant near the university that they visit with friends in the evening, while to others it may be particularly valued for its price.

In reverse, the LV of a customer may differ from one organisation to another. Customers who are expensive or inappropriate for one organisation to maintain may be entirely suitable to another. An excellent example of this is USAA, an insurance firm that focuses on military officers, who are unprofitable for most insurers. By developing specialist knowledge of this group's needs, USAA can make it economically viable to cater to this niche market. The base of USAA's system is a centralised database and a telephone sales force that are accessible from any country, ensuring continuity with the customer if they are redeployed to a different location. Thus customers are retained and the cost of finding new customers is reduced.

Steps to value creation

Based on the discussion in this chapter, the following seven steps are recommended in promoting perceived customer value:

1. Be sure of the core service that your organisation offers and the market position it wishes to adopt. For example, discount stores and department stores offer customer value in different ways, as do campus-based university courses versus Internet-based courses.

2. Within these bounds, decide on the most important customer segments. Usually these will be the most profitable, but other factors may influence the relative importance (as in the case of banks valuing students as customers).

3. Customers and managers have a different view on what contributes to customer-perceived value. The difference in customer-service quality standards, as defined by managers and customers, is well known and contributes to gap 1 of the gaps model of service quality (Zeithaml & Bitner 2000). It is important that customers, not managers, define customer-perceived value. Finding out what customers mean by value is likely to involve market research.

   The organisation needs to measure its own performance compared to its competitors on the key value factors identified by customers. In addition, the relative weights customers put on each element of the value package need to be identified. At the least, informal research should be conducted. Frontline staff will have more accurate knowledge than will managers of what customers perceive as value. Alternatively, informal intercept interviews with customers are an excellent source of information on customer-perceived value. Developing an importance/performance grid identifies which components to focus on.

4. The organisation also needs to distinguish between customers' basic requirements and the aspects of the service that add value for customers. Often it is the core service that is basic, and added value is achieved through the supplementary services. For example, a management consultant may write a report and present a client with the key findings of the study, as specified at the time the study was contracted. However, the consultant may follow up by helping the client with the implementation of the study's recommendations. In contrast, there are some services in which value is tied to the core service. For example, visitors to an art gallery who see a particular exhibition (such as Monet in Japan, which visited Perth and Canberra in late 2001) are likely to be most affected by their experience of the exhibition itself rather than by peripheral products, such as the gallery shop or restaurant. In either case, the components that create value should be the focus of managers and can be used to differentiate the service from competitors.

5. Communicate the value package to personnel, especially frontline staff. Personnel play a vital role in the service delivery, and frontline staff in particular play a 'part-time marketer' role. Frontline staff are 'the organisation' to customers. For example, when a customer says 'the bank told me' the customer means the staff member.

6. Plan the value package to be offered and implement it. Frontline staff can be used in its development, as they were used in step 3. Not only do they understand the customers better than managers but they are also the 'face' of the implementation of value.

7. Performance on the value package items should be measured on a continuing basis to identify any changes over time. Direct measures of value, as described in this chapter, are useful as are related measures such as loyalty, satisfaction, commitment to the organisation and profitability.

Summary

LO1: Define customer-perceived value.

- Perceived consumer value was defined as the consumer's evaluation of the utility of a service based on perceptions of what is received and what is given.
- It is a multidimensional construct incorporating factors such as emotional value and social value as well as perceptions of value for money.

LO2: Describe why value perceptions are so important.

- Value is seen as a strategic imperative for business.
- Offering value leads to a sustainable competitive advantage, through retaining a customer's business. This in turn results in greater profitability.

LO3: Identify how customer value is derived and what it leads to.

- Value is derived from a series of give and get components.
- Get components refer to what the customer receives, which includes service quality perceptions as well as other get components such as the positive impact of other customers.
- Give components refer to what a customer gives up, which includes cost and other negative factors related to the service.
- Value leads to customer satisfaction, which in turn increases favourable behaviours among customers, such as word of mouth and customer retention. This in turn improves business performance.

LO4: Develop a measure of customer value.

- The process of measuring value occurs at three different levels: the attribute level, the consequences or benefits level and the human values level.
- Measurement at the consequences/benefit level is particularly recommended as it enables managers to identify critical valued benefits of the service from which associated attributes can be derived and used in the service design or promotion of the service.

LO5: Describe how we can create value and add value.

The four processes of creating or adding value are:

- adding value through a focus on important dimensions or attributes valued by customers
- adding value through supplementary services
- adding value through the brand name
- adding value through inclusion of the customer in the service delivery process.

LO6: List managerial and marketing applications of value.

- Understanding value as described in this chapter enables managers to use the value concept in various ways. For example, value can be created, as in the previous point, and marketers can segment and position based on value.
- Assessing the lifetime value of a customer is also a useful and sobering exercise, which offers a longer term perspective on customer profitability.

 key terms

Added value: offering benefits, beyond those offered by both the core service and essential facilitating services, that are valued by one or more customer segments (p. 148)

Get components: what the customer perceives they have received when using a service (p. 138)

Give components: what the customer perceives they have given up when using a service (p. 138)

Lifetime value: what customers are worth over a lifetime of their custom (p. 158)

Perceived value: 'the consumer's overall assessment of the utility of a service based on perceptions of what is received and what is given' (Zeithanl 1988) (p. 138)

Supplementary facilitating services (and goods): services and goods that make it possible for customers to use the core service (p. 152)

Supplementary supporting services (and goods): additional services beyond the core and facilitating services (p. 152)

Value package: all aspects that contribute to the perceived value of a service (p. 148)

review questions

1. Why is customer value important?
2. How does customer-perceived value relate to perceived service quality and satisfaction?
3. Value has been described as multidimensional at the benefit level. Describe the dimensions.
4. Why would perceived value vary over the course of using the service — before, during and after use?
5. What are four ways in which value can be added to a service organisation?
6. Describe the customer lifetime value concept. Does the importance of customer LV differ across services? If so, how?

application questions

1. Think of a service you have used recently. Evaluate the service on each of the five dimensions of value described on page 146.
2. Explain four ways in which value can be added and give examples from:
   (a) the tourism industry
   (b) a movie theatre
   (c) your university department or school
   (d) a restaurant
   (e) an ISP provider.
3. Imagine that you are setting up a new service on campus, for example a coffee bar, shoe cleaning service, photocopying shop, typing service, tutoring inquiry centre. What factors would affect your student market's perception of value?
4. Interview a manager or owner of a business. Ask them how they believe their customers perceive value. How do they find out what their customers value? How do they ensure that the customers perceive their business as a valued service?
5. Find a mission statement of a service organisation that directly or indirectly states that they offer value to customers. You could use the Internet to do this. Search for further information to find whether the organisation truly supports this position or whether it appears to be paying 'lip-service' to value.

vignette questions

1. Read the International Issues vignette on page 137. Describe the change in focus that postal services need to take. Do you think that Australia Post or New Zealand Post have changed in this way? (See www.auspost.com.au or www.nzpost.co.nz.)
2. Read the Services Marketing Action vignette on pages 138–9. How do customer value perceptions differ across the three examples?
3. Read the Services Marketing on the Web vignette on page 150. Explain how value is added to independent accounting firms through membership of RAN ONE.
4. Read the profile on page 151. Describe three of the ways of adding value. Why are these particularly appropriate in a professional service scenario?
5. Read the Ethical Issues vignette on page 157. Do you feel it is ethical for retailers to manipulate the service environment through music, colour and other environmental factors to add value to a shopping experience?

recommended reading

Servicescapes are no longer merely a place of economic exchange. This article discusses the extension of the servicescape to a place of social links and communities. This article should be used to address the Ethical Issues vignette:

Aubert-Gamet, V. & Cova, B. 1999, 'Servicescapes: from modern non-places to postmodern common places', *Journal of Business Research*, vol. 44, no. 1, pp. 37–46.

This article shows how a visit to a museum can be broken down into individual stages and how different aspects of value affect satisfaction at different stages of the service process:

de Ruyter, K., Wetzels, M., Lemmink, J. & Mattsson, J. 1997, 'The dynamics of the service delivery process: a value-based approach', *International Journal of Research in Marketing*, vol. 14, pp. 231–43.

This book is helpful in understanding the practice of value. It uses simple case studies to illustrate concepts:

Gale, B. T. 1994, *Managing Customer Value: Creating Quality and Service that Customers Can See*, The Free Press, New York.

Value perceptions can change over the purchase decision process. This article proposes a framework for monitoring customer value at different stages of the process:

Parasuraman, A. 1997, 'Reflections on gaining competitive advantage through customer value', *Journal of the Academy of Marketing Science*, vol. 25, no. 2, pp. 154–61.

Value perceptions comprise more than value for money. This article links various value components with different choice levels (e.g. to smoke or not):

Sheth, J. N., Newman, B. I. & Gross, B. L. 1991, 'Why we buy what we buy: a theory of consumption values', *Journal of Business Research*, vol. 22, March, pp. 159–70.

A multidimensional scale of value is developed in this article. While developed in the context of a high involvement good, the scale can be adapted for service contexts, such as recreational courses, as described in this chapter:

Sweeney, J. C. & Soutar, G. N. 2001, 'Consumer perceived value: the development of a multiple item scale', *Journal of Retailing*, vol. 77, no. 2, pp. 203–20.

The customer value funnel is described in more detail in:

Weinstein, A. & Johnson, W. C. 1999, *Designing and Delivering Superior Customer Value: Concepts, Cases and Applications*, St Lucie Press, Boca Ranton, FL.

This article provides a useful conceptualisation of value, including the customer value hierarchy model. It also suggests how a marketing information system based on customer value can be set up:

Woodruff, R. B. 1997, 'Customer value: the next source for competitive advantage', *Journal of the Academy of Marketing Science*, vol. 25, no. 2, pp. 139–53.

This early conceptual article served to create profound interest in the value concept. It remains important and relevant to discussing and researching value today.

Zeithaml, V. A. 1988, 'Consumer perceptions of price, quality and value: a means-end model and synthesis of evidence', *Journal of Marketing*, vol. 52, July, pp. 2–22.

 references

Aaker, D. A. 1996, *Building Strong Brands*, The Free Press, New York.

Albrecht, K. 1992, 'The only thing that matters', *Executive Excellence*, vol. 9, November, p. 7.

Anderson, J. C. & Narus, J. A. 1999, *Business Market Management: Understanding, Creating and Delivering Value*, Prentice Hall, Upper Saddle River, NJ.

Andreason, A. R. 1983, 'Consumer research in the service sector', in Berry, L. L., Shostack, G.L. & Upah, G. (eds), *Emerging Perspectives on Services Marketing*, American Marketing Association, Chicago, pp. 63–4.

Aubert-Gamet, V. & Cova, B. 1999, 'Servicescapes: from modern non-places to postmodern common places', *Journal of Business Research*, vol. 44, no. 1, pp. 37–46.

Bateson, J. E. G. 1979, 'Why we need services marketing', in Ferrell, O. C., Brown, S. W. & Lamb, C. W. Jr. (eds), *Conceptual and Theoretical Developments in Marketing*, American Marketing Association, Chicago, pp. 131–46.

Beatty, S. E., Kahle, L. R., Homer, P. & Misra, S. 1985, 'Alternative measurement approaches to consumer values: the list of values and the Rokeach value survey', *Psychology and Marketing*, vol. 2, fall, pp. 181–200.

Bishop, W. R. Jr. 1984, 'Competitive intelligence', *Progressive Grocer*, March, pp. 19–20.

Bita, N. 2001, 'Shopping and faking', *The Weekend Australian*, Sydney, July 7–8, p. 23.

Brock, T. C. 1968, 'Implications of commodity theory for value change', in Greenwald, A. G., Brock, T. C. & Ostrom, T. M. (eds), *Psychological Foundations of Attitudes*, Academic Press, New York, pp. 243–75.

China Daily 1999, 'China: posts must cater to new demands', 12 September, p. 2.

Chua, C. 2001, 'An investigation of the antecedents and outcomes of customer participation in recreational services', PhD thesis, University of Western Australia, Perth.

Clemons, D. S. & Woodruff, R. B. 1992, 'Broadening the view of consumer (dis)satisfaction: a proposed means-end disconfirmation model of CS/D', in Gordon, P. J. & Kellerman, B. J. (eds), *Marketing Theory and Applications, Winter Proceedings*, American Marketing Association, Chicago, pp. 413–21.

Dobree, J. & Page, A. S. 1990, 'Unleashing the power of service brands in the 1990s', *Management Decision*, vol. 28, no. 6, pp. 14–28.

Doyle, M. 1984, 'New ways of measuring value', *Progressive Grocer, Executive Report*, pp. 15–19.

Doyle, P. 1990, 'Building successful brands: the strategic options', *The Journal of Consumer Marketing*, vol. 7, spring, pp. 5–20.

Eiglier, P. & Langeard E. 1977, 'A new approach to service marketing', in Langeard, E., Lovelock, C., Bateson, J. E. G. & Young, R. (eds), *Marketing Consumer Services: New Insights*, Marketing Science Institute, Cambridge, MA, pp. 37–41.

Farquhar, P. H. 1990, 'Managing brand equity', *Journal of Advertising Research*, vol. 30, August–September, pp. 7–12.

Francis, I. S. 1991, 'Improving customer quality and shareholder value', *Quality Australia*, September, pp. 35–6, 39–40.

Gopalakrishnan, R. 1996, 'Benefits outweigh the cost of loyalty', *The Hindu*, 15 June, p. 27.

Guiry, M. 1992, 'Consumer and employee roles in service encounters', in Sherry, J. F. & Sternthal, B. (eds), *Advances in Consumer Research*, vol. 19, Association for Consumer Research, pp. 666–72.

Gutman, J. 1982, 'A means-end chain model based on consumer categorization processes', *Journal of Marketing*, vol. 46, spring, pp. 60–72.

Ikea, accessed 17 January 2002, www.ikea.com/about_ikea/our_vision/better.asp.

Keller, K. L. 1993, 'Conceptualizing, measuring and managing customer-based brand equity', *Journal of Consumer Research*, vol. 57, January, pp. 1–22.

Kelley, S. W., Donnelly, J. H. J. & Skinner, S. 1990, 'Customer participation in service production and delivery', *Journal of Retailing*, vol. 66, no. 3, pp. 315–335.

Langeard, E., Bateson, J. E., Lovelock, C. H. & Eiglier, P. 1981, *Marketing: New Insights from Consumers and Managers*, Marketing Science Institute, Cambridge, MA.

Lovelock, C. H. & Young, R. F. 1979, 'Look to consumers to increase productivity', *Harvard Business Review*, vol. 57, summer, pp. 9–20.

McDonald's, accessed 17 January 2002, McDonalds.com/corporate/info/vision/index.html.

Mills, P. K. & Morris, J. H. 1986, 'Clients as partial employees of service organizations: role development in client participation', *Academy of Management Review*, vol. 11, no. 4, pp. 726–35.

Monroe, K. B. 1990, *Pricing: Making Profitable Decisions*, McGraw-Hill, New York.

Murray, K. 1991, 'A test of services marketing theory: consumer information acquisition activities', *Journal of Marketing*, vol. 55, January, pp. 10–25.

Parasuraman, A., Zeithaml, V. A. & Berry, L. L. 1988, 'SERVQUAL: a multiple-item scale for measuring consumer perceptions of service quality', *Journal of Retailing*, vol. 64, spring, pp. 12–40.

Pawlyna, A. 1999, 'HSBC in drive to give customers more value', *South China Morning Post*, 25 March, p. 26.

Reicheld, F. F. & Sasser, W. E. 1990, 'Zero defections: quality comes to services', *Harvard Business Review*, vol. 68, September–October, pp. 105–11.

Rust, R. T. & Oliver, R. L. 1994, *Service Quality: New Directions in Theory and Practice*, Sage Publications, Thousand Oaks, CA.

Schechter, L. 1984, 'A normative conception of value', *Progressive Grocer*, Executive Report, pp. 12–14.

Sheth, J. N., Newman, B. I. & Gross, B. L. 1991, *Consumption Values and Market Choice*, South Western Publishing Company, Cincinnati, OH.

Shostack, G. L. 1977, 'Breaking free from product marketing', *Journal of Marketing*, vol. 41, summer, pp. 73–80.

Slater, S. F. 1997, 'Developing customer value-based theory of the firm', *Journal of the Academy of Marketing Science*, vol. 25, no. 2, pp. 162–7.

Sweeney, J. C. & Soutar, G. N. 2001, 'Consumer perceived value: the development of a multiple item scale', *Journal of Retailing*, vol. 77, no. 2. pp. 203–20.

Sweeney, J. C., Soutar, G. N. & Johnson, L. W. 1999, 'The role of perceived risk in the quality-value relationship: a study in a retail environment', *Journal of Retailing*, vol. 75, no. 1, pp. 75–105.

Veverka, M. 2000, 'Returns: number crunch — what's the value of an Amazon customer? Depends on who's counting', *The Asian Wall Street Journal*, 9 February, p. 2.

Weinstein, A. & Johnson, W. C. 1999, *Designing and Delivering Superior Customer Value: Concepts, Cases and Applications*, St Lucie Press, Boca Ranton, FL.

Woodruff, R. B. 1997, 'Customer value: the next source for competitive advantage', *Journal of the Academy of Marketing Science*, vol. 25, no. 2, pp. 139–53.

Zeithaml, V. A. 1988, 'Consumer perceptions of price, quality and value: a means-end model and synthesis of evidence', *Journal of Marketing*, vol. 52, July, pp. 2–22.

Zeithaml, V. A. & Bitner, M. J. 2000, *Services Marketing: Integrating Customer Focus across the Firm*, McGraw-Hill, New York.

Part 3

Marketing research

Chapter 7   Services research

Mark Gabbott

Chapter 7
Services research

Mark Gabbott

LEARNING OBJECTIVES

After reading this chapter you should be able to:

- develop an understanding of the specific market research problems that are encountered by service organisations
- understand the various research objectives that may be set when research is undertaken
- plan a simple research project
- critically evaluate some popular service research methods
- understand different research methods applied in a services context.

CHAPTER OUTLINE

This chapter deals with services research, which contains a complex and wide ranging set of issues. In marketing, our clear challenge is to respond to customers in such a way as to increase their satisfaction, thereby increasing the probability of their return. In practice, it is sometimes difficult to establish what makes customers satisfied and, equally, what the organisation can do to make them more satisfied. This chapter presents a discussion of services and highlights the main research problems associated with listening to service customers. It then provides a summary of the main research methods that can be applied with a degree of confidence to services research problems. Finally, it summarises two holistic models of service quality and looks at the problems and pitfalls of using online data collection methods.

Introduction

In writing a chapter on services research, there is a natural tendency to merely delimit some generalisable guidelines for research, which the avid reader can take away and apply with little difficulty. However, as practitioners and academics would rightly point out, implementing research in the services domain presents a number of challenges and opportunities that would benefit from the delineation of a unique 'services' approach. In fact, the solution is to take some generalisable principles of research and apply them to the services context with a degree of selection and creativity that fully reflects the nature of the services product. This chapter presents some elements of a common approach and, after pointing out some deficiencies in simple application, describes the main methodologies and issues associated with research in this area.

Why research anyway?

Whatever the focus of research, the objective is to provide reliable and accurate data, which in turn can provide managers with sound information upon which to base market decisions. These decisions then alter the form of the organisation's activity and often change customers' experiences, requiring more research to assess the change and help manage the activity. Chisnall (1986) has characterised this as a two-way process of information flow between the internal organisation and its external environment, and places market research as an ongoing activity rather than a discrete action. In keeping with a **market orientation**, all successful and competitive organisations need to know, in order of specificity: the characteristics of the broad business environment; the market for their products; the precise nature of their current customer base; potential reaction to changes in their offering; and clear organisational and managerial data about their operations. Each of these activities demands different forms of data and information collection, as well as different time horizons for the activity. For example, monitoring the broad business environment is an ongoing activity comprising both **systematised data collection** and **ad hoc data collection**. By contrast, the prediction of potential market reaction to a change in the product can be accomplished with a single ad hoc market study. As a starting point, all organisations should be undertaking research into the following:

- *Broad business environment.* Researching the broad business environment would involve monitoring legal and political change, emergence and decline of new technologies, competitor activity (including new entrants and departures) and demographic and economic trends (including the impact of world events). Examples of recent trends in Australia would be the likely sale of the remaining government stake in Telstra; the impact of September 11 on security services and tourism; the economic outlook on inflation, wages and infrastructure and the implications for service **outsourcing**; and long-term demographic trends toward single person households and available leisure time.

- *Market change.* Within a particular service industry, research might be directed towards understanding service expectations, declining or increasing loyalty, price elasticity, brand tracking and demand forecasting. Examples of detailed research might include forecasting the likely demand

Market orientation: *the pursuit of organisational activity reflective of market demand*

Systematised data collection: *surveys or other research activities that are ongoing and programmed*

Ad hoc data collection: *surveys or other research activities that are one-offs, usually directed at answering or responding to a particular problem*

Outsourcing: *an arrangement in which one company provides services for another company that could, or would normally, be provided by the client company*

for mobile telecommunications; understanding growth or decline in business travel; establishing the times of the day when service consumption occurs; or predicting the likely impact of an additional consumption tax on organisational revenue.

- *Current customer trends.* Depending upon the quality of the marketing information system, organisations might need to know how their customers evaluate competitor offerings; to track changes in taste or expectations regarding service delivery; to understand the changing elements of customer lifestyle; and to examine changes to the process of service procurement or the desire for **service bundling** or unbundling to allow greater flexibility. Examples might include the market response to the opening of a new hotel, the increased number of female consumers, a demand for more or less customisation, increased demand for speed in delivery, or a change to the way in which a large customer procures office cleaning contracts.

> **Service bundling:** *the practice of combining different services and charging a single price*

- *Detailed product review.* Every service organisation needs to undertake a constant review of the detail of their offerings and, in light of the above, may decide to change the price, availability, personnel or format of service delivery. Examples might include an assessment of the detailed response to a new retail environment; the impact of a customer training program for service personnel; an analysis of complaints received to highlight process failure or aggregate data on performance to be used as **benchmark data.**

> **Benchmark data:** *data that is used to compare one's performance with others*

- *Organisational operations.* Depending upon the nature of the organisation, there will be more or less emphasis upon profitability, cost containment or overall benefit relative to investment. In each case, data will need to be collected and communicated, including data on the cost of service (that is, wages and salaries); cost of delivery per customer; inventory held; peak and trough staffing allocation; costs per order received; revenue flow; and the cost of infrastructure, including options relating to technology. This data may then be used to assess the viability of a new offering or to monitor existing offerings.

Palmer (1993) identifies two broad purposes for marketing research. First, it provides management with both market and product-specific information that allows it to plan its activities and minimise risks. Second, it provides a control function, allowing management to monitor overall performance or specific activities once they have been initiated to ensure that they are to plan.

From this brief introduction you should be able ascertain that research activity for any organisation is both central to its competitiveness and, ultimately, to its market orientation. Equally, the scope of potential research is very wide and, depending on the nature of the market, is likely to involve a high degree of investment in time and resources. As a consequence, it is of the utmost importance that the research function is addressed with a great deal of thought and skill. A general approach to undertaking research is contained in the following protocol, in which the stages are considered quasi-linear.

1. Problem definition
2. Research objectives
3. Desk research (gathering secondary data)
4. Research design
5. Research method
6. Sample design
7. Data collection
8. Analysis and interpretation of the data
9. Writing a research report and presentation of findings.

The first and perhaps most important part of this process is defining the problem and, more specifically, the research objectives that are based upon it; that is, what exactly you are trying to find out. There are numerous examples of expensive and comprehensive research studies that have been doomed to failure by a lack of clarity at this stage. Indeed many organisations appear to embark upon research with very little idea about what the problem is they are addressing, or precisely what they are trying to find out. It is desirable to frame the problem and the research objectives in terms that are ultimately **operational outcomes**. For instance, a problem could be stated as 'declining service satisfaction scores'. The research objective might then be stated as 'Determine the reason for declining satisfaction scores among current customers who have stayed at X hotel in the last six months'. The following types of research objectives set in service organisations are merely examples, and the list is not exhaustive.

- To identify customers who are dissatisfied and may defect
- To monitor customer expectations of performance and establish current service delivery levels
- To establish longitudinal benchmark data on service levels
- To undertake an industry review of competitor activity using non-customers
- To monitor the performance of changes to the design of the service, including communications programs
- To establish individual service-provider performance as part of a reward structure
- To establish whether the service requires innovation, deletion or review

In many instances, the data to answer these questions is already held and the first port of call for any researcher is to establish what is already known. That may be done by reviewing published literature or seeking out internal documents and data. In all cases, researchers should try to get their hands on the **raw data** rather than someone else's interpretation of it, thereby avoiding systemic faults. It is not unheard of for a critical error in a published study to be reproduced for many years until the **primary data** has been looked at again. At the end of this process, researchers should be in a position to further clarify the research problem and, conceivably, the research objectives. If the research is to be outsourced, this will be the end of the process. However, many organisations are now conducting research themselves and so have to consider the methods they will employ. With the requisite experience and expertise, the design of a study — including how it should be implemented — will be feasible for most large organisations. Nevertheless, data collection and analysis will still often be handled by specialists.

The problem with services

Before looking at some of the unique characteristics of services research, it is worth spending time clarifying some terminology, specifically the dominant themes of **service quality** and **customer satisfaction**. Service quality and customer satisfaction comprise a series of techniques, assumptions and models that have been used extensively in the services research domain. Quality, in a general sense, refers to conformity, so in a manufacturing context conformity would require that the dimensions of a particular part or component meet the specifications. For example, the tolerance on a drive shaft should be within

---

Operational outcomes: outcomes that can be clearly specified, clearly implemented and clearly measured

Raw data: unprocessed data that has not been organised or analysed

Primary data: data that is collected, for a specific purpose, directly from informants

Service quality: the result of an evaluation process in which the customer compares their perceptions of the service with their expectations

Customer satisfaction: 'the customer's fulfilment response; a judgement that a product or service feature, or the product or service itself, provided a pleasurable level of consumption-related fulfilment, including levels of under- or over-fulfilment' (Oliver 1997, p.13)

0.001 millimetres. However, when it is applied in services it is used as a short-hand term for assessing whether the service meets customers requirements (see Crosby 1980). There are two identifiable dimensions to this assessment: first, what is delivered or, as Grönroos (1991) refers to it, **technical quality**; and second the process through which it is delivered, or **functional quality**. Davies et al. (1999) have suggested a missing dimension that they refer to as 'fit' quality — simply whether the service is optimal for the consumer. As you can see, each of these qualities has the potential to generate considerable research activity.

The other theme associated with service quality is customer satisfaction. The ongoing debate concerning the interaction between quality and satisfaction is beyond the scope of this chapter, but some observations may help to clarify what the debate is about. Quality is by definition about the activities of an organisation, specifically in managing the delivery of a product to customer-described specification. Therefore, in determining what these specifications might be, the organisation would need to talk to its customers. By contrast, satisfaction is a customer-defined outcome; it is not something that emanates from the organisation but definitely resides in the customer domain. Organisations need to find out about levels of customer satisfaction, so there is also a need to talk to customers. For example, one might agree that, based upon the available evidence, a doctor provides a high-quality service experience. However, you may also conclude that your last consultation was highly unsatisfactory. Service quality definitely affects satisfaction but does not determine it. The outcome of all this is that organisations talk to customers about quality (specification) and satisfaction (experience) although much service research, referred to as service quality research, includes both.

A number of authors have identified problems in trying to research service quality and satisfaction. These problems provide some description of the differences in approach required when looking at services as compared to physical goods. Services are dynamic. They change constantly according to who uses them, when they are consumed and whether other customers are present. It is worth recalling the following aspects of services.

- Most services are produced and consumed simultaneously, so interaction is central to **customer perceptions**.
- Services are often situationally dependent. Therefore, while the service may be the same, the context in which it occurs may generate differences of perception.
- Services are often 'people centric' and, as people are invariably different, they react differently to the same thing.
- Service customers generally have a role in the service and their performance of that role will impact on the outcome.
- Service customers approach the service delivery process with different degrees of experience, different sets of personal resources and different desired outcomes.
- Service customers may well not understand what it is they are buying (for example, legal services and, specialist health care) and may not be in a position to evaluate what happened after the service has been delivered.

For all these reasons, researching services is very different from researching physical goods. The sources of variation include time, the customer, the service and the service provider. In such a highly volatile environment, services research presents a considerable challenge to researchers, especially where the outcomes of the research are to be used to generate more change. Lewis (1996) summarises the main problems by classifying them under three headings:

1. methodological problems relating to the dimensions of services
2. variations in customer expectations
3. the nature of measurement.

Each of these will be considered below in some detail.

Service dimensions

Any delimitation of specific research issues in services assumes, often wrongly, that the service component of a particular offering is capable of unique extraction. In other words, that we can deal only with the service component rather than a broader range of attributes that capture the whole customer experience. In today's environment the distinction between intangible services and the physical components of delivery is becoming increasingly blurred, to the extent that even pure services necessarily include some reference to the physical components of delivery. For example, counselling services are often highlighted as pure services; however, there are also elements of the physical in the delivery of counselling services: the service environment (waiting rooms and consulting rooms), billing information and leaflets describing the service. This is the first problem in services research: defining the scope of the activity. We are dealing with a product that, by its very nature, is multidimensional, the dimensions including aspects of the environment, the customer, and variation in process and outcome. Therefore, there is likely to be a large set of possible drivers for any overall service evaluation. Any research that does not take all these components into account is really only dealing with a small subset of the service. For example, many hospitals now recognise that a key determinant of service evaluation is the quality of food that patients receive. Likewise, in restaurants a key determinant is the physical décor, and in airlines it includes the comfort of seats.

The second aspect to this problem is that the dimensions of service which have been described elsewhere in this book are, by their very nature, difficult to assess. Because services are intangible, it is not possible to present an example to potential customers and ask for their views with any degree of reliability. This is not the case for physical products, where a mock-up or a sample can be presented. Similarly, we can measure the performance of many physical goods — exhaust emissions or fuel consumption in the case of a car, or the cooling power of air conditioners — but for a service, measuring performance is problematic. Should we measure the outcome of the service, which may not emerge for many years (as in the case of health care, education and insurance)? Or should we measure the process, such as whether they enjoyed the delivery (as in the case of a visit to the dentist or an interview with a bank manager)? Because of heterogeneity, each customer will view the same service slightly differently, so any aggregation of views, as is usually associated with quantitative measures, will necessarily mask important detail.

Service operations: the system of translating organisational resources into service outcomes

Finally, when directing the focus of research to **service operations**, it is difficult to put precise measures on key aspects of performance such as how much of the service has been delivered, what it cost, or comparative metrics for each encounter. Admittedly, we could generate certain indicators, such as average time per call or per customer, salary cost per customer, or service capacity per hour but these are very rough indicators and often highly unreliable.

Customer expectations

The second broad set of problems emanates from the main data source: customers. Asking questions after the event relies upon detailed memory and a degree of objectivity on the part of respondents that is often superhuman. Research has indicated huge variations in response to the same service when identical questions are asked at different times after the same event. But more importantly, customers assessments may be significantly influenced by different levels of expectation about what will happen, different degrees of interaction during delivery or different resources allowing them to customise or direct the service. Suppose a customer has very low expectations of the service they are about to consume. They experience a superlative service experience like no other they have experienced. Then the researcher asks them to rate the service and, not surprisingly, they give it a very high score indeed. Equally, if a customer has received very high levels of service experience beforehand, but experiences a reduction in some aspect of their experience, then their subsequent ratings will show a drop in satisfaction levels. Because most services provide non-standardised delivery, any potential researcher is dealing with co-variation of the customer, their expectations and individual participation, as well as variation in the service provider's ability to perform consistently over time.

International Issues:
Culture-specific research

It is a mistake to assume that customers will view services similarly across countries and across cultures. For instance, consumers in Taiwan place a great reliance upon face-to-face contact to establish trust. Consumers in Australia are often happy to spend the time of day with a service provider but in Europe extended conversations are unpopular because they hold up the service for others. In each country and in each culture, depending upon the service, you will need to undertake research to discover precisely what drives satisfaction with a service. It is not a good idea to take an existing survey instrument or even a model such as SERVQUAL and apply it without significant risk of missing some key drivers. Look around at the economy or the local market you are operating in and consider the characteristics of best service. These will be your benchmark and are likely to determine customer service expectations.

In a recent survey in the United States, speed and process efficiency were rated very highly in the banking sector. As a consequence, the banks have made great efforts to ensure that speed and process efficiency are paramount, introducing self-use technology (such as Internet banking), call centres and benchmarking. By contrast, Australian consumers value innovation, personal interaction and advice. As a consequence, the US research would have misled marketing managers and potentially caused market dissatisfaction when applied in a different country.

Measurement

Based upon the work of Chakrapani (1997) we can summarise some of the measurement problems associated with service research. Framed in terms of a comparison of physical goods research versus service research, we can identify five important measurement problems.

1. *Regression towards the mean.* If customers get poor service from all financial institutions, then poor service is the norm. Any attempt to measure relative performance will be thwarted, since any scoring will regress toward the mean; that is, scores will tend towards five on a 10-point scale. This does not indicate that the service received is 'average' in relative terms — just that customers see mediocre service as 'normal' and are accustomed to it. In some industries, the situation is even more confusing where, because of long experience in one form of delivery, any attempt to improve the service results in a lower performance score because consumers are moved out of their **comfort zone** and are required to 'learn' the new service.

2. *Artefact of satisfaction.* Any service provision will generate a segment of satisfied customers, which automatically inflates the mean satisfaction score across all customers. Since all customers do not demand or expect the same level of service, there will be some whose expectations are so low that they are quite satisfied. Depending upon the market, this may be a sizeable group, again thwarting any argument to improve or invest in a service on the basis of dissatisfaction.

3. *Limited perceptions.* It is difficult to get customers to identify what would constitute great service, because they rarely think outside their current experience. This problem has been identified before, especially in new product development, where an innovation is highly regarded once introduced but no-one mentioned it as desirable before it was introduced. This is a real problem in new service development. Again, for physical goods it is possible to show the new product, undertake testing, and even comparatively test new livery or new retail locations.

4. *Cultural comparison.* Many large organisations, for reasons of standardisation, adopt services research methods that allow for comparison across many different cities, states or countries. Clearly service will differ from context to context, so there is a contradiction between standardised responses suitable for comparison weighed against local approaches. For instance, service components in South-East Asia are different from the United States and Europe, and so standardised measures may be unreliable indicators for managers.

5. *Mid points.* For many customers a service is satisfactory — it meets all their requirements and they are happy. Applying a 10-point scale to this situation is difficult, since customers tend to rate a service at say five points out of 10 to indicate that they are effectively ambivalent, that is not 'dissatisfied' but also not 'very satisfied'. This confusion in terminology is difficult to break; since we assume that a satisfied customer will put down a 10 out of 10 rating, a mid-point ambivalence is difficult to interpret.

At this point let us recap. We have a product that is integrally bound within the context of its delivery, and exhibits many attributes that are inherently non-standard; we have potential respondents whose responses we cannot rely upon; and we have problems in measuring what they might say anyway — not a great start to a consideration of services research. These are problems, but we should look upon them as opportunities. For the last thirty years or so, academics and practitioners have sought to resolve these inherent issues by various assumptions and techniques to ensure that research in services is both managerially informative and methodologically sound.

Comfort zone: the collection of behaviours, experiences and knowledge with which the customer is wholly familiar

Service research methods

In reviewing the main services research techniques, it is important to remember that, because of the characteristics of services, we are concerned with probably three key objectives:

- understanding customer expectations of service, either real or anticipated
- assessing the performance of service delivery efforts
- monitoring attributes of service outcomes.

The methods described below deal with all of these objectives either individually or collectively. But in undertaking research there will need to be some customisation of questioning, project framing or analysis in order to deal with the precise nature of the problem identified or to reflect different service industries or organisations.

It is not the purpose of this chapter to dwell upon the classic market research categorisations of continuous versus ad hoc, or of quantitative versus qualitative. One can argue that these are misleading dichotomies. Some research is ad hoc in nature but may well be repeated — so is it continuous? Likewise the distinction between qualitative and quantitative research methods can be seen as artificial. On the one hand the interpretation of hard data necessarily involves many qualitative elements. Interpreting cut-off scores for cluster analyses or factor loadings or even mean score analysis may be less than purely objective. Equally, qualitative methods often use agglomeration, in the sense that a view or expression often obtains significance by the mere fact that it appears in many transcripts or is a repeating theme in content analysis. What we do have is a continuum of methods either tending toward the qualitative or quantitative. Along that continuum we can place a series of research activities that are associated with services research. The selection of the topics which follow is not meant to indicate either their uniqueness in this area (they are used in non-services research), or their completeness (there are many other techniques used which are not covered here). Finally, it is wise to consider the full range of service provision and not focus too energetically upon customers as the key source of information. Almost all services use the activities of channel partners, third-party providers, dealers, agents and so on. Researching their needs, expectations or performance as they help serve the end customer is an important part of the process in ensuring the delivery of seamless service quality.

Mystery shopping

Sometimes called 'situation research', mystery shopping describes the activity of an unknown and unidentified individual who acts as a 'shopper' to observe service environments and to interact with the service personnel. This may involve walking into retail outlets and making a purchase or phoning a company with specific requirements or queries. The key to this technique is to ensure that the evaluators are sufficiently well trained and briefed about what should happen, company service guidelines and so on; and they should be able to record their experiences in a meaningful way for subsequent analysis. This technique may provide quantitative information: the number of process points achieved, the number of staff consulted, scoring of service activity, or the timing of sequential service components. Equally, this technique can also provide qualitative information about subtle service delivery attributes: how did the waiting for service feel? did personnel seem concerned? did they manage to convey a degree of empathy? There are many advantages to this technique, since the research can be designed specifically to deal with identified problems, specific locations or times, and can be conducted in relation to competitor activity just as easily as your own.

Mystery shopping can be more informally accomplished by getting marketing executives out into the marketplace to experience their own service first hand and anonymously. Many managers will phone their own offices to ask questions to see how their staff handle the customers, or sometimes walk into a store in which they are not known, just to observe the service or participate in it. For some organisations, this is an important part of familiarising marketing executives with what actually happens at the **service delivery interface**. How many times have you waited to be served, and thought: 'If I were the boss here . . .'.

However, this technique has to be used extremely carefully, and the mere knowledge that mystery shopping surveys are being carried out can demotivate and antagonise service personnel. The ICC/ESOMAR International code of Marketing and Research Practice specifically refers to mystery shopping and cautions researchers against using the technique to assess the performance of individual staff, or invading individual privacy. Often it is important to consult with workplace organisations, unions or work councils to brief them on the general aspects of the activity and to ensure the process is as transparent as possible.

Service delivery interface: the point of interaction between the service organisation and the customer

Ethical Issues:
Mystery shopping dilemma

A retail store chain in the United Kingdom approached a researcher to undertake a series of mystery shopping visits at predetermined outlets. The aim of the research was to assess the levels of service and the transaction and payment systems, as well as satisfaction with their clothing. The research was designed and the mystery shoppers briefed. Just before the research was started, the client company called to ask whether it would be possible to add a few dimensions to the report card. The new dimensions were faxed across and the researcher realised that in fact what the client wanted was to identify each service provider by name and have a named assessment for their performance.

At ensuing discussions between the client and the research team, the client made the point that it wasn't really very helpful to get an overall service evaluation, since there may be weak members of the service team and the client would like to know where development and training should be directed. The researcher, who was in contact with some colleagues in the finance industry, discovered that in fact the retail chain was under some pressure to cut costs, either by reducing staff or by closing outlets completely.

Should the dimensions be included so that the client could achieve what they wanted to, according to the brief? Or should the researcher refuse on the basis that it was unethical to identify staff and potentially lose them their jobs or contribute to the closure of their store?

Complaint analysis

There is considerable confusion regarding the issue of complaint management. Many executives monitor complaints from a summary level, looking at the numbers of complaints received and the possible causes. Intuitively, the more complaints you have, the more problems you have but a closer analysis would suggest that this may be an erroneous assumption. Higher complaint levels could indicate high levels of customer commitment or better complaint facilitation mechanisms. We also know that somewhere between 90 and 95 per cent of customers who are dissatisfied fail to voice this to the organisation, often just leaving and never coming back. Occasionally, customers with unresolved complaints become vociferous critics, which can damage the reputation of a service company forever. So, any increase in complaint reception should actually be treated positively, not only as a source of current market information but also because it gives an opportunity to detect where problems are occurring and, potentially, to recover customers who would otherwise defect.

Most organisations will have an existing complaint resolution system, occasionally outsourced through a call centre, and often providing documented reports. The summary reports give only broad indications of the content, such as personnel, infrastructure and transaction detail. It requires much more detailed analysis to extract the lessons for the organisation in terms of process failure points. These require detailed information about the sequence of events, and the tracking of resources to recreate the circumstances of the event — which service provider, what time of day, how many other customers were present, how a delivery occurred, and events preceding and subsequent that led to the voiced complaint. However, there is a distinction between hard and soft systems. Hard systems are those which are regularised and relatively formal and quasi legal. Soft systems by contrast are not related to any specific issue nor formal in their structure. For example, many organisations use suggestion boxes or some other solicited system to extract comments from customers. This could be an email account, a physical suggestion box or an invitation to fill in a report card. These soft systems are useful in detecting dissatisfaction or receiving complaint information that the customer did not want to voice. They also present an opportunity to solicit positive feedback and suggestions for improvement.

Critical incidents

The critical incident technique (CIT) has been successfully used to provide deep insights into service delivery. The basis of the technique is to elicit from customers written scripts of events that they classify as particularly significant, usually in the form of an example of exemplary service or disastrous service. This is usually achieved by an interviewer who helps construct a written story, which is then analysed and categorised by researchers. This technique, framed around successful service, can help to identify the components that are particularly valued by customers. Equally, when framed around negative events, it can reveal both failure points and what the customer really wanted to happen, which allows for service improvement. The customer reports are highly detailed and quite vivid in their depiction of service experiences. Often, they describe events or incidents at which even some service staff are surprised. A recent study by the author revealed, for instance, that a customer had seen a small rodent running across a restaurant floor but was unable to get anyone to take her observation seriously — they thought she must be joking. In fact the company amended its staff handbook to present a protocol for dealing with this type of complaint.

The value of this type of research is that it is inductive, based on interviews with respondents to record events and behaviours that led to the success or failure of a specific event (Ronan & Latham 1974). An incident is defined as an observable human activity that is complete and allows inferences and predictions to be made about behaviour. It is essentially a classification technique employing content analysis of incidents as data. The use and validity of the critical incident technique (CIT) as a research method in marketing has been examined and used by a number of authors (for example Bitner, Booms & Mohr 1994; Gabbott & Hogg 1996) and the conclusion is that CIT provides a rich source of data, generating accounts that deal with the micro-processes of relationships. However, it is basically a content analysis technique and shares the advantages and disadvantages of such techniques. The main weakness is that the interviewer can filter, misinterpret or unconsciously misunderstand the respondent through the ambiguity of certain word meanings. It is essential, therefore, that in carrying out the data collection and in the classification and interpretation of results, researchers understand the service and are aware of the dangers of influencing respondents with preconceived opinions (Edvardsson 1992).

One aspect of this technique is the ability to undertake more advanced analysis than just the content of the scripts. By categorising the detail of the incidents and combining observation across groups of customers or delivery environments, categorical analysis using log linear regression can be applied to help model determinants of success or failure in particular contexts. The CIT is one of the few techniques that embodies both the depth and colour of qualitative data with quantitative modelling.

Services Marketing Action:
Research in action

In most cross-cultural research, it is usual to compare one set of customers in one country with a similar set in another. An alternative method used is to take the same group of customers and get their responses as they experience services in different countries. This opportunity rarely arises but an international study tour provided all the required resources to undertake this approach. A group of 24 Monash University students from different countries (not those visited) travelled to six different countries over the space of three weeks, visiting international marketing companies. At the end of the stay in each country, each student was interviewed in order to obtain critical service incidents that related to events in that country.

The results revealed surprising differences among the students in terms of their assessment of exceptionally good and exceptionally bad service, based upon their cultural backgrounds. The critical differences were associated with dimensions such as the service environment, where cleanliness and good design rated highly for Australian native students, whereas personal interaction rated very highly for students with an Asian background. Overall the quality of personal interaction was rated low in the United Kingdom and United States relative to Hong Kong and France.

The implication of this research is clearly that different cultural norms apply to service evaluation and, as a consequence, service marketers should be aware of these differences and avoid becoming ethnocentric in their design and delivery decisions.

Deep ethnography

If the objective of research is to understand as accurately as possible the consumer's experience, as well as their service expectations and outcome assessment, it is desirable to get as close to the customer as possible. Much research uses consumers as key informants but an alternative technique is to approach the study from an ethnographic point of view: to immerse oneself in the service and become a customer. In today's multicultural environment it is very dangerous to apply monocultural frames of reference, either from personal experience or drawing upon themes reported from other countries or from other industry sectors. One solution to this problem is to approach the study using **deep ethnography** and study the service in its natural setting, much as an anthropologist might study a remote tribe. The researcher participates and collects information regarding the roles people adopt, the importance of artefacts and storytelling, the assessment of power, and the hierarchy and distance between people. In reality, this is more than just an approach and may require many different forms of data collection, interviews, observation, participation, documentary analysis and social interaction. It will involve the study of the total service experience and illuminate the connections between the consumption environment, other consumers, service personnel and the role of the artefacts or tangibles of the service. In their study of white-water rafting as a service experience, Arnould and Price (1993) observed the role of the tour guides in managing the customers' expectations; the practice of storytelling to transmit specific knowledge; and the ebbs and flows of satisfaction during an extended and often arduous service encounter. They identified how group cohesiveness was formed and the idiosyncrasies of individual reaction to events, as well as expectation change and performance assessment.

Clearly this technique cannot be embarked upon lightly, and requires significant skill as a researcher to avoid undue bias and not to alter the experience by participating in it. While this approach has many applications, both organisationally and socially it requires a degree of objectivity and care in reporting findings that are managerially operational. The data is also context specific, which means that the resultant analysis cannot easily be applied to subsequent or alternative consumption contexts.

Deep ethnography: a methodology that systematically describes the culture of a group of people in terms of activities and patterns

Customer panels

The use of customer panels has long been a feature of retail market research and a number of other industry sectors. Customer panels are a form of continuous market research, where selected customers are brought together as a group on a regular basis to study opinions and experiences of the service provision. Once such a panel has been set up, it can also be used as a test bed to trial new service development plans and to assess new service opportunities. The benefit of the panel approach is that organisations can get regular and systematic market information and have access to a relatively close group of customers. However, this must be traded against a number of disadvantages. A customer panel must be representative of the customers at any point in time and if changes are observed in the actual customer base, then these must be reflected in the panel's composition. This requires constant review and updating, and counts against continuity. Members of the panel may become organisationally conditioned; they may reflect individual rather than typical views and may, because of their involvement, be less than normally critical in their comments. As a consequence, although panels provide a useful mechanism of gaining customer feedback, they should not be used exclusively.

Survey research

Any market research textbook will provide a fair summary of the problems and pitfalls of designing surveys, asking questions, selecting samples and analysing data. The key issue is that, while survey techniques cannot hope to reflect individual detail, they can be administered to large numbers of customers relatively cheaply. With careful design, the detail can be traded off against the scope of the response set. In this section we will consider general surveys and the dominant service quality methodology contained in the SERVQUAL instrument.

Satisfaction surveys

The use of satisfaction surveys is increasing, with many service organisations providing opportunities for customers to comment on their service experience. Comment cards are an unreliable way to collect customer satisfaction data. The **response rate** is usually very low, the customers who complete them are either delighted or seriously unhappy, and the cards have no time boundaries. The only potential value is in picking up occasional issues that can be fed into a more structured data collection activity. These satisfaction surveys appear in locations such as airport lounges and hotel rooms, and come unsolicited through the mail When undertaking more rigorous satisfaction surveys using questionnaires, the key concerns for managers of service oper ations are the type of questions included, the measurement applied and the use to which the subsequent data is put. Rust, Zahorik and Keiningham (1996) suggest three discrete purposes of such surveys:

Response rate: the proportion of consumers who have responded to a survey in relation to the total number surveyed

- to help focus process improvement efforts
- to determine whether previous changes to the delivery have worked
- to uncover strategic advantage or disadvantage.

The big question for the services researcher is 'Who am I going to ask?'. Clearly, the most obvious answer is 'existing customers'. The problem is that sometimes a customer may appear to be current but they may have already signed up with someone else and will not be back. Likewise, the surveys miss those customers who have yet to transact with us. For both these reasons, it is important to focus the activity at the point of transaction. Not only do you get more detailed information because the experience is more immediate, but you can avoid inclusion of past customers and capture new-to-business customers. There may be a problem of bias, though, because we can assume that customers who are transacting are relatively satisfied, which may not give a true picture. As a consequence, current customer activity needs to be matched with past customer activity to get a picture of why customers left. A control group of non-customers who may know about a service but not have experienced it can also be a good source of data, since the organisation may be suffering from some misconception about its service levels. Conceivably, if the sample is large enough, the organisation will pick up some of its competitors' customers too. Other groups might include advanced users (those who are experts and who have considerable experience); customers who are very high value and whom the organisation does not want to lose; or customers who are very low users and might be encouraged to use the service more frequently or more efficiently.

We often assume that satisfaction is solely of concern to customers. However, because of the simultaneity of service production, we should also recognise the role of service providers. Unhappy service staff can have a direct impact upon customers' experiences, so employee or service-provider surveys are a good match for customer satisfaction surveys. Depending upon how such surveys are designed, the organisation can get detailed feedback of customer comments via the employee, or particular issues encountered by staff in trying to resolve customer problems. For instance, a complaint about a cup of coffee may be a serious issue for the customer. The service provider may not have the authority to refund the price or commence service recovery, which can significantly slow down the process of dealing with the complaint, further exacerbating the problem and putting the staff member in a difficult and stressful position.

The second key issue is what the survey is going to ask. In each case the survey instrument must be developed with some understanding of the customer's view. It is no good asking if *the* service provider was friendly if there are 16 service providers within the process. Equally, it is no good asking about a specific service delivery event if what you are interested in is overall outcomes. The development of survey questions is an important and often overlooked activity. If there are rules to abide by, the most important two are that the wording must be clear and unambiguous and that the resulting data are useable. Ask yourself the question, make your own answer and ask yourself 'So what?'. For example: 'Were you satisfied with your visit to this restaurant?'. Do you want 'yes' or 'no' or perhaps a five-point rating scale from 'very' to 'not at all'? The question 'So what?' should be framed as 'So I know that a customer is not at all satisfied — what else do I need to know?'. In most cases, numeric closed answers are easier (that is, 'Choose one and tick the box') but you may wish to offer the opportunity to provide comment or descriptions. These are helpful but need to be analysed differently from simple numeric responses.

Once the design has been finalised, it must be tested on customers to ensure that they understand what is being asked and that the language is clear. Occasionally we use jargon, or special words that have no meaning to our customers; these have to be spotted before the full survey is administered. Finally, some system must be designed to administer the survey and collect the data. Are they to be posted out or left for completion in situ; emailed to a customer database or handed to the providers? Perhaps they are to be administered via interviewers, in which case where and when? These types of questions have to be answered, bearing in mind the objectives of the survey, the budget and the targeted respondent group.

SERVQUAL

Generalisability: the ability to draw, from the research, conclusions that apply to other situations or contexts

Reliability: the ability of research results to be reproduced

Despite the problems with this technique and the conceptual debate about its applicability, **generalisability** and **reliability**, this model has been extensively used to generate managerially applicable activity, and therefore needs to be understood. First published by Parasuraman et al. (1988), the principal architecture of the method is a distinction between what is expected of a service and what is actually experienced or perceived. The difference is operationalised to the organisation by looking at five potential difference points: between what managers think customers are getting and what customers are actually getting, between operational service specification and service delivery, and so on. These have already been described in chapter 4. While each of these gaps is an important research objective in its own right, the most widely used is gap 5: estimating the difference between customer expectations and customer perceptions of performance.

The instrument is in three parts, the first being a series of questions that relate to expectations. These are phrased as 'Excellent companies have . . .' or 'Excellent companies do . . .'. This is the expectation benchmark. Each is scored in terms of agreement on a seven-point Likert scale. Secondly, there is a weighting section which asks the respondent to rank five service dimensions. Finally, the same questions and response categories that appeared in the first part are repeated, but they are worded: 'This company has . . .' or 'This company does . . .'. By matching the expectations to the actual experience, a series of gaps emerges. Customers might agree with a mean of 6.1 that excellent banks 'perform the service right first time'. However, in the matched response it might emerge that, in the case of this particular bank, customers rate its performance as 4.2. The difference is a gap or, more precisely, a service quality gap.

Detailed analysis of this data can reveal where failures are occurring, which dimensions need attention and which are performing well. Specifically, it meets the first research objective. If this method is used repeatedly over time, it is possible to track the organisation's performance and responses to changes in the service delivery; that is, it also meets the second objective. Finally, it can help to identify where the organisation has a competitive service advantage. In this sense it provides a complete and operationally sound method, which may explain the rapid uptake and implementation of the SERVQUAL method in the wider service economy. Adaptations have been made, especially to question wording, to reflect different industry sectors from libraries to IT, and it has adapted relatively well, with the dimensions reproducing reliably.

As with every method there are also a number of problems with SERVQUAL. Buttle (1996) lists these under the headings of Theoretical and Operational. Under theoretical criticisms he lists three things: shortcomings associated with the disconfirmation paradigm (that is, if you get what you expect then you are satisfied); the process orientation explicit in the five-gaps model; and problems with dimensionality (that is, the dimensions should be contextualised to reflect different service activities). Under operational criticisms he lists semantic confusion over what an expectation really signifies; dynamism in how customers assess activities minute by minute; and problems associated with repeated administrations of the same questionnaire instrument. Clearly this method must be used with a degree of caution, although one could argue every method should be used with a degree of caution, and this technique has as many advantages and disadvantages as any other.

Six Sigma process analysis

An alternative way to look at customer service is to track or map processes that contribute to overall customer satisfaction. There are many possible approaches to process mapping, including blueprinting, system mapping and information tracking. Six Sigma is a highly structured and integrated program for developing customer-orientated business processes. The method was developed by Motorola in the 1980s after engineers had concluded that the ability to produce zero defects was one thing but that the product might not actually satisfy their customers, which rather defeated the object of zero defects. Therefore, both quality and customer requirements had to be integrated into a single approach. While grounded in manufacturing, its application has spread to many large service organisations and over the next few years is likely to emerge among some of the major global service providers. Six Sigma relates to the elimination of defects, and the aim is to achieve six sigma deviations, which represents 3.4 defects per million. The reason for its inclusion here is that defects have been broadly defined to include defects in service process, and within the methodology the critical driver is not just to perform without fault but to perform according to customer-determined criteria.

The method is based upon a four-part process: measure, analyse, improve and control. The first stage is dependent upon a 'critical to quality' (CTQ) metric which is the customer's definition of what is most relevant to them. The organisation then determines which activities drive the CTQs and works backwards through its processes to analyse its systems, set performance metrics and implement process controls to ensure customer-orientated performance. For example, when applying the method to a sales CTQ, determined as 'receive the correct order', the company worked backwards to determine the impact of incorrect orders, such as incorrect inventory levels, customer complaint handling, re-ordering and so on. The company then invested in its order system to allow customers to place orders directly and verify before despatch. This reduced costs significantly and, at the same time, reduced customer dissatisfaction. The methodology, however, requires organisation-wide, large structural changes and senior management commitment to re-engineer the organisation around the CTQ processes for customers. The impact of the method has been significant, with clear contribution towards profitability and customer satisfaction.

Online data collection

There is increasing use across the economy of Internet-based surveys. The reasons for this growth are primarily due to its low cost per respondent and its ability to reach geographically dispersed customer groups. In addition, the process of collecting data via a **webform**; the automatic population of a database for **real-time analysis**; and the immediacy of the response are all cited as advantages of using this medium to undertake service research. In some cases, the questionnaire form can be put into the service process. For example, once you have been through an information search, enquiry or FAQ bank or made a transaction, the instrument can appear on screen. It may also be disaggregated so that one evaluation question appears after each step in the service delivery. Other benefits cited include a reduction in response errors, since they can automatically be checked; reduced processing errors, since there is no recoding or rehandling of the data before it goes to the data- base; the absence of interviewer bias; and the opportunity to manage sample distributions.

However, while technology can provide many advantages, and appears to be a highly efficient, low-cost method, Internet-based surveys can have a number of disadvantages too. The first and most important is the self-selection bias that is similar to satisfaction comment cards. Most respondents have polarised views, either good or bad, and the data can be misleading. Similarly, there are all the other problems of Internet communication. Issues concerning security, veracity of responses, and multiple visits all cast doubt upon the reliability of the data. But perhaps the most important problem is that Internet access and use is still confined to a relatively small part of the population, and many attitudes and perceptions are coloured by the medium itself.

Webform: the electronic input that receives customer-entered online data

Real-time analysis: the analysis of data as it is being submitted or recorded

Services Marketing on the Web:
The shopping cart problem

A major online retailer had undertaken some analysis of its server records, and had discovered a problem with abandoned 'shopping carts'. Customers had collected their purchases in a virtual shopping cart and proceeded to the 'checkout' to make payment but at that point they logged out of the site and left the shopping cart abandoned. Further analysis of feedback emails suggested that customers were very dissatisfied with the process of paying — not that they resented paying, but they found it unnecessarily difficult.

The company started a tracking study, following the sequence of actions by customers. By using customer identification technology, which revealed customer log-on details, they were able to identify customers by their email address. After two weeks of collecting the names of customers who had logged on, they then emailed a short questionnaire to try to establish broad drivers of satisfaction with the site and to identify specific problems. The results were confusing. Scores for satisfaction with the site, with the products provided and with the service levels were extremely high but scores for ease of transaction were very low.

By talking to their customers they discovered that when a purchase of a single item was made the transaction was very easy, but as soon as multiple items were purchased the customer was forced to go through the transaction and order confirmation process as many times as there were items in the shopping cart. A simple change to the software allowed all items to be presented at a single view, with a single order confirmation. A later survey, after these changes, found that not only were satisfaction levels with the site, product and service increased by 15 per cent but that the transaction had ceased to be a problem area, and many compliments were received from customers about how easy the system now was.

Summary

LO1: Develop an understanding of the specific market research problems that are encountered by service organisations.

These can be categorised as problems which relate to:
- the dimensions of services — intangibility, inseparability, heterogeneity, perishability and ownership
- variation in customer expectations
- the nature of measurement.

Within each category, services researchers need to assess the extent to which their research is affected.

LO2: Understand the various research objectives that may be set when research is undertaken.

The precise objectives set will depend upon the nature of the research to be undertaken; however, they can be summarised as:
- identifying customers who are dissatisfied
- monitoring customer expectations

- establishing benchmark data, either historical or comparative
- assessing competitor activity
- monitoring performance of the service
- monitoring the performance of individual providers
- identifying innovation of deletion activity.

LO3: Plan a simple research project.

The stages in a research project are:

- problem recognition
- defining the research objectives
- gathering already known information, that is, desk research or secondary data
- designing the research
- selecting appropriate methods
- designing or identifying a sample or selection of informants
- collecting the data
- analysing the results obtained
- presenting the research.

By following this simple process you should be able to plan the research methodically and anticipate the activities you will need to undertake.

LO4: Critically evaluate some popular service research methods.

The methods used to research services are many. In this chapter we reviewed the benefits and problems associated with mystery shopping, complaint analysis, critical incidents, deep ethnography and customer panels.

LO5: Understand different research methods applied in a services context.

In addition to the methods considered under LO4, we have also examined four key research activities that apply to services:

- satisfaction surveys
- the principal service quality methodology SERVQUAL
- Six Sigma process analysis, which focuses upon internal organisational change
- online data collection, which is increasingly being used to obtain data from customers.

 *key terms*

Ad hoc data collection: surveys or other research activities that are one-offs, usually directed at answering or responding to a particular problem (p. 169)

Benchmark data: data that is used to compare one's performance with others (p. 170)

Comfort zone: the collection of behaviours, experiences and knowledge with which the customer is wholly familiar (p. 175)

Customer perception: the process by which customers select, organise and interpret information (p. 172)

Customer satisfaction: 'the customer's fulfilment response; a judgement that a product or service feature, or the product or service itself, provided a pleasurable level of consumption-related fulfilment, including levels of under- or over-fulfilment' (Oliver 1997, p.13) (p. 171)

Deep ethnography: a methodology that systematically describes the culture of a group of people in terms of activities and patterns (p. 180)

Functional quality: the components of the process used to arrive at the service outcome (p. 172)

Generalisability: the ability to draw, from the research, conclusions that apply to other situations or contexts (p. 182)

Market orientation: the pursuit of organisational activity reflective of market demand (p. 169)

Operational outcomes: outcomes that can be clearly specified, clearly implemented and clearly measured (p. 171)

Outsourcing: an arrangement in which one company provides services for another company that could, or would normally, be provided by the client company (p. 169)

Primary data: data that is collected, for a specific purpose, directly from informants (p. 169)

Raw data: unprocessed data that has not been organised or analysed (p. 171)

Real-time analysis: the analysis of data as it is being submitted or recorded (p. 184)

Reliability: the ability of research results to be reproduced (p. 182)

Response rate: the proportion of consumers who have responded to a survey in relation to the total number surveyed (p. 181)

Service bundling: the practice of combining different services and charging a single price (p. 170)

Service delivery interface: the point of interaction between the service organisation and the customer (p. 177)

Service operations: the system of translating organisational resources into service outcomes (p. 173)

Service quality: the result of an evaluation process in which the customer compares their perceptions with their expectations (p. 171)

Systematised data collection: surveys or other research activities that are ongoing and programmed (p. 169)

Technical quality: the outcome of the service (p. 172)

Webform: the electronic input that receives customer-entered, online data (p. 184)

 review questions

1. List five areas that a service company would wish to monitor by undertaking research.
2. List five objectives that may be set by a service organisation undertaking research.
3. Write down the nine common steps in undertaking a research project.
4. What are the five measurement problems faced when undertaking services research?
5. List five service research methods and explain the benefits and problems with each.
6. In order to assess the performance of a specific service outlet, which research technique might you use?

application questions

1. Write down in story form the details of a great service experience and a poor service experience. Try to identify the common and distinct components of each experience set.
2. In a group, identify a service that everyone has experienced. Ask each group member to identify the best things about the service and the worst. Do you all agree? Or are your perceptions different? Why?
3. What is service quality and how is it different from customer satisfaction?
4. Design a short satisfaction questionnaire for a service. What considerations do you need to take into account?
5. Identify a service process, such as paying in a restaurant or taking out insurance, and try to map it. See if you can identify where the process could be amended to increase customer satisfaction.
6. Design a simple satisfaction questionnaire to assess satisfaction of students with their tutor. What factors appear to be important? Discuss the desirability and the ways in which the organisation could increase satisfaction.

vignette questions

1. Read the International Issues vignette on page 174. How do global service organisations cope with differences between the markets they serve?
2. Read the Ethical Issues vignette on page 177. What should the researcher do?
3. Read the Services Marketing Action vignette on page 179. Ask any overseas friends what aspects of a service they particularly value and which parts they particularly dislike. Compare these results with ones obtained after talking to friends from Australia.
4. Read the Services Marketing on the Web vignette on page 185. Visit three customer transaction or online retail sites. Assess how easy it is for you to make a purchase and list three aspects of the site that are good and three that are bad.

recommended readings

The following series of research articles provides examples of how the research techniques are put into practice by academics:

Gabbott, M. & Hogg, G. 1997, *Contemporary Services Marketing Management: A Reader*, Dryden Press, London.

This book is a great collection of articles on research methods, with many references to published work in highly specialised areas:

Chakrapani, C. 2000, *Marketing Research: State of the Art Perspectives*, AMA, Chicago.

The following reference is a practical guide to undertaking services research, and details all the steps in the process:

Johns, J. & Lee, R. D. 1998, *Research Methods in Services Industry Management*, Cassell, London.

references

Arnold, E. J. & Price L. L. 1993, 'River magic: extraordinary experience and the extended service encounter', *Journal of Consumer Research,* vol. 20, June, pp. 24–45.

Bitner, M. J., Booms, B. & Mohr, L. 1994, 'Critical service encounters: the employee's viewpoint', *Journal of Marketing,* vol. 58, no 4, pp. 95–106.

Buttle, F. 1996, 'SERVQUAL: review, critique, research agenda', *European Journal of Marketing*, vol. 30, no. 1, pp. 8–32.

Chakrapani, C. 1997, *How to Measure Service Quality and Customer Satisfaction: The Informal Field-guide for Tools and Techniques,* American Marketing Association, Chicago.

Chisnall, P. 1992, *Marketing Research,* McGraw-Hill, London.

Crosby, P. 1980, *Quality is Free,* Mentor, New York

Davies, B., Baron, S., Gear, T. & Read, M. 1999, 'Measuring and managing service quality', *Marketing Intelligence and Planning*, vol. 17, no 1, pp. 33–47.

Edvardsson, B. 1992, 'Service breakdowns: a study of critical incidents in the airline industry', *International Journal of Services Industry Management,* vol. 3, no. 4, pp. 17–29.

Gabbott, M. & Hogg, G. 1996, 'The glory of stories — using critical incidents to understand healthcare evaluation', *Journal of Marketing Management,* vol. 14, no. 2, pp. 6–17.

Grönroos, C. 1991, *Strategic Management and Marketing in the Services Sector,* Studentlitteratur, Lund, Sweden.

Lewis, B. 1996, 'Customer care in services', in Glynn, W. & Barnes, J. (eds), *Understanding Services Management,* John Wiley & Sons, Chichester.

Palmer, A. & Cole, C. 1995, *Services Marketing,* Prentice Hall, London.

Parasuraman, A. Zeithaml, V. & Berry, L. 1988, 'SERVQUAL: a multiple item scale for measuring customer perceptions of service quality', *Journal of Retailing,* vol. 64, pp. 12–40.

Ronan, W. W. & Latham, G. P. 1974, 'The reliability and validity of the critical incident technique: a closer look', *Studies in Personnel Psychology,* vol. 6, spring, pp. 53–64.

Rust, R., Zahorik, A. & Keiningham, T. 1996, *Service Marketing,* HarperCollins, New York.

Part 4

Marketing strategies

Chapter 8

Managing supply and demand

Meredith Lawley and Tracey Dagger

LEARNING OBJECTIVES

After reading this chapter you should be able to:

- understand the importance of managing supply and demand for services
- describe the role of perishability in managing supply and demand of services
- discuss the strategies that can be used to adjust supply to meet demand in cases of both high demand and low demand
- discuss the strategies that can be used to adjust demand to meet supply in cases of both high demand and low demand.

CHAPTER OUTLINE

Managing supply and demand is important to the management of services, as it is clearly linked to profitability, particularly in the case of services, where demand fluctuations are difficult to predict. An ideal situation for any service business is for demand and supply to be in balance, thus making optimal use of all resources. Unfortunately, this situation does not occur in many service operations, owing to the inability of services to be stored or inventoried; that is, services are perishable. Demand will often follow cyclical or even erratic patterns, resulting in reduced profit. Revenue is lost when customers are turned away because of demand that cannot be satisfied. Similarly, if demand is too low, the services resources will not be fully utilised, which increases expenses. Hence, the purpose of this chapter is to describe strategies that can be used by service firms to better balance supply and demand.

This chapter has three major sections. The first section addresses the reasons for the imbalance between supply and demand in relation to services. Next, various strategies for managing supply to meet high and low demand are discussed, followed by a similar treatment of strategies for managing demand to meet supply.

Introduction

Like Goldilocks, most service providers would like supply and demand to be 'just right', but this is not always the case. In some situations demand is too high: all the tables in the restaurant are full, and unhappy potential customers are turned away while waiters are stressed by dealing with a full restaurant. In other cases demand is too low, tables are empty and waiters are standing around with little to do. The ideal situation is for demand to be just right — a full or close to full restaurant, no customers turned away and waiters working consistently but not at extraordinary levels.

Balancing supply and demand requires considerable effort on the part of managers of service firms, who must plan in advance the strategies needed to achieve this goal. As a basis for this planning, managers must first have a good understanding of the nature of demand for their particular service. Strategies can be aimed at adjusting elements of supply, such as staffing, facilities and equipment, to meet demand or adjusting demand to meet supply, for example stimulating demand in periods of low demand. In many cases a combination of both approaches may be used.

The purpose of this chapter is to explain the reasons for the imbalance between supply and demand, to understand the nature of demand as a basis for planning and to outline various strategies that can be used to manage supply and demand.

The challenge of supply and demand: perishability

Perishability, or the inability of service firms to store inventory for later use, is the fundamental issue underlying the need to manage supply and demand. Consider your local radio station and the advertising time they sell to local business to promote their services. Unused advertising time on one day cannot be resold during the following days. Contrast this to your university bookshop. If the bookshop does not sell all the copies of a particular book during orientation week, it can inventory them and store them for sale during the first few weeks of semester or return them to the publisher for a refund. Thus, managing fluctuating demand for services is much more difficult than managing fluctuating demand for consumer goods. The supply capability of a firm, in conjunction with fluctuations in demand, results in a number of alternative supply and demand outcomes. These alternatives are outlined in table 8.1. It should also be noted that capacity levels and fluctuations in demand affect some services differently from others. For example, crowding may be a desirable part of going to the Big Day Out, because without the crowds and energy they create the atmosphere and experience may be lost. In contrast, if you are on a flight between Brisbane and Perth and the plane is completely full, you may find that the level of crowding may adversely affect your overall experience.

Table 8.1 indicates that there are four potential supply levels at which a firm can operate: greater than maximum supply, maximum supply, optimum supply and less than optimum supply. **Greater than maximum supply** reflects demand that exceeds the absolute maximum level of a firm's supply. Having stretched supply as far as possible, the firm still cannot satisfy demand.

Greater than maximum supply: higher demand than maximum available supply

In this scenario, customers are turned away. **Maximum supply** means that the firm is operating at 100 per cent. This is the maximum level it can operate at without having to turn customers away. **Optimum supply** represents a balance between supply and demand. The firm is operating at a level that enhances the customer's experience and effectively and efficiently uses the resources it has available. Generally, optimum capacity is considered to be 70 to 90 per cent of the maximum supply level. At this level resources are not being overtaxed as they would be if the firm was operating at the maximum supply level. In addition, customers are not being turned away as they are when demand is greater than maximum supply. Finally, demand can sometimes be **less than optimum supply**. In this case there are not enough customers and the firm's resources are being under-utilised. The following section looks at the implications of these four supply levels in greater detail.

Table 8.1   Alternative supply and demand outcomes

Supply	Relationship to demand	Issues
Greater than maximum supply	Higher demand than maximum available supply	• Customers turned away • Lost business opportunities • Resources under great pressure • Service quality suffers • Crowding • Staff and facilities overtaxed • Customers seek competitors' offerings
Maximum supply	Higher demand than optimal supply levels	• All customers serviced • Excess pressure on all resources — facilities and staff • Queuing and long waits • Crowding • Service quality suffers
Optimum supply	Demand and supply are well balanced	• Resources utilised at an ideal rate • Productivity ideal • Service quality delivered • No delays • Pleasant amount of crowding
Less than optimum supply	Lower demand than optimal supply levels	• Resources (staff/facilities/equipment) under-utilised • Productivity decreases • Profitability suffers • Customers receive excellent individual service • Customers have full use of facilities • No waiting • Lack of customers could create negative image or atmosphere

Higher demand than maximum available supply

When demand is greater than the maximum supply level, customers are turned away. This results in lost business opportunities and potential customers who are turned away may never visit the service firm again. Moreover, these customers are likely to seek competitor's offerings. The firm's resources (staff, facilities and equipment) are being utilised at a rate that cannot be sustained for long periods of time. The staff, facility and equipment are under immense pressure. As a result, service quality suffers. Customers who do receive the service may be disappointed by crowding, excessive waiting times, impersonal service and so on. Take the example of visiting Dreamworld to watch a Big Brother eviction. Demand may be greater than the available supply and potential customers may be turned away. In this instance supply is constrained by the facilities available and the number of people that can safely occupy a particular venue.

Higher demand than optimal supply levels

When demand exceeds optimum supply (remember that optimum supply is generally between 70 and 90 per cent of the firm's maximum supply) the temptation is to accept the additional business, even if it means pushing staff, facilities and equipment to the limit. To do this, service firms seek ways to achieve supply flexibility (for example, double-booking tables at a restaurant, squashing in extra seating at a concert). At the maximum supply level the firm is operating at full capacity. Although the level of demand does not exceed the maximum level of supply, as outlined in the previous scenario, the level of demand still exceeds the optimum supply level. All customers are catered for but the quality of the service may be compromised because staff, facilities and equipment are being overused. Customers must deal with issues of crowding, lengthy queuing and waiting periods. As a result, the service organisation finds it difficult to meet customers' expectations and provide exceptional service quality. Customers in turn are dissatisfied and may begin spreading negative word of mouth about the firm. Service firms should consider trying to shift demand patterns to reduce the problems involved with taking on additional business over and above the optimum supply level — problems such as unpleasant crowding, queues and reduced service quality. At the maximum supply level, all customers wanting to attend the Big Brother eviction get tickets. Customers find that they have to spend a long time queuing, they have difficulty finding a parking space, they do not get a good view of the evictee due to the level of crowding, the facilities are overused and the staff feel overwhelmed.

Demand and supply are well balanced

The ideal level of service operation is when supply and demand are well balanced. Resources (staff, facilities and equipment) are utilised at a rate that allows service providers to meet consumers' expectations for service delivery. Staff are not overworked, facilities are well maintained, there are no excessive waiting times or overcrowding. The service provider has allowed some leeway to ensure that facilities, staff and equipment are not overworked. As a result, service quality is at the optimum level and the firm's resources are meeting customers' expectations comfortably. At this ideal or optimum level of supply, supply and demand are well balanced. You get a great view of the Big Brother eviction night stage and the evictee, the facilities are not over used, the staff are not being overworked, the crowding is not excessive, parking is acceptable and you don't have to queue for a long period of time.

Lower demand than optimal supply levels

When supply exceeds demand, resources are under-utilised and productivity decreases. These decreases in productivity result in reductions in profitability. However, customers will receive excellent individual service, having full use of the service's equipment and facilities while not having to deal with issues of crowding and waiting. The impact of excess supply on customer perceptions will differ depending on the characteristics of specific services. Services that depend on a degree of crowding to create atmosphere and enhance the service experience will suffer if there is excess supply. In such situations, customers' expectations may not be met or they may perceive that the service is not popular or not of a desired quality level.

Consider the impact of attending the Big Brother eviction if three-quarters of the venue was empty. There would be no problems associated with parking, queuing or crowding. However, would your experience be as good without the energy and enthusiasm of the crowd?

Adjusting supply to meet demand

As previously indicated, supply and demand are closely linked; manipulating either one impacts on the other. In this section the focus will be on identifying strategies that manipulate or create flexibility in supply in order to help manage both high and low demand.

During periods of high demand service firms seek to expand capacity or supply as much as possible, using the strategies summarised in table 8.2, like increasing staffing levels and acquiring additional space. Conversely, during periods of low demand firms try to reduce the supply of resources such as staff as a way of minimising expenses.

Generally, supply is constrained by one of more of the following four elements (Bitner & Ziethaml 2001):

- *facilities* — the actual building or location from which the service may be offered
- *equipment*, such as pizza ovens, kitchen equipment, crockery and cutlery in a restaurant
- *labour* — the staff, who may range from unskilled to professionals and can be employed on a full-time, part-time or casual basis
- *time* — the hours during which the service is available; for example, a people-based service like an accountancy practice may normally operate between 9 a.m. and 5 p.m. from Monday to Friday, while an equipment-based service like an ATM is available 24 hours a day, seven days a week.

Most supply strategies revolve around these four elements of supply, with some elements being more important than others for different types of services. For example, some professional services such as accounting firms and medical practices require highly skilled and trained staff for core functions. This type of labour is typically not as flexible or as easily manipulated as the relatively untrained staff required for a fast-food restaurant. Hence it is easier for a restaurant to develop a large pool of labour to draw on, whereas the medical practice may not be able to find sufficient labour for peak demand periods. In contrast, an equipment-based service like an ATM has minimal need for labour input.

The first column of table 8.2 highlights the element of supply on which the strategy focuses, while the second column identifies the strategy. From the second column it can be seen that all strategies aimed at adjusting supply focus on increasing the flexibility of all elements of supply. The final columns identify the tactics that can be used when demand is high and supply needs to be increased; and the tactics for when demand is low and supply needs to be decreased.

Table 8.2   Adjusting supply to meet demand

Relevant marketing elements	Strategies for adjusting supply to meet demand	Tactics for high demand	Tactics for low demand
Facilities	Create flexibility in facilities	• Rent additional space • Share facilities	• Decrease space
Equipment	Create flexibility in the service product	• Hire/outsource/rent additional equipment	• Hire/outsource/rent current equipment to other service providers
Labour	Create flexibility in labour capability	• Employ casual or part-time staff • Cross-train employees • Increase staff working hours/ encourage staff to work overtime • Ask staff to specialise in one job role • Utilise third parties/outsource • Reduce interaction of staff with customers	• Ask staff to work in varied job roles • Schedule vacations • Reduce staff working hours • Lay off staff • Plan for staff training
Time	Create flexibility in the process of service delivery	• Extend hours of operation to accommodate demand • Increase customer participation in the process of service delivery • Develop a peak operating procedure	• Reduce hours of operation • Schedule down time for maintenance

Facilities

In this section we consider the facilities used by the service operation; that is, the actual space required to deliver services. Examples include the beauty salon occupied by a hairdresser or the actual location required by a restaurant.

Tactics for high demand

When demand is high, a service operation needs to expand its facilities to cater for this demand. Two possible ways this can be done are by renting additional space or sharing facilities. For example, a restaurant may be able to rent additional space for its peak evening period from a neighbouring shop that does not operate in the evening; or a function centre may be able to put up additional marquees in its grounds to cater for very large functions. This happened at the Commonwealth Heads of Government Meeting (CHOGM) on the Sunshine Coast in Australia in 2002. No conference venue existed that was large enough to accommodate the delegations from over 50 countries, so a two-storey marquee was erected to act as the main conference venue.

Sharing facilities is best undertaken by complementary services such as a beautician and a hairdresser, or an accountancy practice and a mobile book-keeping service. In cases such as these, when demand is high for one of the services, the other can assist by, say, answering the phone and taking appointments.

Think about the last time you went to a sporting match and tried to get a drink or an ice-cream from a food service outlet. These outlets are in very high demand and physically cannot cope with the demand. In such cases these operations may make use of staff who go out into the crowd to sell directly to customers, thereby reducing pressure on the existing facilities.

Tactics for low demand

In periods of low demand, the need is to reduce the supply of facilities or decrease the space required. For example, a hairdresser may sublease space in the salon on certain days and at certain times. In this way facilities that would otherwise be under-utilised are able to produce some income. Similarly, at the sportsground food outlet, when demand is low there would be no additional mobile food sellers and customers would have to go to the central outlet.

Equipment

Equipment-focused strategies relate to creating flexibility in the equipment necessary to produce a service. This strategy is more applicable to services that require a component of equipment, either in their production or their delivery, and is less applicable where reliance on equipment is minimal, as in the case of a doctor or lawyer. For example, a fortune teller or palm reader has very few equipment needs, whereas a hotel requires beds, mattresses, sheets and so on.

Tactics for high demand

The key to managing high demand is to obtain more equipment but in a flexible way, so that the equipment can be returned when demand is lower. For example, many restaurants, resorts and clubs hire additional cutlery, crockery and glassware during periods of high demand such as busy holiday periods. Once the period of high demand is over, the restaurant, resort or club returns the hired products to the hire company. This is a viable option for many service businesses, as they do not have to invest additional capital in purchasing products that will only be used for short periods of time throughout the year. Moreover, these services do not have to worry about storing unused product during low-demand periods. Indeed, even hire companies may sub-hire or lease extra equipment during busy periods.

Tactics for low demand

In periods of low demand, equipment can be moved to areas of high demand or subleased. For example, airlines may lease or sublease their planes to other airlines and a hire company may sub-hire their equipment to other hire companies who have high demand at that time. Moreover, many service providers and contractors such as builders, plumbers and electricians may temporarily relocate to a region that is experiencing a boom in building.

Labour

As mentioned earlier, labour can be made up of full-time, part-time and casual staff, often with a combination of all three types of labour. Again, the focus is on creating flexibility in labour capability so that staffing is always at an optimal level, with extra staff in periods of high demand and fewer staff when demand is lower. Planning for flexibility also needs to take into account the level of skills and training required for service delivery.

Tactics for high demand

In cases of high demand, the following tactics, or combination of tactics, may be considered to increase the supply of staff:
* *Employ casual or part-time staff.* For example, many fast-food restaurants and retail outlets have a bank of casual staff who can be called in for peak

periods like late night shopping or other periods of high demand. These staff can often work for short periods and can stop work when business slows down. Similarly, universities may employ sessional teaching staff to assist full-time staff during teaching periods, letting them go during non-teaching periods. In comparing these two examples, it is often much harder for the university to find sessional tutors than it is for the restaurant to find waiting staff, owing to the different skills and qualifications required to teach at university level.

- *Cross-train employees to increase their flexibility*. This means in very busy times a greater pool of staff can be used. For example, McDonald's ensures that staff are trained in all areas of operation — not just in front counter or drive through, so that the restaurant has greater options for scheduling of staff.
- *Allow staff to specialise in one job role*. In contrast to the previous tactic, this can increase the efficiency and output of an employee in a peak period. This must be balanced against the loss of flexibility.
- *Increase staff working hours/encourage staff to work overtime*. In some cases, particularly if some training or development of skills is required, a good strategy may simply be to ask existing staff to work longer hours or overtime. This must be balanced against maintaining a suitable level of service quality, which could be jeopardised if staff are required to work too long, too often.
- *Utilise third parties*. This outsourcing involves calling on another service provider to supply extra labour for the periods of high demand, as described in the Services Marketing Action vignette below.
- *Reduce the amount of interaction staff have with customers*. This can be done by using self-service options, which take pressure off overtaxed staff and allow labour to perform at an optimal level.

Services Marketing Action:
Innovative and flexible workforce solutions

Manpower is a global employment agency that provides a full range of employment-related services to people looking for jobs and to companies looking for staff. One of its services to businesses is that of providing flexible short-term solutions to staffing needs. For a price, Manpower can provide labour to meet needs on an hourly, daily or weekly basis. It is a service firm catering to the needs of other service firms. Briefly, Manpower operates in over 61 countries and has over 1.9 million temporary staff on its books, providing staffing solutions to over 400 000 customers worldwide (Manpower 2002).

One small business that regularly uses the services of Manpower is Party People, an equipment hire company (the subject of a case study later in this book). Party People relies on a core staff of five people and uses Manpower to fill the gaps in staffing requirements. These gaps could be for a day if one staff member is sick or a particularly big job comes in; for a few weeks to cover annual holidays; or for a few months in peak demand periods such as Christmas. For a small company such as Party People, the use of temporary staffing provides a reliable and worry-free flexibility in its workforce.

Tactics for low demand

Tactics here focus on flexibility in numbers of staff and in skill levels. For example, if staff are trained in all areas of service provision and do not specialise in one area, they are more flexible in periods of low demand as they can fulfil a variety of job roles. Other tactics include getting staff to take holidays during periods of low demand, scheduling staff training in low demand times, reducing working hours where possible, and perhaps laying staff off.

Time

Time strategies consider not only the actual hours of availability of a service but also time taken at various stages of service delivery. The delivery of many services can be broken up into various stages, and bottlenecks or time delays can be identified at each of these stages. For example, the stages of a haircut may be washing, cutting and then drying the hair. Attending a concert may involve getting a ticket, driving to the venue, parking, getting into the venue and obtaining augmented service products such as food, beverages or programs.

Tactics for high demand

The problem of not enough time can be easily resolved by increasing time in peak demand periods. For example, in the weeks leading up to Christmas and particularly in the days before Christmas, retail shopping hours are often extended. Some supermarkets are open 24 hours a day during this period of high demand. Similarly, university libraries often extend their opening hours in exam periods.

Alternatively, customer participation in the process of service delivery can be increased, which saves time and so allows more customers to be served when demand is high. If you have had coffee at a Starbucks coffee shop, for example, you will have noticed that staff do not give you spoons, sugar, chocolate on your cappuccino, or any accompaniments to coffee. All of these additional elements are put on a central serving station within the coffee shop, and customers are encouraged to help themselves. Similarly at McDonald's, customers are encouraged to clear their own tables.

Finally, a peak operating procedure can be developed so that staff know the policy and what to do when demand is very high. Hotels may have a procedure whereby, if too many guests are trying to check in at the same time, they are offered coffee shop vouchers and asked to come back in an hour's time. Notice also the example of Delta Hotels in the Services Marketing Action vignette opposite. In particular, notice how Delta has slightly different procedures depending on whether the customer is part of the hotel's loyalty scheme and is therefore more likely to be a regular customer.

Tactics for low demand

Reducing a firm's hours of operation can be a useful strategy during periods of low demand. For example, university libraries offer very limited hours of operation in non-teaching periods, and many other services on university campuses also reduce their hours of operation or even close entirely. Periods of low demand are also an ideal time to schedule maintenance activities. Many schools, for example, have buildings repaired, painted or refurbished over school holiday periods.

In summary, manipulating the elements of supply requires good planning by managers to predict the variations in demand and be able to implement strategies accordingly. The key elements of supply include facilities, equipment, labour and time, and should all be considered, with the key goal being to develop flexibility in all areas.

Services Marketing Action:
What to do with too many customers

Typically, many large hotels work on an overbooking principle. From experience they know that a certain number of guests will cancel at the last minute or just not show up. To make sure they are still working at full capacity, they overbook by about 5 per cent to cater for this 'no-show' element. But occasionally they get caught. If all 105 customers turn up, each wanting one of the 100 rooms available, then five guests must be refused. As you can imagine, this is not a pleasant task. To make life easier for reception staff, many hotels develop a peak operating procedure that documents exactly how to deal with those last five customers.

An example of such a procedure is from Delta Hotels (www.deltahotels.com). Their procedure for confirmed bookings who cannot be accommodated is to find the guest a room at an equivalent standard hotel, arrange and pay for a taxi to take the guest to the new hotel, and provide a phone so that the guest can call their business or family and notify them of the change in arrangements. In addition, if the guest is a member of the Delta loyalty program, they will also be given a voucher (of around $200) to be spent in Delta facilities such as the bar or restaurant on that day or during their next stay. Having such a procedure in place saves time and frustration for both the hotel staff and the guest.

Adjusting demand to meet supply

In this section the focus turns to identifying strategies that can influence the demand for services, both when demand is too high and when demand is low. Table 8.3 summarises the various strategies that can be used to adjust demand. The first column of this table highlights the element of the marketing mix on which the strategy focuses, while the second column identifies the overall strategy. The final columns identify the tactics that can be used when demand is too high and needs to be reduced, and the tactics for when demand is low and needs to be increased. Again, not all tactics will be suitable for all services. Much will depend on the nature of the particular service and, as with supply, several tactics can be used in combination.

Distribution

Distribution is about how the service gets to the customer. Firms must decide whether it is possible for the service to come to the customer, as in the case of home delivery of dry cleaning or financial planners making house calls; or whether the customer has to go to the service, as they do if going to the movies; or whether the service is to be provided remotely through an agent or technology such as an ATM. Hence, distribution strategies focus on modifying and adjusting the way services are delivered. This strategy is applicable in the case of people-based services like insurance or hairdressing, as well as equipment- or technology-based services.

		Table 8.3 Adjusting demand to meet supply	
Relevant marketing elements	**Strategies for adjusting demand to meet supply**	**Tactics for high demand**	**Tactics for low demand**
Distribution	Modify location of service delivery	• Get consumers to come to service facility (if applicable)	• Bring the service to consumers
Service product: core and supplementary elements	Vary the service offering	• Modify service offering to help facilitate extra demand • Reduce augmented service elements	• Modify the service offering to appeal to different market segments • Increase augmented service elements — value add by developing complementary products
Process of service delivery	Modify the process of service delivery	• Use a reservations system to help manage high demand	
Price	Differentiate on price Use creative pricing	• Increase price to match demand • Charge full-price	• Offer discounts and price reductions
Promotion	Use the promotional mix to shift service usage	• Advertise busy times • Offer incentives to use low demand periods • Advertise benefits of non demand usage	• Advertise to stimulate demand during slow periods

Tactics for high demand

In cases of high demand, a key strategy is to reduce the time involved in the distribution process by using tactics like getting the customer to come to the service facility. For example, in the Party People equipment hire case study (pages 529–32), getting customers to come to the service facility to collect their hire items reduces the time and labour spent delivering the service and frees up these resources, allowing staff to serve more customers. Typically, this reduction in augmented services is accompanied by a reduction in price.

In addition, distribution can be extended to take pressure off service centres or facilities where high demand means there is insufficient space to meet requirements. Restaurants, for example, may extend to home delivery or take-away while hairdressers may add a home service.

Tactics for low demand

Similar strategies can be used to stimulate demand. To make a service more attractive and accessible, a firm can bring the service to time-poor and physically restricted customers, as in the case of a hairdressing service visiting patients in hospital.

Service product: core and supplementary elements

The strategy in this case focuses on varying the service offering (or product) to meet supply constraints. A service product is made up of several levels; for example, the core service and the facilitating and supporting services. Typically, the core benefit will remain unchanged but tactics can be used to manipulate supplementary service components.

Tactics for high demand

When demand is too high, one tactic is to modify the service offering to help facilitate the extra demand. In a food service operation, for example disposable crockery and cutlery can be used to allow more people to be served in a more timely manner, or the variety of menu choices can be restricted to focus on items that are less resource intensive. Similarly, the supporting service elements can be reduced. For example in cases where free delivery is normally included, this supporting service can be withdrawn.

Tactics for low demand

When considering tactics for increasing demand, the focus should be on modifying the service offering to appeal to different market segments. For example, tax accountants can look at providing general bookkeeping services during periods of the year when demand for tax is low; and a resort developed primarily around winter sports like snow skiing can offer services such as mountain bike riding or hiking during the summer months. Similarly, a sailing rental company might be consistently busy during holiday periods and weekends but suffer from low demand during non-holiday weekdays. To overcome this the company might focus on a different target market for this low-demand period, offering sailing courses to local schools, perhaps.

In addition, augmented service elements can be increased, that is, value can be added by developing complementary products. For example, a university or school whose facilities are not used in vacation and break periods could offer short courses during these periods. Also think about the Services Marketing on the Web vignette below, and consider the bundling of services that occurs in package holidays to stimulate demand.

Services Marketing on the Web:
Managing supply and demand online

One of the key benefits of the Internet from a consumer perspective is the ability to compare prices quickly and easily without leaving the comfort of your own home (or wherever you access the Internet). To assist in their management of supply and demand, many service firms have capitalised on this feature of the Internet by promoting and communicating price variations and stand-by rates to prospective customers.

Some companies have taken this concept a step further and combined their loyalty programs, databases and Internet communication to promote excess supply to customers who they already know and who are predisposed to using their services. Take the Qantas Frequent Flyer program: as a member of this program, you can elect to be sent notification of special deals in relation not just to airfares but to the associated accommodation and entertainment packages — all carefully selected by contributing companies to help manage demand and supply.

A slightly different use of the Internet is that adopted by Priceline.com. Here the customer can bid for a range of services including airfares, accommodation, cruises and even home financing. It is then up to the supplier to decide whether they will accept the bid or not — obviously depending on their supply and demand situation at that point in time.

Process of service delivery

The process of service delivery refers to the operational elements that combine to produce the core service and its supplementary services. While the previous section on supply management looked at creating flexibility in the service delivery process, managing demand for the process considers strategies for coping when demand remains high after all else has been tried.

Tactics for high demand

Management could consider using a reservation system to help manage high demand, for example making reservations for a specific time at restaurants. Customers know in advance the availability of the service and the restaurant can plan for demand by knowing how many customers without reservation can be catered for. Within a restaurant setting, a cocktail bar can be used as a pleasant place for customers to wait until a table becomes available. When customers do have to wait for service, various tactics can be used to minimise the dissatisfaction that the waiting period may engender. These tactics are based on principles of waiting lines proposed by Maister (1985):

- *Unoccupied time feels longer than occupied time.* Service providers should try to make sure that if customers have to wait, their time is occupied, as in the case of the cocktail bar in the restaurant. Similarly, waiting rooms for many service providers are filled with magazines, newspapers, television and even complimentary tea and coffee making facilities. Likewise, at Christmas at one local supermarket, all checkouts were busy and had long queues. The store manager walked along the queues apologising for the delays and offering Minties.

- *Pre-process waits feel longer than in-process waits.* The waiting time to buy a ticket to a theme park often seems longer than the wait to go on rides once inside the theme park. Once in the theme park the queue for a ride can often be made entertaining by street performers, or the nature of the queue can be made to seem part of the ride. For example, the queue for the Batman ride at Movie World on the Gold Coast goes through Wayne Manor. Similarly, in some service situations, customers can be given paperwork to complete while they are waiting. This speeds up service delivery and makes waiting time seem less.

- *Uncertain waits are longer than known definite waits.* The message for service providers here is to let customers know honestly how long waiting periods will be. Be realistic and keep customers informed.

- *Unfair waits are longer than equitable waits.* In Australia and New Zealand, we generally expect to be served in turn — first come, first served. Therefore, many service outlets use a numbering system or operate a single queue with customers being served in turn from the single queue.

- *The more valuable the service the longer people will wait.* The media often show people queuing overnight and even longer to ensure they get concert tickets or other valuable items.

Tactics for low demand

When demand is low, various stages of the process can be combined. For example, rather than having customers order food and drinks separately, both may be ordered through one staff member who looks after both.

Price

Pricing is perhaps the most obvious and most frequently used strategy for manipulating demand for services. When demand is high, full price or premiums can be charged, and when demand is low prices can be discounted. However, price is seldom used on its own as there is little point manipulating price if consumers are not made aware of this through promotion and communication.

Service offerings can vary in their price elasticity of demand. If a service shows considerable elasticity of demand, it means that a change in price will result in a change in demand. If a service has relatively inelastic demand, then a change in price will not result in a change in demand. For example, medical specialists such as neurosurgeons have relatively inelastic demand. If you need to see such a specialist then typically you will not shop around on price to find the cheapest. Similarly a change in the price charged by the specialist would probably not affect demand. In contrast, the demand for going to the movies or going to a bar can be greatly influenced by price, so it is clear that these services have elastic demand.

Tactics for high demand

When demand is high, the price charged for a service can be increased to help manage or alter demand. If you have ever tried to book accommodation at a beach resort over the Christmas and New Year period, or priced airfares during this same period, you will have noticed that prices are often quoted for low season, shoulder and peak, which are based on demand. Christmas and Easter ticketing often attracts a surcharge; in other words, a tactic of increasing price to match demand has been adopted.

Tactics for low demand

When demand is low, price can be used to stimulate and increase demand. Have a look at some of the junk mail delivered through your letterbox. Notice the pizza vouchers: discounts are often given for a certain night, such as a Tuesday, when demand is typically low. Discounts are also given for picking up rather than delivering, and many vouchers are only available on certain nights of the week. Cinemas also offer discounts on Tuesdays and companies in the food and beverage sector have managed to piggyback on the success of movies by offering earlybird meal deals to fit with show times; supper packages for after the movie; and meal deals with movie tickets included. Look through a Saturday paper — notice the advertisements for discounts at inner-city hotels at weekends, a time when their normal business clientele do not demand services. Stand-by rates for travel, accommodation and early-bird dining packages, for example, manipulate demand through price. Another example is Mystery flights. These flights are offered at a very low price but consumers have no choice on what time of the day they will fly or their destination. It will be little surprise to find out that such flights are often very early in the morning for the outgoing flight and very late at night flight for the return.

Another example of managing demand through price is priceline.com, a web-based business linking travellers with suppliers of travel. This company allows potential customers to state how much they will pay for airline tickets or for car hire. It is then up to the supplier to decide whether to accept the offer or not. Obviously, if demand is high, they may not accept offers but when demand is low they can accept offers that will mean better utilisation of resources.

Promotional mix

Promotion is the element of the marketing mix in which businesses communicate with their customers. The promotional mix is made up of a variety of elements, including advertising, publicity, personal selling, and direct marketing sales promotions, and all of these elements can be used to manipulate demand. The promotional mix becomes a key strategic tool for businesses to use when trying to manipulate demand. For example, sales promotions such as 'buy one meal, get one to the same value' may be used to get customers to purchase a service at a specific time and location. Similarly, mainstream advertising such as television and radio may be used to communicate alternative methods of service delivery.

Tactics for high demand

In addition to using the promotional mix to communicate other strategies for reducing demand, such as premium pricing and possibilities of queuing and delays, the promotional mix can be used to communicate when times are busy and the benefits of using the service outside high-demand times. For example, in a heavy demand period like Christmas, Australia Post uses television, radio and newspaper advertising to inform customers of the benefits of sending mail early, before peak-demand periods. Australia Post also advertises the possibility of delays or non-arrival by Christmas if mail is posted after certain dates. Similarly, a personal selling approach can be used to sell the benefits of moving to lower demand times, with reception or booking staff and travel consultants trained to point out the benefits of low-demand periods.

Tactics for low demand

The promotional mix can also be used to stimulate demand in slow periods. As noted above, advertising can be directed at letting consumers know when high- and low-demand periods are. Sales promotions, such as incentives, can be used. For example, a free bottle of wine can be offered to early bird diners, free hotel transfers or breakfasts can be given with accommodation packages and children can travel free with adults during low-demand periods.

In summary, all elements of the marketing mix can be used to manipulate demand. The appropriate mix of strategies will vary depending on the nature of the service to be provided. Service providers need to make sure they also consider supply-side strategies to arrive at the best possible outcomes.

Summary

LO1: Understand the importance of managing supply and demand for services.
- Ideally, to maximise profitability, managers of service operations need to match supply and demand at optimal levels: if demand is greater than supply, revenue is lost; and if supply is greater than demand, costs are increased. In both cases profitability is affected.
- In many service operations, demand can be inconsistent and difficult to predict.
- Managers must have a good understanding of the nature of demand for their particular service.

LO2: Describe the role of perishability in managing supply and demand of services.
- perishability, or the inability of services to be stored for later consumption, is the fundamental issue driving the need to manage supply and demand.

LO3: Discuss the strategies that can be used to adjust supply to meet demand in cases of both high demand and low demand.

- Strategies for managing supply centre on creating flexibility within the elements of supply.
- The four major elements of supply are facilities, equipment, labour and time.
- Appropriate strategies will often combine various tactics concerning all elements of supply, and may vary according to the nature of the service.

LO4: Discuss the strategies that can be used to adjust demand to meet supply in cases of both high demand and low demand.

- Strategies for managing demand focus on the elements of the marketing mix, notably product, price, promotion and place.
- Again, strategies may combine tactics from several areas as appropriate for the particular service.

key terms

Greater than maximum supply: higher demand than maximum available supply (p. 193)

Maximum supply: higher demand than optimal supply levels (p. 194)

Optimum supply: when demand and supply are well balanced (p. 194)

Less than optimum supply: lower demand than optimal supply levels (p. 194)

review questions

1. Why is it difficult for services to be inventoried?
2. Briefly explain why managers of services have to be able to manage supply and demand.
3. List and briefly describe the four elements of supply.
4. For each of the four element of supply, outline one tactic for managing supply when demand is too high and one tactic for managing supply when demand is too low.
5. For each element of the marketing mix, outline one tactic for coping with high demand and one tactic for coping with low demand.

application questions

1. For each of the following situations, identify what you consider to be their pattern of demand (daily, weekly, yearly) and, based on this pattern, recommend a combination of supply management and demand management strategies that could be adopted by management to optimise supply and demand:
   (a) a photocopying service located on a university campus
   (b) a theme park (like Movie World or Sea World) located at a coastal resort area
   (c) a tax accountant specialising in small businesses

(d) a cinema complex in a suburban shopping centre

(e) a lawn and garden care service

(f) a coffee shop located in a business/industrial precinct.

2. What is the impact of perishability on service firms? Does perishability impact differently on different classifications of services? Using the services classification scheme in chapter 1, identify the unique supply and demand issues that a service in each classification would face. Also identify supply and demand issues that would be generic across all service types.

3. Think of a service business that is faced with significant fluctuations in demand, such as a local resort. Remember that demand patterns can occur yearly, monthly, weekly, daily and even hourly.

(a) Can you identify all the different demand patterns occurring in this service setting?

(b) What are the causes of these demand fluctuations?

(c) Which of these fluctuations has the greatest impact on the service?

4. Discuss the implications of fluctuating supply and demand on service quality and customer satisfaction. Consider the impact of the different supply levels outlined in table 8.1 on service quality and customer satisfaction.

5. What other examples of using price to manipulate demand (except movie/meal deals) can you think of?

(a) For each case you identified, what other complimentary services could benefit from this manipulation of demand?

(b) Think of examples of service companies not currently using price to manipulate demand who could benefit from this strategy.

vignette questions

1. Read the Services Marketing Action vignette on page 199 and answer the following questions.

(a) What type of service operations could make use of the services of companies like Manpower?

(b) Outline the advantages and disadvantages of service providers utilising this service.

2. Read the Services Marketing Action vignette on page 201 and answer the following questions.

(a) Can you think of any contingencies that the Delta Hotels procedures do not cover? Could these procedures be improved in any way?

(b) As a customer with a confirmed reservation who has been told no rooms are available, how would you react to Delta's procedures? Would you be satisfied? Would you stay with Delta again?

3. Read the Services Marketing on the Web vignette on page 203 and answer the following questions.

(a) Using your favourite search engine, do an Internet search for hotel accommodation. Note the number of hits you get and peruse the first 10 or 20. Note how many of these are promoting special deals or stand-by rates. Have a look at some of the special conditions that apply to these rates.

(b) Have you noticed that accommodation is often cheaper as part of a package deal with airfares? Why do you think hotels are prepared to 'sell' rooms to an airline more cheaply than they do to individuals?

 *references*

Bitner, M. & Zeithaml, V. 2001, *Services Marketing: Integrating Customer Focus Across the Firm*, McGraw-Hill, Boston.

Maister, D. 1985, 'The psychology of waiting lines', in Czepiel, J. A., Solomon, M. R. & Surprenant, C. F., *The Service Encounter*, Lexington Books, MA, pp. 113–23.

Manpower, accessed 3 June 2002, www.manpower.com.

Chapter 9
Relationship marketing and CRM

Chad Perry, Sally Rao, Sarah Spencer-Matthews

LEARNING OBJECTIVES

After reading this chapter, you should be able to:

- define relationship marketing and outline the concept of the ladder of loyalty
- identify and distinguish between the four methods of relationship marketing
- distinguish between social and structural bonds in a marketing relationship and explain the different classifications of marketing relationships
- appreciate the role and place of customer relationship management (CRM)
- discuss where and when relationship marketing can be applied
- discuss how CRM can be applied.

CHAPTER OUTLINE

The aim of this chapter is to explore the principles of relationship marketing in general and how they are applied in CRM in particular. Essentially, we argue that CRM should be the ultimate goal of a services marketing manager, but we also argue that the principles of relationship marketing can be applied in situations where a firm does not have the information technology to support CRM.

The chapter has three parts. Firstly, we define key terms such as relationship marketing and its applications (direct marketing, database marketing and CRM, for example). Then we consider core concepts of relationship marketing, such as the elements of a relationship, and the situations where relationship marketing can and cannot be applied. Finally, we focus on the specific principles of applying CRM.

Introduction

When you phone your bank about your account, you want the person you talk with to know what the last action on your account was and whether that action was an inquiry about linking your account to the Internet, or about an account statement, or a complaint. You do not want to have to explain your history all over again. That is, you want your bank to operate as though they have an ongoing relationship with you, and not to treat you as someone new every time you contact them. If your current bank treats you as a new customer each time you have a transaction with it, there is little to stop you going as a new customer to another bank. This kind of relationship, which most of us want with many organisations, means it must be customer centred. The organisation must also have a computer that remembers how we dealt with the firm in the past and that allows staff in the firm to have access to that information whenever we communicate. Indeed, the recent development of relationship marketing called customer relationship management (CRM) incorporates information technology to make services even more customer focused than ever before.

Services Marketing Action:
Understanding your customers

Jody is a long-term customer of a leading bank. She has four savings and investment accounts along with three loans for both personal and business purposes. She has recently experienced a frustrating series of events where she was trying to get her loans consolidated into one loan, and gain access to another $4000 of credit.

Jody's need for the loan was stimulated by a 'personally addressed offer' from the bank advertising its loan options. In addition, Jody had personally visited the two different branches at which the loans were held, as well as speaking on the telephone to the customer service centre. Her frustration was increased by having to retell her story each time she enquired. Three weeks after her initial enquiries, she still didn't have a clear idea as to who would take responsibility for her requests. The final straw came for Jody when she was doing her daily banking at the branch near her work when the bank teller asked her: 'Have you heard about our loan options?'. Jody became angry and, to the bewilderment of the teller, stormed out

A week later Jody managed to transfer her loans to a new bank. The result for her old bank was a lost customer opportunity, as Jody had lost patience and confidence with their ability to care and look after her needs. The problem was not due to poor product but lack of service, communication and understanding.

Successful CRM is about understanding and anticipating your customer needs in order to develop and maintain ongoing and mutually beneficial relationships. It is about having a total, or holistic, view of your customer.

Defining relationship marketing

We need to know exactly what we are talking about before we go further, so we must first define relationship marketing because it is the underlying idea behind methods such as customer relationship management.

Marketing focuses on exchanges between buyers and sellers. **Transactional marketing** and **relationship marketing** are two ways of looking at these exchanges. Thus, to begin to understand definitions of relationship marketing, it is necessary to distinguish between a transaction and a relationship. The duration of the exchange relationship distinguishes the two. A transactional exchange involves a single, short time exchange with a distinct beginning and ending. In contrast, a relational exchange involves multiple exchanges extending over time. For example, when you buy toothpaste, it is a single transaction, and it does not matter who is serving you at the supermarket checkout. However, a legal service is another matter. When you have medical problems, you prefer to go to a doctor with whom you have an ongoing relationship, who has seen you on many matters before, whom you can trust and whom you do not have to brief all over again about your medical history. The distinction between a transaction and a relationship is actually a continuum, with industrial commodities at the transaction marketing end, then to fast-moving consumer goods (FMCG) and services, and through to business-to-business industrial services at the relationship marketing end, as shown in figure 9.1. Clearly, relationship marketing is particularly applicable to services.

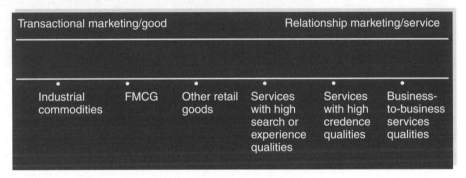

Figure 9.1: The continuum from transactional to relationship marketing (derived from Covielo & Brodie 1998; Grönroos 1994)
Note: FMCG = fast-moving consumer goods

In brief, towards the relationship marketing end of the continuum, we are concerned with multiple exchange relationships. Furthermore, the relationship marketing approach is multifunctional and integrative — it 'views marketing as an integrative activity involving functions across the organization, with emphasis on facilitating, building and maintaining relationships over time' (Coviello, Brodie & Munro 1997, p. 23).

One comprehensive definition of relationship marketing is based on seven conceptual categories of relationship marketing: creation, development, maintenance, interactive, long-term, emotional content and output (Harker 1999). Incorporating these categories, our definition emphasises the management of many relationships: 'relationship marketing occurs when an organization is engaged in proactively creating, developing and maintaining committed, interactive and profitable exchanges with selected customers or partners over time' (Harker 1999, p. 16). The word 'partners' in this definition implies that relationship marketing can refer to many stakeholders in addition to customers, including employees, shareholders and other firms in a strategic alliance. However, the supplier–customer relationship is central to marketing and to this chapter.

This definition emphasises the purpose and benefit of relationship marketing. Note that the definition includes the word 'profitable'. One of the major benefits of relationship marketing is that making another sale to an existing customer can be about five times cheaper than making a sale to a new customer, because of the savings from not having to advertise for and establish rapport with a new customer. This figure can be almost 30 times cheaper in some industries and zero in others, but it averages out to be about five over most situations. Indeed, a baseball park in the United States does not do any advertising at all because it has found that establishing an ongoing relationship with its current baseball watchers, through regular mailings, is cheaper than looking for new customers. In Australia, Mazda managed to stay in the market despite some of its models being 'rebadged' by another car maker and sold more cheaply. Mazda had a warranty system that encouraged Mazda buyers to have their car serviced by Mazda in a strong relationship-building way. For example, the mechanic who worked on the car and the senior mechanic who supervised it would personally speak to the customer about their car's servicing when it was being picked up. That made progression to another Mazda, when it was time to buy another car, almost inevitable. Similarly, some Lexus dealers in some countries have a free light breakfast on Saturday morning for people who have bought a Lexus, including their family. The relationship with the Lexus dealer becomes such an integral part of the buyer's social world that they will almost certainly buy a second Lexus when considering another car. Thus, building a relationship with an existing customer does cost the organisation in terms of customer service time and effort, but it is often cheaper than hunting for a new customer. The end result is more profits.

As well, our definition implies that a relationship has specific states of introduction, growth, maturity and possibly decline in its words 'creating, developing and maintaining . . . over time'. The concept of the **ladder of loyalty** considers this in more detail. Essentially, in a relationship, a party starts out as a suspect, becomes a customer and ends up as a partner, as shown in figure 9.2.

Ladder of loyalty: *the six ascending steps of a relationship from prospect, to first-time customer, to repeat customer, to client/ member, to advocate and to partner*

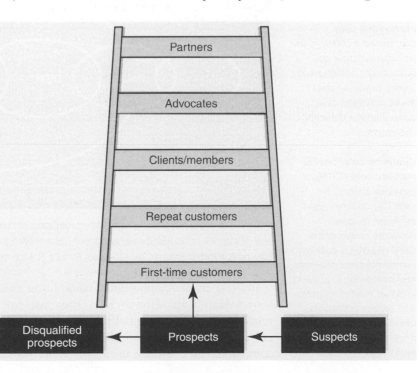

Figure 9.2: The ladder of loyalty (derived from Griffin 1995)

The first few rungs of the ladder of loyalty are straightforward, up to the rung of repeat customer. After a customer has become a repeat customer, they can become better known to staff. For example, at a hotel they can be called by their name without having to give it; they become a client rather than a mere customer. They can also elect to become a member of a 'club' like a frequent flyer program. Next, the client becomes an advocate of the organisation, spreading word-of-mouth recommendations. Finally, the customer becomes a partner and becomes involved in the design and delivery of the product — we call this involvement structural bonding, and discuss it later in this chapter. Note that a person does not need to progress along the ladder in exactly the order shown in figure 9.2. For example, someone could become an advocate after they have gone to a hotel just once, without waiting until they have become a client. Moreover, a customer could even go back down a rung of the ladder. Nevertheless, the ladder of loyalty provides an interesting first glimpse of the states through which a relationship might evolve.

Four methods of relationship marketing

Direct mail: *a promotional tool that uses the postal service to target particular customers*

Direct marketing: *a promotion or marketing communication tactic that involves cross selling; that is, offering an existing customer some other products from the organisation that he or she has not yet bought*

Database marketing: *a method that uses information technology in an organisation-wide process of gathering and storing relational data about individual past, current and/or potential customers*

Customer relationship management (CRM): *a business strategy for selecting and managing the most valuable customer relationships. CRM requires a customer-centric business strategy and philosophy to support effective marketing, sales and service processes, which are supported, not driven, by CRM technology.*

Relationship marketing can be thought of as covering a variety of marketing methods such as **direct mail**, **direct marketing**, **database marketing** and **customer relationship management (CRM)**. These methods show an increasingly strategic application of relationship marketing, as shown in figure 9.3. Let us consider the historical development of relationship marketing through these four methods. There may be other ways of looking at the way relationship marketing has been applied, but this treatment is useful because of its comprehensiveness and modernity.

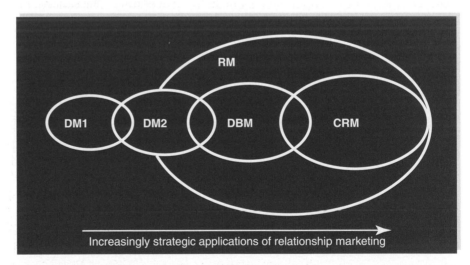

Figure 9.3: How relationship marketing methods of direct marketing, database marketing and customer relationship management have developed out of direct mail (derived from Dawes & Worthington 1996; Coviello, Brodie & Munro 1997)

Interest in developing and maintaining relationships with customers has shown significant growth over the past few years. Tools for developing relationships have essentially revolved around database marketing, which has grown from a narrow tool used for specialist direct mail and direct marketing campaigns to a widely used tool that has company-wide implications for managing relationships with customers. This progression of the application of relationship marketing through different foci, users and issues is summarised in table 9.1. Note that the distinctions between the four methods are not as clear cut as table 9.1 might suggest, for there may be some overlap between the four methods in any one organisation, as shown in the overlapping circles in figure 9.3.

Table 9.1	Four methods of relationship marketing			
Salient issues	Method one: direct mail	Method two: direct marketing	Method three: database marketing	Method four: customer relationship management
Focus	Promotion	Transactions	Relationship over multiple transactions with a marketing focus	Holistic relationship with the whole organisation
Users	Sales	Sales/marketing/ accounting	Multiple individual departments, possibly coordinated by relationship manager (marketing)	Organisation wide
Issues	Lack of real customer focus; organisational bottom line main issue	No integration between departments and/or products; duplication of effort; lack of consistency from consumer perspective; lack of information sharing within organisation	More coordinated effort in terms of marketing communication and transactions with customer; some information sharing but accessibility is limited	Entire organisation develops customer focus; sharing and linking of data; accessibility of customer information at various and appropriate points within the organisation for all staff

Source: adapted from Dawes & Worthington 1996

Method one: direct mail

At first, relationships with customers were conducted by using customer databases as an address source for one-way communications with a customer (DeTienne & Thompson 1996). Marketing or sales departments provided output from their database for the administration of direct mail or telemarketing campaigns (Dawes & Worthington 1996). These campaigns, while oriented towards particular customers, were essentially a promotion tool that was internally focused on short-term, bottom-line objectives.

For example, a charity in Brisbane had an expensive, luxury car to offer as a prize in an art union lottery. A staff member went to the foyer of Waterfront Place, a tall building with the most expensive floor space in the city, and jotted down the names of all the lawyers, consultants and so on that were listed there. A mail-out to those people asking them to buy expensive tickets in the art union provided a very profitable campaign. To top it all off, the charity sold off the mailing list for a considerable profit the next year.

Method two: direct marketing

Relationship marketing has grown from the internal focus of the above method, where the emphasis was on making the promotion activities administratively easier and more profitable, to one which is more market and customer focused (Dawes & Worthington 1996). Common techniques of the second method, direct marketing, are essentially a promotion or marketing communication tactic and involve cross selling; that is, offering an existing customer some other products from the organisation that he or she has not yet bought. This enthusiastic embrace of direct marketing has been driven in part by the increased power of computer technology and the corresponding decrease in the cost of such technology (Buttle 2000a).

However, this popularity of direct marketing may lower the impact of direct marketing when the customer is bombarded with too many 'special offers' from different companies, or even from different departments within the same company. Indeed, this increased clutter can have the unintended effect of encouraging customers to become price sensitive by waiting for the 'right' offer (Rosenthal & McEachern 1997).

Method three: database marketing

The growth in database marketing information systems has seen information become a strategic necessity for business; that is, it is more than just a promotional tactic, and needs to be used for other things such as new product development, market research and customer acquisition (Palmer, McMahon-Beattie & Beggs 2000). Other reasons why database marketing has grown include the fragmentation of markets; increases in purchasing methods and contact avenues within an organisation; increased clutter in the market place; growth in the sophistication of technology; and the increasing availability of data (Evans 1998).

A definition of database marketing should be both strategic and tactical. Moreover, a comprehensive definition needs an emphasis on the relational processes of modern databases and its ability to provide real-time, up-to-date information on customers (Reedy, Schullo & Zimmerman 2000). This trend requires larger investment in information and information technology such as databases (Webster 1992).

A new definition of database marketing is presented here. This definition reflects all the developments in the field above including its progress with information technology (Webster 1992; Evans 1998), customer focus (Colgate & Alexander 1998), relational ability (Reedy, Schullo & Zimmerman 2000), real-time access to data (Reedy, Schullo & Zimmerman 2000; Dawes & Worthington 1996) and implications for the organisation as a whole (Domegan 1996). Therefore, we define database marketing as a method that:
- uses information technology in an organisation-wide process of gathering and storing relational data about individual past, current and/or potential customers
- maintains the integrity of such data by continually monitoring customer
- behaviours and needs
- accesses this information in real-time situations
- uses the information to formulate marketing strategy and fosters personalised contact and relationships with customers.

Database marketing as defined above has four distinct characteristics that differentiate it from traditional marketing methods: the ability to personalise contact, a reliance on information, responsiveness and accountability.

Ability to personalise contact

Database marketing has the ability to contact individual customers. The database as a segmentation tool makes it possible to communicate with specific targets even down to 'a segment of one' (Peppers & Rogers 1997, p. 11). This ability to personalise is attractive because stereotyping customers in segments of two or more customers overlooks some aspects of a customer's individuality (Schneider & Bowen 1999). Moreover, this new ability to segment down to an individual customer is useful for identifying those customers who provide the best value and potential to an organisation (Galbreath & Rogers 1999). Indeed, mass impersonal communication is becoming increasingly ineffective (Webster 1992). In brief, a marketing database can remove this stereotyping and reduce impersonal mass communication.

Reliance on information

This function of personalising communication with a consumer requires access to information, the second characteristic of database marketing. Information on customers can come from numerous internal and external sources, including customer interaction or call centres, customer touch points like a reception area, and mailing lists and response to mailings.

A company can utilise this information for analysis and input into marketing strategies. That is, this information can be used to identify those customers who need to be dropped, encouraged or rewarded. However, it is not just the information that is important to database marketing but how the database is used to 'remember' customer details and needs. The database provides the facility to help the company 'remember' the customer (Pitta 1998). This reliance on information helps the effectiveness of loyalty programs through increased information intensity and customisation (Palmer, McMahon-Beattie & Beggs 2000).

In brief, a useful database must have accurate and current information. However, the iterative nature of the database means that some information on customers may become out of date and incorrect, for example when a customer moves to a new address or gets married. This poor quality of information may result in ineffective and inefficient output from the database. Related to this issue of quality is the quantity of information kept on the customer. Much of the information kept on a database can become superfluous, and this is exacerbated by the increased ability of organisations to collect and keep data.

An outcome of these quality and quantity issues is the concern for privacy by some consumers. More specifically, a database raises ethical issues in relation to accuracy, usage and consent of such information. The growth of database marketing has resulted in the issue of privacy becoming more sensitive (DeTienne & Thompson 1996). Indeed, information technology is a double-edged sword that potentially provides increased value for companies but may be seen by customers as a potential threat to their interests.

Responsiveness

The information contained in a marketing database permits an organisation to respond to customer needs. Given the right information, customer needs can be anticipated through the marketing database (Hochhauser 1992). For example, when you get a film developed, you can ask for the photographs to be matt or gloss. A database allows your preferences to be recorded so that they will be used when you return with another film. In addition, the database provides the potential to individualise offerings and develop two-way dialogues with customers (Peters 1997) using mail, telephone or email.

Accountability

This interactivity and responsiveness paves the way for the fourth and final characteristic of database marketing, accountability. Proponents of database marketing emphasise accountability and measurability as strengths. Different offers, products and segments can be assessed for effectiveness (Hochhauser 1992) enabling expenditure on a campaign to be measured against subsequent campaign results (Schoenbachler et al. 1997). Indeed, in comparison with mass media communication, database marketing is more precise, in that it can assess the effectiveness of strategy (Forcht & Cochran 1999). Furthermore, this tracking of database marketing effectiveness can help to retain those customers who are of value to the company (Schoenbachler et al. 1997). Indeed, database marketing can save costs through targeted strategy, resulting in decreased wasted effort and increased returns (Zineldin 2000). In comparison, the costs of alternative mass marketing strategies have increased remarkably over recent years (Forcht & Cochran 1999).

In summary, database marketing has characteristics that constitute advances on traditional marketing and direct marketing. It therefore provides a base discipline to investigate how customer relationships can be managed.

Method four: customer relationship management

To develop relationship marketing beyond database marketing, computer database information integration has become a key issue (Dawes & Worthington 1996). This issue of integration is being addressed in a new method called customer relationship marketing or, the broader term, customer relationship management (CRM) (Day 2000).

CRM has grown because there has been growth in customer contact services. These are personal communication channels such as face-to-face contact, mail, phone and the Internet, which affect the way a customer may interact with a business (Dawes & Rowley 1998; Galbreath & Rogers 1999; Potter-Brotman 1994). This access must be in real time and be available at all customer contact points, for example whenever a customer phones a hotel to make a booking, arrives, requests room service or pays the bill by mail. At the core of customised customer contact service is this information that may be collected, maintained and retrieved through the marketing database.

More particularly, CRM is a form of database marketing that blends relationship marketing and information technology in a very explicit and focused way. CRM gained currency among computer software builders in the mid- to late 1990s. CRM software should still be considered just a part of relationship marketing, because practitioners emphasise that a software package does not underpin CRM; it rests upon a relationship with a customer and related organisation and work processes, rather than on information technology. It is important to note that, at its highest level, CRM is about more than just information technology (Buttle 2000b), since it also includes systems, structures, organisational culture and staffing. In brief, CRM can be defined as: 'a business strategy to select and manage the most valuable customer relationships ... [and] requires a customer-centric business strategy and philosophy to support effective marketing, sales and service processes' (Thompson 2001a, p. 1) which is 'supported, not driven, by CRM technology' (Lee 2001, p. 1).

Thus the underlying philosophy of CRM acknowledges the need to treat valuable customers individually. With the trend towards CRM, companies need to find ways to capture in the database the elements of the relationship that customers most value (DeTienne & Thompson 1996). However, collecting information on its own does not guarantee success. The information must be used to meet customer needs in a seamless manner by disseminating and acting upon it when and where required. In other words, organisations must address the issue of accessibility to customer information by connecting the customer contacts through the database in a way that facilitates service delivery. For example, a nationwide UK building society introduced an integrated customer information system to replace its more traditional customer management system (Dawes & Worthington 1996). The aim of the system was to provide one-touch services that allowed 80 per cent of customer needs or queries to be attended to wherever the point of contact was made. Issues related to this change included the integration of data from various sources, the need to clean the data, the need for investment by management into the system and the access to data by staff from a variety of locations in order to deliver services.

Even more recently, in 1998 and 1999, CRM was expanded from a focus on relationships with end-consumers to other partners in an industry's supply chain. This expansion was done with **partner relationship marketing (PRM)** software. In PRM, business-to-business (B2B) relationships with a firm's own distributors are given attention, as well as relationships with end-customers, because the distributors are 'partners' in the product's delivery (Thompson 2001b, p. 2). It also includes suppliers as the partners of a business, not just distributors. Like CRM, the focus of PRM is the creation and maintenance of long-term, mutually beneficial relationships with strategically important outside organisations, which provide value for the customer and the company over the longer term in both business-to-consumer and business-to-business contexts. The value perceptions of the people in the other organisation serve as bonds, or exit barriers, which inhibit the search for alternative sources of supply (Buttle 2000a; Buttle & Ahmad 1999). CRM and PRM focus on strategically significant markets: customers or partners with high lifetime values who serve as a benchmark for other customers and who inspire change in the supplier.

The next stage after CRM and PRM will be management of the whole supply chain from suppliers, to producers and distributors, to end-customers (possibly called supply chain relationship management (SCRM)). To stop a confusing blitzkrieg of initials, we will incorporate PRM into CRM in this chapter, because PRM also deals with customer relationships, even though they are in a business-to-business context rather than with an end-consumer.

In summary, CRM requires relationship-appropriate culture, structure, staff and systems (Buttle 2000b), because the goal of CRM is to customise a whole organisation's offerings and interactions to individual customers. Because this is a massive undertaking, even (or especially) for a big business, it is not surprising that many organisations have not fully implemented a true CRM business approach (Colgate & Stewart 1998).

Partner relationship marketing (PRM): a CRM concept applied to business-to-business (B2B) relationships

International Issues:
Customer-centric, consistent financial services

One international bank with 49000 employees in 1500 branches throughout 70 countries uses CRM. In 1998, Dresdner Bank decided it had to shift from a focus on banking products to a focus on continuing relationships with its customers. Its information systems at that time could not support this new approach, so the bank asked Accenture to work with it on becoming a customer-centric global organisation. Accenture is a leading consultant to the financial services industry and in the quickly emerging field of CRM. It operates around the world with one common brand name and business model designed to enable the consultancy to serve clients in the same way around the world. It has more than 5000 consulting professionals around the world with experience of customer service, including call centres and e-commerce. Working in teams, Accenture and bank staff 'aligned processes, people and technology to a customer-centric strategy'. They did this by using technology to acquire information about clients, maintaining that information so that it was up to date, and distributing it to staff when they needed it. This technology allowed information that related to operations and products to migrate through interfaces within the bank. While it was being rolled out and tested, computer-based training prepared the bank staff for the transition to the new system. Now, more than 3500 sales professionals in eight service centres and 305 corporate banking branches are linked together in the customer-service process. Customers are greeted by a bank staff member who can instantly call up information about an account onto a screen, thus producing better customer service. According to Dresdner Bank board member Dr Bernd Fahrholz, 'The system reaffirms our leadership in technology and allows us to concentrate even more on customer care'.

Derived from Accenture 2001

Relationship marketing

The previous section noted how direct marketing, database marketing and customer relationship management are all part of the family of relationship marketing, and this was summarised in figure 9.3. This part of the chapter aims to explore core streams in the evolution of thinking about relationship marketing. Essentially, relationship marketing can involve several relationships built over time, which involve both structural and social bonds, and it is merely a marketing approach rather than an overarching paradigm. We will discuss the elements involved in exchange processes of a relationship and classify types of marketing relationships. The managerial implications of decades of relationship marketing thought are also provided. We cover ideas that apply both to business-to-jbusiness and to business-to-consumer relationship marketing.

Relationship marketing was first investigated in the 1970s, even though it has been a central part of what practitioners have done for millennia (Ridley 1996).

However, it was not until the late 1970s and the 1980s that the term 'relationship marketing' emerged in the marketing literature. Since then, relationship marketing has evolved over the last two decades with emphases shifting to different approaches such as customer relationship management, as described above. We now turn to its core themes, beginning with exchange processes.

The exchange processes in relationship marketing

An 'exchange' in our definition of relationship marketing on page 212 encompasses multiple exchange processes with customers, along with suppliers, internal units, the government and competitors. We use the terms structural and social bonds to describe these processes. **Structural bonds** are forged when two parties adapt to each other in some economic or technical way, as they do when making product or process adjustments (Wilson & Mummaleni 1988). These structural bonds are usually associated with an investment that is dedicated to a relationship. For example, they exist when a windshield wiper manufacturer installs special equipment to suit just one car maker, so that 'just-in-time' deliveries of wipers can be made as required. In contrast, **social bonds** are investments of time and energy that produce positive interpersonal relationships between two parties, although these can range from formal, organisational contacts to informal, personal ones. These bonds are discussed in more detail below. We will limit our discussion to bonds between an organisation and its customers, rather than with government or financiers, for example, because the former are the major focus of this book.

Structural bonds: bonds forged when two parties adapt to each other in some economic or technical way, as they do when making product or process adjustments

Social bonds: investments of time and energy that produce positive interpersonal relationships between two parties, ranging from formal, organisational contacts to informal and personal ones

Structural bonds

Structural bonds have not received as much attention as social bonds, but their importance to competing within markets deserves just as much attention. Structural bonds are forged when two parties adapt to each other by making investments that are difficult to retrieve when the relationship breaks down. These are often strengthened through joint investment in products and process development (Turnbull & Wilson 1989).

Within both business-to-business and business-to-consumer contexts, there can be several sorts of structural bonds. For example, Boeing brings American Airlines people to its plant in Seattle to help design aircraft precisely for that airline's huge fleet. Similarly, a hospital has included patients on some committees to help improve its patient processes. And Griffith University in Queensland has focus groups with second-year students to improve its processes for first year students. Examples of another sort of structural bond include loyalty schemes such as frequent flyer points, and a hardware store that offers credit facilities to long-term customers. Another example of a structural bond is an Australian courier service, Star Track Express, which provides a package tracking service to its clients, so that the courier firm and the customer both know where the package is at any time.

Social bonds

Social bonds are more personal than structural bonds. Trust and commitment are the most mentioned social bonds in the literature. Trust concerns the confidence that one party has in the other's reliability and integrity within a relationship. In turn, trust leads to the commitment to a relationship that results from a party exerting all of their efforts to preserve an important relationship (Morgan & Hunt 1994).

To build this trust and commitment, the film processing company National Photos provides an online description of the company to show that it is long established and knows its processes and customers well. It also provides an updated report of a film's processing online. Each purchase builds up 'frequent buyer discount points' that help cement commitment to the company. Similarly, Heinz contacted new mothers after the birth of their babies and built trust with a personalised message that refers to the company's specialist nursing and dietary staff. They built up commitment so well with follow-up communications and services that Heinz did not bother advertising its baby food on television for several years.

Note that these social bonds are not necessarily independent of structural bonds. For example, the social bond of commitment noted above can be linked to switching costs that 'lock in' at least one party to the relationship. These switching costs are created by investments in the structural bonds of the relationship. For example, if one party in a relationship switches to another supplier, this could involve costly re-engineering of its processes. Generally speaking, opportunities for structural bonding emerge as a result of social bonds first being set in place (Buttle & Ahmad 1999).

In brief, our categorisation of elements of exchange processes into social and structural bonds provides a mechanism for understanding their differences and similarities. It also has implications for management, as explained below.

Classifications of marketing relationships

Our definition of relationship marketing implied that there are many types of relationships in marketing. In this section, several classifications of marketing relationships will be synthesised in a way that incorporates the two types of bonds discussed above.

Relationship development requires at least two actors who are in contact with each other. Based on this simplest relationship, Gummesson (1995) proposed that relationships can be categorised into three classic relationships of marketing: dyad, where the relationship is between a customer and a supplier; triad, which involves a relationship between the customer, their present supplier and competitors; and network, which concerns all members in the distribution chain. In turn, a six-fold classification is developed for this chapter because of its comprehensive acknowledgement of core issues (based on Teale 1999). A range of marketing relationships can be placed in this classification, as demonstrated in figure 9.4, and this is discussed next. Note that these categories do not necessarily have a causal link between them; that is, you do not have to go through box 2 to get to box 4 (figure 9.4), and it is possible to go from box 5 to box 3.

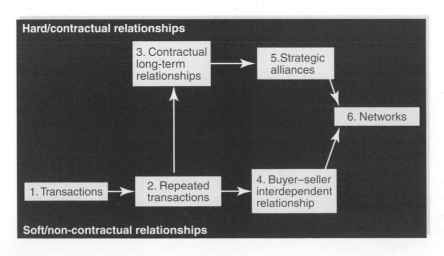

Figure 9.4: A categorisation of marketing relationships, with shading denoting the presence of social/structural bonds
Source: adapted from Rao & Perry forthcoming; Teale 1999, based on Webster 1992

To begin, a single transaction (box 1 in figure 9.4) between two actors, buyer and seller, forms the basis of economic exchange. These transactions are conducted as discrete, market-based exchanges with virtually all the necessary information contained in the price of the product (Houston & Gassenheimer 1987). Buying a one-off load of coal in a spot price market would be a classic example. Within such a pure transactional relationship, profit maximisation is the objective of marketing activities, while credit extensions are not granted, customers are not recognised by the seller, and loyalty does not exist (Webster 1992).

A pure transaction becomes repeated transactions (box 2 in figure 9.4) when firms use different marketing strategies to win customers' loyalty (Grönroos 1994), for example frequent flyer programs offered to customers by airlines. The presence of customer repeat purchases means that the exchange has shifted away from one-off transactions. It can be argued that these loyalty program exchanges are not relationship marketing because there are no social bonds involved — there is no 'affection, fidelity or commitment' (McGoldrick & Andre 1997, p. 74). Nevertheless, they might indicate the beginning of some social bonding in the form of trust and commitment (Pelton, Strutton & Lumpkin 1997). That is, these repeat transactions can be seen as an opportunity to convert repeat purchases into meaningful, ongoing relationships (Grönroos 1994; Webster 1992). However, these transactions are still one-way, in that there is no structural adaptation for particular customers.

In turn, these beginnings of trust and commitment in the repeated transaction classification may become closer social bonds when a contract is signed. These hard, long-term **contractual relationships** (box 3 in figure 9.4) centre on a contract that focuses on shipments and on the resolution of disputes (Webster 1992; Pelton, Stutton & Lumpkin 1997). In contrast, **soft/ non-contractual relationships** (box 4 in figure 9.4) are normally developed from repeated transactions without the existence of contracts.

Next, contractual long-term relationships can be developed into strategic alliances (box 5) that involve more than just shipments and the resolution of disputes — they are comprehensive, contractual relationships similar to those of a vertically integrated firm. For example, Country Road, an Australian clothes company, has alliances with its suppliers. Their structural bonding is high but social bonding may be low because legal rather than social sanctions enforce cooperation. Finally, networks (box 6) are at the end of the continuum and cover more complex relationships, with webs of three or more actors (Coviello, Brodie & Munro 1997). In the exchange processes of networks, there is greater economic and social interdependence than in other types of relationships.

In brief, these six types of relationship evolve through time as each party makes investments in and adapts to the other, and as structural and social bonds emerge and evolve. This classification system captures many of the issues discussed earlier about structural and social bonds and the differences between transactional and relational marketing.

Where and when can relationship marketing be applied?

Relationship marketing theory has evolved in the ways described above. But there is no generally accepted position about its impact on the practice of marketing, so relationship marketing is somewhat troubled in practice. We

Contractual relationships:
relationships centred on a contract that focuses on shipments and on the resolution of disputes

Soft/non-contractual relationships:
relationships that are normally developed from repeated transactions without the existence of contracts

argue that factors such as product/service and situation; customer's orientation; and industry, organisation and management (Coviello & Brodie 1998; Stewart & Durkin 1999) can influence the amount of relationship marketing that is done in practice. These three relationship marketing factors appropriately reflect the traditional marketing management steps of product/market segmentation; the needs of segments; and the development of strategies for the segments.

Product/service and situational factors

Various types of goods and services can be placed along a continuum from industrial commodities to industrial services, as illustrated in figure 9.1. Relationship marketing should be used differently according to where on the continuum a firm's product is placed (Grönroos 1994). In general, some marketers of fast-moving consumer goods (FMCG) may benefit from a transactional marketing approach, while service firms would be better off applying a relationship marketing strategy. This is because customers are more likely to prefer a relationship if products are too complex and involving to be chosen in a clinical, transactional manner.

For example, imagine you are driving home from a funeral in a town far away. You are unlikely ever to return to the town; indeed, you are unlikely ever to drive along this country road again. When you stop for petrol at a service station, you do not need to develop or maintain a relationship; you merely hand over your credit card and do not even bother to look the attendant in the eye (Dwyer, Schurr & Oh 1987). But your local garage or mechanical workshop is another matter. When your car is serviced there, you need to trust the people there and want to commit to them. Thus they wear clean uniforms with a name on the pocket and you try to remember their names. When you take your car in for a service, you talk about the previous service and, when you pick up the car up after a service, you talk about the next one. These people would probably not want to put something unnecessary in your car and charge you for it, because they would lose the stream of your future visits if you ever found out about it.

Customer's orientation

In addition to this product/service factor, the application of transactional or relational marketing may depend on the customer's orientation to a relationship (Anderson & Narus 1990; Garbarino & Johnson 1999). That is, some customers may not want to have a relationship. Even if they do, they vary in the extent to which they wish to develop commercial relationships (Dwyer, Schurr & Oh 1987). For example, for the customers of a New York repertory theatre company, trust and commitment are mediators only for a segment of high-relational customers and not for a segment of low-relational customers (Garbarino & Johnson 1999), thus confirming the idea that customers may or may not voluntarily establish attachments to organisations. Costly relationship marketing efforts to build strong relational bonds may therefore not be necessary if the customer does not desire the relationship. In brief, one firm may need to practise both transactional and relational marketing because of different customer orientations.

Industry, organisation and management factors

Within the context of the two factors above, a firm has to work out whether it is able to establish relationships with customers. Factors such as a firm's size, nature of employees, and size and nature of customer base may all contribute when determining the appropriateness of relationship marketing (Stewart & Durkin 1999). For example, large firms with large customer bases may not be able to have a relationship with each customer (Palmer 1997).

More importantly, organisations need to have various capabilities to make relationship marketing work, for example a pervasive marketing culture (Grönroos 1995), internal marketing (Berry 1995), a business strategy based on services (Christopher, Payne & Ballantyne 1991), strategic customer bonding (Buttle & Ahmad 1999) and capabilities relating to information management (Coviello & Brodie 1998; Perry, Cavaye & Coote 2002).

In brief, judicious and intelligent relationship marketing and management is required. Relationship marketing is a new and important approach that marketers may or may not use to enhance the effectiveness of their practices.

How can CRM be applied?

The previous section covered some of the principles of when and where relationship marketing may be applied. Based on those principles, we need to consider how the method of relationship marketing called CRM can be applied. This section looks at some of the issues in implementing and maintaining a successful CRM initiative in situations where it may be appropriate.

To begin, CRM promotes a holistic approach to marketing that involves the entire organisation. This approach is necessary because CRM recognises that many areas of a business can affect consumer perceptions, which means that CRM is not just the responsibility of the marketing department. The holistic aspect of CRM means that the organisation needs a seamless integration of front office and back office operations. This integration of many diverse functional areas brings with it several issues. One issue relates to technology, as the customer database is usually at the core of a CRM program because it can provide the essential links between the back office and front office functions as well as connecting the IT, sales, marketing and customer service departments. Over the past few years, technology has become more sophisticated and accessible for those organisations implementing CRM. Technology can often provide much of the required automation but, on its own, technology does not constitute CRM. However, technology is only part of the solution for successful CRM. Processes to gather, input, maintain and output data from a wide range of sources are required.

Resources, including both financial and non-financial ones, are another issue. For example, staff need to be trained in the new procedures, and encouraged to share information and develop a customer focus. Implementing CRM is a significant change management project for a business — it involves getting the entire organisation working together on the new philosophy and processes. Time is another resource issue, with many CRM programs taking some years to implement fully. Accordingly, CRM can be expensive in terms of systems and other costs. Some organisations view the financial costs of implementing CRM as an expense rather than an investment, particularly in light of the delay in return on investment. Whatever the costs to the firm, the benefits in terms of improved relationships need to be considered.

Services Marketing on the Web:
'Please call me back.'

A 2001 survey by Aura Consulting in the United Kingdom revealed that approximately half the companies that had a 'call me back' service for customers on their website failed to respond to call-back requests. People logging on to a company's website can sometimes simply leave a message with their phone number and call-back time, or they might also have to provide additional information such as their name, email address and comments. On one occasion, a holiday company responded about one and half hours later to a request for a call-back in five minutes. Moreover, the technology was not being used well. When an operator at a call centre did eventually call back, they often did not know that it was a call-back rather than one of the usual incoming phone calls and so did not know the person's name or why the call was necessary. Surely customers who had already shown their interest in the company's products by logging on to its website should be given more care and a higher priority than those making a phone call to the company's call centre.

However, at one well-managed company, the call-back operators knew the name of the person they were calling, the reason for calling and knew what was in the customer's web shopping trolley at the time of the request for a callback. This meant that the customer did not have to provide a long explanation of the reason for the call and it also presented a professional image on the part of the service.

In brief, companies need to integrate their web and call centre channels, and use the technologies to their fullest extent. Their customers require these services.

Derived from Aura Consulting 2001

CRM can provide customers with immediate, accurate and relevant service by anticipating their needs and providing personalised content to customer interactions. However, in order to deliver this improved service, organisations need relevant and up-to-date data on individual customers. This need for data introduces two issues that require consideration: security of data and a customer's right to privacy. Security is an issue internal to the organisation and is heightened by the information-sharing aspect of CRM. For example, information-sharing by its nature means that staff at all levels have access to data, and this impacts on data security, integrity and accuracy. Indeed, the ease of access to information about individual customers is of concern to many, particularly issues to do with the accuracy of data, who has access to it and not knowing what data is held on an individual (Forcht & Thomas 1994). To this end, concerns about privacy highlight the need for marketers to understand the boundaries of utilising the marketing database. These varying concerns depend upon both internal organisational factors, such as perceptions of trustworthiness with customer data, and external factors such as the method and type of data collected (Long et al. 1999). Furthermore, privacy thresholds may vary because some customers may perceive that information accessibility can deliver benefits to them (Forcht & Pierson 1994). Nevertheless, if organisations are set to gain maximum and long-term benefit from their integrated databases, then customers need to be assured that their data is protected and used with respect.

Managers should also consider whether all their consumers want the type of relationship that CRM can provide. For a start, high-frequency consumers are more likely to want a relationship. Thus, managers need to target these consumers in particular. For example, telephone companies and banks appoint relationship managers to only a few selected accounts, and frequent flyer programs have bronze, silver and gold levels. Many CRM programs have a 'club' format that a customer can elect whether to join or not; for example, the Omomatic Club is for washing powder customers who want to join. That is, different types of customers will require different types of relationships.

If a relationship needs to be built, then an organisation's ability to do this needs to be developed. While creating this development, managers should be aware that relationships can revert to a previous state, or go forward to an advanced state, or even die, as we pointed out in our discussion of the ladder of loyalty (figure 9.2). Indeed, a relationship may become dormant in any state. Therefore, managers should not be too linear or deterministic when trying to manage relationships. Moreover, this management process should not focus only on social bonds but should consider how to integrate social and technical bonds. For example, a car dealer building a relationship with a customer must be aware that the dealership's mechanics and their maintenance procedures inside the workshop are also integral parts of the relationship between the dealer and the customer.

Barriers to implementing CRM

In the year 2000 a survey, by the authors, of industry experts found that while CRM is important for service growth, few Australian companies had successfully implemented CRM. All respondents nominated commitment by top management and the organisation's culture and systems as factors that hinder the integration of customer contact points in delivering customer contact management. This was followed closely by the issue of resources. Very few participants thought that implementation was severely hindered by customer resistance, lack of needs or benefits. Some of the reasons for poor implementation of CRM were:

- commitment by management
- too lengthy a process
- culture
- issues of information sharing
- technology/systems
- company too big or complex
- customer resistance
- structure of the company
- resources
- unwilling to be a pioneer
- lack of knowledgeable staff
- no perceived need
- too big a change.

Listed below are some industry quotes from that survey about barriers to implementing CRM:

- ' . . . being seduced by the mechanics of CRM rather than with people and customer retention'
- 'Systems operate on a product view rather than a customer view.'

- 'All departments need to change for a true customer focus.'
- ' ... needs a cultural learning ... must come from the top'
- 'Smaller organisations are quicker at implementing — larger organisations are more bureaucratic, slow to change, higher failure rate.'
- ' ... biggest issues relate to skills'
- 'Introducing new technology requires behaviour change and people issues in order to get value out of it.'
- 'Data quality is a big problem.'
- 'Organisations don't embrace CRM because they just don't get it ... it is a corporate philosophy and unless the CEO lives and breathes it — it is a whole bunch of technology that will go absolutely nowhere.'
- 'Long-term goals versus short term goals ... may take three or five years to even start yielding results.'
- 'The potential magnitude of data is an issue ... and coding and capturing anecdotal data.'
- 'It is a whole new way of thinking about your customer.'
- ' ... egos, attitudes, politics and culture'
- 'Qualitative issues are often the key to the success of change.'

In brief, there are many barriers to successful implementation of CRM, ranging from a too narrow approach, rather than a whole-of-organisation approach, to technical IT issues.

Summary

LO1: Define relationship marketing and outline the concept of the ladder of loyalty.
- Relationship marketing is a multifunctional and integrative approach to customer management that emphasises long-term relationships with customers, and their needs and values.
- The ladder of loyalty acknowledges that a relationship with a customer can take place over time.

LO2: Identify and distinguish between the four methods of relationship marketing.
- The four methods of relationship marketing range from mainly tactical applications to an increasingly strategic applications.
- Direct mail is essentially a promotional tactic focusing on sales.
- Direct marketing attempts to target customers more personally but is still essentially a promotional and transactional tool.
- Database marketing has grown into a more strategic tool that utilises relational processes to provide more targeted interactions with individual customers. The organisational centre for database marketing is often the marketing department.
- Customer relationship management continues the strategic execution of relationship marketing. Unlike database marketing, CRM has an organisation-wide focus that coordinates and integrates information about individual customers. This customer information is shared, where appropriate, at various points across the organisation. Accordingly, CRM is more than just marketing; it requires relationship appropriate culture, structure, staff and systems.

LO3: Distinguish between social and structural bonds in a marketing relationship and explain the different classifications of marketing relationships.

- Structural bonds are forged when two parties adapt to each other in some economic or technical way such as product or process adjustments.
- Social bonds are investments of time and energy that produce positive interpersonal relationships between the two parties, although these can range from formal, organisational contacts to informal, personal ones.
- Transactions are discrete, market-based exchanges with virtually all the necessary information contained in the price of the product exchange.
- Firms can use different marketing strategies to win customers' loyalty and shift the focus of exchange from one-off transactions. With repeated transactions, there might be some beginning of social bonding in the form of trust and commitment.
- Repeated transactions may become closer social bonds when a contract is signed.
- Soft buyer–seller relationships normally develop from repeated transactions without the existence of formal contracts.
- Long-term contractual relationships can develop into strategic alliances. These are comprehensive contractual relationship similar to those of a vertically integrated firm. Structural bonding is high, whereas social bonding may be low.
- Networks are more complex relationships, with both economic and social interdependence in the exchange processes.

LO4: Appreciate the role and place of customer relationship management (CRM).

- CRM is a customer-centred philosophy and set of actions that a business undertakes in its management of a relationship with a customer.
- CRM usually incorporates IT to deliver more customer-focused service.
- CRM is a dynamic strategy that incorporates real-time analysis.

LO5: Discuss where and when relationship marketing can be applied.

The practice of relationship marketing is influenced by three factors:

- Product/service and situational factors. For example, some marketers of FMCG may benefit from a transactional marketing approach while service firms would be better off applying a relationship marketing strategy because customers are more likely to prefer a relationship if products are too complex and involving to be chosen in a clinical transactional manner.
- Customer's orientation. Some customers may not want to have a relationship and, even if they do, they may vary in the extent to which they wish to develop commercial relationships.
- Industry, organisation and management factors. A firm has to work out whether it is able to establish a relationship with customers. Factors such as a firm's size, nature of employees, and size and nature of customer base may all contribute when determining the appropriate relationship marketing.

LO6: Discuss how CRM can be applied.

- CRM recognises that many areas of business affect customer perceptions, so CRM is not just the responsibility of the marketing department.
- CRM requires seamless integration of front office and back office activities and requires attention to factors such as technology, resources, processes, systems and cultural changes.

Contractual relationships: relationships centred on a contract that focuses on shipments and on the resolution of disputes (p. 223)

Customer relationship management (CRM): a business strategy for selecting and managing the most valuable customer relationships. CRM requires a customer-centric business strategy and philosophy to support effective marketing, sales and service processes, which are supported, not driven, by CRM technology (p. 214)

Database marketing: a method that uses information technology in an organisation-wide process of gathering and storing, relational data about individual past, current and/or potential customers (p. 214)

Direct mail: a promotional tool that uses the postal service to target particular customers (p. 214)

Direct marketing: a promotion or marketing communication tactic that involves cross selling; that is, offering an existing customer some other products from the organisation that he or she has not yet bought (p. 214)

Ladder of loyalty: the six ascending steps of a relationship from prospect, to first-time customer, to repeat customer, to client/member, to advocate and to partner (p. 213)

Partner relationship marketing (PRM): a CRM concept applied to business-to-business (B2B) relationships (p. 219)

Relationship marketing: occurs when an organisation is engaged in proactively creating, developing and maintaining committed, interactive and profitable exchanges with selected customers or partners over time (p. 212)

Social bonds: investments of time and energy that produce positive interpersonal relationships between two parties, ranging from formal, organisational contacts to informal and personal ones (p. 221)

Soft/non-contractual relationships: relationships that are normally developed from repeated transactions without the existence of contracts (p. 223)

Structural bonds: bonds forged when two parties adapt to each other in some economic or technical way, as they do when making product or process adjustments (p. 221)

Transactional marketing: a transactional exchange involving a single, short exchange with a distinct beginning and ending (p. 212)

review questions

1. Explain the difference between relationship marketing and transactional marketing. Provide specific examples.
2. What is meant by the term 'ladder of loyalty'? Give examples to illustrate.
3. What are the four characteristics of database marketing? Provide examples to illustrate.
4. What is customer relationship management? How does CRM differ from other methods of relationship marketing?
5. What factors need to be considered by marketing managers in implementing CRM? Give an example of each of these factors.

application questions

1. Think of an example of relationship marketing that you have observed, and determine where the service involved fits on the continuum (figure 9.1). Can you find other examples at other stages of the continuum?
2. Is it possible for a bank to use relationship marketing? Why?
3. Provide examples that illustrate each of the four methods of relationship marketing shown on page 215.
4. Do you agree that relationship marketing has been a central part of what practitioners have done for millennia? Why?
5. Provide examples of how an organisation could apply each of the six conceptual categories of relationship marketing.
6. What do you see as the 'costs' to a company that practices CRM?

vignette questions

1. Read the Services Marketing Action vignette on page 211 and decide whether Jody's old bank practised CRM. What recommendations would you give to Jody's new bank in regard to CRM?
2. Read the International Issues vignette on page 220. Identify the benefits of going from a product-centred approach to a customer-centred approach for Dresdner Bank.
3. The Services Marketing on the Web vignette on page 226 outlines some experiences of organisations trying to provide customer relationship enhancement through the Internet. What is the main lesson from the vignette? Elaborate on the concept that maintaining relationships with customers cannot be limited to one channel such as the Internet, but should be considered as a multi-channel task that links the Internet, phone, email, mail and personal contact.

recommended readings

Articles from the following websites provide different perspectives, from both academics and practitioners, on CRM and its implementation.

The following two websites were built by groups of CRM consultants who share their experiences and learnings. Their case studies are especially interesting:
www.crmproject.com
www.crm-guru.com

This site is similar, but also includes cutting edge articles by academics:
www.crm-forum.com

An example of a CRM company that provides technology and consultant services, including CRM software, to other companies is:
www.sap.com

The following two sites belong to companies like SAP, but also include small businesses among their targeted market segments:
www.bprmag.com.au/95/4.asp
www.crmexpress.com

references

Accenture, website accessed 2001, 'Gaining business advantages in banking through customer focus', www.crm-forum.com.

Anderson, J. C. & Narus, J. 1990, 'A model of distribution firms and manufacturer firm working partnerships', *Journal of Marketing*, vol. 54, January, pp. 42–58.

Aura Consulting, website accessed 2001, 'Say hello? Wave goodbye!', www.crm-forum.com.

Berry, L. 1995, 'Relationship marketing of services — growing interest, emerging perspectives', *Journal of the Academy of Marketing Science*, vol. 23, no. 4, pp. 236–45.

Buttle, F. 2000a, 'The S.C.O.P.E. of customer relationship management', manuscript, Manchester Business School, UK.

Buttle, F. 2000b, 'The CRM value chain', manuscript, Manchester Business School, UK.

Buttle, F. & Ahmad, R. 1999, 'Bonding with customers', Proceedings of Academy of Marketing Conference, University of Sydney.

Christopher, M., Payne, A. & Ballantyne, D. 1991, *Relationship Marketing: Bringing Quality, Customer Service and Marketing Together*, Butterworth/Heinemann, Oxford.

Colgate, M. & Alexander, N. 1998, 'Banks, retailers and their customers: a relationship marketing perspective', *International Journal of Bank Marketing*, vol. 16, no. 4, pp. 144–52.

Colgate, M. & Stewart, K. 1998, 'The challenge of relationships in services — a New Zealand study', *International Journal of Service Industry Management*, vol. 9, no. 5, pp. 454–68.

Coviello, N. E. & Brodie, R. J. 1998, 'From transaction to relationship marketing: an investigation of market perceptions and practices', *Journal of Strategic Marketing*, vol.13, no. 6, pp. 501–22.

Coviello, N. E., Brodie, R. J. & Munro, J. 1997, 'Understanding contemporary marketing: development of a classification scheme', *Journal of Marketing Management*, vol. 13, no. 6, pp. 501–22.

Dawes, J. & Rowley, J. 1998, 'Enhancing the customer experience: contributions from information technology', *Management Decision*, vol. 36, no. 5, pp. 350–7.

Dawes, J. & Worthington, S. 1996, 'Customer information systems and competitive advantage: a case study of the top ten building societies', *International Journal of Bank Marketing*, vol. 14, no. 4, pp. 36–44.

Day, G. 2000, 'Managing market relationships', *Academy of Marketing Science Journal*, vol. 28, issue 1, pp. 24–30.

DeTienne, K. B. & Thompson, J. A. 1996, 'Database marketing and organizational learning theory: toward a research agenda', *Journal of Consumer Marketing*, vol. 13, no. 5, pp. 12–34.

Domegan, C, 1996, 'The adoption of information technology in customer service', *European Journal of Marketing*, vol. 30, no. 6, pp 52–69.

Dwyer, F. R., Schurr, P. H. & Oh, S. 1987, 'Developing buyer–seller relationships', *Journal of Marketing*, vol. 51, April, pp. 11–27.

Evans, M. 1998, 'From 1086 and 1984: direct marketing into the millennium', *Marketing Intelligence and Planning*, vol. 16, issue 1, pp. 56–67.

Forcht, K. & Cochran, K. 1999, 'Using data mining and data warehousing techniques', *Industrial Management and Data Systems*, vol. 99, no. 5, pp. 189–96.

Forcht, K. & Pierson, J. 1994, 'New technologies and future trends in computer security', *Industrial Management and Data Systems*, vol. 94, no. 8, pp. 30–6.

Forcht, K. & Thomas, D. 1994, 'Information compilation and disbursement: moral, legal and ethical considerations', *Information Management and Computer Security*, vol. 94, no. 2, pp. 23–8.

Galbreath, J. & Rogers, T. 1999, 'Customer relationship leadership: a leadership and motivation model for the twenty-first century business', *The TQM Magazine*, vol. 11, no. 3, pp. 161–71.

Garbarino, E. & Johnson, M. S. 1999, 'The different roles of satisfaction, trust and commitment in customer relationships', *Journal of Marketing*, vol. 63, April, pp. 70–87.

Griffin, J. 1995, *Customer Loyalty: How to Earn It, How to Keep It*, Lexington Books, New York, p. 36.

Grönroos, C. 1994, 'From marketing mix to relationship marketing: towards a paradigm shift in marketing', *Australian Marketing Journal*, vol.2, August, pp. 9–29.

Grönroos, C. 1995, 'Relationship marketing: the strategy continuum', *Journal of the Academy of Marketing Science*, vol. 23, no. 4, pp. 252–4.

Gummesson, E. 1995, *Relationship Marketing: From 4 Ps to 30 Rs*, Liber-Hermods, Malmo, Sweden.

Harker, M. J. 1999, 'Relationship marketing defined? An examination of current relationship marketing definitions', *Marketing Intelligence and Planning*, vol. 17. no. 1, pp. 13–20.

Hochhauser, R. 1992, 'The power of integrated database marketing', *Direct Marketing*, vol. 55, September, pp. 32–6.

Houston, F. & Gassenheimer, J. 1987, 'Marketing and exchange', *Journal of Marketing*, vol. 41, October, pp. 3–18.

Lee, D., website accessed 2001, 'Four steps to success with CRM', www.crmguru.com/content/features/lee02.html.

Long, G., Hogg, M., Hartley, M. & Angold, S. 1999, 'Relationship marketing and privacy: exploring the thresholds', *Journal of Marketing Practice: Applied Marketing Science*, vol. 5, no. 1, pp. 4–20.

McGoldrick, P. & Andre, E. 1997, 'Consumer misbehaviour: promiscuity or loyalty in grocery shopping', *Journal of Retailing and Consumer Services*, vol. 4, no. 2, pp. 73–81.

Morgan, R. & Hunt, S. 1994, 'The commitment–trust theory of relationship marketing', *Journal of Marketing*, vol. 58, July, pp. 20–38.

Palmer, A. 1997, 'Defining relationship marketing: an international perspective', *Management Decision*, vol. 35, no. 4, pp. 319–21.

Palmer, A., McMahon-Beattie, U. & Beggs, R. 2000, 'A structural analysis of hotel sector loyalty programs', *International Journal of Contemporary Hospitality Management*, vol. 12, no. 1, pp. 54–60.

Pelton, L. E., Strutton, D. & Lumpkin, J. R. 1997, *Marketing Channels: A Relationship Management Approach*, Irwin, Chicago.

Peppers, D. & Rogers M. 1997, *Enterprize One-to-One*, Doubleday, New York.

Perry, C., Cavaye A. & Coote, L. 2002, 'Technical and social bonds within business-to-business relationships', *Journal of Business and Industrial Marketing*, vol. 17, no. 1, pp. 75–88.

Peters, L. 1997, 'IT enabled marketing: a framework for value creation in customer relationships', *Journal of Marketing Practice: Applied Marketing Science*, vol. 3, no. 4, pp. 213–29.

Pitta, D. 1998, 'Marketing one-to-one and its dependence on knowledge discovery in databases', *Journal of Consumer Marketing*, vol. 15, issue 5, pp. 468–80.

Potter-Brotman, J. 1994, 'The new role of service in customer retention', *Managing Service Quality*, vol. 4, no. 4, pp. 53–6.

Rao, S. & Perry, C. forthcoming, 'Thinking about relationship marketing: where are we now?', *Journal of Business and Industrial Marketing*.

Reedy, J., Schullo, S. & Zimmerman, K. 2000, *Electronic Marketing: Integrating Electronic Resources Into the Marketing Process*, Dryden Press, Fort Worth.

Ridley, M. 1996, *The Origins of Virtue*, Penguin, Harmondsworth, UK.

Rosenthal, L. & McEachern, C. 1997, 'Getting the holistic picture', *Bank Marketing*, vol. 29, issue 9, pp. 15–21.

Schneider, B. & Bowen, D. E. 1999, 'Understanding customer delight and outrage', *Sloan Management Review*, vol. 41, no. 1, pp. 35–46.

Schoenbachler, D., Gordon, G., Foley, D. & Spellman, L. 1997, 'Understanding consumer database marketing', *Journal of Consumer Marketing*, vol. 14, no. 1, pp. 5–19.

Stewart K. & Durkin, M. 1999, 'Bank relationships with students', *Irish Marketing Review*, vol.12, no. 2, pp. 17–28.

Teale, J. 1999, 'Influences of services quality on relationship development and maintenance in the Australian financial services industry: an in-depth study', PhD thesis, University of Southern Queensland.

Thompson, B. 2001a, 'What is CRM?', *The Customer Relationship Management Primer*, available at: www.crmguru.com.

Thompson, B. 2001b, 'Partner relationship management: bringing indirect channels into CRM', *The Customer Relationship Management Primer*, available at www.crmguru.com.

Turnbull, P. W. & Wilson, D. 1989, 'Developing and protecting profitable customer relationships', *Industrial Marketing Management*, vol.18, pp. 233–8.

Webster, F. E. 1992, 'The changing role of marketing in the corporation', *Journal of Marketing*, vol. 56, October, pp. 1–17.

Wilson, D. T. & Mummalaneni, V. 1988, 'Bonding and commitment in buyer–seller relationships: a preliminary conceptualisation', *Industrial Marketing and Purchasing*, vol. 1, no. 3, pp. 44–58.

Zineldin, M., 2000, 'Beyond relationship marketing: technologicalship marketing', *Marketing Intelligence and Planning*, vol. 18, no. 1, pp. 9–23.

Chapter 10
Communication in services marketing

Rebekah Bennett

LEARNING OBJECTIVES

After reading this chapter you should be able to:

- understand the nature of communication and its complexity
- understand how the characteristics of services influence communication in services marketing
- identify seven strategies for achieving effective communication for services marketing
- demonstrate how to use various communication tools in order to achieve service objectives
- understand the importance of communication with non-customer stakeholders.

CHAPTER OUTLINE

This chapter focuses on the role of communication in services marketing. It includes seven strategies for managing the communications of a service organisation, and examines the tools for implementing these strategies. The chapter commences with the definition of communication, which includes an explanation of the social constructionist approach to understanding communication. This is followed by a discussion of the relevance of communication for services and the strategies for managing communication in a service organisation. Finally, communication tools are outlined for both customers and other stakeholders.

Introduction

Communication:

the creation of shared meaning between participants

Communication is a complex and problematic concept that involves the creation of shared meaning between participants. Miscommunication can occur when meaning is not shared and each party perceives something different in a message, document or context. The main purpose of communication with service customers is to build mutually beneficial relationships that ultimately result in repeat purchase or loyalty. The intangible, inseparable, perishable and heterogeneous nature of services creates special communication requirements and involves risks of miscommunication that are not as evident in the marketing of goods. It is important therefore that service providers carefully manage their communication with potential and existing customers and other stakeholders.

It is important to recognise that there is no broad sweeping strategy for dealing with communication across all services categories. However, there are some common strategies and tools that may be used for effective communication in services marketing.

What is communication?

Transmission model:

a model that views communication through a conduit metaphor as messages that are 'transmitted' from one party to another

The dominant model of communication in the marketing text books and literature to date has been the **transmission model** or conduit model (Shannon & Weaver 1949) of communication which is shown in figure 10.1. This sender–receiver model of communication assumes that communication is an information flow that is created by a message sender, encoded, sent through a channel, decoded, and then received by the message receiver. This model was created by engineers but found wider use. However, it has been widely criticised as being too simplistic an approach for use in the social sciences. In most communication research, it is considered an outdated theory (see Lewis & Slade 2000). The transmission model denies the role of the creation of meaning through interaction between the participants in the communication process. See figure 10.2 for a more detailed list of the problems with using the transmission model of communication.

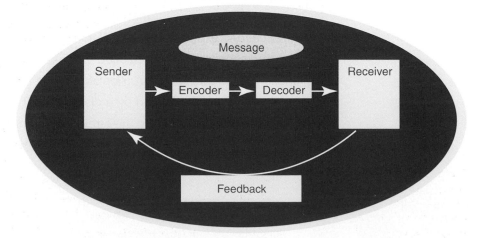

Figure 10.1: Transmission model of communication
Source: adapted from Shannon & Weaver 1949

- It assumes that a message is intended (we can communicate unintentionally).
- It assumes that the source is the decision maker and the receiver is passive.
- It doesn't allow for meaning or interpretation of messages; assumes that meaning is simply extracted from the words not 'constructed' by the receiver.
- It doesn't address conflicting messages between non-verbal and verbal that can be sent simultaneously.
- It doesn't take into account the content of the communication, e.g. the content of a lecture is different from the content of a family discussion.
- The participants are treated as isolated individuals and not as part of a community which shares values (culture).
- Time can change attitudes and thus affect our conversations, so it is not linear.
- It takes into account context, such as noise, but doesn't suggest ways of addressing this to improve communication.
- The relationship between the people is important and may change the communication, e.g. boss to worker, parent to child.
- It considers the medium that is used, not the meaning of the medium and the different effects.
- The transmission model is not an accurate reflection of the complex nature of communication.

Figure 10.2: Criticisms of the transmission model of communication (derived from Reynolds 2001; Chandler 2001)

Given the problematic nature of communication and the inadequacy of the transmission model to provide a clear perspective, it is interesting that most marketing texts still include this model in sections on communication. This may be due to the theoretical base of the marketing discipline. Marketing draws on a number of other disciplines for its base theories, including economics (pricing), psychology (consumer behaviour theory), accounting (pricing) and communication (promotion). Over time, as these base disciplines developed and altered their theories, this information was not necessarily adopted by the marketing discipline.

The transmission model was developed in 1949, about the same time as the marketing discipline was gaining momentum. Although higher-level research was being undertaken on communication, marketing researchers put little effort into retracing the roots and keeping up to date with changes in communication theory.

What then does contemporary communication theory define as communication? Communication is a social dynamic that occurs through the creation of shared meaning. It is the sharing of ideas, knowledge or feelings (Lewis & Slade 2000) and is a network rather than a linear process. It is not a physical object to be transmitted, but rather the process of creating meaning (Ticehurst & Ross-Smith 1998). Contemporary theories on communication are referred to as meaning-based models of communication and include the **social constructionist theory**. This theory views communication not as a process that people do but as the vessel in which participants act (Pearce 1994). The

Social constructionist theory: contemporary communication theory that views communication as the dynamic creation of shared meaning between participants

participants construct their own 'world' of meaning through communication. Each interaction between participants reflects any previous communications they may have had together, the context they are in, their individual traits, and their values and social norms (see figure 10.3). In this theory, communication can be planned or unintentional.

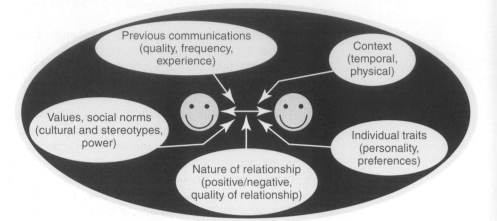

Figure 10.3: Social constructionist model of communication

When communication breaks down, it is not because of a failure on the part of the sender or receiver or in the encoding/decoding of the message; it is because of a failure to create shared meaning. Communication breakdowns are more common than communication successes (Lewis & Slade 2000). Service organisations need to recognise this and actively seek to reduce the incidence. They must also have a back-up plan for when the communication goes awry (Lewis & Slade 2000).

The importance of communication for services

The aim of a communication strategy for a service organisation is to align client perceptions closely to actual deliverables to reduce the incidence of dissatisfaction. Frustration and dissatisfaction can occur for both the customer and the organisation when communication breaks down. There are myriad reasons for communication breakdowns, and these differ according to the situation. Four of the key characteristics of services — intangibility, inseparability, heterogeneity, and perishability — give rise to opportunities for communication problems if not carefully managed. When the problems associated with these characteristics are combined with the problematic nature of communication, there is greater potential for problems to occur than in any other element of the marketing mix or in the marketing of any other type of product. These four characteristics have been explained in detail in previous chapters and will now be explored for the implications they contain for communication.

Intangibility and communication

The intangibility factor makes communication problematic for services marketing. Services cannot easily be displayed, stored or demonstrated for customers (Hill & Nimish 1992), making pre-evaluation of a service difficult.

The fact that you cannot pick up a service and see, smell or taste it increases the perceived risk of buying the service (Zeithaml 1981). Evaluation is based on the identification of qualities possessed by the good or service. As a result of the lack of search qualities (Zeithaml 1981), customers look for proxies of quality such as price, the service-provider, the servicescape, symbols such as branding and any tangible evidence (such as a policy document for house insurance). Organisations can use these proxies to communicate quality images to consumers.

With the lack of pre-evaluation information available to consumers, there is a high need to 'tangibilise' the service; that is, show the physical evidence or proxies (Zeithaml 1981). In advertising, this may mean showing a before-and-after shot of a haircut, or testimonials from happy clients, such as 'We used XYZ lawyers for our personal injury claim and we received much more money than we expected'. Word of mouth and referrals are important sources of information for the pre-evaluation of services, so communication effortys need to be made to influence key opinion leaders in the community. For example, a financial service company could contact a priest at a church and ask them to arrange a session for parishioners on the importance of estate planning and having a will (at which the financial services company would speak). The priest, as an opinion leader for the congregation, could help influence people to attend the session. The financial service company's presentation could have greater credibility because it was at a session suggested by the priest.

Consumers tend to rely on personal sources, such as friends and family, when looking for information about a service. In comparison, both personal and non-personal sources (reports, marketing material, brochures) are used when purchasing goods (Murray 1991). The higher levels of perceived risk generally associated with services usually result in consumers relying on sources of information they can trust, in order to reduce this risk. Non-personal communication sources such as advertising and websites may not be viewed by consumers as reliable sources of information for risk-reduction. For instance, the purchase of a mobile phone service provider can be quite difficult, given the varying criteria between providers and the different plans. The service is highly intangible, in that a consumer cannot pick up the plans and touch and feel them for comparison. Word-of-mouth advice from people known by the customer to have used the mobile phone service provider reduces the risk and anxiety in the purchase decision. Personal selling becomes very important, as this provides an opportunity for a service organisation to demonstrate a service or to develop a relationship with the potential customer (Sharma & Patterson 1999). The customer may use physical proxies such as the clothes the salesperson is wearing, the quality of the sales material and the personability of the salesperson in order to establish information about the quality and riskiness of the service being offered.

Inseparability and communication

Inseparability means that the service provider cannot be separated from the service, so the role of the service provider is important in developing the quality of the service and in managing the perceptions of the customer (Zeithaml, Parasuraman & Berry 1985). Professional services in particular require significant judgement on the part of the service provider. Communication appears to be more problematic for this type of service than for service

Managing expectations

Many organisations overpromise what they cannot deliver, which in turn results in dissatisfaction, complaining behaviour or negative word of mouth (Oliver 1980). A source of dissatisfaction among customers is the disparity between expected and actual outcomes (Oliver 1989). Effective communication can be used to manage the expectations of consumers so that their expectations match reality more realistically (Czepiel, Soloman & Surprenant 1985). For example, many people purchasing tickets for a rock concert for the first time may not be aware that the tickets are usually non-refundable. If the buyer is suddenly unable to attend, they may try to return the tickets, only to find that this is not possible. This can result in a feeling of dissatisfaction with the concert organisers, and the buyer may exhibit complaining behaviour or engage in negative word of mouth.

Communication can assist in managing expectations through promising what can be delivered; presenting clear images of what the service consists of; and focusing on the tangible aspects of the service (for example, stating at the point of purchase, and printing on the back of a rock concert ticket, that the ticket is non-refundable).

Integrating the organisational approach to communication

Communication must be consistent across the organisation and, in particular, the key messages communicated in a marketing campaign must be consistent with the operational aspects of the organisation. If we look at the example of the Telstra positioning statement, 'Making it easy for you', this means that consumers who choose Telstra as their telecommunications service provider are likely to expect their dealings with the company to be 'easy'. If the reality of their contact with Telstra becomes difficult through inefficient processes, then a conflict between the promises and the reality can lead to dissatisfaction. An example of this may be calling Telstra and going through a voice-activated system when you want to speak to a person immediately.

Influencing consumer responses to communication

One of the purposes of communication in a marketing context is to elicit a response from the consumer — the response usually being purchase. The **hierarchy-of-effects** models contain the order of responses consumers may have to communication. These responses include cognition (thinking processes — learn), affect (emotional processes — feel) and conation (behavioural processes — do).

There are three commonly accepted hierarchy-of-effects models: standard learning, dissonance attribution and low involvement (Ray 1973). These hierarchies are not opposing models; rather, they are relevant to different situations depending on the level of involvement, differentiation of alternatives and communication source (Ray 1973). The standard learning hierarchy model (Ray 1973) of learn–feel–do establishes a step-by-step process among the various responses (see figure 10.4). The respondent first develops knowledge (learn) towards the advertised object, then feelings (feel) followed by an intention to act or not act (do). The dissonance attribution model (Ray 1973) of do–feel–learn (figure 10.5) places learning as the final response and is more behaviourist in its approach, in that it does not presuppose any

Hierarchy of effects: *the order of responses a consumer has to a marketing communication*

cognitive processing before purchase. The low involvement model (Ray 1973) of learn–do–learn–feel (figure 10.6), initially proposed by Krugman (1965) puts forward the view that advertising prior to purchase results in some cognitive movement initially but the majority occurs after the purchase and assumes low-involvement levels.

These models are primarily focused on responses to communication about goods, and do not take into account the influence of the characteristics of services. A fourth hierarchy has therefore been proposed as more relevant for the service sector, called the services sector hierarchy (Young 1981). The services hierarchy-of-effects model, of feel–do–learn (see figure 10.7), proposes that buyers in the services sector commence with the emotions. Consumers then progress to the actual purchase, after which they develop knowledge about the service through actual experience. Services are highly emotive experiences regardless of the involvement level; anger and frustration can develop while waiting for a hamburger at McDonald's as well as waiting in the casualty section of a hospital.

Figure 10.4: Standard learning hierarchy

Figure 10.5: Dissonance attribution hierarchy

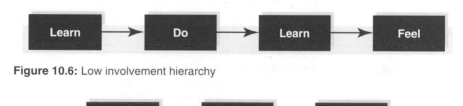

Figure 10.6: Low involvement hierarchy

Figure 10.7: Services sector hierarchy

Young (1981) placed emphasis on the intangible aspects of services and proposed that people anticipate the emotional outcome of the service in advance. When searching for information as part of the pre-evaluation process, individuals are interested in the experience that others have had with the service and how that made them feel.

There is very little information available to assist a consumer in developing an attitudinal intention to purchase the service. As attitudes consist of cognitive and emotional components (Azjen & Fishbein 1980), if there is little information available to stimulate the cognitive components, then the emotional component is likely to be the dominant factor in influencing attitude development (Kim, Lim & Bhargava 1998). Thus the role of emotions in the purchase of services is important, particularly when the consumer has little experience in the service category.

When communicating with users of a service, it is therefore important to understand that feelings play an important role, particularly in the emotional expectations of the experience. Therefore, communications such as advertising should stimulate feelings and emotions that are consistent with the emotional expectations of the target market (Young 1981).

Communication aims to stimulate consumer responses with the ultimate aim of repeat purchase. Using the hierarchy-of-effects model in figure 10.7, customer communication aims to initially generate emotions to develop a positive feeling towards the service provider. This will assist in reducing the perceived risk of dealing with that service provider. Next, communication should aim to encourage switching and trial (actual purchase). The 'do' stage can be generated through marketing communication tools that encourage trial and purchase, such as 'two for one' sales promotions, samples of the service and price discounts. The development of information and knowledge of the service provider is a cognitive process, which can constitute awareness, information search, interest generation and evaluation. Mediums such as advertising, promotional material, post-sale written communication or a website can be used at this stage. Different communication tools can be used to stimulate consumers at each stage of the model with the objective of leading the consumer onto the next stage (see table 10.1).

It is essential that marketing managers understand the order of responses made by consumers so that they may use the various communication tools most effectively. For the services context, it is suggested that consumers commence with an emotional response. If this is positive, they proceed to the action stage, where they trial or purchase the service, and after consumption they have a cognitive response in the form of attitude formation and opinions.

Table 10.1	Summary of hierarchy-of-effects models			
	Standard learning	Dissonance attribution	Low involvement	Services
Responses	Learn	Do	Learn	Feel
	Feel	Feel	Do	Do
	Do	Learn	Learn	Learn
			Feel	

Managing non-verbal communication

While some services are performed without personal interaction, as in the case of ATMs and Internet delivered services, most services involve interpersonal contact between a customer and the service provider.

Non-verbal communication is very important for services because customers' evaluations of a service are often based on the interaction that occurred (Sundaram & Webster 2000). Non-verbal communication consists of paralanguage (pitch of voice, tone, volume), kinesics (body movements such as hand-shaking, nodding), proxemics (distance and relative posture) and physical attractiveness (appearance, clothing). Each of these interacts with the service provider's and customer's verbal communication to create an emotional response (affect) by the customer.

The end result of a positive emotional response is customer evaluation of the service-provider as friendly, courteous, empathetic, competent and credible (see figure 10.8).

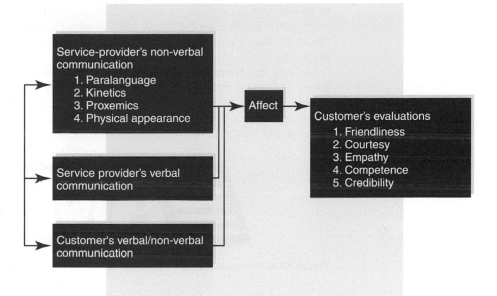

Figure 10.8: Role of non-verbal communication in service interactions
Source: Sundaram & Webster 2000

Sundaram and Webster (2000) suggest there are seven ways that managers can manage the non-verbal communication of their employees to encourage a positive customer evaluation:

1. Ensure all employees understand that non-verbal communication is as important as verbal communication.
2. Train employees to recognise non-verbal cues through roleplays etc.
3. Provide feedback on employee behaviour.
4. Offer voice training to employees so they all convey warmth and empathy.
5. Match employee dress with customer expectations. If a customer expects to see a health practitioner in a lab coat, then ensure they wear one.
6. Conduct research to measure employee communication.
7. Provide incentives to reward employees who adopt the recommended communication behaviour.

Providing tangible cues and symbols and physical evidence of a service

The intangible nature of services means that consumers have difficulty in evaluating what they are buying and this increases the perceived risk. Making the service 'tangible' can give consumers a more concrete grasp of what they are buying, thus reducing the gap between expectations and performance, as well as providing cues for quality. This can be done through the use of slogans that contain concrete objects, such as 'You are in good hands with Allstate'; and through physical evidence, such as written guarantees, policy documents, plastic credit cards and airline tickets, which are proxies (Berry 1980).

Branding

One method for reducing perceived risk is the use of branding as a tangible cue or symbol that can be used to imply quality, as demonstrated by the brand in figure 10.9.

The AMP brand uses the colour blue, which is a traditional, conservative colour (good for financial institutions) and also has the forward moving lines indicating progress.

Likewise, the National Australia Bank logo is easily recognisable and conveys an image of forward movement (the lines) and of being Australian (the star from the Southern Cross). It also has the positioning statement 'Tailored financial solutions'. When customers see the brand, it authenticates the communication as being genuine and from a known and trusted bank.

Figure 10.9: Example of a service brand

A brand also eases the amount of effort a customer has to undertake when repurchasing a product. Consider the purchase of car insurance. The brand purchased on the previous occasion now has some meaning for the purchaser. It could be a brand that conveys images of safety, security and confidence that claims will be paid out, or it could have negative images associated with the brand, owing to some unsatisfactory service received. The next time insurance is required, a purchaser will either automatically repurchase the brand without the effort of searching for alternatives or will look for another service provider. Either way, the choice has been simplified compared to the last purchase. When a brand's image (the meaning that the organisation wants to create) matches the image you have of it, then you have shared meaning.

Third-party endorsements

If a service organisation is not well known under its own brand, it can be useful to use other credible brands as an endorsement of the quality of the service. Even if a service organisation is well known, using logos of industry associations or awards 'borrows' from the credibility of that organisation and reduces the risk of using that service. Strategic Joint Partners Pty Ltd, part of the SJP Group of financial services, has included in all its communications the logo of the Financial Planning Association and the Association of Independent Financial planners (indicating membership) to demonstrate its integrity and adherence to ethical conduct. The inclusion of these logos on all written and electronic communication conveys the message that 'Strategic Joint Partners is a reputable and ethical financial services firm that can be trusted'.

Figure 10.10: Front and back of a Strategic Joint Partners business card

Influencing consumer responses through the servicescape

As a tangible indicator, the servicescape communicates images, benefits, relationships and a host of other meanings to the customer (Bitner 1992). Management of this environment can thus be crucial to establishing mutually beneficial relationships that enhance the positioning of the service and achieve an organisation's goals. After experiencing a restaurant meal, factors that may influence subsequent visits are the consumption experience, the décor, the ambience, the music and the perception of intimacy. In a servicescape environment, music has been found to create associations with past emotional experiences (Oakes 2000) and thus communicates associated images. Music can influence consumers by acting as a trigger for positive emotions or emotions that are consistent with the service. Additionally, the tempo of the music can influence the speed with which diners in a restaurant eat their meal: fast music increases the speed of eating and slow music decreases it (Oakes 2000).

The non-verbal interaction and the servicescape between a customer and service provider stimulates an emotional reaction (Sundaram & Webster 2000) and communicates the positioning of the organisation. This can affect the overall service experience and influence whether that person continues to buy from that service provider.

If, for example, a person seeking tax advice enters an accountant's office where it is dark and dingy, the overall perception that is communicated is likely to be negative, and the consumer may not wish to return to that accountant.

Communication through formal promotional methods, such as advertising, or through informal methods, such as non-verbal interpersonal communication, needs to be planned for effective service marketing management.

Developing service-based positioning and key messages

Positioning: the process of influencing the consumer's perception of a good or service using the marketing mix

Communication can be used to position a service in the consumer's mind. There are seven types of **positioning**: by attribute, benefit, price–quality, use, product user, product class and competition. A commonly used communication tool for establishing positioning is advertising. Examples of campaigns are illustrated in table 10.2.

Table 10.2   Positioning campaigns for services

Positioning strategy	Company	Positioning statement	Tactic
Attribute	Visa	'The world's best way to pay' Visa is positioning itself as the card that is most widely accepted and therefore the best way to pay.	Brands service by payment options
Benefit	Telstra	'Making it easy for you' Telstra recognised that communication is getting very complex and overwhelming for most people.	Brands service by benefit
Price–quality	Midas Car Care system	'Dealership service without the price tag' Midas demonstrates an awareness of public perception that dealership services are high quality but are also accompanied by high price.	Creates a value proposition for low-cost pricing
Use	NIB health insurance	'Health cover for every body'	Brands service as having cover for your body
Product user	Sun Herald Advertising	'For businesses who want to reach people with a taste for the good life'	Targets businesses who want to access high-end consumers
Product class	University of Queensland	'World class — be part of it' Places UQ in a high-status category and implies that UQ is a leading institution.	Creates identification with world-class practices
Competition	Avis car rental	'We try harder' Avis acknowledged that it was number 2 and that's why they try harder.	Differentiates from competitor

The positioning of a service, while it draws on the same principles as the positioning of a good, can be difficult owing to the difficulty in communicating intangible benefits resulting from the four key service characteristics (Ennew, Watkins & Wright 1995). This is demonstrated in research that looked at positioning strategies for credit card services in the United Kingdom and found an emphasis on providing information in communication mediums (Blankson & Kalafatis 1999). Presumably this was to reduce the perceived risk of an intangible product where little pre-purchase information is available (Murray 1991).

Communication tools targeting customers

The promotional element in the four Ps of marketing is the core of marketing communication, which targets customers. It includes the tools of advertising, personal selling, sales promotions, Internet/electronic communication, publicity, sponsorship and word of mouth. These communication tools need to reflect the different characteristics of services and the importance of emotion and the 'whole experience' (Young 1981). This means that some of the accepted notions of marketing communication for products may not easily translate when communicating a service. Additionally, these tools need to reduce the dissonance between expectations and performance and thus create shared meaning.

Advertising

Advertising is the communication tool that most consumers are familiar with, and the one that springs to mind for students when marketing communication is first mentioned. Advertising mediums include broadcast media (television, radio), print (newspapers and magazines), outdoor (billboards, buspaks, vehicles), cinema, directional media (directories) and electronic (Internet, SMS, CDs, kiosks). The purpose of advertising is to create awareness and develop predispositions, positioning or limited knowledge. Advertising can do this by informing, persuading or reminding.

Advertising for a service is different from that for a good. As mentioned earlier, services are a riskier purchase than goods, which means that the role of advertising should be to reassure consumers that the advertised service is lower risk than the alternatives. Advertising can provide information that assists in tangibilising the service and in purchase evaluation (Mortimer 2000). In a study of newspaper advertisements, it was found that advertisements for services were higher in informational content than goods (Grove, Pickett & Laband 1995). Four types of information were identified; price, guarantees, performance evidence and availability. Additionally, a study comparing products and services advertising found differences among the type of information displayed, with services placing more emphasis on informing consumers about the 'contents' of the service (what the service actually is) to make it more tangible (Mortimer 2000). It would therefore be expected that if a service is low in tangibility — investment advice, for example — there needs to be increased information content in its advertising compared to a service that is higher in tangibility, such as a restaurant.

The findings that advertising content for services differs from that for goods supports the positioning research mentioned earlier. However it contradicts the proposed hierarchy response for services, which places cognitive activity last. In the Young (1981) model, the role of emotion is important for services, and reassurance at an emotional rather than a cognitive level is more important for services in the initial stages of the purchase process. Whether advertising for a service should contain information or emotional cues is an unanswered question at this stage, as the little research into advertising for services has focused predominantly on the content of the advertising rather than the effectiveness of the content.

Personal selling

Personal selling: a two-way communication process in which a salesperson engages with a potential customer for the purpose of selling a good or service

Personal selling is usually appropriate for services that are highly complex and require demonstration, customisation or explanation. This is a dominant form of communication in business-to-business markets, owing to the high complexity and transaction values associated with purchases (Morris 1992). In a service environment, the sales process can also provide indicators of quality and pre-evaluation information. For instance, if a consumer is in a sales appointment with an insurance adviser, the level of trust and commitment the consumer has in the adviser provides information about the quality of the insurance service being sold. If the adviser appears trustworthy, or has been in the past, then this is likely to transfer to the services they represent. For services high in credence qualities, there is little choice for the consumer but to rely on their salesperson (Sharma & Patterson 1999).

In particular, the communication skills of the salesperson are important for a service environment, where there is no physical product to evaluate. Financial advisers who are effective in their communication have been found to increase the level of trust and commitment to an ongoing relationship with their customers (Sharma & Patterson 1999). Communication effectiveness, in this study, represents their ability to keep the client informed, to provide clear explanations of financial concepts, to show willingness to provide information when required and to provide a balanced perspective.

Sales promotions

Sales promotion: a promotion that directly stimulates a sale, usually offered at the point of sale

The area of **sales promotion** covers tactics such as competitions, coupons, premiums, pricing discounts, point-of-purchase materials and rebates. While sales promotions have been used extensively with packaged consumer goods, they are not as prolific in the service context (Lovelock & Quelch 1983). Indeed, when examining research into the sales promotion technique of coupons, there is little evidence of coupons being used by service organisations. Sales promotions can assist in creating effective communication through matching its offer with expectations of the service. If the sales promotion overpromises, misperceptions can occur and communication breaks down.

However sales promotions can be very useful for services that experience seasonal demand; reducing the risk of trialling a new service; and introducing some excitement into a stable market. Sales promotions may also be used in conjunction with another communication tool in an integrated marketing communication approach. Sales promotion is not a tool to generate long-term results such as brand loyalty or long-term sales (Ehrenberg, Hammond & Goodhardt 1994). Coupons, in particular, are not effective in generating brand loyalty, but they can induce brand switching or trial of an alternative service by lowering the perceived risk (Slater 2001).

Seasonal demand

Services that have changes in supply and demand experience peaks and troughs. The need to smooth demand is more important for services than goods, because the 'product' is perishable and cannot be stored, and because service delivery capacity is difficult to change (Lovelock & Quelch 1983).

As services rely primarily on people as the service providers, when demand decreases there is reduced need for the personnel to perform the service. For example, a hotel that is operating at full capacity during school holidays needs more room cleaners, waiters, and kitchen staff than it does in the off-season when it may be only half full. It can be very expensive to carry the cost of permanent service personnel on a constant basis. While this increases consistency of service quality and delivery, it increases the overall costs of the organisation, which may lead to higher prices (see chapter 11 for more information on pricing). For example, the hotel could use pricing discounts, two-for-one deals and extra features in low demand periods to help even out demand. Another example is council bus services offering a price incentive for commuters to travel at off-peak times during major city events such as the Olympic Games or football games.

Adding excitement into a stable market

Markets that are stable are usually characterised by repetitive, habitual behaviour, which makes it very difficult for service marketers to gain brand switching. This is especially true if there is little decision making occurring at the point of purchase and if consumers are merely buying their previously bought brand through habit. The use of a sales promotion activates the consumer decision-making process and, once this occurs, a service provider can then attempt to encourage the consumer to switch service providers by trialling their service through the sales promotion. In addition, the sales promotion can reinforce the cognitive and emotional commitment a consumer has for their existing service provider before settling down into an automated pattern of habitual buying. A National Australia Bank campaign (see figure 10.11) is an example of a sales promotion that offers excitement in a stable market. The campaign offers purchasers of National home, contents, car or residential investor insurance the chance to enter a draw to win a $50 000 homewares shopping spree.

Figure 10.11: National Australia Bank competition
Source: National Australia Bank September 2001

A word of caution in offering sales promotions: promotions that focus on price discounting (such as 10 per cent off) rather than value-adding (two-for-one deals or premiums) run the risk of diluting brand equity. Worse, they may even reduce profits if the customer was going to buy the service anyway. However, if you already have a regular discount program, withdrawal of the program may upset existing customers who are used to the deals and expect them — a Catch-22 situation. For example, when Proctor and Gamble abandoned its coupon deals in 1996, it did so on the assumption that the discounts had a negative impact on brand image and did not yield sufficient additional sales (Slater 2001). However, there was a substantial customer backlash. Customers felt they had a 'right' to the coupons, even if they did not use them (only 2 per cent were redeemed), so Proctor and Gamble were forced to reconsider their no-coupon decision and reintroduce them (Slater 2001). In 2002, Coles Myer's decision to withdraw its discount program for shareholders sparked similar dissatisfaction.

Finally, sales promotions are often used in conjunction with other marketing communication campaigns. These present a consistent image, and reinforce the key messages of the other mediums which may include advertising and sponsorship.

Internet and electronic interfaces

Using the Internet for communication can occur through a firm's own website or through advertising on other sites. Organisations can use their own website to communicate branding, products, new information and company background, or they can place advertising on other sites. Other electronic mediums such as email are also used to communicate with customers.

It is the interactive nature of the Internet that allows service users to customise the information they are seeking in a manner not previously seen (Van Doren, Fechner & Green-Adelsberger 2000). This customisation allows consumers to access the information relevant to their context and thus access the communication they need. This assists in the management of expectations. Additionally, many organisations now reduce misperceptions of a service by providing tangible evidence. There are many financial institutions, for example, who provide evidence of tangible outcomes. Loan calculators on their websites are provided to assist in determining repayments. Zurich's website (www.zurich.com.au) contains many calculator tools, including loan repayment schedules, an investment savings calculator, and a retirement calculator.

The benefit of such online tools is that consumers can be discussing a new loan situation with their partner and be able to make decisions jointly with the tools in front of them at home. The 24-hour convenience of the Internet offers key benefits for household decision making.

The Internet can also be used to reduce the uncertainty and perceived risk of a service supplier. Many users will spend a great deal of time searching for information using chat rooms, bulletin boards and third-party sources before making a purchase. Travel, for example, can be a highly risky purchase. If you select a hotel to stay at, it is too late to discover a problem on arrival in peak tourist season. By using sites such as The Thorn Tree at www.lonelyplanet.com.au, which contains objective opinions from other travellers, you can avoid many of the pitfalls that plague unsuspecting travellers. (See chapter 14 for further discussion of e-services.)

Services Marketing on the Web:
Carpet Court New Zealand

by Jacqui Jones, Managing Director WEBENZ, www.webenz.co.nz

Carpet Court New Zealand is a franchise system that supports its franchise members throughout New Zealand by providing marketing activity, systems and training on how to retail carpet in New Zealand. This approach increases the consistency of Carpet Court's marketing message across its franchises.

Traditionally the franchise members would meet two to three times a year to be presented with opportunities and strategies of how to increase the Carpet Court brand awareness, increase sales and market share, improve business productivity and provide retail store benchmarking information. Together, the franchise members would vote on what Carpet Court should implement.

An extranet (an external intranet) system was developed to enable the franchise members, stakeholders and suppliers to communicate more frequently than just at annual conferences. This enables the members from all over the country to log in and actively participate in communication. It also enables the Carpet Court support office to increase its marketing and support services to the franchise members. Some of these services include:

- centralised Library System — allows the members to search, review and download the most up-to-date versions of Carpet Court training manuals and system documents
- surveys — allows the support office to create surveys to benchmark franchise member and supplier performance and to gain opinions from franchise members about what opportunities and strategies should be undertaken for the group. Survey results are published in the system to enable the franchise members, suppliers and stakeholders to view and download the reports.
- marketplace — allows franchise members to view supplier offerings and place an order online before the offer end date. During the offer period, members and suppliers are able to view the accumulation of orders to see if they are meeting minimum order levels. Its access can also be extended right back to the source of manufacture, so adding value and cutting cost for Carpet Court's local distributors.

As Internet communication tools, banner advertising and pop-up features are not as effective as initially thought, because consumers are not as prepared to passively receive advertisements as they are when watching television (Van Doren, Fechner & Green-Adelsberger 2000). The reported click-through rate of banner advertisements varies from only 2.6 per cent (IPRO 2001) to 4 per cent (IAB 2001). Viral marketing is beginning to be popular, with organisations developing advertisements specifically for consumers to email to their friends. Remember the dancing baby? This started off as someone's promotion for their organisation, distributed by email in the mid 1990s. As many people liked the file, it was passed it on, and eventually found its way into other mainstream media, including Coke advertisements. However, who remembers the organisation that started it?

Public relations and sponsorship

Public relations: *the process of managing communications with key stakeholders of an organisation for mutual benefit and a positive outcome*

Stakeholder: *any individual who feels they have a stake in the consequence of an organisation's decisions*

The role of **public relations** has moved from being primarily a publicity-based function to one that focuses on mutually beneficial relationships between an organisation and its **stakeholders** (Gregory 2001). While both communication and marketing disciplines claim ownership of this area, in a marketing model, public relations falls clearly into the marketing communication mix and contributes directly to marketing management outcomes. Public relations can be very effective in managing perceptions and expectations through positive dialogue with the organisation's stakeholders.

A key management issue for public relations is the evaluation of its programs and campaigns. The increasing pressure on organisations to be more accountable also increases the pressure on their internal divisions to deliver tangible accountable outcomes. Thus, evaluation has been a high priority for public relations practitioners in recent times (Gregory 2001). Objectives for a public relations program for a service may be to change or develop attitudes (feel), then obtain behavioural changes (do), and then develop information (learn). These objectives can be broken into three categories: cognitive, affective and conative (as outlined in the earlier section on the hierarchy-of-effects models). From a services perspective, consumers can be influenced in the order of feel, do and learn (Young 1981). Essentially, a public relations program is effective if it achieves these three objectives (Gregory 2001).

Sponsorship: *where an organisation provides funds for an event or another organisation in order to create a positive association*

Sponsorship is a common method for generating publicity and getting the external community involved with the organisation. Its objectives are usually concerned with brand awareness, corporate image and positioning. The Suncorp Metway sponsorship of the Goodwill Games in Brisbane in 2001 demonstrates this well. Suncorp Metway, as part of its corporate sponsorship, received VIP seating with which key clients and stakeholders could be entertained and relationships could be developed. Additionally, the sponsorship allowed Suncorp Metway to link to a positive event that focused on achievement and success, which is consistent with their positioning.

Word of mouth

Word of mouth: *conversations by consumers about a product or service*

Word of mouth is well known as a key factor in influencing consumer attitudes and purchase behaviour. Word of mouth is defined as informal communication between consumers about products and services (Westbrook 1987). The first time a credit card service or mobile phone service is purchased it is likely to involve information from personal sources. Advice from friends or family will probably determine which company a service is purchased from, as friend and family are deemed objective and therefore credible.

While word of mouth is technically not part of the marketing communication mix, as it is outside the control of the organisation, it can be influenced by marketing activities. As stated earlier, word of mouth is particularly relevant for services owing to the low level of pre-purchase evaluation that can be done, and, thus the increased risk associated with this.

Customer referrals are an important outcome of word of mouth as they reduce the dissonance between expectations and performance. This is especially the case for professional services, such as doctors, lawyers, accountants and consultants, which are high in credence qualities. You will notice, for instance, that these organisations rely less on traditional promotion such as advertising and more on the development of networks and referrals.

Many service companies implement referral programs in order to encourage their loyal customers to recommend them to friends, as they recognise the power of word-of-mouth communication. American Express periodically contacts its members and offers gifts to them if they recommend friends or colleagues for the card. RACQ also used a member referral scheme, where members received a 19-piece tool kit if a friend or family member joined RACQ as a result of the referral.

A key issue for the management of word-of-mouth communication is that customers need to be encouraged to speak positively about a service encounter as close to the event as possible. This is because the evaluation of the event is more extreme the closer it is to the encounter (Christiansen & Tax 2000). This could be done by offering a bonus coupon to give to a friend, with the coupon having an expiry date not long after the encounter date.

The level of search qualities determines the importance of word of mouth. Different services have varying search qualities, so word of mouth can be more important for some services than for others. Services that are high in credence qualities make word of mouth very important, so referrals are the main source of business (Christiansen & Tax 2000). Less direct methods of communication, such as word of mouth, may be more effective in influencing consumer purchase in situations of high perceived risk.

It is interesting to note that word of mouth appears to be a common feature across cultures (Christiansen & Tax 2000). Therefore, in the creation of shared meaning between organisations and consumers, word of mouth can be a useful tool both in international marketing and in multicultural societies such as Australia, New Zealand, Singapore and the United States.

Summary of communication tools

Each of the communication tools outlined can be used together or separately to manage perceptions and create shared meaning. Each of the tools has its limitations and benefits and should not be expected to achieve all communication objectives exclusively. The key purpose for each tool is outlined in table 10.3.

Table 10.3 Key purposes for each communication tool

Tool	Key purpose
Advertising	To achieve brand positioning, create awareness, encourage long-term demand, provide information
Personal selling	To create knowledge and information, explain complex or high-value purchases
Sales promotion	To create trial, brand switching, generate short-term sales increase, smooth demand, generate excitement
Internet	To promote the service organisation, provide information about service
Public relations	To create awareness, foster relationships, communicate information
Word of mouth	To increase referrals and new business, minimise customer defection

It is also important to remember that the communication tools need to elicit the feel–do–learn responses of the services sector hierarchy-of-effects model (Young 1981). The initial response to communication about a service is emotional, owing to the limited pre-evaluation information available before purchase. Thus, communication at this stage aims to evoke a positive emotion towards the service and reduce anxiety created by perceived risk. The tools and physical environment that can be used to achieve this are advertising, the servicescape, public relations and sponsorship.

The services sector hierarchy proposes that once a positive emotion towards the service is established, the next consumer response is action (Young 1981). The aim of communication at this stage is to encourage trial of the service (for first-time purchasers) or repeat purchase. This can be done most effectively through sales promotions (half price offers, complimentary services) and personal selling.

The final response after purchase is consumer learning (Young 1981). This is the cognitive evaluation of the service experience and the acquisition of post-consumption experience. At this stage, the aim of communication is to reduce any cognitive dissonance and to develop a positive attitude towards the service. The tools that can achieve this are advertising ('Aren't you glad you bought a ...'), public relations (brochures, telemarketing) and website information (tips, newsletters). The desired outcome at this stage is for the consumer to be satisfied and to engage in positive activities such as word of mouth, referral and repeat purchase of the service.

Communication with other stakeholders

In a service environment, the influence of personal sources of information on customers is high (Zeithaml 1981). It is therefore especially important for a services organisation to have effective relationships with the groups who are likely to influence the purchase behaviour of the service organisation's customers.

This section covers internal customers — employees and shareholders — as well as external stakeholders — opinion leaders, media, community and lobby groups, and government. Management of communication with these external stakeholders is usually the domain of public relations. Given the influence of word of mouth on services, and the likelihood of consumers preferring personal sources of information in their pre-evaluation, the influence of these stakeholders cannot be underestimated. However, the relationship with these stakeholders must be reciprocal and based on respect rather than extortion or manipulation. For example, the website for AMP has a section on its community involvement. It played a major role in the Sydney 2000 Olympic Torch Relay, organising for thousands of Australians to relay the torch around Australia before its arrival in the Olympic stadium. This generated a great deal of publicity and goodwill towards AMP and was a unifying feature of the Olympic Games that brought Australians together.

Recognition of the variety of stakeholders' interests needs to be identified in order for communication to be effective. For example, the media (an external stakeholder) tends not to be as interested in internal company issues or a new service unless it is of interest to its readership/viewers. Thus communication with the media through media releases needs to be mindful of this and should not contain information that is deemed 'irrelevant' by the media. Some of these varied interests are outlined in table 10.4.

Table 10.4	Stakeholders' interests
Stakeholder	**Stake**
Employee	Job security, employment, job satisfaction
Shareholders	Profits/dividends, sense of ownership
Opinion leaders	Sense of responsibility, shared interest
Media	Newsworthy issues, public interest, reporting 'the truth'
Community and lobby groups	Shared interests, protection of rights
Regulatory bodies and government	Compliance with legislation, political implications, social implications

Employees

Employees are a key part of an organisation, so internal communication becomes an essential part of the communication mix. Face-to-face communication is the most effective method of communication with employees, as it allows for non-verbal communication to be taken into account and for feedback to be sought through the interaction (Gamble & Kelliher 1999). Briefing meetings are short, regular meetings where information can be imparted and discussed and staff involvement obtained (Gamble & Kelliher 1999).

In high-contact service organisations where there is a high degree of personal contact between the service personnel and the customer, the relationship between the organisation and personnel is of critical importance (Berry 1980). The service quality that is delivered requires employees to understand marketing in order to deliver the service at the highest standard. This approach is called 'internal marketing' and, in a service context, is defined as 'applying the philosophy and practices of marketing to the people that serve the external customer' (Berry 1980, p. 26).

The importance of service personnel understanding the marketing concept of 'meeting the needs of the customer through the creation of value' cannot be underestimated in a situation where the employees are part of the 'production' process of delivering the 'product' to the consumer (see chapter 12 on service delivery).

Shareholders

Shareholders are one of the more obvious stakeholders in an organisation, owing to their ownership interest. This financial interest means that shareholders are keen to obtain information on a regular basis about the performance of the organisation. This is usually done in the form of an annual report and ad hoc reports. Additionally, share prices are available on a daily basis through stockbrokers, newspapers and the Internet. The use of the Internet has made communication with shareholders a great deal easier, and many companies offer their shareholders the option of an electronic annual report in place of a printed version in order to reduce printing costs.

There are also annual general meetings held between organisations and their shareholders to brief the shareholders on company-related matters.

One of the world's most successful companies is Berkshire Hathaway (www.berkshirehathaway.com), which holds an annual gathering for shareholders that more resembles an evangelical rally than a corporate meeting. The shareholders start the meeting on Friday evening and continue until Sunday with dinners, meetings and festivities. The shareholders have a strong sense of community and many credit CEO Warren Buffet as the man behind their own financial independence.

Opinion leaders

Opinion leaders:
individuals or organisations whose opinions have a key influence on a consumer's purchasing process, products or services

Opinion leaders play an important role in services marketing. Given the increased emphasis on personal sources of information, opinion leaders who are known to the consumer can play either an advocate or adversarial role for an organisation. So too can opinion leaders who are not personally known to the consumer and who have no vested interest in the transaction. This can include industry leaders or associations such as the Australian Marketing Institute, the Law Society and the Australian Medical Association. If these opinion leaders endorse a product, this provides a great deal of credibility and reassurance to the consumer.

Services Marketing Action:
Sensis

Sensis is an Australian organisation that is a majority owned subsidiary of Telstra. While most Australians would not be familiar with the name of this organisation, they are very familiar with the services and products provided, including the Yellow Pages™ and the White Pages™. Sensis has two primary markets for the Yellow Pages products: the business customer who pays for advertising, and the consumer who uses the product.

The Yellow Pages directories generate close to A$1 billion each year from advertising revenue. With more than 80 per cent of the customer base defined as small business, it is important that Sensis has the support of opinion leaders who influence small business. This includes local chambers of commerce, government departments and industry associations such as the Motor Trades Association. In order to maintain goodwill with these groups, as well as provide resources for their advertisers, Sensis has embarked on a number of public relations campaigns to influence opinion leaders. These include the Yellow Pages Business Ideas Grants, and Yellow Pages Small Business Index.

The Yellow Pages Business Ideas Grants is a PR campaign that offers cash grants for people with a good idea that they would like to turn into a business. This campaign is publicised on The Small Business Show on Channel 9. This show presents information relevant to small business and acts as an opinion leader. Thus, when the show reports on the grants, this lends credibility and approval to Sensis, the company responsible for the grants. The Yellow Pages Small Business Index is quarterly research commissioned by Sensis to report on consumer and business confidence. The results of this report are widely reported in the media and used in government papers. The use of these figures by business opinion leaders, such as the media and government, again lends approval and credibility to Sensis.

Media

The role of the news media is to inform the public on issues that are deemed to be relevant. Interestingly, the news media have traditionally perceived their role to be that of a seeker of truth and justice, and many perceive other professional communicators, such as those involved in public relations, as little more than highly paid spin doctors. However, according to the National President of the Public Relations Institute of Australia, almost half the content of newspapers originated from PR sources (Macnamara 2001).

There are some important issues that service organisations must consider if they wish to communicate effectively with the news media. First, it is necessary to build a relationship with the media to find out what the various editors and journalists value in a news story. Second, public relations practitioners need to write media releases with the audience in mind. If the public is not interested in your company's latest cleaning service, then neither is the media. There must be an angle to the story and it must be newsworthy if you want to get it into the media. Being aware of the processes, deadlines and core interests of your target audience (the media) can be the difference between gaining media coverage and not receiving a mention.

Community and lobby groups

Community and lobby groups may consist of members from any of the other stakeholder groups. Community groups are linked not only by their location or government but also by their particular interests, and may not have originally been formed as a lobby group (a local cyclists association, for example). Lobby groups are linked by a particular issue, interest or group of issues, and not necessarily by their location. They have usually been formed with the main intention of influencing government policy or enlisting support for their 'issue'. Community and lobby groups can use their power in both official and unofficial ways, from writing a complaint letter to holding a street protest. Consider the anti-globalisation lobby group. This is a worldwide movement that selected 1 May 2001 as a major day of protest. Outside stock exchanges around the world, members of this lobby group protested against what they claimed was the cultural imperialism of global companies such as McDonald's and Nike.

In some cases, these community and lobby groups establish websites aimed at promoting and disseminating negative word-of-mouth material about organisations. This can be very harmful to organisations and difficult to track.

These groups can have a real impact on an organisation's bottom line, particularly if the issue is of interest to the media. It is important that service organisations identify the key community groups who are stakeholders. This may be anything from the local parents and citizens group to an international movement. Service organisations need to involve them in consultation, open forums, calls for expressions of interest, community panels or advisory boards, all of which can be effective mechanisms for providing two-way communication with these groups. If the organisation has a relationship with the group, it is far more likely to be able to respond and deal with a crisis.

Regulatory bodies and government

Key stakeholders for any organisation are regulatory bodies and the government. They set the legal environment within which all marketing occurs. This includes aspects of pricing and promotion, as well as service delivery issues.

The Australian Securities and Investment Commission (ASIC) oversees the Australian financial services industry. It monitors compliance issues and conducts audits on companies and advisers in the industry. Communicating with this regulatory body is essential in order to understand the compliance issues and legal requirements of day-to-day operations. ASIC's website www.asic.gov.au, provides service organisations with access to this information; publicises scams and illegal deals for consumers to be wary of; and awards the worst scam a Gull of the Month award.

Ethical Issues:
The role of communication

The role of advertising on consumer choices has long been discussed in terms of ethical responsibilities. However, the rest of the promotional mix in marketing also has ethical issues that need to be managed.

Advertising

Does art influence reality or reality influence art? How much of a role does advertising play in influencing the standards of society? Does it set the pace or merely reflect existing trends and attitudes? The portrayal of women in advertising has generated much discussion, as does the use of advertising to encourage smoking and alcohol consumption. Additionally, should marketers be advertising to children who sometimes can't tell the difference between television programs and advertising?

Internet and direct marketing

Privacy is a key issue when using the Internet or direct marketing tools to communicate with customers. The new privacy laws in Australia require organisations to seek permission from customers before they contact them for promotional purposes. There are additional issues regarding privacy and the sale of databases and lists. How would you like to find your details being sold to businesses who then send you offers through the mail?

Public relations

Public relations is in the unenviable position of being in the firing line whenever disaster strikes an organisation. They need to balance the organisation's need to maintain a positive corporate image against the social/public good of other stakeholders. The Public Relations Institute of Australia has a code of ethics for its members that clearly states its requirements. (See www.pria.com.au.)

Sales promotions

In 2001, the retailer Target was in trouble for overuse of disclaimers in its sales promotions. The use of fine-print is necessary for many promotions but how far should it go? Have a look at the promotions offered by mobile phone dealers. There are more conditions than offers. Virgin Mobile identified this as a problem and set about positioning itself as the 'no fine print' service provider.

Personal selling

In many sales oriented organisations, the compensation plans for sales people only reward sales made. This can create a 'win at all costs' attitude rather than a focus on the long term interests of the customer. The pressure of commission-only jobs can encourage sales people to 'promise the world' in order to get the sale, which may be at the expense of satisfying the customer's needs.

Summary

LO1: Understand the nature of communication and its complexity.

- Communication is highly problematic, owing to the complexity of creating shared meaning.
- Influences such as context, personal experience, values, the nature of the relationship, individual traits and previous communication lead to a variety of understandings and perceptions.
- Communication is made more difficult because the core characteristics of a service increase the potential for misunderstanding.

LO2: Understand how the characteristics of services influence communication in services marketing.

- Intangibility creates difficulty for consumers who want to pre-evaluate the service. The role of communication is to reduce the level of risk and increase the costs of switching to another service provider.
- Inseparability increases the importance of one-to-one communication through personal selling, which acts as a method of risk-reduction for the consumer and as source of pre-evaluation information.
- Perishability creates the need for an organisation to communicate additional/different benefits of its service to customers in order to encourage purchase in off-peak times.
- Heterogeneity leads to inconsistency of creating shared meaning. This means that communication is situation specific, and is influenced by the participants in the process.

LO3: Identify seven strategies for achieving effective communication for services marketing.

- Managing expectations using communication can be done through promising what is able to be delivered, presenting clear images of what the service consists of and focusing on the tangible aspects of the service.
- Communication must be consistent across the organisation and, in particular, the key messages communicated in a marketing campaign must be consistent with the operational aspects of the organisation.
- Communication can influence consumers' responses by focusing initially on emotions, then encouraging purchase and, finally, providing information and opinions.
- Effective management of non-verbal communication can result in customer evaluation of the service provider as friendly, courteous, empathetic, competent and credible.
- The use of branding and third-party endorsements in communication reduces perceived risk by establishing credibility.
- The servicescape is a tangible indicator of benefits, quality and images.
- Appropriate positioning strategies can assist in 'tangibilising' the services in the customer's mind.

LO4: Demonstrate how to use various communication tools in order to achieve service objectives.

- There are six key tools for communicating with customers: advertising, personal selling, sales promotion, Internet, public relations and word-of-mouth communication.
- Advertising can be used to provide information, positioning, awareness and long-term demand. It can create perceptions that lead to appropriate expectations.

- Personal selling can be used to explain high-value or complex services and be used to clarify or correct inappropriate expectations.
- Sales promotion can be used to generate excitement or smooth demand to reduce risk for the purchase of a service.
- The Internet can be used to promote a service or provide information about it. This can be tailored to an individual context or experience.
- Public relations assists the organisation in communicating with its stakeholders and creating shared meaning.
- Word of mouth can be used to increase referrals and reduce perceived risk, which is more likely to be higher for the purchase of a service than a good.
- Each of these performs a different function, but they need be co-ordinated into an integrated approach to communicate a consistent message.

LO5: Understand the importance of communication with non-customer stakeholders.
- The influence of employees, shareholders, opinion-leaders, media, government and community groups on the final decision/choice of the customer is very important in a service context.
- The goodwill of those groups who hold a stake in the organisation is important to maintain, particularly in times of crisis.
- The role of employees as service providers affects the performance and delivery of the service.
- Opinion leaders act as personal and credible sources of information to influence purchase decisions.

 *key terms*

Advertising: any paid form of non-personal presentation of ideas, goods or services (p. 249)

Communication: the creation of shared meaning between participants (p. 236)

Hierarchy of effects: the order of responses a consumer has to a marketing communication (p. 242)

Opinion leaders: Individuals or organisations whose opinions have a key influence on a consumer's purchasing process, products or services (p. 258)

Personal selling: a two-way communication process in which a salesperson engages with a potential customer for the purpose of selling a good or service (p. 250)

Positioning: the process of influencing the consumer's perception of a good or service using the marketing mix (p. 247)

Public relations: the process of managing communications with key stakeholders of an organisation for mutual benefit and a positive outcome (p. 254)

Sales promotion: a promotion that directly stimulates a sale, usually offered at the point of sale (p. 250)

Social constructionist theory: contemporary communication theory that views communication as the dynamic creation of shared meaning between participants (p. 237)

Sponsorship: where an organisation provides funds for an event or another organisation in order to create a positive association (p. 254)

Stakeholder: any individual who feels they have a stake in the consequence of an organisation's decisions (p. 254)

Transmission model: a model that views communication through a conduit metaphor, as messages that are 'transmitted' from one party to another (p. 236)

Word of mouth: conversations by consumers about a product or service (p. 254)

 review questions

1. What is the difference between the transmission model and social constructionist theories of communication?
2. How do the four key characteristics of services impact on communication?
3. What is the difference in the role of emotion (feel) between the service hierarchy-of-effects models and the other goods-focused, hierarchy-of-effects models?
4. Why is the servicescape important? How does it communicate?
5. What are the key purposes of each of the six key communication tools for customers?
6. Why is it important to communicate with non-customer stakeholders?
7. If word of mouth is difficult to control, how can it be part of a formal communication program?

 application questions

1. If you were opening a new hair salon, with whom would you communicate and what communication tools would you use?
2. Imagine you are establishing a new medical centre. How would you use communication to overcome the problems associated with intangibility, inseparability, perishability and heterogeneity?
3. Think of a document you recently received from a service provider. Were you satisfied with it as a communication medium? Suggest how it could have been improved.
4. Design a communication campaign for a service organisation with which you are familiar and which uses three of the communication tools outlined. Outline the objectives of each tool.
5. Consider a recent advertisement you have seen. Did it contain emotional or informational content? Was this appropriate? Why or why not?

vignette questions

1. Read the International Issues vignette on page 241. To what extent do you think international companies should localise their communication?
2. Read the Services Marketing on the Web vignette on page 253. Given the lack of personal interaction on the Internet, do you think the extranet of

Carpet Court will reduce the relationship it has with its franchise owners? Why or why not?

3. Read the Services Marketing Action vignette on page 258. How effective do you think the publicity tactics of Sensis are in gaining the confidence of small business opinion leaders? Refer to the Sensis website for details on the programs.

4. Read the Ethical Issues vignette on page 260. How would you overcome some of the negative issues for communication raised in this vignette?

recommended readings

It is important to understand the key differences between goods and services and the implications for marketing. These are outlined in:

Berry, L .L. 1980, 'Services marketing is different', *Business*, May–June, pp. 24–9.

For students more familiar with the transmission model of communication, a discussion of contemporary approaches to communication and comparison with the transmission model is outlined in the chapter 'Theories and models of communication' in:

Lewis, G. & Slade. C. 2000, *Critical Communication*, Prentice Hall, Sydney.

The addition of the services hierarchy of effects is outlined in detail along with the other three hierarchies of effects proposed by Ray (1973) in:

Young, R. F. 1981, 'The advertising of consumer services and the hierarchy of effects', in Donnelly, J. H. & George, W. R. (eds), *Marketing of Services*, American Marketing Association, Chicago, pp. 196–9.

The evaluation process using the model of search qualities is outlined in:

Zeithaml, V. 1981, 'How consumer evaluation processes differ between goods and services', in Donnelly, J. H. & George, W. R. (eds), *Marketing of Services*, American Marketing Association, Chicago, pp. 186–90.

references

Ajzen, I. & Fishbein, M. 1980, *Understanding Attitudes and Predicting Social Behavior*, Prentice Hall, New Jersey.

Berry, L .L. 1980, 'Services marketing is different', *Business*, May–June, pp. 24–9.

Bitner, M. J. 1992, 'Service-scapes: the impact of physical surroundings on customers and employees', *Journal of Marketing*, vol. 56, pp. 57–71.

Blankson, C. & Kalafatis, S. 1999, 'Issues of creative communication tactics and positioning strategies in the UK plastic card services industry', *Journal of Marketing Communications*, vol. 5, pp. 55–70.

Caldow, D. 1998, 'The relational elements of service loyalty: an exploratory study', *Australia and New Zealand Marketing Academy Conference*, Dunedin, New Zealand.

Chandler, D., accessed 3 April 2001, *Communication Theories*, research report, www.aber.ac.uk/media/Documents/short.trans.html.

Chandler, D., accessed March 2002, 'The transmission model of communication', www.aber.ac.uk/Media/Documents/short/trans.html.

Christiansen, T. & Tax, S. S. 2000, 'Measuring word-of-mouth: the questions of who and when?', *Journal of Marketing Communications*, vol. 6, pp. 185–99.

Clemes, M., Mollenkopf, D. & Burn D. 2000, 'An investigation of marketing problems across service typologies', *Journal of Services Marketing*, vol. 14, no. 7, pp. 573–94.

Czepiel, J. A., Soloman, M. R. & Surprenant C. F. 1985, *The Service Encounter*, Lexington Books, Lexington, MA.

Doney, P. M. & Cannon, J. P. 1997, 'An examination of the nature of trust in buyer–seller relationships', *Journal of Marketing*, vol. 61, pp. 35–51.

Ehrenberg, A. S. C, Hammond, K. & Goodhardt, G. J. 1994, 'The after effects of price-related consumer promotions', *Journal of Advertising Research*, vol. 34 no. 4, pp. 11–21.

Ennew, C., Watkins, T. & Wright, M. (eds) 1995, *Marketing Financial Services*, Butterworth-Heinemann, Oxford.

Fournier, S. & Yao J. L. 1997, 'Reviving brand loyalty: a reconceptualisation within the framework of consumer-brand relationships', *International Journal of Marketing*, vol. 14, pp. 451–73.

Gamble, P. R. & Kelliher, C. E. 1999, 'Imparting information and influencing behaviour: an examination of staff briefing sessions', *The Journal of Business Communication*, vol. 36, no. 3, pp. 261–79.

Ganesan, S. 1994, 'Determinants of long-term orientation in buyer–seller relationships', *Journal of Marketing*, vol. 58, no. 2, pp. 1–19.

Garver, M. S. & Flint, D. J. 1995, 'A proposed framework for exploring comparison standards at various stages of the business-to-business relationship evolution', *Journal of Consumer Satisfaction, Dissatisfaction and Complaining Behaviour*, vol. 8, pp. 11–21.

Gregory, A. 2001, 'Public relations and evaluation: does the reality match the rhetoric?', *Journal of Marketing Communications*, vol. 7, pp. 171–89.

Grove, S. J., Pickett, G. M, & Laband, D. N. 1995, 'An empirical examination of factual information content amongst service advertisements', *The Services Industries Journal*, vol. 15, April, pp. 216–33.

Hill, D. J. & Nimish. G. 1992, 'Services advertising: a framework to its effectiveness', *Journal of Services Marketing*, vol. 6, fall, pp. 63–76.

IAB, accessed 13 February 2001, *Measuring Success*, research report, www.iab.net.

IPRO, accessed 13 February 2001, *Ad Leaders Report: Assessing Measurement Systems Online and Off*, www.topicalnet.com/downloads/ipro/ipro_ad_survey.pdf.

Kim, J., Lim, J. & Bhargava, M. 1998, 'The role of affect in attitude formation: a classical conditioning approach', *Journal of the Academy of Marketing Science*, vol. 26, no. 2, pp. 143–52.

Krugman, H. E. 1965, 'The impact of TV advertising — learning without involvement', *Public Opinion Quarterly*, vol. 29, fall, pp. 349–56.

Lewis, G. & Slade. C. 2000, *Critical Communication*, Prentice Hall, Sydney, pp. 2–11.

Lovelock, C. & Quelch, J. A. 1983, 'Consumer promotions in service marketing', *Business Horizons*, May–June, pp. 66–75.

Macnamara, J., accessed 11 October 2001, *The Impact of PR on the Media*, research report www.pria.com.au/papersandresearch.html.

Morgan, R. M. & Hunt, S. D. 1994, 'The commitment–trust theory of relationship marketing', *Journal of Marketing*, vol. 58, no. 3, pp. 20–38.

Morris, M. H. 1992, *Industrial and Organisational Marketing*, Macmillan, Sydney.

Mortimer, K. 2000, 'Are services advertised differently? An analysis of the relationship between product and services types and the informational content of their advertisements', *Journal of Marketing Communications*, vol. 6, pp. 121–34.

Murray, K. B. 1991, 'A test of services marketing theory: consumer information acquisition activities', *Journal of Marketing*, vol. 55, pp. 10–25.

National Australia Bank, accessed September 2001, www.national.com.au.

Oakes, S. 2000, 'The influence of the musicscape within service environments', *Journal of Services Marketing*, vol. 14, no. 7, pp. 539–56.

Oliver, R. 1980. 'A cognitive model of the antecedents and consequences of satisfaction decisions', *Journal of Marketing Research*, vol. 17, no. 4, pp. 460–9.

Oliver, R. L. 1989, 'Processing of the satisfaction response in consumption: a suggested framework and research propositions', *Journal of Consumer Satisfaction, Dissatisfaction and Complaining Behaviour*, vol. 2, pp. 1–6.

Pearce, W. B. 1994, 'Understanding conversations', in *Interpersonal Communication: Making Social Worlds*, Harper Collins, New York, pp. 17–25.

Ray, M. 1973, 'Marketing communication and the hierarchy-of-effects', research paper, Stanford University, no. 180.

Reynolds, K., accessed 3 April, 'Critiquing the Transmission Model', report, www.aber.ac.uk/education/undergrad/ED10510/karenr.html.

Reynolds, K., accessed March 2001, 'What is the transmission model of interpersonal communication and what is wrong with it?', www.aber.ac.uk/media/Modules/ED10510/Karenr.html.

Shannon, C. E. & Weaver, W. 1949, *The Mathematical Theory of Communication*, University of Illinois Press, Urbana, IL.

Sharma, N. & Patterson, P. G. 1999, 'The impact of communication effectiveness and service quality on relationship commitment in consumer, professional services', *Journal of Services Marketing*, vol. 13, no. 2, pp. 151–70.

Silvestro, R., Fitzgerald, L., Johnston, R. & Voss, C. 1992, 'Towards a classification of service processes', *International Journal of Service Industry Management*, vol. 3, no. 3, pp. 62–75.

Slater, J. 2001, 'Is couponing an effective promotional strategy? An examination of the Proctor and Gamble zero-coupon test', *Journal of Marketing Communications*, vol. 7, pp. 3–9.

Sundaram, D. S. & Webster, C. 2000, 'The role of nonverbal communication in service encounters', *Journal of Services Marketing*, vol. 14, no. 5, pp. 378–91.

Ticehurst, G. W. & Ross-Smith, A. 1998, 'Professional communication, organisations and management', *Australian Journal of Communication*, vol. 25, no. 2, pp. 1–12.

Van Doren, D. C., Fechner, D. L. & Green-Adelsberger, K. 2000, 'Promotional strategies on the World Wide Web', *Journal of Marketing Communications*, vol. 6, pp. 21–35.

Westbrook, R. A. 1987, 'Product/consumption-based affective responses and postpurchase processes', *Journal of Marketing Research*, vol. 24, pp. 258–70.

Young, R. F. 1981, 'The advertising of consumer services and the hierarchy of effects', in Donnelly, J. H. & George, W. R. (eds), *Marketing of Services*, American Marketing Association, Chicago, pp. 196–9.

Zeithaml, V. 1981, 'How consumer evaluation processes differ between goods and services', in Donnelly, J. H. & George, W. R. (eds) *Marketing of Services*, American Marketing Association, Chicago, pp. 186–90.

Zeithaml, V. A., Parasuraman, A. & Berry, L. L. 1985, 'Problems and strategies in services marketing', *Journal of Marketing*, vol. 49, pp. 33–46.

Chapter 11
Service product pricing

Tony Ward

LEARNING OBJECTIVES

After reading this chapter you should be able to:

- identify and discuss the fundamentals of pricing service products
- discuss how consumers perceive price and value
- discuss pricing decisions from a market forces perspective
- analyse pricing situations for service products
- identify and discuss the main considerations in determining a pricing strategy.

CHAPTER OUTLINE

There are several factors that determine how organisations set prices for service products and these factors have been arranged in three main sections. Firstly, the fundamentals of the pricing of service products are discussed and seven main elements are identified. Secondly, there is a discussion of nine market force factors that place the pricing of service products in context, and these are factors that must constantly be kept in mind. Finally, pricing strategies, which provide a framework for making the price decision, are identified and discussed.

The chapter is based on the pricing of consumer service products, rather than business-to-business product pricing.

Introduction

The pricing of service products should be determined by the interaction of :

- profit goals
- costs
- the balance of supply and demand
- competition
- market regulation
- what customers are prepared to pay for a given product.

The basic theories of pricing are equally applicable to service products as to goods. However, there are a number of additional factors that contribute to determining the best marketing strategy for pricing service products. These factors are to do with the difficulty customers have in identifying, for example, their needs, determining their perception of value, understanding the product being purchased, and making product comparisons.

This chapter seeks to identify specific issues for the pricing of service products rather than covering too much basic ground on pricing in general. However, there is a brief overview of fundamental pricing factors.

Fundamental pricing factors

There are a number of fundamental pricing factors that need to be discussed before looking at the price decision making process: definitions, pricing goals, costs and break-even point, elasticity, demand and supply issues, and temporal fluctuations in demand. In addition, the final part of this section discusses the price implications of the special characteristics of services.

Price: the amount of money (or some other item that is exchanged or bartered) that a buyer exchanges for a service product provided by the seller

It is appropriate to commence by giving basic definitions of both 'price' and 'pricing'. **Price** is the amount of money (or some other item that is exchanged or bartered) that a buyer exchanges for a service product provided by a seller.

Price is therefore defined as an exchange of values, in which the buyer gives 'an amount of money' (or other item that is 'bartered') to a supplier in exchange for a service product. In theory, the product is thus worth more to the buyer than the price paid, and the money (price paid) is worth more to the seller than the cost of producing the service. Again, in theory, everyone gains utility or value by exchanging something they perceive as being of lesser value for something they perceive as being of greater value. Hence, this simple philosophy reflects the main principle of the 'transaction' or 'exchange' in marketing (and business).

As indicated above, there are occasions where no money changes hands, but there is an exchange of items, as would occur in a barter situation. Some services are 'free', such as many government services, in which case a service may be provided without any reciprocal payment or item being exchanged, in which case no 'price' is calculated or charged.

Pricing: the process by which an organisation decides on the price of a service product

Pricing is the process by which an organisation decides on the price of a service product. Thus, pricing is recognised as a process that an organisation engages in to make a decision on the price (and thus value) it wants for the service product offered for sale. This recognition that pricing is a conscious decision is also fundamental to marketing, and is one of the reasons that setting the price of a service product is so important to businesses. As discussed above, there are situations where there is an exchange of an item for a service. If the service is provided free of charge, there is no price set, but in some situations it is to both parties' advantage that no money changes hands but that there is an exchange of values. The introduction of the GST in Australia has, however, made such transactions rather more complicated, as they may be GST assessable, in which case GST may be levied even though no money has changed hands.

Pricing goals

The first thing that an organisation must do when pricing a service product is to decide on the **pricing goals** of the organisation. These goals are closely related to pricing strategy and force us to focus on the organisation's pricing requirements. There are several overall goals that an organisation could have, and these will be reflected in the criteria for deciding on the price for a service product (or products):

* to maximise profit (short and/or long term)
* to build market share
* to maximise immediate cash flow
* to maximise long-term customer perceptions of value of the product
* to position the product in a certain place in customers' minds
* to target a given segment of the market.

In certain situations, two or more of these goals could be pursued at the same time. For example, an electricity supply company could jointly aim to build market share and maximise immediate cash flow by pricing its service product (electricity) very competitively. The effect of such competitive pricing would be to attract new customers and retain existing customers, so that short-term cash flow and market share are maximised, but at the expense of lower profits in the short term (or even a loss short term). In the late 1990s and early 2000s, the world saw many examples of this motivation for pricing in the Asia-Pacific region by service providers who ultimately rely on high production volumes for success — telecom companies, satellite television services, Internet providers and so on. If they do not obtain high market share, they do not get the advantages of scale and cannot become competitive in the marketplace. Since 1990 there has been a very rapid rise in the provision of Internet services at home by Internet Service Providers (ISPs), using telephone connections. These ISPs have grown at a phenomenal rate in a most competitive industry. In order to be competitive, they initially rely on attracting large numbers of customers at below cost-price levels that are unsustainable in the long term. Thus the organisations were setting prices below cost to achieve the overall goal of attracting customers. Gradually, prices were raised to above cost levels, but many organisations could not attract the volume of business required to make them profitable. Consequently, most of these organisations went out of business between 2000 and 2002. This is a classic case where too much competition (and consequent oversupply) resulted in the marketplace effectively regulating itself, so supply was reduced to match demand. The surviving ISP organisations were those that were best able to match their pricing goals to their ability to perform, largely due to having sufficient financial strength to outlast the competition.

Thus, the pricing goals of an organisation are fundamental, and must be determined prior to making pricing decisions.

Costs and break-even

In the long run, all organisations must make a profit to survive (except charities and other not-for-profit organisations). Whatever the pricing goals and short-term objectives of an organisation, the price must be greater than the total cost of providing the service product. The base cost of a service product thus sets a long-term line above which the price must be set. Short-term considerations may enable a price to be set lower than cost, but this situation can only prevail if the organisation has the finances to survive the ensuing loss.

Costs generally comprise two components: fixed costs and variable costs. The fixed costs are, by definition, unchanging, for example rates, rent, permanent staff salaries and other fixed overheads. In contrast, variable costs vary with the number of service products provided, and include casual staff salaries and consumables. In some organisations the fixed costs are high relative to variable costs, as in capital intensive industries such as electricity supply companies and airlines. In others, variable costs dominate, as in a consultancy where fixed costs are low compared to variables.

A costing technique that has received much attention recently is **activity based costing** (ABC). This technique focuses on the activities that an organisation has to undertake in order to produce a product, which could be either a good or service. The technique essentially targets the activity and the resources expended to complete that activity. Proponents of ABC claim that it is a more accurate way of costing the production of both goods and service products, because it pinpoints the costs associated with different products. Whatever technique is used to compile cost data for products, accurate data is required by all organisations, whether profit or not-for-profit.

It is thus essential to know how the costs of providing a service product are made up, including the fixed component and the variable component. It is also essential to know how variable costs change with volume of business, as many businesses (especially those with high fixed costs) require a high minimum volume level to reach break-even, but they accumulate profits quickly once that volume level is exceeded. Figure 11.1 shows two organisations, one with low fixed costs and high variable costs (Firm A), and one with high fixed costs and low variable costs (Firm B).

Activity-based costing: a costing technique that focuses on the activities that an organisation has to undertake in order to produce a (service) product

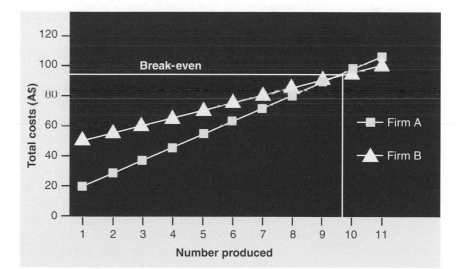

Figure 11.1: Different break-even components

As can be seen in figure 11.1, the break-even points are very similar, but are made up of very different fixed and variable cost components. It is essential for price decision makers to know these components of the service product before commencing the pricing decision process.

Elasticity

*Elasticity: the degree of price sensitivity, relating change in price to the effect on demand for a product

The principle of **elasticity** applies just as much to the pricing of service products as to goods. Demand for a service product is termed 'elastic' if a change in price results in a greater change in demand for the service product. Thus the market is known as price sensitive; that is, a small change in price results in a relatively high change in demand (Danaher & Brodie 2000). Conversely, inelastic demand is the opposite: a small change of price has very little effect on demand. The setting of prices in an elastic market is thus much more critical than in an inelastic market. In reality, the situation is more complex, as there may be situations where the degree of elasticity varies at different pricing levels. In all cases the elasticity of prices for a product must be known (Cracknell & Knott 1995).

The hospitality industry, for example, is subject to seasonal fluctuations in demand. In Australia and New Zealand, demand slumps every February after the summer holiday over Christmas and New Year. To counter this slump, many hotels and resorts offer discounts to attract extra customers. In determining the size of the discount, the hotel must identify how much is required to significantly boost demand without underpricing. A five-star resort may find demand inelastic at its normal room rates of $175 per room per night, so offering a 10 per cent discount has very little effect on demand. Even a 30 per cent discount ($124) has limited effect. However, because February is a very slow month, when a 'February special' of $99 dollars is offered, demand may jump by over 300 per cent. What is happening in this situation is that people who would not normally contemplate spending $175 per night will jump at the chance to stay in a five-star resort for $99. Thus the targeted market segment has been expanded to include price-sensitive customers who are usually outside the target market because of price considerations.

Knowing your target market, and the characteristics of potential customers outside your usual target market, is therefore important. This aspect is all about knowing your customers.

Demand and supply issues

One of the most important issues in economics, the balance between supply and demand, is also critical for marketers when setting prices of service products. If the supply exceeds demand then pricing will be competitive, but if demand exceeds supply, then there is more scope for marketers to raise prices. At the start of the twenty-first century, organisations found a situation in which most consumer goods were in oversupply, not just because of the mild recession then underway, but also because of the tremendous advances of production technology in the last 50 years and low labour costs in many countries. The result was the oversupply of most commonly available manufactured goods, the exceptions being a few new and innovative products. These oversupply market conditions, especially where there are several competitors openly displaying their prices, create perfect market conditions for consumers who can shop around, compare products and prices to get the best value for their own needs, and make an informed purchase decision. The situation is much less clear cut where service products are concerned, for a number of reasons:

1. Mass production techniques, such as the use of robots, are often not applicable to the provision of service products, which generally demand more human effort.
2. Many goods can be manufactured where labour is inexpensive and transported to another country for sale. Many service products cannot be provided that way as they are created in situ, at the time of demand.

3. Fluctuations in demand for many goods can be accommodated by storage of the product. However, for many service products there are diurnal, weekly, monthly or seasonal fluctuations in demand. Moreover, services cannot be stored. Thus service firms must have the flexible capability to provide the service product when and where customers demand.

4. It is generally more difficult for customers to compare the values (product attributes, benefits and price) of service products than of goods, owing to the intangible nature of service products. Therefore service product purchasers have a greater risk of not getting good value than do goods purchasers.

5. Even when a service product market is in oversupply, there are often times and places where there is local undersupply, resulting in the supplier being able to charge a higher price than normal.

6. Convenience service products are often priced at a premium. You can get a hire car at an international airport without booking, but the rental will be significantly higher (often twice the daily rate) than if you had pre-booked.

Thus, although the ratio of supply and demand are important considerations in setting prices, local conditions and the type of product offered may be much more influential in setting the price of service products.

Temporal fluctuations in demand

One of the traditional characteristics of service products, which differentiate them from goods, is that they cannot be stored. There are some exceptions. For example, electricity supply companies often generate excess electricity in off-peak periods, store that power, and have it available for peak periods. Likewise, insurance organisations, banks and finance companies provide insurance cover and 'store' money 24 hours a day. However, for many service product providers there is no storage capability. For example, a vacant seat on an aircraft is lost forever, and, if the doctor's queue is too long, patients will go elsewhere or go unattended. As discussed above, demand fluctuates for many service products, resulting in local over- and under-supply conditions. Such fluctuations can be quite challenging for the service provider; they must have enough staff on duty when demand is high, but not too many when supply is light. Demand is not always predictable, as customers tend to arrive at random intervals, creating overdemand and underdemand within the space of only a few minutes.

Temporal fluctuations in demand: *variations in demand over time, often within a time span of a few minutes*

How an organisation deals with such **temporal fluctuations in demand** will have a significant influence on customer perceptions of the quality of the service product provided. In some cases it is only a question of having sufficient staff available but, in many situations, certain facilities are also required that may be expensive to provide. There is thus a trade-off required between the level of service quality provided and the cost of maintaining that level of quality. All of these considerations affect the cost of provision and thus the price charged for the service product. Therefore, as most service products cannot be stored, temporal fluctuations in demand must be accommodated by the service product provider, and appropriate trade-offs made between the cost of providing a certain level of service quality (including queue length) and the convenience to the customer.

Pricing implications of the special characteristics of services

Only one of the five characteristics of services presents specific challenges for marketers when setting prices: intangibility. A brief review is given here of the potential implications of intangibility when setting prices.

One of the great difficulties for customers is how to determine whether or not a given service represents good value. The main reason for this difficulty is that if the service is not well understood, it is difficult to evaluate. Many goods are relatively easy to evaluate, as a buyer can view the product, sometimes test it, and assess its performance prior to purchase. Marketers refer to such products as being high in search qualities; that is, many attributes of the product can be determined prior to purchase, thus taking much risk out of the purchase decision. However, some goods are not so easily evaluated and need to be experienced before they can be evaluated. For example, the only way of determining whether or not a new breadmaker performs well is to purchase one, take it home and make the type of bread you like; that is, the product must be used or experienced before an evaluation can be made. Likewise, many service products need to be experienced before they can be properly evaluated, which is one reason why we refer to the experiential nature of services.

However, there are some services that are very difficult to evaluate, because even when they are performed well, the customer may not know just how well. An example would be the service of an investment fund manager. One can look at past performance, but every investor knows that such an indicator is no guarantee of future performance. Very often the decision is made on a 'credence' basis. That is, the customer relies on the credentials of the fund manager, or any recommendation made by a credible person such as a solicitor or bank manager, or some other factors that add credence to the decision. Such service products are said to be high in credence values, making it difficult for the customer to independently evaluate the service. In this example, it is only with the passage of time that the customer will be able to evaluate whether the choice was a good one or not, based on the long-term performance of the fund.

The intangibility factor is not only apparent to purchasers when trying to choose the 'best' service for their needs, but also in determining what price represents good value for that service. For more on value issues and, in particular, customer perceived value, see chapter 6.

Setting prices

The process of setting prices varies between organisations, and there is no universal method. However, there are a number of principles that can be applied to the process. A six-step guide is given below for the pricing of a new product.

- *Step 1 — know costs.* It is essential for an organisation to know how much a product costs to produce. This is no easy task in any organisation, but in many service organisations there are specific difficulties associated with identifying exact costs for each service product, particularly when many different products are offered. Irrespective of other considerations in setting a price, an organisation must have a reasonably accurate knowledge of how much each product costs.

- *Step 2 — know competitors' costs.* Virtually every marketplace today is highly competitive. Customers have a range of products to choose from, and these come from direct competitors. In addition, some tasks can be achieved by customers using an alternative service from indirect competitors. For example, when booking a flight, the customer has the choice of booking by telephone, on the Internet, in an airline office, or through a tour operator, travel agent or some other tourism organisation. In each of these cases there are different suppliers competing for the customer's business. For example, there are several travel agents in most towns and cities. It is essential, therefore, to collect competitor's prices, both for direct competitors and indirect competitors.

- *Step 3 — identifying fundamental pricing factors.* Earlier in this section we identified and discussed fundamental pricing factors. It is essential to know the impact of each one on the price set, as it will guide decision making on prices and price variability (as when catering, say, for weekly fluctuations in hotel room prices, or the difference between elastic and inelastic products). In addition, pricing goals must be identified by this step.
- *Step 4 — identify market forces.* Market forces are discussed in the next section. All of these factors are important, but their relative importance will vary case by case. Usually one or two of these factors will be dominant, while the others are of secondary importance. Identifying the dominant factors is critical in each pricing process.
- *Step 5 — pricing strategy.* The four steps above are all processes that must be completed before a pricing strategy is developed. The factors that need to be incorporated in this step are described in the section on pricing strategies later in this chapter.
- *Step 6 — the pricing decision.* Finally a price needs to be set. Normally there is much more to pricing than just setting a single price for a product. Typically, an organisation will issue a set of accompanying rules or guidelines to staff, covering such issues as:
  - variability with size of order
  - variations arising from any source (such as variations in demand with time, special events)
  - discounting policy (in general or for specific customers such as shareholders)
  - degree of empowerment for service providers and their supervisors to reduce prices in given situations
  - remediation, including but not limited to compensation, when mistakes are identified or when customers complain
  - any other factor requiring specific policy and/or pricing decisions.

As can be seen, the setting of prices is no simple task. In addition, once the guidelines have been set, an organisation will need to monitor the marketplace continuously to identify changes in competitor prices, demand from forecasts, and so on. Markets are dynamic entities, changing continuously, and as the price charged for a service is one of the easiest marketing variables to change, so marketers need to be forever vigilant of prices set and associated policies.

Market force factors

There are a number of market forces within a marketplace, and each needs to be considered during the price decision-making process. These market forces are discussed below under the following headings: perfect price knowledge, competition, product comparisons, customer needs, customer perceptions of value, regulation, service quality, DIY versus purchase, and segmentation.

Perfect price knowledge

Most consumer goods are marketed in an open market system, where the products and prices of competitors can be compared, and consumers often use a reference price as a basis for comparison (Niedrich, Sharma & Wedell 2001). In contrast, for many service products, especially professional ones, there are often no visible prices for comparison, resulting in purchase decisions being made without knowing exactly what the eventual price will be for the service. Thus, the customer cannot make a fully informed purchase decision (Taylor & Bearden 2002).

However, this effect goes deeper because customers do not know what is being charged, and nor do competitors. With goods, for example, most petrol stations display their prices openly; many now have electronic displays that can be changed from within the pay booth and, as one company changes price and changes its display, competitors can follow — or not. They all know exactly what the others are charging for a litre of fuel. For service products this is often not the case, as competitors' prices are often not well known. If an organisation does not know exactly what a competitor's prices are, it is difficult to price one's own service on a competitive basis. This effect is compounded when competitors vary their prices frequently, particularly as most consumers cannot remember the price they paid previously (Turley & Cabaniss 1995).

Thus, during the pricing decision-making process, it is not unusual for an organisation to have to set a price without knowing exactly what competitors are charging.

Competition

The business world gets more competitive every day. This unmistakable trend in world markets has been a driving force for over a hundred years, but the pace at which competition has advanced has accelerated over the last 50 years, largely due to huge production efficiencies, internationalisation, communication effectiveness and speed, and the lowering of real transportation costs. The overall effect has been the creation of markets that are closer to being perfect than ever before. This competitive effect has been seen in some service product markets such as telecommunications, but is not so marked in other areas such as professional services. Where competitor prices are not well known, extra caution is required when setting prices of service products.

Product comparisons

As shoppers of consumer goods, most people have developed their skills in shopping around for the brand that best suits their particular needs, especially for large purchases. Making product comparisons, irrespective of price, is important to most consumers, as most people like to think they are getting a good deal when they buy. When purchasing service products, however, making such comparisons is more difficult, largely because of the intangible nature of service products. This effect is made worse when many organisations do not describe their products very well. Not being able to accurately compare service products makes the purchase decision difficult for consumers.

Consider, for example, the purchase of a superannuation policy. Research shows that a typical superannuation policy in Australia has about 300 attributes (Ward 1995), of which only about 30 are of real significance to a potential purchaser. Most people do not understand the superannuation policy they buy because the product is intangible and the subject matter unfamiliar. Consequently; they tend to make their purchase decision based on the personality of the salesperson. In contrast, a modern automobile has many thousands of components and attributes, but most people feel they have a good enough understanding to make an informed purchase decision.

Ethical Issues:
Executor to a will

James was 39 when his father passed away. There seemed to be an endless list of jobs that had to be done. One of the most important and difficult tasks was for James to act as executor to his father's will, but he had never had to do anything like that before, and had no knowledge of what was required or what his responsibilities were. At his first meeting with his father's solicitor, James explained that he was new to the process and was apprehensive about his responsibilities. He then asked exactly what the solicitor actually did for his considerable fee. The solicitor immediately took offence. Apparently no-one had ever asked him to describe his service before, and he interpreted the question as a challenge to his professional status and integrity.

When he had recomposed himself, the solicitor tried to put together a list of activities and regulatory requirements, but after several minutes said it was too complicated and he would have to 'think about it'. Clearly the solicitor had not sat down and simply listed the actions and responsibilities involved in executing a service that he had provided many hundreds of times before.

Such situations are not atypical of many professions, which leaves the customer with the impression that it is all done with 'smoke and mirrors'. Clients should have some idea of just what they are paying for. To help people like James, it would be quite simple for a solicitor to prepare a short overview of the legal requirements and processes, thereby giving the client/executor some idea of what was involved and what were the respective responsibilities of the solicitor and executor.

The ethical issue is: should professionals make a greater effort to describe the service they are delivering and the responsibilities of lay people (their clients) in such circumstances?

Customer needs

Customer needs: the customer's perception of the need that is satisfied by purchasing the product

Virtually all marketing decisions should include an element of customer focus — what does each customer need? Pricing service products is no different; **customer needs** are paramount. If the price of a service product is set too high for customers, they will go elsewhere or do without; if too low, the organisation may not make a profit, and will certainly not optimise profits.

Consumers do compare prices. Almost everybody is price conscious — except some of the very rich. Due to the non-material nature of service products, it is more difficult for customers to compare products offered by competing companies. This in turn makes it difficult for marketers to set a price, because they are uncertain how consumers will perceive the pricing structure. When customers compare prices, they do so from the value they perceive the product has to them. This customer self-orientation is one of the most difficult things for marketers to understand, not in terms of it happening, but in terms of understanding the customer's particular perspective of the needs and the price they are prepared to pay to satisfy those needs — that is, the value to the customer.

In summary, prices must be set in a range that customers consider:

- competitive — service providers must be competitive with other providers, not necessarily by being the lowest priced, but being in a similar range in a given market segment
- affordable — if the product is perceived by customers to be beyond their range of affordability, they will go elsewhere, do without or look for cheaper alternatives
- good value — in all cases customers must perceive that the product offered at a given price represents good value for money (see next section).

Customer perceptions of value

Value: the customer's perception of whether or not the service product represents good value for money; that is, a trade-off between the attributes and benefits of the product against the price paid

All organisations must be seen by their customers to offer good **value**, a combination of appropriate service quality and reasonable price, in the long term (Zeithaml 1988). Research has shown quite conclusively that an organisation's image is seriously damaged by customer perceptions that it is not offering good value (Ward & Smith 1998).

One person can stay at a caravan park for $40 a night, while another can stay in a five star hotel for $250, and both consider they have received good value for their money. Why? Simply because they have different needs and different perceptions of what represents good value to them as individuals (Ajora 1996). Considerable research has shown that customers will not make repeat purchases unless they perceive that they get good value from an organisation for their service products. Further, it is clear that in order to nurture a strong relationship with customers, service firms must ensure that customers perceive that they get good value. If they do not consider they are getting good value from a service provider, customers will switch providers.

One of the difficulties with customer perceptions of what represents good value is that customers are all different. Therefore, setting a price for a service product that will be perceived by customers as good value requires considerable research. This area is a typical situation where market research is required in order for organisations to determine the price range for a particular service that the target segment of customers considers to be good value.

While judging the quality of a service product can be very difficult for consumers, judging the value is usually even more difficult. This is definitely an area where the marketer needs to make sure that the customer can 'see' or determine the value easily. This is not too difficult for some service products, such as a haircut, where the results are discernible (although not until after the hairdresser has finished). However, for an insurance policy, it is often not until the customer has a claim that the 'real' value of the product can be ascertained. If market research shows that the range of prices considered by consumers to be good value is lower than the supplier can economically support, radical changes are required either to the service or how it is provided.

One of the factors that needs to be considered, with respect to value, is positioning — the position the product has in the customer's mind. If a golfer on holiday wanted to play a variety of courses the relative quality of the courses, would be inferred from the price charged. A green fee of $80 might be quite acceptable for playing a championship course that is well maintained, while $20 for playing a short local club course might not be at all attractive. The price the golfer is prepared to pay is thus largely determined by the position the respective courses occupy in the golfer's mind.

Services Marketing on the Web:
Different values offered by a stockbroker

Since about 1980, the number of people owning stocks and shares has risen dramatically. One of the barriers to owning stocks was the commission charged by stockbrokers (often over five per cent to buy and sell a stock), a barrier that kept many individuals out of the market. How things have changed! Today many stockbrokers have a variety of offerings to match a diverse group of investors. For example, Get-Rich-Quick stockbrokers (GRQ) now offer three different levels of service:

- *Full service*. Clients get weekly 'tip' sheets, market alerts, phone consultation and monthly economic commentary. The minimum transaction fee is $150, plus one per cent of contract value over $5000 (buy or sell).
- *Telephone service*. Clients can give their orders over the phone and get occasional advice. The minimum transaction fee is $50, plus 0.5 per cent of contract value over $10 000.
- *Web service*. Clients can give their orders over the Internet but get no advice. The minimum transaction fee is $20, plus 0.1 per cent of contract value over $10 000.

All three services have the same core service product — the purchase or sale of shares — but are targeted at different segments of the market, since clients have different needs and different perceptions of value. Thus, GRQ have made the service product affordable by stripping out features that some customers do not want or need. GRQ have found that these three levels of service product cater for the majority of investor needs, and though they are very different, they still represent 'good value' to each market segment.

Examples of online stockbrokers are found at www.tdwaterhouse.com.au, www.instinet.com and www.commsec.com.au.

A typical online stockbroker may offer the following services:
- news and research on individual firms
- international share trading
- trading in both the stock and bond markets in Australia
- a watchlist facility where real-time quotes for a portfolio of shares can be accessed
- access to trading in managed funds, unit trusts, etc.
- a margin facility for increasing the leverage of a portfolio
- loans with long-term repayments for purchasing shares.

Mostly, there is no provision for advice such as when to purchase a specific stock. Moreover, the services are usually available to Australian residents only.

Regulation

Pricing regulations: a set of laws that restrict the setting and movement of prices

In many service industries, there are **pricing regulations** that must be observed. Such legislation is usually designed to protect consumers from unfair pricing practices, and often applies in the professions. Regulations are also often used where safety issues are of paramount importance; thus, minimum charges apply in order to provide sufficient finance for equipment maintenance.

A classic example is the airline industry, in which maximum prices in Australia were 'fixed' by government and operators by agreement, while in many countries minimum prices are also agreed on for safety reasons. The airline industry grew up in the twentieth century as a heavily regulated industry, and when deregulation commenced in Western countries in the early 1980s, it caused havoc that resulted in many airlines going bankrupt — they just could not cope with a free marketplace. In Australia, we saw this fate befall Ansett in 2001. The airline business just got too competitive and the less efficiently run carriers tended to fall.

Price fixing: *a (generally) illegal activity where two or more organisations conspire to fix prices of competing products in an uncompetitive manner*

Price fixing is an activity where apparently competing organisations fix prices in such a manner that they create an artificial price floor, below which nobody goes. Price fixing is illegal in many countries, as it is anti-competitive and generally not in consumers' interests. However, it is very difficult in most cases to establish that price fixing has actually occurred. Take, for example, four motels on the edge of a country town on a busy main road. Every morning, the manager of each motel walks outside and looks at the prices displayed by the other three motels, and then makes any required adjustment to his own displayed price. Is this price fixing? Unless it can be proven that some form of communication took place between the managers in which they conspired to fix their prices, they cannot be charged with price fixing. There is a general feeling that this form of price setting borders on price fixing, but it is in a grey area, and price fixing cannot be proven.

Factors such as government watchdogs, government policy, political and social considerations all contribute to regulating price fixing, but there are no total controls. Many professional service industries follow **self-regulation** practices that are implemented to maintain standards — and generally, healthy profit margins.

Self-regulation: *a practice whereby an industry relies on all organisations voluntarily adhering to a set of rules or a code of conduct, rather than on legislation, to regulate business practices that reflect customer rights*

Service quality

Service quality was discussed in chapter 4, but a brief consideration is required with respect to pricing. As discussed above, customers need to see they are getting good value. With goods, this goal is sometimes difficult to achieve, as customers do not always know exactly what quality of product they have purchased, and what they 'should' have paid for it. With service products, the situation is worse, as customers generally find it more difficult to judge the quality of a service, thus making the value judgement more prone to error. Of course, it is the customer's perception of service quality that is paramount, and this perception may be different from reality. Thus, an organisation may be offering an 'ordinary' service product, but if the customer perceives it as 'excellent', then all will be well (unless they eventually tumble to the actual situation).

One of the techniques used in services marketing is to help the customer to perceive the product as excellent by making certain attributes or benefits more tangible. For example, an accountant may advertise herself as being 'accredited', indicating that she is recognised by a professional association, implying some level of minimum training and a certain standing in the profession. In this way the customer has a certain level of trust in the accountant's abilities and degree of professionalism, and knows that there is a means of appeal if too much is charged or poor advice given.

Thus, if marketers can help customers to appreciate the quality of their product, then in determining the price they can take into account that level of customer-perceived service product quality.

Do-it-yourself (DIY) versus purchase

Many service products can be termed 'convenience' services — that is, they can be performed by the customer but they choose instead to purchase the product from a specialist provider. Typical examples of this kind of service are grass cutting, laundries and house cleaning. Many of these types of services are performed by part-time providers who often offer very competitive prices.

In setting a price, the customer may not consider what is good value from an objective viewpoint; that is, whether the quality of the product at a given price represents good value. Instead, they may make a judgement that they are prepared to pay as much as is required in order not to have to do the job themselves. When setting prices in these cases, we must look at the customer's perceptions of value from a replacement viewpoint, rather than from a strictly product-value viewpoint.

Segmentation

Segmentation is one of the most underrated constructs in marketing. It is absolutely fundamental for marketers to know all they can about the target segment or segments. What may be good value to customers in one segment of our market may not be perceived as good value, or even affordable, by another segment. The earlier example of the overnight stay in a caravan park versus a five-star resort is a case in point. Know your customer, and segment the market according to how customers can be grouped, or segmented. It is not intended to go into much detail here, other than to emphasise the point that segmentation is as fundamental to pricing as it is to marketing in general.

Pricing strategies

The basics of pricing and the forces discussed above have established a base for a discussion of a number of pricing strategies that can be used by service providers. In this section it is assumed that an organisation can be competitive selling at a price over the cost of providing a service product, because if this were not the case, the long-term future of the business would be in doubt. The section discusses three major strategic considerations: price leadership, fixed versus variable pricing, and differentiation through price, followed by examples of pricing applications to specific service product categories.

Price leadership

Price leader: the organisation that leads or dominates price selling in a market segment (usually the organisation with highest market share)

One of the main tasks when deciding on a pricing strategy is to ascertain whether your organisation and product occupy a leadership or follower position in the marketplace. Most often the position of **price leader** in a market is determined by market share. The product with the highest market share in a market segment will generally have price leadership in that segment. Thus, almost by default, all other products will be price followers. While there will occasionally be cases where this rule does not apply, such cases are rare and are usually associated with a transition situation, as when an old, dominant organisation (or service) is just about to be 'passed' by a new, more dynamic organisation (or service).

Being the price leader in a market is usually a distinct advantage for several reasons:

- The general level of prices can be set at a point where a comfortable profit can be realised.
- Being the largest producer should result in also being the lowest cost provider (at a given product quality).
- Customers will tend to use the market leader as a barometer of what pricing (and service quality) levels to expect.
- The price leader can vary prices (within limits) as and when it suits them, and the remainder of the market can then choose whether or not to follow.

Skimming

Skimming: a practice whereby early adopters of new products are charged a high initial price for the opportunity to own the new product soon after release

Price **skimming** is quite common for goods, and is generally applied when a new, innovative product is first launched when the manufacturer has limited or no direct competition. Examples of this are the launch of a new computer or next-generation mobile phone. The principle is that early adopters of new products are prepared to pay a premium for the new product (often new technology), so the manufacturer 'skims' those early adopters by charging a premium before the market for the new technology becomes competitive.

For service products, the use of skimming is not so common or so pronounced, largely because there are fewer opportunities for offering a new product that is so different or desirable. However, there are some examples, such as the recent introduction of new body-scanning machines that provide better, more detailed scans of the human body, with immediate diagnostic benefits. These machines offer faster and more detailed scans to patients, thus providing greater diagnostic performance with substantial medical benefits to the patient. Patients are prepared to pay a premium for access to such new technology in the hope that early detection of certain diseases will enable a complete and early recovery. As more and more competing service providers are able to offer the same scanning quality, so the element of skimming is reduced.

There is no doubt that price skimming for certain service products is a legitimate and effective marketing strategy. However, care must be taken not to alienate those segments of the market that cannot, or will not, pay the higher price during the skimming period.

Penetration pricing

Penetration pricing: a pricing technique for promoting a newly launched product at a heavily discounted price to boost initial sales

When new products are launched, organisations often use a technique known as **penetration pricing** (sometimes called cost leadership penetration) to boost sales in the critical period at and immediately after launch. A typical example was the spurt in growth of Internet service providers with launch prices that were always very competitive and mostly under cost. This was done in order to try to lock in customers and gain significant market share — essential for businesses that require high-volume sales. The intention was then to slowly raise prices so that profits would flow after two to five years. Many such companies were not able to gain the market share required and have subsequently gone out of business (OneTel, for example).

This technique is quite common and can be employed very effectively. However, in all cases long-term success depends upon being able to slowly raise prices without losing too much market share.

Fixed versus variable pricing

In a supermarket, a particular brand of product in a given size will usually be offered at exactly the same price for all customers at a particular time. In practice it would be difficult to vary prices for each customer, except where there is some form of discount for shareholders or members, but such discounts are not usually visible to other shoppers. This uniformity of price may not be the case in business-to-business situations, but that discussion is outside the scope of this chapter.

With consumer service products there is much more scope for varying prices, largely due to lower price visibility. Why would a service provider wish to vary prices to customers who are purchasing exactly the same service product? There are a variety of reasons, discussed below.

Tickets to an event are frequently offered at a discount to early purchasers, thus encouraging purchasers to buy early. This practice offers benefits to the organisers, such as cash flow and the security of having sufficient advance sales to justify continuing with the event. People who show up on the night may have to pay slightly more in return for not having to make up their minds about attending until the last minute, thus trading off convenience against price.

Another example is a firm of solicitors handling a court case for a client. There is usually a standard hourly fee, plus an additional element known as 'care and consideration'. Care and consideration fees are levied depending on how difficult the case is for the legal team, thus if there are many complications and some concerns about the case for the lawyer, an additional fee, commensurate with the difficulties, will be charged.

An important area where prices of service products are varied is where there is limited capacity at a particular time. For example, there are reports of all 300 people in economy class on a jumbo jet paying a different price for their ticket, even though they get the same level of service in the airport and on board, get the same food and drinks, and travel from the same place to the same destination at the same time. Why? The answer is more complex than the question, as there are a number of factors that affect the price:

- *How you book.* If you book through a travel agent, then a booking fee or commission (about nine per cent) has to be paid by the airline to the travel agent. If you book by telephone direct with the airline, such a commission is not due, thus lowering the costs on the airline (although some airlines, by agreement with travel agents, do not lower prices for bookings made by phone). If you book over the Internet, some airlines offer their lowest price, as the cost of booking is less.
- *Demand/supply.* If you want to travel at a peak time, prices are generally higher than at off-peak times. This is simply a supply versus demand situation in which the organisation is responding to market forces.
- *When you book.* Generally, the earlier you book, the lower the price. The reason here is that if the service provider knows well in advance what the load factor is likely to be, adjustments to pricing (and promotions) can be made as the event time nears, to maximise revenue. The technique used is called 'yield management' and is discussed below.

Yield management

Consider again the case of an airline. If the airline knew that they could always fill every seat on every aircraft, then they could charge the same price for each seat in each class — say three different prices for economy, business and first class. In theory, they could set the price for each class just high enough that the last seat is just sold for each flight, thus maximising profits. Life, however, is never that certain or simple. Running an airline is a competitive business and, if an airline took the single-fare per class approach, they would soon find themselves undersold by some of their competitors and flying with empty seats, or priced so low they could not make a profit — not a good business approach (Heuslein 1993). Further, demand is not constant from one day to another, one month to another, or at different times of each day. The objective (as ever for commercial organisations, at least) is to price their products so that they can make the maximum long-term profit from a given capital outlay.

Airlines now use **yield management** to help price each seat on each aircraft for each flight. This technique usually involves computer software that

Yield management: *the use of variable pricing techniques to obtain optimum return from a temporal event with limited capacity*

calculates the optimum price derived from a set of assumptions and objectives supplied by the airline. The software takes into account the number of seats booked, the time to go before the flight, the anticipated demand for that flight, expected competition, and so on. The algorithms in the software then calculate an optimised price day by day on demand from a travel agent or customer, right up to the time that the flight closes (unless all seats are sold). Virtually all airlines now use such techniques, and are very unlikely to answer questions about such matters, as they are considered strategic tools that supply a tangible competitive advantage. Yield management is now used in many service industries (Harris & Peacock 1995) and is considered a key tool for services pricing. The technique is closely linked to the development of a pricing strategy (Desiraju & Shugan 1999).

An example of the pricing structures resulting from an airline using yield management can be seen at the Qantas website, www.qantas.com.au.

Figure 11.2 shows a typical yield management price curve for a motel. The rate charged varies with 'time to go', from $100 per night if booked the week before, to only $55 if booked seven or more weeks in advance.

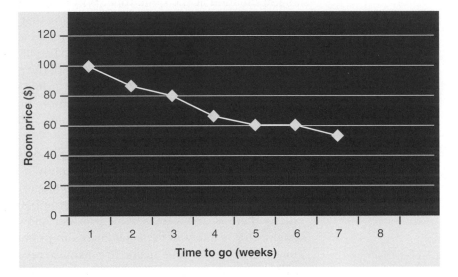

Figure 11.2: A typical yield management price curve

Even in simpler situations, marketers use a variety of techniques to manipulate prices of service products in order to suit market conditions. Thus, for many years business hotels have offered special packages at weekends, when demand is low, in order to help maintain occupancy rates. Likewise, hire-car companies (generally a business-dominated industry) do the same at weekends to maintain usage rates. A website showing variable prices for hotel rooms can be found at www.wotif.com.au.

Note also how much lower the prices are when booked online compared with the 'normal', full room rate. Likewise, for many inner-city hotels that mainly cater for business travellers, the rates at weekends tend to be the lowest offered. Such off-peak rates are offered to help boost utilisation rates for quiet nights. Yield management software thus enables service providers who offer timed events, such as airline flights and hotel rooms, to maximise long-term revenue and, therefore, profits. Generally, yield management programs are only used by large businesses (or large franchises), because the cost of buying and adapting the software and then using it is beyond most small businesses.

Services Marketing Action:
Motel pricing

After Frank retired from the bank, he and his wife Gina bought a 50-room motel. After a while, it became clear that charging a flat rate for each room, irrespective of advance booking and fluctuating seasonal demand, was not optimising total return or profit.

Gina started to read about different pricing techniques and came upon yield management. The idea seemed perfect but the cost of acquiring and setting up a computer system was prohibitive for their small operation.

There were three options: join a franchise (which they did not want to do) in order to access yield management software cheaply; design their own simplified system; or do nothing (which was not really an option). They decided to develop their own system without using complex computer software (which they could not do). They felt they could develop a set of rules for pricing that allowed prices to vary according to how long in advance a room was booked and the expected demand for that night, taking weekly and seasonal demand fluctuations into account. The rules went as follows.

- Expected demand, one of three states: low (under 50 per cent utilisation)
  - medium (51 to 80 per cent utilisation)
  - high (over 81 per cent utilisation).
- Booking time, one of four states:
  - over eight weeks in advance
  - between one and eight weeks in advance
  - book less than one week in advance
  - walk in on the night.

Price in $	Over 8 weeks	1–8 weeks	Less 1 week	Walk in
Low	50	55	60	70
Medium	55	60	70	80
High	65	75	90	110

While relatively unsophisticated, this table provided Frank and Gina with a guide to pricing based on expected demand and time of booking, and at no significant cost. It allowed them to significantly raise their total revenue without creating a situation where they were overpriced relative to their competition. This solution was thus a simple application of an advanced technique most small motel operators thought was out of their grasp.

__Overbooking:__ a technique used in temporal demand situations where more bookings for units of a product are taken than are available, to counter potential loss of business due to late cancellations

Overbooking policy

Although not strictly concerned with fixed versus variable pricing, **overbooking** is a common occurrence where yield management techniques are used, with or without formal computer software. The practice is widespread in airlines, hotels and motels, and is designed to maximise profits by minimising the number of empty seats and beds due to late cancellations. Quite simply, a hotel with, say, 100 rooms will accept 110 bookings for a night. They do this because they anticipate that at least 10 people will cancel their reservations. Thus, instead of booking 100 rooms and having 10 cancelled, leaving only 90 occupied, the hotel will book 110, have 10 cancellations, and still have all 100 rooms occupied, thus maximising utilisation of the hotels capacity.

The downside with overbooking is that when the number of cancellations is fewer than usual, customers who arrive late find there is no room available. The hotel is thus required to find a room in another hotel (possibly a competitor) and offer an apology and some form of compensation for the inconvenience. Such activities often lead to customers perceiving that the hotel has broken the relationship of trust, and are very prone to switching to another hotel chain.

In the United States, overbooking is aggressively applied by some airlines, giving rise to an interesting culture. If there is a late arrival who absolutely insists on flying on a given flight, the airline will ask for a volunteer (who already has a seat allocated) to surrender their seat in return for a free ticket. Many travellers on limited budgets book on a flight, arrive early enough to get a seat allocated and then hover around the desk in the departure lounge waiting to be the first volunteer. These travellers are thus trading off a free seat against the additional time they will take on the journey. In some cases, where passengers are actually on board and in their seats when asked to volunteer to surrender their seat in return for the free ticket, and there is usually someone who is happy to do so.

Service providers in these situations must thus make conscious decisions about overbooking, not only from the revenue maximisation perspective, but also from a customer relations perspective. There are some challenging trade-offs that must be considered, and decisions should always focus on the long-term performance of the provider, rather than on short-term profit gain.

Differentiation through price

Many organisations differentiate their products through price, using a variety of techniques such as brand value, bundling and exclusivity. Eight such techniques are discussed below.

Brand value

Brand value: an intangible amount that an organisation places on its brand name

One of the fundamental concepts in marketing is **brand value**. Normally an organisation can charge a slightly higher price for a branded product than a non-branded product of the same actual quality (rather than perceived quality) (Erdem, Swait & Louviere 2002). Service products are branded in exactly the same way as goods. There is, for example, a value attached to the Hertz brand of rental cars that a local 'no name' rental company does not have. The branded rental will probably be slightly more expensive, but there is assistance if required, the perceived risk of breakdown is lower, and so on. Thus, the customer pays for having confidence in the level of service that will be provided, and in there being little risk of a major negative occurrence.

One of the difficulties with goods, as well as service products, is how much the brand is name worth, or how much extra can be charged for a branded product without overpricing. There is, of course, no easy answer, except trying a variety of differentials with the competition, to see what works and what does not work. In effect, this technique involves trying different prices and plotting against sales revenue (and profit), then correcting for known fluctuations such as weekly or seasonal variances. In this way, records will show the size of price differential that optimises turnover and profit.

The size of the optimum differential will then show exactly how strong the brand image is, and how much the brand is actually worth. Such a calculation is only valid for a limited time, as marketplaces are not static. They are dynamic entities in which competing organisations vary prices according to the level of competition, supply and demand. Service providers must therefore keep a constant monitor on their prices and the value of their brand.

Price bundling

Price bundling: a practice in which several service products are combined and offered at one price (often at a discount compared to separate purchase)

Price bundling is a commonly used strategy, often a disguised form of discounting, though there are instances where the reverse is true. For service products, especially in tourism, there are package deals offering accommodation, meals, activities and transportation for a total or 'all inclusive' price. Advantages are that customers know (or think they know) the total price, so price risk is reduced. That is, they know fairly accurately just how much a holiday will cost. Additional advantages are that the tour operator does all the organising and booking, reducing the administrative load on the customer; and the operator knows where cost effective accommodation and facilities can be found, and the best regions and places to visit. The downside of a package tour for many people is that there is a reduction in flexibility, and the unknown element of fellow travellers, although this factor does not apply to all price-bundled services.

Price bundling can be a very useful tool for promotions, filling the hole in demand caused by seasonal fluctuations, and for generally promoting two or more service products in one advertisement (such as accommodation and transport). With bundled prices, customers generally do expect a good deal; that is, they expect a discount on what they would pay for purchasing the same basket of individual services separately (Soman & Gourville 1998). However, bundling is sometimes undertaken to confuse the customer by putting together a bundle for which there is no direct competitor for comparison. The technique of bundling can also be applied to non-profit organisations (Ansari, Siddarth & Weinberg 1996)

International Issues:
The total eclipse

On 21 June 2001, the first total eclipse of the sun in the twenty-first century (and third millennium) took place. Bart and Susan were determined to see this eclipse, as it would also allow them to see the big game animals in Africa. A characteristic of solar eclipses is that they typically cover only about 0.3 per cent of the Earth's surface, so for most people they have to travel to see the eclipse. The best place to see this particular eclipse was southern Africa, either in Zambia or Zimbabwe — both countries that were undergoing significant internal political turmoil. This made personal safety an important issue. Further, there was a fuel shortage in Zimbabwe; hire car bookings could be unreliable; hotels were of an unknown standard; and Bart and Susan had never been to southern Africa before.

Bart and Susan had to make a choice: should they make their own travel arrangements or go on a specialist package tour? The former would be cheaper and would allow greater flexibility and independence, but would require much research to ensure safety. A package would be more expensive, but would have the advantage of being safer and more convenient. The greater safety was inferred, as none of the available package tours promoted themselves on the basis of guaranteed safety.

Bart and Susan eventually chose to go with a package tour where there was price bundling: they would have an all-inclusive week's holiday, with visits to game parks and Victoria Falls as well as travel to a site with optimum views of the eclipse. Although this choice was much more expensive, the tour was a complete success in every way, so they had an overriding sense of value derived from the more expensive price-bundled option.

Cross selling

Cross selling: trying to sell a second, or ancillary, product once the first purchase decision has been made by a customer

Most customers are familiar with **cross selling**, as they are exposed to it most times they shop. It is sometimes known as the 'will you have fries with that?' technique, developed for the sale of fast food. The strategy is common in the marketing of service products, and is often closely related to bundling; that is, both strategies are used in concert. Generally, the principle is that the core service product is priced relatively competitively while the 'real' profits are made from the add-ons — the cross selling. An example would be a resort offering special reductions on room rates during quiet periods to attract customers who would normally find the prices too high, but still charging the same for meals, drinks and activities. Thus, the additional customers contribute to the ongoing cost of rooms and enable profits to be maintained from restaurants, bars and other facilities.

Price segmentation

Price segmentation: the use of different price brackets where different segments of the market are prepared to pay different prices

Price segmentation is commonly used for service products, and refers to the situation in which different segments of the market are prepared to pay different prices. A classic example of market segmentation by price is airline travel, where all customers travel on the same plane at the same time, but passengers in economy, business and first classes all pay very different prices for different seat sizes, food, drinks and entertainment. The airline can charge these different prices because there is a combination of holiday and business travellers, and within both of these market segments there are travellers on different budgets. Experience has shown that these three classes of seat cover most price segments of the market, irrespective of whether business or leisure travel is involved. A fourth class has recently been introduced by some airlines on long-distance flights — an upgraded economy class featuring the same level of service as economy, but providing a slightly better seat with more leg room, but at only a 25 per cent premium over economy (compared to about double for business class).

There are five features required for effective price segmentation:

1. The segments must be identifiable. There must be a clear way in which customers (as well as the service provider) can differentiate between segment offerings.
2. It must be possible to price them differently. There must be readily discernable attributes and benefits associated with each segment.
3. Each group of customers must respond differently to the different price groupings. There must be a real demand in the marketplace for the different price segments.

4. Customers should not be confused by the different segments. Thus each segment should be clearly differentiated from the others.
5. It must be cost effective for the provider to offer each separate segment. There is no benefit to the provider if the cost of offering the segments is higher than the additional return obtained.

Special events pricing

When special events are staged, there is always the opportunity for charging a higher price. In Sydney, during the 2000 Olympic Games, some people were renting out their houses at astronomical prices. Care must be taken not to charge too much of a premium, as such an action could put people off and prove counterproductive. This was kept in mind with the 2000 Olympic Games. The New South Wales government limited the price increases of many service products, especially hotels, motels and resorts. Limits were put in place to avoid perceptions of exploitation of limited supply in an over-demand situation. This action also helped to ensure that visitors left with a good impression of New South Wales and Australia.

Special event pricing of service products requires care, as it usually entails a substantial price rise for a limited period. If profit is to be maximised for the duration of the event, it must do so without damaging overall brand image, or damaging the relationship with long-term customers who may provide regular revenue after the special event is over.

Special event pricing: a pricing technique that is limited to the time span of a special event, during which very high demand is expected

Availability premium

For some service products, there is a benefit in offering an **availability premium**, or discount. For example, during peak travel periods, day-return train tickets may be fully priced as demand is high and many people do not have any practical alternative travel mode. In contrast, people travelling during non-rush-hour times can get a discount, thus encouraging usage during the quieter periods of the day. Similar discounts may be offered at weekends, when there is limited commuter traffic. In a similar way, cinemas may offer discounts during the day to children and senior citizens.

Generally, the same degree of care is required in setting availability premiums and discounts as other segmentation strategies, but they can be very useful in boosting use of facilities that are subject to widely fluctuating demand, but that have relatively fixed supply.

Exclusivity pricing

Many services can be effectively differentiated in the minds of customers by setting a very high price, so that the price itself implies quality and exclusivity — this is known as so called **exclusivity pricing**. The strategy could also be termed 'communicating quality through price'. One classic case in marketing is Giorgio perfume, which was initially priced below the traditional French perfumes, with little success. The price was then doubled so that it was the most expensive, implying that is was better and more exclusive than the top competition. Sales exploded — purchasers wanted to buy the best for their partners, and the best was obviously the most expensive!

Exclusivity pricing: a pricing technique where the high price of the product indicates the degree of 'exclusivity' that the product may have in customers' minds

Many five-star hotels and resorts try to differentiate themselves by using the strategy of exclusivity pricing, which is an interesting technique, as it is assumed by some that a high room price:
- will ensure that 'undesirable' people are discouraged from staying, thus raising the general level of the clientele

- will guarantee high levels of service quality
- will ensure a high level of tangible physical surroundings (buildings, room décor, grounds, etc.)
- has a certain 'snob' value that will impress their friends, and so on.

However, marketers need to be careful how they promote exclusivity. Generally, sales staff should let customers make their own judgements on the benefits they will gain, rather than stating them too overtly. They would state the attributes of the resort rather than be too open about what benefits potential customers may or may not be seeking.

As is commonly found in marketing, image is everything, and if an organisation is marketing a high-quality, exclusive service, then this pricing strategy can pay definite dividends.

The management of price setting

Although not strictly a pricing strategy, the management of the price setting process is of great importance, yet surprisingly it is one of the activities that is often poorly performed by organisations. There are generally three areas in which organisations set prices in an inadequate manner:

1. *Not knowing customers well enough.* When setting prices, marketers must know the range of prices that customers are prepared to pay. If they price too low, the organisation could put people off, as they will perceive the service product to be inferior. If they price too high, the organisation becomes uncompetitive.

2. *Market knowledge.* In any given market segment, marketers need to know what their competitors are offering. As discussed earlier, service product prices are not always readily visible for easy comparison (by either marketer or customer), but marketers should have some knowledge of competitors' practices and take these into account. In addition, marketers need to be aware of the balance between supply and demand, and how it is fluctuating.

3. *Decision-making team.* There is often a tendency for senior managers (especially in large organisations) to make pricing decisions without seeking input from staff with particular knowledge, such as the sales team member who interfaces with customers on a regular basis. In some organisations, the finance department puts specific restrictions on minimum prices; sometimes such practices are justified and sometimes not. It is essential for all parts of an organisation that have relevant input to be involved with pricing decisions, even though the actual pricing decision may be made by a very small team of senior managers.

Summary

LO1: Identify and discuss the fundamentals of pricing of service products.
- It is important to understand the definitions of price and pricing before discussing the seven fundamental pricing factors. Price is defined as the amount of money (or some other item that is exchanged or bartered) the buyer exchanges for a service product provided by the seller. Pricing is defined as the process by which an organisation decides on the price of a service product.

- The following seven factors form a background of important considerations that must be kept in mind during the price decision-making process, as they will collectively have a major impact on price decisions:
  - pricing goals
  - the costs of producing a service
  - elasticity of price
  - demand/supply issues
  - temporal fluctuations in demand
  - the intangible nature of services
  - the six-step process for setting prices: knowing the costs of producing the product; knowing the cost of competitors' products; identifying which pricing factors are relevant to a pricing decision; identifying which market forces are of most importance; deciding a pricing strategy; and making the pricing decision within a strategic framework and with all relevant facts available.

LO2: Discuss how consumers perceive price and value.

- Marketers must recognise that it is essential that service products meet customers' needs and wants.
- Customers must be able to see that they are getting value for their money, otherwise there is little chance they will make a repeat purchase.

LO3: Discuss pricing decisions from a market forces perspective.

- In theory customers should have perfect price knowledge prior to making a purchase decision. This objective is often difficult for customers of services.
- Competition in business is increasing all the time, and organisations must be able to respond to ever changing and ever more competitive market conditions.
- It is often difficult for purchasers of services to make product comparisons, largely due to the difficulty of getting information about competing products, and of assessing the value (to the purchaser) of those products.
- There are some service industries in which regulation has a marked impact on pricing.
- In general, customers will respond positively to high service quality and, in the long term, this perception will often allow the organisation to charge higher prices.
- There are a number of services where significant competition comes from customers not purchasing a service but performing that service themselves.
- Segmenting a market into specific and identifiable segments is fundamental to marketing all products, including services.

LO4: Analyse pricing situations for service products.

Many examples and vignettes are given throughout the chapter that illustrate typical pricing situations for service products, such as:

- a solicitor having difficulty communicating his services to the executor of a will, which raises the ethical issue of whether a professional service provider should be able to explain their product to clients
- the specific values offered by a web-based stockbroker, showing how share trading costs have been reduced
- the owners of a motel using a self-generated yield management model for motel pricing
- an overseas trip to Africa, which illustrates how price bundling can provide substantial benefits to customers, even when it is at greater cost than if the customers had made their own arrangements.

LO5: Identify and discuss the main considerations in determining a pricing strategy

- There are five techniques that can be used to achieve price leadership:
  1. skimming of prices when a new product is launched to take advantage of early adopters
  2. the use of penetration pricing to raise market share at new product launch (effectively the opposite of skimming)
  3. the need to decide on whether to have a fixed or variable pricing policy
  4. the use of yield management techniques to vary price with demand
  5. the use of overbooking to maximise utilisation.
- There are seven techniques discussed, which can be used to establish differentiation through price:
  1. brand value — charge more for a branded product than an unbranded one
  2. price bundling
  3. cross selling
  4. price segmentation
  5. special events pricing
  6. availability premium
  7. exclusivity premium.
- The management of price setting is one of the most important tasks in an organisation with respect to pricing.
- Without properly thought out pricing goals and strategies, it is doubtful whether an organisation can optimise revenue and profit in the long term. The above provides a checklist of essential items you should know and be able to discuss.

key terms

Activity-based costing: a costing technique that focuses on the activities that an organisation has to undertake in order to produce a (service) product (p. 271)

Brand value: an intangible amount that an organisation places on its brand name (p. 286)

Cross selling: trying to sell a second or ancillary, product once the first purchase decision has been made by a customer (p. 288)

Customer needs: the customer's perception of the need that is satisfied by purchasing the product (p. 277)

Elasticity: the degree of price sensitivity, relating change in price and the effect on demand for a product (p. 272)

Exclusivity pricing: a pricing technique where the high price of the product indicates the degree of 'exclusivity' that the product may have in customers' minds (p. 289)

Overbooking: a technique used in temporal demand situations where more bookings for units of a product are taken than are available, to counter potential loss of business due to late cancellations (p. 285)

Penetration pricing: a pricing technique for promoting a newly launched product at a heavily discounted price to boost initial sales (p. 282)

Price: the amount of money (or some other item that is exchanged or bartered) the buyer exchanges for a service product provided by the seller (p. 269)

Price bundling: a practice in which several service products are combined and offered at one price (often at a discount compared to separate purchase) (p. 287)

Price fixing: a (generally) illegal activity where two or more organisations conspire to fix prices of competing products in an uncompetitive manner (p. 280)

Price leader: the organisation that leads or dominates price setting in a market segment (usually the organisation with highest market share) (p. 281)

Price segmentation: the use of different price brackets where different segments of the market are prepared to pay different prices (p. 288)

Pricing: the process by which an organisation decides on the price of a service product (p. 269)

Pricing goals: goals that are set to guide the pricing process in order to help the organisation achieve marketing objectives and overall goals (p. 270)

Pricing regulations: a set of laws that restrict the setting and movement of prices (p. 279)

Self-regulation: a practice whereby an industry relies on all organisations voluntarily adhering to a set of rules or a code of conduct, rather than on legislation, to regulate business practices that reflect customer rights (p. 280)

Skimming: a practice whereby early adopters of new products are charged a high initial price for the opportunity to own the new product soon after release (p. 282)

Special event pricing: a pricing technique that is limited to the time span of a special event, during which very high demand is expected (p. 289)

Temporal fluctuations in demand: variations in demand within time, often over a time span of only a few minutes (p. 273)

Value: the customer's perception of whether or not the service product represents good value for money; that is, a trade-off between the attributes and benefits of the product against the price paid (p. 278)

Yield management: the use of variable pricing techniques to obtain optimum return from a temporal event with limited capacity (p. 283)

 review questions

1. Identify one fundamental pricing factor that must be completed before setting prices for a service product. Explain why this factor is so important.
2. Explain why cost and break-even figures are required by a team of managers who are about to set prices for service products.
3. Explain why the theory of perfect knowledge is just theory when marketing service products.
4. Why is it so important for marketers to take customer needs into account when setting the price of service products?
5. In some situations, customers can decide whether to do something themselves or purchase a service product instead. Identify one example of a personal service product and explain what criteria a customer might use to decide whether to do the task themselves or to purchase a service product instead.
6. Explain why price bundling and cross selling are often closely related pricing strategies.
7. Explain why overbooking can result in annoyed customers.

1. Explain how you would go about producing a break-even curve for a general practitioners business in a rural environment.
2. What options would you have if the costs associated with a rent-a-flower business (flowers, shrubs and small trees in pots) were above the price your competitors were charging to their clients?
3. Identify and describe an example in which a service product can be stored (other than the examples in the text) to accommodate fluctuations in demand. How could you benefit from the storage capability of the provider?
4. Talk to a few companies offering superannuation and ask them how super-annuation is regulated in your country. Make a list of the benefits that customers get from this regulation.
5. Take an insurance policy (any policy that you hold will do) and read it. Then identify the main attributes of the policy. Make a list of the attributes that you find easy to identify and a second list of those you find difficult. Having made the two lists, what conclusions can you make about your understanding of your policy? Has making the two attribute lists helped you to understand the policy better, or made you confused? Do you now need to talk to the insurance company to clarify any aspects of the policy?

vignette questions

1. Read the Ethical Issues vignette on page 277. Think of an example of your own where you have encountered a service provider who is reluctant to describe the product offered. How did you resolve the difficulty you faced? Could you resolve the problem better now?
2. Read the Services Marketing on the Web vignette on page 279.
   (a) Describe how different users of online stockbrokers could find value in each of the three trading options offered by GRQ.
   (b) As a group, identify another example where different values are offered for the differing needs of customers. Each group member should then make their own set of goals for that product, and then decide which value option they would choose. In turn, report back to the group and identify the similarities and differences in value perceptions within the group.
3. Read the Services Marketing Action vignette on page 285. Identify and describe a situation where yield management techniques are used. How does the use of yield management increase the revenue of the organisation?
4. Read the International Issues vignette on page 287. Identify the main trade-offs involved in deciding to pay extra for a price-bundled tour in comparison to making your own arrangements.

recommended readings

It is important to understand the basics of pricing for marketers. A good overall description of pricing, from a European perspective with Australian inputs, is given in:

Baker, M. J., Graham, P. G., Harker, D. P. & Harker, M. C. 1998, *Marketing: Managerial Foundations*, Macmillan, Melbourne, pp. 311–32.

Another very good overall description of pricing, this time from an American rather than European perspective, is given in:

Kotler, P., Armstrong, G., Brown, L. & Adam, S. 1998, *Marketing*, Prentice Hall, Sydney, pp. 412–41.

 references

Ajora, R. 1996, 'Influence of price and variety of services on consumer intention to use the services: an experimental investigation', *Journal of Professional Services Marketing*, vol. 15, no. 1, pp. 105–20.

Ansari, A. S., Siddarth S. & Weinberg, C. B. 1996, 'Pricing a bundle of products or services: the case for nonprofits', *Journal of Marketing Research*, vol. 33, February, pp. 86–93.

Cracknell, D. & Knott, M. 1995, 'The measurement of price elasticities. The BT experience', *International Journal of Forecasting*, vol 11, no. 2, pp. 321–29.

Danaher, P. J. & Brodie, R. J. 2000, 'Understanding the characteristics of price elasticity for frequently purchased packaged goods', *Journal of Marketing Management*, vol. 16, pp. 917–36.

Desiraju, R. & Shugan, S. M. 1999, 'Strategic service pricing and yield management', *Journal of Marketing*, vol. 63, no. 1, pp. 44–56.

Erdem, T., Swait, J. & Louviere, J. 2002, 'The impact of brand credibility on consumer price sensitivity', *International Journal of Research in Marketing*, vol. 19, no. 1, pp. 1–20.

Harris, F. H. & Peacock, P. 1995, 'Hold my place, please', *Marketing Management*, vol. 4, fall, pp. 34–46.

Heuslein, W. 1993, 'Carl Icahn is out. Can Al Checchi and Gary Wilson be far behind?', *Forbes Magazine*, January 4, p. 178.

Niedrich, R. W., Sharma, S. & Wedell, D. H. 2001, 'Preference price and price perceptions: a comparison of alternative models', *Journal of Consumer Research*, vol. 28, December, pp. 339–55.

Soman, D. & Gourville, J. T. 1998, 'Transaction coupling: the effects of price bundling on the decision to consume', Marketing Science Institute working paper, no. 98–131.

Taylor, V. A. & Bearden, W. O. 2002, 'The effect of price on brand extension evaluations: the moderating role of extension similarity', *Journal of Academy of Marketing Science*, vol. 30, no. 2, pp. 131–40.

Turley, L. W. & Cabaniss, R. F. 1995, 'Price knowledge for services: an empirical investigation', *Journal of Professional Services Marketing*, vol. 12, no. 1, pp. 39–52.

Ward, A. 1995, 'Service product knowledge', PhD thesis, Queensland University of Technology.

Ward, A. & Smith, T. 1998, 'Relationship marketing: strength of relationship time versus duration', *European Marketing Academy Conference Proceedings*, vol. 1, Stockholm, Sweden, pp. 569–88.

Zeithaml, V. A. 1988, 'Consumer perceptions of price, quality and value: a means-end model and synthesis of evidence', *Journal of Marketing*, vol. 52, July, pp. 2–22.

Chapter 12

Service delivery: the role of personnel and customers

Liliana Bove

LEARNING OBJECTIVES

After reading this chapter you should be able to:

- describe a service process in terms of its complexity and divergence
- blueprint or flowchart a service
- appreciate the type and potential outcome of role stressors typically experienced by service employees
- understand what is meant by customer participation in service production
- identify the benefits of customer participation
- recognise the factors that determine the consumer's willingness to participate in service production
- discuss methods that a firm can use to encourage customer participation
- classify services according to customers' willingness to participate and their requirements for customisation
- appreciate the negatives of increased customer participation in service delivery.

CHAPTER OUTLINE

The aim of this chapter is to comprehend a service process and understand what is meant by complexity and divergence. We also examine the role of participants in the service encounter. First, the role of the service worker is examined. The various types of stressors typical of the service worker's role are considered. Managerial practices to manage role stressors to an acceptable level are discussed.

Second, the role of the customer as a participant in service production and delivery is examined, including the factors that govern customer participation.

Finally, the customisation versus self-service matrix is offered as a typology by which service providers can segment their market.

Introduction

As previously discussed, services, unlike goods, are simultaneously created as they are consumed. This simultaneity of production and demand means that the buyer of the service normally participates in the specification and delivery of the service as it is being performed (Zeithaml 1981). This chapter focuses on the customer–worker interface in an attempt to provide a better understanding of the role of high customer-contact jobs, such as those performed at the organisational boundary by service workers. In particular, we examine the potential stressors of emotional labour, role conflict, ambiguity and overload, which are common to boundary spanning roles. Further, the chapter looks at the role of customer participation, where customers provide a source of production input through information or their labour.

Process

Typically described as the fifth P of the services marketing mix, process includes the actual procedures, tasks and the sequence of activities followed in order to produce and deliver the service. Customers always like and expect the service delivery process to be simplified so that they can receive the service without problems, hiccups or undesired questioning by service providers.

Complexity and divergence

Complexity: *the number and intricacy of steps required to perform a service*

Divergence: *the degree of freedom or variability of steps required to perform a service*

Processes may be described in terms of **complexity** — the number and intricacy of the steps required to perform the service — and **divergence** — the degree of freedom, judgement, discretion, variability or situational adaptation allowed in a process step (Shostack 1987). For example, compare two hairdressing salons. One offers haircuts, colour and styling only, while the other offers the additional services of waxing, nail therapy and tanning. The first salon is low in complexity, as it has a narrow service offering. The second salon is high in complexity because it offers a broader, more extensive full-service alternative.

Increasing complexity can increase the revenue generated by each customer as they use the multiple services offered. However, complexity is increasingly difficult to manage and the overall perceived service quality can fall as a result of a poor experience in one of the service offerings. For example, although you like your hairdresser, the beautician who waxed your legs was very rough, which lowered your overall opinion of the hairdressing salon. Increased process complexity is not always preferred by customers. Highly bureaucratic services, typically found in the public sector, frequently have complex processes that defy logic and frustrate the customer. For example, subject enrolment used to be a nightmare exercise at universities, because students were physically forced to go through multiple stations at different sites within the university and fill in a number of confusing forms. Contrast this with the situation now, where enrolment may be conducted from the comfort of your own computer at home.

A highly divergent service is one in which nearly every performance of the process is unique. That is, a considerable amount of judgement, discretion and situational adaptation is required by the service worker, because the service is customised to the preferences of the customer. A service of low divergence is one in which the steps are standardised and there is little room to accommodate individual customer needs. For example, some restaurants have no modifications that can be made to the menu, no half serves available, no omissions or additions to an item possible. Orders are accepted electronically by the kitchen via the waitress, who enters the customer's selection on the register by selecting the item's designated number. This system is designed to generate a limited number of standardised meal offerings. Contrast this to a restaurant where the waitress manually takes the customer's order to the kitchen and discusses the customer's requirements with the chef. Considerable discretion is allowed to the waitress and chef, which may result in a heterogeneous final product. Half serves are accepted, entrées can be upgraded to a main course size, and omissions or additions ('No parmesan on my pasta please') can be made to any item.

The first scenario represents a service that has been industrialised, that is, only one permissible manner and order of the service is offered. Low divergence offers the advantages of high reliability and consistency, increased productivity and lower costs to the service provider. Inventory can be ordered in larger, more economic quantities and service workers do not have to be very skilled. These benefits are usually transferred to consumers in the form of lower prices and greater service availability. However, some customers find the lack of flexibility and choice frustrating, and may reject a highly standardised service even if it is offered at a lower price. Greater customisation and flexibility tend to command a higher price because a divergent service is more difficult to manage and control, since inventory requirements are variable and therefore difficult to predict. Furthermore, service quality is highly dependent on the service worker's correct interpretation and ability to meet the customer's need. The service worker who works in a service that is high in divergence has to be more skilled, and is given more discretion to make decisions than a service worker who works in a service low in divergence. Not only is their job more interesting, but they usually can command a higher wage. For example, compare a chef who works at the Hyatt with one who works at McDonald's. In fact, services of low divergence, where there is 'routinisation' of the service delivery process, have been shown to diminish the service worker's autonomy and skill, undermining both their bargaining power and their pride in their work (Leidner 1999).

Blueprinting the service experience

Service blueprinting is also commonly known as service mapping or service flowcharting. It is a visual graphical approach that offers managers a useful tool by which they can gain a holistic view of their service and an insight into the nature of a customer's experiences. In constructing a blueprint, a customer perspective is taken and the sequence of events that it documents are those that the customer passes through in acquiring the service. Each step includes visible and invisible aspects of delivering the service to the customer. There are four steps in drawing up a service blueprint:

1. Identify in sequence all the principle functions required to create and distribute the service. Indicate the degree of divergence offered in each step.
2. Define the **zone of visibility** (frontstage) — processes that are visible to the customer and in which the customer is likely to participate; and the **zone of invisibility** (backstage) — processes that are hidden from the customer's view.
3. Show the current average timing of each principle function and identify which is the relevant department or personnel responsible for each function or whether the customer is expected to perform the function.

Service blueprinting: a visual, graphical approach that maps out the steps in service acquisition from a customer's perspective. All invisible processes (backstage) are included, as well as those that the customer sees (frontstage).

Zone of visibility: frontstage processes or activities that are visible to the customer and in which the customer is likely to participate

Zone of invisibility: backstage processes that are hidden from the customer's view but are part of the production or delivery of the service

4. Show the acceptable tolerances in timing for each function such that customers' perception of quality will not be adversely affected.

Steps 3 and 4 may be omitted when the objective of the blueprint is to communicate the general nature of the service rather than to diagnose and improve the service delivery process.

Figure 12.1 (on following page) gives an example of a blueprint for a café. A blueprint provides valuable information to the service manager. It illustrates how the service is initiated by the customer and what actions the customer must take to acquire the service. It also identifies which service personnel interact with the customer, how long and how often. But more importantly perhaps the service blueprint makes it easier for the service manager to try to improve service quality. For example, the blueprint may identify bottlenecks (where customers have to wait too long) or failure points (where the customer does not receive what they expect) in service delivery. Alternatively, the blueprint may highlight functions for which no person in the organisation appears to be accountable. Processes may be sped up and service personnel freed up by weeding out superfluous steps that add no value for the customer. A blueprint also makes it very clear where frontstage activities depend strongly on backstage activities and where weaknesses lie. Once the offending activity is identified, it can be isolated, and an individual blueprint of that activity can be constructed that will provide greater detail needed to isolate the problem.

Re-examine figure 12.1. Can you find the bottlenecks? It is clear that the major bottlenecks occur in the preparation of food: entrée, main and dessert. Waitress staff are working well within the customer tolerance times, but the time between food order and delivery is simply too slow. This would be noticed by customers, because it exceeds their tolerance times. Management needs to blueprint the current processes in the kitchen to work out why there is a delay in the preparation of customer selections. Are tasks being done that are not necessary during peak meal times? Or are there simply not enough kitchen staff to meet meal demands?

Service blueprinting is not only useful in the evaluation of existing service processes, but can also be used in developing and designing new services or new service delivery processes. Innovations in services often arise from changes in the service delivery process made possible by technological developments.

Boundary spanning employees and service delivery

The organisational members who interface with customers are at the **organisational boundary**, and are referred to as **boundary spanners**. In industries such as banking, restaurants and retail, the boundary spanners are the tellers or call centre staff, the waiters, and the sales assistants respectively. These roles are typically the least skilled, lowest paid positions in the organisation. In other industries, boundary spanners are well paid and highly educated professionals, for example accountants, doctors, dentists, lawyers, consultants and even your lecturers.

There are essentially two functions performed by boundary spanners: information processing and external representation. First, boundary spanners obtain information from and about the environment, filter it, and pass it along to other organisational members. Second, boundary spanners represent the organisation as it acquires inputs and distributes outputs (Tansik 1985).

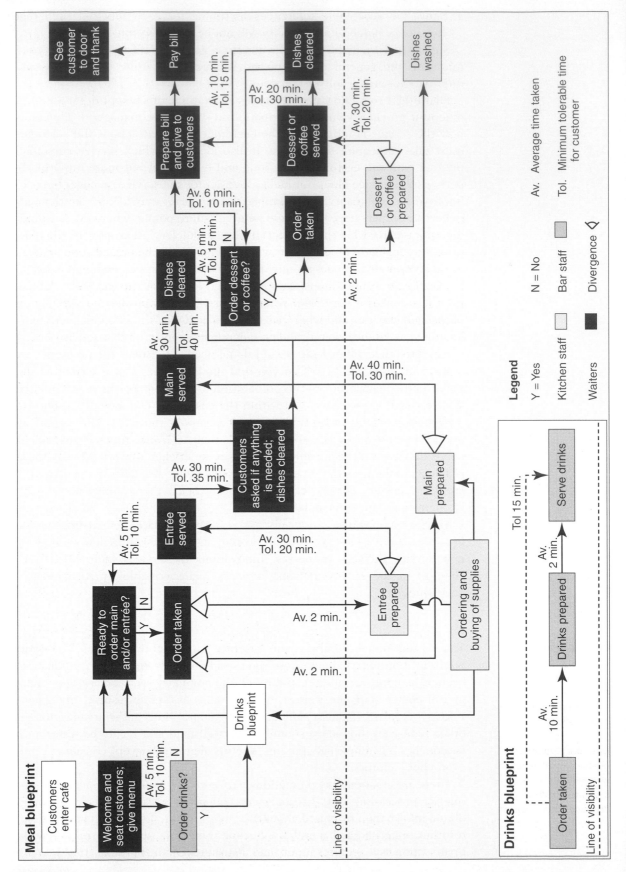

Figure 12.1: Service blueprint for a café

Boundary spanning employees deliver the promises of the firm, create an image for the firm, and promote the firm's services (Bettencourt & Brown 1997). They play a crucial role in linking a firm with its customers and contribute significantly to customer satisfaction, service quality perceptions and loyalty. Therefore, it is imperative that we understand what factors affect their performance, job satisfaction, organisational commitment and quitting intentions.

Role stressors

It has been found that boundary-spanning employees experience the greatest role stress when they perceive their management as being primarily concerned with bureaucratic requirements (following rules and procedures) rather than servicing customer needs (Bowen & Schneider 1985). It is precisely those employees who are committed to a service orientation that experience the greatest frustration at management's tendency to put efficiency ahead of service (Schneider 1995).

There are four main sources of role stress for boundary spanners:
1. *emotional labour* — the degree to which felt emotions are controlled so that socially desirable emotions are expressed
2. *role conflict* — the degree of incompatibility of expectations associated with the role
3. *role ambiguity* — the degree to which clear information is lacking on the expectations associated with the role and consequences of role performance
4. *role overload* — the degree to which the role expectations are far greater than the individual's abilities and motivation to perform a task.

Extreme role stress results in **burnout** and in the subsequent erosion of performance and job-related attitudes such as satisfaction, commitment and turnover intentions, as illustrated in figure 12.2.

Burnout: a stress syndrome that includes feelings of emotional exhaustion, depersonalisation and non-accomplishment

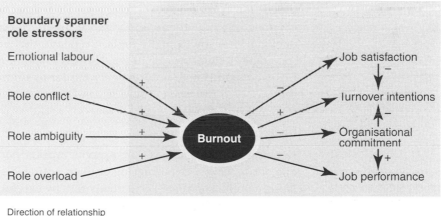

Direction of relationship
+ The linear relationship is increasing.
− The linear relationship is decreasing.

Figure 12.2: The effect of role stress on role performance and attitude

Emotional labour

Emotional labour: the degree to which felt emotions are controlled so that socially desirable emotions are expressed

People at work play organisational roles (Argyle 1992), and the role of boundary spanners generally involves high degrees of social interaction and the performance of **emotional labour**, that is 'the management of feeling to create a publicly observable facial and bodily display' (Hochschild 1983, p. 7).

For example, producing a consistent smile for customers requires a type of effort on the part of the service worker that is not asked of other types of workers. When rules for emotional management are dictated by one's job or employer, and the central aspect of a job is to manage one's own emotions for the good of the organisation, then emotional labour is being performed (Shuler & Davenport-Sypher 2000).

Societal norms provide general rules regarding how and what emotions should be expressed by boundary spanners during service encounters. Generally, the greater the power and status of the service worker compared with the customer, the greater latitude they have to modify the degree of compliance with societal norms (Ashforth & Humphrey 1993). Further, in contrast to professionals involved in service work, the emotional labour of low- to middle-level boundary spanners is likely to be guided by employers rather than by professional norms. It is in interactive service work that managers are most likely to intervene directly in aspects of workers' selves not generally regarded as their business, because it is here that the satisfactory completion of work tasks frequently cannot be distinguished from the emotional quality of interactions (Leidner 1999). For example, service personnel are required by their managers to suppress inappropriate emotions and at times heighten or actually change the emotion they are experiencing (Hochschild 1983). Hence, just because a sales assistant displays or expresses customer-oriented or social behaviour by surface acting (Hochschild 1983), does not mean that the individual feels or experiences the social emotion. The display of socially desirable behaviour may just indicate the sales assistants role training or desire to provide good service, obtain positive feedback, avoid management punishment or make a sale. This notion of prescribed and supervised emotions is a defining characteristic that distinguishes emotional labourers. Boundary spanners must often 'psych themselves' into assuming the emotional stance they portray for the public in much the same way that actors psych themselves for a role. Think, for example of sympathetic and sombre funeral director or priest, the hostile debt collector, the friendly flight attendant, the enthusiastic tour guide, and the empathetic doctor or nurse. However, spontaneous feeling and genuine involvement become progressively harder to summon with each iteration of the script, to the point where it can become emotionally exhausting (Ashforth & Fried 1988).

Surface and deep acting

Hochschild (1983) argues that a service worker performs emotional labour in one of two ways: **surface acting** or **deep acting**. Surface acting involves simulating emotions that are not actually felt, by careful display of verbal and non-verbal cues such as facial expression, gesture and voice tone. In this way, the service worker pretends to feel the emotions that are publicly shown, which may include the apparent absence of emotion. In other words, the emotion displayed by the service worker differs from their felt emotion. For example, a medical receptionist may smile while inwardly cursing patients and the doctors. An example of surface acting is given in the following transcript of a male supermarket cashier (Tolich 1993, p. 373):

Surface acting: display of emotions that are not actually felt

Deep acting: attempts to actually experience or feel the emotions displayed

> I can psych myself up to — I can trick my brain into believing something that might not be true, or vice versa. I can smile, and it's not a sincere smile. You

> just learn to do it — it takes practice. And I've found over the years — and probably the worst ones are older people who might be senile and they've had a bad day or whatever, and they come in and they just want to complain and what — and it's your fault. And when I know it's not my fault — but I can't argue with her and tell her it's not my fault. I just have to — the best way to deal with it is just smile and take the complaints. It physically does not hurt me. And I'm not so proud as to let it hurt my feelings because in the back of my mind, I might say, 'Well she has had a hard day, and she's not getting paid for it'. And here I am making $14 an hour and all that I have to do is smile.

In contrast, deep acting involves attempts to actually experience or feel the emotions that one wishes to display (Hochschild 1983). There are two ways of doing deep acting: one is by directly suppressing or shaping feeling; the other is by making use of a trained imagination (Hochschild 1983). Deep acting can therefore be viewed as deceiving oneself as much as deceiving others, whereas surface acting involves deceiving others about what we feel but not ourselves (Hochschild 1983).

As surface acting focuses directly on one's outward behaviour, it requires less effort than deep acting, which focuses directly on one's inner feelings (Hochschild 1979). Further, just as the performances of actors vary in quality, so too does the quality of emotional labour across service workers and across service encounters for a given service worker.

Functions and dysfunctions of emotional labour

Roles involving emotional labour provide pleasures as well as dangers for workers. Given the dynamic and emergent nature of many service encounters, emotional labour provides a critical means of regulating interaction and therefore increases self-efficacy (the belief that one can successfully fulfil task requirements) and task effectiveness (Ashforth & Humphrey 1993). Also, by fulfilling social expectations, emotional labour makes interactions more predictable and satisfying if the customer perceives expression of emotion as sincere (Ashforth & Humphrey 1993). Shuler and Davenport-Sypher's (2000) study of 911 emergency services dispatchers demonstrated that emotional work, although clearly stressful and demanding, was also the social dimension that connected employees and made their work enjoyable. Emotional labour was intrinsically connected with the best and most rewarding parts of a dispatcher's job, and had a central role in making highly stressful, repetitive, and tedious work more manageable and enjoyable. For example, the emotional labour of having to remain emotionally neutral functioned as comic relief when there were 'stupid' or 'crazy' callers; it provided an adrenaline fix in the case of dangerous events, especially crimes in progress; or sometimes just offered the opportunity for a dispatcher to go above and beyond normal service — to engage in altruistic service.

Notwithstanding the positive aspects of emotional labour, its dark side has been well researched. First, it is difficult to control by the organisation. Managers cannot mandate an emotional rapport between service workers and customers. However, they may attempt to control it via a combination of surveillance methods such as direct oversight by supervisors, periodic monitoring of telephone work or the use of mystery shoppers. Second, emotional labour is affected by external factors such as time pressure and stress caused by peak levels of customer demands. Third, its evaluation is subjective, owing to the diverse expectations of customers (Ashforth & Humphrey 1993). Finally, what is functional for the organisation and customer may well be dysfunctional for the service worker. Hochschild (1983) argues that maintaining a difference between feeling and feigning over the long run (surface acting) creates a sense of strain that may cause the individual to feel false and hypocritical, leading to eventual personal and work-related maladjustment, such as poor self-esteem, depression, cynicism and alienation from work. Also, sustained deep acting may impair the individual's sense of authentic self, and this expressive inhibition and distortion may impair the individual's ability to recognise or even experience genuine emotion and well-being (Ashforth & Humphrey 1993). Ironically, while employers and customers may prefer workers whose emotional displays seem genuine, this sincerity ultimately may increase their risk of burnout (Wharton 1999). The long-term masking or reworking of authentic emotions has been linked to psychological and physical dysfunctions such as physical illness, emotional numbness and burnout (Parkinson 1991).

Role conflict

Role conflict: the degree of incompatibility of expectations associated with a role

The nature of the boundary spanner role is such that service workers are likely to become as close psychologically to the firm's customers as they are other service workers (Bowen & Schneider 1985). **Role conflict** arises when boundary spanners are expected to satisfy incompatible expectations or demands from the organisation and customers. Take the example of Lisa who works as a beautician in a very busy Ella Baché store. She has her regular customers who she likes to please. Occasionally a customer, while having her waxing or electrolysis done, decides on an additional service. The manager at the store has every minute accounted for and on most days there is very little slack between appointments. Lisa is torn between providing good service to her clients, which involves complying with their requests, or sticking by the strict appointment times set by her manager, which would involve encouraging the client to make another appointment for the additional service. Lisa feels bad when she tells her client that they need to return, as they perceive her to be inflexible and not very helpful. At times she has complied with a client's request and has been reprimanded by her manager for going over time and delaying subsequent appointments. When a client compels her to be flexible or when she simply cannot ask her client to defer the additional service, she complies and tries to make up for the time by working harder or shortening her break. Many times she has skipped her lunch so that later appointments would not be delayed. Whatever action Lisa decides on she simply cannot win!

Conflict of this nature is especially troublesome to boundary spanners, who are caught between the demands of legitimate authority (their manager or organisational policy) and the demands of customers, with whom they usually identify psychologically (Rafaeli 1989). Whereas management has a remote influence over boundary-spanners, customers have an immediate influence because of their physical proximity to service workers; the amount of time they spend together; the amount of feedback and other information customers provide; and the fact that service workers know how critical customers are to the organisation and to their jobs (Chung & Schneider 2002). Therefore, although boundary spanners place a priority on taking care of customer needs (especially if they directly rely on the customer for income in the form of tips or commission), they become strained if they fail to complete tasks assigned to them by their supervisors. When faced with this conflict, the first response of the customer-contact worker is typically to work harder (Weatherly & Tansik 1993). When boundary spanners are unable to reconcile incongruent expectations, role theory suggests that high levels of distress, frustration and anxiety are generated. This, in turn, results in emotionally charged role environments, where high levels of effort are required to perform tasks. If this persists, boundary spanners may experience burnout (Singh et al. 1994).

Role ambiguity

Role ambiguity: the degree to which clear information is lacking about expectations associated with the role and/or consequences of role performance

Role ambiguity is the degree to which clear information is lacking on the expectations associated with a role, methods for fulfilling role expectations, and/or consequences of role performance for self and others (Singh et al. 1994). It is characterised by uncertainty about expected behaviour in the job, and it reduces performance through diminished effort and delays in taking action. Many boundary spanners work in complex task environments, where it is difficult to provide clear policies and guidelines for all possible situations and contingencies. Furthermore, boundary spanners commonly do not have sufficient resources or power to implement satisfactory solutions. Both factors lead to role ambiguity (Singh et al. 1994).

Some role ambiguity is desirable, because it allows the service worker some latitude in job performance. However, chronic role ambiguity requires excessive levels of energy and mental resources, which may also lead to burnout (Singh et al. 1994).

Role overload

Role overload: the degree to which the expectations of a role are far greater than the individual's abilities and motivation to perform a task

Boundary spanning positions are susceptible to **role overload** because at peak demand times, the flow of tasks is often uncontrollable, causing long customer queues. Furthermore, boundary spanners must interact with large numbers of customers, as well as with many internal employees and supervisors. Consequently, demand exceeds the abilities and resources of the individual (Singh et al. 1994). The service worker's attempts to maintain performance standards despite insufficient time and staff, may lead to an excessive expenditure of time and emotional energy, resulting in emotional exhaustion, a component of burnout (Cordes & Dougherty 1993).

Burnout: the outcome of multiple role stressors

While any single role stressor may not be dysfunctional, their combined effect may exceed the person's capacity to cope, and may initiate the burnout process (Singh et al. 1994). Burnout, therefore, is the result of the cumulative effect of multiple stressors (emotional labour, role conflict, ambiguity, overload), and describes a specific three-component psychological condition in which people suffer emotional exhaustion, tend to depersonalise others, and experience a lack of personal accomplishment (Cordes & Dougherty 1993; Fogarty et al. 2000). Emotional exhaustion is the first stage of burnout, and is characterised by a lack of energy and a feeling that one's emotional resources are used up. A common symptom is dread and anxiety at the prospect of returning to work for another day (Cordes & Dougherty 1993). Depersonalisation is characterised by treating customers as objects rather than people. Service workers display emotional detachment and even callousness, becoming increasingly cynical toward co-workers, customers and the organisation (Cordes & Dougherty 1993). The final component of burnout, diminished personal accomplishment, is characterised by a tendency to evaluate oneself negatively, to the point where there is a perception of lack of progress or even lost ground. Feelings of job competence are reduced (Cordes & Dougherty 1993).

Burnout occurs only when role stressors are great enough to collectively overwhelm the resources of the individual. The costs of burnout are high for the individual and the service organisation alike. Burnout has a direct, dysfunctional influence on psychological and behavioural job outcomes (job satisfaction, organisational commitment, turnover intentions and job performance) (Babakus et al. 1999; Fogarty et al. 2000; Wolpin et al. 1991). For example, burnout is negatively related to organisational commitment — the strength of an individual's identification with and involvement in their organisation (Mowday et al. 1979). Boundary spanners caught in a burnout syndrome generally view the organisation in adversarial terms, and tend to withdraw psychologically from it. Initially, this withdrawal may take the form of absenteeism, physical isolation and extended breaks, as the worker avoids contact with the organisation's members and customers (Singh et al. 1994). Burnout also affects job performance — the degree to which employees execute their job tasks, responsibilities and assignments adequately (Wetzels et al. 2000). This is because it reduces the boundary spanner's energy and leads to reduced efforts at work. Individuals who exhibit burnout symptoms stop taking the usual degree of care in their work, and lower levels of quality may result (Fogarty et al. 2000). Burnout also directly affects performance, as the individual perceives little or no control over the job situation, and their confidence in tackling work-related problems declines (Singh et al. 1994).

If burnout persists, service workers will likely seek permanent avoidance by leaving the position, the firm or even their career (Fogarty et al. 2000). Moreover, unhealthy consumption behaviours, including smoking, drug and alcohol use, usually increase (Cordes & Dougherty 1993). Not only does the individual suffer as a consequence of burnout, but so too do the service worker's family and friends, the organisation and the people with whom the service worker interacts during working hours (customers and co-workers). High role stress and the incidence of burnout is typical among boundary spanners who have high frequency and intensity of interpersonal contact, for example social workers, customer service representatives, school teachers and nurses (Cordes & Dougherty 1993).

Boundary spanners as 'partial customers'

Partial customers: the portrayal of service employees as customers of the organisation

Many boundary-spanning jobs are highly routinised and are not intrinsically motivating. If boundary spanners were managed as **partial customers**, individuals deserving the same courteous treatment that management wants the organisation's customers to receive — their motivation to treat customers in an equal fashion would increase. Service organisations can ill afford to treat their service employees as a disposable resource. They must strive to treat them with respect and dignity while promoting fairness in their compensation, rules and interactions. When service employees view their organisation's human resource practices favourably, their customers will view the service they receive favourably. This is because when boundary spanners feel well treated by management's human-resource practices, they can devote their energies and resources to serving customers effectively (Bowen & Schneider 1985).

In an attempt to reduce the level of role stress, management first needs to evaluate the work environment for boundary-spanning positions and ask: Do these positions require the suppression of true emotions on a sustained basis? Is there a discrepancy between perceptions of the behaviours that management rewards and perceptions of what customers expect? Are customer-contact staff overwhelmed by their jobs? Do they have adequate resources to meet job demands?

Once the level and type of role stressor has been determined, there are various things a manager can do to reduce the level of role stressors if it is established that they are too high. One key action is to give boundary spanners increased perceived control in their role, as this reduces their level of stress. The need for personal control is considered a basic human drive (Wrzesniewski & Dutton 2001) and one way a boundary spanner can achieve it is by ensuring both management and customers follow the scripts that are expected of them. For a service encounter to be successful, the participants must be able to predict the actions and behaviours of the other role occupants (Solomon et al. 1985). Even if customers choose not to follow scripts, organisations can recruit and train service workers to be high 'self-monitors' — to have a high sensitivity to interpersonal cues, be adaptive to situations, and have a diverse repertoire of appropriate response programs (Ashforth & Fried 1988). This way, they would not feel as though they have lost perceived control of the service encounter. Boundary spanners who score high on self-monitoring are better able to avoid burnout than those who lack this ability (Wharton 1999). Further, management needs to re-examine and modify existing organisational policies and practices that may place the boundary spanner in difficult situations with the customer, thereby minimising role conflict. Management needs to identify the behaviours that boundary spanners believe customers want them to perform, and needs to set up systems that reward them for engaging in those behaviours (Chung & Schneider 2002).

The negative effects of emotional labour on the personal well-being of the service worker are moderated by the extent to which the demands of the role are consistent with the service worker's social or personal identity (Ashforth & Humphrey 1993). The more the service individual identifies with the role (or the values and norms of the role), the greater the positive impact on the individual's psychological well-being, which is brought about by fulfilling expectations via emotional labour. Individuals develop a sense of who they are, what their values, goals and beliefs are, and what they ought to do (Ashforth & Humphrey 1993). Certain types of individuals self-select occupations that require particular types of emotional labour. For example, social workers may be motivated by concerns about people and making the world a better place to live in, whereas teachers may be motivated by getting individuals to achieve their best. If the service individual has assumed a social or personal identity that is contrary to those required in the customer-contact role, then emotional labour will have a negative impact on the individual's well-being (Ashforth & Humphrey 1993). Therefore, it is crucial that employers select applicants for boundary-spanning positions on the basis of their interpersonal skills, and that individuals seek jobs that are compatible with their personality.

In addition to treating boundary spanners as partial customers, establishing scripts, and ensuring personality–job fit, managers should allow as much true emotion to emerge from their employees as possible without jeopardising customer satisfaction. In work situations in which customers are generally positive, it should be appropriate and easy for service workers to express their true feelings. On the other hand, when encounters consist mostly of negative customer emotions as they do at, say, the Australian Taxation Office or Centrelink, then excessive latitude is not the answer, because service workers' true feelings will not be appropriate. In these situations, managers may want to provide more extensive training on how service workers can alter their feelings to make it easier for them to display the appropriate emotion. Alternatively, managers can provide opportunities for emotional expression, allowing employees to share real feelings away from the customer at the back office. Boundary spanners may be rostered for periodic backstage duties to allow them an opportunity to 'step out of character' and relax. Ultimately, managers need to ensure that felt emotions are not unduly suppressed in the long term, to the point of stressful consequences.

Managers can also help reduce the likelihood of burnout by providing social support (Wharton 1999). Greater perceived social support from co-workers and supervisors in the form of reassuring words, to the effect that the service worker is capable of successful performance, has a buffering effect on burnout (Cordes & Dougherty 1993).

Finally, not all role stressors are detrimental. They actually provide some energising benefits that come from accomplishing challenging tasks (Singh et al. 1994). What service managers need to do is control excessive role stress that may result in burnout when employees' coping mechanisms are overwhelmed. This may be achieved by closing the gap between job demands and worker skills through effective recruitment, job competency training, stress management training and job rotation. The message for service managers is clear: spend less time supervising customer and service worker interactions and more time cultivating an environment that is 'a great place to work' (Varca 1999). Boundary spanners will make the effort to service customers well if their views of the work environment are positive and they are treated as partial customers by their organisation.

Service delivery and the customer

A key difference between service and manufacturing firms is that customers are often physically present as the service is offered, whereas manufacturing firms rarely have customers present during production. Not only are service customers present, but they often participate in the production of the service, particularly when services are performed directly on the customer. When this occurs, both customers and employees constitute the human resources of the service firm (Bowen 1986).

Customers as co-producers or partial employees

Although customers do not think of themselves as members of service organisations, Lengnick-Hall (1996) argues that if customers are treated as **partial employees**, and are provided with the direction, ability and motivation to contribute to the production process, they will feel free to participate more fully in producing quality outcomes. The more that customers behave as co-producers, the more influence they have on quality resulting from work activities, and the more they provide service firms with a means of improving productivity — something not available to manufacturing firms.

Distinguishing between customer contact and customer participation

Customer **participation** is the degree of effort and involvement, both mental and physical, necessary to produce and deliver the service (Silpakit & Fisk 1985). This concept is not the same as customer contact, which is simply the physical presence of the customer in the service delivery system, as, for example, with a medical examination or haircut. Customer contact is a situational concept that emphasises how conditions of high contact and low contact affect the service operation. In contrast, customer participation is a behavioural concept that emphasises the active role the customer plays in the service encounter. Another important point about customer contact and customer participation is that they do not necessarily take place simultaneously in the service encounter. Reducing customer contact often leads to increased customer participation. For instance, compare Internet banking (high participation, low contact) with teller-assisted banking in a branch (low participation, high contact).

Extent of customer participation

'Participation refers to the types and level of behaviour in which buyers actually engage in connection with the definition and delivery of the service (or value) they seek' (File, Judd & Prince 1992, p. 6). Customers participate by supplying labour and/or knowledge to the service creation process. The quality of the service delivered is influenced by that labour (effort) and knowledge (information). The level of customer participation may vary from simply providing the required information to the service provider, to joint production with the assistance of the service worker, to situations where the customer is the sole producer — that is, self-service.

Consider the following service encounters in which the customer simply provides knowledge:

- When applying for a loan or a credit card, customers of financial institutions are required to provide detailed financial information.
- Small business clients of accounting firms must provide details of receipts, payments and GST transactions before a business activity statement (BAS) can be submitted.
- Clients at hairdressing salons provide their hair stylist with hair colour or style preferences.
- Patients provide their doctors with a detailed description of symptoms so that an accurate diagnosis may be made.

Partial employees: temporary participants in the service delivery process, who contribute resources to the service organisation in the form of information or effort

Participation: the extent of effort and involvement needed to produce and deliver a service

Joint production occurs when both service personnel and customers participate in service production. In these situations, the effective delivery of the service depends on the customer specifying needs, providing information and cooperating with the service provider. Consider a medical patient who is late for his appointment, reports his symptoms inaccurately, does not follow instructions concerning diet and exercise, and refuses to take his medication!

Self-service is defined as the customer performing all aspects of a specific service encounter. At its purest form, self-service does not involve any assistance from service personnel; only technology supports the customer. Examples include automatic teller machines, e-trade, online ticketing, laundrettes and do-it-yourself car wash stations.

Benefits to the firm

Customer co-producers are an effective way of increasing productivity and reducing costs in the production and delivery of services, as they reduce the need for paid labour. For example, insurance agencies offering online self-service options have been able to free staff for more productive work. Up to 60 per cent of customer phonecalls to agencies can be reduced simply by allowing customers access to their billing histories online. This allows staff to spend more time in consultative selling, attending to their customers' future needs and portfolios, improving claims service, and strengthening client relationships (Morgan 2001).

Increased participation by consumers is also associated with increased ratings of quality and feelings of satisfaction (Cermak, File & Prince 1994). For example, Dean (1997) found that there was a significant relationship between customer participation and perceived service quality in health care. This is because when service personnel are involved, customer perceptions of good service rely on more than just the outcome. They hinge on the extent to which the service worker conveys a sense of genuine sensitivity and concern (Ashforth & Humphrey 1993). Further, the ability of the service worker to comply is often externally constrained by physical and resource limitations, peak levels of customer demand, and conflicting and ambiguous role demands from customers, peers and management (Ashforth & Humphrey 1993). Therefore, as a result of co-creating the service, the customer becomes more accountable for the service performance, and he or she accepts some responsibility for how satisfying the ensuing results will be (Mills, Chase & Margulies 1983).

Benefits to the customer

Although the customer is involved through their participation in the service creation, the customer's orientation is toward consumption of the output, not its production (Mills & Morris 1986). While the effort that customers put into the service (for example, clearing food trays and placing wrappings in the bin at a fast food restaurant) may increase productivity for the service provider, customers are more interested in consumption outcomes that affect them, such as satisfaction, service quality or service value.

Greater perceived control of the service encounter

Perceived control is the amount of control a customer feels they have in a service encounter, and is used a means of reducing stress. Customers like to be in charge of their own actions, so they participate in order to control or contribute to their own satisfaction as part of the production process of the service (Mills & Morris 1986).

Cook-your-own (CYO) stations operate in colleges around the United States, and consist of easy-to-use induction cook-tops with assorted pans and semi-prepared ingredients. Students select from a limited number of ingredients such as pre-chopped meats for stir-fries, waffle batter, beaten eggs and pasta. They prepare their meals according to their specific tastes and nutritional needs. The only role the service employee has is restocking ingredients and plates, keeping mess to a minimum and assisting customers with basic cooking techniques and recipe ideas. Cook-your-own stations are especially popular among international students, because they like to cook their own food but do not like the preparation and clean-up work. They perceive this food as fresher because they prepare it themselves and like to be in control of the way their food is cooked (Food Management 2001).

Greater convenience

Using self-service technologies, customers can access services when and where they want, as they usually have wider availability and longer, more flexible hours of operation (Bitner, Brown & Meuter 2000). Being able to produce and consume the service when and where needed was found to be an important contributor to customer satisfaction (Bitner, Brown & Meuter 2000). For example, parents can do their banking and shopping after their children have gone to bed for the night, without having to leave the family home. This increased convenience may also encourage more transactions to be performed; for example, Internet banking transactions can be made daily, whereas a trip to the bank is unlikely to be more than a weekly event.

Greater perceived time savings

Customers participate more in service production in order to reduce perceived waiting time. For example, in order to save time, some of us may swipe our bankcard and select the method of payment, including cash out, while the supermarket cashier is scanning our groceries. McDonald's is switching to do-it-yourself drink stations, as customers get the satisfaction of walking away from the counter much more quickly if they don't have to wait for a drink. Never mind the time it takes to draw it! We all know from personal experience that if we are occupied while waiting, the time seems to pass more quickly. Hence, people often prefer to participate in service production because 'doing something' helps reduce perceived waiting time.

Lower prices/fees

Service providers commonly reward customers for their participation with lower prices, reduced fees or loyalty points. For example, Alaska Airlines gives its customers 500 bonus frequent-flyer miles if they use electronic check-in (Schwartz 2000).

Greater customisation

The use of self-service technologies allows customers to define the service more clearly and deliver it in a manner that better suits their own needs (Bitner, Brown & Meuter 2000). Internet retailers such as Amazon.com allow customers to search for books (among other things) the way they want, get the type of information they want (such as reviews, excerpts) and even choose how they pay (online versus over the telephone), all of which are forms of customisation.

Customer participation drivers

There are a number of factors that govern customer participation efforts. These may be broadly classified under three headings: customer, process and service.

The customer

A customer's disposition to participate refers to how active a role the customer tends to play in supplying labour or information to the service production process (Larsson & Bowen 1989). The greater the customer's disposition to participate, the more work can be shifted to the customer. This is in line with suggestions of using customers as partial employees in order to take advantage of customer motivation, competencies and labour (Bowen 1986).

Level of involvement in the process

The higher the degree of subjective importance and personal relevance invested in a service, the greater the levels of participation. Consider childcare co-operatives, kindergartens or schools, where some parents participate in the management and functioning of the organisation for no payment and very little recognition. Some parents have a high degree of personal involvement in a service that encourages their voluntary participation.

Ability

Certain classes of potential customers such as the uneducated, the elderly, those with intellectual or physical disabilities and minority groups, may not possess the abilities necessary for performing a production role.

Motivation

There appear to be two sources of customer motivation for increased participation. First, the customer may find doing it for themselves intrinsically attractive, even without monetary or time-saving benefits (Bateson 1983). Second, customers may feel that their active involvement is necessary in order to guarantee service quality (Larsson & Bowen 1989). In fact, some customers believe they can provide the service more effectively than the firm's employees; worse still, some customers perceive the service workers as a nuisance to be avoided (Meuter et al. 2000). Take the handyman who refuses to call on tradespeople to do any house repairs or maintenance, as he feels he can do a better job. In the meantime, his partner waits for over a year for the kitchen painting to be finished, the laundry tap to stop leaking and the cracked bedroom window to be replaced. Heard the story before?

Economic expectations

Offering a lower price can induce customers to provide some of the service labour themselves. For instance, banks impose higher fees for teller-assisted transactions than for telephone banking, ATM or Internet banking transactions. Alternatively, there may be a penalty for not participating; for example, customers in some supermarkets do not get their gold coin reimbursed unless they physically return their shopping trolleys to the designated trolley bays.

Traits

Increased participation has been linked to customer traits such as youth, education, impatience, having a dislike of waiting in lines, having a liking for playing with machines, and being male (Langeard et al. 1981). Further, there is a segment of customers who would prefer not to have to interact with service personnel in order to achieve the service outcome (Meuter et al. 2000).

The process

To encourage customer participation in service delivery, service processes should be made less complex. There should also be assistance and guidance in the form of accessible service personnel; clear directional or illustrative signs; well-written simple instructions; and easy-to-use self-service technologies

Well-defined service roles, scripts and tangible cues

If customers know what they are expected to do and how they are expected to perform, they are more likely to do what is needed (Bowen 1986). In do-it-yourself applications, the customer needs to learn how to use the system, and will benefit from simple and carefully designed interfaces (Dawes & Rowley 1998). Scripts provide customers with the knowledge of what to do for effective participation in service production. Lack of knowledge forces the customer either to invent what to do, follow others who appear to know what to do, or be told by service personnel what to do. Therefore, customers need to understand their roles clearly and follow their scripts so that the service can be performed effectively.

Tangible cues can also be used to assist customers. For first-time users, the presence of highly explicit signs prevents them being disorientated in the service setting. Likewise, clearly written instructions regarding what is expected of customers leads to more customers using the service correctly. For example, McDonald's uses a highly visible counter, tray racks and rubbish bins, to inform customers that they need to give their order at a centralised location and clean up after themselves. Video previews of a service delivery offer another way in which customers can be made aware of their co-production roles, so that they engage in productive behaviours. This is a common method used by service providers of adventure or high-adrenaline experiences.

Self-service technologies

Technology-based services have made new service delivery options available to firms, making customer participation more widely possible. 'Self-service technologies (SSTs) are technological interfaces that enable customers to produce a service independent of direct service employee involvement' (Meuter et al. 2000, p. 50). Self-service technologies may be broadly classified into three groups, based on the purpose of their use, as shown in figure 12.3 (on the following page):

1. Customer service — allows customers to query accounts, pay bills, view frequently-asked questions, and track deliveries.
2. Direct transactions — allows customers to locate, view and place an order, and buy and exchange resources with companies without any direct interaction with their employees.
3. Self-help — allows customers to learn, receive information, train themselves, and provide their own services at their convenience. Examples include health information websites, tax preparation, CDs and software, self-help videos, and telephone-based information lines.

INTERFACE / PURPOSE	Telephone/interactive voice response	Online/ Internet	Interactive kiosks	Video/CD*
Customer service	• Telephone banking • Flight information • Order status	• Package tracking • Account information	• ATMs • Automated hotel checkout • Order, pay and go self-service kiosks for fast-food restaurants	
Direct transactions	• Telephone banking • Prescription refills	• Retail purchasing • Financial transactions • Online share trading	• Pay at the pump • Hotel checkout • Car rental • U-Check or U-Scan self-checkout for supermarkets	
Self-help	• Information telephone lines	• Internet information search • Distance learning	• Blood pressure machines • Tourist information	• Tax preparation software • Television/ CD-based training

Figure 12.3: Categories and examples of SSTs in use
Source: adapted from Meuter et al. 2000

Self-service assisted by technology is welcomed by customers in industries that meet the following criteria (Corlett 2001):

- the right staff are in short supply
- staff are resistant to training, or training is ineffective because of turnover
- staff are counterproductive to perceptions of service, as in checkout clerks
- the tasks are simple, requiring little customer expertise and training.

The service

The nature and situational context of the service influences the customer's need and desire to participate in service delivery. Where the outcome of the service depends on the quality of customer's input, then the customer is more willing to participate. However, if the service is complex and requires a high level of expertise, or the service occasion is very important, the customer is more likely to leave it to the professionals.

Type of service and usage occasion

Human services, such as health care, consulting and education, are characterised by the fact that the customer is the key outcome of the transformation activities (Lengnick-Hall 1996). Hence, there is a strong source of motivation for customers to participate actively in service production in order to obtain intrinsic rewards or, through their effort or information, receive adequate problem solving throughout service production (Larsson & Bowen 1989).

Where services require a high level of expertise, or the purchase occasion is of significant importance, most customers would prefer to have the service performed for them. For example, wealthy people are likely to use a lawyer to draw up their will rather than do it themselves. The parents of a bride are likely to call on the services of a professional photographer rather than take photographs themselves. Similarly, for services that are new and unfamiliar, the majority of customers do not perceive benefits in performing the service themselves.

Have you ever waited in a supermarket checkout queue, wondering anxiously when the cashier was going to get that price check for the customer in front of you, or finish counting out her till money? Well you may never need to wait again if you are prepared to take the role of the cashier and check out your own groceries with the help of U-Check or U-Scan self-checkout scanning technology. This technology is currently replacing cash register employees in the United States, allowing supermarkets to reduce their overall labour costs, which account for 50 to 60 per cent of overheads (Heun 2001). The reduction in labour costs allows supermarkets with the self-checkout technology to offer lower prices, giving them a competitive edge over other supermarkets. Furthermore, the technology reduces the ongoing problem for supermarket managers — that is, finding and keeping good employees. In an industry dominated by casual employment practices and low pay, cashiers tend to be juniors looking for part-time work. Turnover is high and reliability can be poor. U-Check and U-Scan technology work 24 hours, seven days a week and never call in sick! But what of customers? What is the appeal of processing their own purchases? The main benefit of the technology is that it allows customers to get in and out of the store quickly. Moreover, customers are able to pay more attention to the price of the scanned good, allowing errors to be identified more easily. How many times have you gone home to find that the item you purchased on sale was scanned at its original price and not its sale price? Increased perceived control of the service transaction is the overriding benefit customers receive from the U-Check and U-Scan technology. It more than compensates customers for having to weigh, scan and place their groceries in bags and miss out on the cashier's 'How are you today?' or 'Have a nice day!'.

Experience has shown that where the self-checkout technology is present within the supermarket, about a third of the customers tend to use it. Self-checkout is primarily applied in express lanes, where customers have few items, bagging requirements are minimal and convenience is a primary concern (Reid 2001). U-Check and U-Scan identifies each item by weight. Customers at the checkout scan their items and place them in a separate cart attached to a scale. The scanner shuts off if items are placed inside the second cart without having been scanned, as the scale senses the new weight. Software calculates the weight of each item based on its barcode, and checks that bagged items match the expected weight. Further, cameras above each lane and one employee monitor the systems for performance and theft and check customer IDs for alcohol and cigarette purchases (Heun 2001). Typically, one cashier can walk new users through the process and oversee four self-service registers (Rosen 2001). Consumers pay for their purchases by inserting a card into a machine, similar to an ATM, located at the end of the self-checkout aisle. The machine also accepts cash, dispenses change for cash purchases and receipts for cards. Online debit card users can get cash out up to $100 (Credit Card Management 2001). Alternatively, customers can pre-register their credit or debit cards and fingerprints, then just scan their purchases and touch the screen to check out (Rosen 2001). The package costs US$25 000 to US$35 000 per lane (Heun 2001).

How can a firm encourage customer participation?

Service managers must understand what customers need to know in order to participate effectively in the service delivery process. Once they understand this, there are two major ways that a service provider can encourage customer participation: by selling the benefits of increased participation to the customer, and by organisational socialisation.

Show customers the benefits

Customers must be sufficiently motivated to play the role of the partial employee. Service firms can motivate their customers in this role by reinforcing participating behaviours. This is done by providing the customer with benefits that are directly traceable to their participation. In other words, management must make the connection between participation and desirable outcomes, such as increased control over the terms of service delivery, time savings, monetary savings or greater customisation, which is highly visible to customers. As expressed by Bitner (2001 p. 10) the challenge with self-service technology is 'getting customers to use the technology in the first place, and then providing them with the level of service that ensures they come back.' Further, when self-service alternatives are first introduced, service workers must be available to demonstrate the equipment and answer questions, particularly when there is potential customer resistance to change. In fact, the firm must provide convincing evidence of the benefits of the technology, not only to customers but also to employees who may feel threatened by the technology and fear the loss of their jobs. For example, when Alaska Airlines first sought to introduce customer self check-in it actively sought input from its traffic staff. The technology was sold to staff as a means by which they could perform their roles more effectively, giving them more time to deal with the passengers who needed their help (Schwartz 2000).

Customers are often frustrated by poorly designed systems that are difficult to follow or technologies that are difficult to use and understand. In such situations, customers decide that the hassle of self-service is not worth the potential benefits, and they return to the traditional option of personal service delivery, where that is available. Alternatively, they may switch to a service firm that offers the personal delivery option. The success of the ATM can be attributed to its simple, clear, step-by-step prompted instructions, which make it easy to use. Further, bank personnel are always willing to provide a demonstration. In fact, some people would argue that it is easier to use than the interpersonal service option. Could you envisage living without an ATM today? Do you ever want to interact with another teller in a bank and face the long queues?

Socialise the customer

In many service delivery situations, customers may not know exactly what they are supposed to do or say, or when they are supposed to do or say it (Manolis et al. 2001). Organisational socialisation of customers is a process by which customers gain an appreciation of the firm's values; develop the abilities necessary to function within the firm; gain an understanding of what the organisation expects of them; and gain the knowledge necessary to interact with employees and other customers (Kelley et al. 1990). There are a number of methods available to service firms for socialising their customers as partial employees so that the customers perform the behaviours needed for service production and delivery. These include formal orientation programs, organisational literature, environmental cues, reinforcement and observation of other customers (Kelley, Donnelly & Skinner 1990). For example, many gymnasiums formally train new members on how to use their equipment. They also use environmental cues such as signs requesting users to 'Please wipe down machines after use'. AMP socialises its members on organisational values by distributing pamphlets and annual reports. Banks, supermarket delicatessens, airlines, Centrelink and some hotels use environmental cues such as ropes, tickets and signs to indicate appropriate queuing behaviours to customers. Customers can also be socialised through positive and negative reinforcement. For instance, banks use lower transaction fees to encourage customers to participate in service delivery through telephone, ATM and Internet banking. Finally, customers are socialised through the observation of other, more experienced customers. For example, fast-food customers may decide to clean their own table after observing the behaviour of other customers.

Customer socialisation not only encourages participation in service delivery, but also avoids negative service experiences. Informed customers require less attention from service workers, make fewer mistakes, feel more secure and perceive more control (Manolis et al. 2001). Customers who do not understand the process and what is expected of them will tend to hold up service delivery and negatively affect their own as well as other customers' service perceptions. For example, have you ever stood behind someone who obviously did not know how to use an ATM? You wish they would let you help them, or stand aside and practise in their own time!

Customer organisational socialisation is most applicable for services that are highly customised. This is because in order to customise a service it is generally necessary for service workers and customers to exchange resources in the form of information or effort. When services are not customised, there are limited resources required from the customer, so the participatory role of the customer is diminished (Kelley, Donnelly & Skinner 1990).

Services Marketing on the Web:
Web community addresses self-service industry

Touchpoints (www.self-service-touchpoints.com) is a global online community that aims to stimulate debate among banks, retailers, dot coms and consultants who have an interest in the evolving self-service market. The site provides a forum where individuals can exchange ideas and information on self-service issues. Features of the site include:

- an update on new technologies and the self-service industry from around the world
- articles by industry leaders on the self-service industry
- case studies that demonstrate how organisations have implemented self-service technology to keep pace with the demands of customers
- notification of new legislation, rules and regulations that affect the self-service industry
- latest polls, whereby a visitor to the site can register the level of agreement on a self-service issue and view the cumulative results, by asking, for example: 'Do you think a standard operating system, such as Windows, is the way forward for self-service?'.

The customisation versus self-service matrix

Larsson and Bowen (1989) designed a service delivery typology based on two dimensions: the level of customer demand diversity (and hence the need for customisation); and the customer's disposition to participate in the service production process. This framework can guide market segmentation and the provision of suitable service designs to these segments.

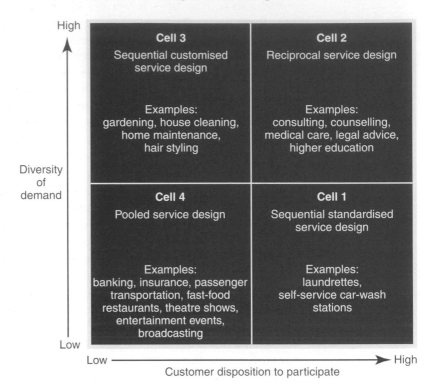

Figure 12.4: A typology of customer demand diversity, and customer disposition to participate
Source: adapted from Larsson & Bowen 1989

As shown in figure 12.4, four specific designs can result from the typology:

- *Cell 1 — sequential standardised service design.* Situations of high customer disposition to participate and low diversity of demand (and therefore low requirement for customisation of service) allow the bulk of the workload to be placed on customers. This means that clear and tightly specified customer scripts must be designed. The benefit for the customer is reduced price for the service. The benefit for the service provider is that they can mass-produce inexpensive services. The service design is labelled 'sequential standardised' because customers service themselves after service personnel have provided the goods and facilities needed for self-service. Typical examples of this service design include laundrettes and car-wash stations.

- *Cell 2 — reciprocal service design.* This represents situations of high customer disposition to participate but high diversity of demand, because customers have complex and unique problems (and therefore high requirement for customisation of service). In this scenario, the customer is not motivated by economic rewards to participate in service production, but rather by intrinsic rewards or in order to monitor the quality of the service. This leads to interactive service production between the customer and service worker, which is typical of professional services such as consulting, counselling, medical care, legal advice and higher education. The service design is given the label of reciprocal service because the output from the customer becomes the input for the professional service worker and vice versa. The script in this case is loosely defined because of the continuous transmission of new information or feedback. However, the script does emphasise the customer's assisting role in terms of providing adequate information concerning the problem and acceptance of instructions for how to participate effectively in problem solving.

- *Cell 3 — sequential customised service design.* This represents situations of high diversity of demand (and therefore high requirement for customisation) accompanied by low customer disposition to participate. However, unlike cell 2, where customers lack the expertise to perform the service themselves, in this case customers may prefer the unique services to be done for them because of increased convenience, lack of time, or the customer's low intrinsic motivation to participate in menial services. The service design is labelled 'sequential customised' because customer specification of the demanded services precedes employee performance of the service. Given low disposition to participate, the customer plays a limited part in the service performance, for their own convenience, and the bulk of the workload is placed on service personnel, as in the case of gardening, housekeeping, home maintenance and hairdressing.

- *Cell 4 — pooled service design.* The last cell represents situations of low demand diversity (and therefore low need for customisation of service) and low customer disposition to participate in service production. Customers are not motivated to participate in service production either because there is no need to monitor the quality of standardised services or because of their inability to perform large-scale services. The term 'pooled service design' is applied because although each customer has little need to interact with service personnel (or fellow customers being served simultaneously), they engage in the sharing of resources that makes the mass service possible. The customer script is tightly specified, as this service design benefits from imitative customer role behaviour in order to standardise customer conduct during service provision. Examples of services that typically apply this service design include banking, insurance, passenger transportation, fast-food restaurants, broadcasting, theatre shows and other entertainment events.

A service provider can use several different service designs simultaneously to address the differences in customers' diversity of need and desire to participate. For example, a bank that has a predominantly pooled service design can incorporate a sequential standardised service design via ATMs that fit a segment of customers who are motivated to participate and who have low demand diversity. Furthermore, the bank could use a reciprocal service design by offering professional financial services to meet the needs of a customer segment that had diverse demands and a disposition to participate. Where multiple segments exist, it is wise that a service firm provides customers with traditional low-tech, high-touch service deliver as well as the high-tech, low-touch alternative. Enabling customers to select freely between technologically or interpersonally based encounters allows them to experience the encounter as desired. It is a dangerous strategy to force customers to use technology in the service encounter without viable options (Bitner, Brown & Meuter 2000).

Potential problems of customer participation

Customer participation is not problem free. Potential issues include loss of quality control by the service firm, lack of social bonding between the customer and service workers, the changed nature of the service worker's role, and heavy technology reliance.

Loss of quality control

Customers who participate in the ongoing service delivery process raise the level of uncertainty in production activities. The organisation must therefore develop mechanisms for managing these customers in order to ensure that they behave in ways that facilitate the service encounter (Kelley, Donnelly & Skinner 1990). However, this is difficult because firms do not have the same degree of freedom regarding customer co-producers as they often have with employees. They are not able to reward or reprimand partial employees as they do traditional employees. Further, if pushed too far, customers may abdicate their role as co-producers, preferring firms that do not place additional burdens upon them.

Loss of social bonding and support

On-site service encounters bring service workers close to the customer, both physically and psychologically. Service workers listen to, sympathise with and share information with customers, which is conducive to social bonds being formed. Many customers are not driven exclusively by economic needs, and may enjoy interacting with service workers who provide a significant source of casual conversation, social comparison, or confidential self-disclosure (Adelman, Ahuvia & Goodwin 1994). Relationships with service workers add value to the service encounter and service workers even provide customers with a source of delight when they exceed their expectations. This may be contrasted to SSTs, which may delight customers on their first use but from then onwards merely satisfy customers when all is functioning well, or highly dissatisfy customers when unexpected technical failures occur. Furthermore, service worker relationships provide customers with confidence benefits, social benefits and special treatment benefits (Gwinner, Gremler & Bitner 1998). Social support benefits in particular are playing an increasingly important role in society as the number of single household and elderly consumers increase. The personalised nature of service encounters provides these groups with a sense of community and social integration (Adelman, Ahuvia & Goodwin 1994). SSTs do not offer customers benefits beyond those labelled as functional. The lack of relationships and derived benefits under SST conditions would suggest that 'true' loyalty, defined by both a positive attitude and repeat purchasing behaviour (Dick & Basu 1994), may be more difficult to establish when the service encounter is devoid of customer interaction with service workers. For example, compare the person who has a newspaper home delivered by the local newsagency with the person who buys it daily from the newsagency. Which of the two consumers is more likely to be loyal to the newsagency?

Changed role of service worker

Opportunities for social interaction at work are generally experienced as positive and authenticating for service workers (Wharton 1999) and customer contact may be one of the primary attractions of a service job. Service workers build relationships with customers at work to enhance the meaning of their work and create more positive work identities (Wrzesniewski & Dutton 2001). Informal social interaction with customers also provides an important source of variety in a boring job (Sutton & Rafaeli 1988). By getting the customer to do more with the assistance of technology, service workers are moved to backstage functions that alter the design of their job and the social environment in which they work. Alternatively, their job shifts from a predominantly service role to an active sales role. These changes are unlikely to suit the current service employee workforce. Further, it will become increasingly difficult to keep employees in the job for any length of time, adding to the current service labour shortage.

Increased reliance on technology

In cases where technology plays a large role in making enhanced customer participation possible, there is a risk that the technology will fail to perform. We have all come across situations where machines are out of order or have been vandalised, PINs or passwords have failed, servers are down, and so on. These technology failures are especially frustrating for those of us who have come to rely on being able to perform transactions 24 hours a day from wherever we want. Sometimes customers can directly contribute to their own service failure in situations of self-service delivery. They lose or forget their PIN or password, they fail to provide information as requested, or they enter the wrong information. Because service-recovery systems are often nonexistent when the process or technology fails, the customer typically has no choice but to call or come in person to the service firm, which is exactly what they were trying to avoid by using the self-service technology in the first place. Alternatively, the customer may simply decide to forgo using the service or postpone it to another time. The worst scenario is that the customer simply switches service providers. As Meuter et al. (2000) found, although customers produced the service themselves using SST, few were prepared to share the blame when the service failed.

Summary

LO1: Describe a service process in terms of its complexity and divergence.
- Complexity refers to the number and intricacy of the steps required to perform the service.
- Divergence refers to the degree of freedom, judgement, discretion, variability or situational adaptation allowed in a process step.

LO2: Blueprint or flowchart a service.
- Blueprinting or flowcharting a service involves presenting a visual map to gain a holistic appreciation of the sequence of steps required in service delivery.
- There are four steps to drawing up a service blueprint:
  1. The sequence of all the principle functions required to create and distribute the service is identified.
  2. Processes that are visible to the customer are separated from those that are hidden from the customer's view.
  3. The current average timing of each principle function and the corresponding responsible personnel are identified.
  4. The acceptable customer tolerances for each function's timing are stated.

LO3: Appreciate the type and potential outcome of role stressors typically experienced by service employees.

- Boundary spanning employees (service workers who interface with customers at the organisation's external boundary) are subject to a number of potential role stressors, namely emotional labour, role conflict, role ambiguity and role overload.
- When role stressors are great enough to collectively overwhelm the resources of the boundary spanner, burnout results.
- Burnout describes a psychological condition in which people suffer emotional exhaustion, tend to depersonalise others and experience a lack of personal accomplishment.
- Burnout has a direct, dysfunctional influence on psychological and behavioural job outcomes such as job satisfaction, organisational commitment, turnover intentions and job performance.

LO4: Understand what is meant by customer participation in service production.

- Customer participation is the active role a customer plays in the service encounter.
- Customers participate by supplying labour (effort) and/or knowledge (information) in the service creation process.
- The level of customer participation may vary from simply providing the desired/required information to the service provider, to joint production with the assistance of the service worker, to situations where the customer is the sole producer — that is, self-service.

LO5: Identify the benefits of customer participation.

- Benefits to the firm of customer participation in the production and delivery of services include increased productivity and reduced labour costs.
- Benefits to the customer include greater perceived control of the service encounter, increased convenience, perceived time savings, lower prices/fees and greater customisation.

LO6: Recognise the factors that determine the consumer's willingness to participate in service production.

- The factors that govern customer participation efforts can be broadly classified into three areas that concern the customer, process or service.
- Customer issues include their level of involvement in the service, their physical or intellectual ability, their motivation, their economic expectations and their traits.
- Process issues include the availability of well-defined service roles, scripts and tangible clues and the presence of self-service technologies.
- Service issues concern the type of service and usage occasion.

LO7: Discuss methods that a firm can use to encourage customer participation.

- A firm can encourage customer participation by selling the benefits of increased participation, and by socialising customers to the organisation so that they gain the confidence to perform the required behaviours to accomplish service production and delivery.

LO8: Classify services according to customers' willingness to participate and their requirements for customisation.

- Customers may be segmented in a 2×2 matrix according to their need for customisation and their disposition to participate in service production.

- Cell 1 — sequential standardised service design — depicts situations of low need for customisation and high disposition to participate. Examples are laundrettes and car-wash stations.
- Cell 2 — reciprocal service design — represents situations of high need for customisation and high disposition to participate. Examples are medical care, legal advice, consulting and counselling services.
- Cell 3 — sequential customised service design — represents situations of high need for customisation and low disposition to participate. Examples are housekeeping, gardening, home maintenance and hairdressing.
- Cell 4 — pooled service design — depicts situations of low need for customisation and low disposition to participate. Examples are banking, insurance, passenger transportation and fast-food restaurants.

LO9: Appreciate the negatives of increased customer participation in service delivery.

- Service organisations must acknowledge that increased customer participation does come with a price that may not be immediately apparent.
- Potential problems include loss of quality control, diminished opportunities for social bonding and support, loss of appeal of the service worker's position and increased reliance on technology.

 *key terms*

Boundary spanners: organisational members who interface with customers at the organisation's boundary (p. 299)

Burnout: a stress syndrome that includes feelings of emotional exhaustion, depersonalisation and non-accomplishment (p. 301)

Complexity: the number and intricacy of steps required to perform a service (p. 297)

Deep acting: attempts to actually experience or feel the emotions displayed (p. 302)

Divergence: the degree of freedom or variability of steps required to perform a service (p. 297)

Emotional labour: the degree to which felt emotions are controlled so that socially desirable emotions are expressed (p. 301)

Organisational boundary: zone where the external customer and environment meet the internal operations of the organisation (p. 299)

Partial customers: the portrayal of service employees as customers of the organisation (p. 306)

Partial employees: temporary participants in the service delivery process, who contribute resources to the service organisation in the form of information or effort (p. 309)

Participation: the extent of effort and involvement needed to produce and deliver a service (p. 309)

Role ambiguity: the degree to which clear information is lacking about the expectations associated with the role and/or consequences of role performance (p. 305)

Role conflict: the degree of incompatibility of expectations associated with a role (p. 304)

Role overload: the degree to which the expectations of a role are far greater than the individual's abilities and motivation to perform a task (p. 305)

Service blueprinting: a visual, graphical approach that maps out the steps in service acquisition from a customer's perspective. All invisible (backstage) processes are included, as well as those that the customer sees (frontstage). (p. 298)

Surface acting: display of emotions that are not actually felt (p. 302)

Zone of invisibility: backstage processes or activities that are hidden from the customer's view but are part of the production or delivery of the service (p. 298)

Zone of visibility: frontstage processes or activities that are visible to the customer and in which the customer is likely to participate (p. 298)

review questions

1. What does a service blueprint show? How can it be used by managers?
2. Define emotional labour. What is the difference between surface acting and deep acting?
3. How can the potential for burnout in boundary spanners be minimised?
4. How do customer contact and customer participation differ? Provide two examples in which an increase in customer participation has led to a decrease in customer contact.
5. In what ways do increased participation in service delivery benefit the customer?
6. Discuss methods by which a service organisation can encourage customers to participate in service production.
7. Describe the customisation versus self-service matrix and how it can be used by service organisations.
8. What are some of the potential problems of increased customer participation in service production and delivery?

application questions

1. Blueprint the service process of a traditional florist and a standardised florist service such as Interflora. Compare and contrast the level of structural complexity and divergence in service provision.
2. Provide a list of six occupations that you believe require emotional labour. Justify your selection.
3. Emotional labour is what service workers perform when they are required to feel, or at least project the appearance of, certain emotions as they engage in job-relevant interactions. Describe the emotional displays you would expect in your dealings with the following service workers: flight attendants, policemen, child care workers, 000 emergency dispatchers, debt collectors, funeral attendants, medical specialists and priests/ministers.

4. The process of customer organisational socialisation provides marketing managers with a means of conveying to customers their desires concerning the service encounter. What socialisation methods would you use if you were to set up a cook-your-own station at the university you attend?

5. You are setting up a fast-food restaurant and want to minimise the number of service employees you need to recruit. What strategies could you implement to encourage customer participation in service production and delivery?

6. One of the potential negatives of increased customer participation is the likely erosion of organisational 'true' loyalty. Explain why this is a possibility and how an organisation may counteract this.

vignette questions

1. Read the Services Marketing Action vignette on page 315.
   (a) Self-checkout is a novel concept internationally. When the technology comes to Australia, where do you think it should be introduced first? Why?
   (b) Is such participation desired by all market segments under all situations? What about a parent with a couple of screaming children and $200 worth of groceries piled in a trolley?
   (c) A cashier scans groceries much faster than a shopper — some say twice as fast — yet customers perceive self-checkout as faster. Why?
   (d) What goods typically purchased at supermarkets may not yet be suited to the self-checkout concept?

2. Read the Services Marketing on the Web vignette on page 317 and access the Touchpoints website.
   (a) What do you think is the objective of Touchpoints?
   (b) Who is its target market?
   (c) How would the site encourage/discourage customer participation in the production and delivery of services?

recommended readings

For a discussion of the role of boundary spanners and their treatment as a firm's partial customers see:

Bowen, D. E. & Schneider, B. 1985, 'Boundary-spanning role employees and the service encounter: some guidelines for management and research', in Czepiel, J. A., Solomon, M. R. & Surprenant, C. F. (eds), *The Service Encounter: Managing Employee/Customer Interaction in Service Businesses*, Lexington Books, Toronto, pp. 127–47.

For an excellent review of role conflict, ambiguity, overload and the outcome of burnout, see:

Fogarty, T. J., Singh, J., Rhoads, G. K. & Moore, R. K. 2000, 'Antecedents and consequences of burnout in accounting: beyond the role stress model', *Behavioural Research in Accounting*, vol. 12, pp. 31–67.

The original reference and explanation of the concept of emotional labour is found in:

Hochschild, A. 1983, *The Managed Heart: Commercialization of Human Feeling*, University of California Press, Berkeley.

The following article provides an excellent discussion on the role of the customer as a 'partial employee' of the service firm:

Lengnick-Hall, C. A. 1996, 'Customer contributions to quality: a different view of the customer-oriented firm', *Academy of Management Review*, vol. 21, no. 3, pp. 791–824.

The following articles present a good review of the role of technology in assisting customer participation in service production and delivery:

Bitner, M. J., Brown, S. W. & Meuter, M. L. 2000, 'Technology infusion in service encounters', *Journal of the Academy of Marketing Science*, vol. 28, no. 1, pp. 138–49.

Meuter, M. L., Ostrom, A. L., Roundtree, R. I. & Bitner, M. J. 2000, 'Self-service technologies: understanding customer satisfaction with technology-based service encounters', *Journal of Marketing*, vol. 64, July, pp. 50–64.

For a more detailed explanation of the customisation versus self-service matrix, see:

Larsson, R. & Bowen, D. E. 1989, 'Organisation and customer: managing design and coordination of services', *Academy of Management Review*, vol. 14, no. 2, pp. 213–33.

references

Adelman, M. B., Ahuvia, A. & Goodwin, C. 1994, 'Beyond smiling: social support and service quality', in Rust, R. T. & Oliver, R. L. (eds), in *Service Quality: New Directions in Theory and Practice*, Sage Publications, Thousand Oaks, CA, pp. 139–71.

Argyle, M. 1992, *The Social Psychology of Everyday Life*, Routledge, London.

Ashforth, B. E. & Fried, Y. 1988, 'The mindlessness of organisational behaviors', *Human Relations*, vol. 41, no. 4, pp. 305–29.

Ashforth, B. E. & Humphrey, R. H. 1993, 'Emotional labor in service roles: the influence of identity', *Academy of Management Review*, vol. 18, no. 1, pp. 88–115.

Babakus, E., Cravens, D. W., Johnston, M. & Moncrief, W. C. 1999, 'The role of emotional exhaustion in sales force attitude and behavior relationships', *Journal of the Academy of Marketing Science*, vol. 27, no. 1, pp. 58–70.

Bateson, J. E. G. 1983, 'The self-service customer — empirical findings', in Berry, L. T. (ed.), *Emerging Perspectives on Services Marketing*, American Marketing Association, Chicago, pp. 50–3.

Bettencourt, L. A. & Brown, S. W. 1997, 'Contact employees: relationships among workplace fairness, job satisfaction and prosocial service behaviors', *Journal of Retailing*, vol. 73, no. 1, pp. 39–61.

Bitner, M. J. 2001, 'Self-service technologies: what do customers expect?', *Marketing Management*, pp. 10–11.

Bitner, M. J., Brown, S. W. & Meuter, M. L. 2000, 'Technology infusion in service encounters', *Journal of the Academy of Marketing Science*, vol. 28, no. 1, pp. 138–49.

Bowen, D. E. 1986, 'Managing customers as human resources in service organisations', *Human Resource Management*, vol. 25, no. 3, pp. 371–83.

Bowen, D. E. & Schneider, B. 1985, 'Boundary-spanning role employees and the service encounter: some guidelines for management and research', in

Czepiel, J. A., Solomon, M. R. & Surprenant, C. F. (eds), *The Service Encounter: Managing Employee/Customer Interaction in Service Businesses*, Lexington Books, Toronto, pp. 127–47.

Cermak, D. S. P., File, K. M. & Prince, R. A. 1994, 'Customer participation in service specification and delivery', *Journal of Applied Business Research*, vol. 10, no. 2, pp. 90–6.

Chung, B. G. & Schneider, B. 2002, 'Serving multiple masters: role conflict experienced by service employees', *Journal of Services Marketing*, vol. 16, no. 1, pp. 70–87.

Cordes, C. L. & Dougherty, T. W. 1993, 'A review and an integration of research on job burnout', *Academy of Management Review*, vol. 18, no. 4, pp. 621–56.

Corlett, C. 2001, 'Self-service: the ultimate service', *Vital Speeches of the Day*, pp. 626–30.

Credit Card Management 2001, 'Self-checkout moves to the passing lane', vol. 14, September, issue 7, p. 10.

Dawes, J. & Rowley, J. 1998, 'Enhancing the customer experience: contributions from information technology', *Management Decision*, vol. 36, no. 5, pp. 350–7.

Dean, A. M. 1997, 'The impact of consumer participation on perceived service quality', Working Paper 24/97, Monash University, Australia.

Dick, A. S. & Basu, K. 1994, 'Customer loyalty: toward an integrated conceptual framework', *Journal of the Academy of Marketing Science*, vol. 22, no. 2, pp. 99–113.

File, K. M., Judd, B. B. & Prince, R. A. 1992, 'Interactive marketing: the influence of participation on positive word-of-mouth and referrals', *The Journal of Services Marketing*, vol. 6, no. 4, pp. 5–14.

Fogarty, T. J., Singh, J., Rhoads, G. K. & Moore, R. K. 2000, 'Antecedents and consequences of burnout in accounting: beyond the role stress model', *Behavioural Research in Accounting*, vol. 12, pp. 31–67.

Food Management 2001, 'Self-service with a twist', vol. 36, pp. 28, 30.

Gwinner, K. P., Gremler, D. D. & Bitner, M. J. 1998, 'Relational benefits in services industries: the customer's perspective', *Journal of the Academy of Marketing Science*, vol. 26, no. 2, pp. 101–14.

Heun, C. T. 2001, 'Grocery checkout goes self-service', *Information Week*, pp. 61–2.

Hochschild, A. R. 1979, 'Emotion work, feeling rules, and social structure', *American Journal of Sociology*, vol. 85, no. 3, pp. 551–75.

Hochschild, A. R. 1983, *The Managed Heart: Commercialization of Human Feeling*, University of California Press, Berkeley.

Kelley, S. W., Donnelly, J. H. J. & Skinner, S. J. 1990, 'Customer participation in service production and delivery', *Journal of Retailing*, vol. 66, no. 3, pp. 315–35.

Langeard, E., Bateson, J. E. G., Lovelock, C. H. & Eiglier, P. 1981, *Services Marketing: New Insights from Consumers and Marketing Managers*, Marketing Science Institute, Cambridge, MA.

Larsson, R. & Bowen, D. E. 1989, 'Organisation and customer: managing design and coordination of services', *Academy of Management Review*, vol. 14, no. 2, pp. 213–33.

Leidner, R. 1999, 'Emotional labor in service work', *Annals of the American Academy of Political and Social Science*, vol. 561, January, pp. 81–95.

Lengnick-Hall, C. A. 1996, 'Customer contributions to quality: a different view of the customer-oriented firm', *Academy of Management Review*, vol. 21, no. 3, pp. 791–824.

Manolis, C., Meamber, L. A., Winsor, R. D. & Brooks, C. M. 2001, 'Partial employees and consumers: a postmodern, meta-theoretical perspective for services marketing', *Marketing Theory*, vol. 1, no. 2, pp. 225–43.

Meuter, M. L., Ostrom, A. L., Roundtree, R. I. & Bitner, M. J. 2000, 'Self-service technologies: understanding customer satisfaction with technology-based service encounters', *Journal of Marketing*, vol. 64, July, pp. 50–64.

Mills, P. K., Chase, R. B. & Margulies, N. 1983, 'Motivating the client/employee system as a service production strategy', *Academy of Management Review*, vol. 8, no. 2, pp. 301–10.

Mills, P. K. & Morris, J. H. 1986, 'Clients as 'partial' employees of service organisations: role development in client participation', *Academy of Management Review*, vol. 11, no. 4, pp. 726–35.

Morgan, R. 2001, 'While clients want service from agents, many seek self-service opportunities', *National Underwriter*, pp. 30–1.

Mowday, R. T., Steers, R. M. & Porter, L. W. 1979, 'The measurement of organisational commitment', *Journal of Vocational Behavior*, vol. 14, April, pp. 224–47.

Parkinson, B. 1991, 'Emotional stylists: strategies of expressive management among trainee hairdressers', *Cognition and Emotion*, vol. 5, no. 5/6, pp. 419–34.

Rafaeli, A. 1989, 'When cashiers meet customers: an analysis of the role of supermarket customers', *Academy of Management Journal*, vol. 32, no. 2, pp. 245–73.

Reid, K. 2001, 'Technology update: removing the cashier', *National Petroleum News*, pp. 18–22.

Rosen, C. 2001, 'More retailers to tell customers, do it yourself', *Information Week*, p. 29.

Schneider, B. 1995, 'The service organisation: climate is crucial', in Payne, A., Christopher, M., Clark, M. & Peck, H. (eds), *Relationship Marketing for Competitive Advantage: Winning and Keeping Customers*, Butterworth-Heinemann, Oxford, pp. 97–113.

Schwartz, A. C. 2000, 'Do-it-yourself check-in', *Air Transport World*, p. 19.

Shostack, L. 1987, 'Service positioning through structural change', *Journal of Marketing*, vol. 51, January, pp. 34–43.

Shuler, S. & Davenport-Sypher, B. 2000, 'Seeking emotional labor', *Management Communication Quarterly*, vol. 14, no. 1, pp. 50–89.

Silpakit, P. & Fisk, R. P. 1985, 'Participatizing the service encounter: a theoretical framework', in Bloch, T. M., Upah, G. D. & Zeithaml, V. A. (eds), *Services Marketing in a Changing Environment*, American Marketing Association, Chicago, pp. 117–21.

Singh, J., Goolsby, J. R. & Rhoads, G. K. 1994, 'Behavioral and psychological consequences of boundary spanning burnout for customer service representatives', *Journal of Marketing Research*, vol. 31, November, pp. 558–69.

Solomon, M. R., Surprenant, C., Czepiel, J. A. & Gutman, E. G. 1985, 'A role theory perspective on dyadic interactions: the service encounter', *Journal of Marketing*, vol. 49, winter, pp. 99–111.

Sutton, R. I. & Rafaeli, A. 1988, 'Untangling the relationship between displayed emotions and organisational sales: the case of convenience stores', *Academy of Management Journal*, vol. 31, no. 3, pp. 461–87.

Tansik, D. A. 1985, 'Nonverbal communication and high contact employees', in Czepiel, J. A., Solomon, M. R. & Surprenant, C. F. (eds), *The Service Encounter: Managing Employee/Customer Interaction in Service Businesses*, Lexington Books, Toronto, pp. 149–61.

Tolich, M. B. 1993, 'Alienating and liberating emotions at work: supermarket clerks' performance of customer service', *Journal of Contemporary Ethnography*, vol. 22, no. 3, pp. 361–81.

Varca, P. E. 1999, 'Work stress and customer service delivery', *The Journal of Services Marketing*, vol. 13, no. 3, pp. 229–41.

Weatherly, K. A. & Tansik, D. A. 1993, 'Tactics used by customer-contact workers: effects of role stress, boundary spanning and control', *International Journal of Service Industry Management*, vol. 4, no. 3, pp. 4–17.

Wetzels, M., de Ruyter, K. & Bloemer, J. 2000, 'Antecedents and consequences of role stress of retail sales persons', *Journal of Retailing and Consumer Services*, vol. 7, no. 2, pp. 65–75.

Wharton, A. S., 1999, 'The psychosocial consequences of emotional labor', *Annals of the American Academy of Political and Social Science*, vol. 561, January, pp. 158–76.

Wolpin, J., Burke, R. J. & Greenglass, E. R. 1991, 'Is job satisfaction an antecedent or a consequence of psychological burnout?', *Human Relations*, vol. 44, no. 2, pp. 193–209.

Wrzesniewski, A. & Dutton, J. E. 2001, 'Crafting a job: revisioning employees as active crafters of their work', *Academy of Management Review*, vol. 26, no. 2, pp. 179–201.

Zeithaml, V. A. 1981, 'How consumer evaluation processes differ between goods and services', in Donnelly, J. H. & George, W. R. (eds), *Marketing of Services*, American Marketing Association, Chicago, pp. 186–90.

Chapter 13
Service recovery

Janet R. McColl-Kennedy

LEARNING OBJECTIVES

After reading this chapter you should be able to:

- understand the importance of service recovery to organisations
- explain and provide examples of the different types of service failure
- outline complaint behaviour
- discuss what the service recovery process is
- describe the three aspects of justice theory
- outline fairness theory and its application to service recovery
- describe counterfactual thinking
- understand the role of emotions
- outline the key elements of successful service recovery.

CHAPTER OUTLINE

The aim of this chapter is to provide an overview of the process of service recovery. First, the importance of service recovery is introduced, followed by a discussion of the nature of service failure. Attention is then focused on complaint behaviour, including e-complaining. Next, a conceptual model of complaint behaviour is presented and the recovery process outlined. Following this, discussion centres on theoretical frameworks for service recovery. In particular, attention is focused on fairness theory, as it provides an integrative framework for understanding service failure and recovery. The role of emotions, both of the customer and service provider, in the service recovery process is discussed. Finally, attention is drawn to the key elements of successful service recovery.

Introduction

Customers today are generally better informed, more assertive and more demanding than ever before. This in turn has led organisations to become increasingly concerned about customer satisfaction levels (Smith, Bolton & Wagner 1999), as it is well documented that customer satisfaction is linked to success and profit (Brown, Fisk & Bitner 1994; Heskett et al. 1994). Because of the unique characteristics of services — lack of ownership, intangibility, inseparability, heterogeneity, simultaneous production and consumption and perishability — **service failures** are commonplace, despite attempts to deliver high-quality service. Packages occasionally get delivered to the wrong address, planes are sometimes delayed, bank clerks are sometimes rude, and frequently customers have to wait a long time to see a professional service provider such as a doctor or a dentist.

Service failure: a breakdown in the delivery of a service

It is critical to realise that although services typically involve a number of individual activities or steps, it may take just one service failure at one of these steps for customers to be dissatisfied with the particular service and with the organisation. In chapter 4 we discussed service quality, specifically the gaps model, which identifies potential gaps between customer expectations and perceptions. Dissatisfaction occurs when there is a significant difference between what customers expect and what they perceive was delivered. If this dissatisfaction is left unaddressed, customers may decide to look for another service provider to deliver the service. If this occurs, the service provider loses the customer and their business. It is important, therefore, for organisations to attempt to recover dissatisfied customers. However, how should organisations go about this recovery process? This chapter outlines the importance of attempting to recover dissatisfied customers, and the key elements of the service recovery process. But in order to carry out the recovery process, organisations need to know that customers are dissatisfied with the service and to understand the nature of the dissatisfaction. Customer complaints thus play a critical role in providing this information.

Different types of service failure and different causes

Customer dissatisfaction occurs when service failure takes place. Service failure is a breakdown in the delivery of a service. This may be a large failure, such as not delivering the service at all; not undertaking a medical procedure when scheduled; not having some aspect of the service available; not being able to undertake a complete service on a motor vehicle because the mechanic ran out of time, and so on.

When contemplating the most appropriate service recovery, it is important to understand the nature of the service failure. As shown in table 13.1, service failures can result from four key areas:
1. the service itself
2. service providers
3. things outside the service provider's control
4. customer related.

An example of a failure with the service itself is when a customer receives an overcooked or undercooked meal in a restaurant or café, or receives someone else's order. Sometimes a service fails because the service provider behaves inappropriately: being rude to a customer, not looking at the customer while serving them, speaking to a fellow employee about what happened to them at the weekend, and not attending to the needs of the customer. Sometimes service failures are outside the service provider's control. For instance, an electrical power cut affects the delivery of services that rely on electrical tools, such as dental work. Likewise, poor weather, thunderstorms, hailstorms, cyclones, air traffic controllers' strikes are outside the service provider's control, and can affect outdoor concerts and airline flights. Finally, service failures can result from customers themselves.

Table 13.1	Service failures identified by customers

Category 1 — service

Unavailable service:	Examples:
Wrong product	Didn't get business class seat
	Overcooked/undercooked meal
	Meal too cold
	Rat in room
	Didn't get drinks
	Overbooked (seats on plane)
	No jet skis, despite a booking
Wrong price	Had to pay more than expected
	Had to pay extra for parking
Unreasonably slow service:	
Waiting too long	Room not ready
	Wait on meal delivery

Category 2 — service providers

Unprompted and unsolicited employee actions:	Examples:
Truly out-of-the-ordinary employee behaviour	Humour
	Offensive humour/jokes
	Rudeness
	Other actions (e.g. things said, tone of voice)
	Employee had an off-day

Category 3 — things outside the service provider's control

Environmental factors	Examples:
Non-human causes	Wet weather
Behaviour of other organisations	Power cut
	Delayed flight

(continued)

Table 13.1 *(Continued)*

Category 4 — customer related	
	Examples:
Unavoidable customer behaviours	Tired
	Accident (automobile rental)
	Sick/heart attack
	Too short for theme park ride
	Guest injured
Avoidable customer behaviours	Guest arrives early
	Guest loses wallet
	Wants automobile for another day but didn't book it
	Missed bus
Behaviour of other customers	Intoxicated customers
	Loud behaviour

Sources: Bitner, Booms & Tetreault 1990; McColl-Kennedy & Sparks 2003

Extracts from service failure diaries

The following extracts highlight one example from each of the four categories of service failure. The first illustrates a core service failure (service failure 1, where the *service* is unavailable).

> I met a client at Café Stromboli to talk about a marketing contract. We ordered a skinny flat white and a cappuccino. Both coffees came out lukewarm and during our meeting, no staff member followed up to find out if we enjoyed our coffee or if we required any other refreshments. When we paid at the counter, I said to the waitress that our coffees were not hot enough and that there may be a problem with the machine. She apologised and refunded our money. I was initially disappointed at having a meeting in a coffee shop that served lukewarm coffee, and made a mental note never to have a client meeting there again. However, as the waitress apologised and refunded our money, I would be happy to try the coffee at this café again (Throssell 2002).

Service failure 2 is out-of-the-ordinary behaviour, namely rudeness of the *service provider* (employee), as demonstrated in the following script.

> I was looking through racks in a women's dress shop and accidentally knocked one of the dresses off the coat hanger. I was just about to bend down and pick it up when I heard a loud voice behind me calling out for me to leave it. The shop assistant not only raised her voice but ran over to where I was and made such a fuss about the dress falling to the floor, saying that the dress was very expensive and that customers should be more careful. Other customers immediately looked over at me and clearly the whole situation made me feel very uncomfortable in the store. I vowed that I would never go back there and would tell my friends and acquaintances of the situation.

The third category of service failure is a failure that is *outside the service provider's control*. This is demonstrated in the next script:

> We had saved up for a considerable time [and] now we had the money and time to go on a dream holiday to a beautiful island and get away from all the

> hustle and bustle of city life. With our bags all packed, we excitedly waited for the taxi to pick us up from the house and take us to the airport. The taxi arrived on time and we drove to the airport only to find that there was an air traffic controllers' strike and that all flights out of Sydney were cancelled indefinitely.

The fourth category of *customer related* failure is illustrated in the following script:

> We arrived at the theme park early. He had been waiting for this trip to the theme park for months. My son was particularly excited about getting on the Tower of Terror ride. We all lined up and waited twenty minutes. Finally, it was our turn. When my son eventually got close to the ride, to his disappointment he discovered that he was two centimetres short of the required height for the ride. You can imagine how awful he felt!

Complaint behaviour

As discussed in chapter 5, dissatisfaction occurs when expectations are not met. When customers are dissatisfied, they have several choices. Broadly speaking, the customer may take action or take no action (Day & Landon 1977). Even when no action is taken, it is likely that the customer has a less favourable attitude towards the organisation than before the service failure occurred (Hart, Heskett & Sasser 1990). Actions can take several forms. The most common forms are:

- make a complaint
- intend discontinuing the service
- give a warning to friends
- take legal action
- exit or boycott.

If customers do not complain and simply exit without saying anything to anyone within the organisation, then the organisation loses in a number of key areas. First, the organisation does not know that the problem exists so it cannot rectify it. Second, the organisation loses the opportunity to rectify the problem and retain the customer (Hirschman 1970). Third, the organisation can expect a loss of revenue. Fourth, there is no marketing information on how to prevent the problem occurring again, as the organisation does not know what the problem is or why it occurred (Fornell & Wernerfelt 1987). Fifth, the firm's reputation can be damaged from negative word of mouth (Richins 1983; Stephens & Gwinner 1998). Therefore, good managers will want to know why customers are unhappy; speak to those who are prepared to voice their complaint; and speak to those who do not wish to complain formally.

Complaints: expressions of dissatisfaction or disapproval

Complaints may be defined as expressions of dissatisfaction or disapproval. Because of this, service providers do not like to receive them. However, complaints should be viewed positively rather than negatively, as they give an organisation a chance to find out what the problem is, why there is a problem, and provide an opportunity to do something to rectify it and restore a high level of customer satisfaction. If customers do not complain directly to the organisation, they may tell their friends and acquaintances negative things about the organisation and the service specifically. They may also complain to third parties such as Consumer Affairs or Internet complaints forums such as complaints.com. If a customer complains to a third party such as Consumer Affairs or a complaints website, the organisation may incur more costs through litigation, and they certainly cannot rectify the problem immediately. Furthermore, the organisation may never be able to fully rectify the problem, as they are sometimes not given specific information regarding who made the complaint, nor the details of the complaint.

Figure 13.1: Consumer Affairs follows through on customer complaints. *Source:* Ministerial Council on Consumer Affairs, 2002

Negative word of mouth is more powerful than positive

People in the main like to tell negative stories rather than positive ones about their experiences with organisations and the individuals involved. Indeed, the TARP (1995) study found that dissatisfied customers told nearly twice as many people their negative word-of-mouth story than satisfied customers told people about their positive experiences. On average, dissatisfied Australian consumers tell nine other people a negative story about an organisation. Several research studies support this view, with up to two-thirds of customers not reporting any dissatisfaction with the organisation, even though they have experienced dissatisfaction (see, for example, Day & Landon 1977; Richins 1983; Anderson 1985). It appears that most customers would prefer to switch to another service provider than tell their current service provider that they are unhappy with the service, and many may also engage in negative word of mouth (Singh 1988).

How can organisations get customers to complain?

Complaints can be obtained by organisations through a variety of means. Some organisations display complaints boxes, sometimes referred to as suggestion boxes, in a prominent place in the foyer or reception area of the organisation, making it is easy for customers to complain. Another way is through customer-complaint forms. A third way organisations can encourage complaints is through a dedicated phoneline. Centrelink, for example, advertises a free call number 1800 050 004 for customers to phone and register a complaint. Faulding, a large pharmaceutical company, puts a freecall number on the packaging of their products so that customers can complain directly to the organisation with little cost or inconvenience. In one case a customer rang the freecall number because the sunscreen she had bought leaked, owing to the top of the tube not having been properly crimped. The customer's call was answered by a very helpful person who wrote down the customer's details. The customer was then asked to return the tube of sunscreen to a reply paid address. About ten days later the customer was informed that an investigation had been conducted and that the reason the tube had not been crimped properly was that sunscreen at the top of the tube had prevented the ends from sticking. The customer was then told that she would receive a replacement bottle. The replacement bottle arrived a couple of days later along with a bonus tube of Banana Boat aloe vera gel. The customer was very happy with the outcome, as the complaint did not cost anything, thanks to the free phonecall and free postage. Moreover, the customer's complaint was well received and followed up promptly with two complimentary items.

Another way for organisations to obtain complaints is through satisfaction or exit surveys and comment cards. It is common for hotels to place survey forms or comment cards in guests' rooms, often on the individual guest's bed. Sometimes firms offer an incentive, such as entry into a prize draw to win a night's free accommodation if the customer fills out the form. These and other commonly used research methods were discussed in chapter 7.

Finally, employees can be another good source of information on customer complaints. Sometimes customers cannot be bothered or feel that they do not have the time to write a formal complaint to the organisation. However, they may say to the person serving them that they were not happy with a particular aspect of the service. They may convey this in a casual manner, not wishing to offend the person serving them, by saying, 'Well, I thought I was never going to get in to see you'. It is important that organisations understand the importance of informal complaining and set up procedures for receiving employee feedback.

Services Marketing Action:
Centrelink

Centrelink is serious about providing excellent customer service, stating very clearly that it is committed to becoming a customer-driven organisation delivering 'best in the world' service (Centrelink 2000). They have a customer charter that states very clearly how to contact Centrelink (see below). Furthermore, Centrelink has Customer Service Managers (CSMs) who manage the process of identifying customer needs and values and delivering on customer values. There is at least one Customer Service Manager per service centre, call centre or program. The primary role of CSMs is to provide leadership to the organisation by promoting continuous improvement in service delivery. The

Customer Service Managers are supported internally by a CSM support team that provides 'training, development and keeping up with worldwide innovations in customer-driven organisational behaviours and techniques' (Centrelink 2000, A8 p. 17). These CSMs are generally characterised as having a 'friendly, outgoing and positive personality'; have a 'personal commitment to, and believe in, excellence in customer service and quality'; have good problem solving skills, being 'able to generate options with lateral thinking' (Centrelink 2000, A8 p. 18).

In addition, each Centrelink office has customer service officers, and a regular monthly customer satisfaction survey is undertaken. Very high levels of customer satisfaction have been achieved throughout Australia. However, to improve on these very high scores, Centrelink seeks feedback from its customers and has put in place a whole range of processes to make it easy for customers to complain. For example, Centrelink has customer comment forms in each of its offices throughout the whole of Australia (a copy of the form is shown in figure 13.2). The customer comments have been used to help improve customer service in Centrelink.

Tell us what you think

1 Which office or service are you commenting on?

2 Who served you? (optional)

3 What payment/s are you enquiring about?

4 If you have a complaint, compliment or idea about our service then please write in the space provided giving the date and time of your contact with the office.

Date ____ / ____ / ____   Time _____

5 Would you like a reply?   No ☐   Yes ☐   ▶ If yes, please ensure you complete your contact details below (your name and address are optional).

6 Given names

Surname

Address

Postcode

Telephone   (   )   Date   /   /

Thank you for taking the time to fill in our Customer Comments Card. All information will be treated as confidential.

| Information in languages other than English **Phone 13 1202** | TTY Customer Relations Line **Freecall™1800 000 567** Only for people who are deaf or who have a hearing or speech impairment. A TTY phone is required to use this service | If you are dissatisfied with our handling of your concern, you may contact an office of the Commonwealth Ombudsman. |

C0003.0207

Figure 13.2(a): Centrelink customer comment form

In addition to comments boxes being available in all Centrelink offices, Centrelink runs value creation workshops which try to determine what things customers are particularly unhappy about and how service could be improved. As part of Centrelink's commitment to being a customer-driven organisation, the value creation process helps the organisation to keep in touch with its customers and ensures that it receives continuous feedback on the quality of service that is delivered by Centrelink. A value creation facilitator and a technician are attached to each geographical area, and are responsible for running the workshops as required. The value creation team runs the workshops to ensure quality feedback.

Centrelink has a customer charter which states:

'We want you to find Centrelink easy to deal with. This customer charter outlines:
• what we do
• how to contact us
• the type of service you can expect
• your basic rights and
• how to give us feedback.

Figure 13.2(b): Cover of the comment form

If you are happy or unhappy with our service, there are four ways you can tell us:
• talk to any of our staff
• complete a customer comment card
• telephone our customer relations line or Freecall 1800 050 004 or the tele-typewriter (TTY) service on Freecall 1800 000 567
• visit our website at www.centrelink.gov.au.'

E-complaining

E-complaining is voicing dissatisfaction through an electronic website. There are several electronic complaints websites such as Complaints.com, eComplaints.com, NotGoodEnough.org, and PlanetFeedback.com. These act as a third party with no direct links to any particular organisation, and offer unhappy customers the opportunity to complain to the world. These sites post customer complaints for free on their websites, assist the customer with writing a complaint letter, send the details to the target organisation and can even help customers and organisations work out disagreements. Essentially, they provide an open forum for customers to complain.

Services Marketing on the Web:
Is e-complaining for you?

by Nichola Robertson, La Trobe University

Many believe that sites such as Complaints.com, eComplaints.com, NotGood Enough.org, PlanetFeedback.com and Fightback.com will eventually take over from the traditional complaint avenues, such as Consumer Affairs, becoming the preferred way of complaining to a third party about an organisation. Disgruntled customers can certainly get greater exposure if they use these electronic third parties rather than the more traditional means of making a complaint.

Complaint sites offer a range of services to customers. For example, Complaints.com posts customer complaints free on its website. However, it only sends complaints along to the offending organisation if their email address is provided by the customer, and provides no follow-up on complaint resolution. In contrast, eComplaints.com, in addition to posting the complaint, helps the customer to write a complaint letter; offers a step-by-step guide and form letter; finds the offending organisation's address; sends the complaint to the targeted organisation; and provides some follow-up to the complaint made. Fightback.com and OnlineResolution.com go one step further by helping customers and businesses work out disagreements.

The decision of whether or not to complain about a dissatisfying experience has been thought to depend on how much effort the customer expects is needed to lodge the complaint. Customers who perceive difficulty in voicing their complaint, perhaps because of a lack of complaint channels, are unlikely to directly voice their grievances to the offending organisation. Therefore, the ease and convenience of complaining is the key to the popularity of these independent complaint sites. For instance, PlanetFeedback.com makes it easy for customers to complain by providing a form letter and the offending company's address. It is also available and accessible to customers whenever it is needed. PlanetFeedback.com claims to lower the thresholds to feedback: time, access and information. All customers must do is to supply the problem!

Customers' propensity to complain is also based on their perceived ability to effectively voice a complaint to redress a dissatisfying experience. Many customers simply do not know where or how to complain. Some customers do not feel comfortable writing a complaint letter, as they do not know what information to include, and they don't know where to send it. On the eComplaints.com site, writing a complaint letter is as easy as clicking a button and filling in a form letter, with a range of sample letters also provided to assist.

Finally, some customers use complaint sites to regain some power and control in the complaint process. Customers wishing to communicate a complaint must believe that their complaints will lead to adjustments that sufficiently compensate for their dissatisfaction. These complaint sites give customers expanded power to express their dissatisfaction, provide leverage to wronged customers, and connect individuals to each other to increase their influence. eComplaints.com even includes a little cartoon character named Louis. Frustrated customers can click on Louis, who in turn lets out a loud scream, and suddenly a caption pops up: 'Whew, I feel much better now'.

Although these sites may be perceived as a new form of word of mouth or third party complaint, as opposed to being a direct voice to the organisation, this complaining behaviour seems far more accessible and, some may argue, controllable by the organisation. Complaints.com and others inform the offending organisation that the given customer complaints have been posted for public view. eComplaints.com promotes the fact that it can help interested organisations improve their service and recover customer relationships by acting as an independent third party.

Although the number of customers who currently use independent complaint sites on the Internet may be relatively small, there is no doubt that they are extremely vocal and powerful, as they have the ability to tell the world whether they like or dislike a particular service.

Some customers never complain

'I find it hard to say anything when I'm unhappy [with a purchase]. It takes talking to myself all the way to the store. I say, How do I say that? I practice it. If I can get my husband to do it, I will' (Stephens & Gwinner 1998, p. 172).

Although we tend to tell our friends and acquaintances negative stories about organisations or individual service providers, we do not tend to complain directly to the organisation concerned. A recent study by AC Nielsen found that only two per cent of dissatisfied customers actually voiced their complaints to the organisation itself. Why do some customers never seem to complain, even when they are not happy with the service being provided? One reason customers do not complain is that they do not think anything will be done by the organisation to fix the problem. A second reason is that it takes time to write letters, make a phone call or go to a store in person. Thirdly, some consumers say that they do not know how to go about making the complaint. Specifically, they may not know exactly who to contact, or where to send the letter to, or how to get the contact details of the person they should be speaking to. The fourth main reason customers do not complain is that some are discouraged by other customers who have complained in the past without success. These findings are borne out by the 1995 TARP study, which found that 27 per cent of households did not complain because they did not think contacting the organisation would do any good. A further 38 per cent felt that it wasn't worth the time or trouble and another 14 per cent felt that they did not know to whom to complain.

Cognitive-emotive conceptual framework

Stephens and Gwinner's (1998) model of consumer complaint behaviour helps us to understand why some customers complain to an organisation when they are dissatisfied while others do not. As shown in figure 13.3, when a customer experiences a dissatisfying experience, they will first assess the significance of the situation to their own well-being. For instance: Does this affect me in terms of what I want to achieve (goal relevance)? Is it relevant to what I want to achieve (goal congruence)? How does it affect my self-esteem (ego-involvement)? Each of these concepts is illustrated in figure 13.3.

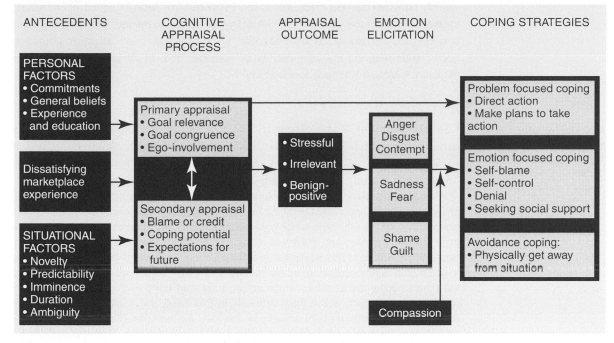

Figure 13.3: Cognitive-emotive model of consumer complaints
Source: Stephens & Gwinner 1998

Goal relevance

Goal relevance: the extent to which a problem is perceived to be relevant to the customer's well-being

Goal relevance is the extent to which a problem is perceived to be relevant to the customer's well-being. If a situation arises that has no implications for an individual's well-being, it is appraised as goal irrelevant (Lazarus & Folkman 1984). In this no-goal-relevance situation, there will be no emotion (Lazarus 1991b). The intensity of the emotional response also depends on goal relevance (McColl-Kennedy & Sparks 2003). The greater the goal relevance, the greater the negative emotions experienced by the customer. For example, if a customer discovers that an amount of money that was supposed to be transferred into an account has not yet appeared, this is likely to be assessed as goal relevant, particularly if the customer had planned to use the money for a special purpose at that specific time. If the money is not there, then the customer presumably cannot make the planned purchase. This event is likely to result in the customer experiencing anger (Nguyen & McColl-Kennedy forthcoming).

Goal incongruence

Goal incongruence: the extent to which an event does not meet the desires of the customer, or is judged to be inconsistent with the customer's wants

Goal incongruence is the extent to which an event does not meet the desires of the individual, or is judged to be inconsistent with what they want (Lazarus 1991b). For example, the following illustrates goal incongruence in a service setting. A patient has been waiting forty minutes to see a doctor at a medical centre. When the customer approaches the counter to complain, she is informed that the doctor is caught up in an emergency. The customer then asks to be transferred to another doctor because she sees that patients of other doctors are being attended to and they have arrived after her. However, the person on the front desk makes no attempt to offer options to the customer. The customer ends up waiting for an hour. By this time she is feeling very annoyed, not because of the waiting time per se, but because of the inflexibility or lack of concern or training shown by the person on the front desk. The customer expected that the front desk service provider would be able to offer an alternative, such as seeing another doctor, thus allowing the customer to achieve her goal of being seen by a doctor (Nguyen & McColl-Kennedy forthcoming).

Ego involvement

Ego involvement: *the extent to which a situation touches an individual's ego-identity, which involves self-esteem, social esteem, personal value, moral value, meanings, ego and ideas*

Ego involvement is the extent to which a situation touches an individual's ego-identity, which involves self-esteem, social esteem, personal value, moral value, meanings, ego and ideas (Lazarus 1991b). If one's self-esteem is threatened, anger is likely to occur (Nguyen & McColl-Kennedy forthcoming).

A customer makes a booking in a restaurant for a very important date. When he arrives with his friends and family, no seats are available. Somehow the booking was not recorded. This situation is not only goal relevant, and goal incongruent, but also included ego involvement: the event has implications for the customer's self-esteem, because he selected this particular restaurant for an important date. Not being able to get a seat is embarrassing, as his friends and family may think that he did not take the time to make the booking, which in turn may lead them to think that he does not really care that much about them after all. In this case, the customer might experience anger, although it might actually be his fault for being late for the booking time, or perhaps other factors, such as a traffic jam, made him late. The anger might be directed at himself, or he might blame the restaurant for the problem. In short, ego-involvement might lead to anger as well as other negative emotions (Nguyen & McColl-Kennedy forthcoming).

In this example and in the previous ones, there is evidence of a combination of cognitive appraisals and emotions being felt by the customer who has experienced the service failure.

When the consumer assesses the experience as being positive or irrelevant to their well-being, no coping strategies are needed (Stephens & Gwinner 1998). However, when the situation is assessed as being stressful to the consumer's well-being; the customer will experience negative emotions. Typical situations are those that affect the consumer's health (being served a meal which is 'off' or being prescribed inappropriate medicine); those that result in financial loss (being given financial advice that recommends investment in an organisation that later goes bankrupt); or those that result in social loss (being given a haircut that is too short).

The type and intensity of the negative emotion is thought to result from the attribution that the customer makes (Izard 1977; Smith & Ellsworth 1985). For example, if the source of the problem is attributable to something that could have been avoided, the person is likely to experience a negative emotion such as anger or dislike (Roseman, Spindle & Jose 1990). Lazarus (1991a) argues that when an external person or object can be blamed, the result is outwardly directed anger. When one blames someone rather than just holds them responsible for the action, this suggests that the person could have done something differently to fix the problem. If the cause of the problem was considered to be internal — that is, the customer — then this is likely to result in shame or guilt. For example, 'I should have made the booking earlier so as to avoid this situation of not being able to get a seat at the restaurant'. If no-one can be blamed, either externally or internally, then sadness is likely to be experienced. These outcomes are illustrated in figure 13.4.

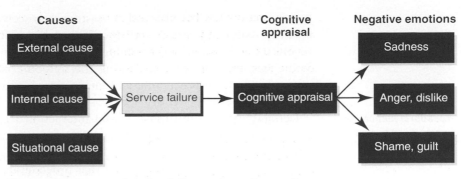

Figure 13.4: Causes of service failure and negative emotions
Source: Nguyen & McColl-Kennedy 2002

Service recovery process: how it is done is critical

Service recovery is the action, or series of actions, a service provider takes in response to a service failure (Grönroos 1988). When an organisation is given information about a customer's dissatisfaction with the service, the organisation has the opportunity to recover the customer. If an organisation goes about recovering the customer in an appropriate manner, then it is possible that the customer will return to a state of satisfaction that is higher than before the failure. However, if the organisation goes about the service recovery process in the wrong way, the customer will become even more dissatisfied. The negative result will be magnified through first having the service failure and then having the organisation fail again. This is called the **double deviation** from expectations (Bitner, Booms & Tetreault 1990). We will look at two theories used by researchers to understand the service recovery process, and then examine the roles that people, emotions and cultural differences play in service recovery. The Australian Standard for Complaints handling is also discussed.

Justice theories

Justice theories have been used by several researchers (Tax, Brown & Chandrashekaran 1998; Sparks & McColl-Kennedy 1998, 2001; Smith, Bolton & Wagner 1999) as a theoretical framework for understanding the service recovery process. The central idea is that a customer's level of satisfaction and their future loyalty depends upon whether they felt that they were treated fairly — that is, whether justice was done (McColl-Kennedy & Sparks 2003). Three forms of justice are thought to operate:

- distributive justice
- procedural justice
- interactional justice.

Within a service recovery context, **distributive justice** may be defined as the outcome of the recovery process — that is, what the customer receives at the end of the recovery. Examples include a free drink voucher for missing out on an earlier booking at a show, and waiving of room charges if a stay in a hotel was considered unsatisfactory (McColl-Kennedy & Sparks 2003). Judgements of distributive justice are formed by comparing what the cus-

Service recovery: the actions a service provider takes in response to a service failure in order to 'put right' the service

Double deviation: a situation in which the organisation fails again in service recovery after having failed in the first place

Distributive justice: what the customer receives as an outcome of the recovery process

tomer received with what other customers received. However, it is not always possible in a service setting to know what another customer may have received for the same service failure. Therefore, Van den Bos, Vermunt and Wilke (1997) argue that evaluating the outcome is difficult, so customers may rely more on procedural and interactional justice actions to assess the overall fairness of the recovery process.

Procedural justice: the process used to resolve the problem

Certainly, **procedural justice** and interactional elements of justice have been found to be particularly important in services settings (Clemmer 1993; Sparks & McColl-Kennedy 2001; Tax, Brown & Chandrashekaran 1998). Folger & Cropanzano (1998) found that procedural and interactional justice moderate the evaluation of the outcome failure. That is, being treated fairly during the recovery process means much more than simply receiving a fair outcome (distributive justice). What matters is how the customer was treated rather than what was received. Procedural justice focuses on the process used to resolve the problem (McColl-Kennedy & Sparks 2003). This includes formal policies and structural considerations. Structural considerations include process control, such as allowing customers to 'voice' their concerns verbally or in writing (Bies & Shapiro 1988). Voicing allows customers to articulate exactly what they are thinking and feeling, thus letting the customer 'have their say'.

Interactional justice: the manner in which the problem is dealt with and the interactions between the service provider and the customer

Interactional justice is the manner in which the service problem is dealt with by service providers and the specific interactions between the service provider and the customer (Sparks & McColl-Kennedy 2001). Examples of specific elements of this are interpersonal sensitivity, treating people with dignity and respect, and providing explanations of the events. Service researchers such as Clemmer (1993) and Sparks & McColl-Kennedy (2001), have demonstrated the impact of interactional justice on the recovery process. Interestingly, Tax, Brown & Chandrashekaran (1998) found that interactional justice was the strongest predictor of trust in a service and the strongest predictor of a customer's overall satisfaction.

Fairness theory: an integrative framework

Although justice theories help us to understand how customers assess service recovery, fairness theory offers an integrative framework for understanding service failure and recovery, and it includes much of the justice research (Folger & Cropanzano 1998). In essence, fairness theory argues that negative perceptions of fairness associated with procedural justice, interactional justice and distributive justice are linked with the idea of accountability (Folger & Cropanzano 1998). This means that when a customer assesses the recovery process (that is, the procedural, interactional and distributive justice elements) as being unfair, the customer seeks to blame someone for the problem, including the motives and intentions of the person responsible for the offence (Folger & Cropanzano 2001). There are three components of accountability:

1. A negative event needs to occur that results in damage or harm to the customer (for example, a service failure that results in the customer experiencing damage such as damage to self-esteem).
2. There is some degree of volitional control in relation to the actions taken by the service provider (for example, the service provider could deal with the problem in a number of ways).

3. The actions of the service provider violate some type of moral principle (for example, the service provider does not give the customer their money back, even though the problem occurred because the organisation could not carry out the service requested by the customer and promised by the organisation when the service was ordered).

Figure 13.5 illustrates this fairness-based approach.

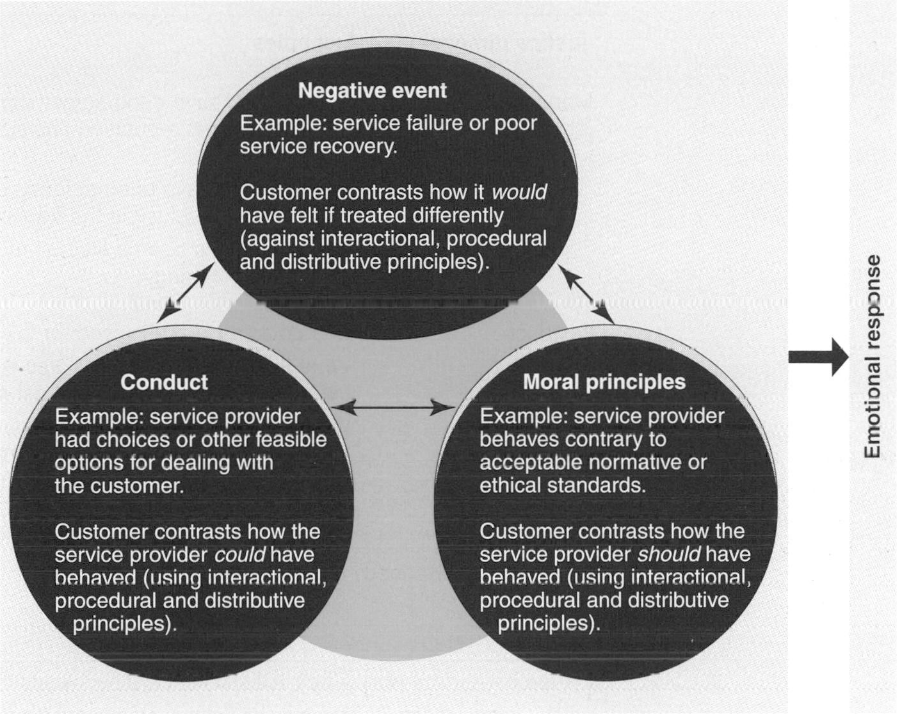

Figure 13.5: Fairness-based framework
Source: McColl-Kennedy & Sparks 2003

Counterfactual thinking

Counterfactual thinking:
thinking that is contrary to the facts

An important element of fairness theory is **counterfactual thinking** (Folger & Cropanzano 1998), which is thinking that is contrary to the facts (Roese 1997). In service failure or recovery situations, a customer may be able to imagine a sequence of actions that differs from what actually took place. In doing this, the customer is providing a contrastive framework about how things might have been if things had been done differently. Folger & Cropanzano (2001) argue that customers will use counterfactual thinking when assessing accountability for an event. Negative events such as service failures are especially likely to produce counterfactual thinking (Morris & Moore 2000). For instance, a customer who has been rudely treated by an insurance company representative may think to herself 'if only the rep had been polite to me, and had made an effort to look at me rather than look at the computer, I would have felt so much better'. Thus, in making this evaluative assessment the customer looks at who is accountable for how she is feeling. During this evaluation, McColl-Kennedy & Sparks (2003) argue that the customer engages in three contrastive actions: what *could* have occurred (the representative treating the customer with respect by looking at her and speaking politely); what *should* have occurred (looking at the customer and treating her politely — here, a moral judgement is being made); and how it *would* have felt had alternative action been taken (feeling happier).

As shown in table 13.2, the customer thinks of things that the service provider should have done. When a customer can think of actions that could have been undertaken by the service provider but were not, the customer feels that they were not treated properly, and further negative feelings are likely to result.

Table 13.2   Customers' counterfactual thinking examples for justice dimensions

Justice dimensions	Examples
Moral principles (should)	'They *should* have done something; I cannot imagine that a restaurant of that reputation and size would not have something vegetarian.'
	'There *should* have been at least a letter of apology that said "Sorry you were stuck in the transit lounge for 24 hours."'
	'He *should* have been a little bit more empathetic, a little bit more understanding.'
Conduct (could)	'She *could* have apologised for taking down the wrong order.'
	'What they *could* have done was so simple; it could have been just to go into the kitchen and get me some decent food.'
	'What they *could* have done … the responsibility thing is huge … if someone says, "Look you're right, we screwed up", that to me takes half the problem away; that takes all the stress and you go, "Okay, I don't have to fight with you to get something."'

Source: McColl-Kennedy & Sparks 2003

Service providers play a key role in service recovery

Service providers play a key role in service recovery. They can make customers feel the same, better or worse. But often these employees are not well trained in service recovery techniques and do not know what to do when a failure takes place. Should they do something straight away or wait until the customer gets really annoyed? Should they apologise? Should they give the customer what they want? What will the boss say? Some managers expect service providers to know what to do without giving them any training in service recovery. If service recovery is to be implemented within an organisation, there needs to be full commitment from top management, and service providers need to be given the training and ability to carry out service recovery in their work areas. (The importance of training was stressed in chapter 1 — see figure 1.5.) Training needs to take place in two key areas. First, service providers need to understand what the customer concerns are. Having the service provider think from the customer's perspective is helpful. It is easier for the service provider to understand what the customer is feeling if they put themselves in the customer's shoes. How does it feel to have missed a flight? How does it feel not to get the hotel room overlooking the beach that you thought you had booked and paid for?

The second area is understanding what the organisation is prepared to do to recover the customer. How much effort does the organisation want the service provider to put into recovering the customer? Often the organisation must let the frontline service provider make on-the-spot decisions about how much compensation to offer the customer and how much effort to go to for the customer. The international hotel chain Ritz Carlton is well known for its policy of empowering frontline staff to resolve problems on the spot.

Australian standards for complaints handling

In 1995, Standards Australia published AS4269 Complaints Handling to provide businesses with guidelines on how to effectively handle complaints in order to improve customer satisfaction. The standard specifies the crucial elements of an effective complaints-handling process, and how to successfully implement such a process. It also details complaint-handling procedures that frontline employees can apply when addressing a customer's complaint.

First, the standard states that there should be commitment at all levels of the organisation and that this commitment should be demonstrated in the distribution of documented policies for complaints resolution. Second, the standard states that the complaints process should be fair. The extract below outlines what a customer should do to ensure they are treated fairly (Australian Standard Complaints Handling 1995):

- be heard
- check that the organisation's product/service guidelines have been followed
- provide all relevant material
- be informed of the process criteria and avenue for review
- be informed of the response
- be informed of the reasons for the decision
- know that the complaint will be viewed by an independent person/body

In addition, the standard also says that customers should have access to information; explanatory information through such things as brochures, interviews and correspondence; a response; and remedies such as refunds, replacements, repairs and substitutes.

An international customer service standard (CSIA 2002) has recently been made available. This document has been developed by the Customer Service Institute of Australia, and may be applied to non-profit as well as for profit and government organisations.

Role of emotions

At the time of a service failure (as illustrated in the extract from the service diaries at the beginning of this chapter) and during service recovery attempts, customers are likely to experience strong emotions such as anger, frustration, rage, joy and delight. Service researchers are just beginning to study emotions during recovery (Smith & Bolton 2002, Andreassen 1999). Customers are not the only ones to experience heightened emotions during service failure and recovery; service employees are also likely to experience emotions. The impact of employee emotions on the customer and on their levels of satisfaction with the service recovery attempt has to date been neglected.

Emotional intelligence: *'the ability to perceive emotions, to access and generate emotions so as to assist thought, to understand emotions and emotional knowledge; and to reflectively regulate emotions so as to promote emotional and intellectual growth' (Mayer & Salovey 1997, p.5)*

However, considerable attention has been given to the role of emotions by organisational psychologists. There is certainly evidence that emotion experienced by the employee does affect the service provider directly and this in turn affects others around them (Bass 1990; Conger & Kanungo 1998; Lewis 2000). Service providers not only need to be aware of the customer's emotions, but also need to be able to control their own emotions. '**Emotional intelligence** is the ability to perceive emotions; to access and generate emotions so as to assist thought; to understand emotions and emotional knowledge; and to reflectively regulate emotions so as to promote emotional and intellectual growth' (Mayer & Salovey 1997, p. 5).

Emotionally intelligent service providers will be able to recognise when a customer is feeling annoyed and will respond appropriately. Showing concern, providing an apology and allowing a customer to voice their feelings will be related to whether the service provider has the ability to appropriately read a customer's emotions and level of dissatisfaction, and whether the service provider has the ability to appropriately respond to the emotionally laden situation (Mayer, Caruso & Salovey 1999).

Some cultures are more reticent about expressing their emotions than others. It is well documented that individualistic Western cultures such as Australia, New Zealand, the United States, Canada and Britain tend to be more expressive than collectivist Asian cultures such as Japan, Korea, Taiwan, and China (Markus & Kitayama 1994; Matsumoto 1989). Individualistic cultures place particular importance on needs and goals of self, exhibiting behaviours that emphasise separatedness. Further, they believe that the individual is autonomous and that individual behaviours are emotionally detached from the collective. In contrast, collectivist cultures tend to emphasise collective needs and goals (Triandis 1988).

Markus and Kitayama (1991) argue that ego-focused emotions such as anger, frustration and pride tend to be associated with an individual's own needs and goals. Other-focused emotions such as empathy, shame, peacefulness and indebtedness tend to be associated with other people's needs and goals. Other-focused emotions will tend to be expressed by interdependent cultures, whereas emotions that focus on an individual's own self (anger, frustration and pride) will tend to be expressed in Western, individualistic cultures. (See also chapter 1 on the role of emotions in services marketing.)

Successful recovery in practice

For successful service recovery, services providers need to recognise how the customer is feeling; for instance, does the customer appear to be annoyed, frustrated or angry. Emotion can be identified through one's facial expressions. For example, when a person is feeling happy they tend to smile, when concerned they tend to frown and when angry they tend to look very serious. They may start to go red in the face or neck and exhibit other physiological expressions. Next, the service provider should listen attentively to what the customer is saying and note the customer's body language, as it often reflects how someone is feeling. If the customer is not saying anything, then the service provider could ask if the customer is happy with everything so far. Next, it is important for the service provider to think of feasible alternatives and offer these to the customer. If the customer can think of feasible alternatives (by engaging in counterfactual thinking) and the service provider does not offer any of these, then the customer will feel that the organisation has not done the right thing by them and has not put in any effort. This is likely to be interpreted as lack of interest or concern for the customer (McColl-Kennedy & Sparks 2003). This in turn is likely to result in more negative emotions, such as frustration, anger and possibly even rage, because the customer's ego and goals have been affected. Throughout the process it is important that the service provider show concern about the situation and the customer particularly (Sparks & McColl-Kennedy 2001). If compensation is offered, the compensation should be commensurate with the problem. Offering too much may appear to be an overreaction to the problem, and will seem strange and inappropriate. Above all, there should be consistency between process and outcome. Customers are not only interested in what they will get out of the organisation, but also how they are treated by the organisation and by the individual service providers during the service recovery process.

The following is a checklist for successful service recovery:

1. Recognise emotions in the customer and in one's self.
2. Listen to what the customer is saying.
3. Show concern.
4. Allow the customer to voice their feelings and views.
5. Offer feasible options and check back with the customer for understanding.
6. Offer an apology.
7. Consider compensation.
8. Put effort into the recovery process.
9. Think from the customer's perspective.

Summary

LO1: Understand the importance of service recovery to organisations.
- It is important to attempt to recover dissatisfied customers, as customer satisfaction is linked to organisational success.
- If organisations go about service recovery in an appropriate manner, they can restore customer satisfaction and may even be able to raise the level of customer satisfaction to a level that is higher than it was before the service failure.

LO2: Explain and provide examples of the different types of service failure.
- Service failure is a breakdown in the delivery of a service. This can result from four key areas:
  1. the service itself
  2. service providers
  3. things outside the service provider's control
  4. customer related.

LO3: Outline complaint behaviour.
- Customers have several options, including:
  - making a complaint
  - intending to discontinue with the service
  - giving a warning to friends
  - taking legal action
  - exiting or boycotting.
- If customers do not complain, the organisation loses the opportunity to fix the problem, so it is important to encourage customers to complain.
- Complaints can be obtained by organisations through a variety of means, including:
  - complaints boxes
  - complaint forms
  - dedicated phone lines
  - satisfaction and/or exit surveys and comment cards
  - directly, through the customers themselves.
- E-complaining — voicing dissatisfaction through an electronic website — represents the latest form of complaining and may eventually take the place of more traditional avenues such as Consumer Affairs.
- The Stephens and Gwinner (1998) model of consumer complaint behaviour is useful in that it helps us understand why some customers complain to an

organisation when they are dissatisfied, while others do not. They argue that customers assess the dissatisfying experience in terms of whether it affects their well-being, particularly in terms of goal relevance, goal congruence and ego-involvement.

LO4: Discuss what the service recovery process is.

- Service recovery is the actions a service provider takes in response to a service failure (Grönroos 1988).
- Service recovery can return the customer to a state of satisfaction that is higher than it was before the failure.
- If the service provider goes about the service recovery in the wrong way, the customer can become even more dissatisfield.
- The service recovery process is not just about outcomes (distributive justice), but also includes process elements (procedural justice) and interactions with the customer (interactional justice).

LO5: Describe the three aspects of justice theory.

- Justice theories have been proposed as a framework for understanding service recovery.
- Three forms of justice are thought to operate:
  1. distributive justice
  2. procedural justice
  3. interactional justice.

LO6: Outline fairness theory and its application to service recovery.

- Fairness theory offers an integrative framework for understanding service failure and recovery, and it includes much of the justice research.
- Essentially, fairness theory argues that when a customer assesses the recovery process as being unfair (that is, in terms of procedural, interactional and distributive justice elements), the customer seeks to determine who is accountable and may engage in counterfactual thinking.

LO7: Describe counterfactual thinking.

- Counterfactual thinking is thinking thoughts contrary to the facts.
- During the customer's evaluation of the recovery process, the customer engages in three contrastive actions:
  1. what *could* have occurred
  2. what *should* have occurred
  3. how it *would* have felt had alternative action been taken.

LO8: Understand the role of emotions.

- Emotions are heightened during service failure and recovery, with customers likely to experience strong emotions such as anger, frustration, rage, joy or delight.

LO9: Outline the key elements of successful service recovery.

- A checklist for successful service recovery is:
  1. recognise emotions
  2. listen
  3. show concern
  4. allow customer voice
  5. offer feasible options
  6. offer apology
  7. consider compensation
  8. put in effort
  9. think from the customer's perspective.

key terms

Complaints: expressions of dissatisfaction or disapproval (p. 334)

Counterfactual thinking: thinking that is contrary to the facts (p. 345)

Distributive justice: what the customer receives as an outcome of the recovery process (p. 343)

Double deviation: a situation in which the organisation fails again in service recovery after having failed in the first place (p. 343)

E-complaining: voicing dissatisfaction through a website (p. 338)

Ego involvement: the extent to which a situation touches an individual's ego-identity, which involves self-esteem, social esteem, personal value, moral value, meanings, ego and ideas (p. 342)

Emotional intelligence: 'the ability to perceive emotions; to access and generate emotions so as to assist thought; to understand emotions and emotional knowledge; and to reflectively regulate emotions so as to promote emotional and intellectual growth' (Mayer & Salovey 1997, p. 5) (p. 347)

Goal incongruence: the extent to which an event does not meet the desires of the customer, or is judged to be inconsistent with what the customer wants (p. 341)

Goal relevance: the extent to which a problem is perceived to be relevant to the customer's well-being (p. 341)

Interactional justice: the manner in which the problem is dealt with and the interactions between the service provider and the customer (p. 344)

Procedural justice: the process used to resolve the problem (p. 344)

Service failure: a breakdown in the delivery of a service (p. 331)

Service recovery: the actions a service provider takes in response to a service failure in order to 'put right' the service (p. 343)

review questions

1. Why is it important to recover dissatisfied customers?
2. Some customers never complain. Why?
3. What are the key options customers may use when complaining?
4. Define service failure.
5. Outline the key elements of successful service recovery.

application questions

1. With reference to table 13.1, into which category would you put the following service failure?

   As a family of three (mother and two daughters), we went to a restaurant on impulse after attending a school gymnastics event. We arrived at 7.30 p.m. without a booking and were shown to a table in the restaurant's courtyard, as all the tables inside were taken. We were invited to select a table outside and advised that we would be moved inside as soon as a table became vacant. Our dinner order was taken promptly and we were given water to drink, as we requested. The entrée of garlic bread arrived within 15 minutes. As it became colder and colder outside, we checked to see if any tables had become vacant inside and were reassured that we would get the first available table. By 8.30 p.m. our meals had not arrived and we were becoming restless. Other patrons outside had also not received their meals and were getting annoyed. Again I went inside and spoke to the staff who advised me that our meals would be ready soon. At 9 p.m. we were shown to a table inside the restaurant. We were reassured once more that our meal would be ready soon. Inside the restaurant I noticed that other patrons who had arrived earlier than us were only just getting served. At 9.30 p.m. we decided to leave. I offered to pay for the garlic bread but the waitress apologised and said they would waive the cost. They apologised for the delay and we left. I felt disappointed with the way we were treated at the restaurant, particularly that no-one came to explain that they were extremely busy and that there would be a long wait. Sitting outside the restaurant looking through the glass at those eating inside was very uncomfortable and isolating. When the children began to act that they were begging for food from other patrons behind the glass window, I felt embarrassed and disappointed that our 'girl's night out' was spoilt. However, the children regarded the evening as a great success and a huge joke. I was relieved that my husband wasn't there to witness the disaster (Johnston 2001).

(a) In your view, what brought about these failures?
(b) How would you evaluate the response taken by the service providers?
(c) How would you recommend going about recovering these failures? Justify your response.

2. How would you go about recovering a customer who is really angry? Justify each step.

3. Think about a service recovery attempt that you felt was handled very badly. Outline the steps the service provider took. Why was this unsatisfactory?

4. Roleplay an interaction with a service provider and a customer who has just tried to check into a five-star resort that is overbooked. The customer has flown into the resort from interstate. It is 10 o'clock on a Friday night. How would you suggest the resort recover this very tired and angry customer? Be specific.

5. Try to recall a very satisfactory service recovery that you have experienced. Why was this so successful? To what extent were elements of the checklist (page 349) used?

 vignette questions

1. Read the Services Marketing Action vignette on pages 336–38 and answer the following questions:
   (a) Do you know of another organisation that has 'customer service champions'? List any organisations that could benefit from putting in place a similar process to that of Centrelink.
   (b) What are the key benefits of:
      • customer service champions
      • value creation workshops
      • customer complaint boxes?

2. Read the Services Marketing on the Web Vignette on pages 339–40. Visit one of the complaint sites identified. Choose one customer complaint made online regarding a dissatisfying service experience.
   (a) In your view, what is the essence of the problem?
   (b) What are the benefits of using an electronic complaints site for this particular complaint?

 ## recommended readings

For an overview of justice theory applied to service recovery, see:

Sparks, B. & McColl-Kennedy, J. R. 2001, 'Justice strategy options for increased customer satisfaction in a service recovery setting', *Journal of Business Research*, vol. 54, pp. 209–18.

This article focuses on the importance of *how* service recovery takes place. It provides an overview of justice theory, including procedural, interactional and distributive justice, and their importance to customer satisfaction:

Tax, S. S., Brown, S. W. & Chandrashekaran, M. 1998, 'Customer evaluations of service complaint experiences: implications for relationship marketing', *Journal of Marketing*, vol. 62, April, pp. 60–76.

For a concise overview of the service recovery literature, see:

Tax, S. S. & Brown, S. W. 2000, 'Service recovery: research insights and practice', in Swartz, T. A. & Iacobucci, D. (eds), *Handbook of Services Marketing & Management*, Sage Publications, Thousand Oaks, CA.

 ## references

Andreassen, T. W. 1999, 'What drives customer loyalty with complaint resolution', *Journal of Service Research*, vol. 1, no. 4, pp. 324–32.

Anderson, A. R. 1985, 'Consumer responses to dissatisfaction in loose monopolies', *Journal of Consumer Research*, vol. 12, pp. 135–41.

Australian Standard Complaints Handling 1995, AS4269.

Bass, B. M. 1990, *Bass and Stogdill's Handbook of Leadership*, Free Press, New York.

Bies, R. J. & Shapiro, D. L. 1988, 'Voice and justification: their influence on procedural fairness judgments', *Academy of Management Journal*, vol. 31, pp. 676–85.

Bitner, M. J, Booms, B. H. & Tetreault, M. S. 1990, 'The service encounter: diagnosing favorable and unfavorable incidents', *Journal of Marketing*, vol. 54, January, pp. 71–84.

Brown, S. W., Fisk, R.P. & Bitner, M. J. 1994, 'The development and emergence of services marketing thought', *International Journal of Service Industries Management*, vol. 5, pp. 21–48.

Centrelink 2000, *Customer Service Champion Manual*.

Clemmer, E. C. 1993, 'An investigation into the relationship of fairness and customer satisfaction with services', in Cropanzano, R. (ed.), *Justice in the Workplace: Approaching Fairness in Human Resource Management*, Lawrence Erlbaum Associates, Hillsdale, NJ, pp. 193–207.

Conger, J. & Kanungo, R. 1998, *Charismatic Leadership in Organizations*, Sage, Thousand Oaks, CA.

CSIA (Customer Service Institute of Australia), accessed September 2002, *International Customer Service Standard 1999–2002*, www.csia.com.au/standards.asp.

Day, R. L. & Landon, E. L. 1977, 'Toward a theory of consumer complaining behaviour', in Woodside, A. G., Sheth, J. N. &. Bennett, P. D. (eds), *Consumer and Industrial Buying Behaviour*, North Holland, New York, pp. 425–37.

Folger, R. & Cropanzano, R. 1998, *Organisational Justice and Human Resource Management*, Sage, Thousand Oaks, CA.

Folger, R. & Cropanzano, R. 2001, 'Fairness theory: justice as accountability', in Greenberg, J. & Cropanzano, R. (eds), *Advances in Organisational Justice*, Stanford University Press, California, pp. 1–55.

Fornell, C. & Wernerfelt, B. 1987, 'Defensive marketing strategy by customer complaint management: a theoretical analysis', *Journal of Marketing Research*, vol. 24, November, pp. 337–46.

Grönroos, C. 1988, 'Service quality: the six criteria of good service quality', *Review of Business*, vol. 9, winter, pp. 10–13.

Hart, C. W. L., Heskett, J. L. & Sasser, W. E. 1990, 'The profitable art of service recovery', *Harvard Business Review*, vol. 68, July–August, pp. 148–56.

Heskett, J. L., Jones, T. O., Loveman, G. W., Sasser, W. E. & Schlesinger, L. A. 1994, 'Putting the service–profit chain to work', *Harvard Business Review*, March/April, pp. 164–72.

Hirschman, A. O. 1970, *Exit, Voice and Loyalty*, Cambridge University Press, Cambridge, MA.

Izard, C. E. 1977, *Human Emotion*, Plenum, New York.

Johnston, M. 2001, personal communication.

Lazarus, R. S. 1991a, 'Cognition and motivation in emotion', *American Psychologist*, vol. 46, April, pp. 352–67.

Lazarus, R. S. 1991b, *Emotion and Adaptation*, Oxford University Press, New York.

Lazarus, R. S. & Folkman, S. 1984, *Stress, Appraisal and Coping*, Springer, New York.

Lewis, K. M. 2000, 'When leaders display emotion: how followers respond to negative emotional expression of male and female leaders', *Journal of Organizational Behavior*, vol. 21, pp. 221–34.

Markus, H. R. & Kitayama, S. 1991, 'Culture and the self: implications for cognition, emotion and motivation', *Psychological Review*, vol. 98, no. 2, pp. 224–53.

Markus, H. R. & Kitayama, S. 1994, 'The cultural construction of self and emotion: implications for social behaviour', in Kitayama, S. & Markus, H. R. (eds), *Emotion and Culture: Empirical Studies of Mutual Influence*, American Psychological Association, Washington, DC.

Matsumoto, D. 1989, 'Cultural influences on the perception of emotion', *Journal of Cross-Cultural Psychology*, vol. 20, no. 1, pp. 92–105.

Mayer, J. D., Caruso, D. & Salovey, P. 1999, 'Emotional intelligence meets traditional standards for an intelligence', *Intelligence*, vol. 27, pp. 267–98.

Mayer, J. D. & Salovey, P. 1997, 'What is emotional intelligence?', in Salovey, P. & Sluter, D. J. (eds), *Emotional Development and Emotional Intelligence*, Basic Books, New York.

McColl-Kennedy, J. R. & Sparks, B. 2003, 'Application of fairness theory to service failure and service recovery', *Journal of Service Research*, vol. 5, February.

Ministerial Council on Consumer Affairs, accessed June 2002, www.consumer.gov.au.

Morris, M. W. & Moore, P. C. 2000, 'The lessons we (don't) learn: counterfactual thinking and organisational accountability after a close call', *Administrative Science Quarterly*, vol. 45, pp. 737–65.

Nguyen, D. T. & McColl-Kennedy, J. R. 2002, 'Customer cognitive appraisal and anger in the service recovery context: a conceptual framework', paper presented at International Services Marketing Conference, Brisbane, 4–5 July.

Nguyen, D. T. & McColl-Kennedy, J. R. forthcoming, 'Diffusing customer anger in service recovery: a conceptual framework', Special Issue, *Australasian Marketing Journal*.

Richins, M. 1983, 'Negative word of mouth by dissatisfied consumers: a pilot study', *Journal of Marketing*, vol. 68, pp.105–11.

Roese, N. J. 1997, 'Counterfactual thinking', *Psychological Bulletin*, vol. 121, no. 1, pp. 133–48.

Roseman, I. J., Spindel, M. S. & Jose, P. E. 1990, 'Appraisals of emotion-eliciting events: testing a theory of discrete emotions', *Journal of Personality and Social Psychology*, vol. 59, pp. 899–915.

Singh, J. 1988, 'Consumer complaint intentions and behaviour: definitional and taxonomical issues', *Journal of Marketing*, vol. 52, pp. 93–107.

Smith, A. K. & Bolton, R. N. 2002, 'The effect of customers' emotional responses to service failures on their recovery effort evaluations and satisfaction judgments', *Journal of the Academy of Marketing Science*, vol. 30, no. 1, pp. 5–23.

Smith, A. K., Bolton, R. N. & Wagner, J. 1999, 'A model of customer satisfaction with service encounters involving failure and recovery', *Journal of Marketing Research*, vol. 26, August, pp. 356–72.

Smith, C. A. & Ellsworth, P. C. 1985, 'Patterns of cognitive appraisal in emotion', *Journal of Personality and Social Psychology*, vol. 48, no. 4, pp. 813–18.

Sparks, B. & McColl-Kennedy, J. R. 1998, 'The application of procedural justice principles to service recovery attempts: outcomes for customer satisfaction', *Advances in Consumer Research*, vol. 25, pp. 156–61.

Sparks, B. & McColl-Kennedy, J. R. 2001, 'Justice strategy options for increased customer satisfaction in a service recovery setting', *Journal of Business Research*, vol. 54, pp. 209–18.

Stephens, N. & Gwinner, K. P. 1998, 'Why don't some people complain? A cognitive–emotive process model of consumer complaint behaviour', *Journal of the Academy of Marketing Science*, vol. 26, no. 3, pp. 172–89.

TARP 1995, *American Express–SOCAP Study of Complaint Handling in Australia*, Society of Consumer Affairs Professional in Business, Australia.

Tax, S. S., Brown, S. W. & Chandrashekaran, M. 1998, 'Customer evaluations of service complaint experiences: implications for relationship marketing', *Journal of Marketing*, vol. 62, April, pp. 60–76.

Throssell, G. 2001, personal communication.

Triandis, H. C. 1988, 'Collectivism and individualism: a reconceptualization of a basic concept in cross-cultural social psychology', in Verma, G. K. & Bagley, C. (eds), *Personality Attitudes and Cognitions*, Macmillan, London.

Van den Bos, K. R., Vermunt, R. & Wilke, H. A. M. 1997, 'Procedural and distributive justice: what is fair depends more on what comes first than on what comes next', *Journal of Personality and Social Psychology*, vol. 72, no. 1, pp. 95–104.

Part 5

Specialisation

Chapter 14
E-services

Judy Drennan

LEARNING OBJECTIVES:

After reading this chapter you should be able to:

- explain what is meant by e-services
- describe what companies need to do to create customer-effective e-services
- illustrate how digital technology has affected the services industry
- describe the services trends in online distribution channels
- discuss the value for customers in e-financial services
- demonstrate an understanding of online privacy and security issues.

CHAPTER OUTLINE

The aim of this chapter is to examine the impact of the Internet on the service industry, and describe the strategies that service companies are implementing to attract and retain customers in an online environment. It examines both web-based and mobile-directed delivery of services, and discusses the development of new opportunities in the electronic distribution channel. Most importantly, it considers the value of online services for consumers and highlights online privacy and security issues.

First, the chapter introduces and defines e-services, then examines the growth of e-services around the world. The impact of digital technology on the services sector is described, and issues relating to disintermediation and the emergence of new intermediaries are discussed. Service trends in online distribution channels are explored, and examples of broker-based, agent-based and aggregator services are discussed. Next, e-financial services are described, and specific examples relating to e-banking and online insurance are provided. The next section focuses on online consulting, and discusses new directions in online legal services and e-health. Finally, privacy and security issues are examined.

Introduction

Consider this scenario. You plan to meet with your friends to go to a concert in the city. Unfortunately, you're running late and, in your haste, you trip over a crack in the footpath. Sprawled on the ground, you come to the conclusion that you've either twisted or broken your ankle. Unsteadily, you sit up, pull out your mobile device and press the speed-dial connecting you to your doctor. The receptionist, on taking your call, asks for your personal code, which you key in. With this information, the receptionist is able to pull up your records immediately on screen, check your insurance cover, and send your details down the line for you to confirm. Upon confirmation, he can then refer you to the doctor, who will question you about your symptoms, arrange for interim medical attention to arrive and have you transported to the nearest medical facility. Wireless digital technology has enabled your doctor's surgery to provide an online service regardless of your whereabouts.

Services Marketing Action: HealthDirect

One example of an innovative e-health program is the HealthDirect service that was set up by High Performance Healthcare and the Health Department of Western Australia in 1999. This service, which is used as a 'frontline' tool, matches consumer needs with the most appropriate and cost effective health-care services by using the latest telephone and information technology. The three main technology components are:

1. a flexible PABX which is combined with special call management software that makes it easy to route the calls and enables the performance of the call centre to be measured and reported
2. a strong local area network that is able to cope with demand 24 hours a day, seven days a week, 365 days a year
3. a case management system that has guidelines built into it to make sure that the decisions made by the nurses about patient care are consistent in all cases.

This allows the nurse to search by the caller's identified symptoms for an appropriate guideline; determine through a series of questions the appropriate disposition and self-care advice (such as 'See your GP within 24 hours'); and then provide the caller with information about service provider availability. Callers can be directed to appropriate providers through the nurse's access to a database of all health service providers, including GPs. It is envisaged that a voice response system and web-agent technology will allow 'intelligent' access to nurse agent advice via the web.

Source: adapted from NOIE 2002a

Mobile portal offerings now include voice capability, compression, security and quality of service, and enable access to enterprise resource planning, customer relationship management, database, e-mail and voicemail content, as well as integrated payment systems to enable secure electronic transactions over wireless devices (Duffy 2000). It can be seen from the twisted ankle scenario that a traditional bricks-and-mortar professional service can grasp

We can see that the population is geared up for e-services, but what about businesses? A breakdown of Internet use by industry in Australia shows that, in June 2000, the electricity, gas and water supply industry was in the lead, with 79 per cent of its companies online. Other well-represented industries included property and business services (76 per cent), finance and insurance (71 per cent), and cultural and recreational services (63 per cent). In terms of growth, the accommodation, cafés and restaurants sector recorded the highest rate of increase from 14 per cent to 40 per cent between June 1998 and June 2000. As shown in figure 14.2, all industries showed increases in Internet access except the communication services. As an indicator of this substantial growth in Internet access, the US-based Economic Intelligence Unit (EIU) moved Australia from sixteenth place in May 2000 to second place in May 2001 in its publication of E-business Readiness Rankings for over 60 countries (Economic Intelligence Unit 2001). These rankings are based on a set of indicators under the following categories: connectivity; business environment; e-commerce consumer and business adoption; supporting e-services (online intermediaries, Internet-hosting companies, application service providers, website developers, etc.); and social and cultural infrastructure.

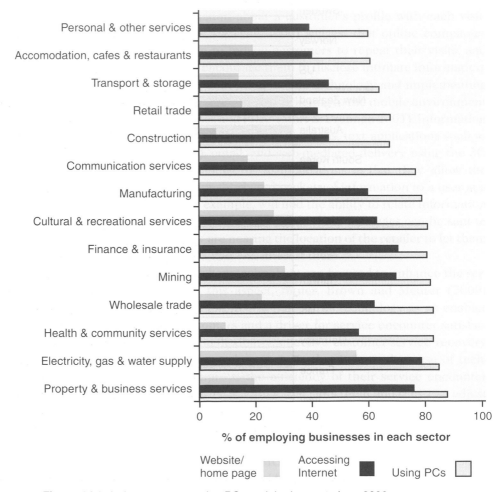

Figure 14.2: Industry sectors using PCs and the Internet, June 2000
Source: NOIE 2002b; Business Use of Information Technology, ABS 8129

Impact of digital technology on the services industry

The impact of digital technology on the services industry has been vast. This section takes a broad perspective to give you an understanding of how digital technology has affected the service sector overall. Within this sector, large organisations such as banks, financial service institutions, airlines, utilities and government organisations have been major buyers of information technology (IT). They have also been involved in the initial design, financing and dispersal of the technology.

You can understand how an IT push by large, influential organisations would have affected the smaller companies that act as **intermediaries** (those companies that play a role in transferring a product, service or information between the supplier and consumer) in their distribution channel. Generally, they were required to adopt the technology themselves if they wanted to stay part of the group of companies within the channel (Alexander 1992, Quinn 1992). Thus, there was widespread penetration of digital technology in service industries, and this in turn broke down the boundaries between them. Airlines, for example, no longer competed just against those within the airline industry itself; they also competed against travel agents, tour groups, and retailers of products sold through in-flight catalogues (Quinn 1992). To illustrate, we have seen how airlines such as Virgin Blue now offer highly competitive prices to customers who book their own tickets online rather than go through a travel agent.

A further outcome of the introduction of digital technology was that many of the tasks undertaken by intermediaries were automated. Moreover, as seen by our previous example, customers were now able to connect directly with airlines via the Internet. This led to concerns that the Internet would cause disintermediation — a term that will be explained in the following section.

Intermediaries: those companies that play a role in transferring a product, service or information between the supplier and consumer within their distribution channel

Disintermediation

Disintermediation is the process whereby traditional intermediaries are eliminated (Alba et al. 1997; Quinn 1992). For example, the online selling of software, compact disks or books directly to the consumer squeezes out the traditional retailers. If it is possible to bypass intermediaries, profit margins along the value chain can be redistributed to producers and consumers (Lewis & Talalayevsky 1997). One of the major fears for intermediaries such as travel agents is the ability of customers to connect directly with airlines. The concern is that the intermediary may be at risk of being 'squeezed out' of the value chain. Airlines' direct consumer accessibility to computer reservation systems and to computerised frequent-flyer programs, which build brand loyalty to one airline can reduce the use of travel agents. However, travel agents represent an important intermediary between airlines (the producer) and consumers, because they provide expertise. Interestingly we are seeing the advent of the online travel agent, which suggests that disintermediation has not occurred; rather, an online intermediary has emerged.

Disintermediation: the process whereby traditional intermediaries are eliminated

Survival of the smartest

As exemplified by travel agents, smart intermediaries will use IT to strengthen their bonds with suppliers and customers. However, they may have to radically reinvent their business in order to survive. For intermediaries to gain competitive advantage and success in this electronically driven market place, there will need to be a significant shift in the value-adding that they bring to the supply chain. Further, customers must perceive the value offered by the intermediary to be essential. For some intermediaries, this may involve an alteration in the scope of their business (Cort, Stith & Lahoti 1997).

Intermediaries most likely to survive and gain competitive advantage are those that adapt successfully to IT (Cort et al. 1997). They need to focus on achieving efficiencies in internal functions and redesign business processes to take advantage of IT to serve their customers' needs. Further, they must have a strategy for creating value by using IT effectively to leverage knowledge and redesign relationships in the networks (Venkatraman 1994).

A particularly successful strategy has been the replacement or supplementation of traditional intermediaries with their online equivalents (Strauss & Frost 2001). Many retailers (such as www.colesonline.com.au), real estate agents (such as www.raywhite.com.au) and tax agents (such as www.hrblock.com) have successfully added an online service to their traditional services. Other intermediaries choose to operate solely as an online presence because there are none of the overhead expenses of a bricks-and-mortar company. For example, online groceries such as www.aussie-shopper.com.au and www.fooddirect.com.au can gain take advantage of their lowered costs to deliver fresh food to time-poor customers at prices that are relatively competitive with their bricks-and-mortar counterparts. Therefore, we can see that an e-service can be an augmentation of a traditional service or it can represent a core service in itself. Both these types of online services will be discussed in more detail in the next section.

Service trends in online distribution channels

In our discussion on disintermediation, we saw that some intermediaries were under threat of being squeezed out of the value chain by new technological developments. To counter this perceived threat, many firms augmented their traditional services with online services. One of the most exciting new trends has been the development of new kinds of intermediary roles in e-services. One such example is the mobilemediary. Wireless technology allows the **mobilemediary** to break into the value chain at any point to provide information and transactional capabilities to customers at the time and place that they are ready to purchase a service or buy a product. Importantly, the mobilemediary will be more about context (where you are and what you want to do) rather than content (Kenny & Marshall 2000).

One example of a company that is offering a mobilemediary service is Gadget-Space Inc. This service will 'mobilise' applications of any vendor for any mobile device, and will enable users to pull information from a range of applications. Such users may include salepersons who need to build up a view of a customer's account before a meeting, by accessing data from the customer database, the company's inventory and accounts systems (Wexler 2002).

Another example can be found in the financial services area. In order to reduce the frustration felt by consumers who must deal with a third party, such as a bank, to transact over the Internet, AZYGO Inc states that it has developed a payments

Mobilemediary: a new kind of intermediary that uses wireless technology and can break into the value chain at any point to provide information and transactional capabilities to customers at the time and place that they want to buy a product or service

platform that will impact on Internet billing. It is downloaded from a customer's financial institution, and embeds in their web browser so that it can be accessed with one click anywhere online. This allows the financial services institute to become a mobilemediary that can break into the value chain at any point and bring secure transaction capability to customers whenever and wherever they are ready to buy (AZYGO 2002).

Other online intermediary activities that have developed as a result of the Internet and e-commerce capabilities include exchanges, auctions and **aggregators**. Exchange activities are commonly undertaken by **brokers** and **agents**, and we will now examine these two types of intermediaries to consider their online service strategies.

Broker-based services

Brokers normally work on commission and they create markets in which both buyers and sellers of services are able to complete transactions online. It is important to note that they do not represent either the buyer or the seller, but merely provide the services to make exchange and negotiation possible (Strauss & Frost 2001). In the online world, the most recognised brokerage models are exchanges and auctions.

Online exchanges and trading

Predictions were made that more than 20 million people would be trading stocks, bonds, mutual funds and commodities online by 2002 (Turban 2000). In the United States alone, households using an online trading service rose from 2.7 million in May 1999 to 3.5 million in January 2000, representing a 30 per cent increase (Morrison 2001).

An example of online exchange or trading is E*Trade (www.etrade.com) which offers services such as an investor network, bookstore and personalised home page on Internet-enabled phone or handheld computers (PDAs) to access mobile wireless financial services. For buyers, the value-added services provided by online brokers include convenience, speed, lower prices, decreased search time and reduced frustration in locating appropriate sellers. For sellers, there are lowered transaction and customer acquisition costs (Strauss & Frost 2001). The E*Trade website stands as a message of affordable trading for the mass market, while also supplying a product that enables customers to research companies, make investment decisions and customise their stocks (Mohammed et al. 2001).

Online auctions

Online auctions, which started in 1995 (Turban et al. 2000) have also become extremely popular, and eBay (www.eBay.com.au), in particular, has been innovative in delivering an enormous range of product categories, appraisal services and electronic payment to its customers. More importantly, it provides value by facilitating easy exchange between sellers and buyers. For example, eBay developed a relationship with e-Stamp, which is a US postal service product that allows individuals to purchase and print stamps online to save sellers time and effort. It also has a relationship with iShip to enable buyers to estimate shipping costs. Other partnerships are with Tradenable, which is an escrow service to take custody of the money for the buyer until set conditions are met, and Billpoint, which provides secure online credit-card transactions (Mohammed et al. 2001). The Internet makes it possible to execute auctions more cheaply and with larger numbers of buyers and sellers all around the world. However, two major limitations are the inability to see the items physically and the possibility of fraud (Turban et al. 2000).

It is also possible to have a **reverse auction** where the website serves as a purchasing agent for individual buyers. Here, it is the buyer who specifies a price and the sellers bid for the buyer's business. An Australian example of a reverse auction site is Lowestbid (www.lowestbid.com.au), which is a trading exchange for energy supplies in the business-to-business market. It is also worth looking at Priceline (www.priceline.com) as an example of a reverse auction in the business-to-consumer market for a range of products such as airline tickets and home finance.

Reverse auction: where the website serves as a purchasing agent for individual buyers who specify a price, and the sellers bid for the buyer's business

This leads us to discuss other agent-based services that have developed on the Internet over the last few years.

Agent-based services

Agents can represent either the seller or buyer, and will represent the interests of whichever has hired them. Examples of online, agency-based services are in employment placement, real estate and the travel industry. These will be discussed to examine how they operate and provide value for their customers.

Online travel and tourism services

As the public has become more confident in using the Internet, websites that offer travel agent services with cost savings for the consumer have become popular (for example www.oztravel.com.au, www.traveland.com.au, www.travel.com.au, www.airfare.com.au). These online travel agencies provide information regarding trips, accommodation, entertainment, reservations, interactivity and purchasing of tickets. In addition, they may provide tips from seasoned travellers, fare comparisons, world news, chatrooms, bulletin boards, specials and frequent-flyer deals (Turban et al. 2000). Intelligent agents can also help customers to find a match for their destination, budget and other special requirements.

It can be seen that these online travel services offer real value to customers in terms of access to free information from any place and at any time. Customers are also able to learn from other travellers and gain useful information and advice in an electronic form of word of mouth. However, limitations exist if customers are not comfortable in the web environment or if their travel arrangements are particularly complex and require the specialist skills of a travel agent.

Online employment placement agencies

Another service that has been adapted to the online environment is that of matching prospective employees and employers. For example, Mycareer (www.mycareer.com.au) specialises in jobs in the insurance industry and offers services such as job alerts, customised folders to store jobs, résumé assistance, videos with interview advice, and mentoring (see figure 14.3). Another site that you may like to visit is www.seek.com.au, which specialises in university students and recent graduates. It also offers an application tracker that logs the details of every online job application lodged and organises them in a user friendly format — a free, automatic service for registered users.

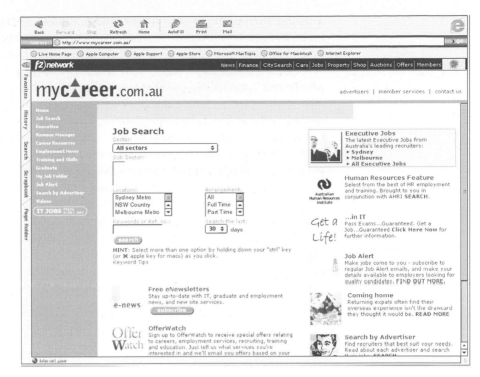

Figure 14.3: Mycareer homepage
Source: Mycareer 2001

The job market is one of the largest in the world, and the Internet offers the following advantages for job seekers, who have the ability to:

- find information on an enormous number of jobs around the globe
- communicate quickly with employers
- write and post résumés for large-volume distribution
- obtain free support services
- learn to handle interview situations.

The use of the Internet for global recruiting purposes has expanded. In 1998, 29 per cent of *Fortune* magazine's Global 500 companies used the Internet for recruiting, but by 2001 this had grown to 88 per cent. This was led by a strong growth in Asia-Pacific companies (Pastore 2001).

Advantages of Internet recruiting for employers are that they are able to:

- advertise globally to large numbers of job seekers
- save on advertising costs
- decrease processing costs by using electronic application forms (Turban et al. 2000)

However, there are also perceived drawbacks, and these are cited as lack of quality candidates, too many responses, cost, and the inability to screen and track responses (Pastore 2001).

Both employees and employers can also use intelligent agents. For example, www.jobsleuth.com is a free service that allows job seekers to put in their profiles and receive daily emails alerting them to job opportunities from online job placement sites; and www.resumix.com enables employers to find résumés that match their job descriptions (Turban et al. 2000).

Online real estate services

A third example of an online agent can be found in the real estate industry, where a radical transformation is taking place. The Internet has made real estate markets more efficient, as it has increased the quality and quantity of information available to both buyers and sellers (Jud & Roulac 2001). It is also an excellent tool for real estate, because it enables potential property buyers to view a wide range of places from their computer, thereby saving travel time and costs.

A good representative site is www.realestate.com.au, (see figure 14.4), which encourages potential buyers to develop a wish list that describes the qualities of their ideal home, including preferred location, price and features. They are then alerted by email about properties that meet their criteria. Another feature of the site is detailed information on house buying, including house inspections, negotiating a deal, contracts, conveyancing and the moving process. Helpful information is also provided for sellers. The site also provides 3D virtual tours, a loan mortgage calculator and a comparison of lending agencies. At this stage the site does not allow for real estate transactions, but legislation in the United States suggests that changes are taking place to enable sellers and buyers to do this. In the United States, the federal E-SIGN bill became effective from 1 October 2000, which effectively allowed people to use electronic signatures in place of traditional pen and paper signatures where a legally enforceable signature was required (Brice 2001). This suggests that documentation such as mortgage applications and contract approvals can be completed online in real time.

Figure 14.4: Real estate web page
Source: Realestate.com.au 2001

Aggregators

The Internet has provided many opportunities for inventing new services, such as the aggregation of existing services to create a new service category. Other new services include **matchmaking services**, where buyers' needs are matched with products and services from sellers; and **notification services**, which let you know when a service becomes available, when it goes on sale or when it is cheaper (Lawrence et al. 1999).

Matchmaking services: services that match buyers' needs with products and services from sellers

Notification services: services that let customers know when a service becomes available, when it goes on sale or when it is cheaper

Aggregators perform the task of bringing together products from multiple suppliers to provide consumers with a range of choices in one location. In the virtual world, the products or services that are brought together are organised and displayed on a user's computer screen or PDA. Online examples of these aggregators include shopping agents such as Pricescan (www.pricescan.com) and **metamediaries** such as Edmunds (www.edmunds.com.au) (see page 372), but can also include portals such as Yahoo! (www.yahoo.com.au). These act as aggregators by enabling customers to obtain, for example, cheaper Visa cards and gain cheaper insurance products through trading within the site (Lawrence et al. 1999). Let us examine two specific examples: comparison shopping services and metamediaries.

Metamediaries: sites that connect customers with goods and services that fill their needs for life events or major asset purchases

Comparison shopping services

A new service that has evolved from online purchasing is that of price-comparison shopping services, or **electronic shopping agents**. A price-comparison engine is either a robot or agent shopping tool or artificial intelligence technology that does automated searches of all online stores that sell products. It does this in real time and then compiles a list of the URLs of vendors, along with their products and prices.

Electronic shopping agents: software tools that assist users to search the Internet for products and services by providing items matching the search criteria, as well as prices and direct links to the site

It is estimated that 60 per cent of online shoppers would not make a major decision without first researching it for information on the best prices available and for the best value (NOIE 2002b). As price is not the only factor that consumers consider when they intend to make a purchase, these shopping services may also have the following features:

- *Product information hub.* This content includes such things as prices, photos, product features and retailer services. It also has links to other databases of reviews and ratings.
- *Consumer-written ratings and reviews.* These sites are created exclusively by consumers as a way for new or potential buyers to find out what others think about products, and are called **second generation shopping agents**. One site of interest is BizRate (www.bizrate.com), which provides a report card on online merchants, based on customer feedback (see figure 14.5).
- *Industry reviews.* Professional reviews, written by experts and supplied by leading content providers, may also be included.

Second generation shopping agents: sites that are created exclusively by consumers as a way for new or potential buyers to find out what others think about products

Other trends include a combined comparison-shopping/group-buying service such as MobShop (www.mobshop.com), which finds the price that moves the highest amount of products to the most people. These services benefit consumers, who get the best price, and retailers who improve their inventory turnover (NOIE 2002b).

These comparison-shopping sites earn advertising revenue from retailers, but additional revenue can be obtained from one or more of the following sources:

- a percentage of transactions generated
- fees for lead referrals (the fees paid for each customer that the service directs to a retailer's website)
- affiliate programs in which online retailers pay a comparison-shopping site in order to be included in the service or to get a preferred position
- licensing fees, whereby some services, such as Deja.com and BizRate.com, license their databases of product ratings and proprietary technologies to other companies for a fee

- sale of customer information, where the comparison shopping site sells the marketing research that it gathers from consumers, at the point of sale, to retailers or other parties.

Figure 14.5: BizRate home page
Source: BizRate 2001

Metamediaries

The complexity of online trading has created a new breed of intermediaries called 'metamediaries'. Mohanbir Sawhney coined this term, and he suggests that metamediaries work in '**metamarkets**' (virtual trading spaces) that connect customers with goods and services that they require in order to fill their needs for life events or major asset purchases (Strauss & Frost 2001). Life events that can be used to construct metamarkets include weddings, childbirth, education, career changes and retirement (Sawhney 2000). For example, if a couple wanted to get married, they might purchase flowers, food and beverages, and hire cars and a reception hall. Sawhney (2000) suggests that a good example of an metamediary is Edmund's in the automobile market (www.edmunds.com.au). It has created a valuable data franchise by giving away information about prices of new and used automobiles, dealer costs, reliability, automobile buying advice and reviews. Interested customers are referred to Autobytel for negotiation and dealer search; Aussie Car Loans for financing; Price Auto Outlet for off-lease used cars; JC Whitney for auto spare parts; Geico for insurance; and Warranty Gold for extended warranties.

The function of the metamediary is to link all these together electronically so that customers can use the one site location to have their needs met. Also providing fertile ground for metamarkets are home ownership and financial assets. From this description, we can see that metamediaries are agents that represent the content providers, e-tailers and manufacturers. The proposition

Metamarkets:
virtual trading spaces

offered by metamediaries is that they broker, as a trusted third-party, the often complex process of integrating disparate suppliers into a standardised online trading environment (Sey 2001). They are valuable to consumers because they help them make better decisions for a cluster of activities. They also assist in reducing search times; they provide trusted advice, quality assurance and information about vendors; and facilitate transactions for a group of purchases. For suppliers, they offer access to multiple buyers and markets.

We have seen how intermediaries have taken advantage of the Internet to develop, expand into or develop new online services. In many cases, this has been a response to the threat of disintermediation, and is an essential strategy for retaining their value to consumers and suppliers in the distribution chain. Let us now consider how and why other service companies have developed a web presence.

E-financial services

The financial services industry is generally responding to digital technology at varying rates, with some sectors adapting better than others to e-business. E-banking and brokering are making enormous strides, while the insurance sector is moving a little slower. However, e-services that provide comparison of insurance and loan rates, investment information and analytical tools, for example, are now offered to customers as a result of the Internet. The demand for this service has also led to some of the leading Internet companies such as AOL Finance and Yahoo!Finance, which were not traditional financial service companies, to act as online financial portals and become significant players in the industry.

E-banking

E-banking: *online banking; the provision of banking services through means other than traditional branch banking*

E-banking or online banking are terms that are used to describe the provision of banking services through means other than traditional branch banking (Liao et al. 1999). However, it should be noted that this service is provided by both bricks-and-mortar branches and virtual banks (Orr 2001).

As banking is an information intensive business, IT can be used very effectively. In the 1960s, IT was employed to automate the back-office, but it was eventually implemented in the front-office until the division between the front- and back-offices became less relevant. IT also had an enormous impact on the way customers could deal with their finances. For example, they could use credit cards and automatic teller machines (ATMs), which enabled them to bypass the branches (Liao et al. 1999). Now, banks provide online services that include electronic bill payment, smart cards, and autoloans. Customers can view their account balances and transactions, transfer funds between authorised accounts, initiate loan payments, request stop payments on cheques, order personal cheques, and download transaction information onto their computer or PDA. For example, the Commonwealth Bank of Australia (www.commbank.com.au) offers NetBank. The number of customers using this service tripled to 322 000 in the year after a browser-based version was introduced in March 2000 (Commonwealth Bank of Australia 2000).

As with most online services, all these activities can take place anywhere or at any time, and fees for online transaction are generally cheaper than for teller-assisted transactions. Therefore, electronic banking saves time and money for customers, and is perceived as useful if customers' expectations of accuracy, security, network speed, user friendliness and convenience are met

(Liao & Cheung 2002). For the banks, it offers a cheaper alternative than the use of physical bank branches, and enables them to attract and deal with remote customers (Turban et al. 2000).

Customers' reaction to online banking has changed markedly since its inception. Generally, they were extremely cautious, mainly because of their concerns about security. However, Internet banking has since experienced a strong growth in Australia with more than one in 10 bank customers now using online banking. Even more interesting is the fact that the number of online users aged over 50 has almost trebled (Tobler, 2001). Demand has changed to such an extent that banks have reported losing clients or being unable to compete for specific business because they lack a particular Internet function (Forman & Shafer 2000).

In addition to physical banks that are adding online services, virtual banks have emerged that have Internet transactions as their core activity. In October 1997, New Zealand's first virtual bank, BankDirect, was launched. With no physical branches, BankDirect was able to reduce overhead costs while still providing a complete set of services to customers. One of their most difficult challenges, however, was to build relationships without the face-to-face environment. To do this, they implemented an advanced customer management system to enable them to offer a competitive customer service (Atterby 2001). One of the major challenges for new players is that they must build up trust with consumers. Existing banks in Australia, for example, have a head start in terms of their brand recognition and size which is difficult for smaller players to emulate (Wade & Hughes 2000).

Finally, an example of how one-on-one marketing can work for online banking is Bank of America's 'Build Your Own Bank'. Online customers who use this service first provide the bank with basic personal details on their age, gender, occupation, income, place of residence, whether they rent or own a home, and the types of accounts that they have with the bank. Next, they give an indication of financial interests and priorities. The bank then responds with money tips and news items related to the customer's interests, and sends special offers for services prioritised by the customer. Both customer and bank benefit from this mechanism. The customer gains tailored offerings, a personal site with up-to-date information about balances in each account and a snapshot of their bank holdings. The bank, on the other hand, has opportunities to cross-sell products and services (United States Department of Commerce 2001a).

The mobile phone is also an important vehicle for online banking services. For example, a Scandinavian bank introduced stock trading and bank transfer via wireless devices and allowed customers to use their phones to buy movie tickets by debiting purchases directly from the bank account (Echikson 2001).

Online insurance

It is possible for people to access information online about insurance policies and then purchase policies from insurance carriers, banks, securities brokerages and car marketplaces. The insurance industry has begun to use the Internet in order to meet the challenges from new competition and deregulation, to address changing customer preferences, and to lower distribution costs.

In their attempt to be more innovative through IT, insurers are using the Internet not merely as a distribution tool or a place to display their promotional materials, but also as a customer-centred communication tool. Customers can use online policy information and online financial tools to determine the policy that is suitable for their purposes. They could then complete an application and, if they chose, purchase the policy online. A direct online sale by the carrier avoids agent commissions, and a sale through an online agent reduces the commission by half.

Other savings can be gained in the application and underwriting processes, which are made more efficient by electronic communication. Electronic links with third parties, such as hospitals, medical technicians and the Department of Motor Vehicles, reduces the time and effort previously involved in these processes (United States Department of Commerce 2001b).

An Australian example of an online insurance company is WWW Insurance Agencies (www.insuru.com.au), which provides Internet insurance services for domestic and business markets and the medical profession. It allows customers to obtain online quotes; change the details on any of their policies; lodge details of valuable items; and lodge serial numbers associated with their motor vehicle, which, in the event of its loss (or loss of memory) they may need to recover in the future. On the website, WWW Insurance Agencies provides the history of the company and reasons for going online, stating that the agency has existed for nearly 30 years, having started in Woomera in 1975. The company embraced the Internet in 1996 in view of its potential to enhance their communication efficiently and cost-effectively. It anticipated that the Internet would be important for meeting the needs of its clients and began to design its website at this time.

With the development of new portal markets for insurance, customers can not only purchase their policies online, but also access and review their policies at their convenience. Customers can update their own customer profiles and track the status of a claim. In the insurance industry, there is a heavy reliance on customer information. The electronic exchange of information not only saves time and money, but can provide customer information that can be mined and used to determine customer preferences and needs. Innovative companies can use IT to pursue the customer and to make significant savings.

Online consulting

Online consulting is a field that is growing rapidly (Turban et al. 2000) and appeals to consumers who need medical, managerial or legal advice without exorbitant fees and without leaving home.

Online legal services

The Internet is also changing the way that lawyers work. There are now a growing number of solicitors offering legal services online. Some use simple email services that allow you to send information by email, which is worked on by lawyers who then reply to you by email (for example, www.nzlawyers.co.nz/services/). An interesting Australian site (see figure 14.6) hosted by the National Children's and Youth Law Centre (NCYLC) is targeted at people under 18. It provides them with the opportunity to ask legal questions via the Internet and to obtain advice and information (free of charge) from specialist children's solicitors at the Lawstuff site (www.lawstuff.org.au). This service commenced in October 1998 and has been receiving approximately 20 email enquiries per week. It appears to be reaching its target market, with the most frequent users being 16- and 17-year-olds, Australia wide. More than 50 per cent of users are young women likely to be accessing the service from home. Most of their questions tend to be related to schooling, family law, child protection and the legal process. Interestingly, the majority of the respondents had never sought legal advice before, but they reported that they received more information than they expected and they found out exactly what they wanted to know (Willett 2000).

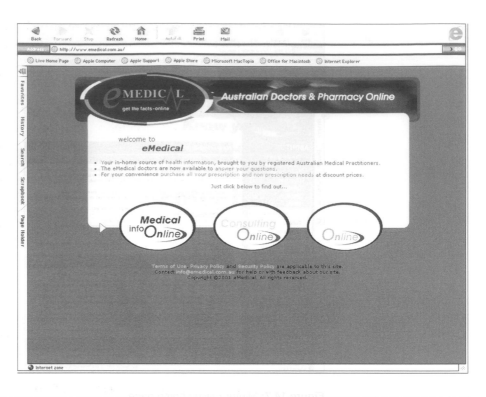

Figure 14.8: eMedical website
Source: eMedical 2001

Services Marketing Action:
Using a mobile phone to examine ECGs

When an 84-year-old woman collapsed at home and was brought to the emergency department of Concord Hospital, she was given an ECG. It is common for hospitals to be staffed by junior doctors on weekends and evenings, and they may have limited experience in interpreting the subtleties of changes in ECG waveforms. Normally, the junior doctor will telephone the cardiologist on call and will need to describe the ECG verbally. Obviously, in some cases, it would be desirable for the cardiologist to actually view the ECG, and the development of a system that enables the transmission of the ECG to a mobile phone has made this an actuality. This system, set up by Professor Ben Freedman of the University of Sydney, allows staff to transmit urgent ECGs from the emergency department of the Concord Hospital to the cardiologist on call.

In this particular case, the house staff at the hospital were able to use the system to check the results of the ECG with the specialist cardiologist who was sailing on his yacht in Sydney Harbour at the time. They first made contact with the cardiologist via a long-range pager and were then able to transmit the ECG to his mobile phone. He then alerted house staff to possible problems that required more aggressive early management.

This system may be particularly valuable for hospitals in rural or remote areas where a doctor is not immediately available. It would then be possible for nurses to use it in cases of suspected acute heart problems.

Source: adapted from Freedman 1999

In the pharmacy sector, the emergence of virtual pharmacies can represent a potential threat to bricks-and-mortar pharmacies that fail to offer an online service. For example, Mychemist (www.mychemist.com.au) offers pharmaceutical advice, pharmaceutical products and other beauty and fragrance products. This online company advises that all their orders are encrypted and securely transferred behind a firewall, and delivery is free for all Australian orders except large bulky items.

Internet pharmacies offer customers/patients easier access, speed and convenience, but also raise concerns regarding issues of privacy and safety (Landis 1999). In the United States, for example, the Internet has opened doors for profiteers to sell medications to anyone with or without a prescription (Ukens 1999). However, efforts have been made by the US Food and Drug Administration to control the increasing use of the Internet to obtain prescription drugs without the adequate supervision of a physician or proper pharmacy intermediary, by enlisting the assistance of physicians and pharmacists (Marwick 1999).

Online privacy issues

We have discussed several scenarios in this chapter that demonstrate the extent to which e-health services have enabled patients to communicate about health issues. An important fallout from this technological development is the issue of patient privacy. If emails are used between patients and doctors, for example, they become part of a medical record and need to be protected from unwelcome observers, as stored emails may contain information that could be embarrassing if they were revealed publicly (Spielberg 1999). It is not only in the health area that privacy in an issue, however. In general, the last three decades have seen new technologies that have put consumer privacy at risk in many different ways.

Technologies such as computerised databases, Internet data devices like cookies and Internet bugs, and electronic processing of information enable all personal information to be collected, collated, transferred, matched and mined. Data is gathered from our EFTPOS and credit card transactions, through reward schemes such as frequent flyer programs or Fly Buys, and through our Internet activities. The volume, detail and accessibility of the electronic storage of this information is such that it is perceived as constituting a risk to privacy that needs to be managed.

To understand more about electronic monitoring, it is useful to know that 'cookies' are small data structures sent by a host website or server to reside in the user's computer. They allow websites to 'remember' information about users, and originated, before the development of the Internet, as a way of storing password codes. The initial idea was not to gather knowledge about users, but to provide them with the convenience of remembering their password. As the Internet was developed, they were adapted for use with shopping carts carrying electronic purchases and for tracking activity on the website. Eventually, Internet marketers developed the ability to use them for monitoring and profiling users across multitudes of websites. Now they are able to link the histories of particular individuals through both voluntary user action and industry-wide database consolidation (Charters 2002).

A conundrum for marketers is that data collected on consumer behaviour and demographics helps them to target consumers in individualised ways, but this comes at the cost of consumer privacy. For marketers, technology has become a commodity that is of commercial value. It has even created a new service, which compiles and rents lists of personal information, such as income, recent purchases, sex, age and known interests, in order to facilitate target marketing. This has also led to holdings of personal information being considered as company assets. The danger of this view for consumer privacy is demonstrated in the vignette below.

Ethical Issues:
Toysmart.com

In May 2000, US Internet retailer Toysmart.com ceased operations and became one of the first high-profile dotcom toy retailers to succumb to the dotcom shakeout resulting from low or no profits. More dramatically, it also found itself in the middle of an uproar involving privacy issues. During its operation, Toysmart had collected personal information about visitors through its website — names, addresses, shopping preferences, billing information and family profiles that included names and birthdates of children (Federal Trade Commission 2000a). To assure its customers that this data would never be shared with third parties, the retailer had posted a privacy policy on its website. Moreover, it had been licensed by TRUSTe, a non-profit privacy seal organisation.

Despite this policy, Toysmart requested approval to put all its assets up for sale as part of its bankruptcy proceedings. Its assets included its customers' records — names, addresses and credit card numbers and so on. Toysmart advertised in the newspaper its intention to sell its assets and indicated that its customer lists were also on sale (Greenburg 2000). TRUSTe reported this possible violation of its own privacy policy to the Federal Trade Commission (FTC). An investigation was undertaken and a lawsuit filed. Eventually, the FTC and Toysmart agreed on a settlement that protects customers of Toysmart from any privacy policy changes in the future by a bankruptcy purchaser (Federal Trade Commission 2000b).

The realisation that customer data is a saleable asset is one that concerns many consumers, who fear that the problem could become worse with so many dotcoms going bankrupt. For example, Voter.com, which is a defunct political portal, has announced a plan to sell 170 000 email addresses and party affiliations (Green 2001). Ethically, it would seem that companies should respect the privacy rights of consumers who have provided their personal details in good faith.

It is argued that consumers need to be fully informed about the way that organisations handle information, and that they must have the right to forbid organisations to supply or sell personal information to other parties without explicit consent. In Australia, the development of a privacy webseal not only assures consumers of the privacy credentials of a company, but also:

- enables consumers to opt out of any direct marketing communication from the outset of the customer relationship
- provides advice on how to access and correct one's personal records
- facilitates the complaints process by identifying the code adjudicator and providing a complaint form, or advice about how complaints can be made

- provides details of the industry privacy code, if any, that applies to the company
- provides the complaints statistics of the applicable code
- provides clear and unambiguous advice about the information handling practices
- provides a link to the website of the Federal Privacy Commission.

The Department of Communications, Information Technology and the Arts suggest that even if a customer is happy about a purchase item and the price, and is ready to order, there are a number of privacy questions that should be considered before clicking the purchase into the shopping trolley.

By undertaking the following steps (DCITA 2001), customers can ensure that they have greater privacy on the Internet:

- Deal with companies that have a clear, comprehensive privacy policy that is easy to find on the website. If they don't, think again before sending your details.
- Check to ensure that the website provides an email address or phone number so that you can ask for more detailed information about privacy policy.
- Make certain that the company's privacy policy conveys what the merchant intends to do with your data.
- If the company plans to share your personal details with other companies, does it give you the option of declining this 'offer'?
- Be aware that not all of your personal details are of equal value. Your tax file number and mother's maiden name are much more sensitive than your name and telephone number, which may be found in any phonebook.
- Don't provide password information (for example, the one you use to access your Internet connection) to anyone. Be very wary about a company that asks for you to provide them with any password data.
- Ask yourself whether the information requested by the company is really necessary. Provide only the personal information necessary for the transaction.

Impact of privacy issues on customer uptake of online services

This practice of gathering personal customer data and building databases that can be used, sold or revealed is one that has kept many consumers from shopping online (Turban et al, 2000). A PricewaterhouseCoopers (PwC) study reported that 60 per cent of US Internet users would shop more online if they could be assured that retail sites would not do anything with their personal information (Mohammed et al. 2001). Figure 14.9 shows more detailed results of consumer attitudes towards online privacy.

Interestingly, some consumers are also taking advantage of the opportunities in personalised marketing, and are trading off aspects of their privacy for benefits such as reward points, tailored advertising or customised service. Others are paid by infomediaries to rent space on their computer screen, which is then sold to advertisers who welcome the chance to use one-on-one marketing strategies (Strauss & Frost 2001). The introduction of GPS (global positioning system) technology in mobile phone handsets will let individual consumers be tracked. Australia's biggest SMS portal, BlueSkyFrog, has 1.8 million members signed up to receive free SMS alerts for films, shows and other activities. Half the invited customers opt for text messaging, and BlueSkyFrog is careful to send messages that are value-added, offering discounts or bonuses (Bita 2001).

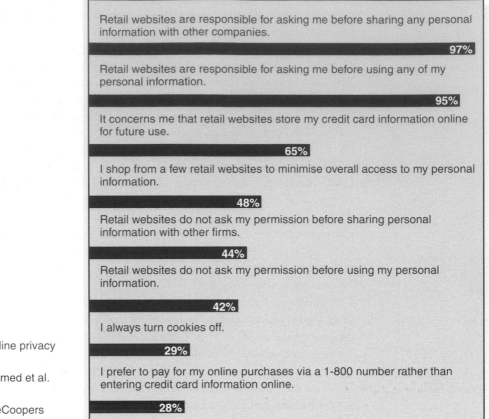

(% of online users in the US who agree/strongly agree)

Retail websites are responsible for asking me before sharing any personal information with other companies.
97%

Retail websites are responsible for asking me before using any of my personal information.
95%

It concerns me that retail websites store my credit card information online for future use.
65%

I shop from a few retail websites to minimise overall access to my personal information.
48%

Retail websites do not ask my permission before sharing personal information with other firms.
44%

Retail websites do not ask my permission before using my personal information.
42%

I always turn cookies off.
29%

I prefer to pay for my online purchases via a 1-800 number rather than entering credit card information online.
28%

Figure 14.9: Online privacy attitudes
Source: Mohammed et al. 2001, based on PricewaterhouseCoopers data

Security

Concerns about security are a leading deterrent to e-commerce, and financial institutions and organisations with online services have been trying to find solutions (Brown 2001). A key issue that customers consider when deciding whether or not they can trust a website is its security. In particular, potential users need to be able to trust the site to manage their credit card and, if this trust is violated, it has repercussions, not only for the company itself but also for the industry in general (Mohammed et al. 2001). Despite the increase in e-commerce transactions, some buyers are avoiding the use of payment cards on the Internet to avoid the risk of losing their money.

No matter what the size of business, two key security factors need to be considered: systems reliability and e-commerce security (Pugliese & Halse 2000). Online service companies also have security concerns in terms of fraudulent use of credit cards. Visa International, for example, has had many disputes over goods bought online by someone posing as a client. Therefore, authenticating whether the person is who they say they are has become a key problem faced by financial institutions that conduct e-commerce. Visa has attempted to address this problem with its Visa Authentication Payment (VAP) program, which allows the bank that issued the card to identify both buyers and sellers engaging in online financial transactions. By matching the same level of security afforded in the physical world, VAP is instrumental in improving consumer confidence (Brown 2001).

In addition to authentication, there are other parameters for the operationalisation of online security (Wilson 1999). These include:

- *integrity:* the extent to which the document is believed to be genuine and unchanged from when it was first written
- *non-repudiation:* the extent to which the document's originator can deny responsibility for it and any terms and conditions stated on it
- *confidentiality:* the extent to which the document can be secured against a third party viewing it without permission of the signing parties
- *availability:* the capacity of the document to be delivered and the archive document to be accessed in the future.

All these security measures are important in give customers a sense of security if online companies hope to succeed in using e-commerce. As Dann and Dann (2001) rightly comment, however, fraudulent card use is actually more common offline, and the act of faxing a purchase form with name and credit card number, personal details and signature is no more secure than the Internet.

However, if Internet users do not have confidence that their communications and data are safe from unauthorised access or modification, it is unlikely that they will use the Internet on a routine basis for commerce. A secure site requires:

1. secure and reliable telecommunications networks
2. effective means for protecting the information systems attached to those networks
3. effective means for authenticating and ensuring confidentiality of electronic information to protect data from unauthorised use
4. well-trained users who understand how to protect their systems and their data (United States Department of Commerce 2001a).

Unfortunately, there is no single 'magic' technology or technique that can ensure a site will be secure and reliable. It is necessary to use an array of technologies such as encryption, authentication, password controls and firewalls that are supported globally by trustworthy key and security management infrastructures. For e-services to be fully embraced, consumers must perceive security risks to be low and, more importantly, their perceptions should match reality.

Summary

LO1: Explain what is meant by e-services.

- E-services can be broadly defined as those services made available over the Internet in a user-friendly way.
- These services may be accessed through web browsers, mobile devices or even embedded devices such as automobile navigation systems.

LO2: Describe what companies need to do to create customer-effective e-services.

Firms offering e-services need to:

- define broadness of offerings
- make online processes convenient
- integrate the Internet where customer services cannot be met offline
- define the total customer experience to be provided online
- make informed decisions on key customer activities to be supported online, and key pieces of utility

- make service processes transparent to e-customers
- consider serving customers in real time
- ensure efficient flow of transaction process
- communicate service levels to customers before and after they complete a service request.

LO3: Illustrate how digital technology has affected the services industry.

- Large organisations such as banks, airlines and government organisations were influential in dispersion of technology within the service industry.
- Many tasks undertaken by intermediaries were automated, and led to concerns that the Internet would cause disintermediation.
- To avoid the threat of disintermediation, smart intermediaries use IT to strengthen their bonds with suppliers and customers.
- There is a need for a significant shift in the value-adding that intermediaries bring to the supply chain.
- Intermediaries need to focus on achieving efficiencies in internal functions and to redesign business processes so that IT serves customers' needs.
- Some traditional intermediaries have been replaced or supplemented with online equivalents.

LO4: Describe the services trends in online distribution channels.

- Exciting new trends include mobilemediaries.
- Online intermediary activities include online exchanges and trading, online auctions, online travel and tourism services, online employment agencies, online real estate services, comparison shopping services and metamediaries.

LO5: Discuss the value for customers in e-financial services.

- Online banking enables customers to perform their banking activities from home or via their PDA seven days a week, 24 hours a day.
- Online insurance makes it possible for customers to access information about insurance policies, determine policy that is suitable for their purposes, and purchase them from insurance carriers, banks and securities brokerages.

LO6: Demonstrate an understanding of online privacy and security issues.

- Technologies such as computerised databases, Internet data services such as cookies and web bugs, and electronic processing of information enable personal information to be collected, collated, transferred, matched and mined.
- Many consumers are concerned that their personal details may be sold or used for purposes for which they have not given permission.
- Attempts have been made by government to assure consumers of the privacy credentials of a company by means of webseal.
- Concerns about security are a leading deterrent to e-commerce.
- Parameters for operationalisation of online security include authentication, integrity, non-repudiation, confidentiality and availability.

key terms

Agents: online businesses that can represent either the seller or buyer and will represent the interests of whichever has hired them (p. 367)

Aggregators: online businesses that perform the task of bringing together products from multiple suppliers to provide consumers with a range of choices in one location (p. 367)

Brokers: online businesses that do not represent either the buyer or the seller, but provide the services that make exchange and negotiation possible (p. 367)

Co-producers: those who do the work of inputting data and undertaking transactions that would normally be carried out by an organisation (p. 360)

Disintermediation: the process whereby traditional intermediaries are eliminated (p. 365)

E-banking: online banking; the provision of banking services through means other than traditional branches (p. 373)

Electronic shopping agents: software tools that help users to search the Internet for products and services by providing items matching the search criteria, as well as prices and direct links to the site (p. 371)

E-services: those services made available over the Internet in a user-friendly way (p. 360)

Intermediaries: those companies that play a role in transferring a product, service or information between the supplier and consumer within their distribution channel (p. 365)

Matchmaking services: services that match buyers' needs with products and services from sellers (p. 370)

Metamarkets: virtual trading spaces (p. 372)

Metamediaries: sites that connect customers with goods and services that fill their needs for life events or major asset purchases (p. 371)

M-marketing: the application of marketing to the mobile environment of mobile phones, smart phones and PDAs (p. 362)

Mobilemediary: a new kind of intermediary that uses wireless technology and can break into the value chain at any point to provide information and transactional capabilities to customers at the time and place that they want to buy a product or service (p. 366)

Notification services: services that let customers know when a service becomes available, when it goes on sale or when it is cheaper (p. 370)

Reverse auction: auction where the website serves as a purchasing agent for individual buyers who specify a price, and the sellers bid for the buyer's business (p. 368)

Second generation shopping agents: sites that are created exclusively by consumers as a way for new or potential buyers to find out what others think about products (p. 371)

 review questions

1. Many of our traditional services such as banking, insurance and legal services are offered to us online. What advantages are there for traditional companies to invest in delivering services online? What benefits are there for customers?
2. Describe what is meant by disintermediation. Give an example.
3. How have intermediaries added value through the Internet within the distribution channel? Give examples.
4. What are the limitations of online travel and tourism services?

5. What are the advantages for employers and jobseekers from online recruiting agencies? How do these agencies make a profit?
6. What is the role of an aggregator? Give two examples.
7. How can marketers show respect for the privacy of consumers while trying to build up as much information about their customers as possible?
8. What are five parameters for the operationalisation of online security?

application questions

1. It is sometimes said that customers are becoming more demanding with regard to online services. Do you agree? What type of demands are they making? What type of demands do you make?
2. E-health sites have become very popular. Why do you think this is the case? Go online to see if you can find some examples of online services provided by pharmacists and dentists. What value do you think they are providing to their online customers?
3. Check out AussieShopper (www.aussieshopper.com.au) or an e-tailer of your choice. How does this site attempt to reassure its customers about the security of purchasing online?
4. What examples can you find online of legal companies that offer both an online and an offline service? Compare the online services provided by two different sites. Is one providing more benefits than the other? Which one would you be more likely to use? Why?
5. Mobilemediaries can deliver their messages to you on your mobile phone or PDA. What incentives do you think are necessary to encourage customers to sign up to these types of services? Give an example.

vignette questions

1. Read the Services Marketing Action vignette on page 359.
   (a) What service does HealthDirect provide? What are the three main technology components?
   (b) Give an example of how the HealthDirect service could be employed.
   (c) Do you foresee any problems that may arise from this service for patients or the medical profession?
2. Read the Services Marketing Action vignette on page 378.
   (a) Describe how the specialist cardiologist was able to diagnose a patient while sailing on his yacht in Sydney Harbour. Do you have any comments about this scenario?
   (b) In what other cases do you think mobile technology would be beneficial for medical diagnosis?
3. Read the Ethical Issues vignette on page 380.
   (a) How did Toysmart.com destroy consumer trust?
   (b) What are the ethical issues involved in the Toysmart.com story?
   (c) Do some online research to follow up the case of Toysmart.com. How has recent United States legislation affected the company?
   (d) What long-term impact do you think the behaviour of Toysmart.com will have on consumer confidence in privacy policies? How can online service companies deal with it?

recommended readings

For details on the technology infusion matrix, see:

Bitner, M. J., Brown, S. W. & Meuter, M. L. 2000, 'Technology infusion in service encounters', *Journal of Academy of Marketing Science*, vol. 28, no. 1, pp. 138–49

For an Australian perspective on strategic e-marketing, see:

Dann, S. & Dann, S. 2001, *Strategic Internet Marketing*, John Wiley & Sons, Brisbane, Australia.

To gain an overview of the impact of the ubiquitous Internet, see:

Kenny, D. & Marshall, J. F. 2000, 'Contextual marketing', *Harvard Business Review*, vol. 78, no. 6, p. 119.

For a general overview of e-marketing issues, see:

Mohammed, R., Fisher, R. J., Jaworski, B. J. & Cahill, A. M. 2001, *Internet Marketing: Building Advantage In the Networked Economy*, McGraw-Hill/Irwin, Boston.

Strauss, J. & Frost, R. 2001, *E-Marketing*, 2nd edn, Prentice Hall, Upper Saddle River, NJ.

references

Alba, J., Lynch, J., Weitz, B., Janiszewski, C., Lutz, R., Sawyer, A. & Wood, S. 1997, 'Interactive home shopping: consumer, retailer and manufacturer incentives to participate in electronic marketplaces', *Journal of Marketing*, vol. 61, no. 3, pp. 38–53.

Alexander, M. 1992, 'Disintermediation — redefining the role of corporate headquarters', *Long Range Planning*, vol. 25, no. 6, pp. 110–12.

Atterby, M., accessed 7 November 2001, 'Virtual customers you can bank on', www.crmmagazine.com.au.

AZYGO, accessed September 2002, 'Building face-to-face transaction trust into the Internet', www.azygo.net./azygo/white_paper.html.

Bita, N. 2001, 'Undercover agencies', *The Australian*, 27 September, Features, p. M03.

Bitner, M. J., Brown, S. A. & Meuter, M. L. 2000, 'Technology infusion in service encounters', *Journal of Academy of Marketing Science*, vol. 28, no. 1, pp. 138–49.

Bizrate, accessed October 2001, www.bizrate.com.

Borck, J. R. 2000, 'Transforming e-business: e-services', *InfoWorld*, vol. 22, no. 41, pp. 75–9.

Brice, B., 2001, 'E-signatures in the real estate world: there's more to it than the technology enables and the law allows', *Real Estate Issues*, vol. 26, no. 2, pp. 43–6.

Brown, B., accessed 24 September 2001, 'Industry tries to allay fears about security', www.theaustralian.news.com.au.

Button, V., accessed 16 November 2000, 'Dot-com doctor set to see first patient', www.theage.com.au.

Charters, D. 2002, 'Electronic monitoring and privacy issues in business-marketing: the ethics of the doubleclick experience', *Journal of Business Ethics*, vol. 35, pp. 243–54.

Commonwealth Bank of Australia 2000, Report to Shareholders 2000, www.commbank.com.au.

Cort, S. G., Stith, R. M. & Lahoti, D. 1997, 'Industry corner: motivators and inhibitors', *MIS Quarterly*, vol. 32, no. 4, pp. 55–8.

Cyberatlas, accessed 14 October 2002, 'The world's online populations', http://cyberatlas.internet.com/resources/archives.

Dalgleish, J. 2000, 'Create customer-effective e-services', *e-Business Adviser*, vol. 18, no. 12, pp. 26–34.

Dann, S. & Dann, S. 2001, *Strategic Internet Marketing*, John Wiley & Sons, Brisbane.

DCITA (Department of Communications, Information Technology and the Arts), accessed October 2001, 'Shopping on the Internet: facts for consumers no. 5', www.dcita.gov.au.

Duffy, J. 2000, 'Nortel unveils "wings of light" wireless plan; allies with HP, unveils software to foster untethered Internet access, mobile e-services', *Network World*, June 19, p. 14.

Echikson, W. 2001, 'The dynamo of e-banking', *Business Week*, no. 3728, p. 10.

Economic Intelligence Unit accessed 21 November 2001, 'Global business intelligence for the digital age', www.ebusinessforum.com.

eMedical, accessed October 2001, www.emedical.com.au.

Engler, N. 1997, 'A wholesale survivor', *Software Magazine*, vol. 17, no. 9, pp. 28–39.

Federal Trade Commission, accessed 10 July 2000a, 'FTC sues failed website, Toysmart.com, for deceptively offering for sale personal information of website visitors', www.ftc.gov/opa/2000/07/toysmart.htm.

Federal Trade Commission, accessed 21 July 2000b, 'FTC announces settlement with bankrupt website, Toysmart.com, regarding alleged privacy violations', www.ftc.gov/opa/2000/07/toysmart2.htm.

Forman, L. & Shafer, D. 2000, 'From doubt to adoption...', *AFP Exchange*, fall, pp. 104–7.

Freedman, S. B. 1999, 'Direct transmission of electrocardiograms to a mobile phone for management of a patient with acute myocardial infarction', *Journal of Telemedicine and Telecare*, vol. 5, no 1, pp. 67–9.

Gates, B., Myhrvold, N. & Rinerason, P. 1995, *The Road Ahead*, Viking, New York.

Green, H. 2001, 'Your right to privacy: going ... going ...', *Business Week*, 23 April, no. 3729, p. 48.

Greenburg, P. A., accessed 13 July 2000, 'Toysmart flap triggers Privacy Bill', www.ecommercetimes.com/perl/story/3766.html.

Harrington, L. H. 1997, 'New approaches to channel strategies', *Transportation and Distribution*, vol. 38, no. 5, pp. 49–52.

Hoffman, D. & Novak, T. 2000, 'How to acquire customers on the web', *Harvard Business Review*, vol. 78, no. 3, pp. 179–86.

Jud, G. D. & Roulac, S. 2001, 'The future of the residential real estate brokerage industry', *Real Estate Issues*, vol. 26, no. 2, pp. 22–30.

Kenny, D. & Marshall, J. F. 2000, 'Contextual Marketing', *Harvard Business Review*, vol. 78, no. 6, p. 119.

Landis, N. T. 1999, 'Virtual pharmacies boast easy access, privacy safeguards', *American Journal of Health System Pharmacy*, vol. 56, no. 12, pp. 1174, 1177–9.

Lawrence, E., Corbitt, B., Fisher, J., Lawrence, J. & Tidwell, A. 1999, *Internet Commerce: Digital Models for Business*, 2nd edn, John Wiley & Sons, Brisbane.

Lawstuff, accessed October 2001, www.lawstuff.org.au.

Lewis, I. & Talalayevsky, A. 1997, 'Logistics and information technology: a coordination perspective', *Journal of Business Logistics*, vol. 18, no. 1, pp. 141–57.

Liao, Z. & Cheung, M. T. 2002, 'Internet-based e-banking and consumer attitudes: an empirical study', *Information and Management*, vol. 39, no. 4, pp. 283–95.

Liao, S., Shao Yuan, P., Wang, H. & Chen, A. 1999, 'The adoption of virtual banking: an empirical study', *International Journal of Information Management*, vol. 19, no. 1, pp. 63–74.

Marwick, C. 1999, 'Several groups attempting regulation of Internet Rx', *The Journal of the American Medical Association*, vol. 281, no. 11, p. 975.

MinterEllison Lawyers, accessed October 2001, www.minters.com.au.

Mohammed, R., Fisher, R. J., Jaworski, B. J. & Cahill, A. M. 2001, *Internet Marketing: Building Advantage In the Networked Economy*, McGraw-Hill/Irwin, Boston.

Morrison, M. 2001, 'E-commerce, web design and development: e-commerce trends', www.niacc.cc.ia.ua/admin/academic/scroll/trends/html.

Mort, G. & Drennan, J. 2001, 'Mobile digital technology: emerging issues for marketing', *The Journal of Database Marketing*, vol. 10, no. 1, pp. 9–24.

Moschella, D. 1999, 'HP's e-services strategy stands out from the pack', *Computer World*, Nov 29, p. 29.

Mycareer, accessed October 2001, www.mycareer.com.au.

NOIE (National Office for the Information Economy), accessed 14 October 2001, 'Readiness: international benchmarking: population, household readiness and demographic characteristics', www.onlineaustralia.net.au.

NOIE (National Office for the Information Economy), accessed 21 October 2002a, 'Further Australian e-health case studies', www.onlineaustralia.net.au.

NOIE (National Office for the Information Economy), accessed 16 October 2002b, 'The current state of play April 2002', www.onlineaustralia.net.au.

Orr, B. 2001, 'E-banking: what next?', *ABA Banking Journal*, vol. 93, no. 12, pp. 40–6.

Osman, H. 2001, 'More lawyers offer online legal services', www.wwlegal.com.

Pastore, M., accessed 2001, '6 million Australians used net in '99', Cyberatlas, http://cyberatlas.internet.com.

Peattie, K. & Peters, L. 1997, 'The marketing mix in the third age of computing', *Marketing Intelligence and Planning*, vol. 15, no. 2/3, pp. 142–51.

Pugliese, A. J. & Halse, R. 2000, 'SysTrust and WebTrust: technology assurance opportunities', *The CPA Journal*, vol. 70, no. 11, pp. 28–35.

Quinn, J. B. 1992, *Intelligent Enterprise*, Macmillan, New York.

Realestate.com.au, accessed October 2001, www.realestate.com.au.

Rust, R. T. & Lemon, K. N. 2001, 'E-service and the consumer', *International Journal of Electronic Commerce*, vol. 5, no. 3, pp. 85–101.

Sawhney, M., accessed March 2000, 'Making new markets', www.business2.com.

Sey, J., accessed 28 February 2001, 'Get2Connect — information intermediaries', www.computerweek.co.za.

Smith, D. 2000, 'E-services vision starts to take shape', *Internetweek*, April 17, p. 37.

Spielberg, A. 1999, 'Online without a net: physician communications by electronic mail', *American Journal of Law and Medicine*, vol. 25, no. 2/3, pp. 267–95.

Strauss, J. & Frost, R. 2001, *E-Marketing*, 2nd edn, Prentice Hall, Upper Saddle River, NJ.

Thompson, B. 2002, *eService Strategies for Success in the Customer Age*, RightNow Technologies, USA

Tobler, H. 2001, 'Over-50s lead stampede to net banking', *The Australian*, 26 September, Finance, p. 24.

Turban, E., Lee, J., King, D. & Chung, H. M. 2000, *Electronic Commerce: A Managerial Perspective*, Prentice Hall, Upper Saddle River, NJ.

United States Department of Commerce, accessed 21 November 2001a, 'Framework for global electronic commerce', www.ecommerce.gov/framewrk.htm.

United States Department of Commerce, accessed 21 November 2001b, 'The emerging digital economy', www.ecommerce.gov/Append4.pdf.

Ukens, C. 1999, 'Internet pharmacies', *Drug Topics*, vol. 143, no. 10, pp. 63–70.

Venkatraman, N. 1994, 'IT-enabled business transformation: from automation to business scope redefinition', *Sloan Management Review*, vol. 35, no. 2, pp. 73–87.

Wade, M. & Hughes, A., accessed 31 July 2000, 'Missing in action: the virtual revolution', www.smh.com.au.

Weiner, E. & Brown, A. 1995, 'The new marketplace', *Futurist*, vol. 29, no. 3, pp. 12–6.

Wexler, J., accessed April 2002, 'Cool middleware services', www.nwfusion .com/newsletters/wireless/2000/1002wire1.html.

Willett, J., accessed 2000, 'Youth speaks — an evaluation of the LawMail service', www.lawfoundation.net.au/resources/lawmail/lawmail.html.

Wilson, S. 1999, 'Digital signatures and the future of documentation', *Information Management and Computer Security*, vol. 7, no. 2, pp. 83–7.

Chapter 15
Services marketing issues in tourism and hospitality

Beverley Sparks and Carmen Tideswell

LEARNING OBJECTIVES

After reading this chapter you should be able to:

- understand the unique marketing challenges encountered by tourism and hospitality organisations
- identify the types of information search processes used by travellers when choosing their holiday destination
- appreciate the growing role of the Internet in marketing tourism and hospitality services
- understand the importance of service quality and customer satisfaction to the tourism and hospitality industry
- recognise the role of service recovery in hospitality marketing and identify service recovery strategies in various hospitality settings
- discuss the ways in which hospitality organisations can foster loyalty among their customers.

CHAPTER OUTLINE

This chapter discusses some of the challenges facing service marketers. The discussion focuses on the application of some key services marketing concepts to the tourism and hospitality industry — an industry that relies heavily on the delivery of positive service experiences to customers.

Topics in this chapter include information search, the role of the Internet, customer satisfaction, service failure and recovery, and customer loyalty. Information search and the role of the Internet highlight marketing issues in the pre-purchase phase, further emphasising the difficulties of distribution and evaluation of service products. As the hospitality and tourism industry is so much about customer experiences, a lot of marketing attention is given to understanding how the consumer evaluates the product and how this affects loyalty or return patronage.

Introduction

The tourism and hospitality industry offers a broad range of services, including accommodation, food and beverages, transport (air, ground and sea), tours and attractions (natural and built). As highlighted in earlier chapters, service industries are given special attention because they are said to differ from those producing manufactured goods. Similarly, the services provided within the tourism and hospitality sector have unique service characteristics that distinguish them from the products offered by manufacturing and other commercial sectors. For example, tourism and hospitality services are relatively intangible, cannot be inventoried and involve simultaneous production and consumption. Thus, it is difficult to observe tourism and hospitality services in advance and even harder to 'try before you buy'. Furthermore, when considering tourist destinations, the marketing challenges become even greater. Much evidence (for example, Plog 2001) has been produced to show that the character of a tourist destination changes over time as the destination matures. This produces a challenge to marketers, as there tends to be a shift in which the original market segments that were attracted to the destination look elsewhere for new experiences.

As already highlighted, the area of tourism and hospitality is quite complex, and is a field of study in itself. As a result, it is beyond the scope of this chapter to cover all the unique features of the industry. Nevertheless, there are several key topics that deserve consideration. First, given the complexity and experiential nature of tourism products, the topic of how consumers search for, and make decisions about, the tourism or hospitality product is elaborated. Related to search processes is the increase in the use of the Internet; this topic is explored through some of the positive benefits that are brought to potential tourists as a result of electronic advancements. In particular, the Internet has enabled tourists to get a better appreciation of destinations prior to travel, thus increasing the tangible dimensions of the tourism and hospitality product.

Another challenge to all tourism and hospitality firms is the maintenance of a quality product. This is particularly highlighted by the simultaneous nature of production and consumption and the experiential nature of the products.

Similarly, understanding and measuring customer satisfaction is vital to the industry, so the chapter highlights the importance of service quality and customer satisfaction. However, services sometimes fail and service personnel and managers require a good understanding of service recovery tactics. Thus, the chapter elaborates on specific research findings on service recovery within the industry.

Finally, understanding customer loyalty is also important to managers and this chapter explores what this means within the tourism and hospitality sector.

Overview of the tourism and hospitality industry

The tourism and hospitality industry is quite diverse in its composition. The industry is made up of many products such as restaurants, accommodation, transport, museums, natural attractions (such as rainforests and snowfields) and built attractions (such as theme parks). Table 15.1 illustrates some of the tourism and hospitality products and the implications for marketing.

Table 15.1   Examples of tourism and hospitality products

Tourism/hospitality product	Unique characteristics — examples	Implications for marketing — examples
Accommodation	Mix of tangible and intangible factors	Quality assurance vital Loyalty schemes important Word of mouth important
Airlines	Difficult to manage capacity	Need to find ways to balance demand and supply such as yield management Loyalty schemes important
Cruises	High emphasis on experience	Service delivery and interactions vital
Tours	Complex range of service provided	Customers may engage in extensive search behaviour to identify the best tour
Tourist destinations	Complex interrelated range of products	Difficult to manage and maintain product

Customer information search processes

Possibly one of the most challenging tasks for those involved with marketing tourism and hospitality services is to understand where and how consumers search for information on tourist destinations, hospitality services and individual attractions.

Information search: an expressed need to consult various sources of information prior to making the final purchase or destination selection decision

Moutinho (1987) has defined **information search** as an expressed need to consult various sources prior to making a purchase decision. Information search occurs as a result of consumers either being highly motivated to learn fully about a new product or fearing that it is risky to try an unfamiliar product (Raju 1980). When a traveller is planning their tourist itinerary, they have an expressed need to find out what travel opportunities exist, where these opportunities are available and at what cost (Raitz & Dakhil 1989). These information search strategies are an integral factor in ensuring that a successful trip is planned, and that the risk of a poor trip experience is minimised. In summary, the process of information search is an overt behaviour adopted by the tourist in order to reduce the risk and uncertainty associated with undertaking their travel itinerary (Fodness & Murray 1997).

How much information do travellers want?

Some travellers are happy to visit an unknown destination even though they have very little information gathered on its attractions and tourist facilities; others are known to conduct an extensive search for relevant information prior to their departure. The latter, referred to by Snepenger et al. (1990) as 'destination naive tourists', view the collection of a large range of information prior to departure as a way of minimising the risk of the unknown, particularly when travelling to an unfamiliar destination. The level of information search conducted by travellers has also been found to positively correlate with the distance travelled to the primary destination (Gitelson & Crompton 1983). In this context, travellers to long-haul destinations are expected to exhibit higher degrees of information search than their shorter-haul counterparts when planning their itineraries. Van Raaj & Francken (1984) argued that more intensive information search behaviour is undertaken when the traveller is considering unfamiliar destinations. Data collected by the Bureau of Tourism Research (1999a) supports this idea. When considering the information search behaviour of different country of origin markets, just 24 per cent of visitors from New Zealand indicated that they collected any information on Australia before their visit. Meanwhile, a much greater proportion (60 per cent) of visitors from the long-haul market of Scandinavia indicated that they had collected some form of tourist information before to their visit 'down-under'. Clearly, New Zealanders have a fairly good knowledge of Australia and its tourist attractions, which explains why so few visitors stated that they gathered much information when planning their visit. Visitors from Scandinavia, however, generally need to consult a variety of information sources as their knowledge of Australia is not as great.

Yacoumis (1989) suggested that a traveller's awareness of destinations is affected not only by their own knowledge and experience, but also by the information provided by external sources such as travel agents, airlines and so on. Typologies of information sources have been classified in several ways. The most common classification, however, is 'internal' versus 'external' search.

Internal search: destination familiarity and previous travel experience

Internal search:
information retrieved from one's own memory based on past experiences with a product or service

Internal search refers to information retrieved from the tourist's own memory, based on past experiences (Fodness & Murray 1997). Visitors who are planning to return to a past vacation destination will rely on their recollections of the previous trip (either to the same destination or a similar one) when planning their repeat visit.

For tourist destinations, the importance of ensuring that a visitor has a satisfactory first experience of a destination, its attractions and its service providers cannot be overstated. Given that tourists initially turn to their own recollections of previous trips when considering their next travel destination, destinations cannot be too careful in 'getting it right the first time'. No amount of marketing through glossy tourist brochures or elaborate websites can overcome the problem of convincing a traveller to return to a destination at which they have previously encountered poor service and had an unsatisfactory tourist experience. For this reason, tourist destinations must attempt to understand how many of their future visitors are likely to be repeat visitors who will largely rely on internal information when deciding whether or not to return to a region in the future; and they must also understand what perceptions and images those former visitors have of their tourism products and services. Such information can be best obtained through market research studies such as those conducted by Tourism Queensland on the popular Sunshine Coast region.

Services Marketing Action:
Past visitors' perceptions of the Sunshine Coast

In September 1999, Tourism Queensland commissioned research into Australian residents' awareness and opinions of the Sunshine Coast, a popular resort area in Queensland (Tourism Queensland 2000). Amongst other objectives, the study aimed to obtain insights into how past visitors felt about the region as a tourist destination. Through focus groups conducted in the key domestic origin markets of Brisbane, Sydney and Melbourne, some encouraging results were found. Sydney and Melbourne residents in particular were extremely enthusiastic in endorsing the Sunshine Coast as a tourist destination that closely met their holiday ideals and desires. Past visitors to the Sunshine Coast claimed that they intended to return as a result of their positive experiences. They appeared to be undoubted ambassadors for the region and were found to be a very powerful source of positive word of mouth, presenting the Sunshine Coast as an attractive destination to other potential visitors.

Interestingly, those who had not previously visited the Sunshine Coast lacked any specific knowledge about what the region had to offer as a holiday destination. Their perceptions were limited to quite vague descriptions of beaches and beach activities. Meanwhile those who had previously visited areas such as Noosa clearly identified the region as offering much more than sand and surf. They placed a lot more emphasis on describing the Sunshine Coast as offering an attractive 'lifestyle', which visitors could experience during their stay.

Based on these findings, Tourism Queensland was able to identify the clear benefits of ensuring that visitors' 'internal information search' mechanisms result in positive recollections being retrieved. These positive experiences not only greatly increase the likelihood of a particular visitor returning to the Sunshine Coast, but also provide a clear source of positive word of mouth to other potential visitors. Information that may not be clearly obtained through **external information sources** such as tourist brochures can be easily relayed by a past visitor, who is able to describe their positive tourist experiences in a clear and enticing manner.

External information sources: *sources other than one's own memory or past experiences (such as travel agents, tourist brochures and so on)*

External information search

When a person has no previous travel experience of a destination or a similar destination, any impressions must be formed by acquiring information from a variety of sources (Etzel & Wahlers 1985; Seaton & Bennett 1996). Tourists' use of promotional materials is, in part, a mechanism used to reduce the perceived risks associated with the travel decision-making process (Seaton & Bennett 1996; Vogt & Fesenmaier 1998). The act of acquiring and absorbing information about potential tourist destinations undoubtedly results in the traveller becoming more familiar with the area in question. It has been suggested that there is an inverse relationship between past travel experience of a given destination and the level of other information obtained (Etzel & Wahler 1985). However, overall travel experience (that is, not just of one destination), was also shown in the same study to increase the amount of information sought. This suggests that the more experienced travellers are aware of the benefits of acquiring destination-related information when planning travel to new places.

What types of information do tourists require?

Gitelson and Crompton (1983) suggested that the information search process involved in selecting an international tourist destination is predominantly external, and that a variety of information sources are used when vacation travel is being planned. It is well known that travel agents and the multitude of travel brochures they stock are one of the most popular sources of information referred to by people in the early holiday planning stages. But what type of information are they looking for? And what decisions are made first? Studies that have looked at the travel decision-making process have shown that one of the first decisions made by the potential traveller is the particular region to be visited (Hyde 1998). Brochures and other materials are scanned to determine what types of travel experiences are available in different countries. At this stage information on the general destination is of interest, but equally important is information about the travel packages that are available. Packages will generally range from short weekend breaks of two nights' accommodation including transportation to extensive tours of up to several weeks in duration.

Further information may also be sought from specific tourist information providers associated with a region. For example, the Gold Coast Tourism Bureau is a local tourist marketing authority, which makes available to visitors a wide range of promotional materials on the Gold Coast region. Tourism Bureaus provide a variety of brochures on particular attractions, accommodation and other hospitality services in a region. They also act as advisers to local industry operators on how to maximise the effectiveness of their marketing strategies for both domestic and international markets.

Individual tourism operators, including hotels, airlines and restaurants, must make themselves aware of the key sources of information referred to by visitors when planning their holidays. For this reason, many of the marketing activities of hospitality operators are conducted on a somewhat cooperative basis. For an individual operator, promotion of their services in the brochures of well-established tour operators and travel agents is a much more cost-effective marketing strategy than relying on direct distribution of their own promotional materials. For example, a resort hotel in Cairns that wishes to target the Japanese market, which accounts for almost 20 per cent of Australia's international visitors (Bureau of Tourism Research 1999a), must work on developing marketing alliances with key Japanese wholesalers such as the Japanese Tourism Bureau (JTB) and Jalpak. These operators have the distribution systems in place to pass on information to a high volume of potential visitors. The hotel by itself would incur an unbearable cost if the same amount of exposure was attempted by producing and distributing its own promotional materials.

While travel agents, visitor information centres, government tourism authorities and individual hospitality operators provide a realm of information to the potential traveller, it is impossible to discuss the distribution of tourism and hospitality marketing materials without giving some consideration to the role of the Internet.

The role of the Internet

The Internet has opened up endless opportunities for potential travellers seeking information on potential destinations. The advantages of being able to access information on travel and hospitality services via the Internet include:

- ease of accessibility (speed and amount of travel information obtainable)
- freedom to search for destination and travel product information without being influenced by an agent to whom commissions are payable
- the ability to follow through the information search process by making online bookings.

From the customer's point of view, the ability to book travel accommodation and other services via the Internet often means that a better rate is available due to the absence of a travel intermediary such as a travel agent, who tends to add a minimum 10 per cent commission to all bookings made. From the hospitality provider's perspective, these commissions need not be paid to a third party (unless the bookings are made via a commissionable online reservations site such as Utell or Lexington Services). Furthermore, many hotels in particular are utilising their websites to capture valuable information on those who visit the site. Many are moving towards using the Internet as much more than a mere system of distributing product information. Some hospitality and tourism providers are implementing direct marketing strategies via the Internet by providing special incentives to travellers to book via the Internet. For example, Virgin Blue, who entered the Australian domestic airline industry in 2000, offers many airfares that are cheaper than its competitors. It does this by providing special ticket prices that are available only to travellers who book via the Internet. The use of electronic brochures is also quite common, and provides an effective means of communication between, say, a hotel and its guests without the need for copious quantities of brochure stock. Sites such as that described in the Services Marketing on the Web vignette below generally incorporate some mechanism for gathering the email and other contact details of those who visit the site.

Services Marketing on the Web:
Power up for the next frontier in services

In recognition of the growing use of the Internet as an information source for potential visitors, Tourism Queensland has developed a series of websites specially designed to appeal to specific international markets.

Imagery: *a set of visual cues, such as pictures, colours, words and associated personalities or attractions, that are typical of a travel destination or service provider*

The **imagery** and content of each website has been designed to target the needs of the market represented. For instance, the website directed at the UK market (www.queenslandholidays.co.uk) features an image of a 'typical Aussie bloke' welcoming visitors to the site with the Australian greeting of 'G'day'.

The Tourism Queensland websites include destination information, attraction and product information, and links to regional tourism organisation websites. The feature attractions listed on the front page of each international site vary depending on the types of attractions that different markets perceive as 'must see or do' icons of Australia. The UK site, for example, highlights the Great Barrier Reef as one of the 'world's great natural wonders'. Meanwhile the site aimed at the North American market has a feature article highlighting the Australian Outback as the location of the American reality-TV series 'Survivor II'. The site targeted at the Singapore market places a strong emphasis on promoting Australia's Gold Coast region, along with a variety of natural attractions such as rainforests, a trip on the Skyrail in tropical North Queensland, and the Tangalooma Wild Dolphin Resort. Clearly the imagery used on each version of the website is carefully chosen to appeal to the tourist interests and desired experiences of particular international markets.

Figure 15.1: The Tourism Queensland website for the United States market

Service quality: the result of an evaluation process in which the customer compares their perceptions of the service with their expectations

Customer satisfaction: 'the customer's fulfilment response; a judgement that a product or service feature, or the product or service itself, provided a pleasurable level of consumption-related fulfilment, including levels of under- or over-fulfilment' (Oliver 1997)

Service experience: the time in which the customer is directly using or consuming the service

The role of service quality and satisfaction

At the core of much services marketing research are **service quality** and **customer satisfaction** issues. The marketing and management perspective on service quality generally points to a discrepancy between customers' perceptions and expectations in defining service quality (Parasuraman, Zeithaml & Berry 1988). As customers participate in the **service experience**, they make judgements about the quality of the core service and interaction. These judgements are primarily based upon the messages communicated to the customer during the service delivery, while the exchange will be influenced by an array of individual differences and experiences. In particular, ethnic background, motives for using a service (for example, staying at a hotel for business or pleasure) and the experiences associated with different classes of services (for example, a five-star compared to a three-star hotel) can be major influences upon expectations of how an exchange should proceed and what constitutes quality service.

More recently, researchers (such as Gremler & Gwiner 2000) have turned their attention to social dimensions of service interactions as a way of further investigating service quality and customer satisfaction. Gremler and Gwiner (2000) argue that rapport has an important role to play in influencing feelings of satisfaction, word of mouth and loyalty to a firm. Similarly, Butcher, Sparks and O'Callaghan (2001) found that, within the restaurant industry, feeling comfortable and relaxed with a service provider impacted positively on service quality and satisfaction evaluations.

Service quality and satisfaction evaluations are important to managers and marketers because evidence has shown that these relate to business and consumer behaviour factors such as profit, word of mouth and loyalty. Research by Bowen and Chen (2001) demonstrated that, for hotels, as customer levels of satisfaction increased so did likelihood of return and positive word of mouth. Moreover, an important finding of Bowen and Chen (2001) was that a minor change in satisfaction can lead to a major change in loyalty to the hotel. However, a minor drop in satisfaction was also found to lead to a major drop in willingness to recommend the hotel to others.

Kimes (2001) undertook a study to investigate the relationship between profit and product quality within a hotel. She undertook her study by investigating the hotel franchise company Holiday Inn. In order to measure the operating performance of hotels, Kimes used an indicator known as **RevPAR** (revenue per available room). To assess quality, she used Holiday Inn's quality assurance reports that evaluate a range of aspects of properties. The focus of her study was on the physical qualities of the properties, such as the hotel lobby, dining facilities and guest rooms. Kimes found that there was a clear relationship between product quality and the hotel's financial performance. Indeed, she reported that, on average, hotels with defective products had a RevPAR of approximately $3 less than hotels without non-defective products.

In summary, service quality and satisfaction are vital to the tourism and hospitality industries. Evidence shows that an investment in ensuring high levels of customer satisfaction will potentially provide good returns in terms of repeat business and recommendations to other potential customers.

Measuring service quality and customer satisfaction

A number of researchers (Parasuraman, Zeithaml & Berry 1988; Grönroos 1984) have proposed various approaches for conceptualising and measuring service quality. As explained in chapter 4, one of the most widely used is SERVQUAL (Parasuraman, Zeithaml & Berry 1988). The **SERVQUAL** scale is the result of extensive work by these researchers and comprises two sets of 22 multi-item questions, that measure customer expectations and perceptions of service. Their model of the dimensionality of service quality consists of tangibles, reliability, responsiveness, assurance and empathy. Practitioners and researchers are also interested in monitoring and managing customer satisfaction. The Services Marketing Action vignette below provides an overview of a study that investigated consumer satisfaction with a tourist destination.

RevPAR: *a term used in hotels to indicate revenue per available room*

SERVQUAL: *a 44-item instrument used to measure customer expectations and perceptions according to five service quality dimensions: responsiveness, tangible aspects, assurance, empathy and reliability*

The tourism product is multifaceted, comprising many different elements. As a result, the satisfaction of visitors to a destination can be affected by a range of tourism experiences, which may be derived from many sources, such as accommodation, use of natural attractions, restaurants and so on. Similarly, when using any one tourism product, there are many aspects that influence satisfaction: the treatment provided by service personnel, the physical environment, and the ease with which a visitor can access the product. In an effort to better understand and manage satisfaction, a study was commissioned by an Australian tourist destination (Sparks 2000a). A working party was established to identify the key factors to be investigated.

Tourism dimensions

Based upon a review of existing satisfaction literature, some preliminary pilot studies and focus group discussions, it was decided to focus on measuring tourist satisfaction with five key dimensions for a range of tourism objects (products). Figure 15.2 provides an overview of these. Each dimension was measured using two items (questions) that were deemed to be indicators of the dimension under consideration. This was determined through previous research and pilot testing procedures. *Value for money* was measured using visitors' perceived value of a product and assessment of the prices paid for that product. *Access* was designed to measure views on how accessible a tourism object was, as well as its hours of operations. *Service* was measured using two questions that sought information on visitors' perceptions of overall service levels and consistency of service delivery. The *physical environment* dimension sought information about the actual physical set-up (or environment) of the tourism object, as well as the visitors' perceived level of safety. Finally, *communication* was primarily concerned with seeking feedback on visitors' assessment of service personnel's communication style and helpfulness. This final dimension may overlap somewhat in the service dimension, but here the emphasis is on personality and empathy, whereas the service dimension emphasises reliability and consistency.

Tourism objects

Because the tourism product is made up of a range of objects such as accommodation, restaurants, shops, amusement parks and beaches, each of these was included in the survey. The decision about which objects to include was made after pilot testing the questionnaire and consultation with some members of the working party. An issue for researchers is that it is not always possible to cover all objects within the tourism system, and that was the case with this study. However, the aim was to include those objects considered most salient for the destination.

Method of data collection

A self-administered questionnaire was developed and implemented. The population of interest was any domestic (Australian resident) tourist who had spent at least two nights at the destination at the time of contact. Wherever possible, tourists were sought as they completed their stay at the destination. This approach was taken in order to optimise 'top of mind' experiences with the tourism product. Information was collected and then analysed using statistical approaches. The next sections discuss the predictors of satisfaction with tourism objects and overall satisfaction with the destination.

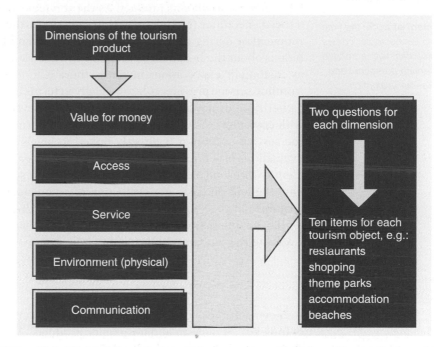

Figure 15.2: Model of dimensions used for measuring satisfaction with each tourism object

Results on the predictors of satisfaction with various tourism objects

For restaurants and cafés, the best predictors of overall satisfaction were, in order of importance, service, communication, value, environment and accessibility. In order of importance, satisfaction with the shopping object was best predicted by communication, value, environment, service and accessibility. In order of importance, theme park/wildlife satisfaction was best predicted by environment, service and value. Satisfaction with this object was not reliably related to communication or accessibility. For the accommodation element, the best predictors of satisfaction were, in order, service, communication, environment, value and accessibility. Finally, the environment (physical), service (which included information about conditions) and value dimensions (value of the beaches as part of the holiday destination) respectively were the best predictors of satisfaction with the destinations' beaches. Satisfaction with beaches was not related to the respondents' ratings of accessibility and communication.

Results on predicting overall satisfaction with the tourist destination

When considering the overall satisfaction people felt with the tourist destination, four of the five tourism objects were most important. In particular, the objects that made a significant contribution to respondents' overall satisfaction in order of importance were accommodation, restaurants, beaches and shopping.
Source: based on Sparks 2000

The service encounter

Service encounter: *interaction between customer and service provider involving exchange, and varying in complexity and duration*

Moment of truth: *the time when the customer comes into contact with a service or service personnel and makes an evaluation*

The next section focuses specifically upon the **service encounter**, which is often referred to as the **moment of truth**. The service encounter involves the time that the consumer directly interacts with the personnel, physical facilities and other tangible elements of the organisation (Shostack 1985). The hotel industry relies heavily on the quality of service (or the moment of truth) in the delivery and differentiation of its product. As the service encounter is first and foremost a social encounter (McCallum & Harrison 1985), the nature and quality of communication during this encounter establishes and confirms customer expectations about the hospitality product. Brown, Fisk and Bitner (1994) argue that as customers' expectations increase, there is a need to better understand the frontline service provider role, especially in terms of solving customer problems, gathering information on customer needs and developing ongoing relationships with customers. As others note (for example, Bitner 1990; Czepiel et al. 1985), the service encounter is directly linked to levels of customer satisfaction and evaluations of service quality. In the Brown, Fisk and Bitner (1994) paper, they identify three major areas of service encounter research: the role of the physical environment on customer evaluation of an encounter; the involvement of the customer in the service delivery process; and the management of customer–employee interactions, including the outcome evaluations. Each of these areas is vital to the tourism and hospitality industry.

The need for service recovery

Achieving 100 per cent error free service delivery is quite difficult, given the complexity of tourism and hospitality products. As a result, service failures do occur and need to be understood. A **service failure** or service breakdown will be defined as that which does not meet the customer's expectations. **Service recovery** is the attempt to 'put right' the service and regain the customer's satisfaction. This section will discuss some of the likely causes of service failure in the tourism and hospitality industry. This will be followed by a discussion of key service recovery tactics.

Service failure: *a breakdown in the delivery of a service*

Service recovery: *the actions a service provider takes in response to a service failure in order to 'put right' the service*

Causes of service failure in tourism and hospitality products

There are several potential causes of service failure and a limited set is discussed here (see Sparks 2001 for wider discussion). A service may fail because the core product is defective. For example, customers are likely to perceive that a service has broken down if the steak is tough or their flight is unsafe. In the case of a hotel, cleanliness, bed comfort and functioning of appliances within the room are often key indicators of the core product quality. Similarly, other research investigating failure within the restaurant industry (Hoffman, Kelley & Rotalsky 1995) found defective food product, such as cold, soggy, burnt or poorly cooked items, was a significant source of dissatisfaction.

Service failures sometimes occur because the core product is not available. Examples of this would be a family going to a theme park only to find a particular ride was out of service; or certain dishes advertised on a restaurant's menu no longer being available. Similarly, failure may occur if critical details of a service are not provided to the customer at the time of sale; for example, a customer might book a hotel room and finds on arrival that the property is in the midst of renovation. A cancelled flight or a room service meal that does not arrive are other examples of service failures due to omission.

Another common cause of service failure relates to timing issues. Most timing problems can be categorised as either too slow (delays or wait times) or too fast (inappropriate timing). For instance, in a study of restaurant patrons, 38 per cent of respondents indicated failures attributable to time delays (Sparks 1998). Timing failures also include waiting in line to check in or out of a hotel. In a study of service failures using airlines as the focal point, Edvardsson (1992) found that delayed or cancelled flights accounted for 82 per cent of customer dissatisfaction.

Peripheral aspects: the non-core components of a service

Quite frequently the cause of service failure is directly related to more **peripheral aspects** of the product, such as the service provider. The interpersonal or communication skills of the service provider often contribute to customers feeling less than satisfied. Indeed, Keaveny (1995) found that many service failures were attributed to some aspect of the service employees' behaviour or attitudes, such as being uncaring, impolite or unresponsive. Similarly, in recent research into service recovery (Sparks 2000b), several focus-group discussions highlighted the importance of the interpersonal dimension of service recovery. For instance, a common theme to emerge was the comment that in a service failure/recovery situation the provider should be 'a bit more understanding', 'a bit more sympathetic and communicative'. Indeed, clear evidence existed that while some firms might rectify the core service failure, it is the additional interactional dimension that makes a difference between regaining the customer's satisfaction or not.

The vignette presented below demonstrates the importance of showing evidence of concern beyond the mere rectifying of the core service.

Services Marketing Action:
The importance of peripheral dimensions

On one of her regular trips back to her home city, Natalie, a receptionist, waited patiently for her luggage to come out on the baggage carousel. It was an evening flight, the last one for the day into the terminal, and it had landed just before 10 p.m. As it was reasonably busy, Natalie was not surprised to have to wait a while for her baggage to come out. She waited and waited until finally the carousel stopped and everyone had left the area. Realising that her baggage was not going to appear, Natalie immediately proceeded to the baggage master to report her lost bag. There were two or three other passengers milling around, but Natalie wanted to be the first, and moved quickly to grab the baggage master's attention. She described her luggage to the baggage master, and he replied that he would go and look for it. He took a few other inquiries and then disappeared into the back-of-house area. He appeared to be in a hurry, and Natalie could see a few of the other luggage handlers apparently looking around for the luggage lost from the last flight. After about two minutes the baggage master returned and said, 'Oh, we can't find it'. As the terminal was almost completely empty, and staff were obviously preparing to close up for the night, Natalie just had to accept his word. There didn't seem to be anyone else she could turn to, which she found frustrating.

Natalie was also getting very concerned because she had all her clothes in the bag, as well as some little gifts and items for her family. She was concerned mostly about the value of what she had in the luggage, even though she knew that she had insurance. Natalie completed a form about the missing bag and informed the airline where she could be contacted. Before she left the air terminal, she said to them, 'I know that there are people here all night, so I want a phonecall when you find my luggage, and I don't care what time of the night it is'.

When Natalie arrived at her parents' home an hour later, she received a phonecall from the baggage master. He said that he had found her bag; it was on the tarmac. The next morning, a taxi brought the bag to Natalie's parents' house.

However, Natalie was not satisfied: she wanted to know how this situation had happened. Therefore, the next day, Natalie called the airline, and determined that the baggage master was on again that evening. When she finally spoke to him, she introduced herself and explained that she was wondering if he could tell her where her bag was found. The baggage master replied, 'Oh, it was on the tarmac'. Natalie asked, 'Can you tell me how it got there'?. The baggage master said abruptly, 'It fell off a cart'. Natalie then asked how it could have fallen off, to which the baggage master replied, 'Oh, they were probably, like, just not watching — it's dark and everything'. After this exchange, Natalie was even more dissatisfied.

Understanding what makes for a fair service recovery

As outlined in chapter 13, considerable attention has been given to understanding what makes for a fair service recovery. Typically researchers have used what is referred to as a justice framework for gaining further insight into how people feel about service recovery. Three key sorts, or dimensions, of justice are generally agreed to exist. These include distributive justice, where the focus is on evaluating fairness based on what compensation is provided to customers; procedural justice, where the focus is on evaluating fairness by considering the procedures used; and interactional justice, where the focus is on the interpersonal behaviour of the service provider. Figure 15.3 illustrates each dimension of justice, with examples from the tourism and hospitality industry.

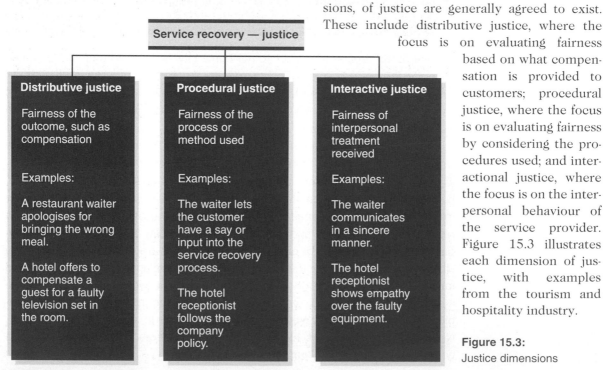

Figure 15.3:
Justice dimensions

Service recovery tactics for the tourism and hospitality industry

A range of actions can be taken to recover service failures. A brief overview is presented here.

Taking responsibility

Staff empowerment: the latitude in decision making and support from management that gives staff the power to take whatever action is necessary to fix a problem

Management should ensure service personnel can take responsibility for the problems. Issues of **staff empowerment** and flexibility may come into action here. Some researchers argue that the best way to recover from service failure is for frontline workers to identify and solve problems, even if this means breaking rules. Hence, it is suggested that effective service recovery requires latitude in decision making and ultimately support from management to take whatever action is necessary to fix the problem. As the tourism and hospitality industry relies so heavily upon the actions of frontline service employees, attention to careful policy development and training in empowerment is important.

Overt display of effort

Service personnel should use demonstrations of effort to communicate concern and respect to customers. This is a service recovery tactic that is easy to implement, and, if done in a genuine manner, it can go a long way towards making an aggrieved customer feel better. In a study of tourism and hospitality service personnel responses to service failure (Sparks & McColl-Kennedy 2000), it was found that it is possible to turn an aggrieved customer into a delighted one by 'doing a little bit extra'. Similarly, other hospitality research (Sparks 1999) found that one of the most important aspects of service recovery is customers feeling they are 'treated with respect'. The following example presents a story that was told by an airline worker and highlights an example of such an action. 'We had a lady in Adelaide who was taking her dog to Melbourne over the Christmas holidays . . . and there are rules and regulations about the carriage of animals, so we explained all those to her, and we're not too sure where it broke down, but when she got to Melbourne the dog wasn't with her, but the dog arrived a couple of hours later, and it was delivered to her place. But the bottom line to her was that she was ringing to complain to say we'd given out the wrong information, so one of the operators had seen in the supermarket Christmas stockings for animals, so they sent her a $4 Christmas stocking for her dog, and she just thought that was the greatest.'

Providing an explanation

Providing an explanation for a service failure is sometimes a helpful approach to managing them. However, the overall effectiveness of explanations as a means of service recovery is still unclear and, to some degree, under-researched. It has been reported (Tax, Brown & Chandrashekaran 1998) that the provision of information had both positive and negative outcomes for customer perceptions. It seems the manner in which the information is perceived makes a considerable difference. For instance, when information was perceived as an excuse to mitigate an organisation's accountability, it was seen as negative. In contrast, information that increased understanding about the problem and led to a quick resolution was perceived favourably. Similarly, within a hospitality setting it has been found

(Sparks & Callan 1995) that accepting responsibility by providing an explanation and being prepared to back this up with some form of compensation was evaluated very favourably in a service failure situation. It seems customers want an explanation but not an excuse.

Providing compensation

Another service recovery action is to provide the customer with financial recompense, such as a refund, in recognition that the service was defective. Some research has found (Goodwin & Ross 1990) that customers preferred to receive a tangible outcome, even a token refund, when there was a breakdown in service delivery. Using a hotel setting, research by Sparks and Callan (1995) found that an offer was perceived more or less favourably depending upon other factors such as the explanation provided for the breakdown. Blodgett, Hill and Tax (1997) found that compensation only made a positive difference to satisfaction when accompanied by high levels of courtesy and respect. This implies that if the recovery process involves a rude service provider, then no amount of financial compensation will make up for the service failure.

Developing customer loyalty to hospitality organisations

While hotels, restaurants, airlines and other members of the hospitality industry place a great deal of emphasis on exceeding the expectations of customers and ensuring that satisfaction levels are maintained, there is no guarantee that a satisfied customer will continue to visit an establishment. A visitor from Brisbane who stays at a hotel in Perth may be extremely satisfied with his stay at this property, but will not stay there again because he has no plans to return to Perth in the future. Alternatively, if he does decide to visit Perth again, he may very well want to stay at a different accommodation property as a means of satisfying a need for variety in his travel experiences. Or perhaps, as often happens in the hospitality industry of today, the visitor has simply been lured away by another hotel property that has offered him an extremely competitive rate.

It is clear, therefore, that not all satisfied customers will become repeat users or exhibit any form of loyalty to the hospitality enterprise. As a result, it is important for hotels, restaurants and other hospitality operators to understand which of their customers are loyal and to consider ways in which they can tailor their services to reward loyal customers for their valuable commitment to the business.

Benefits of customer loyalty

Customer loyalty:
'a deeply held commitment to rebuy a preferred service consistently in the future, despite situational influences and marketing efforts having the potential to cause switching' (Oliver 1997)

Customer loyalty in the hospitality industry is not just about getting customers to return to the same hotel or restaurant in the future. Repeat patronage is just one benefit associated with establishing a loyal customer base. The fact that a guest keeps returning to the same hotel year in year out on their annual vacation is not just of benefit to the property because of the additional revenue generated from return visits. Further benefits associated with loyal customers are presented in table 15.2.

Table 15.2 Benefits of loyal customers in the hotel sector

Benefit	Example
Positive word of mouth	Loyal hotel customers tell an average of 12 people about the hotel they are committed to. Twenty per cent of guests claim they go out of their way to mention their favourite hotel when discussing hotels with friends and colleagues.
Positive complaint behaviour	Loyal customers are more likely to tell hotel management about a potential problem, in the hope that it will be rectified, than to switch to another property.
Useful feedback to hotel management	Loyal guests are often willing to serve on hotel advisory boards to provide guest feedback to management.
Increased profitability	Loyal guests are more profitable for a hotel than first-time guests owing to the lower marketing costs required to secure bookings.
Less sensitivity to price increases	Loyal guests are more willing, within reason, to accept an increase in room rates than are disloyal guests.

Source: adapted from Bowen & Shoemaker 1998

Antecedent factors to hotel loyalty

Before a hotel or restaurant can work towards rewarding loyal customers for their patronage, the factors that lead to loyalty among hospitality consumers must be fully understood.

Satisfaction

Clearly, as discussed previously, a customer must be sufficiently satisfied with past service encounters at a restaurant to be tempted to eat there again in the future. With the variety of restaurants available to diners these days, providing a satisfactory service experience is not enough to guarantee that a customer will become loyal to the establishment. This provides a particular challenge for restaurants situated in tourist destinations, such as Adelaide in South Australia, where visitation to the region is highly seasonal. Many restaurateurs in a region such as Adelaide must focus heavily on creating a loyal customer base from within the local community to ensure a steady flow of diners during the low tourist seasons. Similarly, hotels often find themselves in the same situation, and the local resident population of an area is a critical market needed to maintain occupancy levels during tourist downturns. Following the September 2001 terrorist attacks in the United States, hotels in regions as far away as Australia found themselves struggling for business. They faced cancellations of conference bookings from overseas and the postponement of major events such as the Commonwealth Heads of Government Meeting, which was due to be staged in Brisbane in October 2001. Global terrorism affected Queensland hotel occupancy levels, as it had throughout the world and, to make matters worse, the Australian airline industry crisis, in which Ansett was forced to close, left many Queensland properties in a state of chaos. It was not surprising, therefore, that many hotels, faced with escalating cancellation rates and dismal occupancy levels, turned to the local market with a variety of special offers used to stimulate patronage of their properties. Five-star hotels who were expecting the high occupancy levels associated with CHOGM in October 2001 were instead forced to turn to their local markets for support, and advertised extremely attractive offers in local newspapers as a result.

The role of trust and commitment

Previous studies have investigated the type of emotional attachments hotel guests exhibit towards the properties where they stay on a regular basis (Bowen & Shoemaker 1998; Dube & Reneghan 1999). Other studies have also looked at the type of loyalty strategies used by airline operators (Ostrowski, O'Brien & Gordon 1993; Dube & Maute 1998). Two antecedent factors that were shown to be prerequisites in gaining the loyalty of hotel guests were a high level of trust between the guest and hotel management, and a feeling of commitment between themselves and the hotel (Bowen & Shoemaker 1998). It has been clearly shown that although hotels may offer a wide range of financial incentives (such as reward programs and discount rates) to promote loyalty among their customers, loyalty is not something that can be gained on such incentives alone — not in the hospitality industry. Because of the very nature of hospitality services, where the role of people is critical to guaranteeing a successful service encounter, it is of utmost importance that guests come to feel that a hotel is trustworthy and is committed to servicing the needs of its repeat customers above and beyond other customers. For example, it has been shown that one of the top three factors that hotel guests indicated was highly important in maintaining their commitment to a particular hotel was that the hotel uses information from prior stays to customise services for you (Bowen & Shoemaker 1998). Another key factor raised was that 'employees communicate the attitude that (guests') problems are important to them'. Interestingly, the availability of a frequent guest program was ranked just twelfth out of 18 strategies that hotel guests felt were important to fostering their loyalty to the property (Bowen & Shoemaker 1998). It is clear, therefore, that for hotels to maintain and extend their list of loyal guests, strategies aimed at strengthening the emotional attachment of guests to a property are more important than the traditional financial incentives.

The crises mentioned earlier highlight the importance of maintaining a loyal customer base who will remain committed to patronising hospitality enterprises in times of good and bad. Satisfying the needs of loyal customers requires some unique marketing tactics to be used by hotels, airlines and restaurants alike, who need to reward guests for their commitment and continuing patronage. An example of the tactics used by hotels to foster loyalty is discussed below.

Strategies used by hotels to foster guest loyalty

Traditionally, many hospitality operators have based their loyalty-building strategies on the assumption that customers or guests could be won over by offers of rewards such as frequent user points systems, whereby guests earned points towards some 'reward' such as a free night's stay or a free dinner for two after having reached a certain level of expenditure at a hotel or restaurant. Such incentives are referred to as 'transactional tactics'. Today, however, having recognised that loyalty to a hospitality service is based on much more emotive aspects, as well as financial rewards, most hotels and restaurants are incorporating a wider range of 'emotional tactics' to foster guest loyalty.

Transactional tactics

Transactional tactics: strategies used by service organisations to reward customers for their loyalty, usually through some form of frequent user rewards scheme

As noted previously, **transactional tactics** are used primarily as an inducement for customers and guests to choose a particular hospitality establishment on an ongoing basis. For instance, many hotels have introduced some form of loyalty card whereby, after so many stays at their property or on reaching a certain expenditure level, customers are rewarded with some free or upgraded service. The Marriott International chain was one of the first international hotel chains to introduce such a system. Today their 'Marriott Rewards' program has a membership of over 20 million guests worldwide. Guests earn 10 rewards points for each dollar spent at one of the 2000 participating hotels. A guest who has earned 5000 points can upgrade their room to a larger suite or to one with their preferred view at selected properties (Marriott 2001).

However, the difficulty with relying solely on such incentives to foster guest loyalty lies in the fact that once the reward has been redeemed by guests (they have used, say, their free weekend stay for two) and all points revert back to zero, the guest may choose to discontinue their association with the property, as there is nothing to be gained in the short term. While they could commit to rebuilding their points under the rewards system, it generally takes a guest some time to reach their next reward level. In such cases, it is tempting for customers to switch to another hotel, which may be equally appealing and may have a better rewards system.

In essence, hotel guests are often loyal to the incentive program, not to the hotel in itself. Dowling & Uncles (1997) describe this type of loyalty as 'deal loyalty' rather than true loyalty to the organisation. Ultimately, if transactional tactics are used in isolation from other loyalty inducing strategies, there is a danger that a loyal guest may sever ties with a property if the incentive scheme is withdrawn. Having recognised this in the 1990s, many hotels have now moved towards addressing the non-financial benefits that guests seek from a hotel to which they have formed an attachment.

Emotional incentives

Since it has been clearly established that loyalty to organisations cannot be 'bought' solely by offering financial incentives or frequent user points systems, hospitality providers must turn their attention to securing the emotional attachment of their customers. **Emotional tactics** should be employed to entice guests to return, knowing that their special needs will be met by the hospitality enterprise. Such tactics may require a hotel to keep an extensive database on loyal customers, which provides service staff with critical information on special requirements of a particular guest. For example, when Mr Morrison checks into his favourite hotel on his next visit to Sydney, the receptionist will have noted from the guest history database that he always requires 10 extra coat-hangers in his wardrobe and that he prefers to have the *Sydney Morning Herald* delivered to his room no later than 7 a.m. before he leaves for his business meetings. The fact that the hotel has pre-empted his needs assures Mr Morrison that his patronage is of value to the property and that his needs are catered for in a way that he may not encounter if he stayed at a competitor's property. Another simple tactic that should be fostered by hospitality operators to secure the emotional bond between the hotel and its loyal guest is the courtesy of recognising valued and loyal customers by name. Nobody wants to keep staying at the same hotel time after time, year after year, only to be greeted by

Emotional tactics: strategies used by service organisations to reward customers for their loyalty, usually through non-financial rewards such as service upgrades or services especially tailored to the customers' needs

the vague look of staff who clearly do not recognise them, let alone know their particular needs. While such strategies do not require a great deal of financial commitment on the part of the hospitality operator, they do provide repeat visitors with a sense that they hold some special value to the business. The distribution of periodic newsletters or updates on special offers to loyal customers is a further tactic that can be successfully used in the hospitality industry to increase the level of commitment customers feel to an establishment. A simple email update informing Mr Morrison of special events or discounted rates available to him again confirms the fact that the hotel values its customers and is taking steps to keep them informed of relevant matters. Similarly, newsletters can keep loyal customers up to date on happenings at the property.

Services Marketing Action:
Conrad Jupiters Casino Rewards

Conrad Jupiters is a luxury five-star hotel and gaming facility on Queensland's Gold Coast. Many of the hotel's guests are attracted to the property by its lively atmosphere and the thrill associated with a win at a gaming machine or table. The hotel and casino have worked closely together on devising a program that rewards guests and locals alike for their patronage of the gaming facilities. The program, known as 'Casino Rewards' offers a combination of tactical and emotional incentives to encourage customers to continue to visit the property. Three levels of Casino Rewards membership can be awarded — White, Silver or Gold — depending on the extent of play on the gaming machines, table games and Keno. This covers both Conrad Jupiters and an associated property, the Treasury Casino in nearby Brisbane. Casino Reward members receive not only financial rewards in the form of weekly prize draws and cash giveaways, but also a special bimonthly newsletter that keeps them informed of current gaming, accommodation, and food and beverage offers available to them. Members who have achieved Gold level status are invited to a monthly $10 000 superdraw and cocktail party function in one of the hotel's prime convention facilities. Special promotions are often made available to Casino Reward members, such as a 15–25 per cent discount on food and beverages in several of the hotel's restaurants. Other incentives offered to encourage Reward members to choose Conrad Jupiters as their preferred accommodation venue include special accommodation rates. Members are given a clear message that their continued use of the casino's gaming facilities is highly valued by the management of Conrad Jupiters and, as such, a host of benefits are provided that are not available to non-member guests.

Summary

LO1: Understand the unique marketing challenges encountered by tourism and hospitality organisations.
- Tourism and hospitality services are unique in that they involve a mixture of tangible and intangible factors.
- It is often difficult to manage capacity because of the seasonal effects of tourism travel.

- Tourists and hospitality customers place a very high level of importance on the overall experience encountered during the delivery of the service.

LO2: Identify the types of information search processes used by travellers when choosing their holiday destination.

- When planning a trip to a tourist destination, travellers will generally begin their destination selection process by relying on their own memories and previous travel experiences (internal information search).
- External information search (for example, visiting a travel agent or ordering a tourist brochure) is commonly used after the internal search process has not provided sufficient information for the traveller to select their travel destination or hospitality service.

LO3: Appreciate the growing role of the Internet in marketing tourism and hospitality services.

- The Internet presents a variety of advantages to tourism and hospitality consumers compared to more traditional forms of marketing.
- The Internet enables faster access to a wider variety of information about tourism and hospitality services.
- It also provides the ability to retrieve information 24 hours a day from anywhere in the world.
- Consumers of tourism and hospitality services now have the ability to book services directly without paying commissions to third party agents.

LO4: Understand the importance of service quality and customer satisfaction to the tourism and hospitality industry.

- The tourism and hospitality industry relies heavily on experiential products. As a consequence, the quality of service received is important when customers form overall evaluations of the product.
- SERVQUAL is frequently used to conceptualise and measure service quality.
- Understanding and measuring customer satisfaction for tourism destinations is multifaceted, because a range of objects and experiences will make up satisfaction evaluations.

LO5: Recognise the role of service recovery in hospitality marketing and identify service recovery strategies in various hospitality settings.

- There is a need to understand how service failures affect customers and their future behaviour.
- By understanding potential service failures and recovery options, tourism and hospitality firms can better manage their businesses through improved satisfaction levels and positive word of mouth.
- Managers can implement service recovery strategies by focusing upon procedural, interactional and distributive dimensions of service, such as policy, communication and compensation.

LO6: Discuss the ways in which hospitality organisations can foster loyalty among their customers.

- Hospitality organisations can encourage guest loyalty through the use of emotional or transactional tactics, or a combination of both.
- Emotional tactics rely more on making the customer feel that the organisation treats them in a special manner in recognition of their continued patronage (by means of, say, special gifts on arrival at a hotel).
- Transactional tactics rely solely on offering customers some form of financial incentive program (such as frequent flyer points) to encourage them to use the service on a regular basis.
- Emotional tactics are more successful in engendering true guest loyalty in the longer term than are transactional tactics.

Customer loyalty: a feeling of commitment towards a service provider, which results in positive benefits to the organisation such as repeat patronage, lower price sensitivity, willingness to refer other customers to the business and a greater tolerance for mistakes that may occur in the service encounter (p. 406)

Customer satisfaction: 'the customer's fulfilment response; a judgement that a product or service feature, or the product or service itself, provided a pleasurable level of consumption-related fulfilment, including levels of under- or over-fulfilment' (Oliver 1997) (p. 398)

Emotional tactics: strategies used by service organisations to reward customers for their loyalty, usually through non-financial rewards such as service upgrades or services especially tailored to the customers' needs (p. 409)

External information sources: sources other than one's own memory or past experiences (such as travel agents, tourist brochures and so on) (p. 395)

Imagery: a set of visual cues, such as pictures, colours, words and associated personalities or attractions, that are typical of a travel destination or service provider (p. 397)

Information search: an expressed need to consult various sources of information prior to making the final purchase or destination selection decision (p. 393)

Internal search: information retrieved from one's own memory based on past experiences with a product or service (p. 394)

Moment of truth: the time when the customer comes into contact with a service or service personnel and makes an evaluation (p. 402)

Peripheral aspects: the non-core components of a service (p. 403)

RevPAR: a term used in hotels to indicate revenue per available room (p. 399)

Service encounter: interaction between customer and service provider involving exchange, and varying in complexity and duration (p. 402)

Service experience: the time in which the customer is directly using or consuming the service (p. 398)

Service failure: breakdown in the delivery of a service (p. 402)

Service quality: the result of an evaluation process in which the customer compares their perceptions of the service with their expectations (p. 398)

Service recovery: the actions a service provider takes in response to a service failure in order to 'put right' the service (p. 402)

SERVQUAL: a 44-item instrument used to measure customer expectations and perceptions according to five service quality dimensions: responsiveness, tangible aspects, assurance, empathy and reliability (p. 399)

Staff empowerment: the latitude in decision making and support from management that gives staff the power to take whatever action is necessary to fix a problem (p. 405)

Transactional tactics: strategies used by service organisations to reward customers for their loyalty, usually through some form of frequent user rewards scheme (p. 409)

review questions

1. What are the two types of information search processes that tourists may conduct when selecting their next travel destination?
2. What are the main advantages to travellers of being able to access information on hospitality organisations via the Internet?
3. What reasons can you think of to explain why a guest who has had a satisfactory experience with a hotel they recently stayed in may never visit the same property again?
4. What are the key benefits to a restaurant of fostering loyalty amongst its customers?

application questions

1. Why must organisations involved with marketing tourism and hospitality enterprises understand the information search processes used by their potential customers? Describe how this search process will differ between a tourist who is highly familiar with a region (they have been there before or have relatives living there) and one who is considering visiting a remote, exotic location to which they have limited prior exposure.
2. Talk to your friends about their tourism or hospitality experiences. What makes for a satisfying experience? What makes for a dissatisfying experience?
3. Evaluate and discuss how customer satisfaction of tourism destinations can be undertaken.
4. Develop a service recovery strategy for a restaurant or hotel. What are likely failures? What can be done to minimise failures?
5. Repeat visits to a hospitality operation are just one characteristic of a 'loyal customer'. Consider a restaurant or hotel in your own region and provide an overview of the other benefits to that organisation of fostering loyalty among its patrons.
6. Discuss the advantages and disadvantages a hotel faces in using tactical versus emotional incentives to foster loyalty among its guests.
7. Discuss what might make exceptional service recovery in the tourism and hospitality industry.

vignette questions

1. Read the Services Marketing Action vignette on page 395. What are the implications for the future marketing of the Sunshine Coast?
2. Read the Services Marketing on the Web vignette on pages 397–8. Alternatively you can visit the UK website at www.queenslandholidays.co.uk. Discuss how effectively imagery has been used to capture the attention of potential overseas visitors to Queensland, Australia.
3. Read the Services Marketing Action vignette on page 400. Why is a multi-dimensional and multi-object approach taken to investigate customer satisfaction?

4. Read the Services Marketing Action vignette on pages 403–4.
    (a) Why was the customer not satisfied, even though her luggage was found and delivered to her?
    (b) Can you think of cases where the peripheral service matters as much as or more than the core service?
5. Read the Services Marketing Action vignette on page 410. Comment on how effective the Conrad Jupiters Casino Rewards program is in developing loyalty to the accommodation services available at this property.

 recommended readings

This article discusses the relationship between customer satisfaction levels and loyalty towards a hospitality service:

Bowen, J. T. & Chen, S. L. 2001, 'The relationship between customer loyalty and customer satisfaction', *International Journal of Contemporary Hospitality Management*, vol. 13, no. 5, pp. 213–17.

This article identifies current gaps in what hotel guests believe are important rewards for loyalty compared to how well they perceive hotels actually provide such benefits:

Bowen, J. T. & Shoemaker, S. 1998, 'Loyalty: a strategic commitment', *Cornell Hotel and Restaurant Administration Quarterly*, February, pp. 12–25.

This article reviews the key requirements of a successfully implemented customer loyalty program:

Dowling, G. R. & Uncles, M. 1997, 'Do customer loyalty programs really work?', *Sloan Management Review*, summer, pp. 71–82.

This article compares the use of value-added versus value-recovery strategies on customer satisfaction and loyalty in the airline industry:

Dube, L. & Maute, M. F. 1998, 'Defensive strategies for managing satisfaction and loyalty in the service industry', *Psychology and Marketing*, vol. 15, no. 8, pp. 775–91.

This article discusses the impact of hotel performance in key functional areas on guest loyalty:

Dube, L. & Reneghan, L. M. 1999, 'Building customer loyalty — guests' perspectives on the lodging industry's functional best practices', *Cornell Hotel and Restaurant Administration Quarterly*, October, pp. 78–8.

This article provides some insight into the importance of building an understanding with your customer:

Gremler, D. D. & Gwiner, K. P. 2000, 'Customer–employee rapport in service relationships', *Journal of Service Research*, vol. 3, no. 1, pp. 82–104.

This article expands on the important topic of the link between quality and profitability using hotels as an example:

Kimes, S. E. 2001, 'How product quality drives profitability', *Cornell Hotel and Restaurant Administration Quarterly*, vol. 42, no. 3, pp. 25–8.

This chapter elaborates on the structure of service failure and sets out recovery tactics for the hospitality and tourism industry:

Sparks, B. A. 2001, 'Managing service failure through recovery', in Kandampully, J., Mok, C. & Sparks, B. A., *Service Quality Management in Hospitality, Tourism and Leisure*, Haworth Press, New York.

Australian Bureau of Statistics 2001, *Regional Population Growth — Australia and New Zealand*, cat no. 3218.0, ABS, Canberra.

Bitner, M. J. 1990, 'Evaluating service encounters: the effect of physical surroundings and employee responses', *Journal of Marketing*, vol. 54, pp. 69–82.

Blodgett, J. G., Hill, D. J. & Tax, S. S. 1997, 'The effects of distributive, procedural and interactional justice on postcomplaint behavior', *Journal of Retailing*, vol. 73, no. 2, pp. 185–210.

Bowen, J. T. & Chen, S. L. 2001, 'The relationship between customer loyalty and customer satisfaction', *International Journal of Contemporary Hospitality Management*, vol. 13, no. 5, pp. 213–17.

Bowen, J. T. & Shoemaker, S. 1998, 'Loyalty: a strategic commitment', *Cornell Hotel and Restaurant Administration Quarterly*, February, pp. 12–25.

Brown, S. W., Fisk, R. P. & Bitner, M. J. 1994, 'The development and emergence of services marketing thought', *International Journal of Service Industry Management*, vol. 5 no. 1, pp. 21–48.

Bureau of Tourism Research 1999a, *International Visitor Survey*, Bureau of Tourism Research, Canberra.

Bureau of Tourism Research 1999b, *Domestic Visitor Survey*, Bureau of Tourism Research, Canberra.

Butcher, K., Sparks, B. & O'Callaghan, F. 2001, 'Evaluative and relational influences on service loyalty', *International Journal of Service Industry Management*, vol, 12, no. 4, pp. 310–27.

Czepiel, J. A., Solomon, M. R., Surprenant, C. F. & Gutman, E. G. 1985, 'Service encounters: an overview', in Czepiel, J. A., Solomon, M. R. & Surprenant, C. F. (eds), *The Service Encounter: Managing Employee/ Customer Interaction In Businesses*, D. C. Heath, Lexington, MA.

Dowling, G. R. & Uncles, M. 1997, 'Do customer loyalty programs really work?', *Sloan Management Review*, summer, pp. 71–82.

Dube, L. & Maute, M. F. 1998, 'Defensive strategies for managing satisfaction and loyalty in the service industry', *Psychology and Marketing*, vol. 15, no. 8, pp. 775–91.

Dube, L. & Reneghan, L. M. 1999, 'Building customer loyalty — guests' perspectives on the lodging industry's functional best practices', *Cornell Hotel and Restaurant Administration Quarterly*, October, pp. 78–88.

Edvardsson, B. 1992, 'Service breakdowns: a study of critical incidents in an airline', *International Journal of Service Industry Management*, vol. 3, no. 4, pp. 17–29.

Etzel, M. J. & Wahlers, R. G. 1985, 'The use of requested promotional material by pleasure travelers', *Journal of Travel Research*, vol. 23, spring, pp. 2–6.

Fodness, D. & Murray, B. 1997, 'Tourist information search', *Annals of Tourism Research*, vol. 21, no. 3, pp. 503–23.

Gitelson, R. J. & Crompton, J. L. 1983, 'The planning horizons and sources of information used by pleasure vacationers', *Journal of Travel Research*, winter, pp. 2–7.

Goodwin, C. & Ross, I. 1990, 'Consumer evaluations of responses to complaints: what's fair and why?', *The Journal of Consumer Marketing*, vol. 7, pp. 39–47.

Gremler, D. D. & Gwiner, K. P. 2000, 'Customer–employee rapport in service relationship', *Journal of Service Research*, vol. 3, no. 1, pp. 82–104.

Grönroos, C. 1984, 'A service quality model and its marketing implications', *European Journal of Marketing*, vol. 18, pp. 36–44.

Hoffman, K. D., Kelley, S. W. & Rotalsky, H. M. 1995, 'Tracking service failures and employee recovery efforts', *Journal of Services Marketing*, vol. 9, no. 2, pp. 49–61.

Hyde, K. F. 1998, 'Building a model of independent traveller decision-making for choice of vacation itinerary', PhD thesis, University of O tago, New Zealand.

Keaveney, S. M. 1995, 'Customer switching behaviour in service industries: an exploratory study', *Journal of Marketing*, vol. 59, April, pp. 71–82.

Kimes, S. E. 2001, 'How product quality drives profitability', *Cornell Hotel and Restaurant Administration Quarterly*, vol. 42, no. 3, pp. 25–8.

Marriott, accessed 21 October 2001, *Marriott Rewards*, www.marriott.com.

McCallum, J. R. & Harrison, W. 1985, 'Interdependence in the service encounter', in Czepiel, J. A., Solomon, M. R. & Surprenant, C. F. (eds.), *The Service Encounter: Managing Employee/Customer Interaction In Service Businesses*, Lexington Books, Lexington MA, pp. 35–48.

Moutinho, L. 1987, 'Consumer behaviour in tourism', *European Journal of Marketing*, vol. 21, no. 10, pp. 5–44.

Ostrowski, P. L., O'Brien, T. & Gordon, G. L. 1993, 'Service quality and customer loyalty in the commercial airline industry', *Journal of Travel Research*, fall, pp. 16–24.

Parasuraman, A., Zeithaml, V. & Berry, L. 1988, 'SERVQUAL: a multi-item scale for measuring consumers' perceptions of service quality', *Journal of Retailing*, vol. 64, pp. 12–41.

Plog, S. 2001, 'Why tourism destination areas rise and fall in popularity', *Cornell Hotel and Restaurant Administration Quarterly*, vol. 42, no. 3, pp. 13–24.

Raitz, K. & Dakhil, M. 1989, 'A note about information sources for preferred recreational environments', *Journal of Travel Research*, vol. 27, no. 1, pp. 45–9.

Raju, P. S. 1980, 'Optimum stimulation level: its relationship to personality, demographics and exploratory behavior', *Journal of Consumer Research*, vol. 7, December, pp. 272–82.

Seaton, A. V. & Bennett, M. M. 1996, *Marketing Tourism Products: Concepts, Issues, Cases*, International Thomson Business Press, London.

Shostack, G. L. 1985, 'Planning the service encounter', in Czepiel, J. A., Solomon, M. R., & Surprenant, C. F. (eds), *The Service Encounter*, Lexington Books, New York.

Snepenger, D., Meged, K., Snelling, M. & Worrall, K. 1990, 'Information search strategies by destination naive tourists', *Journal of Travel Research*, summer, pp. 13–16.

Sparks, B. A. 1998, *Service Failures and Justice in a Restaurant Setting*, Working Paper, Griffith University, Australia.

Sparks, B. A. 1999, 'Service problems and perceptions of procedural justice in the hospitality industry', *Convention Proceedings 1999 International Council on Hotel, Restaurant and Institutional Education*, pp. 137–47.

Sparks, B. A. 2000a, *Tourist Satisfaction Survey Gold Coast: Project 2.3 of the Gold Coast Visioning Project*, CRC for Sustainable Tourism, Griffith University, Australia.

Sparks, B. A. 2000b, *Customer Perspectives on Service Failures in the Tourism and Hospitality Industry*, CRC for Sustainable Tourism, Griffith University, Australia.

Sparks, B. A. 2001, 'Managing service failure through recovery', in Kandampully, J., Mok, C. & Sparks, B. A., *Service Quality Management in Hospitality, Tourism and Leisure*, Haworth Press, New York.

Sparks, B. A. & Callan, V. 1995, 'Dealing with service breakdowns: the influence of explanations, offers and communication style on consumer complaint behaviour', *Proceedings of the World Congress Seventh Bi-Annual Marketing Science Conference*.

Sparks, B. A. & McColl-Kennedy, J. 2000, *Service Providers' Perspective On Service Failures in the Tourism and Hospitality Industry: An Exploratory Investigation*, CRC Sustainable Tourism Working Paper, Griffith University, Australia.

Tax, S. S., Brown, S. W. & Chandrashekaran, M. 1998, 'Customer evaluations of service complaint experiences: implications for relationship marketing', *Journal of Marketing*, vol. 62, no. 2, pp. 60–76.

Tourism Queensland 2000, *Trends Newsletter*, issue 18.

Van Raaij, W. F. & Francken, D. A. 1984, 'Vacation decisions, activities and satisfactions', *Annals of Tourism Research*, vol. 11, pp. 101–12.

Vogt, C. A. & Fesenmaier, D. R. 1998, 'Expanding the functional information search model', *Annals of Tourism Research*, vol. 25, no. 3, pp. 551–78.

Yacoumis, J. 1989, 'South Pacific tourism promotion: a regional approach', *Tourism Management*, vol. 10, no. 1, pp. 15–28.

Chapter 16
Franchising

Lorelle Frazer

LEARNING OBJECTIVES

After reading this chapter you should be able to:
- appreciate the important contribution of franchising to the economy
- explain why franchising is regarded as a service, and describe the various characteristics of the service
- identify the core product and supplementary services of a franchising service strategy
- identify the factors that contribute to a successful franchising relationship
- understand the contractual arrangements involved in the franchising relationship, including the pricing strategies available in terms of franchise fees
- describe the most common methods of achieving growth and development in franchising.

CHAPTER OUTLINE

The aim of this chapter is to analyse franchising from a services marketing perspective. The analysis will demonstrate that many of the characteristics of services marketing apply to franchising arrangements. In addition, this chapter will illustrate the important contribution of service industries to the franchising sector.

The chapter firstly explains the nature of franchising. Next, the various characteristics of the service of franchising are explored; that is, franchising is analysed from a services marketing perspective. We then look at how and why a franchising service strategy is important. The contractual nature of the relationship is also discussed in terms of the pricing strategy of franchise fees. Finally, methods of developing and expanding franchise systems are considered.

Introduction

Franchising: an
agreement under which a
franchisor grants exclusive
rights to a franchisee for
distribution and/or sale of
a service or product, in
return for payment and
conformance to quality
standards

Franchising is an efficient method of distributing goods and services. Since its rapid expansion in the Asia-Pacific region in the 1980s, the franchising sector of most countries has continued to grow and mature. Franchising is itself a provision of services to facilitate the distribution of products. This chapter will explore many of the important characteristics of franchising in the context of services marketing.

What is franchising?

Franchising is the 'cloning' of a successful business concept, enabling relatively inexperienced investors to operate under the umbrella of an established, proven system. Under a franchise agreement, the owner, producer or distributor of a service or product grants exclusive rights to an individual for the local distribution and/or sale of the service or product, and in return receives some form of payment and conformance to quality standards.

Most franchises offer a business format under which the franchisor markets a unique business system under a trade name. Franchisees then adopt the standardised procedures to run their own businesses. **Business format franchising** is characterised by the adoption of unique business and marketing systems, ongoing support and training, and standardised outlets. It is found across a wide range of industries such as fast food, retail, real estate, business services, education and construction.

*Business format
franchising:* a common
form of franchising
characterised by the
adoption of unique
business and marketing
systems, ongoing support
and training, and
standardised outlets

Some franchisors offer a complete 'turnkey' operation, providing franchisees with full start-up assistance for commencing their new outlets, thus enabling investors with no prior experience to have access to the industry. Franchises such as Fastway Couriers or Aussie Pooch Mobile offer turnkey operations.

A recent survey of the sector revealed the percentage of franchising that occurs in certain industries in Australia, as illustrated in table 16.1.

Table 16.1 Distribution of franchising in Australia	
Industry	**Percentage of franchisors**
Retail trade — non-food	31
Property and business services	20
Retail trade — food	14
Personal and other services	7
Construction and trade services	6
Accommodation, cafés and restaurants	4
Education	4
Cultural and recreation services	4

(continued)

Table 16.1	(continued)	
Industry	**Percentage of franchisors**
Unclassified	3
Manufacturing and printing	3
Finance and insurance	2
Transport and storage	1
Communication services	1
Total	**100**

Source: Frazer & McCosker 1999

The service sectors of property and business services and construction and trade services are witnessing the most rapid growth in franchising. This growth surge is due to a greater outsourcing of service activities to specialists.

Services Marketing Action:
Service industry boom

In the 1980s a new Australian franchise in residential cleaning was formed: Bizzi Beez. The franchisor already ran a carpet and fabric dry-cleaning franchise and he was able to transfer his experience to the new venture. He recognised that a niche market in household cleaning existed. Two-income families were becoming more common and these working couples were too busy to spend time on household chores. Their increased income levels meant they could outsource these household duties in order to maintain a more balanced and better quality lifestyle.

This was the beginning of the home services industry boom. Franchising was an ideal format for distributing household cleaning services because of the professional standards maintained by franchisees. Potential clients expect minimum levels of product quality to be performed by franchise organisations. In addition, the franchisee is normally an owner-operator who has an incentive to provide a high level of service so that customers will return. Moreover, house cleaning requires the franchisee to visit the client's home to perform the service, and the visibility of 'servants' on the premises may satisfy the client's ego needs.

Bizzi Beez is now Australia's largest residential cleaning company, with more than 350 franchised units across the country. The company has also expanded into the commercial cleaning market under its Bizzi Beez After 5 commercial cleaning franchise. It is joined by competitor organisations such as The Jim's Group, VIP Home Services and Absolute Domestics, which are also franchised, indicating the suitability of this method of distribution for domestic and commercial cleaning services.

Although the franchising sector covers both service and retail industries, franchising itself is a service function. It can be argued that McDonald's is in the business of franchising as well as the business of fast food. Hamburgers are the tangible product with which consumers are concerned but, in addition, McDonald's distributes the product through its franchise system, thus providing an intangible service to its thousands of franchisees. Hence, most franchise organisations will balance themselves equally between products and services on the service continuum, as shown in figure 16.1.

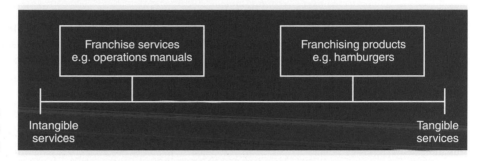

Figure 16.1: The position of franchise organisations on the service continuum

Why franchise?

Have you ever wondered why some companies franchise and others do not? Consider the hairdressing chain Stefan or the telecommunications company Fone Zone, which are fully company owned. Both organisations have many outlets spread throughout the country. Compare them to companies such as Just Cuts and Optus World which are both franchised organisations. Why have these companies chosen different organisational structures in order to expand?

The answer is actually very complex and may depend on a number of relevant factors. Two of the most commonly cited reasons for franchising are resource constraints and efficiency. Some companies begin franchising so that they can obtain more rapid market penetration without needing access to capital markets, because the franchisees provide the necessary capital (Caves & Murphy 1976; Norton 1988); in other words, resource constraints motivate them to franchise. An alternative view is that it is more efficient to expand via a network of franchisees because these owner-operators have a greater incentive to succeed than do employee-managers (Rubin 1978; Brickley & Dark 1987). Both these views have some merit, and franchising is probably a result of both issues.

Characteristics of the franchising 'service'

The franchisor has a dual role of promoting and distributing its product (for example, fast food, accounting services or lawn mowing) and administering the franchise system that supports its network of franchisees. The franchise system includes the brand name and intellectual property associated with the company; the start-up, ongoing and marketing assistance provided to franchisees; and the monitoring and quality control of the product. Under a franchising arrangement, the franchisee is the 'customer' of the franchisor and consumers are customers of the franchisee.

Franchising may be classified according to a number of characteristics that are common to many service activities:

- There is an intangible bundle of franchise management services.
- The franchisee is involved in the process.
- There is a high degree of customisation of service.
- The nature of service is continuous.
- The degree of contact with franchisees varies.
- There are electronic and physical delivery channels.

Intangibility

The franchisee 'customer' in the franchising relationship is not purchasing a tangible product such as furniture. In fact, the franchisee is often not even purchasing a clearly defined service, such as a haircut, which has an identifiable outcome. Franchising services resemble promises via a contractual arrangement, so they are intangible in nature.

The following are the main types of support provided by reputable franchisors:

Established brand name. Names like Snap Printing, Eagle Boys Pizza and Jim's Mowing are the product of many years of successful operation and exposure to the marketplace. The names signify quality, longevity and success to both end consumers and prospective franchisee investors. New franchisees can expect to attract business on the strength of the brand alone, thus giving them a better start to their new venture. An established brand name often forms a large portion of the intangible benefits of joining a franchise system, and franchisors are rewarded for their brand recognition by the higher entry fees payable by franchisees. Although an established brand name is normally a signal that a franchise is reputable and successful, there have been cases where large, well-established franchises have collapsed. Two such franchises in Australia were Cut Price Deli and Great Australian Ice Creameries, which were regarded as franchising icons. However, the impact of litigation by franchisees led to their ultimate demise.

- *Intellectual property pertaining to the operation of the franchise system.* One of the most important reasons for joining a franchise is that it allows a relatively inexperienced operator to perform under the umbrella of an established business. The franchisor provides know-how and training for people without the specific industry background to operate successfully. Normally, the procedures for running the business are carefully documented in operations and training manuals, which act as guides for franchisee operators. These confidential operations manuals represent years of development and fine-tuning of the franchise system.
- *Quality control.* The provision of standardised products and services across franchise systems is one of the characteristics of franchising. Customers are able to visit any store in the network and know that the goods they choose and the service they receive will be of a similar, familiar standard. This is because the franchisor monitors its franchisees for expected quality levels. The reputation of the system relies greatly on the ability of the franchise to supply products and services of a consistent quality across all outlets.

  Franchisors may choose to monitor their franchisee operations in a number of ways. For example, some employ field staff to visit stores and report on set criteria such as cleanliness, product quality and adherence to the system. Others use mystery shoppers who are able to observe and report on store operations. The Coffee Club franchise has a philosophy of 'catching people doing things right' rather than 'catching them doing things wrong'. Members of their corporate office regularly visit franchisees in their stores to provide support and encouragement, rather than to check on the franchisee's level of compliance. This more consultative approach helps to build positive relationships between franchisor and franchisee.

- *Support services.* A feature of franchising that is absent from independently operated businesses is the extensive initial and ongoing support that is normally provided by the franchisor. One of the reasons for joining a franchise network is that the inexperienced franchisee has access to these support services. Typical initial support services include site selection, pre-opening training and access to comprehensive operations manuals. Ongoing support is provided over the life of the agreement and includes field visits from head office personnel; ongoing training as new products and systems are developed; access to communication channels such as an intranet; regular newsletters; franchise meetings and conferences; and computerised booking services for allocating customer orders.

In summary, many of the services that are provided in a franchise network are intangible in nature. However, they are crucial to the success of individual outlets and play an important role in maintaining the reputation of the franchise.

Franchisee involvement in the process

As with other service industries, but unlike retail businesses, the customer plays a role in the production process. In the case of franchising, the franchisee is the recipient of franchising services and also participates in the production of those services. Just as a client must help the accountant prepare a tax return by supplying relevant financial details, so too must the franchisee assist the franchisor. For instance, a communication system will only be useful to the franchise network if individual franchisees participate by reading notices, attending meetings and networking with other franchisees in the system. This two-way partnership explains why the franchising relationship is often compared to a marriage — the success of the union depends upon the cooperation and interdependency of the two parties.

High degree of customisation of service

Although most services require some degree of customisation to suit the consumer, many are quite standardised. Consider the level of customisation required by a medical consultation as compared to a dog shampoo, as shown in figure 16.2.

Highly customised	Medical consultation
	Franchising services
	Haircut and colour
	Restaurant meal
Highly standardised	Dog shampoo

Figure 16.2: Level of customisation of service

Many of the services provided by a franchisor are highly customised. New franchisees enter the network throughout the year and they are often individually trained and supported in the initial stage of the relationship. Over the term of the agreement, the franchisor will not only provide continuing assistance as required by individual franchisees, but also general support for the entire group, such as a national marketing campaign. On the whole, franchising support activities are characterised by a high degree of customisation of service.

Continuous nature of service

Some service activities are single experiences — for example, the use of an ambulance after an accident. Others, including franchising, provide a continuous supply of services. Franchisees will therefore demand certain levels of performance based on their expectations at the outset of the relationship. This is where many franchising arrangements fail, because the franchisor may not deliver the level of service expected by the franchisee.

What motivates a franchisor to supply continuous support to its franchisees? Why not just take the initial entry fees and then leave the franchisees to their own devices? Of course, the franchisor has an incentive to maintain its reputation. By helping franchisees to run their businesses successfully, the image of the entire network will be enhanced. In particular, by charging franchisees ongoing fees for support services, the franchisor will have an even greater incentive to assist them, particularly if the fees are linked to franchisee sales levels.

Degree of contact with franchisees varies

Services are sometimes classified according to the level of contact with customers. In a franchising arrangement, the initial contact between franchisor and franchisee is concentrated, because a franchisee needs most assistance in the early stages of setting up the outlet. Over time, the franchisee needs less assistance, so the level of contact between the two parties tapers off as the franchisee becomes more independent — similar to a parent–child relationship.

However, the nature of the particular franchise business is related to the amount of support and contact required, as shown in figure 16.3. Generally, simple franchise systems such as lawn mowing are easy to run, so they require less ongoing support than complex systems such as a printing franchise, which is dependent on technology and characterised by rapid change. High-contact franchises that require a lot of interaction between the parties require more franchisor resources and commitment.

High contact	Printing services franchise
Medium contact	Coffee shop franchise
Low contact	Lawn-mowing franchise

Figure 16.3: Degree of contact with franchisees on an ongoing basis

Electronic and physical delivery channels

Due to technological advancements, the franchising sector has embraced the use of both electronic and physical methods of delivering services to franchisees. Help with the day-to-day operation of the business is provided by field staff, who visit the franchisee's premises and provide hands-on advice. Similarly, some monitoring activities such as the use of mystery shoppers require a physical presence.

However, there is an increasing trend towards providing some services electronically. Many franchises communicate by an intranet because franchisees are often located all over the country or the world. For example, New Zealand and South-East Asia are the most common destinations for Australian franchisors who export their systems, so electronic methods of communication are invaluable in these franchises. In addition, the franchising sector in Australia is regulated by the Franchising Code of Conduct, which requires franchisors to supply their franchisees with particular documentation (for example, a disclosure document containing detailed information about the franchise). To keep this paperwork up to date and to minimise costs, many franchisors distribute it electronically. We can expect to witness a greater use of electronic channels in supplying services to franchisees in future.

Developing a franchising service strategy

The previous section described the characteristics of franchising services. The discussion will now extend to the development of a franchising service strategy. Such a strategy enables the franchisor and franchisees to provide superior service to their clients. The franchising service strategy is a means of acquiring greater market share in a competitive environment.

Core, supplementary and augmented products in franchising

Core product: *the core services offered by the franchisor to franchisees as part of the franchising agreement*

Supplementary product: *the extra services provided by the franchisor to franchisees in addition to core services*

All products and services consist of the **core product** plus the **supplementary product**, which produce the total or augmented product as shown in figure 16.4.

Figure 16.4: Augmented product of a pet grooming franchisee

The core product of a pet grooming service might be the shampoo and the treatment of a dog's coat for fleas. For this core product, customers might expect a mobile service provided by a pet-friendly operator for a set fee. In addition, the service operator might provide supplementary services such as nail clipping, blow drying in winter, and the sale of dog food. These additional services are like the icing on a cake — they are not necessary but are nice to have. Supplementary services may distinguish one service provider from another, so they are powerful marketing tools.

As for the pet grooming franchisor, it is not only in the business of pet grooming, but is also providing franchising services to its franchisees to enable them to operate effectively in their own pet grooming businesses.

Like other products and services, franchising also offers various levels of service, as illustrated in figure 16.5. The core product of the franchisor might include start-up assistance such as site selection and initial training; monthly field visits from head office staff to monitor adherence to quality standards; and ongoing marketing support such as national advertising. The supplementary product, such as an annual conference or rewards and incentives for high-performing franchisees, are additional value-adding services that go beyond mere support and help to differentiate the franchise from others in the market.

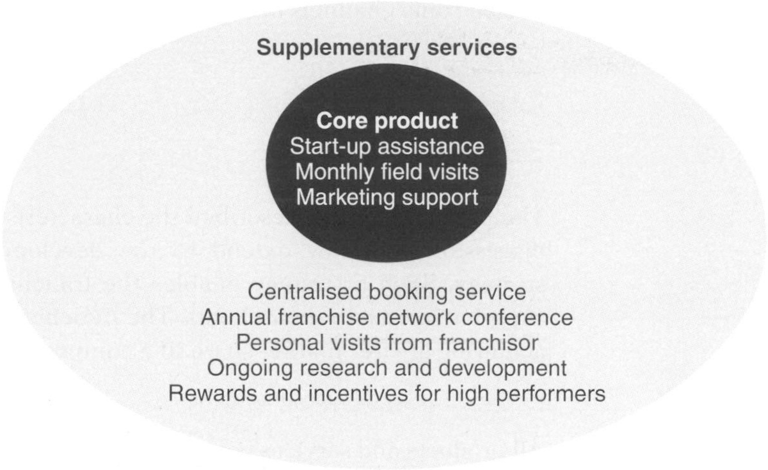

Supplementary services

Core product
Start-up assistance
Monthly field visits
Marketing support

Centralised booking service
Annual franchise network conference
Personal visits from franchisor
Ongoing research and development
Rewards and incentives for high performers

Figure 16.5: Augmented product of a pet grooming franchisor

A key factor in the success of a franchisor's service strategy is the ability to offer prospective franchisees a level of service that is superior to that offered by other franchises. The franchising sector is highly competitive, and research has shown that attracting and recruiting new franchisees is becoming increasingly difficult (McCosker 2000). It is also known that prospective franchisees do not research franchising opportunities very thoroughly, often choosing a system without comparing many alternatives, such as other franchises in the same or different industries, or independent business ownership.

Hence, the challenge for franchisors is to be able to communicate to prospective investors that they offer many intangible services and benefits that are not directly observable to normal consumers. Many use their websites as a means of showcasing their support systems, providing separate 'franchising' sections on their commercial websites. For example, if you browse the Wendy's website (www.wendys.com.au) looking for its nearest ice-cream store, you will also have the opportunity to view information about its franchise operations, which include 'supplementary' services such as computer technology for delivering superior management support tools.

In summary, franchisors offer an augmented product consisting of core services for franchisees plus supplementary services that differentiate their system from others on the market. Given that franchising enables inexperienced operators to enter virtually any industry, the provision of value-added supplementary services may help to attract prospective investors.

Relationship management in franchising

A good franchise system relies on the strength of the relationship between the franchisor and franchisees. Unlike most service encounters, which are relatively short term, the franchising relationship may exist over a number of years. The average length of franchise agreements is five years (McCosker & Frazer 1998), so it is imperative that franchisor and franchisee establish and build a strong working relationship. There are several factors that contribute to successful franchising relationships:

- trust
- commitment
- franchisee satisfaction
- communication
- financial bonds
- length of time
- competitor comparisons.

Trust

A necessary quality of a successful franchising relationship is the ability of the parties to trust one another, because they are mutually dependent. The franchisor needs a reliable network of franchisees to achieve market penetration and brand recognition and to enhance its reputation. Likewise, franchisees rely on the franchisor to help them establish and grow their businesses and remain at the cutting edge of the industry.

Such an interdependent relationship assumes a high level of trust between the parties at all stages of the association, including the precontractual discussions during which the decision to enter a business relationship is made. For example, the Australian Franchising Code of Conduct ensures that certain minimum information must be disclosed by the franchisor to potential franchisee investors so that they may make informed decisions. This legal requirement actually enhances the franchising relationship, as it provides some reassurance that accurate information is being exchanged.

Commitment

All relationships require commitment, and the franchising relationship is no exception. In fact, because franchise agreements last for several years, both parties need to be striving for similar goals such as maintaining system quality and uniformity and achieving improved market share.

Franchisee satisfaction

Marketers know that satisfied customers remain loyal to the organisation. Similarly, satisfied franchisees will be loyal to the franchisor, resulting in a stronger franchise network that is free from conflict.

Communication

Just as the three most important rules of real estate are 'location, location, location', the most important rules of franchising must surely be 'communication, communication, communication'!

Franchisors who communicate effectively with their franchisees experience fewer disputes and therefore suffer less disruption in their operations (Frazer 2001). The Australian Franchising Code of Conduct recommends that a mediation process be used to resolve disputes and conflict before resorting to litigation. This conciliatory process has been effective in reducing the amount of litigation in the franchising sector (Lim & Frazer 2001), presumably resulting in more harmonious franchising relationships.

Financial bonds

The franchising relationship is characterised by a contractual agreement involving the payment of fees by the franchisee to the franchisor. Although arrangements may differ among franchise systems, generally the franchisee pays an initial fee for entry to the system as well as some form of ongoing fees in return for franchisor support (for example, marketing assistance, product development and quality control).

Franchise fees are thought to be important in creating financial bonds between the two parties. As well as recouping start-up costs through the initial fee, many franchisors believe it is important that the fee includes an element of risk, commonly referred to as the 'hurt factor'. The reasoning behind this is that franchisees will not try hard enough to make the business succeed unless they personally contribute a substantial investment into the franchise.

In addition, the ongoing fees paid by franchisees provide an incentive to the franchisor to ensure quality standards are maintained and to help franchisees increase their sales. This financial interdependency between the two parties is a unique feature of franchising that ensures franchisee and franchisor pursue a set of shared goals.

Length of time

Franchising agreements are normally effective for a number of years, so both parties in the arrangement are usually motivated to maximise the experience. Renewal of the agreement depends upon both the franchisee and franchisor meeting their contractual obligations (such as complying with the franchise system in the case of a franchisee or providing agreed levels of support in the case of a franchisor).

Franchisee loyalty may be recognised and rewarded by the franchisor in order to strengthen the relationship. For example, high-performing franchisees may be granted additional franchise units because of their proven performance record.

In brief, franchising relationships need to be sustained over a long period of time. Their success depends upon the cooperation and synergy of the two parties.

Competitor comparisons

A positive franchising relationship should begin in the pre-contractual stage while the negotiations are taking place. Prospective franchisees will often 'shop around' for a suitable investment. Franchisors are competing for franchisees in a marketplace that is progressively contracting because good franchisees are difficult to attract and select. A potential franchisee might be simultaneously assessing whether to invest in a lawn-mowing franchise, a courier delivery franchise, an independent retail store or the share market. Franchisors must compete for franchisees and, in so doing, they should nurture and develop a relationship with franchisees that will last for many years. Hence, it is important to begin managing the franchising relationship from the earliest opportunity.

The unique, long-term, interdependent nature of franchising relationships means that the usual features of relationship management such as trust, commitment and customer satisfaction are of great importance for the ultimate success of both parties. Franchisors should aim to achieve the highest possible level of relationship with franchisees, as shown in figure 16.6.

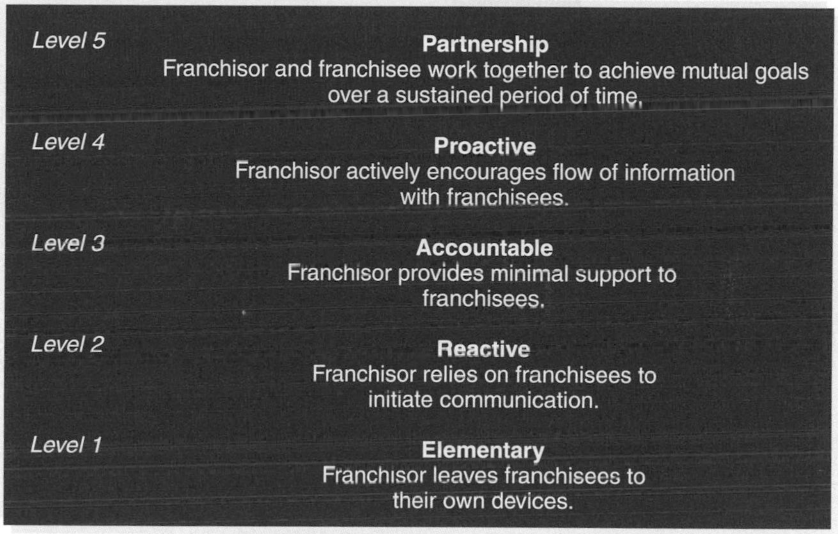

Level 5	**Partnership** Franchisor and franchisee work together to achieve mutual goals over a sustained period of time.
Level 4	**Proactive** Franchisor actively encourages flow of information with franchisees.
Level 3	**Accountable** Franchisor provides minimal support to franchisees.
Level 2	**Reactive** Franchisor relies on franchisees to initiate communication.
Level 1	**Elementary** Franchisor leaves franchisees to their own devices.

Figure 16.6: Levels of franchise relationships
Source: adapted from Justis & Judd 2002

However, the interdependency between franchisor and franchisee takes time to develop fully. In fact, early in the relationship franchisees are normally heavily dependent on the franchisor and the system. Over time, franchisees strive to become more independent but ultimately the franchising relationship will thrive if both parties cooperate and make use of the synergies of the franchise network (Nathan 2000). This gradual progression has been studied by Nathan (2000), who has identified six stages that franchisees typically experience, as illustrated in figure 16.7. These stages are described below:

- *Glee stage:* franchisees are excited and optimistic about the franchise in the first few months.
- *Fee stage:* franchisees begin to resent paying ongoing fees to the franchisor.
- *Me stage:* franchisees attribute their success to themselves rather than to the franchise system.
- *Free stage:* franchisees desire greater independence and freedom from the franchise system.
- *See stage:* following conflict and tension, many franchisees realise that the franchise system plays a critical part in their success.
- *We stage:* franchisees move towards interdependency as they become more experienced, mature and businesslike.

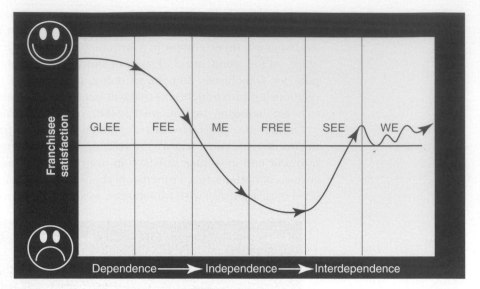

Figure 16.7: The Franchise E-Factor — six stages that franchisees experience. (See www.franchiserelationships.com for more information about the Franchise E-Factor.)
Source: Nathan 2000, p. 79, © Greg Nathan 2002

In brief, franchising is all about creating, developing and maintaining positive relationships. Relationship management in franchising is important because of the long-term association between the parties. In the next section, the impact of the contractual relationship will be discussed.

Pricing strategy

The contractual nature of the franchising relationship means that franchise fees are used to bond the two parties in their pursuit of common goals. These are fees that franchisors require as payment for the services they provide to franchisees. Although there is a great deal of variety in franchise fee structures, there are typically five main fees:

- initial franchise fee
- franchise services or management fee
- marketing levy
- renewal fee
- transfer fee.

Initial franchise fee

Initial franchise fee: a fee normally paid by the franchisee, granting entry to the franchise system

An **initial franchise fee** is usually paid by the franchisee when the franchise is granted. Various reasons have been offered in the franchising literature to describe the purpose of the initial fee. It is regarded by some as a fee for entering the organisation, which normally has a proven or well-developed business concept (Lafontaine 1992). Others view the initial fee as a means of recovering the costs expended in opening the franchisee's outlet, including the cost of advertising for and screening potential franchisees, and providing initial services such as training (Forward & Fulop 1993). Payment of an initial fee is sometimes viewed as entitling a franchisee to participate in the reputation and goodwill of the franchise, or as the franchisor's compensation for granting the use of established trademarks and trade secrets (Terry 1989; Sherman 1993). Another view is that initial fees are a bond paid by the franchisee to discourage them from shirking contractual obligations (Norton 1988; Rubin 1990).

Franchise services or management fee

These ongoing fees (sometimes referred to as royalties) may be in the form of a flat weekly or monthly payment or, more commonly, a percentage of turnover (McCosker 1988).

Franchise services or management fees are collected by the franchisor to reflect the costs incurred in providing various ongoing services to franchisees (Terry 1989; Mendelsohn 1993). The services provided typically involve field visits from head office, regular newsletters, telephone hotlines, ongoing training, franchise advisory councils and annual conferences. Ongoing payment of fees incorporates a bonding mechanism between the two parties and ensures that the franchisor will maintain the overall quality of the franchise (Rubin 1978; Sen 1993).

Some franchisors either substitute or complement a continuing franchise fee with profits made on the sale of products, known as product mark-ups (Dnes 1992). The franchise agreement may specify that the franchisee must buy products from the franchisor or from preferred suppliers. In the former case, the franchisor obtains income by marking up the price of the product. In the latter, the franchisor may choose to take advantage of rebates offered by suppliers. Because product rebates reflect the bulk purchasing power of the system, some franchisors distribute them to the franchisees.

Marketing levies

Franchise agreements often require franchisees to contribute to a central marketing fund through a **marketing or advertising levy** (Terry 1991). Sometimes, part of the continuing franchise fee is set aside by the franchisor and used for this purpose (Mendelsohn 1993). Generally, the franchisor does not directly profit from marketing levies as they are spent on promotional activities that benefit the whole system. However, the franchisor may benefit indirectly through associated goodwill and an enhanced reputation (McCosker 1988).

Renewal fees

A **renewal fee** is sometimes charged by a franchisor before granting a new contract term to a franchisee (Sherman 1993; Frazer & McCosker 1995/6). Franchisees who have fulfilled their contractual obligations can expect to be granted a new term upon expiry of the original agreement. This provides an opportunity for a franchisor to charge a fee at the time of renewal. The franchisor is not faced with screening, selection, or set-up costs as they are with a new agreement. However, there may be legal and administrative costs involved in drafting a new agreement.

Transfer fees

A **transfer fee** may be charged to an exiting franchisee who sells the outlet to another person (Sherman 1993). Transfer fees are often necessary because a franchisor may have invested considerable effort and capital in selecting, training and setting up a franchisee in an outlet. When a franchisee decides to sell the outlet to a new franchisee, the franchisor will most likely need to invest further effort and capital in ensuring that the new person is a suitable and capable operator. To maintain standards, the franchisor has an incentive to screen the new buyer carefully before authorising the sale. It will also be necessary to train the new franchisee fully. A new franchise agreement will

---

Franchise services or management fees: *ongoing fees paid by franchisees to a franchisor over the term of an agreement in return for ongoing franchise support*

Marketing or advertising levy: *the ongoing levy collected by a franchisor from franchisees for promotional activities benefiting the whole franchise network*

Renewal fee: *the administrative fee sometimes charged by a franchisor when granting a franchisee an additional term of operation*

Transfer fee: *an administrative fee sometimes charged by a franchisor when an existing franchisee sells an outlet and leaves the system*

have to be prepared for the incoming franchisee, resulting in further legal and administrative costs. Hence, a transfer fee enables a franchisor to recoup the costs incurred in the sale of an existing outlet.

Franchise expansion and development

Various techniques are employed in franchising to enhance the efficient development of systems and to expand the size of the network. Rapid market penetration is a key goal of many franchise systems. The most important expansion strategy techniques are:

- multiple units, concepts and systems
- co-branding
- conversion franchising
- mobile and home-based franchising
- white collar franchising
- interstate expansion
- international franchising.

Multiple units, concepts and systems

The original model of franchising was the entrepreneur-franchisor enlisting 'mom and pop' franchisees who each held a single franchise unit (Kaufmann 1996). It was thought that owner-operators have a greater incentive to succeed than employee-managers because of the difference in the way they receive compensation. Franchisees directly benefit from profits earned, whereas employees normally earn wages. However, expansion under this method can be slow and ineffective, as large numbers of franchisees need to recruited, selected and trained.

A more efficient method of expansion is to offer suitable franchisees multiple units in the franchise network. **Multiple unit franchising** can be used to reward good operators by allowing them the opportunity to increase their investment in the franchise and thereby provide a greater management challenge. In addition, this practice enables the franchisor to limit the network to a desired number of individual franchisees, thus making communication easier and more effective. The problem of finding enough good franchisees is also overcome by allowing multiple unit ownership.

Multiple unit franchising: the practice whereby a single franchisee holds multiple units within a franchise system

Another method of increasing the size of the franchisor's network is to offer **multiple concepts** under the one umbrella. The franchisor often starts with a single franchise concept but then expands the offering to include similar, but not competing, franchise concepts.

Multiple concepts: the technique used by a franchisor to offer several complementary franchise systems under one central administration

For example, Jim's Mowing started as a single mowing franchise. It is now one of a suite of franchises in The Jim's Group, which offers separate franchises in residential cleaning, lawn care, pet grooming, bookkeeping and so on.

Multiple concept franchising enables franchisors to achieve a larger size by offering similar franchises under a single brand name. This is particularly important in countries such as Australia and New Zealand, which have a small population base. The franchisor's resources can be spread more efficiently over the range of concepts, thus economising on administrative and franchise support costs.

Multiple systems: diversification through ownership of several franchise systems

Franchisors may also expand their activities by offering **multiple systems** under a single brand name. This is not yet very common in the Asia-Pacific region, but we can expect to see it happening more in future. The idea is similar to that of multiple concepts except that the franchisor offers completely different franchises.

An example of multiple system franchising is The Care Group, which operates both the Car Care and Housework Heroes franchises in Australia. Economies of scale enable the franchisor to spread expertise, support and administration across the two systems.

Co-branding

Co-branding is another franchising expansion technique that is growing in popularity. Although co-branding has been adopted in the United States since the 1980s, it is relatively new to the Asia-Pacific region. Co-branding is the side-by-side positioning of two or more brands, each providing different goods or services and each having a different owner (Ishani 1999). It is also known as dual branding (if two concepts are involved), multi-branding and combination franchising.

Some examples of co-branding in Australia are Starbuck's and the Commonwealth Bank, and McDonald's located in service stations. Sometimes the franchises operate side by side; in other cases one franchise is located inside another.

The adoption of co-branding introduces new benefits as well as new complexities to the operation of franchise systems. The advantages and disadvantages of co-branding are listed in table 16.2.

Table 16.2   Advantages and disadvantages of co-branding in franchising

Advantages	Disadvantages
Increased brand recognition	Different franchisors working together (problems with different philosophies)
Customer loyalty	Location of the co-branded unit (often in the middle of another outlet)
Customer convenience	Franchise system uniformity being compromised
Access to desirable locations	Franchisees needing training in two or more systems
Reduced initial and operating expenses	
Better use of limited resources such as parking and customer seating	
Increased sales	
Use of cross promotions and advertising	

Conversion franchising

Conversion franchising occurs when an existing, independently owned business joins a franchise network. It is a common method of rapid expansion in the marketplace by a franchisor. Examples may be found in the pizza home-delivery industry, travel agencies and real estate businesses.

Various strategies may be used to enter the overseas market. As with inter-state expansion, master franchising arrangements remain popular. However, other alternatives include joint ventures with an overseas partner, licensing arrangements, direct investment in company-owned stores overseas, and exporting the manufactured product overseas.

International Issues:
International franchise expansion

In a study of Australian franchisors who have expanded internationally, it was found that the majority experienced *reactive* rather than *proactive* expansion (McCosker & Chadda 2001). Proactive expansion implies that franchisors adopt a deliberate and planned strategy to move overseas, whereas reactive expansion results in franchisors responding to unsolicited overseas enquiries. This situation is not unique to Australia; many other regions with mature franchising sectors, such as the United States, Canada and Europe, report a similar pattern.

Some interesting differences occur between proactive and reactive franchisors. Franchisors who are proactive about entering international markets have more experience domestically (10 years as opposed to five years) than reactive franchisors (McCosker & Chadda 2001). In addition, proactive franchisors decide to expand internationally when the domestic market becomes saturated, whereas reactive franchisors merely respond to overseas requests. Hence, proactive franchisors plan where they will target internationally, with New Zealand being the most common choice because it is close and has similar culture to Australia. However, reactive franchisors tend to enter a country where interest is expressed.

Although little research has been done on international franchising, it appears that a proactive strategy may be linked to greater research and commitment, and improved franchising relationships and level of performance.

In summary, franchising is a growth sector for nations in the Asia-Pacific region, and service industry franchising in particular is outstripping other industry growth. A unique feature of franchising is the two-way relationship between franchisee and franchisor, who must work together to maximise their own system.

Summary

LO1: Appreciate the important contribution of franchising to the economy.
- Franchising enables inexperienced investors to own and operate their own business via an established, proven system.
- Throughout the Asia-Pacific region, franchising is experiencing rapid growth.
- Property/business and construction/trade services are the fastest growing industries in the franchising sector due to the increase in outsourcing of service activities.

LO2: Explain why franchising is regarded as a service, and describe the various characteristics of the service.
- Franchising is used in both retail and service organisations. However, the activity of franchising is a service function in which the franchisor provides ongoing support to its franchisees.

- The franchisor has a dual role of promoting and selling its product as well as administering the franchise system.
- Under a franchising arrangement, the franchisee is the customer of the franchisor.
- Franchising is characterised by the intangible bundle of franchise management services, the interdependent relationship of the franchisor and franchisee, the high degree of customisation, the continuous nature of the franchising service, and the use of electronic and physical delivery channels.

LO3: Identify the core product and supplementary services of a franchising service strategy.

- The core product of a franchisor is its actual product, and includes support such as initial training, site selection, monitoring of franchisee activities, and ongoing product development and marketing support.
- Supplementary services include additional types of support by the franchisor, such as the use of incentives to reward high-performing franchisees.
- Franchisors offer an augmented product (core plus supplementary services) to franchisees to differentiate their systems.

LO4: Identify the factors that contribute to a successful franchising relationship.

- Successful franchising relationships are a result of trust and long-term commitment between the parties; franchisee loyalty and satisfaction; good communication; quick resolution of problems; and the financial bonds formed by the contractual relationship between the parties.
- Franchisees typically progress through a number of stages in the franchising relationship, ranging from initial euphoria at joining the system, to the desire for greater independence and ultimately the realisation that a successful partnership requires the cooperation of both parties.

LO5: Understand the contractual arrangements involved in the franchising relationship, including the pricing strategies available in terms of franchise fees.

- An initial franchise fee is often paid by the franchisee upon entry to the system.
- Initial franchise fees may be used to recover costs incurred by the franchisor in setting up new franchisees; to compensate the franchisor for use of its brand name and trade secrets; and to encourage franchisees to work hard at becoming successful.
- Franchise services or management fees are ongoing fees normally paid by franchisees over the life of an agreement.
- Franchise services or management fees are used to compensate the franchisor for support services provided to franchisees.
- Marketing levies are used to promote the entire franchise system.
- Renewal fees are sometimes charged when a franchisee is granted an additional franchise agreement term.
- Transfer fees are sometimes charged when a franchisee sells an outlet. The fees compensate the franchisor for the cost of inducting a new franchisee into the system.

LO6: Describe the most common methods of achieving growth and development in franchising.

- Franchisees may achieve growth by holding multiple units within a single franchise system.

- Franchisees and franchisors may achieve growth by investing in multiple franchise systems.
- A franchise system may adopt multiple concepts involving complementary activities under the one administration system in order to achieve growth.
- Complementary franchise systems may deliberately locate near each other to achieve greater synergy through their co-branding efforts.
- A franchise system may achieve rapid growth by converting similar independently owned businesses to franchises within the system.
- Two growth areas in services franchising are mobile and home-based systems and white collar franchises.
- Franchisors wishing to expand interstate may do so through the adoption of master franchisees. Similarly, international expansion may occur through joint venture arrangements, licensing agreements, exporting or direct investment strategies.

key terms

Business format franchising: a common form of franchising characterised by the adoption of unique business and marketing systems, ongoing support and training, and standardised outlets (p. 419)

Co-branding: the side-by-side positioning of two or more different franchises (p. 433)

Conversion franchising: the conversion of an independently owned outlet to a franchised outlet within the same industry (p. 433)

Core product: the core services offered by the franchisor to franchisees as part of the franchising agreement (p. 425)

Franchise services or management fees: ongoing fees paid by franchisees to a franchisor over the term of an agreement in return for ongoing franchise support (p. 431)

Franchising: an agreement under which a franchisor grants exclusive rights to a franchisee for distribution and/or sale of a service or product, in return for payment and conformance to quality standards (p. 419)

Home-based franchise: one in which the franchisee works from a home office instead of holding a separate fixed outlet (p. 434)

Initial franchise fee: a fee normally paid by the franchisee, granting entry to the franchise system (p. 430)

Marketing or advertising levy: the ongoing levy collected by a franchisor from franchisees for promotional activities benefiting the whole franchise network (p. 431)

Master franchisees: franchisees (or sub-franchisors) who provide the services of a franchisor in remote locations (p. 435)

Mobile franchise: one in which the franchisee drives to the customer to provide the service, instead of holding a fixed outlet (p. 434)

Multiple concepts: the technique used by a franchisor to offer several complementary franchise systems under one central administration (p. 432)

Multiple systems: diversification through ownership of several franchise systems (p. 432)

Multiple unit franchising: the practice whereby a single franchisee holds multiple units within a franchise system (p. 432)

Renewal fee: the administrative fee sometimes charged by a franchisor when granting a franchisee an additional term of operation (p. 431)

Supplementary product: the extra services provided by the franchisor to franchisees in addition to core services (p. 425)

Transfer fee: an administrative fee sometimes charged by a franchisor when an existing franchisee sells an outlet and leaves the system (p. 431)

White collar franchising: franchising in the professional services industries (p. 434)

review questions

1. Describe the two main reasons why companies choose to franchise their operations rather than retain company outlets.
2. Investors are willing to pay a premium to enter a successful franchise system. Describe four benefits or services that franchisees can expect to receive by joining a reputable franchise.
3. Describe six stages that franchisees typically progress through on their journey from dependence to interdependence.
4. What is the purpose of a renewal fee?
5. Some franchise systems achieve rapid growth by converting independent operators in their industry into franchisees. Why would an independent operator consider joining a franchise?
6. Under what circumstances is the use of a master franchising arrangement appropriate?

application questions

1. Describe the augmented product (that is, the core and supplementary services) offered by a car detailing franchisor.
2. A franchisee in the initial 'glee stage' of the franchising relationship might remark: 'I'm so excited about starting my coffee shop. I know it's going to be a huge success!'. Write typical statements that a franchisee might make in each of the remaining five stages that franchisees experience.
3. One lawn-mowing franchisor charges a flat ongoing fee structure of $500 per week per franchisee. Another lawn-mowing franchisor applies a fee of six per cent of gross sales. What are the benefits and drawbacks of each system from both the franchisor's and franchisee's point of view?
4. Discuss why a franchisor might charge a franchisee a transfer fee of $5000 upon the sale of the outlet to a new franchisee.
5. The franchisor of a bookkeeping franchise wants to develop multiple franchising concepts under a central head-office administration. Think of three more concepts that would complement the bookkeeping service.

vignette questions

1. Read the Services Marketing Action vignette on page 420 and answer the following questions.
   (a) Bizzi Beez has expanded successfully from the domestic market to include the commercial cleaning market also. Some franchisees would like to take up multiple units in these systems. Under what circumstances should the franchisor consider granting multiple units to franchisees?
   (b) A competitor in the domestic cleaning franchise market wants to be the market leader. Recommend some strategies for achieving rapid market penetration and growth.
2. Read the Services Marketing on the Web vignette on pages 434–5, and answer the following questions.
   (a) The Dymocks case illustrates the potential conflict for franchise organisations that introduce e-business strategies. What advice would you give to a franchisor who is considering introducing e-business activities, on how to overcome any possible encroachment on franchisee territories?
   (b) Name three other franchise organisations (in different industries) that might benefit by introducing e-business strategies. Explain how franchisor and franchisee business activities may be enhanced.
3. Read the International Issues vignette on page 436. An investor located in India has approached a cleaning services franchisor and asked for the master franchising rights for that country. India has a huge population, so the franchisor finds the proposal initially attractive. What action should the franchisor take?

recommended readings

The most up-to-date data on franchising in Australia is provided in:
Frazer, L. & Weaven, S. 2002, *Franchising Australia 2002*, Griffith University/Franchise Council of Australia, Brisbane.

For a focus on franchising in the United Kingdom, see:
Mendelsohn, M. 1999, *The Guide to Franchising*, Cassell, London.

A recommended United States text on franchising is:
Justis, R. T. & Judd, R. J. 2002, *Franchising*, 2nd edn, Dame Publications, Houston, TX.

A comprehensive discussion of the nature of franchising relationships is provided in:
Nathan, G. 2000, *Profitable Partnerships*, Nathan's Corporate Psychology, Brisbane.

references

Brickley, J. A. & Dark, F. H. 1987, 'The choice of organizational form — the case of franchising', *Journal of Financial Economics*, vol. 18, pp. 401–20.
Caves, R. E. & Murphy, W. F. 1976, 'Franchising: firms, markets, and intangible assets', *Southern Economic Journal*, vol. 42, April, pp. 572–86.

Dnes, A. W. 1992, *Franchising: A Case-Study Approach*, Avebury, Aldershot.

Forward, J. & Fulop, C. 1993, 'Elements of a franchise: the experiences of established firms', *The Services Industry Journal*, vol. 13, no. 4, October, pp. 159–78.

Frazer, L. 2001, 'Life-cycle stage is associated with disruption in franchise organisations', *Journal of Business Research*, vol. 54, no. 3, December.

Frazer, L. & McCosker, C. 1995/6, 'An exploratory analysis of the use of franchise fees in Australian franchises', *Small Enterprise Research: The Journal of SEAANZ*, vol. 4, nos. 1 & 2, pp. 78–94.

Frazer, L. & McCosker, C. 1999, *Franchising Australia 1999: A Survey of Franchising Practices and Performance*, University of Southern Queensland/Franchise Council of Australia, Toowoomba.

Ishani, M. G. K. 1999, 'Co-branding explained', *Franchising*, Nov./Dec., pp. 57–8.

Justis, R. T. & Judd, R. J. 2002, *Franchising*, 2nd edn, Dame Publications, Houston.

Kaufmann, P. J. 1996, 'The state of research in franchising', *Franchising Research: An International Journal*, vol. 1, no. 1, pp. 4–7.

Lafontaine, F. 1992, 'Agency theory and franchising: some empirical results', *RAND Journal of Economics*, vol. 23, no. 2, summer, pp. 263–83.

Lim, J. & Frazer, L. 2001, 'The effect of regulation: an analysis of the Australian Franchising Code of Conduct', Fifteenth Annual International Society of Franchising Conference, Las Vegas, 2001, pp. 1–16.

McCosker, C. 1988, 'The development and practice of franchising in Australia,' in Pengilley, W. (ed.), *Franchising: Law and Practice in Australia*, International Business Communications, Sydney, pp. 3–27.

McCosker, C. 2000, 'The quest for quality franchisees: an exploration of franchisors' performance', *Franchising — Quo Vadimus? 2000 International Society of Franchising Annual Conference*, San Diego, pp. 1–11.

McCosker, C. & Chadda, R. 2001, 'Australian franchisors abroad', in *Franchising + Own Your Own Business*, Jan./Feb., pp. 118–19.

McCosker, C. & Frazer, L. 1998, *Franchising Australia 1998: A Survey of Franchising Practices and Performance*, University of Southern Queensland/Franchise Council of Australia, Toowoomba.

Mendelsohn, M. 1993, *The Guide to Franchising*, 5th edn, Cassell, London.

Nathan, G. 2000, *Profitable Partnerships*, Nathan's Corporate Psychology, Brisbane.

Norton, S. W. 1988, 'An empirical look at franchising as an organizational form', *The Journal of Business*, vol. 61, no. 2, April, pp. 197–218.

Rubin, P. 1978, 'The theory of the firm and the structure of the franchise contract', *Journal of Law and Economics*, vol. 21, April, pp. 223–33.

Rubin, P. 1990, *Managing Business Transactions*, The Free Press, New York.

Sen, K. C. 1993, 'The use of initial fees and royalties in business-format franchising', *Managerial and Decision Economics*, vol. 14, pp. 175–90.

Sherman, A. J. 1993, 'Building a foundation for the responsible development of a franchising program', in Dant, R. P. (ed.), *Excellence '93: A Bridge to Success: Proceedings of Society of Franchising Seventh Annual Conference*, Society of Franchising, Minneapolis.

Terry, A. 1989, 'Franchising fever', *Australian Accountant*, July, pp. 29–34.

Terry, A. 1991, 'Business format franchising: the cloning of Australian business', *Business Format Franchising in Australia*, Legal Books, Sydney, pp. 1–16.

Chapter 17
Sport marketing

Jane Summers

LEARNING OBJECTIVES

After reading this chapter you should be able to:

- discuss the dichotomy of sport in terms of whether it is a good or a service
- define sport marketing
- explain the unique characteristics of sport
- explain the difference between the marketing of sport and marketing using sport
- discuss the various sport publics and their impact on sport marketing
- examine the major strategic marketing issues associated with sport marketing implementation
- discuss the importance of sport to the economies of many countries.

CHAPTER OUTLINE

This chapter clarifies the unique characteristics of sport that make it an important area for specialised marketing study. In addition to this, the different perspectives of sport marketing — that is, marketing of sport versus marketing using sport — are discussed. The chapter also addresses some of the more complex marketing issues facing sport marketers, and concludes with a review of the importance of sport to both the social and economic profiles of most Western countries. In summary, this chapter provides students with a comprehensive introduction to the concepts involved in sport marketing and clarifies how its application compares to that of traditional marketing principles.

Introduction

So what is sport marketing? Is it just a new buzz word that marketers have developed to gain the attention of consumers or is it a valid area of study and practice in its own right? What you will learn in this chapter is that sport marketing is a $30 billion industry worldwide, and that makes it an important topic.

Much of the material you have already studied in this book will be extended in this chapter. While sport has many of the characteristics of a service, such as intangibility, inseparability, perishability and heterogeneity, it also has some of the more tangible elements of a good. This dichotomy provides unique challenges for marketers, who need to apply strategies of both services and goods marketing to sport.

Similar to service encounters in other industries, consumers' satisfaction with sporting events is largely determined by the quality of their experiences. Further, these experiences are affected by other consumers, by the physical surroundings (servicescape) and by the consumer's moods or feelings. As you are aware from your earlier reading, marketers cannot control or predict a consumer's emotions (moods and feelings) or the interaction of others in the consumer's consumption experience, and in many cases they are only able to exert limited control over the physical surroundings. The same is true in the context of sport consumption. Thus, sport marketers must make marketing decisions in an environment where the outcomes of those decisions are unpredictable. However, this issue does not seem to discourage companies from utilising sport as part of their marketing strategy.

Indeed, there are no limits to the sorts of organisations that get involved with sport as part of their marketing strategy. Even Lego, the Danish toy company, joined the move to sport marketing with the signing of a one-year deal with Major League Soccer to launch a new range of soccer-themed products. This deal represented the brand's biggest global launch for the year and represented their initial foray into the area of sport-themed products and sport marketing (Lefton 1999).

Before we examine the importance and pervasiveness of sport in more detail, we must first understand more about the nature and structure of sport.

Sport — a good or a service?

One of the most challenging aspects of sport is that it has the characteristics of both a good and a service. That is, sport has **tangible** components that are produced, distributed and then purchased, as well as **intangible** elements that cannot be stored for future sale (perishability), and production and consumption occur at the same time (inseparability) (Gilson et al. 1999).

The actual consumption of a sporting event is also closely related to other types of service encounter discussed earlier in this book, where the experience varies from consumer to consumer and with each different consumption event. Thus, sport is often considered to have a number of layers or components that have characteristics of both goods and services. These components interact in many different ways to provide the ultimate end product for the consumer. These are illustrated in figure 17.1.

Think of the sport product as an apple. At its core is the **competition** itself. Without competition of some form, sport would not exist, and the level and intensity of the competition affects the final sport product. Like an apple, the size and age of the core affects the quality of the apple, and you don't know

Servicescape: the environment in which a service is produced and delivered

Tangible: describes something that can be seen, touched or tasted

Intangible: describes something that cannot be seen, touched or tasted

Competition: the struggle and rivalry between opponents that is the central component of a sport product

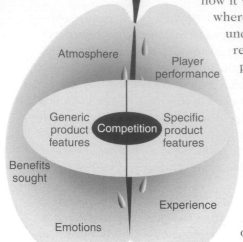

Figure 17.1: The sport product

how it will affect the apple until you bite into it. The same is true of sport, where the quality of competition is unknown until the sporting event is underway. Similarly, external physical cues about quality — the shiny red skin in the case of the apple and the large excited crowd and high-profile players in the case of sport — can be unrelated to the actual quality of the experience: the apple can be tasteless or floury and the sporting event can be disappointing and unpleasant.

From this core, the sport product has both tangible features (like goods) and intangible elements (like services) that combine in a unique way to give each sport product its individual flavour and appeal (the way different varieties of apples all have a similar core). In addition, no two sporting experiences are the same, even though the tangible elements can be stable (just as no two apples are the same, even though they may both be green and of the same variety).

Competition

Competition, by its very nature, means that there must always be a winner and a loser, and this win/loss ratio of sporting teams is totally uncontrollable. In fact, the unpredictability of this core element of sport is the key to the passionate and committed following of many sports fans. Spectators at sporting events can be satisfied with their experience even if their team does not win, as long as the quality and intensity of competition is high.

The implication of this for sport marketers is that they cannot focus on winning as the central theme of their efforts to attract spectators, because they cannot guarantee the outcome of the competition. Rather, sport marketers can only use the past performance or the history of the team or players, and even then this can be awkward if the result is contrary to the high billing. The example of the Australian Cricket Team in the 2001/2002 summer season is a classic situation, where the team — billed as the world champions — failed to make the finals of the competition, which in turn led to customer dissatisfaction and loss of credibility with sponsors.

If a team loses continuously, then the marketing campaign can also lose credibility and create long-term image problems for both the marketer and the team. As in many other service industries, sport marketers are best not to overexcite the expectations of consumers by promising a level of performance that they have no control over. The performance of a sporting team is generally the domain of the coach, who is more interested in the tangible elements of the product, such as player fitness levels, skill development and injury issues.

Tangible elements

At the next level of the sport product, there are the tangible elements, which are the generic and specific features of the sport being defined. **Generic features** are the things that all sports have in common, such as players, administration and management, rules, equipment and facilities and the athletic skills required by players. The fact that these must exist in all sports makes them generic.

The **specific features** of the sport product are those unique aspects of a particular sport that differentiate it from other sports. For example, rugby league has a different administration, requirements, regulations, field size, ball type and shape and even numbers of players from soccer, and it differs more significantly from golf or tennis or horse racing.

Generic features: the largely tangible things that all sports have in common

Specific features: the unique aspects of a particular sport that differentiate it from other sports

Intangible elements

The outer layer of the sport product comprises the intangible components, or the more service-like attributes. We will consider here things like the benefits each participant seeks from the sport, and what motivates spectators to continue consuming sport products. These benefits or motives could be anything from a desire to be healthy and fit, to a need for social interaction, to a desire for **vicarious violence**. All of these benefits are unique to both the sport and the individual and thus contribute to the **heterogeneity** of the sport experience.

Associated with motives are the emotions or feelings induced by sport spectating and participation. Happiness, the thrill and adrenalin rush of the win, and the depressing emptiness of the loss all contribute to a sport consumer's feelings of satisfaction. Similarly these emotions are **ephemeral** and cannot be replicated. Some sports are inherently violent, which is attractive to some participants and some spectators, while other sports are more passive. The nature of the sport, the level of aggression and contact, the actual performance of the players and the involvement of the audience are also intangible elements that affect the overall sport product. These vary from sport to sport, resulting in sport products being **perishable** and heterogeneous experiences for each consumer each time they consume.

Finally, the past experiences of the participants will also effect their current perceptions of the sport product. For example, people who have played a particular sport themselves will have a different view of a game from those who have only ever been spectators. For example, people who have previously played a golf tournament at a particular course will know where the best parking is, what to bring and how to maximise their experience, whereas first-time spectators are more likely to have some levels of dissatisfaction due to their lack of experience.

This duality of sport creates unique challenges for sport marketers, who must understand both goods and services marketing in order to develop sustainable and successful marketing strategies for sport. Before we examine the specific challenges for marketers, we need to clearly define what sport is and introduce some of the relevant terminology.

Sport marketing defined

There is often misunderstanding about the use of the terms sport and sports. **Sports** are defined as a collection of separate man-made recreational and/or physical activities in which participation can be professional, observational, health-related or social. This means that 'sports' refers to activities such as golf, football, tennis, soccer, horseracing, darts and so on. Thus, **sports management** is the management of sports activities and **sports marketing** should be the marketing of individual sports activities.

In contrast, **sport** is a broader term and more accurately refers to the management of people, activities, relationships, businesses and organisations involved with producing, facilitating, promoting, organising and maintaining sports activities and products. Thus **sport marketing** can be defined as all activities designed to meet the needs and wants of **sport publics** through the exchange process. In this chapter we will generally refer to the broader view and use the term 'sport', as we are discussing the management function of sport in general rather than the management of a particular sport.

Vicarious violence: experiencing violence second-hand, through another person

Heterogeneity: a difference or variability in a service

Ephemeral: transient or fleeting, short lived

Perishable: likely to decay or perish

Sports: a collection of separate man-made recreational and/or physical activities in which participation can be professional, observational, health-related or social

Sports management: the management of sports activities

Sports marketing: the individual marketing of individual sports activities

Sport: the management of people, activities, businesses and organisations involved with producing, facilitating, promoting, organising and maintaining sports activities and products

Sport marketing: all activities designed to meet the needs and wants of sport publics through the exchange process

Sport publics: those key groups of individuals who affect sporting organisations and who can include customers, shareholders, employees, suppliers and investors

Sport industry: *the market in which the products offered to buyers are related to sports, fitness, recreation or leisure, and these may be activities, goods, services, people, places or ideas*

Finally, the **sport industry** then can be defined as the market in which the products offered to buyers are physical sports, sporting experiences, fitness, recreation or leisure, and these may be activities, goods, services, people, places or ideas (Pitts & Stotlar 1996).

Sport has both goods and service attributes, and it also has a number of unique qualities that resulted in standard marketing applications being only minimally successful for early sport marketers. Many of these early sport marketers believed that once you knew how to successfully market any product, then you could simply transfer that knowledge to the sport industry — not true, as they found out. There are generally five main areas of difference that sport marketers need to consider, and these can largely be grouped under the 5P classifications used for services: that is, the people (market characteristics), the product, the price, the promotion, and the place (distribution). Table 17.1 highlights these factors and summarises their main characteristics. All warrant close examination, and will be discussed in more detail next.

Table 17.1	Differentiating characteristics of sport
Category	**Specific differences**
People	There is a high degree of personal identification by sport consumers. Many different motivations are satisfied simultaneously in the consumption of sport. Consumer demand fluctuates widely in relation to sport. Satisfaction is affected by social affiliation.
Product	The sport product has universal appeal and pervades all elements of people's lives. The sporting product has many service qualities. Sporting organisations simultaneously compete and cooperate. There is no control over the composition of the core product and only limited control over product extensions. Sport products can be classified as both consumer and industrial products.
Price	The price of sport products is small in comparison to the total cost paid. Indirect revenues are greater than direct operating revenues. Many sports are operated on a not-for-profit basis.
Promotion	Widespread media exposure has resulted in emphasis on sport sponsorship and sport promotion versus sport marketing. High visibility of sport is attractive to businesses through sponsorship. Promotion and marketing emphasise the product extensions rather than the core product.
Place	Sport does not physically distribute its product. Electronic distribution allows the large volume of indirect consumption to exist.

People

Personal identification: *a state of mind in which consumers feel that they 'know' the sports participants and the administration of sports sufficiently to express opinions about how things should be done*

As with many other service-like experiences, the personal interaction between customers and a firm's employees is an important aspect in the ultimate satisfaction of consumers. In the case of sport, the interaction occurs at a distance and in a group setting where the involvement of the media and others creates a 'virtual' interface. Consumers feel they 'know' the players and the sport managers, and yet intimate contact is rare. This high degree of **personal identification** with sport has four main consequences for marketers: expert knowledge, differing motivations, wide fluctuation in consumer demand and the impact of social affiliation.

Expert knowledge

The sport industry is unique in that there is a considerable level of personal identification with both the sports participants and the administration of sport by consumers. Sport consumers feel they have a right to an opinion about who plays the game, where and when it is played, who the referees or officials are, and how the game is administered and organised. Everyone is an expert, particularly after the event!

The prominence and public exposure of all sporting transactions and decisions has a major impact on this phenomenon. All sporting issues, down to the player's personal details and lifestyle, are considered fair game for the media and the public at large. This means that sport marketers have to consider not only the game and its extensions as their product, but also each player or participant. Just cast your mind back to the drama in the life of AFL superstar Wayne Carey. Here was a great player, the captain of his team and a superstar in his sport, forced to resign because of an affair he had with the wife of his best friend (and team-mate). How many other occupations have to consider this hazard? Maybe only movie stars and rock stars.

The concept of managing those who deliver the product to the end consumer in order to ensure successful 'moments of truth' is not a new one for marketers. However, the degree of interest and involvement in this process by the customer is unique to the sport context. Can you imagine people knowing or caring so much about the person serving them on the front desk of a hotel that they would take part in a national discussion about that person on talk-back radio? While individuals may have some interest or concern in this situation, there is certainly not the level of public awareness of other service delivery exchanges as there is in a sporting context. The Services Marketing Action vignette about the marketing of the All Blacks clearly illustrates this issue.

Services Marketing Action:
Branding sport products?

The All Blacks have been known for more than a century as one of the most distinctive international sporting brands, and yet the All Blacks name has only been registered for the last 20 years of the team's 120-year history. Even the sponsors of the team (Adidas, Phillips and Coca-Cola) are well known and take some of the tough All Blacks image to their own products.

Obviously there are some particularly challenging issues involved in treating a sporting team as a brand. One of the most obvious is the divergence in the values of both the team and the brand. The team values are to do with winning, whereas the brand values are related to respect, humility, power, heritage, inspiration and commitment — nothing at all about winning (Rusch 2001). Everything from the team logo to individual players' websites and endorsements is strictly managed to ensure consistency and continuity of the brand image. Interestingly this image management becomes most difficult when the team is not winning. 'When the team is strong, the brand is strong; when the team loses, it's a challenge', says Fraser Holland, NZRFU Marketing Manager (Rusch 2001).

This represents the most difficult aspect of attempting to brand a sports team. When making branding decisions about products, the marketing manager can pretty much control the way the product looks, its price, its distribution and how it will behave in the marketplace. The trick for marketers in creating a great brand is to develop an emotional link with their audience while delivering functional benefits. This is particularly challenging with sporting teams. The creation of emotional links is easy, almost too easy, with some fans becoming obsessive about their favourite team. Delivering the functional benefits is the hard part with sport products, as the marketer has no control over the result.

Another challenge for brand managers is that individual sports figures are notoriously hard to control on and off the field, and the image of the All Blacks as a whole has not always been friendly. All external communications from brochures to television programs must be approved to ensure that it conforms with the team's brand values. This holistic branding process also means that the team members' promotional activities, such as websites, interviews and book deals, are all monitored (Rusch 2001).

Individuals who believe that they are stronger than the team are dropped. This distinguishes the All Blacks from many American sports teams, for example, where very often the individual is allowed prominence over the team, no matter how bad their behaviour (Rusch 2001). Think about Denis Rodman and his outrageous behaviour and media personality. This sort of activity would never be tolerated in the All Blacks. Their unique branding approach of putting the team before individual players allows the NZFRU to avoid some of the unsettling trends affecting other professional sports.

Differing motivations

Because sport consumption is a personal activity, many different motives can be satisfied with the one consumption act. Sport marketers need to understand the motivations of their intended consumers and then focus on the main ones so that they can encourage and support these people to purchase their product.

For example, consider a large tennis tournament. People will attend for a range of reasons:

- they love the sport of tennis
- they play tennis and want to pick up some tips from the masters
- they are part of a social group that is going to the tennis even though they personally are not all that excited by tennis
- they like watching fit, good-looking athletes at close range
- they want to be seen by others or to show off their ability to purchase expensive seats
- they hope to meet someone special

... and the list goes on.

In a major game, where 30 000 people are at the stadium and an additional 100 000 may be watching on television, consumers have many different motives for consuming that event, so there are many possibilities in terms of satisfaction. The challenge for sport marketers is to uncover these different motives and then use them as themes in their promotional campaigns.

Australian Swimming has recognised the different motives of its meet audience, and its current television advertising reflects this. You may remember the theme, 'dangerous when wet' on the togs of swimmers in its ads. They show not only nail-biting finishes, but also lots of shots of well-toned athletes in brief swimming togs, and scenes of the crowd having fun, dressing up, cheering and singing songs. This ad appeals to a range of consumer motives, and is designed to attract different groups of people to attend the meet or to watch it on television.

The demand for sport is erratic and unpredictable. People like to associate with and demand popular winning sports people and teams. However, this can quickly change according to changing fortunes, injuries and incidents totally unrelated to sport. The effects of the September 11 terrorist attacks affected not only the tourism industry and international trade, but also sport. In the United States at that time, many sporting events were cancelled due to security concerns and the unwillingness of sport participants to travel. The rugby league tour of the United Kingdom was postponed; rugby union games planned at the same time in Europe were modified; and many golf tournaments in the United States were cancelled. None of this was controllable or predictable. Thus, consumer demand for sport is difficult to predict.

Some sport players and teams are more attractive to consumers than others; an individual may be more charismatic and a team may be more exciting. However, sporting stars and teams continually have to compete with others to earn their place, and their success is not a certainty. Ian Thorpe is a great drawcard, but if he did not do well at trials he would not qualify for the Australian Swimming Team. Cathy Freeman had this problem when she almost missed qualifying for the Commonwealth Games. A quick revision of the rules was required to allow her to join the team and prove her fitness at a later date.

Sport marketers often have to begin marketing an event, creating ticket sales and advertising their product before the final competitors are known (because qualifying rounds are required). Frequently, their hopes for the best players or teams, from a sales perspective, are not realised.

Ethical Issues:
Winning and losing

The media love to make heroes and villains out of the winners and losers in sports. The full-page photograph or video clip of the illegal head-high tackle or the weeping, defeated team captain are regular features in print and television media. They make great visuals, but are they responsible journalism? The article below asks whether the media has a greater responsibility, when reporting on sports, than just selling sensational news to its customers.

The winning game

by James Wakelin

People say that winning is not everything — it is the only thing. If the sports pages are anything to go by, this is definitely the case.

Mainstream media has an obsession with winners. Winning and losing, and certainly not how you played the game, is what journalists focus on.

It has been argued since day dot that journalists simply present what the public wants to know about. And sports pages, if the readership is any indication, do just that. Despite making up only a small portion of the paper's content, sports pages represent a large contingent of a paper's readership.

(continued)

But at the risk of sounding prudish, what about the improvement of the game or the improvements of people's interaction with each other through sports. Do we, as the media, have a responsibility to encourage a slightly different level of thinking?

Remember the famous Greg Chappell 'grubber' incident? February 1, 1981. It had been a long hot summer for Greg Chappell and his Australian team but they had made it through to the World Series Cricket final only to lose to New Zealand in the first of the best-of-three competition.

To cut a long story short, as most of you will recall, the then Australian Captain Greg Chappell made his brother Trevor bowl an underarm delivery to New Zealander Brian McKechnie. The decision won Australia the game but the furore that erupted after the game said a lot about the way sport is supported and commented on in Australia.

Greg, at the time of the incident, had thought 'there may be a few "tut, tuts" and perhaps a few "not the done thing"'. But the reaction to the incident was unprecedented. Chappell had won the game but he had not played 'in the spirit of the game'.

The Press went to town. Headlines varied from 'Cricket's Day of Disgrace' to 'Chappell the Axe' and even 'Chappell Brother Joins in Fury'. The story that went with that last headline was written by former Australian Captain and brother to Greg, Ian, who incidentally was fined and banned from broadcasting for three months after swearing on air during the match.

Chappell was under siege from the media and continued to be so for much of the season. Keith Miller, commentator and former Australian player, said: 'Yesterday one day cricket died and Greg Chappell should be buried with it'.

It was typical of the ludicrous overreactions reported in media at the time and typical of the immediacy that sometimes plagues us. In the ensuing years, the famous 'grubber' incident has simply become part of sports history, along with countless other incidents. Many of you, before reading this article, would not have thought of it for almost a decade.

Greg Chappell continued to captain the team for another two seasons and finished his illustrious playing career as Australia's leading run scorer before being overtaken by another sporting icon, Allan Border, but nevertheless Chappell's reputation remains intact.

Once again we could say that the public wanted the news, so we gave it to them; or, to use the old editor's favourite, 'it sells papers'.

An even better example of the media's focus on sport is Mike Tyson. Three years ago a villain, today he is on the verge of one of the most remarkable boxing comebacks in history. Everyone loves a winner or perhaps, more accurately, everyone loves to read about a winner. So the fact that Mike Tyson is a convicted rapist does not count. It could be said that it should not, either. The man has done his time.

But can we so easily forget what was written of Mike Tyson when he went to prison? The man was nothing and, what's more, he was finished. So is it because Iron Mike is now back in the winner's circle that the world, and most sections of the media, are back with him again?

I do not know. But I do know that 99 per cent of sports stories are interested purely in the outcome. Sure there is some dissection of how they won, who played well, who the individual winners were in a team.

Have a good look at the sports stories you are viewing and see if they have an outcome and if they focus almost purely on the winner. It constantly amazes me that a team can win a game by one goal and though they may have only scored three per cent more than their opponents, they are depicted as being far superior to the other team.

Winners are grinners; losers barely get a mention.

Source: The Cyber-Journal of Sport Marketing, www.cjsm.com

Social affiliation

All sport is consumed in a public setting and usually in the company of others. Rarely does someone attend a sporting event on their own. However, if this does occur, it is even less likely that they will be the only spectator. The level of enjoyment of sporting events is generally dependent on the interaction with others who are experiencing the event. It has also been found that many people attempt to recreate this social setting even if they are consuming sport indirectly. This involves watching sport with others and, in extreme cases, consumers have been known to attempt to recreate a stadium effect with seating and a large number of friends. Many people comment on how the atmosphere at finals matches for example, or at large international events adds to the pleasure of watching the game.

Customer mix: the optimum combination of customer types that will complement the service provision and provide the fewest negative effects on other customer groups

The impact of others can also have a negative impact on a consumer's experience. Key tasks for sport marketers are to determine the best **customer mix** and to manage customer behaviour in order to enhance the experience of all. The diverse motivations for sport consumption create difficulties in achieving a harmonious customer mix, as there are often large and profitable segments of customers who will most definitely offend other segments of customers. Differential seating plans, ticket prices and other physical interventions can help to manage this problem.

Product

There are five key factors that differentiate the sport product from other goods and services. These are:
- the universal appeal of sport
- the service-like qualities and experiential nature of the product
- the fact that sporting organisations must simultaneously compete and cooperate
- the lack of control over the core product
- the fact that sport products are both consumer and industrial products.

The universal appeal of sport

Sport is found in one form or another in every geographic location on Earth. It involves people from all ages, sexes, income levels, occupations and religions. It is generally associated with leisure and motivation, which are considered to be basic needs by nearly all groups in society. The worldwide appeal of sport means that the potential market for it is very large and most people have some interest in sport in one form or another. This level of interest leads to the personal identification with sport discussed earlier, and also makes sport a very attractive product to investors such as sponsors and the media.

The service-like qualities of sport

Service characteristics of perishability, heterogeneity, intangibility and inseparability of production and consumption all relate to the sport product. Like services, consumers do not obtain actual ownership of sport, and the involvement of others in the consumption of sport is an important part of the product experience. The fact that sport consumption is defined as **experiential consumption** is also an important element in differentiating it from other services and goods. Products are said to be experiential when they must be experienced by the consumer in order for them to be consumed. Other experiential products are concerts, theatre productions and festivals.

Experiential consumption: intense consumption experiences providing identifiable levels of emotion that are appealing to consumers

As a product, sport is highly perishable in that it is not possible to keep an inventory of sporting events. If tickets are not sold for a particular event, then that revenue cannot be realised at some future time. The emergence of strong media coverage of sporting events has helped to minimised this factor, by allowing games to be broadcast at times that are more convenient to both spectators and media planners, thus extending the life of these events and making the potential audience size far greater than the capacity of the sporting venue.

As mentioned earlier, the experience of a sporting event will differ for each person and each time the event is consumed (heterogeneity) and the consumption of the event and its production are intrinsically linked (inseparability). Like many other entertainment products, the consumption of sport is experiential, and the benefits of playing, watching or generally being involved in sport will be different for different people. These experiences are also difficult to describe to others, have different meaning for each consumer and are thus difficult to market.

For example, you may love watching cricket and you manage to secure prized seats to the final test match between Australia and England. You organise the time off work, book and pay for accommodation near the ground and are all set for a great five days. The first day is fantastic, the sun shines, the batters hit the ball all over the park and Australia are playing well. The second day is just as good in terms of the play, but the seats next to you are occupied by a couple of loud-mouthed English supporters who get drunk, fall down, vomit on your shoes and generally make the day unpleasant. The third day arrives and the unwelcome visitors have not returned. All is going well except that Australia are in trouble and look like they may lose the game. The fourth day is a nail biter and then . . . it rains and rains and rains. You get wet, the taxi queue is miles long, the hotel advises you that the restaurant is not open tonight and you have to go back out in the rain to get dinner. The final day of the match is also rained out and the match is a draw.

Most of these experiential factors were out of the hands of the cricket marketers, but all combined to affect your degree of satisfaction with this sporting experience. For the person who has experienced this, how satisfied they are will depend on how much they love cricket, their expectations and many other factors that are unique to the individual.

Sporting organisations simultaneously compete and cooperate

As previously illustrated, the very essence of sport is competition, and in order to provide organised and structured competition, sports teams need to cooperate with each other in some form of association or league. Things like competition schedules, awards, rules, game structure and even fundraising have more effect if controlled and organised cooperatively. Thus sports organisations simultaneously compete and cooperate with each other, and it is this cooperation that differentiates it from other industries.

In most industries, there may be advantages in belonging to industry associations or professional bodies, but this membership is not a *requirement* of their operation. For sports organisations it is. If an organisation is not a member of the National Basketball League, for example, then the team cannot play in this competition. With membership come rules, game structures and other requirements that mean teams have to cooperate and work together even as they compete passionately.

Lack of control over the core product

External, situational factors play a significant role in the delivery and experience of a sporting product. In the cricket example, the rain was one such factor. Even the participants themselves will be inconsistent in how they play the game; after all, they are people, and people are inconsistent. This means that the core product, the game itself, is generally out of the control of sport marketers. Things like the game schedule, player performance and the eventual outcome — who wins and who loses — cannot be influenced by the sport marketer.

Sport products are both consumer and industrial products

End users: *final consumers*

Organisational consumers: *those who take the product and then on-sell it or use it as a component in the production of another product*

The sport product is delivered both to **end users** (consumer product) and **organisational consumers**. It also forms part of new products (industrial product) such as endorsements by sporting figures, sponsorship, broadcasting and corporate boxes. This has implications for marketers when they are attempting to understand how their markets make decisions to buy sport products or participate in sporting events, as each group will have very different motives for their participation.

Price

The price for sport can be determined both in terms of actual ticket sales and in terms of time or opportunity costs. For many who decide to consume sport, particularly through an indirect channel such as television, the price they pay is time — time they could have spent doing something else. Sport marketers therefore need to consider that other leisure activities are direct competitors. In addition, there are three other aspects of pricing that are unique to sport:
- The price of sport products is small compared to the total costs paid.
- Indirect revenues are greater than direct revenues.
- Many sports are operated on a not-for-profit basis.

The price of sport products is low compared to total costs

The price of sport products to consumers is generally quite low per individual, but when you multiply this amount by the numbers who attend live events (100 000 at the Gold Coast Indy in 2001; 86 000 people at the Bledisloe Cup final in Sydney in 2001), then the total cumulative price paid by consumers is high relative to the actual cost of providing that event. This makes sporting events very attractive for many potential investors and sponsors.

Indirect revenues are greater than direct revenues

Indirect revenue: the money realised from selling advertising and merchandising rights to sporting events

The money realised from selling advertising and merchandising rights to sporting events — **indirect revenue** — can be many times greater than the direct operating revenue of the event itself. Sporting events have the unique ability to have many product extensions, and these often have significant value for the marketplace. The Olympic Games is a good example of the power and importance of indirect revenue, as shown in table 17.2. You can see that the revenue from sponsorship, television rights and advertising would have far outweighed the actual revenue received from ticket sales.

Table 17.2	2000 Sydney Olympic statistics
Sydney Olympics	**Statistics**
Expected number of viewers	3.5 billion
Number of extra visitors to Sydney 1994–2000	1.5 million
Visitors to Sydney for the Olympics	250 000
Number of countries competing	200
Number of athletes	10 200
Number of condoms provided to the athletes village (16 000 athletes and officials)	100 000
Expected revenue from advertising rights	A$800 million
Expected revenue from television rights	A$954.6 million
Expected number of media personnel in Sydney for the games	15 000
Revenue from licensing program for Olympic merchandise	A$900 million
Sponsorship of sport in Australia 2000	A$907.1 million and A$1.6 billion including television rights

Source: adapted from the Sydney Olympic FactFile, 25 July 2000

Many sports operate on a not-for-profit basis

It is only at the national and elite levels that most sports operate on a profit-making basis (Barker 1990). Even then, some sports still require their elite athletes to be non-professional. This perspective results in sport using many volunteers in both operational and management roles, which in turn causes many difficulties in attempting to achieve a professional management perspective. The volunteer nature of the sport industry makes it unique in both its structure and the way many sporting organisations are forced to operate. Marketing particularly suffers in this environment, with the focus of marketing efforts largely being on promotion and brochure-ware.

Promotion

Until recently, the sporting industry has been in something of a seller's market, in that consumers had little power over what sport they participated in, as a spectator or a viewer. Their choices were dictated by geography, climate, historical interests and facilities. There are three other aspects to promotion that uniquely affect sport marketers: the increased emphasis on marketing principles; the attractiveness of sport to business investment; and the emphasis on product extensions.

Decreased emphasis on marketing principles

With increased money and professionalism in many sports, resulting in more aggressive and professional marketing, there is more choice for consumers. Consequently, there is a need to apply marketing principles more vigilantly to maintain and increase customer support. However, for some sport marketers the emphasis remains on sponsorship and merchandising at the expense of other marketing mix elements (Berick 1995; Dolahenty 1997). This can result in the development of disjointed and sometimes ill-conceived marketing strategies.

The application of marketing and promotional savvy can be taken to the extreme, and this is not always successful, as the Services Marketing Action vignette illustrates. In this case, the marketers of XFL (Extreme Football League) overmarketed the product, emphasising the intangible elements. They forgot that the tangible elements, such as player skill and the core product of sport — the competition, also need to be considered and developed.

Services Marketing Action:
No Tears for the XFL

In 1999, the World Wrestling Federation (WWF) and NBC sports joined forces to present XFL — Extreme Football League. Just three years later, the creators of XFL pulled the plug. Why didn't this product take off? It had a target market of football fans and young men who enjoy the circuses put on by the WWF. It had the best publicity, it had sponsors, airtime, and a television audience that was primed and ready for this next generation in football. But it was not to be. Audiences of just under 14 million who tuned in for the first game had declined to just under 4 million a year later, which in US television terms was disastrous. In fact, NBC had to give away nearly 30 per cent of the game's advertising slots because of plummeting ratings. It seems that the brand did not meet the market needs, and products that do not match the marketing hype are nearly always doomed to fail.

The basic premise of the game was to have American football played under the same rules as the national game, but with hundreds of cameras on, around and over the field to allow vision and replays from every angle. Players, coaches and referees had microphones and all conversations were encouraged to be 'bad', 'bold' and controversial. All this was complemented by beautiful, scantily clad women who would hold up score cards, give cheering demonstrations and generally add some aesthetic atmosphere to the game.

What could go wrong? After all, this was a tried and tested formula that was successful in the WWF arena. The problem of course was that people were expecting wrestling on the football field and they got second-tier NFL players playing football by the same rules. There was too little shock value for the WWF fans and too little football for the football fanatics.

So what went wrong? It was a great idea but the good-looking cheerleaders and pseudo-violence were not enough to hold the audience. The viewers wanted substance, not just a pretty package. The publicity surrounding the opening was so great that people's expectations were higher than the product could meet.

When the mask was pulled away, people were disappointed, creating the classic gap between consumer expectations and service delivery capabilities. In short, the game suffered from too much hype and confusion about its purpose. XFL couldn't decide whether it wanted to be more about sport or spectacle.

The lesson for marketers here is not to get too carried away with the power of promotion and persuasion without being able to deliver on promises. In the case of male viewers, who were the target audience of XFL, it turns out that they were interested in more than just staged violence and sex — they also wanted entertainment and skill when it came to sporting events. In this case, the XFL promised too much and couldn't deliver.

Attractiveness of sport to business investment

The widespread appeal of sport and the high levels of personal identification with it make it an attractive medium for business investment. When one considers the revenue figures for international events and the earning capacity of some of the best known sporting stars, it is obvious that there is considerable business potential in sport. Internationally, golf is one of the highest earning sports, with golfers accounting for 11 out of the 50 highest earning sports people in Australia. Greg Norman tops that list, earning an estimated $37.3 million a year (Shoebridge 1998). In the United States these sorts of earnings are only topped by high-profile NBL and NFL players. In Australia and New Zealand, cricketers are our next highest money earners, with swimmers and football players (regardless of the code) coming third. Although these sports are popular, they do not produce many big earners, and only a very few sportspeople have the opportunity to attract big money sponsorships.

Most high-earning sports stars in Australia and New Zealand make their money through sport sponsorship and product endorsement. In the United States, many are paid large salaries to play their chosen sport in addition to sponsorship opportunities.

Sponsorship of sporting stars and sporting events offers marketers a unique opportunity in that sponsorship is four-dimensional. Print is seen as one-dimensional (sight only), television as two-dimensional (sight and sound), events as three-dimensional (sight, sound and audience involvement) and sport as four-dimensional (sight, sound, audience involvement and emotional involvement). The emotional elements involved in sport allow marketers to gain significant leverage for their products, since they can transfer emotion and liking from the sport to the brand. (In contrast, events tend to be more transient in nature and therefore any emotional involvement is shortlived.) In addition, successful sponsorship brings with it the opportunity to develop relationships with consumers based on these emotive responses (Lloyd 2001a). All of these benefits are extremely attractive to businesses that are trying to find new ways to connect with their clients.

Emphasis needs to be on product extensions

Promotion is obviously one element of the marketing mix that has a very obvious appeal for the sporting industry. It is also very easy to see the promotional applications of sport, through sponsorship, merchandising, advertising and publicity elements. However, as marketers have little or no control over the core product (the competition), they must concentrate their efforts on the product extensions. These are things like the facilities, pre- and post-game entertainment, merchandise, souvenirs and parking, of which they can control the quality, along with other servicescape elements.

Distribution (place)

Many sport products are consumed where they are produced, and spectators often travel long distances to participate. Increasing and improved media exposure and coverage of a larger array of sporting events has resulted in this physical constriction being less of a challenge for the sport consumer. Each of these distribution issues is discussed in the following sections.

Sport does not physically distribute its products

The experiential nature of sport has always meant that its distribution has been restricted to physical facilities that can cope with the event, forcing consumers to travel to the location or miss the event. Sporting organisers have traditionally arranged their events in locations that suit players or participants and where they can access the largest audience. In addition, sporting organisers also have to consider the sporting history of a location for suitability. For example, when Australian rugby union wanted to expand the audience for rugby in general it looked to Melbourne, and the large facility provided by the Melbourne Cricket Ground (MCG). This venue could seat thousands more people than equivalent grounds in Brisbane or Sydney — the traditional homes of rugby — and so made expansion of rugby into Victoria very attractive. Unfortunately, Melbourne people, and Victorians in general, were AFL supporters and many had never seen a game of rugby. The first game held in Melbourne was reasonably successful, mainly because of the novelty of the event, but subsequent games were less well attended, as spectators did not understand the game, and so could not appreciate the level of competition — the core product.

Electronic distribution facilitates indirect consumption

Improvements in technology have meant that electronic distribution channels can now deliver sporting events to consumers, so they are no longer forced to come to the event. Increasingly, sport events can be delivered at the time and place consumers dictate (particularly with the advent of interactive television). Video streaming has further expanded the delivery options of sport to consumers worldwide. IBM paid US$100 million for its sponsorship of the 2000 Olympics, and it has fine-tuned this delivery mechanism, making audiovisual footage of the games available on the Internet.

However, for many large sport events such as the Olympics, tightly written sponsorship agreements with traditional media still restrict the coverage of sport on the Internet. Television broadcast rights often restrict the content and coverage of sport on the Internet, as was the case with the 2000 Olympics and with the Australian Open Tennis (Hannen 2001). Therefore, even though IBM paid big dollars for exclusive web-casting rights, it was quite restricted in what it could show, and when. In an attempt to protect the delayed television programs only real-time results could be shown — not actual finals.

In spite of these tight sponsorship restrictions on the use of the Internet for sport broadcasting, many sporting organisations are making good use of the Internet. New Zealand company Snowco is one such example, recently winning a prestigious award for its website design and content.

Services Marketing on the Web:
Snowco serves niche audience

The industry-focused Snowco website (www.snow.co.nz) provides up-to-date information on New Zealand's ski fields, including hourly snow reports, an accommodation guide and news and events. One of Snowco's innovative features is the use of webcams to show the conditions at various snowfields throughout New Zealand. It has won numerous awards, including NetGuide's 2001 Best Sports and Recreation Site and Best Sports and Recreation Website at the 2000 ANZ Interactive New Zealand awards.

The judges for the NetGuide awards commented that Snowco has an edge on the competition because it provides exactly the information its niche audience requires. Snowco's advertising and marketing manager said that the site's success was achieved because of the quality, first-hand information it receives from industry operators, which it then distributes to the public in a user-friendly manner.

New Zealand's exceptional 2001 skiing and snowboarding season contributed to a 36 per cent increase in user numbers on the website, continuing Snowco's track record of over 30 per cent growth each year since 1997.

Recently the AFL (Australian Football League) signed a $500 million, five-year deal with a consortium led by News Corporation, which will give it a serious competitive edge over other football codes in Australia by harnessing the power of Australia's two biggest media companies — PBL-Nine and News Corp. The biggest challenge for this type of sponsorship deal in the future will be the emerging technologies such as digital television, pay TV, datacasting, the Internet, multi-channelling and narrow casting, and how these will change the viewing habits of sports lovers brought up on free-to-air television (Stenshol & Way 2001).

Sport marketing in perspective

Professional and amateur sporting bodies in Australia and New Zealand are beginning to include marketing personnel and practices in key operational areas of their sports. Nevertheless, sport sponsorship is still seen as the most prevalent form of sport marketing. In Australia, sport sponsorship now ranks third ($1.6 billion) behind press ($3.36 billion) and television ($2.75 billion) in the money that marketers are paying for exposure. The growth of sponsorship has outstripped all other mainstream media advertising, even taking into account the increase in spending in 2000 due to the Olympics (Lloyd 2001). This trend is also noted in other developed countries such as New Zealand.

This use of sport in the marketing efforts of firms is termed **marketing using sport**. This is where strategic decisions are made to incorporate sport as a vehicle into the marketing strategy of the firm in order to gain attention,

Marketing using sport: any strategy that aims to associate a product, service, idea or company with the emotive force of a sport, sports association or sporting event in order to appeal to target markets in a way that traditional promotion cannot achieve

develop a particular brand or corporate image or perhaps to communicate specific benefits of the product or service to a particular target group.

In contrast, the **marketing of sport** is just one element of the sports management process. Thus, just as the management of a company such as Coca-Cola involves the elements of staffing, production, accounting and marketing, so too does the management of a sporting club or association, regardless of its size or profile. In this context, marketing activities are used to help achieve corporate goals and objectives and to communicate with their various publics. We need to explore these different aspects of sport marketing in more detail.

Marketing of sport: the coordination and facilitation of the delivery of the sport 'product' and extensions in order to satisfy the goals of various stakeholders

Marketing using sport

Approximately $1.6 billion is currently being invested in sport sponsorship in Australia. This investment could be in the form of cash sponsorship for a club, team or player; the purchase of licensing or catering rights; or donation of products and services. In addition to the sponsorship of high-profile teams by large companies, there exists a vast network of local sporting teams and clubs who solicit support from small local businesses every year.

So why do companies and small businesses wish to link their name, or the names of their products and services, with sport? The basic philosophy is that people are very emotional about sport whether they are participants or spectators. Sporting publics can be fiercely loyal to their favourite player, team or club and businesses hope that this loyalty will extend to the goods and services that are seen to publicly support them.

The most recognised use of sport as a marketing tool is in promotion, through sales promotion and sponsorship. Displaying logos and advertisements in sporting venues and on team apparel is a common example of marketing using sport. Using celebrity sports people in mass media campaigns is also a popular promotional strategy using sport. Use of sport as a promotional tool can also overlap to form part of the product and distribution strategies. For example, some companies may produce limited edition products to commemorate a particular sporting event or may adapt or develop a product specifically for a target market. The special Olympics edition mobile phones and Holden cars are examples of this type of marketing activity. Similarly, the purchasing of catering or licensing rights is not only a promotional tactic but can also form part of a company's distribution strategy.

Corporate involvement in sport in Australia and New Zealand is increasing and many brand names are now well entrenched in our sporting culture. Table 17.3 provides some recent Australian sponsorship investment figures. Here, you can clearly see this investment is growing rapidly, apparently immune to economic factors that have effected other advertising spending. Interestingly, although exact figures are not available for New Zealand sponsorship investment, it appears that rugby union, cricket, sailing and yachting attract the most sponsors' dollars.

These figures clearly show the growing interest in sport as a marketing vehicle and confirm the relative 'newness' of it. Sponsorship figures in 1998 for many of the sports listed in table 17.3 are far lower than current expenditure. Even 'niche' sports like ice hockey ($124 000 in sponsorship), archery ($700 500 in sponsorship), cycling ($4.14 million in sponsorship) and baseball ($7.5 million in sponsorship) are now attracting large sponsorship dollars.

Table 17.3 The top 10 sports by value of sponsorship funds received (including TV rights)

Ranking	Sport	2000 ($000)	1999 ($000)	1998 ($000)
1	Motor racing (including Formula One)	652 183	582 142	230 050
2	Australian rules	90 465	90 461	62 461
3	Rugby league	78 465	71 186	62 089
4	Horse racing	70 000	69 000	N/A
5	Rugby union	43 675	42 521	38 509
6	Golf	43 647	43 610	21 637
7	Basketball	41 945	41 168	26 014
8	Sailing	34 414	32 269	N/A
9	Hockey	28 359	27 215	5 933
10	Surf lifesaving/surf events	25 281	24 404	21 832

Source: Commercial Economic Advisory Service of Australia 2000

Identifying a brand or product with sporting celebrities is also a popular strategy. Firms attempt to match the personality of those celebrities with the desired images for their products. Table 17.4 shows the most popular sporting personalities in Australia and New Zealand today. **Sport sponsorship**, unlike other marketing tools, is often quarantined from economic factors, causing companies to trim their other advertising activities.

Sport sponsorship: investment by companies in sport participants, sporting teams or sporting events in return for promotional media coverage; for access to particular client groups; and for special privileges such as celebrity endorsements, corporate entertainment and so on

Table 17.4 Australia's and New Zealand's most popular male and female sporting celebrities, 2002

Top five female sporting celebrities		Top five male sporting celebrities	
Australia	**New Zealand**	**Australia**	**New Zealand**
Susie O'Neil	Barbara Kendall	Ian Thorpe	Gavin Larsen
Cathy Freeman	Sarah Ulmer	Pat Rafter	Stacey Jones
Dawn Fraser	Irene van Dyk	Lleyton Hewitt	Jonah Lomu
Karrie Webb	Beatrice Faumuina	Greg Norman	Craig Monk
Tatiana Grigorieva	Susie Pryde	Steve Waugh	Cory Hutchings

In spite of this, many companies fail to measure the return on their investment, and money can be frittered away on sport to no effect. Only a small proportion of corporate sponsors understand what they are buying and why, and some organisations use sport just to be on the bandwagon (Lloyd 2001). Given that most other marketing decisions in the firm are made from measured, even scientific, perspectives, it is a paradox that sport sponsorship still appears to be an emotive decision for many marketing executives.

This is partly owing to the fact that decision makers have little readily available information on the value of sponsorship, not even from the sporting industry itself. When a company buys advertising on television or in the press, it knows the ratings of a program or the circulation of a newspaper. In sport, only anecdotal evidence exists about levels of exposure. This, in turn, results on the focus shifting from the strategic level to a more operational or tactical level.

Sport sponsorship can make a big contribution to building a brand's image, but too many companies think that a logo on player's arm is enough to build brand awareness and emotive support. Of course this is not so. Exposure in itself is not the same as image and attitude building.

One of the best case studies on how to make best use of sponsorship is the Westpac sponsorship of the 2000 Olympics. It is estimated that the bank spent $50 million to $70 million on its involvement in the games. Westpac was careful to study the return on this major investment using both qualitative research (brand recognition) and quantitative methods (sales generation before and after). Westpac had three main objectives associated with its sponsorship:

1. to gain more business from the existing customer base and new customers
2. to build its brand image in the community
3. to improve staff morale.

Westpac's research showed that its image as a good corporate citizen rose from eleventh to fifth place during the games, its revenue targets for business generation were exceeded and staff morale improved. Not all companies have the resources and the know-how to be as effective in the measurement of their sponsorship investment.

Marketing of sport

The marketing of sport can be traced back to sports management principles. Sport marketing, in its most basic form, has existed since the time of ancient Greeks, but the management of sporting activities has evolved since then as societies and economies have changed. This evolution has resulted in sport being a highly competitive industry in its own right, both on and off the field.

The unique aspects of the sport product, as discussed in the last section, help us to understand the difficulties in marketing such an inconsistent and largely intangible product, with its complex, multiple publics. The definition of the marketing of sport is then the coordination and facilitation of the delivery of the sport 'product' and extensions to satisfy the various stakeholders involved in sport.

Players and spectators have always been the core exchange participants in sport. However, business publics have become increasingly important because there is increased pressure on clubs and associations to generate revenue and broaden exposure in order to remain competitive.

The sport industry in general is gradually moving to a more market-oriented position, because the increased level of corporate interest and the emerging technologies allow consumers to become more involved with their sport. Interestingly, this progression has been almost exponential, with little change occurring for many years and rapid change occurring now.

Whether marketing a particular sport or conducting marketing using sport, end-consumers are only one of the various publics that organisations may target. Generally there are five main groups that marketers need to consider, and often the demands of these groups conflict with one another. Managing the various publics is a difficult job for sport marketers.

Sport publics

As with any industry, identification of relevant publics — those key groups of individuals who affect the organisation — is important. The sport industry has to consider and attempt to satisfy a diverse group of publics who often have conflicting demands on the organisation. There are five main groups relevant to sporting organisations:
1. government publics
2. business/media publics
3. support products and services
4. spectators
5. the players themselves.

Once these key groups have been identified, their relative impact on the organisation needs to be determined. Is their impact of a **supply** nature? That is, do they supply goods and services to the organisation and are they unable to influence the form and structure of the product? That is, do they simply supply goods and services to facilitate the product offering? Or is their impact of a **demand** nature? That is, do they take goods and services from the industry (customers) and are they therefore able to influence the form and structure of the product for their own agenda? It is also important to determine the relative power of each group. That is, what is the impact of their withholding transactions from the organisation?

Supply: the supplying of goods and services to an organisation without influencing the form and structure of the product

Demand: the purchasing of goods and services from an industry, thereby influencing the form and structure of the product

The sport industry has a number of publics that do not fit clearly into either a supply or a demand classification; rather, they have elements of both. Let us examine this more closely by first defining the relevant publics and examining their supply and demand effects on the sport product.

Player or participant publics

Player or participant publics: the players or participants in a particular sport

At the centre of any discussion regarding sport marketing publics is the core sport product itself, and part of this core product is the **player or participant publics**. This, as discussed earlier, takes into account that sport is essentially about competition, and the sport participants or the players and administrators are located here. They have both a supply and demand effect on the product.

Traditionally, without this public, there would be no 'sport' product. However modern marketing has seen new 'sport' products created especially to support and sell other goods and brands previously thought of as product extensions. Examples of this are the extreme sports created by the Pepsi Company to sell soft drink. The entire culture, development of participants and design of the sport has been engineered to suit the needs of a soft drink company. Other sports such as championship bull riding and pro rodeo have also been created using this model.

Business/media publics: *those publics that look at investing in or are involved in the sport product for a business purpose*

Business/media publics also tend to have both a supply and a demand impact on the sport product. Business publics are those that look at investing in or are involved in the sport product for a business purpose (usually with the long-term aim of making a profit). Media publics are those that use the sport product from a media perspective, usually in terms of a profit objective also.

These publics require the sport product to be structured in such a way that they can generate a required return for their investment (demand effect). In the case of business publics, these groups may affect things like competition draws (who plays whom and where) and possibly also the administration of a sport to ensure that significant decisions made in relation to the future and the structure of a sport are made with their requirements in mind. Media publics also have demand effect on the sport product through their influence on things like schedules and venues (schedules designed to suit viewing audiences and venues that are best designed for telecasts).

In terms of their supply effects, both of these publics provide essential services and resources that allow the sport product to function. In the case of business publics, the investment and support they provide often allow a sport to attract a higher profile and thus become more profitable and successful. In the case of media publics, they allow the sport product to be delivered to the various spectator publics at a time and place other than the game venue (through television broadcasts and print coverage of the sport events and issues).

Support goods and services publics

Support goods and services publics: *those organisations and individuals who provide essential support goods and services to those at the core of the sport product*

Support goods and services publics appear on the supply side of the industry diagram and consist of those organisations and individuals who provide essential support goods and services to those at the core of the sport product. These publics include catering services; player and worker unions; manufacturers and suppliers of sporting equipment and clothing; security personnel; and transport companies that bring the spectators or participants to and from a sport event.

These publics generally do not have any influence on the form or function of the sport product, so they have only a supply effect in the sport industry. They simply react to the changes and demands of those involved at the core of the sport product.

Government publics

Government publics: *government interests at local, state and national levels, including both funding bodies (supply function) and regulating bodies (demand function)*

Many sports in Australia and New Zealand are, to varying degrees, funded by local or state and federal governments. **Government publics**, while they may not directly fund high-profile sports, are often involved at the community level of many sports. They provide infrastructure investment in things like facilities, coaching clinics and sporting scholarships, and generally help to encourage sport as a worthwhile and valuable part of community life. The total Australian government investment in sport in 2000 was just over $2000 million, while the New Zealand government spent $534 million in the development of sport (Statistics New Zealand 2000). Both countries aim to invest even more in future years as they recognise the contribution of sport to their national economies. In Australia the contribution is about 1.2 per cent of GDP and in New Zealand this figure is about 0.9 per cent (ABS 2000; Statistics New Zealand 2000).

Government publics, like business/media publics, have both a supply and demand impact on the sport product. They have a supply function in terms of their funding and support for the generation and infrastructure of sport. They also have a demand impact, in that governments require consideration for their involvement in the form of votes or general political mileage.

Spectator publics

Spectator publics: *those who watch sport in either a live or indirect form*

The final group that needs to be considered when looking at the sport industry is the **spectator publics**. They are probably the most important, because without them the sport product would not usually have a viable future. These publics encompass spectators of the sport in all forms, including live game spectators and those who participate through the media, both in electronic and print form. These publics have a demand effect on the sport product because, ultimately, any sport becomes devalued and loses its importance, both from a business and participant perspective, if it loses its spectator publics. Spectators, therefore, through their opinion and influence, can affect the form of a sport, its rules and regulations, its venue and even who participates in the sport.

Many of the demand publics attempt to influence the sport product through their financial involvement in the sport. In contrast, the supply publics provide essential goods and services to the sport industry to allow it to function efficiently. As mentioned previously, the conflicting needs of both the demand and the supply publics are difficult for sport marketers to manage. They need to think strategically about how they satisfy these groups within the constraints of the marketing mix.

Strategic decisions in relation to sport marketing

Sport is a complex product with multiple publics, and it requires careful planning, and strategic manipulation of the marketing mix variables. Figure 17.2 shows a model of the relationship between the marketing mix variables and the sport publics. This model clearly indicates that the marketing mix functions and strategic decisions need to consider the impacts and demands of the various sport publics in order to be effective. The demand effect of many of the publics can affect the core product itself, and the supply publics in turn need to adapt to any resulting changes in the core product. The implications for strategic marketing management in terms of the marketing mix are discussed next.

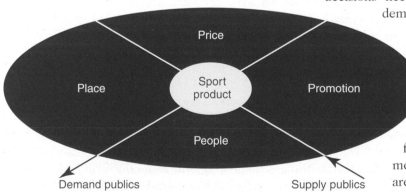

Figure 17.2: A model of sport marketing

Strategic product decisions

The strategic use of 'product' in the sport marketing mix refers not only to the sport but also to product extensions. Product extensions are the truly marketable components of the sport product. Every level and every element of the sporting product can be extended. There are four major components of the product that attract strategic decisions. These are: the game form, the merchandising, the ticketing, and the venue or facility.

Game form

The competition itself can be extended via betting competitions (footyTAB), send-up games (celebrity matches, silly equipment and so on), board games and many other innovative options. The form of the game can also be altered to widen interest and to attract new audiences. For example, short-course and team triathlons and short-course half marathons were all designed to attract new participants and to provide the sports in a form that could be televised. Horse racing at night is another example of a sport that has been modified to suit different market needs. The XFL example provided earlier is a classic case of where changes to the game form were not successful.

Merchandising

Merchandising: the selling of goods related to the sport experience as a means of extending the product

The use of **merchandising** is the most successful form of product extension for many sports. Using this form of promotion, the specific elements of the sport — those attributes unique to the sport — can be extended. The list of potential merchandising options is almost endless, and includes clothing, equipment, posters, cards, books, pictures, music and more. Almost anything that can have a team logo stamped on it is fair game for merchandising.

Even the intangible elements of the sport can be extended through merchandising. The experiences, emotions and benefits of being a direct spectator can be extended via video footage, action photos and audiotape, so that fans can forever recreate that ultimate winning moment.

Merchandising, therefore, is a very flexible promotional tool that can be used by sporting organisations at any level to generate revenue and to foster team spirit, morale and fan loyalty. Licensing arrangements can not only be financially attractive to sport marketers, but also build a strong and loyal customer base, which is important for the long-term survival of the sport.

Ticketing

Tickets to games are also considered a sport product extension. Although the function of tickets seems quite obvious, the form and structure of the ticket is also important. The ticket should provide the relevant information for the purchaser, and should also be designed with specific pricing and packing options in mind. The main objective of tickets is to build value for the purchaser. That is, tickets should include the game plus entertainment, or a portion of the ticket could be redeemable for a sponsor's product or items at the venue. Some tickets are even designed as souvenirs and collector's items.

Strategic packaging of tickets can also help to alleviate uneven demand for the product. For example, in the case of a basketball team, there are bound to be matches scheduled for the home stadium that are not popular with the potential audience. By offering these games as a package with highly popular games, possibly with preferential seating or some other advantage, the sport marketer is more likely to maximise revenue for unpopular games and still have satisfied customers.

The venue or facility

The generic elements of a sport can also be extended by maintaining the quality of the facilities themselves. This minimises the potential of any negative factors that may affect the customer's experience of the sport product. Providing covered, comfortable seating, having easily identifiable team colours, and providing sufficient transport options and parking areas are all examples of this.

Strategic people decisions

The service qualities of sport ensure that people are an important component of the sport marketing mix. Athletes, coaches, referees, administrators and support personnel all play a key role in sport marketing. High-profile personnel such as athletes, coaches and referees need to be trained to deal with the public, as they are commonly subject to media appearances. In fact, many sporting clubs find it desirable to have their players and coaching staff write regular columns for newspapers, and specialty magazines and appear on television, perhaps giving the sporting commentary on the news or as part of a speciality show (such as *The Footy Show*). When recruiting these professionals, consideration must be given to the personality that comes with the talent. They should be selected not only for their skills but also for their suitability as a provider of the sports image and goals.

Administrative and support personnel are important for the same reason; that is, they are representatives of the sport body or club and should always aim to satisfy customers' needs and meet the standards of customer service set by management. The sport body should also emphasise internal marketing where promotional communication is directed not only to consumers but also to employees. They must have the required knowledge to pass onto consumers and should also have a genuine desire to promote the sports philosophy. A sporting body that looks after its employees is also far more attractive to potential athletic and coaching recruits.

Strategic promotional decisions

Sport marketing is believed by some to mean only the promotion of sport. While this is not the case (as can be seen in our model of sport marketing), it does highlight the topical and critical role that promotion has been seen to play. There are three broad strategic promotional issues that need to be considered. These are promotion of the sport, sponsorship and media management.

Promotion of sport follows the same basic principles as promotion of any good or service. A game, competition, series, club, association or sport message can be promoted through any combination of advertising, publicity, sales promotion, personal selling and direct marketing. Examples of sport advertising are abundant in Australia and New Zealand, with television, radio, billboard and print commercials for many sports being very common.

Publicity for individual teams, clubs and sports in general is a much sought after commodity. There is strong competition for free media attention, with every opportunity taken to have athletes and officials receive exposure on television, radio and in print. Organised publicity events such as charity days and celebrity appearances are also used to maximise public exposure and increase awareness of both the sport and the athlete.

Sales promotion can be used as an incentive for both final consumers and channel members. A booking agent, for example, may be given a special incentive to sell tickets to a game and a final consumer could be given a free cap with every ticket purchased in advance. In fact, tickets to the event itself are commonly used as a sales promotion, with a sizeable percentage of tickets often reserved as free tickets for sponsors and spectators.

Personal selling is critical to revenue generation in sport. This applies both to selling tickets and memberships and to securing corporate sponsorship.

Direct marketing can also be used in campaigns aimed at increasing memberships, selling merchandise, pre-selling game tickets, selling corporate boxes and selling season tickets.

As mentioned earlier, the annual sport sponsorship budget in Australia is estimated at approximately $1.6 billion. It is slightly less in New Zealand, which has been slower to respond to sponsorship opportunities in sport. Most corporate sponsors are attempting to reach a mass target market, and they use sponsorship as a non-traditional technique for introducing their brand to new consumers. The motivations for becoming involved in sport sponsorship are varied, and may include increasing brand awareness, localising a product/ service, corporate image promotion, sales promotion, opportunities for research, market segmentation strategies and mass marketing strategy.

Indeed, the choice of which sport to sponsor is also a major decision, with most corporations attempting to match the fan-base profiles with those of their actual or desired target markets. The decision to use sport in a marketing campaign needs to be a strategic one, devoid of emotional reasoning. The organisation should have clear and measurable objectives, and these need to be monitored just as advertising does.

On average, larger companies in Australia receive as many as ten proposals a day for sport sponsorship (Phillips 1994). It is therefore essential that sport marketers are able to communicate very real benefits of sponsorship. They must also be strategic in their selection of a sponsor, and should target that sponsor with a well-developed proposal. In addition, organisations need to clearly establish their sponsorship with their target market; actively promote it; try to own it rather than simply support it; stick with it; and, above all, make sure it is an integrated part of the total marketing mix (Phillips 1994).

Finally, media management is becoming increasingly important for sporting administrations. As the media industry and its role in sport become more complex, professional media personnel are becoming essential additions to the organisational structure of larger sport administrations. The media are singled out here because of their dramatic impact on sport. For example, live spectators, once the most important sport consumers, have increasingly become less important because television takes sporting events live to local, national and international communities.

Strategic distribution (place) decisions

Distribution is an often forgotten marketing variable in service marketing. However, the importance of distribution in sport marketing is evident for several key reasons. Firstly, to maximise attendance, exposure and profile, the physical location of sport events and the venues or facilities used must be viewed strategically. This physical distribution or delivery of the sport requires decisions regarding parking, amenities, seating design and control and transport.

Secondly, the distribution strategy for ticketing must align with other sport marketing variables to make tickets to the sport available at the right time, in the right place and in the right form. Finally, the distribution of the sport product extensions must be planned. Merchandise, for example, is commonly sold in retail outlets, and marketers must decide which outlets best suit the image of the sport and the target market. The timely distribution of merchandise for limited season sports or special events is also crucial.

Strategic price decisions

The cost of organising and staging sporting events is immense. Marketers can use two basic strategies in sport: to try to reduce the costs or to generate more funds. Sport marketers can help to reduce the cost of sport through strategic alliances with channel members such as airlines and sport apparel companies.

The generation of funds is what constitutes the price element of the sport marketing mix. Pricing decisions must be made on ticketing, product extensions and memberships. The other large groups from whom funds are generated are sponsors and media (who may own the rights to very large events). As discussed previously, marketers must decide what price should be attached to different levels of sponsorship. For example, many tangible and intangible elements of sport may be broken up and sold in separate sponsorship agreements — naming rights, uniform rights, stadium signage and so on. In addition, media rights for telecasting events that have large audience appeal can be very lucrative, as the figures relating to the Olympics in table 17.2 attest.

Regardless of whether the fund generation is through final consumers, corporate sponsors or media, marketers must carefully analyse the price element of the marketing mix. It must take into account the cost of the sport, the comparative positioning of other sports or teams, and the overall marketing objectives (that is, profit maximisation versus growth). As mentioned already, sport can generate considerable funds and engage a large number of support services. It therefore has a major impact on many country's economies. This dimension of sport will be examined next.

The economic importance of sport

Sport plays an important role in the economies of many countries. Just look again at the Olympic statistics in table 17.2 — and these do not include the tonnes of food and drink supplied to the athletes and visitors (over 60 000 meals per day) or the salaries paid to cleaners, security personnel, builders, architects and others who were involved in this event. In Australia alone, sport employs 58 500 people, accounts for a further 113 000 volunteers, and generates approximately $2517 million in income (ABS 2000). In New Zealand, sport and active leisure support 31 000 jobs and generates $967 million in household expenditure (Statistics New Zealand 2000). In addition, sport tourism in New Zealand contributes an additional $120 million a year when tourists take part in or watch sport (about four per cent of all New Zealand tourists).

Even apart from the large sponsorship deals and corporate spending on sport, individuals also contribute to the economic value of sport. Just over $2.7 million was spent on organised sport and physical activity by participants in Australia in 1999. In a recent survey, 85 per cent of New Zealanders over the age of 15 indicated they regularly engaged in some form of physical exercise (Statistics New Zealand 2000). Participation by adults in activities organised by clubs or associations was highest in aerobics/fitness, golf, tennis, netball and lawn bowls. On average, this means that people who participate in organised sport spend $693 per annum on things such as clothing, fees, memberships and transport (ABS 2000). Sport participation appears to vary according to geography, climate and age, with increasing numbers of people worldwide competing in their senior years.

Just looking at the Olympics alone, the 2008 Olympics in Beijing are predicted to bring profits of US$19 million to China after taking into account the $20 billion being spent on giving the city a facelift and building the necessary infrastructure. At the same time, Beijing has already contracted US$1.2 billion for television rights and sponsorships, and GDP is expected to rise by 0.3 per cent per year between now and 2008. In addition to the huge marketing and profit potential of the games, there is also evidence of increased tourism, which will further sustain economic growth in China (Barnet 2001). There's no doubt that sport is indeed big business.

In spite of this overwhelming evidence of the importance of sport, both economically and socially, sport marketing in Australia and New Zealand has only recently gained recognition as an integral component of sport and sports planning. Sport in Australia and New Zealand has only just begun to move from its non-profit, largely amateur status to a more professional position where business and marketing skills, as well as athlete skills, are recognised and rewarded. In 1997 only seven per cent of those involved in sport received payment for their effort. In New Zealand, approximately 344000 people (13 per cent of the population) are volunteers in this industry, and similar proportions are noted in Australia (Hillary Commission 2000). Since then, the number of people who receive payment for sport participation and involvement has more than doubled, yet this amount is still far lower, as a proportion, than for our United States or other Western counterparts (ABS 2000).

Sport is clearly an important product that has national and international appeal. However, there is still confusion about what it is and why it is unique in marketing terms. Moreover, most companies lack a fundamental understanding of what makes it effective (Lloyd 2001b). Having studied this chapter, you should have a better understanding of the unique attributes of sport and how to use marketing strategies more effectively in relation to sport.

Summary

LO1: Discuss the dichotomy of sport in terms of whether it is a good or a service.
- One of the most challenging aspects of sport is that it has the characteristics of both a good and a service concurrently.
- Sport has tangible components that are produced, distributed and then purchased.
- It also has intangible elements that cannot be stored for future sale (perishability), and production and consumption occur at the same time (inseparability).

LO2: Define sport marketing.
- When considering the use of the term 'sport', one needs to remember that it implies a collection of separate activities rather than the broader meaning of the collective term 'sports'. In contrast, sport is a broader term and refers to the management of people, activities, relationships, businesses and organisations involved with producing, facilitating, promoting, organising and maintaining sports activities and products.
- Sport marketing can be defined as all activities designed to meet the needs and wants of sport publics through the exchange process.

LO3: Explain the unique characteristics of sport.
- Sport as a product is complex and has many of the characteristics of both a good and a service, with both tangible and intangible attributes.

- There are five main characteristics that result in sport being unique:
  1. the unique market for sport products and services
  2. the sport product itself
  3. the pricing of sport
  4. the promotion of sport
  5. the complex distribution of sport.
- One of the main challenges for sport marketers is that the core of the sport product is the competition itself, which is uncontrollable and intangible.

LO4: Explain the difference between the marketing of sport and marketing using sport.

- When discussing or researching sport, we need to be clear on whether we are approaching the concept of sport marketing from the position of marketing using sport or marketing of sport.
- Marketing using sport is where organisations incorporate sport into their marketing activities in order to assist them in achieving corporate goals.
- Marketing of sport is where sporting organisations attempt to manage their marketing activities.

LO5: Discuss the various sport publics and their impact on sport marketing.

- Sporting organisations serve multiple publics (those key groups of individuals who affect the organisation), and this often places conflicting demands on the organisation.
- The sport industry has to consider and attempt to satisfy diverse publics who often have conflicting demands on the organisation.
- There are five main groups relevant to sporting organisations:
  1. government publics
  2. business/media publics
  3. support products and services
  4. spectators
  5. the players themselves.
- These publics also need to be considered in light of the supply or demand impact they have on the organisation.
- In the case of sporting organisations, some publics have both supply and demand impacts.

LO6: Examine the major strategic marketing issues associated with sport marketing implementation.

- The integrated model of sport marketing presented in this chapter includes the five elements of the marketing mix and outlines the strategic marketing decisions that specifically relate to sport.
- The service qualities of sport ensure that people are an important component of the sport marketing mix.

LO7: Discuss the importance of sport to the economies of many countries.

- Sport is both socially and economically important to modern societies.
- Sport is the most pervasive of all leisure activities and transcends all boundaries of race, culture, language and religion.
- There is considerable evidence that the sport industry in Australia and New Zealand is slowly becoming more professional and is beginning to adopt a more market-oriented focus.
- The increasing investment in sport has resulted in sport marketers needing to use more sophisticated marketing tools to design and measure the incorporation of sport into their marketing programs.

Business/media publics: those publics that look at investing in or are involved in the sport product for a business purpose (p. 463)

Competition: the struggle and rivalry between opponents that is the central component of a sport product (p. 443)

Customer mix: the optimum combination of customer types that will complement the service provision and provide the fewest negative effects on other customer groups (p. 451)

Demand: the purchasing of goods and services from an industry, thereby influencing the form and structure of the product (p. 462)

End users: final consumers (p. 453)

Ephemeral: transient or fleeting, short lived (p. 445)

Experiential consumption: intense consumption experiences providing identifiable levels of emotion that are appealing to consumers (p. 452)

Generic features: the largely tangible things that all sports have in common (p. 444)

Government publics: government interests at local, state and national levels, including both funding bodies (supply function) and regulating bodies (demand function) (p. 463)

Heterogeneity: variability in a service (p. 445)

Indirect revenue: the money realised from selling advertising and merchandising rights to sporting events (p. 454)

Intangible: describes something that cannot be seen, touched or tasted (p. 443)

Marketing of sport: the coordination and facilitation of the delivery of the sport 'product' and extensions in order to satisfy the goals of various stakeholders (p. 459)

Marketing using sport: any strategy that aims to associate a product, service, idea or company with the emotive force of a sport, sports association or sporting event in order to appeal to target markets in a way that traditional promotion cannot achieve (p. 458)

Merchandising: the selling of goods related to the sport experience as a means of extending the product (p. 465)

Organisational consumers: those who take the product and then on-sell it or use it as a component in the production of another product (p. 453)

Perishable: likely to decay or perish (p. 445)

Personal identification: a state of mind in which consumers feel that they 'know' the sports participants and the administration of sports sufficiently to express opinions about how things should be done (p. 446)

Player or participant publics: the players or participants in a particular sport (p. 462)

Servicescape: the environment in which a service is produced and delivered (p. 443)

Specific features: the unique aspects of a particular sport that differentiate it from other sports (p. 444)

Spectator publics: those who watch sport in either a live or indirect form (p. 464)

Sport: the management of people, activities, businesses and organisations involved with producing, facilitating, promoting, organising and maintaining sports activities and products (p. 445)

Sport industry: the market in which the products offered to buyers are related to sports, fitness, recreation or leisure, and these may be activities, goods, services, people, places or ideas (p. 446)

Sport marketing: all activities designed to meet the needs and wants of sport publics through the exchange process (p. 445)

Sport publics: those key groups of individuals who affect sporting organisations and who can include customers, shareholders, employees, suppliers and investors (p. 445)

Sport sponsorship: investment by companies in sport participants, sporting teams or sporting events in return for promotional media coverage; for access to particular client groups; and for special privileges such as celebrity endorsements, corporate entertainment and so on (p. 460)

Sports: a collection of separate man-made recreational or physical activities in which participation can be professional, observational, health-related or social (p. 445)

Sports management: the management of sports activities (p. 445)

Sports marketing: the marketing of individual sports activities (p. 445)

Supply: the supplying of goods and services to an organisation without influencing the form and structure of the product (p. 462)

Support goods and services publics: those organisations and individuals who provide essential support goods and services to those at the core of the sport product (p. 463)

Tangible: describes something that can be seen, touched or tasted (p. 443)

Vicarious violence: experiencing violence second-hand through another person (p. 445)

 review questions

1. What is the difference between the marketing of sport and marketing using sport?
2. List the main characteristics that differentiate sport from other products.
3. Who are the four publics involved in the sport industry, and what is their role in the marketing of sport?
4. How can distribution be used as a strategic marketing tool, and what are the main issues involved in its use?
5. What is meant by the term 'game form', and how does it form part of a strategic product decision?
6. Why is sport such an important part of many countries' economy and social structure?
7. What do companies need to be aware of when using sport sponsorship as part of their promotional program?
8. What is meant by the term 'product extensions' in sport marketing?

application questions

1. Consider the information contained in table 17.3 in relation to sport sponsorship. Pick any two of these sports, identify their major sponsors (the answer here may be country specific) and comment on how well each of these sports and sponsors are matched.

2. Table 17.4 provides a list of the top five male and female sports stars in Australia and New Zealand. Pick one from each country, review their endorsement program and comment on the match between the celebrity and the products/services they endorse. Make any recommendations for improvements.

3. There are almost as many Internet sites for rugby as there are world teams. Have a look at those in the following list. All of these sites have spent considerable money on developing their website.

   (a) Comment on the incorporation of the marketing principles. Particularly look for opportunities to interact with the site and the organisation. Do any of the sites motivate you to return? Why or why not?

   (b) Looking particularly at the Australian, New Zealand and international rugby sites, what suggestions could you make and why? Do you think any of these sites copy each other?

   (c) Which is the best in terms of marketing principles and which is the best in terms of audience and visitor appeal? If the answer to this question is two different sites, what does this mean?

International Rugby Board	www.irb.org
Australian Rugby	www.rugby.com.au
New Zealand Rugby Union	www.nzrugby.co.nz
Rugby Heaven	www.rugbyheaven.com.au
World of Rugby	www.worldofrugby.com
Planet Rugby	www.planet-rugby.com
Scrum	www.scrum.com

vignette questions

1. Read the Services Marketing Action vignette on pages 447–8, then answer the following questions.

   (a) What marketing principles have the All Blacks management employed to make them so successful?

   (b) Comment on the marketing of the team as a brand. Do you think this is a good principle and would it work for all sporting teams? Why or why not?

   (c) Visit the All Blacks website at www.allblacks.com. Can you see any of the branding principles in operation here? What other comments can you make about the usefulness and functionality of the site?

2. Read the Ethical Issues vignette on pages 449–5, then answer the following questions.

   (a) Do you agree or disagree with the points made in this vignette about the responsibility of the media? Why or why not?

   (b) Organise a debate about these issues within the class group to see what others feel about media rights and responsibilities.

(c) Another criticism of media in relation to sport reporting is that it favours men's sports and only focuses on the glamorous female sports such as beach volleyball, where two-piece costumes are worn. Comment on this issue and debate each side of the argument.

3. Read the Services Marketing Action vignette on pages 455–6, then answer the following questions.

    (a) Do you think that this sort of sporting product would work in Australia or New Zealand? Why or why not?

    (b) One of the main reasons given for the failure of the XFL was that it did not have any 'grass roots' fans and development base. This is often said to be an important element for any sport. Choose your favourite sport and examine its fan and development base. Comment on how the sport developed and whether a high-gloss media image would work or not, and why.

4. Read the Services Marketing on the Web vignette on page 458, then answer the following questions.

    (a) Visit www.snow.co.nz and comment on whether the site attracts you or not. Would you return and why?

    (b) What improvements could you suggest for this site?

    (c) Visit a couple of other sporting websites and compare their offerings. How are they different and what lessons could they learn from this site?

recommended readings

For general reading about the sport industry in Australia, New Zealand and America, *Sport Marketing Quarterly* is a good journal. It is aimed at the practitioner level, but also contains some scholarly articles. It will give students the best access to research in the sport marketing field.

The *Journal of Sport Management* is a more scholarly journal and contains mainly empirical research into issues of sport marketing and management. This journal would provide excellent support material for assignments and research-based papers.

Another good source of scholarly articles about issues in sport marketing is the *Journal of Sport and Social Issues*. This journal is based in the United Kingdom and offers perspectives that differ from some of the more prevalent United States journals. It is also a good one to source for assignment information.

A recent sport marketing text by Nigel Pope from Griffith University will provide a good support reference for those interested in exploring the issues addressed in this chapter. See:
Pope, N. & Voges, K. 2001, *Sport Marketing*, John Wiley & Sons, New York.

This United States text is an excellent reference for those looking for a more practical guide to sport and event marketing. It is comprehensive and very helpful:
Stedman, G., Goldblatt, J., Neirotti, L. & Ebersol, D. 2001, *The Ultimate Guide to Sports Marketing*, 2nd edn, McGraw-Hill, Boston.

Another practical guide on 'how to implement sport marketing' is:
Stotlar, D. 2001, *Developing Successful Sport Marketing Plans*, WCB Publishing, Madison, WI.

references

Australian Bureau of Statistics 2000, www.abs.gov.au.

Barker, W. 1990, 'Professionalism and sports marketing: an overview', *Sports Management and Marketing Conference Proceedings*, 21–22 May, Sydney.

Barnet, K., accessed 9 November 2001, 'Beijing stretches its image to fit through the Olympic rings', www.brandchannel.com.

Berich, J. 1995, 'Winning is everything: sponsorhip in the 90s', *Australian Professional Marketing*, May, pp. 12–17.

Commercial Economic Advisory Service of Australia 2000, in Lloyd, S., 'Sponsorship: taking a sporting chance', *Business Review Weekly*, 6 July 2001.

Dolahenty, A. 1997, 'Experts: sports sponsorship needs the proper backing', *B&T Weekly*, vol. 47, February, p. 12.

Gilson, C., Pratt, M., Roberts, K. & Weymes, E. 1999, *Sport Seen As a Product*, HarperCollins.

Hannen, M. 2001, 'Sport: advantage television', *Business Review Weekly*, no. 23, p. 5.

Hillary Commision, accessed 2000, www.hillarysport.org.nz.

Lefton, T. 1999, 'Lego heads to the field with soccer toys and first sports marketing ties', *Brandweek*, 22 November.

Lloyd, S. 2001a, 'Sponsorship: taking a sporting chance', *Business Review Weekly*, no. 26.

Lloyd, S. 2001b, 'Brand power', *Business Review Weekly*, no 23, p. 47.

Phillips, M. 1994, 'Good sports with money', *Australian Business Monthly*, vol. 13, May, no. 7, pp. 58–62.

Pitts, B. G. & Stotlar, D. K. 1996, *Fundamentals of Sport Marketing*, Fitness Information Technology, Inc., Morgantown, WV.

Rusch, R., accessed 30 April 2001, 'The world's best sports brand?', www.brandchannel.com.

Shoebridge, N. 1998, 'Selling sponsorships — an Olympian Games task', *Business Review Weekly*, 12 June, pp. 76–8.

Statistics New Zealand 2000, www.stats.govt.nz.

Stenshol, J. & Way, N. 2001, 'Football's king hit', *Business Review Weekly*, no. 23, p. 14.

Chapter 18
Public sector and government marketing

Susan Dann and Anthony J. McMullan

LEARNING OBJECTIVES

After reading this chapter, you should be able to:

- understand what is meant by the term 'public sector marketing' and the scope of its application
- determine that marketing has an important role to play in the public sector, particularly in improving the effectiveness of service delivery
- identify the reasons why marketing is increasingly being used within the public sector
- identify the difficulties associated with the application of marketing in the public sector
- discuss the potential future for public sector marketing.

CHAPTER OUTLINE

This chapter provides an overview of the marketing of services within the public sector. It defines what is meant by the term 'public sector marketing' and explores the scope of marketing activities within this sector, incorporating the vital elements of successful marketing of services, namely the nature and relationship between the marketing, human resources and operations functions. This chapter also examines the situational factors that have resulted in the marketing discipline being used across the public sector. It raises the issue of just how effectively marketing is being used to improve the delivery of government services to the Australian community. In doing so, problems associated with the introduction of marketing are discussed. The marketing principles referred to in this chapter apply equally to all three levels of government in Australia: federal, state and local.

Introduction

Services form a part of our everyday life. We receive services from not only the private sector but also the public sector — services such as:

- motor vehicle or boat licences from the Department of Transport
- camping permits for a national park (Department of National Parks and Wildlife)
- social welfare benefits such as a Family Assistance Payment from the Federal Government's Centrelink
- reminders of the benefits of driving safely on our roadways (Department of Transport)
- mammogram testing for women and prostate care for men (Department of Health)
- dog and cat registration with a local government authority.

All of these services are provided by government organisations. Some are 'free', others involve a direct financial cost, but all can benefit from the application of appropriate marketing activities. Despite the growing importance of marketing to public sector and government organisations, relatively little has been written on this topic. Although the core principles and tools of marketing can be used in a variety of situations, the unique culture and limitations of the public sector mean that to use marketing effectively, the practice needs to be not only adopted, but also adapted to meet these special needs. This chapter gives an overview of some of the key issues surrounding the use of marketing in a public sector environment.

Importance of government marketing

The marketing of government activities has had a long and varied history, from political campaigns through to various health, educational and social programs. Despite this, it is only in recent years that any attempt has been made to integrate strategic marketing into the mainstream of public sector management. Today we find the techniques of marketing used widely across portfolios, from units responsible for the developing policy to units that perform their activities along commercial lines similar to the private sector. However, many issues prevent marketing from being fully implemented within government. Among these issues are the failure of marketing to move beyond the use of individual techniques, such as promotion and research, to embrace more of an integrated marketing mix approach; and the associated issue of agencies failing to adopt a marketing orientation (culture) agency wide. For some, the value of marketing in the public sector is beyond question. For others, marketing's application within the public sector has only lukewarm support. This is because, although it is intuitively appealing, there are special issues in the public sector that limit how well marketing can be implemented.

The current view is that while it may be problematic, it is nonetheless possible to fully implement marketing in this environment. Effective service delivery depends on the integration of the marketing, human resources and operations aspects of an organisation into its day-to-day service delivery. Before we can discuss how marketing is used in the public sector, it is important to understand the basics of how government operates in Australia and New Zealand.

Government today

Government in Australia and New Zealand is founded on the British system of government known as the **Westminster system** — not surprising given our history as colonies of Britain. Although New Zealand is referred to as a **unitary system** of government and Australia as a **federation**, there is more than one level of government in both countries. In New Zealand, there is a national government and a number of local governments, whereas in Australia there are three levels of government: federal, state and local.

According to the principles of the Westminster system, the public service should be politically neutral. Its role is to advise on and implement the policies of the current government, regardless of who is in power. The public service itself is made up of departments that are responsible for implementing portfolio-specific policy and achieving objectives made by the minister responsible for the portfolio. With the public sector reforms of the last 20 years, the structure of public sector departments has changed to reflect a move away from their traditional role. Today, in addition to the policy function, departments are likely to have business units to deliver the service or program and to have motives similar to the private sector. Equally, some public sector activities have, throughout this period, been the subject of government agendas such as privatisation, (of the Commonwealth Bank, for instance). Other traditional government activities, such as the Totalisator Agency Boards (TAB) and state railway authorities, have been corporatised with the objective of returning a financial dividend to the government stakeholder.

As a result of a number of reforms implemented in both Australia and New Zealand, differences between public sector and private sector management are now not as obvious as before. For most people the notion of public servants and the work they performed was that they were 'concerned with procedures over results and paperwork rather than people, being introspective and resistant to scrutiny, and excessively risk averse' (Sedgwick 1994, p. 344) — all aspects that have had to change. The catalyst for the new face of government management has been the commitment by various governments (at all levels) over the last 20 years to a reform agenda whose core belief is that private sector practices (fundamentally the application of market principles to the public sector) will help to make the public sector more efficient and effective. At the centre of a government's attempt to transform itself into a set of client-focused organisations is the adoption of the private sector management approach of marketing orientation. The discipline of marketing provides a framework by which the needs and wants of citizens can be collected and subsequently developed into effectively implemented policies.

Public sector marketing

Today's public sector, with the benefits of the reform agenda behind it, has witnessed the introduction and acceptance of the marketing discipline within government. This is evidenced by the growth of marketing-related positions within the public sector and the plethora of marketing campaigns undertaken by government — campaigns promoting the virtues of health, exercise, quitting smoking, medical gap insurance, the unacceptability of domestic violence and the privatisation of the TAB.

What is public sector marketing?

Public sector marketing: *any marketing activity undertaken by government-owned or government-managed organisations*

Public sector marketing is defined differently depending on who you ask. Many critics of public sector marketing do not fully understand either the marketing orientation or how it can be applied in the public sector. For some, marketing equals communication, and the link to meeting the needs of clients is not particularly strong. For others, marketing is selling, leading to the question 'What would the government have to sell us?'. Those working in the public sector can sometimes be suspicious of the value of marketing, with some seeing it as an unnecessary expense and, therefore, a waste of scarce resources.

While there is no formal definition of public sector marketing approved by a marketing body such as the AMA, it can be referred to in the broadest sense as any marketing activity undertaken by government owned or managed organisations. This includes **government departments**, **government-owned corporations** and **statutory authorities**. Organisations receiving government funding (non-profit organisations) are excluded from this definition, as they are not strictly government instrumentalities because they may receive funding from a range of sources and set their objectives according to the needs of private organisations and individuals.

Government departments: *traditional public service departments under the control of a minister*

Government-owned corporations: *corporatised organisations, often former monopolies, in which the government is the major shareholder (for example, electricity authorities)*

One of the problems associated with defining public sector marketing relates back to a more fundamental issue — defining the **public sector**. Government and the public sector are not part of a single organisation, nor do all elements of the government have the same objectives. In many units, objectives are based on social outcomes such as improved education. However, since the 1980s and the introduction of 'user-pays' services, elements of the public sector are increasingly focusing on the generation of profits. In general, the greater the similarity between the objectives of the public sector organisation and the objectives of similar private organisations, the easier it is to implement marketing, and the more relevant it is considered to be.

Statutory authorities: *organisations created by a government statute (for example, universities)*

Public sector: *a combination of government departments, government-owned corporations and statutory bodies*

A formal definition of public sector marketing needs to take the range of activities and the flexibility of the sector into consideration. One definition is that public sector marketing is the 'simultaneous adoption of the marketing philosophy as a guiding framework, and the adaptation of specific marketing tools and tactics, to assist in the implementation of policies and programs designed to maximise efficiency and effectiveness with the aim of best serving the public interests as defined through the political process' (Dann 1999).

The important points to note from this definition are that:

- both the marketing philosophy (that is, customer orientation) and specific tools of marketing must be adopted together
- the tools of marketing may need to be modified to suit public sector conditions rather than just being transposed, as is, from the private to public sectors
- marketing's role focuses heavily on improving the implementation of policies and programs
- marketing can assist in maximising both efficiency and effectiveness by providing clients with the services they need in a way that suits them.
- marketing serves the political interest as interpreted by the political process, not the process itself.

Marketing fundamentals in the public sector

As in the private sector, modern public sector management benefits from the planned approach that the marketing discipline provides. The long-term success of government departments and agencies is being built around some core marketing principles. These include the following.

Marketing management

How effectively the needs of target groups are being met while still achieving organisational objectives (that is, matching customer and organisational objectives) applies not only to private sector organisations but also public and non-profit organisations.

Marketing concept

A basic marketing premise is that the consumer is the focal point of all transactions undertaken. In government terms, the word 'client' is used instead of customer.

The marketing concept consists of four basic foundation stones. These are:
- *a consumer orientation* — the practice of researching and meeting the needs of the client group
- *continuous market research* — the process by which client needs are determined on a regular basis
- *integration of all organisational activities* — marketing, human resources and operations to serve the identified needs of the client
- *customer satisfaction and loyalty to return for repeat business* — the end result of a focus upon the customer, a culture of continuous market research and an integration of organisational effort.

Evidence of the use of the marketing concept with government is growing. For example, in Queensland QFleet, the government's motor vehicle fleet manager adopted the marketing concept by recognising that QFleet existed to serve clients. Subsequently, QFleet began an ongoing research program and used the information gathered to design a more appropriate marketing mix. It also integrated all organisation activities, particularly human resources (client service training and client friendly job descriptions) and operations (improved client service delivery based upon a client service standard) to achieve client satisfaction (as measured by performance against the client service standard). QFleet's approach is discussed in more detail in Services Marketing in Action vignette.

Services Marketing Action:
QFleet quality fleet management

Traditionally, individual government agencies in Queensland owned and operated their own motor vehicle fleets. However, in 1991 a decision was made by Cabinet to establish a central unit within the Administrative Services Department (ASD) that would provide fleet management to government departments and statutory authorities. The new unit, QFleet, provides a total fleet-management service including:
- funding and acquisition of vehicles
- leasing and hiring of vehicles

- maintenance of vehicles
- comprehensive insurance for vehicles leased and hired
- management information to help agencies manage their vehicle assets
- disposal of vehicles by public auction.

QFleet management recognised, from the start, the importance of listening to the client. To understand its customers better and to measure their satisfaction with QFleet's service, a strategy was developed to coordinate an external survey. The outcome from such information gathering would result in improved quality of service to clients, in line with their expectations. The major objective of the survey was to provide QFleet management with information that would clarify the service expectations and perceptions of its client base. The way this was achieved was by implementing a range of marketing research tools including SERVQUAL, glovebox surveys, telesurveys and non-structured programs such as client liaison visitation programs.

In early 1995, QFleet conducted the first of what was intended to be an annual service quality survey. It was found that QFleet clients place a huge (92 per cent) importance on the intangible (people related) service attributes of providing service quality. It was within these key dimensions that QFleet had the greatest opportunity to differentiate itself from competitors.

Analysis of the survey data revealed that what clients of QFleet required most of all from their fleet manager was reliability — QFleet's ability to perform the promised service dependably and accurately. Responsiveness, or the willingness of staff to help customers and provide prompt service, was also seen by clients as an area in which QFleet needed to improve.

An intended outcome of the survey was the development of a client service standard by which to set performance standards for improving the quality of service afforded to clients. The standard is consistent with the marketing philosophy of reflecting the clients' service expectations. An education program communicating what clients could expect and what staff should deliver was built around the standard. At an organisational level, the achievement of superior service quality requires a strong commitment by the senior executive. QFleet's senior management fully supported the introduction of SERVQUAL, and its findings and subsequent marketing strategy development to remedy service gaps.

Today QFleet's client service standard is a guiding mechanism for the delivery of superior service to clients and is used as a means of recruiting and training personnel to the level of service expected by clients.

Derived from McMullan 1996

Other government organisations that have implemented the marketing concept include the Queensland Department of Families' 'Families First' program; the Department of Women in the Northern Territory with its domestic violence campaign; New South Wales Fisheries' partnering in order to market a new fishing licence fee; the Victorian Traffic Accident Commission's HELP program — an integrated approach to youth road safety; the Western Australian Government's 'Freedom from Fear' campaign; the Federal Government's Defence Force Recruitment Program; and programs by various local government authorities to encourage economic development through the use of marketing.

Exchange theory

A fundamental principle of marketing is its foundation upon the process of exchange between parties and the transaction that makes up that process. Without an exchange taking place, marketing does not exist. Public sector marketing deals with exchanges that take place within the government environment. Some critics dispute that exchange takes place in the relationships that government has with the public. **Simple economic exchanges**, where, for example, A gives money to B for a loaf of bread, form the basis of most private marketing activities. In government, this also happens regularly in commercially oriented organisations such as the Australian Bureau of Statistics, where members of the public can purchase information or reports for a fee.

Simple economic exchanges: situations in which one person exchanges money for a product or service

In other areas, however, such as health and social welfare, the exchange is less obvious. Bagozzi (1975) extended the idea of exchange to include a range of indirect and **complex exchanges** more suited to the public sector environment. For example, anti-smoking campaigns exchange a stop-smoking message, and the services that support it, for improved public health. Get-fit and weight-reduction campaigns similarly exchange their information about good health for the benefits of a community with a more active way of life.

Complex exchanges: situations in which the exchange between provider and user is part of a complex relationship and does not involve simply handing over money for goods and services

However, while the benefits of not smoking are well known, it could be that for one target group — stressed single mothers — the simple pleasure associated with cigarette smoking may outweigh the long-term negative consequences. Such a group may consider the ability to take a five-minute break from the full-time pressures of looking after children worth the risk of longer term poor health. The exchange continues to be complex when, in 20 years time, the smoker is refused medical treatment because the hazards of smoking were well known and free medical treatment cannot be extended to 'self-imposed' illnesses.

For successful exchanges to occur, five conditions must be satisfied.

- At least two parties must be present.
- Party one must have an item of value sought by party two.
- All parties can communicate intent and deliver to each other.
- There is an assumption that all parties are free to accept or reject the offer.
- All parties must find the exchange to be appropriate and desirable.

For government, this services exchange theory is sometimes problematic. It is easy to argue that the conditions of exchange have not been met. For example, take the previous case of the single mother whose only respite from the rigours of raising her two under-five children is stealing five minutes to have a cigarette. In this scenario, the virtues of an anti-smoking program would falter upon condition 2. Similarly, anti-drinking and anti-drug campaigns ask consumers to give up a pleasurable activity from which they derive some social value.

Condition 4 is even more problematic. The single mother in the above scenario is free to accept or reject the offer being made. However, rejecting it will mean she has a heavier tax burden than people who do not smoke, because each packet of cigarettes is taxed by the government. In this scenario, the price of smoking may also take the form of being refused medical treatment in future because of her smoking habit. Although marketing is based on an assumption of voluntary adoption of products, whether they are physical products, services or ideas, the reality of many government campaigns is that the state can impose penalties on citizens who choose not to adopt the product. Examples of this include compulsory education up to the age of 15, incarceration of offenders in prisons, drink driving penalties, car registration and the payment of taxes.

Broadened domain of marketing

Broadened domain of marketing: the use of marketing in non-commercial areas

The idea that marketing could move from its traditional goods-oriented, private sector roots to the service-oriented public sector is based on Kotler and Levy's (1969) and Kotler's (1972) assertions that the principles of marketing could be applied to any organisation, regardless of its ultimate objectives. The **broadened domain of marketing** which Kotler proposed is often referred to as the generic model of marketing. Government organisations like the Government Printer and departments like Families, Health, Education and Defence have either social or economic exchanges with clients whose needs can be better met through the planned approach of the marketing discipline. The prevalence of marketing within these types of organisations in today's public sector suggests that the concepts and models found in marketing are in fact a useful framework for the achievement of individual and organisational goals.

This broadened domain of marketing provides the public sector marketing manager with exchanges that produce mutual benefits for all parties involved. It means that for all public organisations, marketing is relevant to their organisational endeavour. Marketing can be seen to exist at three levels (Walsh 1994):

* marketing as a business philosophy that puts the customer/client at the centre of the decision making process — for example, Centrelink
* marketing as a strategic tool to help set the policy and direction of the organisation — for example, Department of Families Queensland
* marketing as a series of tactics such as advertising and promotion aimed at achieving specific, often short-term outcomes — for example, transport authorities across the nation and the Department of Defence (Federal Government).

The marketing mix elements in a public sector setting

The marketing decisions undertaken by public sector managers revolve around the traditional marketing mix elements of product, price, distribution and promotion. In addition, given that the main business of government agencies is to deliver services, the three additional Ps of people, process and physical evidence need to be considered as well.

Product (services)

A fundamental part of any marketing strategy is the need for a clear definition and understanding of the product or service to be offered. From a government perspective, services can be difficult to define and explain, although in others it is quite straightforward. For instance, the government car fleet has a clear product. It offers its client the service product of professional fleet management. In other instances, the core role of the government agency is policy development. Much of the marketing work done in the policy-oriented departments involves social marketing and is beyond the scope of this text.

In some cases, however, a social marketing campaign can have a distinct service element, as occurred with the Department of Families, Youth and Community Care with its campaign 'Putting Families First'. This policy initiative was designed 'to provide families in Queensland with easy access to information to help them meet the challenges of family life' (Department of Families 2002). In this instance the policy, along with its various features and services, is the product on offer to the target group. One element of the total product mix was a telephone helpline for families under stress. This is clearly a standard service product that could benefit from all the advances in services management that have been made in profit-oriented, private sector scenarios.

Price

Price is typically expressed in terms of a monetary exchange, as occurs in a simple exchange. For example, a monetary value is assigned to students undertaking a university or TAFE course. For some government services, such as driver safety campaigns and community renewal programs, determining a price for such a service is harder to express.

Price can be valued in terms other than a monetary unit. For instance, what is the cost of not undertaking the initiative for which the marketing program is designed? The cost to the taxpayer-funded health system incurred as a result of people smoking far outweighs the cost to taxpayers today of any anti-smoking marketing campaign. Similarly the price paid by future taxpayers in terms of social breakdown will be much higher if marketing programs for community renewal initiatives are not undertaken today to improve the quality of life, image and confidence of disadvantaged communities. (For more information on community renewal programs, refer to Department of Housing, www.housing.qld.gov.au.)

Place (distribution)

Basic marketing theory refers to distribution as the channel by which the service is delivered from the point of production to the point of consumption. Goods and services can be delivered either directly or indirectly from the original government source. For example, to pay for your car registration you could go to the local transport department office. Alternatively, you could take advantage of technology and pay online or use an intermediary such as a post office agency, which allows people to purchase a number of government charges in the same distribution outlet. Similarly, a public sector marketing campaign with the aim of making people aware of the benefits of healthy living can be marketed to target audiences by promoting to 'a distribution channel' — principally health professionals (doctors, nurses) — as the means of achieving the desired goal.

Distribution, the third P of the marketing mix, aims to maximise accessibility of the means by which the public service is produced by the service provider and consumed by its target audience.

The types of decisions that government organisations need to make include where to build or rent offices to make it easier for clients to use the service; whether to automate some services so that they can be accessed 24 hours a day, seven days a week; whether or not the service, such as a health or welfare service, is best delivered in the client's home rather than at a central location, and so on. Centrelink has recognised the need to use the Internet to improve both access to and communication of its service benefits.

Services Marketing on the Web:
Making Centrelink more accessible

Centrelink was formed in 1997 as a result of the Federal Government's decision to create a one-stop-shop for the delivery of a range of government services (Conn & Ninham 2001). These services include social security payments, financial information services and social work services. Overall, the organisation has 6.1 million customers (about a third of the Australian population), employs 21 000 staff and receives approximately 22 million phone calls a year to the 24 call centres nationwide. This means that there are over 100 million service interactions conducted by Centrelink each year.

Despite the massive size of the organisation and its role, Centrelink has, from the outset, sought to develop a strong culture of service delivery. From the initial stages of development, Centrelink has articulated a vision of client service that has permeated the whole of the organisation (Jongen 2000).

Although Centrelink is a massive organisation, it strives to offer personalised service to its millions of customers. It has achieved this through the development and implementation of the one-to-one service delivery model. All clients are allocated an individual Centrelink service delivery officer, who becomes their main point of contact with the organisation. By having a single officer knowledgeable about individual cases, the potential for higher quality, customised services is enhanced.

New technologies and improved systems mean that Centrelink customers have better access to information. While much of the focus to date has been on improving call centres and telephone systems, increasingly Centrelink is using the Internet to facilitate service delivery.

The Centrelink website was established in 1997 and experiences nearly 200 000 views per month. Currently Centrelink processes more than 11 million transactions a day or approximately 2.5 billion annually. All paper forms are now accessible on the website, which makes applying for and receiving benefits simpler for clients. As part of the integrated customer service strategy, online processing of claims and inquiries is set to expand in line with the organisation's business and services plans.

Within Centrelink, the Netlink system allows staff to use the Internet innovatively to improve customer service. Using Grouputer technology, in which a central computer is linked to a number of screens, staff are able to interact in real time to solve specific customer service problems. The procedure allows significant amounts of data to be collected instantly and gives all participants the potential for equal input into problem-solving processes. Using a combination of internal and external delivery and communications, Centrelink is showing how government organisations can use online technologies to improve services for customers nationwide.

Derived from Conn & Ninham 2001

Promotion

Promotion is the best known of all elements used in the marketing of public services. Promotion is about communication between buyers and sellers. In a government environment, the seller is the service provider (Department of Housing, Energex, transport authorities) and the buyer is the service purchaser (welfare recipients, public transport users and motor vehicle drivers). Therefore, mass communication channels (television, radio, cinemas) are used to communicate the message and promote the service being offered. Communication in government tends to stand out from other promotion because of the nature of the campaign. For example, road safety and AIDS awareness campaigns use fear and shock to market their message to target groups. Moreover, critics of government can claim that the campaign is not providing a service of public information but is an exercise in seeking political advantage for the government of the day. In addition, there is higher than normal sensitivity and scrutiny associated with government communication. The costs of such campaigns and allegations of wasting taxpayers' funds are often reported in the media and in Parliament.

Focusing too heavily on advertising and publications, however, does not fully address how public sector marketers effectively communicate with their publics and clients. Public sector marketing often happens in an environment of very strict budgets and controls, so effective communication often has to be innovative and integrated into the overall activities of the department or organisation. For many sections of the public sector, the main communication happens on a one-on-one basis (see People) as the service is being delivered. Other 'free' forms of communication occur when staff attend public meetings, address community groups or become involved in community initiatives such as a local environmental issues committee. Increasingly, as a way of raising awareness, government agencies are sponsoring community initiatives or co-branding with other related organisations.

Despite the above issues, the activities associated with the use of the fourth P — advertising, public relations, media releases and direct mail — fit well within the context of the public sector environment. Such a fit is due to the belief that one of the public sector's traditional roles is as the disseminator of information to the public.

People

People play an important role in the marketing of government services because the production and consumption of services often occurs simultaneously. People are therefore an integral part of the service delivery. Public employees such as bus drivers, rail ticket sellers and platform staff all make the public sector service experience memorable, hopefully exceeding what the client had expected in terms of service delivery. Frontline staff such as administrators and teachers in local schools, nurses in the public health system, phone counsellors (Parentline, Lifeline, Kidshelp) and emergency service personnel all form part of the marketing mix.

Even where staff are unaware of it, or are not trained as marketers, they are undertaking a marketing function every time they represent the department that they work for. A typical home visit by a social worker will result in the client being made aware not only of that agency's services, but also of those offered by related departments. An elderly man who has suffered a fall, for example, may be visited by a social worker who then informs him of the availability of home help services, health services, alternative accommodation options and even additional pension payments that he is entitled to but may not be aware of. Marketing is part of everyone's job.

Process

A large focus of public sector reforms in recent years has been to reduce waste and to focus on cost savings and 'efficiency'. Many of the changes that the public sector has made to its services have, therefore, focused on the process of service delivery.

To maintain a true marketing focus, it is important that when changes are made to the process of service delivery, they are made with the client in mind, rather than just the organisation's budget. Of course no department or organisation can afford to deliver services inefficiently. However, unless some basic market research is done into how clients use the service, then what appears to be a cost saving may have the opposite effect if it discourages people from actually coming in and interacting with the department. When the Australian Taxation Office decided to improve the process of lodging tax returns by incorporating an online submission facility, this was a move that increased both the efficiency and effectiveness of service delivery because a large number of clients, particularly businesses, had access to the Internet and were comfortable with using it.

For Centrelink, however, a move into the online environment for submitting payment forms may improve the efficiency of the process from the Department's perspective, but diminish the service for certain clients. A large proportion of people who rely on social security are either elderly (a group which has limited experience and access to the Internet); economically disadvantaged and therefore unable to afford the basic infrastructure of a computer and online access; or socially disadvantaged, possibly to the point of having poor education and therefore lacking the literacy levels needed to effectively navigate the Internet. In this case it would be essential to retain many of the traditional service processes to ensure that no group of clients was unduly disadvantaged.

When changes are made to process, the fundamental principle of marketing applies — it should lead to a situation that is mutually beneficial for both the organisation and the clients it serves.

Physical evidence

Government is often seen as a generic organisation regardless of individual functions. Comments like 'the government should do something about violence' don't attempt to focus on what level of government, what department or who in particular should 'do something'.

Partly as a result of this tendency to group all government agencies into a single mass, most departments and agencies now have clear branding strategies that not only help communicate their existence, but also give a tangible reminder of who provided what service. The Greater London Council in England became famous for its use of this branding technique prior to its abolition in the mid 1980s. After market research revealed that few people in London knew what the council actually did, they embarked on a campaign whereby all services provided by the council were tagged with the slogan 'GLC — Working for London'. By putting stickers on rubbish bins to indicate their sanitation obligations as well as on public transport and other service delivery vehicles, a tangible reminder was given to citizens every time they used one of the council's services.

Branding and logos are only one aspect of providing physical evidence. Increasingly, innovative reminders are used in campaigns to reinforce a message and remind people of government services. An excellent example is the Western Australian Government's 'Freedom from Fear' campaign, which printed service details, including a helpline number, on a range of materials, including beer mats, aimed at its target market.

International Issues:
The ever changing rules of public sector marketing

One of the biggest problems associated with the study and implementation of public sector marketing programs is that there are no steadfast rules. What is acceptable for one government is entirely inappropriate or unacceptable for another. Consequently, training for government marketing is done on a country-by-country, government-by-government basis. Even within countries like Australia, Canada and the United States, where there are multiple levels of government through the federation of states, limits of acceptable behaviour will vary between governments.

While there are no hard and fast rules as to what the limits and appropriate use of government marketing are internationally, some countries have greater similarities than others owing to their common heritage. In particular, those countries that share a common heritage, such as former British colonies with a Westminster style of government, have more in common. For example, in Australia, New Zealand, Britain and Canada, the public service is supposed to be politically neutral. This means that there is always pressure on public sector marketers to remain neutral and to focus primarily on information-based, rather than persuasive, campaigns. In the United States, however, there is an overtly politicised public service. This means that whenever the government changes, so do the key public servants, so there is less pressure to be politically neutral. This gives public sector marketers in the United States more freedom to express opinions that could be construed as having positive political outcomes for the government of the day.

In trying to compare public sector marketing in different countries, further difficulties arise because the responsibilities of governments vary according to what political system they are operating in. For example, in Australia and New Zealand there is fairly strong participation by governments in social marketing campaigns such as anti-smoking, sun protection and safe sex. In other countries, however, such campaigns are the province of privately funded foundations or charities.

Managerial challenges

Despite the use of marketing across government agencies at all levels, there remain a number of managerial challenges to its full implementation, some of which exist on a philosophical rather than practical level. Some critics have expressed opposition to the use of marketing in the public sector on the basis that it has failed society by the promotion of the individual at the expense of community values (Sturdivant 1981). Ryan (1991, p. 152), while an advocate for marketing's role in the public sector, acknowledges that, 'the whole idea of marketing in the sphere of government seems problematic'. The good news is that public sector managers are addressing these challenges as they tackle the objective of ensuring that the services they provide are delivered and consumed not only efficiently but, most importantly, effectively.

The key challenges associated with the introduction of marketing into the public sector can be summarised as follows.

Determining who the customer is

The public sector has traditionally not had customers. Rather, its objective has been to serve all citizens in a fair and equitable manner. The concept of customer or client can be traced to the beginnings of the management reform to which we referred earlier. The belief that importing these private sector reforms into the public sector would enhance service efficiency and effectiveness was based on serving the needs of a customer.

The concept of customer, though, is complex in the public sector environment. For instance, public servants often say that senior executives such as the Chief Executive and Minister are the only customers that need to be satisfied. On the other hand, the public servant's immediate manager expects staff to deliver efficient and effective services to the 'client' who wants to renew a boating licence, or who seeks information on access to a government program. This creates the dilemma of whether to serve the client, as the private sector model would predicate, or serve the needs of the senior executive — a no-win situation. In addition to this dilemma is the issue of clients' choice. Do target audiences of government programs, for example regulatory programs like anti-speeding, provide clients with any real choice when the program is consumed by them?

Overcoming organisation centredness

Traditionally, the public sector is organisationally centred and not customer centred. Before the reforms of the 1980s, government departments and organisations focused their activities upon the program (the product) on offer. Developing a program that suited the individual needs of a client group was not paramount in the pre-reform public servants' mind-set. The design of separate marketing mixes for separate target markets was rarely considered necessary, as it tended to be more expensive than simply implementing a generic 'one size fits all' program.

Marketing at this time was only ever seen as a one-way communication function — not as a two-way relationship involving ongoing interactions with the clients. Market research into client needs and wants was very rare. Personnel working in the public sector in marketing roles were typically employed to perform the role of communicator (Graham 1994). Such an organisational structure was referred to as 'organisationally centred'.

Fortunately, modern public sector management is changing. Today's public sector is increasingly using all the tools of marketing, albeit individually rather than in an integrated approach (Dann, Davidson & McMullan 2001). There is a much greater emphasis upon the client, with an equally strong reliance upon research before programs and services are designed and implemented. Increasingly, the function of marketing is being seen as more than just communication, and is resulting in services and programs becoming more effective in meeting the needs of client groups.

Attitudes towards marketing

There still exists, in many areas of the public sector, an unfavourable connotation towards the word marketing. As stated previously, marketing means many things to many people. In this regard, the public sector is no different; the term is used to describe anything from selling (and what does the public sector have to sell?) to a manipulative process that undermines the basic notion of public service in a democracy and that forces people (the public) to purchase programs they don't really want in the first place. In broad terms, it is fair to say that the public sector has had a sceptical attitude towards marketing's application. This is due to the long-held view that government service delivery is about delivering to all members of the community. The thought of segmenting target markets with the aim of more effectively delivering a service runs counter to this viewpoint. It is also due to the fact that past marketing campaigns have resulted in significant amounts of scarce resources — time and money — being spent on advertising campaigns with little objectivity (the campaign had a political agenda) and no ultimate good coming from the campaign in terms of objectives being set and met.

Marketing = communication?

Marketing is still often understood to be only about communication and not a set of integrated tools. Perceptions of marketing in the public sector are often misunderstood as being nothing more than a communication function, with a majority of marketing roles being focused purely on communication and having reference to other marketing mix elements (Graham 1994).

As public sector managers become better educated in the field of marketing, more are turning to the complete mix of marketing elements to determine the best possible strategy for improving service effectiveness. For public sector managers, the use of all marketing mix elements in an integrated fashion is not without problems. This is due to the difficulty of defining the product; the intangible nature of the product (for example law enforcement); the process of product development being interrupted by the political process — principally the minister's or government's right to determine policy; and the need to modify distribution and pricing strategies to suit the unique nature of the public sector. As mentioned previously, the communication function had a traditional role to play in the public sector environment and thus fits well within the culture of government. Examples where such an integrated approach has taken place include the National Drugs Offensive, the Department of Immigration's naturalisation campaign and VTAC's road saftey campaigns.

In addition to the above, other key challenges are worthy of comment. These include:

- the lack of marketing awareness within the public sector, including a lack of education/training of public servants in how marketing can be used to make service delivery more effective (Dann, Davidson & McMullan 2001)
- the fact that marketing is not being marketed within the public sector
- the fact that, owing to government planning cycles (principally election cycles), marketing in the public sector is operational, yet its strategic nature is its real strength.

The future for public sector marketing

Currently, the focus of debate about marketing's application to the public service is on how the marketing concept and the marketing function can be better integrated into government activities in order to make government services more effective. Marketing is increasingly being used within public sector organisations, but in many it remains misunderstood and underutilised.

To help public sector executives to overcome some of the barriers to the implementation of the marketing orientation, and to assist organisations in becoming more marketing focused, the following seven-step framework is suggested.

- *Step 1.* Senior public sector management needs to be educated to understand and appreciate the concepts of the marketing function and the marketing department.
- *Step 2.* Senior management needs to understand the role of the marketing department and the role the marketing manager.
- *Step 3.* The senior manager (CEO) for the department, division or business unit should be responsible for the total marketing function, with assistance from the marketing manager, in the newly created position of board member who coordinates the marketing function of the organisation.
- *Step 4.* The marketing department should be relatively small and not responsible for *all* marketing activities. Rather, all staff, irrespective of department, division, branch or discipline, should be responsible for different aspects of the marketing function.
- *Step 5.* Senior management needs to become marketing-aware through structured training.
- *Step 6.* The traditional hierarchical structure needs to be supplemented by a more flexible, organic, service-driven structure.
- *Step 7.* To facilitate the coordinating role performed by the senior manager (or marketing manager), there is a strong need to communicate to middle management and frontline staff the virtues and key elements of a customer-oriented organisational structure through structured training.

Summary

LO1: Understand what is meant by the term 'public sector marketing' and the scope of its application.

- Public sector marketing applies to the adoption of a marketing orientation and explicit use of marketing tools in the environment of government-owned organisations. These organisations include:
  - public service departments
  - statutory bodies
  - government-owned corporations.
- Public sector marketing campaigns often have a social marketing component and include:
  - health promotion
  - information dissemination
  - road safety, and so on.

LO2: Determine that marketing has an important role to play in the public sector, particularly in improving the effectiveness of service delivery.

Marketing's benefits for the public sector include:
- information dissemination through advertising and other forms of mass communication
- costs savings and improved efficiency
- development of customised services giving people what they actually need and want, thereby improving effectiveness.

LO3: Identify the reasons why marketing is increasingly being used within the public sector.

The expansion of marketing in the public sector has been in response to:
- the reform agenda
- increased competition for many government agencies
- corporatisation and privatisation of former government monopolies
- public pressure for increased effectiveness
- public pressure for increased efficiency.

LO4: Identify the difficulties associated with the application of marketing in the public sector.

Marketing in the public sector is difficult to apply for four key reasons:
- The complex exchanges involved in government marketing often make it difficult to identify exactly who the customer is.
- Most public sector organisations have a strong organisation focus rather than customer focus.
- Negative attitudes towards marketing persist in the public sector.
- For many in the public sector, marketing is equivalent to communications.

LO5: Discuss the potential future for public sector marketing.

Marketing in the public sector is likely to expand because of:
- increased pressure for efficiency and effectiveness
- increased deregulation and competition
- improved education about marketing in higher levels of management
- better understanding of the benefits of marketing for the public sector.

key terms

Broadened domain of marketing: use of marketing in non-commercial areas (p. 483)

Complex exchanges: situations in which the exchange between provider and user is part of a complex relationship and does not involve simply handing over money for goods and services (p. 482)

Federation: a type of system of government based on a group of states that form an alliance under a common national government (p. 478)

Government departments: traditional public service departments under the control of a minister (p. 479)

Government-owned corporations: corporatised organisations, often former monopolies, in which the government is the major shareholder (for example, electricity authorities), (p. 479)

Public sector: a combination of government departments, government-owned corporations and statutory bodies (p. 479)

Public sector marketing: any marketing activity undertaken by government-owned or managed organisations (p. 479)

Simple economic exchanges: situations in which one person exchanges money for a product or service (p. 482)

Statutory authorities: organisations created by a government statute (for example, universities) (p. 479)

Unitary system: a system of government with a single national government (p. 478)

Westminster system: the system of government from Britain on which both the Australian and New Zealand systems are based (p. 478)

review questions

1. What are five services that are marketed through public sector organisations?
2. What aspects of the marketing exchange process do not always easily translate into public sector marketing transactions?
3. Account for the recent growth in public sector marketing in Australia and New Zealand.
4. What is meant by the term 'broadened domain of marketing'?
5. What are some of the issues involved with applying the price element of the marketing mix to public sector marketing?
6. How does the 'people' element influence the success of public sector marketing campaigns?

application questions

1. There are many critics of public sector marketing, who see the marketing of government services as a waste of public money. How would you convince these critics that marketing is a beneficial activity?
2. What are the main challenges that currently face public sector marketing? How can these be overcome?
3. Product definition in the public sector is often very difficult. How would you define the 'product' of the Health Department or the Transport Department?
4. What factors need to be taken into consideration in the pricing of government services as opposed to the pricing of private services?
5. Do public servants face greater problems as service providers than profit-oriented service staff? Justify your answer.

vignette questions

1. Read the Services Marketing in Action vignette on page 480.
    (a) How did QFleet measure customer satisfaction? What other methods could they have used?
    (b) Given the importance of QFleet's vehicles — a tangible element of service in its operations — how do you account for QFleet's customers' strong emphasis on intangibles when judging service quality?

2. Read the Services Marketing on the Web vignette on page 485.
   (a) From the consumer's point of view, how could the increased use of the Internet improve service delivery at Centrelink? What elements of Centrelink's services are best suited to provision online?
   (b) In your opinion, what types of barriers might Centrelink face in increasing its online, as opposed to traditional, delivery of services?
3. Read the International Issues vignette on page 488.
   (a) In your opinion, is it important for public sector marketing campaigns to be primarily information based and avoid any hint of political bias? Why?
   (b) What are the implications of developing politically biased, public-funded marketing campaigns?

 recommended readings

There is very little published in the field of public sector marketing. A literature search will rarely reveal more than a dozen articles, some of which are close to 20 years old. The majority of work done in this area is available only through conference proceedings and, in particular, through the Australian Marketing Institute's annual Government Marketing Conferences. There are two publications, however, which are currently available and address the key issues in public sector marketing. The following monograph is available online from www.ipaa.org.au under Queensland, Research Grant Results. It reports on a study funded by the Institute of Public Administration (Australia) on the understanding and use of marketing in the senior executive of the Queensland public service:

Dann, S. J., Davidson, C. & McMullan, A. J. 2001, 'The use and acceptance of marketing in the Queensland public sector', *Institute of Public Administration Australia*, November.

The following recent article discusses the problems of transposing the exchange model into the public sector. Based on Dutch research, the examples may not always be identical to those in Australia and New Zealand but the concepts are. It discusses in detail the nature of public sector exchange process, the participants and outcomes:

Buurma, H. 2001, 'Public policy marketing: marketing exchange in the public sector', *European Journal of Marketing*, vol. 35, no. 11/12, pp. 1287–300.

 references

Bagozzi, R. P. 1975, 'Marketing as exchange', *Journal of Marketing*, vol. 39, October, pp. 32–9.

Conn, P. & Ninham, E. 2001, 'Making the intangible, tangible: Centrelink, innovation and the balanced scorecard', *Innovation and Imagination at Work*, McGraw-Hill, Sydney pp. 132–51.

Dann, S. J. 1999, 'Public sector marketing: issues and trends', address to Australian Marketing Institute Government Marketing Conference, Gold Coast, July 27.

Dann, S. J., Davidson, C. & McMullan, A. J. 2001, 'The use and acceptance of marketing in the Queensland public sector', *Institute of Public Administration Australia*, November.

Graham, P. 1994, 'Marketing in the Australian public sector: classification of the use of marketing positions', PhD thesis, James Cook University.

Department of Families Queensland, accessed January 2002, www.families.qld.gov.au.

Jongen, H. 2000, 'Centrelink: the business and the brand', address to the Australian Marketing Institute Government Marketing Conference, Sydney, July 27–28.

Kotler, P. 1972, 'A generic concept of marketing', *Journal of Marketing*, vol. 36 , April, pp 46–54.

Kotler, P. & Levy, S. J. 1969, 'Broadening the concept of marketing', *Journal of Marketing*, vol. 33, January, pp. 10–15.

McMullan, A. 1996, 'Towards a marketing orientated public sector', MBA thesis, Griffith University.

Ryan, B. 1991, 'Circulation matters: towards a model of public sector marketing', in O'Fairchellaigh, C., Graham. P. & Warburton, J. (eds), *Service Delivery and Public Sector Marketing*, MacMillan, Sydney.

Sedgwick, S. T. 1994, 'Evaluation of management reforms in the Australian public service', *Australian Journal of Public Administration*, vol. 53, no. 3, September.

Sturdivant, F. D. 1981, 'Marketing, the state, and legitimacy', in Mokwa, M. P. & Permut, S. E. (eds), *Government Marketing: Theory and Practice*, Praeger, New York.

Walsh, K. 1994, 'Marketing and public sector management', *European Journal of Marketing*, vol. 28, no. 3, pp. 63–71.

Case studies

Case study cross-references

The following case studies describe real or typical organisations, and identify services marketing challenges. The 18 cases are intended to provide you with the opportunity to apply your services marketing knowledge to the real world. The cross-references below indicate the chapters to which each case study most strongly relates. The chapters representing the major focus of each case appear in bold.

Number and name of case study	Chapter cross-references
1. AMD Business Services	**1**, **3**, 12
2. Being a patient: health care service quality	1, **2**, **4**, 13
3. Singapore Shield	**3**, 7, 9, 10, 12, 13
4. Citibank	1, **4**, **5**, **7**
5. Value measurement in practice	**6**
6. Party People: managing supply and demand	1, 2, 3, **8**
7. Management information principles	**9**
8. AMP 'time poor' marketing communications campaign	2, 7, 9, **10**, 14
9. Funding participation for people with an intellectual disability	3, **10**
10. Freedom from fear	7, **10**, 11, 12, **18**
11. The perfect holiday	8, 9, **11**
12. Is it worth the wait? Sizzler restaurants	6, 8, 10, 11, **12**
13. E-complaining: the world of online complaint sites	5, 7, **13**, 14
14. Driving online legal services at Minters	6, 8, 12, **14**
15. Rejuvenating a mature tourist destination	5, 7, 8, **15**, 18
16. Just Cuts	10, 11, **16**
17. Branding of sports stars	1, 10, **17**
18. The Perc Tucker Regional Gallery	2, 7, 10, 11, 12, **18**

AMD Business Services

By Anne-Marie Huartson Offer

A multi-skilled consulting team had achieved a high level of local awareness, inquiry and client satisfaction — growth was increasingly on the basis of referral. But it had not all been smooth sailing.

New potential

Over a breakfast of fresh fruit and juices, a newly expanded alliance of business consultants brainstormed the opportunities their pooled efforts promised. Anne-Marie Offer, the marketing consultant within the group, paused to reflect on the evolution of AMD Business Services. In two years, this division of a country accounting firm had expanded from an in-house, financial management advice service to a multi-disciplined team that spoke with confidence of transforming businesses across south-western Australia. The team had earned a solid reputation in the region, and recruitment of new clients was by referral.

At the discussion was the two-man team from Jojara, a team development business based in Margaret River. Jojara runs tailored programs that include workshop discussion, problem-solving exercises, games and physical challenges. Courses range from workshops at clients' premises to adventure challenges held in a choice of destinations. In combination with the existing finance, marketing and human resources consultants, the group felt that their joint efforts could deliver a whole-of-business approach to serving clients, including individual and workplace wellbeing.

As exciting as this development was, Anne-Marie was mindful of the performance of the current team in delivering services to budget. As part of an accounting firm that billed by six-minute units, the productivity of the division had been less than desired. Indeed, several client projects had overrun the budget — the hands-on approach to developing clients' businesses was exhausting. Anne-Marie listened to the group's ideas for new activities in client programs designed to overcome the time control problem by better motivating and supporting clients, allowing them to achieve change for themselves. She thought to herself: 'We give our clients so much now, and they can still fail to implement initiatives. If we do much more for them, we'll be the ones needing business advice!'.

AMD Business Services beginnings

AMD Business Services is the business consulting division of AMD Chartered Accountants, based in Bunbury, Western Australia. The largest accounting firm in WA outside of Perth, AMD has a team of around 40, delivering accounting, auditing, business and marketing planning, superannuation, taxation, company secretarial and IT systems support services. The City of Bunbury has a population of around 30 000 and is the commercial centre of the south-west region. A tapestry of industries feature in the region, including agriculture, mining and tourism. Population growth has been strong in recent years along the coastal strip from Bunbury to Dunsborough.

AMD Business Services was formed in October 1999, and by July 2001 had grown to a team of six. The division was initiated by Justin Bunter, a financial specialist with worldwide experience managing projects for the likes of AMP, the London Stock Exchange, British Rail and British Telecom. Justin had moved to the region with his young family for a better lifestyle and, like many other professionals relocating to the region, believed his skills and experience could benefit local businesses.

In May 2000, Anne-Marie Offer was appointed to the Business Services division. Having performed a variety of marketing management roles, she brought practical skills, media experience and new ideas to the firm. A new resident of the south-west region, Anne-Marie embraced the opportunity to apply her skills to a diverse range of projects. Together, Justin and Anne-Marie developed business and marketing planning methodologies to compete for clients against consultants based in Perth, and increasingly, in south-western Australia. The service offering now included marketing consulting, business planning, feasibility studies, financial management advice and business viability reports for third parties such as banks. Comprehensive business and marketing plans the core products, although many clients requested ongoing assistance after plan completion to partly outsource implementation and monitoring.

The alliance approach

People Management is a home-based business founded by Allan McGillivray, and also provides business planning. Allan is an excellent communicator and holds accreditation as a Registered Training Organisation. For business plans, Allan had always delivered essentially a human resources plan with sparse financial or marketing coverage, while AMD had found human resources issues in businesses a common barrier to the effectiveness of their plans. An alliance between AMD and Allan McGillivray was soon under discussion, and the first combined consulting work took place at the beginning of 2001. By August 2001, Allan McGillivray had taken office space at AMD, and the People Management logo was added to building signage. It was agreed that fees would be split between AMD and People Management, based on the number of hours on each project. Through the alliance, significant appeal was added to AMD proposals in the competitive business planning market.

The small business improvement program

A network of government sponsored Business Enterprise Centres (BECs) operates throughout Western Australia, supporting small businesses with information and assistance. Alison Lannin leads the Leschenault BEC in Bunbury, one of the most active centres state-wide. Alison is well known locally and has introduced the benefit of formal planning to many businesses.

BECs coordinate the Small Business Development Corporation's Small Business Improvement Program (SBIP). Under the SBIP, businesses receive government financial assistance to engage a private sector consultant for business or marketing planning. Coverage to 65 per cent of the consultant's fee up to $5000 is available for each service, with a total limit of $10000 per business. To qualify, business owners require fixed-price quotations from three consultants, and must submit these with their application and selection of the successful consultant. The BEC does not influence the choice of consultant. Should a business engage a consultant prior to funding approval, support will be denied. Each new service necessitates a fresh three-quote process, and there is no cost coverage toward primary research or plan implementation.

The SBIP had provided a beneficial boost to many businesses, and the AMD team ensured all eligible potential clients were aware of the program (to introduce the opportunity for partial fee reimbursement). AMD maintained a close relationship with Alison Lannin, as she was a trusted point of referral to businesses in finding a consultant.

A popular package

A majority of local business plans are under SBIP and, because of the three-quote requirement, consultants from Perth through to Albany compete for new clients. Competition had intensified between 1999 and 2001 in the area, due to an influx of professionals who believed consulting offered an appealing working lifestyle. Marketers, advertising and graphics firms, career senior managers, accountants and even franchised business coaches began to deliver SBIP services. Some of these new entrants used the SBIP as a selling tool to reduce risk and hesitation. Indeed, the AMD team began to screen all new quote requests carefully. Where the business requesting a quote did not seem to be genuinely evaluating a choice of consultants, the team usually declined to quote, as the time involved in meeting and preparing a tailored proposal was unlikely to be recovered if the business owner has pre-selected another consultant.

The price puzzle

As all SBIP plans must correspond to standard terms of reference, minimum guaranteed content appears very similar on paper. Competition thus became centred on added extras, relationship building and price. A predictable benchmark price was the point that maximised SBIP funding. With 65 per cent coverage up to $5000, the total price would be around $7690. The AMD team had sought the advice of Alison Lannin on this issue, as new entrants were discounting below this level to establish a client base. With the costs of a team effort to cover, delivering plans to the promoted standard within the benchmark price was difficult.

The AMD service quality standard was an in-depth, well-justified strategy that was either already implemented, or well on the way to being implemented by the time the final invoice was sent. Clients differed markedly, and the time needed to achieve these outcomes was often in excess of budget. The team had difficulty predicting the quality of information the client could provide, and their ability to participate effectively in planning and implementation. Without support at a hands-on level, many plans tended to end up 'in the third drawer', and a selling point of the AMD service was the delivery of tangible results and 'living plans'.

According to Alison, first-time buyers often select on the basis of price, assessing consultants' charge rates and the number of hours included in the proposal. Alison had quoted rates from as low as $55 per hour to $120 per hour in recent SBIP applications, but emphasised that the quantity of hours, the quality of work and the depth of content varied enormously. Despite these inconsistencies, Alison stated that virtually all SBIP clients reported high levels of satisfaction during a post-plan interview. As the average charge rate of the AMD team was $140, with some consultants billed at $170 per hour, AMD proposals did not disclose rates and hours. Instead, the proposals emphasised value for money based on team capabilities and a tailored planning process.

A typical planning process is described by the flowchart in figure 1A.

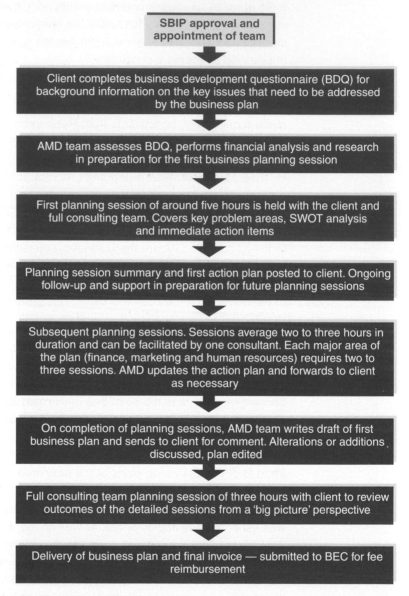

Figure 1A: Typical planning process

Proposal development

The AMD team revised and tested different planning proposals and cost structures over four months from January 2001 to try to make the process more controllable and profitable. Cost structures were based on competitive parity and on the time and resources included in each package. The many redrafts centred around three core package options:

1. *Basic business plan.* This covered the minimum requirements of the SBIP terms of reference, and provided a brief practical introduction to dedicated financial, marketing and human resource planning. This package was promoted as an 'introductory' process for those with small businesses or those with no previous exposure to formalised planning processes. The quoted fee averaged $8000, so that after SBIP reimbursement the net cost was $3000.

2. *Basic business plan plus options.* This package essentially offered the basic business plan plus the client's choice of options based on their perceived needs. For each additional financial management, marketing or human resources plan option, approximately $4000 was added to the $8000 base fee. The maximum SBIP reimbursement under this package was $5000.

3. *Comprehensive strategic business plan.* The premium package was promoted as an investment in achieving sustainable results. It provided in-depth strategy development with a sound foundation in research and analysis. Practical implementation assistance was included free of charge. In fact, this was the package the team felt they had been delivering all along under the guise of the SBIP. As an incentive for client commitment, the team capped the quoted total price for the comprehensive package at $17 500. After deducting SBIP reimbursement, the net cost was $12 500.

By March 2001, the team had gathered sufficient evidence from tracking conversion rates and post-quote feedback to indicate that most potential clients wanted all of the resources and outsourcing opportunities the comprehensive strategic business plan offered but, as first time buyers, they were prepared to pay only for the basic business plan. Unwilling to compromise on service quality, the team searched for fresh solutions to the time budget issue.

Back at the café

As the start time for the first six-minute unit of the day drew nearer, Anne-Marie asked the group for their thoughts on controlling time under the new 'transformational' package. The answers from the team reflected their technical interests.

Allan McGillivray said, 'The boys from Jojara could boost motivation and create a greater sense of the clients' responsibilities to achieve change. By guiding clients through a vision-setting process and acceptance of the hard work ahead, the clients may be less likely to avoid challenging decisions and more committed to plan execution'. He commented that this was sure to affect the bottom line through saving consulting time.

Justin Bunter commented on AMD Business Services team growth and the opportunity to 'leverage down' the research, the client follow-up and the implementation-support areas of the plans to more junior staff with lower charge rates. 'If we invest in training now, in the future we'll be able to reduce our plan completion costs', he said. The team agreed to trial the two initiatives and scheduled their next planning breakfast for the following month.

1. What are the core issues and challenges faced by the team in this case?
2. How effective do you think the two new initiatives will be? Can you offer any alternatives?
3. What suggestions would you give the team for balancing short- and long-term goals?
4. Can you suggest any other initiatives to achieve better time management? How would these be implemented?
5. What approach would you suggest for pricing the business plans?
6. From the perspective of a first-time client, describe how a business planning consultant may be selected.
7. How may a first-time client make a judgement about value in business planning services?
8. Does AMD view customer's perceptions of value in the same way as customers actually perceive value?

Being a patient: health care service quality

By Meredith Lawley and Tracey Dagger

On his GP's recommendation, Arthur Smith nervously rang the hospital clinic to make an appointment. The receptionist promptly scheduled him in for the following week at 1 p.m. She also informed him that the treatment would take about two hours and checked that he knew where the clinic was located.

After an apprehensive week thinking about his treatment, Arthur arrived at the hospital well before his appointment only to find that the multi-story car park was full. Eventually, he found a park in a back street quite a distance from the clinic. The street was marked with a 4-hour parking limit sign. He felt confident that he would make it back in time to move his car well before the four hours were up. After trying to locate the clinic for some time, without any success, Arthur was becoming increasingly nervous, anxious and stressed. Finally, at 1.05, having asked for directions twice, he located the clinic with a great sense of relief. Walking into the clinic, Arthur was beginning to feel anxious about the treatment that lay ahead.

Upon entering the clinic Arthur's first impression was of pleasant surroundings — the clinic was nicely furnished, the walls were a warm colour and the lighting was soft and relaxing. With a renewed sense of confidence, Arthur approached the reception desk and told the receptionist his name, his appointment time and the name of the doctor he was seeing. The receptionist greeted him warmly and told him, in a pleasant manner, to take a seat.

Selecting a seat at the back of the waiting room, Arthur looked around at the other patients and noticed that they were all busy reading or talking softly to each other. He also noticed a number of nurses appearing from around the corner of the reception room carrying trays with different medical equipment on them. Again his apprehension of what lay ahead increased and he felt too nervous to concentrate on trying to read any of the outdated magazines he could see on a bookshelf nearby.

For the next 30 minutes Arthur watched other patients coming and going. What struck him the most was that when many of the patients went to the reception desk, the receptionist appeared to know their names automatically. Moreover, when the doctors came out to greet their patients they often did so with a warm handshake or even a hug. Patients and doctors referred to each other by their first names.

Looking at his watch, Arthur noticed that almost 45 minutes had passed since his scheduled appointment time. Once again he began to feel apprehensive and frustrated at having to sit for so long. As the waiting room became increasingly crowded, Arthur admired the efficiency with which the office staff did their jobs. However, it was not long before he looked at his watch again and was annoyed to find that he had been waiting for one hour. As a professional with a busy work schedule, Arthur began to wonder if being a 'patient' meant that your time and life outside clinics and hospitals didn't matter to anyone but yourself.

Arthur could easily hear the conversations of the people around him. Some of them were talking about their treatments and the side effects of their treatments in great detail. The procedures and reactions they were describing sounded horrible, and Arthur once again became nervous and apprehensive. To calm himself Arthur looked around the clinic and began focusing on the other patients who were waiting in the clinic. Some were laughing, smiling and chatting between themselves but many looked weak, frail and very unwell. Arthur felt a sense of sombreness and sadness but more than anything he began to feel increasingly frightened about the future.

He looked at his watch — 2.15 p.m., he hoped that the doctor would come out soon and call his name. He decided that if he wasn't called by 2.30 p.m. he would go up to the receptionist and make sure that he hadn't somehow been forgotten. For the next 15 minutes he was apprehensive about having to ask the receptionist about his appointment time. After all, she looked busy and he didn't want to be seen as a complaining patient. Finally, at 2.30 he went nervously to the front desk and asked the receptionist how long before he would see the doctor. Using a slightly agitated tone, the receptionist informed him that the clinic and the doctors were very busy and that he would be called when it was his turn. Feeling a little chastened, he returned to his seat.

Arthur noticed that many other patients had also been waiting as long if not longer than he had. He wondered why they looked so relaxed and at ease when he could not stop his mind and pulse racing. As he looked around he noticed for the first time that some patients were listening to CDs, some were reading thick novels, others were doing crossword puzzles, some were having cups of tea and something to eat, and a couple were working on laptops or madly scribbling on pads of paper resting on briefcases. They did not seem worried or agitated about the long wait.

As the next 30 minutes passed Arthur felt angry and frustrated at being kept waiting for so long and anxious about the coming treatment. He wondered if he should approach the receptionist again — after all, perhaps there had been a simple mistake. However, after his last attempt at getting information about times he was reluctant to be chastised again. Arthur wondered why he bothered getting so stressed about being late for his appointment.

Finally at 3.10 p.m., two hours and 10 minutes after his scheduled appointment time, Arthur was greeted by the doctor with a handshake and ushered into his consulting rooms. With a mixture of relief and trepidation he took his seat across from the doctor. The doctor explained the treatment process thoroughly and showed a great deal of empathy and understanding of Arthur's concerns. The doctor listened carefully to Arthur's questions and answered them in great detail. Upon leaving the doctor's office, Arthur felt confident about his treatment and the skill of his doctor, even though he didn't really understand all the clinical elements of his treatment.

When the treatment process was underway Arthur was amazed at how well all the different medical centres (that is, x-ray, pathology, pharmacy and the clinic) worked together to provide his treatment. The nurse watching over his treatment took her time explaining what was happening in a friendly, happy and empathetic way. She told him to ask her any questions he might have and that if she couldn't answer them she would find someone who could. Watching the nurse work, he noticed the skilful and efficient manner she used to administer his treatment. He began to relax for the first time in the past week.

Arthur noticed that the treatment room itself was a buzz of activity, the nurses working together with a sense of comradeship. The nurse assigned to him checked on him constantly, spending time to make sure everything was all right and that he was comfortable and happy. In the cubicle next to him, Arthur could hear a patient talking with her nurse about complex clinical drugs and the correct way for them to be administered. The patient in the next cubicle seemed to know a lot about the clinical side of her treatment. In fact, Arthur overheard the patient telling the doctor and the nurse that she did not want a particular drug any more and wanted it to be substituted for a different drug. After much discussion and consultation between the nurse, patient and doctor they all agreed to stop using the current drug and begin using the alternative that the patient suggested. Arthur was amazed that the patient had the nerve to tell the doctor and nurse to change the drug; after all, it was the doctor who has the knowledge about what was best for the patient — not the patient. He could not believe that the patient in the next cubicle questioned her doctor and the prescribed treatment.

After hearing these conversations, Arthur, who believed that doctors are like gods, vowed to himself that he would always do exactly what the doctor suggested and would never question decisions he wasn't qualified to comment on anyway! When his treatment was finished, his nurse reminded him that if he had any questions or needs, to see one of the doctors over the weekend and that there was always someone at the clinic 24 hours a day, seven days a week. On his way out a number of nurses said goodbye to him. At reception, Arthur made a booking for his next treatment and asked about billing procedures. Although the receptionist was busy she took considerable time explaining the process to Arthur and together they discussed a time and day for his next appointment that fitted around his work commitments. Arriving at his car he noticed a parking ticket stuck to his windshield and cursed under his breath — if the clinic had been running on time he wouldn't have got the fine. When he got home he was tired and was unsure how he felt about his clinic visit.

Six months later Arthur now considers himself a regular at the clinic. He confidently finds a parking space and walks to the clinic. His appointment is at 7 a.m. (these days he tries to book the earliest appointment time available) and he happily chats to Emily at the reception desk. Before he sits down he asks if she can fill his mug with hot water so that he can make himself a cup of tea with the tea bags and sugar he carries in his clinic bag. Arthur sits in his usual chair with a cup of steaming tea in his hands and is happy that the waiting room is almost deserted. He takes out his portable CD player and pops in his favourite music. He also takes his laptop from his bag and begins to catch up on a report that needs to be completed by the end of the week. He feels relaxed and at ease. The time passes quickly and before he realises it he is being ushered into his doctor's consulting room and then into the treatment room. As he goes down the corridor he happily chats with the nurses and exchanges weekend stories. While the nurse is getting him prepared for treatment, he makes sure that she is administering the correct drugs and at the right flow rate. He reminds himself that as soon as the doctor drops in he will ask to be changed to that new drug he has read about that seems to be giving patients fewer side effects than the one he is currently on. After treatment he makes another appointment for the following week. Unfortunately, he has to make it an afternoon appointment, so he mentally makes a note to bring in some extra work to do in the waiting room. He heads home.

On the way home he thinks about the clinic visit and laughs to himself about the joke one of the nurses told him (he'll have to tell his children!). Immediately he begins to look forward to his next treatment. Although the drugs sometimes make him feel really unwell, he enjoys coming to the clinic and always feels positive when he leaves.

Questions

1. Discuss the importance of the five dimensions of service quality, as described by Parasuraman, Zeithaml and Berry (1985), in relation to the health care service described in the case. Which of the following service features did the health care consumer in the case use to judge or assess quality at his first visit to the clinic?
   • Reliability
   • Responsiveness
   • Assurance
   • Empathy
   • Tangibles
   What about his visit to the clinic six months later? Consider whether some features are more important than others.
2. How did the health care clinic perform on these dimensions? Identify when a dimension was successfully filled or not fulfilled by the clinic at each point (initial visit, six months later).
3. Bitner and Hubbert (1994) suggested that service quality comprises three dimensions: technical quality, environmental quality (servicescape) and interpersonal quality. What role do these dimensions play in the context of the scenario depicted in the case?
4. Why do you think that six months into his treatment Arthur felt so much more positive about going to the clinic, even though he had to wait when he arrived? Use service quality theories to help you answer this question.
5. Use service quality theories to make recommendations that would improve the service quality of the clinic.

References

Bitner, M. & Hubbert, A. 1994, 'Encounter satisfaction versus overall satisfaction versus quality', in Rust, R. & Oliver, R. (eds), *Service Quality: New Directions in Theory and Practice*, Sage Publications, Thousand Oaks, CA.

Parasuraman, A., Zeithaml, V. & Berry, L. 1985, 'A conceptual model of service quality and its implications for future research', *Journal of Marketing*, vol. 49, fall, pp. 41–50.

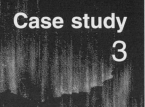

Case study 3

Singapore Shield[1]

By Janelle McPhail and Cynthia Chong

Introduction

> If I had my way, I would write the word 'INSURANCE' over the door of every cottage and upon the blotting book of every public man because I am convinced that for sacrifices which are inconceivably small, families can be secured against catastrophes which otherwise would smash them up forever. It is our duty to arrest the ghastly waste, not merely of human happiness but national health and strength which follows when, through the death of the breadwinner, the frail boat in which the fortunes of the family are embarked founders, and women and children are left to struggle helplessly on the dark waters of a friendless world.
>
> Sir Winston Churchill

The adage that insurance is sold and not bought rings as true today as it ever did. This case study offers an overview of the challenge confronting today's insurance providers. Insurance products and services are sold in an environment that is never static, where markets and consumer preferences are constantly changing and technology is always developing. Being part of the financial service industry, the insurance industry struggles with the other service providers for market share in a business environment characterised by intense competition and changing technology.

Current scenario

It is the monthly senior management meeting attended by the senior managers of the corporate group life and health insurance division at Singapore Shield. This core division has been able to retain its overall position as number one among local companies in Singapore for the past 10 years, as shown in table 3A. As a direct insurer, Singapore Shield has a number of local competitors, namely NIC and Asia Health, and one major foreign competitor, International Insurance, operating in the Singapore market. The need for group life and health insurance continues to grow, with some 431 new policies being issued by local companies in the year ended 31 December 2000. There is further movement in the market, with companies terminating their policies and then seeking a new provider.

---

[1]Singapore Shield is a fictitious name. However, the information in this case study is based on data from the Singapore insurance industry.

Table 3A	Group life and health insurance policies in force in Singapore insurance funds as at 31 December 2000		
Companies	No. of policies	No. of lives insured	Annual premiums ($000)
Local			
Singapore Shield	1 863	370 296	27 210
NIC	854	481 948	19 046
Asia Health	986	318 760	16 581
GE Life	1 081	74 315	9 583
SE Asia Protection	1 321	106 422	7 971
APA	518	40 872	6 968
Foreign			
International Insurance	8 121	418 710	69 917

Singapore Shield has been able to attract a significant proportion of new business (new policies), but in terms of annual premiums it is ranked second to Asia Health, as shown in table 3B.

Table 3B	Group life and health insurance — new policies issued in Singapore insurance funds during the year ended 31 December 2000		
Insurers	No. of new policies	No. of lives insured	Annual premiums ($000s)
Local			
Singapore Shield	261	92 361	5 865
Asia Health	352	202 526	8 384
APA	167	13 875	3 273
SE Asia Protection	659	28 921	3 017
GE Life	201	27 391	2 971
NIC	139	34 981	1 991
Foreign			
International Insurance	2 132	57 079	5 319

Given intense competition from existing traditional insurance providers and new non-traditional providers, and regulatory changes in the Singapore financial services environment, many insurance providers seem to have made price cutting their top priority at the expense of service quality, long-term relationships with customers and profitability. Comparisons of industry figures shown in table 3C also indicate that Singapore Shield has had more than its fair share of terminations and transfer of policies of 'old' customers.

Table 3C	Group life and health insurance — terminations and transfer of policies in Singapore insurance funds during the year ended 31 December 2000			
Insurers	No. of policies	No. of lives Insured	Amount of insured ($000)	Annual premiums ($000)
Local				
Singapore Shield	231	58 737	2 483 701	3 982
Asia Health	319	95 843	2 549 931	6 105
APA	43	12 077	383 472	1 583
SE Asia Protection	514	13 312	179 461	1 412
GE Life	142	23 419	1 106 470	2 102
NIC	99	39 619	494 561	159
Foreign				
International Insurance	1483	69 172	1 875 835	5 319

The general manager (GM) of Singapore Shield does not think that it has to be reduced to a price war. As a practising medical doctor as well, the GM believes there are people in the Singapore market who will not compromise on service quality and will pay a premium for reliable and comprehensive health and medical care. The key is not to focus on price alone but to build on established relationships with existing customers and to retain and increase the loyalty of such 'profitable' customers. Supporting this argument, evidence from several studies indicates that the costs of seeking out new customers were five to ten times greater than keeping existing customers (Bateson & Hoffman 1999). Further, the long-term value of customers, calculated from the predicted financial services needs across their lifetime, is a further reason to retain customers. Also, evidence from industry reports indicates a shift towards a customer focus in the insurance industry, further supporting the GM's argument. However, it was still going to be a difficult meeting.

The senior managers did not view customer defection as a major issue. Customers come and go. Associated with government-linked organisations in its infancy, the company operated in a semi-protected environment. Statutory boards, government-linked organisations and even multinational companies preferred doing business with Singapore Shield. Hence, the company had a competitive advantage during its early years of operation. The company is well positioned as the industry's leading group insurer, with good products and distribution channels and a well-known brand name. Occasional failures in service delivery were not viewed with great concern, since even the best companies make mistakes in the way they deliver services to their customers.

Quite simply, things can go wrong when least expected and it is impossible for any company to provide flawless service. The problem of losing customers had been on the agenda of several previous meetings, but price competition had always been declared the panacea in such discussions. The GM, however, was determined to provide evidence to the contrary; she was convinced that relationship management with corporate customers was the key to inspiring the business customer loyalty. The company has to put these customers first in terms of quality of service, customised design and packaging of products to suit the individual corporate client, and the value-added services required by them.

Industry perspective — Singapore financial services industry

The financial services industry is important to the economy of Singapore. In recent years the industry has grown at rates ahead of Singapore's overall growth and now accounts for 12 per cent of GDP (Monetary Authority of Singapore 2000). The importance of the industry and the economy as a whole is reflected in changes in the regulatory environment designed to ensure the industry can operate and compete in the global marketplace to meet the changing needs and behaviour of customers.

Insurance industry in Singapore

Singapore aims to be the premier insurance hub in Asia by the year 2003. It is already a major insurance centre, home to a rich mix of leading insurance providers, reinsurers, captives and brokers. In 1999, there were 59 direct life and general insurance providers, mostly foreign owned, serving a relatively small domestic market. In addition, there are 101 reinsurers and captive insurers, writing mainly regional offshore business. The 2000 total premiums of the insurance industry amounted to S$7.8 billion. For the life insurance industry, total premiums amounted to S$5.1 billion, while the general industry amounted to S$2.7 billion (Monetary Authority of Singapore 2000).

Global trends in the financial sectors

As an integral part of the financial services industry, the insurance sector is exposed to changing global trends that are blurring traditional demarcations among financial products. Distinctions between the banking, insurance, securities and fund management industries are diminishing. Traditional product-oriented approaches to sales in businesses like stockbroking, insurance, banking and fund management are giving way to new business models centred on the *customer*, both individual and corporate, and aimed at providing total risk solutions and financial planning services.

E-commerce

Technology, competition and cost imperatives are driving the emergence of alternative distribution channels. Traditional distribution models now face growing competition from infomediaries and other e-commerce intermediaries. The Internet permits a vastly increased richness of consumer choice and accelerating consumer knowledge and expectations. Internet-savvy consumers can purchase a widening range of financial services, anywhere and at any time, at the click of the mouse. Products offered are currently targeted at the individual consumer, but it will only be a question of time before products are targeted at the corporate consumer, too.

Deconstruction of the traditional value chain of financial services

There is a growing separation of the firm's back-office, front-office distribution and the way operations are structured. New non-traditional players are emerging, specialising within segments that they can deliver competitively and outsourcing others. Further, regulatory initiatives introduced in 1999 allow new players into the market and raise standards of disclosure. Government-linked organisations will have to compete on their own merits. Expenses are likely to be important drivers for the introduction of alternative and more efficient methods of distributing products to match international best practices and enable Singapore to be a leading centre for insurance services in the Asia-Pacific region. In summary, the opening of markets and blurring of borders in financial services will mean increased competition, new issues in risk management and new challenges for industry participants of insurers, distribution channels and customers. These are all issues that Singapore Shield must deal with if it is to retain its position in the Singapore insurance industry.

Company perspective — case background

Singapore Shield was established in the late 1960s as a local composite insurance company. Three major companies combined resources to become the principal shareholders of the organisation. In the early 1980s one of the larger companies sold its shares to the other major shareholder, which made Singapore Shield a subsidiary of the shareholders' banking operation. The Bank is considered a government-linked bank, appointments to the board of directors being controlled by the Singapore Finance Ministry. Recently, the Bank purchased all the shares from other shareholders and Singapore Shield became a wholly owned subsidiary of the Bank.

Singapore Shield

According to its mission statement, Singapore Shield aims to provide comprehensive, one-stop insurance solutions along with quality service, innovative products and total customer satisfaction. Singapore Shield's structural advantage is its composite nature, with the life, general, and group life and health components interlinked to provide a diverse range of products and services. In the group life and health division, the markets and business lines are very distinct and serve a clearly defined set of corporate clients rather than individual customers. Among its clients are organisations such as Singapore International Airways (SIA), the Mass Rapid Transfer Corporation (MRTC), Seagate Technology and the Singapore Armed Forces (SAF). Given the corporate nature of its customers, such clearly defined market segmentation gives the division the advantages of adopting a long-term focus in these relationships.

Who is the corporate customer?

Given that customers are group policyholders of large and small corporations, statutory boards, government-linked corporations, multinationals and service industries rather than individuals, it is pertinent to establish who the customers are. They are the senior management and/or human resource personnel who hold the decision-making power and buy group insurance products and services for their employees and personnel termed 'group members', as illustrated in figure 3A. Such corporate customers are known as third-party administrators (TPAs), as they also administer such group insurance policies for the group members within their organisation (Jones & Long 1989). TPAs are important because they can influence the group member's decision on whether to continue doing business with Singapore Shield or switch to another provider.

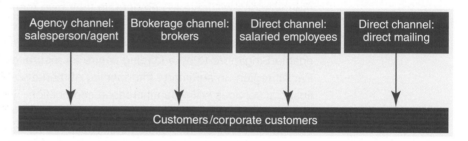

Figure 3A: The corporate customer

Who provides customer service?

Within Singapore Shield's organisation, customer service representatives employed in a specific department that serves as a centralised resource help corporate customers. They frequently have both an administrative and a customer service function in financial transactions that relate to policy values (such as policy loans and cash surrenders). They inform group members of developments that affect their policies and process policy changes (such as adding riders, changing beneficiaries and reinstating lapsed policies). Although these customer service representatives are often the most visible, they are not the only people responsible for providing service to Singapore Shield's corporate customers.

What are the distribution channels?

Brokers and agents are considered by group members and third-party administrators (corporate customers) as a link to Singapore Shield. Consequently, when customers need to contact Singapore Shield, they often do so through their broker or agent to help them obtain a policy loan, make coverage or beneficiary changes and other policy transactions. The various channels are illustrated in figure 3B.

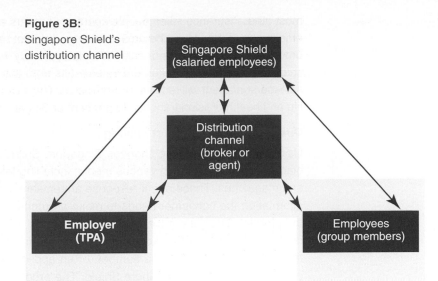

Figure 3B:
Singapore Shield's distribution channel

Singapore Shield (salaried employees)

Distribution channel (broker or agent)

Employer (TPA)

Employees (group members)

Agency channel

An insurance salesperson/agent typically must enter into an agency relationship with at least one insurer. An agency relationship is a legal relationship by which one party, the salesperson/agent, is authorised to perform certain acts for another party, the principal/insurer (Jones & Long 1989). In the personal selling distribution system, the salesperson/agent is authorised by Singapore Shield to act on its behalf in distributing insurance products. The salesperson/agent's authority to act for Singapore Shield is spelled out in an agency contract. Singapore Shield generally grants a salesperson/agent the authority to act for the insurer in soliciting applications for insurance and collecting premiums. The agency contract also describes other aspects of the agreement, such as how the salesperson/agent will be compensated, each party's duties and responsibilities, and specific terms of employment. This channel transacts about 15 per cent of Singapore Shield's life and health business portfolio.

Brokerage channel

The brokerage distribution channel relies on the use of brokers to deliver the insurer's products. In a legal sense, the term *broker* refers to an individual who is not under contract to any insurer and who is acting as an agent of the client rather than the insurer (Jones & Long 1989). In the Singapore milieu, brokers are allowed to transact insurance products and services of more than one insurance provider. Their obligation is to maintain strong relationships with their clients, to understand the clients' businesses and to add value to the clients rather than to the insurer. Use of the brokerage channel by insurers thus varies widely. Some organisations actively seek brokerage business, as is the case with Singapore Shield. In fact, brokers transact 50 per cent of Singapore Shield's group life and health business. Other insurance organisations accept but do not encourage such business, and other channels provide a larger portion of their business acquisition.

Direct channel — salaried employee

The sales distribution channel relies on Singapore Shield's employees to sell and service insurance products. These employees are paid a salary and, typically, also receive bonuses and commissions based on their job performance. By contrast, most other insurance sales people/agents or brokers are not considered employees of the insurance organisation and do not receive a salary. In selling group insurance products, a salaried employee may work either alone or with a salesperson/agent or broker. If a sale results from this collaboration, the salesperson/agent will receive a commission. The salaried employees of the group life and health division transact 30 per cent of Singapore Shield's group business.

Direct response — direct mailing

Using the direct response channel, Singapore Shield promotes its products by placing advertisements in various media, including television, radio, newspaper and magazines. These direct response advertisements generally contain all the information the consumer needs to make a purchase decision and to apply for the product. Thus, the advertisement will include either instruction for the consumer to contact Singapore Shield for more information, for example through a toll-free telephone number, or an application for the consumer to complete and mail to Singapore Shield. The products sold through direct response are therefore fairly straightforward and easy to understand, as the sales do not involve face-to-face discussion and explanation. Only 5 per cent of total business is transacted through this channel.

What are the principles of group insurance?

The benefits offered by group insurance schemes include life insurance, health and medical insurance, and retirement plans. Such a scheme forms part of the benefit plan with which an employer (or TPA) provides its employees (group members) in addition to their salary package. In a group insurance plan the contract insures a number of persons under a single insurance contract called a *master group insurance contract*. In order to form a valid group insurance contract, the employer (TPA) and the insurer must each agree to the contract's terms, must both have contractual capacity, must exchange legally adequate consideration (a signed contract) and must form the contract for a lawful purpose (Jones & Long 1989).

The employer (TPA) is also responsible for making all premium payments to Singapore Shield, although the policy may require that the group members contribute some or all of the premium amount. If the insured group members are not required to contribute any part of the premium for the coverage, then the group insurance plan is a non-contributory plan. If the group members must contribute some of the premium in order to be covered under the group insurance policy, then the plan is a contributory plan. A contributory plan covering employees typically requires the covered employees to pay their contribution through payroll deduction.

Group insurance underwriting and requirements

Payment of premium is not the only consideration. The goal of group underwriting is to determine whether a group of people presents an average risk and whether the group's loss of experience will be predictable and acceptable to Singapore Shield. When evaluating a group, the underwriter seeks to prevent anti-selection and to ensure that the administrative costs involved in providing the insurance are as low as possible. The underwriter will then assign the group a risk classification and determine the appropriate premium rates to charge for the group insurance.

Risk characteristics include the reason for the group's existence, the size of the group, the flow of new members into the group, the stability of the group, the required percentage of eligible group members who must participate in the plan, and how benefit levels will be determined (Jones & Long 1989).

All these characteristics are important in the assessment of risk and the determination of pricing. The insurer generally guarantees the group's premium rate for only a year, and may change the premium rate at the beginning of each policy year or on any premium due date.

Types of group life and health insurance

A group life and health insurance policy is a contract between the insurer and the group policyholder — that is, the employer or other official representative of the organisation/group (corporate customer) purchasing the group insurance coverage. The insured members of the organisation/group are not parties to this contract and are not given individual policies. Instead, each insured group member is given a certificate or benefit booklet that provides information about the group health and medical insurance coverage. Generally, there are two major types of group insurance — group life insurance and group health insurance. The group life insurance covers death and total and permanent disability due to any cause. The cover is renewable annually and the rates are based on the weighted average age of the group. Retirement plans are also established under the group life insurance plan, through which the employer sponsors the employee with group retirement benefits (Jones & Long 1989).

Corporate customer perspective

The GM decided that she needed to commission a market research study, which she hoped would provide direct evidence from customers to help her to build a strategy to retain more of the corporate customers who were terminating their policies.

The report provided by the research firm examined and summarised the data obtained from four in-depth interviews. The interviewees were drawn from the company's existing pool: two were customers who had previously defected to competitors, while two were from the company's existing customer databank. In order to ensure probity and ethical considerations, the interviewees were referred to as case A through to case D, as shown in table 3D. The interviewees were selected from the customer profile of a multinational organisation and a small to medium enterprise (SME). The selections were also drawn from the two main distribution channels of Singapore Shield — that is, from the broker's and the salaried employee's customer pool.

Table 3D	Selection criteria for corporate customers	
Customer profile channel type	Small to medium enterprise (smaller premium)	Multinational organisation (larger premium)
1. Broker	Case A — terminated	Case B — continuing
2. Salaried employee	Case C — continuing	Case D — terminated

Case A is an SME dealing in marine brokerage. Case B is a multinational merchant banker that deals with offshore investment, corporate financing and private banking. Case C is a foreign-owned SME dealing with steel building products. Case D is a multinational company that deals in manufacturing and technical training.

A series of prior categories were used to tabulate the main reasons for terminating or continuing the life and health insurance corporate business with Singapore Shield, as illustrated in table 3E.

| Table 3E | Summary of the findings for the termination and continuation cases |

Service termination and continuation categories	Case A: Terminated broker/SME	Case D: Terminated salaried employee/ multinational	Case B: Cont'd broker/ multinational	Case C: Cont'd salaried employee/ SME
Pricing				
High price		X		
Price increases		X		
Unfair pricing		X		
Reasonable price			X	X
Fair pricing			X	X
Inconvenience				
Waiting for service response (panel doctor not efficient)	X			
Location/restrictive panel of doctors and hospitals	X	X		
Administration inconvenience (paperwork, reams of forms)	X	X		
Core service failure and response to service failure				
Service mistake				
Negative response	X	X		
No response, follow up	X			
Service encounter failures				
Unresponsive (broker and/or staff)	X	X		
Uncaring (from broker and/or staff)	X	X		
Unknowledgeable/inflexible	X	X		
Others				
Competition		X		
Ethical problems, involuntary switching and Internet, e-commerce and other forms				
Creating a customer franchise				
Customised medical package			X	X
Experience refund			X	X
Priority medical cards			X	X
Internet, e-commerce and other forms				
Defection management				
Effective service recovery			X	X
Customer satisfaction strategy			X	X

The results from the interviews support the GM's view that price may not be the only factor for defection. Further evidence provides support that the trigger for a price comparison was unhappy incidents or experiences rather than price itself. Service encounter failures were often cited as the cause for policy termination. For continuing corporate customers, creating a customer franchise was cited as a reason for satisfaction and hence the propensity of corporate customers to stay with Singapore Shield. Further comments made by corporate customers interviewed are documented in table 3F.

Table 3F	Corporate customers' interviews comments	
Problem	Comments from customers with teminated life and health insurance policies	Comments from customers with continuing life and health insurance policies
Inconvenience • Location, restrictive panel of doctors • Administrative inconvenience	The staff were unhappy they had to visit the clinics in the panel list only, instead of being allowed to visit their own family doctor and having freedom of choice. Our employees' productivity level decreased as the recovery period was lengthened because they were not permitted to go to their own family doctor rather than Singapore Shield's panel of doctors. Singapore Shield requires staff to fill in a six page hospitalisation claim form. They should go paperless.	Previously, Singapore Shield insisted on their panel list of hospitals. Now they have revamped their policy to include Gleneagles Hospital and Mount Elizabeth. Our staff are now satisfied. Brokers are a big administrative help. They help to process the paperwork on our behalf. They keep all our administrative records. We at HR redirect the staff to the broker. We have outsourced the admin function and can now concentrate on other areas.
Pricing • High price • Price increase • Unfair pricing	We were very angry that after all these years we had to ask Singapore Shield for a decrease in premium and when they came back the reduction was substantial. We felt cheated. We did not ask International Insurance and yet they gave us a 20 per cent price reduction.	Singapore Shield has a rebate system. We have stayed with Singapore Shield for the past two years, as upon renewal there are more savings to be gained. So we have continued our renewals with them and we are happy with the terms.
Core service failure & response to service failure • Service mistake • Negative response • No response	The insurance program was in place for a number of years and we saw no reason to change. Two years ago our company improved its bottom line, so we wanted better employee benefits for our staff at the various levels. We contacted the brokers for information and a further quote, but they did not come back to us for a while. Eventually they informed us it was too early to discuss it. We were not happy. The brokers delayed until our group insurance policy had nearly expired. We asked for an extension and the bill came from Singapore Shield for a quarter term, not one month. We exchanged emails until Singapore Shield agreed, but we were too angry already and took our business to another insurer.	We are generally very happy with the staff servicing us. When there was a claim problem, the staff followed up to process the claim pretty well and on time. So far, we have had no unhappy encounters.

(continued)

Table 3F *(continued)*

Problem	Comments from customers with teminated life and health insurance policies	Comments from customers with continuing life and health insurance policies
Service encounter failures • Unresponsive • Uncaring • Unknowledgeable	We waited for the broker to come back with a quote for better terms, but they took their time. Why should we place our business with the broker who cared more for business volume rather than existing business? They probably earn more from new customers.	Over the years coverage has been reviewed and on top of the normal benefits Singapore Shield have given us better terms (i.e. 30 days to 60 days for hospitalisation claims). When we ask for an improvement in medical panels they responded with additional panels.
Other • Competition • Ethical problems • Involuntary switching • Internet, e-commerce	We had to go to International Insurance, as our headquarters wanted to rationalise their global structure. We thought it was a global instruction from HQ to use Singapore Shield. Hence, all these years we stuck with Singapore Shield and did not negotiate for better terms. We did not receive anything from them — not even a credit note for good experience. Since we are not computer literate, we will not try to secure the group package deal through the Internet. In fact, given the need to negotiate on the package and price, we would prefer a face-to-face interaction rather than negotiating over the Net!	Singapore Shield has one of the best rates in town. They are well established in the market. We do not mind going the route of technology if Singapore Shield has the capability to provide services via the Internet.

Further internal issues

Pricing

Singapore Shield typically establishes prices (group insurance premium rates) on a case-by-case basis, depending on how important the corporate customer is. Singapore Shield generally guarantees the group pricing for only a year, and may change the pricing at the beginning of each policy year. Significant corporate customers are retained through lower prices and/or price maintenance. Therefore, when threatened with possible competition, Singapore Shield resorts to a price reduction as the main option.

Service quality measurement

While competitors routinely measured customer satisfaction and service quality, Singapore Shield had been lax in that area. Although the number of compliments and complaints received were regularly tracked and analysed, these figures were not matched against the percentage of customers leaving the company altogether. When a TPA of an organisation decided against renewing their contract upon renewal, no exit interview was held to ascertain the true cause of departure. The distribution channel of Singapore Shield would attribute the outcome to better rates offered by competing providers.

Compensation

Brokers, salespeople/agents and salaried employees receive a commission and/or bonus earnings for acquiring new corporate accounts. The focus of sales, the management budget and expenditure is on finding new corporate policyholders. In short, the rewards to the distribution channels that brought in a new corporate customer far surpassed the rewards of renewing an existing organisation's account. Thus, less consideration is given by both staff and the distribution channel members to service recovery and ensuring satisfaction of existing customers.

So what now?

At the management meeting, the managing director was disturbed by the data presented and commented that the future survival of Singapore Shield was indeed an issue. The other senior management team mirrored his reaction. All present looked towards the GM for further comments on the future direction of the group life and health division. The GM, who had anticipated this reaction, outlined several strategic options revolving around implementing a defensive strategy culture for client relationships with the main emphasis on minimising customer defection, maximising customer retention and instituting an effective retention strategy. Before long the GM was tasked to spearhead the service changes and to appoint team leaders for the various areas.

When the meeting ended, it was already long past seven in the evening. As she made her way to her office, the GM heaved a sigh of relief that the meeting had created the desired outcome, but she knew that implementing and realising the planned changes would be an even bigger challenge.

Questions

1. Why do existing corporate customers choose to remain loyal to Singapore Shield? Which aspects of the service are most important to these corporate customers?
2. Why should Singapore Shield concentrate on building customer relationships? What benefits are there for the company?
3. How have the brokers and agents influenced the business relationship between the corporate client and Singapore Shield? What implications are there for Singapore Shield?
4. What roles do the employee group members play in influencing the policy renewal process? Consider the interaction that employees could have with all three parties in the network.
5. As the general manager, you are required in the next month to develop an effective retention strategy to reduce the number of policies being terminated. Outline the main elements of this plan and provide justification.

References

Bateson, J. & Hoffman, K. D. 1999, *Managing Services Marketing,* 4th edn, The Dryden Press, USA.

Jones, H. E. & Long, D. L. 1989, *Principles of Insurance: Life, Health and Annuities,* LOMA, USA.

Monetary Authority of Singapore 2000, accessed 30 November 2001, 'Data room', www.mas.gov.sg.

Citibank

By Mark Gabbott

Citibank is part of the much larger Citigroup, and its goal is to be the premier international finance company for the twenty-first century. To achieve this ambitious target, the Citibank management team had to implement quality initiatives that satisfied its customers quickly and flawlessly at every Citibank around the world. In banking, service is a critical component of competitive advantage and, when assessing Citibank's business, it had to viewed on an organisation-wide basis rather than piecemeal; that is, business unit by business unit.

Citibank discovered through customer satisfaction surveys, both by phone and by mail, that its customers were not happy. Through its customer data collection activities, it was clear that Citibank was carrying dissatisfied customers and that, if it were not for the difficulty of moving accounts to other banks, Citibank was likely to see large defections in future. The research indicated that the dominant views were:

- that the bank was too difficult to do business with
- that every process seemed to be constructed for the bank's convenience rather than the customer's
- that the bank 'didn't fix my problems' — that is, the organisation seemed to have very little control over what it did, and even where problems were identified it couldn't upset the system
- that their systems were not state of the art.

This reflected a widely held belief that customers were actually comparing their service experiences between different industry sectors. In reality, they weren't competing, in service terms, with other banks but with all other retail outlets, fast-food restaurants, airline travel systems and utility companies. The clear message was that they were 'too slow and complicated'. The responses from customers were clearly worrying, and Citibank had to work out how to achieve its stated goal when its customers were feeling so negative about the business.

One approach was to look in more detail at the reasons for customer satisfaction; to try to determine what customer expectations were in the wider marketplace, and then map those onto Citibank's service delivery system. But it appeared that overall attitudes to the bank were positive. What it was picking up was a crisis in its processes rather than dissatisfaction with its staff. As a consequence, the bank was looking for a mechanism to alter processes, improve satisfaction and empower its employees to take responsibility for service quality.

The bank investigated a number of organisation-wide programs but eventually chose Six Sigma as the basis for its approach. Six Sigma refers to the distribution of defect rates, with three sigma equalling 66 807 defects per million and six sigma equalling 3.4 defects per million. By talking to customers and understanding the precise detail of what parts of the service were most closely associated with perceptions of quality, Citibank developed a set of 'critical to quality' characteristics or attributes. These included speed of transactions, turnaround times, processing speed and accuracy. The next step was to map its processes by describing functions involved in each step of a particular function, including loan applications, account transfers, investment instructions, mortgages, new accounts and so on. Having established a full audit of bank systems, it developed two sets of process maps for each, described as 'as is' and 'should be'. The bank then used the customer-determined CTQ attributes to assess each one. A large number of individual counter service staff were involved in the exercise, since they were the face-to-face deliverers of service and knew intimately both the real processes involved and the types of problems and delays the customers were experiencing. By using employee-based research, they assessed the accuracy of the maps and then went about stripping out non-value-adding steps. At each stage, Citibank involved both the service providers and customer groups.

Through its customer research activity and the Six Sigma method, the bank redeveloped processes to make them more customer focused. For instance, when customers wanted to transfer funds from one account to another, they would call their bank and then fax, phone or mail a verified request to have the transfer processed. Because this system inside the bank was so complex, customers were complaining mainly about the length of time it took to complete the transfer. They discovered that because the request wasn't top priority, it would often get held up on the receiving desk before it was put through the system to process. They also discovered that once there was a delay, a key cost in the process was the call back to the customer to check whether they still wanted the transfer to take place and to confirm any changes. The bank managed to cut call-back incidents from 8000 calls to 1000 calls and eliminated call-back completely for over 73 per cent of their process requests. A similar approach was used when assessing the process for opening a bank account. This process revision was based upon reducing cycle time, reducing the handling of paperwork and eliminating data defects.

Having achieved success in using customer research to drive a redevelopment of its processes, and having tracked increased satisfaction and customer retention rates, the next task was to monitor the performance of the changes Citibank had made. This too was based upon the Six Sigma methodology. Having determined precisely the changes they had made to their systems and processes, Citibank embarked on a program of customer consultation to monitor performance over time and to continue to update the critical-to-quality drivers that were centrally embedded in the system. While the research it conducted early on highlighted some clear problems for the bank, it had been able to devise a response that directly addressed customer satisfaction and established an ongoing process for monitoring and reporting changing customer attitudes to its service. In hindsight, the application of a service-quality framework built around the interactions between customer and service provider had reshaped its business. It removed things that customers didn't value and improved things that customers thought important. In effect, it had used customer expectations to drive the re-engineering of customer experience in a virtuous circle that still continues today.

Derived from www.baldridgeplus.com and www.iqa.com.

Questions

1. Identify the key customer problems faced by Citibank.
2. What are the advantages for an organisation of Six Sigma as compared to SERVQUAL?
3. Identify the meaning of 'defects' in a service context.
4. How might Six Sigma methods be applied to education services?
5. Think of a simple service and try to map the processes involved in that service. Assess where the main problems might be in achieving customer satisfaction.

Value measurement in practice

By Jillian Sweeney

The City of Cockburn, in Western Australia, has one of the fastest growing populations in the state, increasing from 60 000 in 1996 to 74 000 in 2001. It is expected to reach 120 000 by 2015. The growth has created demands on local services and infrastructure. In addition, there are many urban and environmental issues that need to be addressed. These can be summarised as follows:

- urban redevelopment of established older residential areas
- market gardens are replaced by urban developments
- a string of environmentally sensitive wetland areas running north and south through the city, and needing to be protected from urban development
- old industrial areas becoming a visual and environmental blight on the landscape
- residents of new urban areas expecting a high level of community facilities and service provision.

How does a local government determine its priorities and the level of service delivery, given these often conflicting demands? How does a local authority allocate its limited resources to ensure that current and future needs are met?

Cockburn City Council is constrained in terms of its resources. Therefore, the council sought to identify practical solutions to council expenditure. This was done by allocating realistic costs or cost reductions to improving or reducing the level of service provided; and by asking ratepayers (business and residential) to trade off the services to achieve their desired mix of services. It was important for ratepayers to understand that increasing the level of service and introducing new services could add significantly to their rates, unless they accepted a reduction in other services. The study therefore ensured that the respondents considered the value of the services offered rather than providing a 'wish list' of demands that could not all be met.

The following extract from the questionnaire asks ratepayers to undertake the trade-off without increasing the level of rates.

Imagine you could change the service described by the shaded boxes, but only as long as the service you end up with costs the same. So, if you want to improve in some areas, you must reduce the service in other areas to balance it up.

You don't have to make any changes but if you want to change the service either up or down from the shaded boxes, please make a circle in the box you want to move to. On each line you need to circle one box, even if there is no change (circle the shaded one). Remember, you must balance the total of the plus dollars with the total of the minus dollars to equal $0. INTERVIEWER: MAKE SURE TOTAL IMPROVEMENTS ADD TO WITHIN $3 OF TOTAL SAVINGS

(continued)

Figure 5A: Sample question from questionnaire (14 of the potential 26 options listed)

Options available

Service	Options available			
1. Response to vandalism and graffiti	Limited response — problems addressed within 48 hours $0		24-hour-a-day response to vandalism and graffiti +$5	Proactive service, including prevention +$10
2. Safety and security for people living and working in the area	Quite a lot of areas or situations where people might feel unsafe $0		A few areas or situations where people might feel unsafe +$10	Virtually no areas or situations where people might feel unsafe +$30
3. Footpaths	Poor condition, potentially dangerous -$10	Reasonable condition $0	Good, problems tackled promptly +$5	Excellent condition, ongoing maintenance prevents problems +$15
4. Appearance of local parks	Poor and uncared for -$30	Clean and tidy with no increase in landscaping $0	Well maintained, reticulated with some landscaping +$10	Well maintained, manicured, attractive landscaping +$40
5. Rubbish-tip passes	Central sites to which you take your own excess and pay as you go -$30	Each household receives 2 free tip passes per annum for excess rubbish -$15	Each household receives 6 free rubbish tip passes p.a. for excess rubbish $0	Each household receives 10 free tip passes p.a. for excess rubbish +$15
6. Bulk and green waste rubbish collection	No service provided -$10	One free annual collection plus one free green waste collection -$5	One free annual collection plus 3 free green waste collections $0	Two free annual collections plus 3 free green waste collections +$5
7. Roads	A less than satisfactory condition -$15	Good condition, problems tackled promptly $0		Excellent condition — ongoing maintenance prevents major problems +$15
8. Facilities at Coogee Beach	Basic toilets and showers, car park and grassed area and playground facilities -$5	Plus beach cleaning 3–4 times a year $0	Plus additional toilets and shower facilities +$5	Plus development of café/restaurant facilities +$30

Figure 5A: (*continued*)

Service	Options available			
9. Planning and building approvals	Slow service −$10	Mediocre service −$5	Good service +$0	Excellent service +$5
10. Information and consultation about council plans and activities	Little information available −$10	Information provided in response to a specific request −$5	Plus some proactive information and consultation $0	Extensive information provided to the community and extensive consultation +$10
11. Recreational programs	Limited traditional recreational programs i.e. active reserves for sport −$10	Wide range of traditional recreation programs including targeted programs for aged, youth, and specific events −$5	Plus specific projects aimed to enhance healthy living. Purpose-built facilities for BMX and skate-boarding building in progress $0	Plus high profile education program aimed at greater percentage of population engaging in healthy activities +$5
12. Community facilities	Two large community and leisure facilities (South Lakes and Spearwood) and fewer neighbourhood facilities −$5	Two large community and leisure facilities (South Lakes and Spearwood) and many smaller facilities in neighbourhoods $0	More large, quality community and leisure facilities as well as smaller community and recreation facilities at the neighbourhood level +$15	Lots of larger, quality community and leisure facilities and many smaller community and recreation facilities at the neighbourhood level +$30
13. Welfare support services	No services −$5	Range of support services for families, children, young people and the frail aged $0		Additional services for children and families aimed at supporting the family in the community including community education projects +$5
14. Environmental management	Seasonal program of midge reduction and mosquito monitoring susceptible areas −$55	Year-round program of midge and mosquito reduction in susceptible areas $0	Plus rehabilitation or improvement of bushland/wetland areas on a gradual, scheduled basis +$15	Plus rehabilitation or improvement of bushland/wetland areas on a high-priority basis +$40

Owing to the complexity of the data and the variety of service options, the data was modelled using an approach similar to neural networks. This identified the gaps between expectations and the current level of service provided, and identified priorities for the city council. Additionally, the process identified where savings could be made so that these improvements could proceed within an existing budget. Priorities for improvement were:

- safety and security — one of the key demands placed on local government by residents and ratepayers in recent years
- parks and footpaths — appearance and maintenance
- communication — informing ratepayers. In particular, there was concern that the city would lose its unique blend of rural and urban lifestyle and become a dormitory suburb, and that the council should communicate its direction and policy in this regard. Communication would thus help ratepayers feel proud and interested in the future growth of the city.

Ratepayers were prepared to reduce or sacrifice the following services to cater for the above improvements:

- reduce the number of bulk rubbish and green waste collections each year from four to two
- reduce the number of rubbish tip passes from six to two
- reduce the level of recreation programs to focus on programs that target the aged, the youth and special events
- halt the program of traffic calming devices.

While reducing the level of recreation programs would initially save money, the council realised that by reducing these services it would create problems in other areas, such as vandalism.

Improvements for the future

The research also identified service improvements for the city to consider in future budgets. These included:

- comprehensive facilities for youth at risk
- activities and programs for the aged, including a senior citizens' centre and aged day care
- extension of local library opening times from 4.5 days a week to six days a week.

Source: Adapted from Avard, R. & Munro, N. (City of Cockburn & Research Solutions) 2001, 'Optimising the service mix in local government', paper presented at the Market Research Society of Australia Conference, Perth, Western Australia, 22 August.

Questions

1. How did the City of Cockburn and the research team conceptualise value from the ratepayers point of view?
2. What were the key issues and constraints in offering value?
3. Describe how value was measured. Why is this approach necessarily different to approaches discussed in 'Measuring customer-perceived value' in chapter 6?

Party People: managing supply and demand

By Tracey Dagger

The service

Party People is an event and party hire company located on the Sunshine Coast in Queensland. The Sunshine Coast is one of the fastest growing regions in Queensland. The service provided by Party People involves two key elements: the equipment hired and the customer service provided.

The hire equipment includes a wide range of products, as illustrated in the list below. Party People can supply equipment for events of up to 1500 people. The equipment hired by Party People is good quality and is maintained in good condition. The company continually seeks product innovations and assesses market demand for new product lines. Party People also carries a range of disposable party items such as balloons, streamers and sparklers.

Party People product range

Marquees — various sizes

Chairs — various colours and styles

Tables — round, square, rectangle

Roasting spits

Barbeque equipment

Catering equipment including pie ovens, bain-maries, urns, chafing dishes

Mobile cold rooms

Conference equipment including electronic white boards, flip charts, OHPs, slide projectors, video screens, televisions, videos

Video cameras — various kinds

Public address systems

Sound equipment

Display panels

Helium gas and balloons

Crowd control

Eskies — various kinds

Lighting equipment

Disco equipment

Pool tables

Flooring

Staging and dance floors

Glassware

Cutlery and crockery

Serving accessories — jugs, vases, carafes, silver platters, punch dishes

Braziers and heaters

Wedding equipment

Jukeboxes

Linen

Disposable items — napkins, sparklers

Red carpet runners

Umbrellas

Party People offers free delivery as part of its service. However, customers often pick up their hire equipment from the Party People warehouse. All equipment is checked before it is sent out for hire. If possible, the company tests the product in the presence of the customer to demonstrate that it is in good working order and to discuss any technical instructions. Detailed instructions are also included with all products to assist the customer using the equipment. All equipment complies with safety regulations and is checked regularly, according to government guidelines.

While most hire equipment does not require additional service elements above those involved in hiring and delivering the equipment, some items require Party People to provide extra services and labour. For example, large functions require Party People not only to hire but also to erect marquees, staging, lighting, flooring and so on. Thus, the company does much more than simply hire equipment, and it strives to provide a consistently high level of customer service.

Competition

Although Party People has a number of competitors, it has the largest range of equipment available on the Sunshine Coast. Because the event and party hire industry is subject to seasonal and weekly variations in demand, competition is often most fierce during the slower demand periods. During this time, some competitors cut prices to increase sales.

Customers

The company's customer base is diverse. However, two target markets are readily identifiable: these are business-to-business customers and private consumers.

The business-to-business market may include restaurants, schools, resorts and hotels. These customers are generally repeat purchasers. These consumers have prior experience with the products and the services provided by Party People. They generally hire larger quantities of equipment than the private consumer market. Many of the events serviced by Party People are held annually or bi-annually, which aids in forecasting future demand and allocating capacity.

The private consumer market tends to hire equipment for parties, weddings and other private functions and events. Although these consumers are often repeat hirers, the amount of repeat hiring and volume of equipment hired is substantially less than in the business-to-business market. Often, private consumers are one-off purchasers. This market often purchases disposables and extra party items from Party People. Demand in the private market is difficult to predict, except on major public holidays such as Christmas and New Year. These consumers often organise hire equipment at the last minute.

Marketing

Party People's main marketing tool is the Yellow Pages. The company uses different Yellow Pages advertising to target its different markets. Advertisements can be found under the party hire section of the Yellow Pages and in other relevant sections such as catering equipment, video camera hire, audiovisual equipment hire, balloon displays, and so on. Party People uses more Yellow Pages advertising than its competitors.

Staffing and equipment hire

As a small business, Party People operates with a core staff of five employees. All employees are multiskilled and are required to perform a number of varied tasks as part of their job description. When additional staff members are required, Party People uses a labour hire company. Large events often require additional labour, which presents a challenge to Party People.

Location and hours of operation

The Party People warehouse and showroom are located in an industrial estate. This is typical for this type of organisation, owing to the large warehouse space required for storing the equipment. The company has easy access to the main motorways running along the Sunshine Coast, and is located in the business centre of the Sunshine Coast — Maroochydore.

The company opens Monday to Friday 8 a.m. to 4 p.m. and Saturday from 9 a.m. to 12 noon. These hours reflect the retail showroom's opening hours. Deliveries of hire equipment may be conducted outside these hours if requested by the customer or if demand is particularly heavy. Because of the nature of the events and party hire-industry, events are often set up and pulled down on the weekends.

The challenges facing Party People

The demand for hire equipment varies tremendously. Party People operates a computerised hire system that aids in forecasting future demand and allocating capacity. The demand for hire equipment has a number of distinct cycles. These include seasonal variations and weekly variations. These variations and the challenges facing Party People are outlined below.

October to January

From about October until the end of January, demand for all products is extremely high, often exceeding available stock levels (despite the large amount of stock carried by the company). This is primarily due to private and business-to-business Christmas and New Year functions. During this period, Party People is stretched to its limit in terms of time, labour, equipment and facilities. Hire equipment is often being turned around on the same day. Equipment is picked up from one location, returned to the warehouse for cleaning and then delivered to another location. The management of time is a major issue during these months, because of the quantity of equipment being hired.

Labour also presents a problem. The office/showroom is exceptionally busy, making it difficult for one person to manage. The level of product knowledge needed and the amount of time it takes to train office and sales staff mean that it is not feasible to hire someone just for the October–January period. The same problem exists in the delivery side of the business. During these times, Party People needs extra employees with extensive product knowledge, but the company could not offer year-long employment.

Although Party People has a large amount of stock available throughout the year, it often has a problem supplying the demand for some stock items during October–January. Owing to the high capital cost of many items, such as marquees, purchasing additional equipment for use only in this period is not considered a viable option. Yet the organisation does not like having to turn customers away.

Party People's facilities are at capacity during this time. Space becomes a major problem because of the high turnaround of equipment and the need for most items to be cleaned mechanically or by hand. This also affects labour capacity. At this time of year, more delivery vehicles are necessary than at other times during the year. As there is not enough demand during the other months of the year to support the addition of another vehicle, this presents a problem during the busy Christmas and New Year period.

February to March

During February and March, demand drops considerably. There is an oversupply of capacity. The need for labour decreases and employees hours are reduced. Demand is slow and office staff have periods when there are no customers to serve. During this period, there is excess capacity and under-utilisation of equipment. Similarly, the facilities of Party People are not being used to their full capacity. During this period, overheads must be kept low to cope with the slump in demand.

April to September

April through to September is characterised by constant demand. The need for labour is relatively constant. Staff are kept consistently busy but not at the maximum capacity rates that characterise the Christmas and New Year periods. Equipment is still under-utilised with excess capacity. Utilisation of facilities is adequate.

Cycles within cycles

In addition to these seasonal cycles, Party People experiences a number of other fluctuations in demand. First, most equipment hire is over the weekends. Second, demand increases over long weekends and short public holidays. Interestingly, school holidays often have a negative impact on demand. Thus, managing demand, forecasting demand and dealing with capacity constraints can be a seasonal, weekly and even daily challenge.

Questions

1. Use services marketing theory to classify this service.
2. How do the characteristics of services marketing affect this service business?
3. What are the major challenges relating to managing capacity and demand for Party People?
4. What strategies would you recommend for managing capacity and demand in this business?
5. How would you manage the seasonal fluctuations evident in the case study? How would you manage the demand fluctuations that occur within the overriding seasonal fluctuations?

Management information principles

By Chad Perry

Alex Brown, the marketing manager for a law firm, had just come out of a meeting with the partners of her firm. She was convinced that what this medium-sized law firm needed was to practise real customer relationship marketing (CRM). One of the partners said he had heard that a firm called Management Information Principles (MIP) was able to provide customised CRM. He had given Alex the following newspaper article. Alex started reading the article but was concerned that perhaps this was really only a sophisticated databank after all. Could it really offer this law firm the benefits of true customer relationship management? Alex pondered the article. Would the law partners learn customer relationship marketing skills from MIP? She was convinced that she needed to ask the rep. from MIP a number of questions. She started jotting them down . . .

CRM neglects integration test

by Jennifer Foreshew

About 70 per cent of customer relationship management (CRM) vendors are overlooking the need for data integration, resulting in a high rate of system failure, an industry expert has warned.

Management Information Principles (MIP) managing director Steve Hitchman said the real cost of introducing CRM was about five times more than the price of the software.

'A lot of CRM vendors out there promote a campaign management system or call centre system, and that's only 20 per cent of the actual delivery of CRM,' he said.

'The biggest issue is data integration. About 70 per cent of CRM vendors don't appreciate they need to do it, but they're waking up to it now.'

MIP, founded in the UK in 1992 and established locally in 1994, builds corporate data warehouses and analyses the data to extract business management information.

Mr Hitchman said research had shown that a company spending $2 million on a CRM system would have to spend another $800 000 a year for customisation.

'It's a constant cost because a business is always changing, so the CRM system needs updating. And a data warehouse is needed, there is no way around that.

'But there are many companies out there with CRM systems that don't work.'

He said a study of 200 CRM projects in the US last year found 30 per cent delivered no return to the business.

(continued)

About 90 per cent of companies were not aware of the need to use data warehouses to house customer-centric information, he said.

MIP is working on CRM-related projects with AAPT, RAMS Home Loans and Vodafone.

Mr Hitchman said predictive modelling, which allowed a company to undertake detailed profiling of a customer, would be crucial to CRM.

'You need to be able to predict what your client is going to do and how you can interact with them properly,' he said.

MIP is working on predictive modelling with major telcos, banks, and finance and utility companies.

The company plans to commercialise its intellectual property, with the first offering on telecommunications churn and loyalty due to roll out in about eight months.

The Australian, 12 June 2001

Questions

1. Discuss why integration is a key component of successful CRM.
2. According to the article, facilities such as campaign management systems account for only 20 per cent of CRM. What does the remaining 80 per cent of CRM delivery constitute?
3. Prepare a list of questions that you would like to ask the rep. from MIP if you were Alex Brown.
4. In what ways can organisations benefit from implementing a CRM project? What benefits are there to customers?
5. What are some of the factors that should be considered before implementing a costly CRM system?

AMP 'time poor' marketing communications campaign

By Kathy Gard and Genevieve Mezger, AMP

Company background

AMP is a leading international financial services business, providing wealth management products and services to around eight million customers worldwide. Principal activities include retirement savings, funds management, life and general insurance, financial planning and banking services. AMP operates in 20 markets around the world, with a significant and efficient domestic presence in its three home markets of Australia, New Zealand and the UK. AMP has around 13 000 employees and planners worldwide, manages assets of more than A$265 billion and has a market capitalisation of approximately A$16 billion.

AMP is in the business of wealth creation and management. It aims to be the customers' window to the financial world, providing easy access to financial solutions that will build and protect their wealth. The AMP vision is to offer customers excellent advice and innovative financial solutions appropriate for every stage of their lives. Financial solutions are created both from AMP's products and from outside AMP. AMP's corporate strategy of driving growth and value for shareholders is by:

- *focusing* on providing wealth creation and protection solutions and services
- *building* and maintaining leading market positions in the corporate and retail sectors in its home markets
- *expanding* regionally from its home markets by leveraging expertise in selected new markets
- *aggressively* building a pre-eminent global asset management business through expansion into North America, Europe and Japan.
  For more information on AMP, visit their website at www.ampgroup.com.

Time poor campaign

In 2000, AMP developed a campaign targeting a fast-growing segment, Generation X: those born between 1966 and 1981, and who make up 8.3 per cent of the population (McCrindle in Matterson 2001). This segment was identified as a priority for AMP, and an integrated marketing campaign was developed.

To ensure the appropriate wealth creation and management proposition was delivered, the campaign was conducted across many business units, including financial services and banking, with multiple access points: financial planner, phone, Internet and interactive centres.

Why Generation X?

AMP has a major strategic initiative — to become a customer relationship specialist. AMP recognises the need to build long-term relationships with current and potential customers, and has identified an opportunity to do so with the Generation X (or Gen X) segment; right now they're young, so they have the opportunity to grow with AMP.

While Gen X appeals to AMP, AMP also has the potential to appeal to Gen X. Their broad product, service and distribution options make AMP a relevant financial services provider. From entry level to competitive banking products to more complex investment and asset-protection solutions, AMP has much to offer. Combine this range of services with the different marketing channel access points (by phone, online or through personalised expert advice), and the AMP–Gen X relationship is set to flourish.

Generation X and AMP

Research indicates that members of Gen X are thinking about wealth creation, debt management and their future, but because they're busy and focused on their day-to-day life, lack of time is a factor in preventing them doing anything about it. This is a generation that wants to invest and needs the various channels of information and distribution that AMP has to offer — Internet, phone and face to face.

AMP started by commissioning some market research into this segment. The findings showed that while their degree of financial awareness varies, they appreciate the importance of planning and working toward financial security. This makes them an attractive target market. Some of Gen X's beliefs about their finances are that:
- money is serious
- security brings freedom
- property brings security
- debt management is important
- financial planning is important
- managing finances is too hard and time consuming.

This was the first time AMP had targeted the Gen X segment — a group that makes up 21 per cent of their existing customer base and represents 7.6 per cent of the total Australian Gen X population. One of the challenges was to gain significant market share.

Brand relevance versus awareness

Brand awareness is not a problem for AMP, but relevance can be, depending on the audience. Research conducted in mid-2001 showed that Gen X knew that AMP had a wide range of products and services, but did not know exactly what they were — though they suspected that they were long-term products for older people. AMP didn't rank in their consideration set, however the AMP brand was known to Gen X as 'trusted and credible'.

AMP wanted members of Gen X to think about their financial needs and consider AMP as a financial solutions provider who is relevant to them. AMP had to prove its relevance by demonstrating that it has products and services for people like them. The challenge for AMP was to position itself as being relevant to Gen X and being able to provide solutions to the financial aspirations of this important segment. The 'time poor' campaign was the first step in that process. This campaign acknowledges that Gen X members have busy lives, which often leaves them short of time to organise their finances.

Getting the business ready for Gen X

It is imperative for AMP to achieve cohesion within the organisation between the different AMP business units, and to deliver, from the customer's perspective, 'one AMP'. How does this happen? For this campaign, all parts of the business were engaged early in the process — a cross-functional, cross-divisional team was gathered to fast-track the development of the campaign and ensure business readiness.

The team looked at the end-to-end customer experience to establish how AMP could live up to a brand promise of being 'easy to deal with'. This is what would really make the difference. Once AMP caught the attention of Gen X, how would it treat them once they walked in the door? A number of initiatives were implemented that would enhance and improve this customer experience. The initiatives included processes that make it easier for customers to deal with AMP, such as automatically registering new customers for online assistance and creating ease of transfer between the banking call centre and other customer call centres within AMP.

Financial solutions for Gen X

The approach was to look at things from the Gen X point of view: consider their financial priorities and position AMP as an organisation that understands and can provide solutions in an integrated way.

Table 8A		AMP's solutions to Gen X priorities		
	Saving	**Investing**	**Advice**	**Access /easy to deal with**
Priority	Many members of Gen X want to stop wasting money on rent and buy a property.	Members of Gen X want to invest in property.	Financial planners should be independent and should help people identify the right investments, not focus on a particular brand.	Some members of Gen X want to deal with an organisation that offers them the option to receive information and purchase products over the telephone, Internet and face to face.
Solution	AMP Banking's eASYSAVER account can help them save for a deposit faster and get their loan with AMP online or via the telephone.	AMP Henderson offers a range of indirect property investments, including property managed funds, listed property trusts and property securities.	AMP's financial planners will be promoted as having access to the best financial products in the market — not just AMP's.	AMP will be promoted as offering Gen X different marketing channels for different sub-segments — the option to deal with AMP over the telephone, via www.amp.com.au and via AMP financial planners.

The challenges for AMP in building an appropriate campaign were:

- to create a brand with 'relevance', not just awareness
- to combine a 'retailing' message with a brand message
- to position AMP as different — 'not my parents' company'
- to choose a theme that can gain the attention of a media savvy generation
- to achieve 'cut-through' with a limited budget
- to communicate multiple messages about access, products and services on offer
- to ensure business readiness for effectively servicing this target market.

The campaign: 'Time poor? It's no excuse for not growing rich.'

The challenge was to communicate a valuable consumer insight and reinforce existing brand values across several business divisions. AMP Financial Services Marketing teams worked with Sydney agency Leo Burnett, who developed the creative platform and produced the majority of the campaign components. 'Time poor? It's no excuse for not growing rich' was the theme for the campaign. This theme was chosen because the campaign needed a common message that would appeal to a variety of sub-segments. When tested through focus groups prior to launch, the theme resonated well with Gen X. Being 'time poor' is a common problem, whether you're 25 and single or 35 with a partner and two kids. This was combined with the use of non-traditional financial-services advertising and direct-marketing mediums to 'cut through'.

The campaign was launched in September 2001, and comprised 20 different components, including a launch for staff to build enthusiasm.

Time poor?
It's no excuse for not growing rich.

To see how AMP can help you grow rich through managed funds, banking products and financial planning, see your adviser or financial planner, or contact us today for a free 'Wheel of Wealth'.

1800 800 883
amp.com.au/timepoor

≡AMP

For the first time, AMP advertised in cinemas. AMP and Channel 10's *The Secret Life of Us* also ran a competition, with the winner receiving $100 000 in an AMP eASYSAVER account. Advertisements and advertorials appeared in magazines not typically associated with AMP, including *Marie Claire*, *Men's Health*, *Wheels*, *Ralph*, *Who*, *She*, *Australian Gourmet Traveller* and *Mother and Baby*. An interactive direct mail pack was sent to subscriber lists of some of these magazines.

Special landing pages were also developed for the AMP website, with Gen X appeal in design and content. AMP had also launched their new interactive centres in locations such as the Queen Street Mall in Brisbane, and these had a strong visual and service appeal to Gen X customers.

Figure 8A: Advertising campaign — grass execution

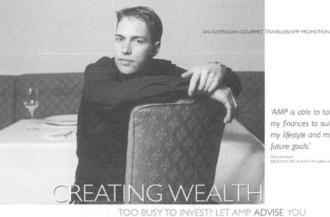

Figure 8B: Advertising campaign — advertorial

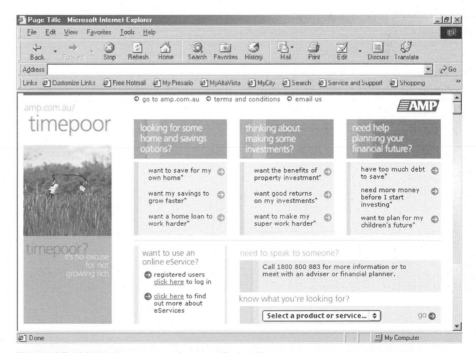

Figure 8C: X Website — campaign specific landing page

Results

By December 2001, there were some good early indicators from web visits and research that AMP had succeeded in appealing to Gen X in both tone and message. As this is the first stage in a long process of becoming relevant to this group, AMP can take what it has learned from this campaign and use it to improve future communications and business practices that will benefit future AMP customers.

References

McCrindle, M. cited in Matterson, H. 2001, 'X marks the spot in study of super', *Weekend Australian*, 7 April, p. 34.

Mackay, H. 1997, *Generations*, Pan Macmillan, Sydney.

Questions

1. What are the key considerations for AMP delivering multiple messages and maintaining existing brand values?
2. Define the key business drivers AMP used in developing an appropriate campaign to target the Generation X market.
3. List three reasons why Generation X is a difficult segment to target.
4. If you were a marketing manager for AMP, what strategies would you implement to encourage Gen X-ers to engage in positive word of mouth and referral?

Funding participation for people with an intellectual disability

By Paul Bradshaw, Chief Executive Officer, Q-RAPID

Introduction

The Queensland Recreation and Sport Association for People with an Intellectual Disability Inc. (Q-RAPID) was formed in 1984 because of concerns that while the needs of people with intellectual disabilities were being addressed in the areas of health, education, housing and employment, the provision of services in the areas of recreation and sport was low. In line with the Disability Services Act, Q-RAPID believes that people with an intellectual disability have a right to access sport, recreation and leisure opportunities others in the community take for granted.

Q-RAPID is now recognised as the leading provider of sport and recreation programs for people with an intellectual disability in Queensland. The association is linked to a national association, with other state- and territory-based members working at various levels.

Q-RAPID works at two levels:

1. *With the community.* The association assists state sporting organisations and other community groups to develop appropriate programs for people with an intellectual disability.
2. *With individuals.* Q-RAPID offers a wide range of programs directly to people with an intellectual disability to enable them to participate in sport and recreational activities within the community. Q-RAPID also assists people to ensure they have the skills, confidence, friends and support to access community-based sport and recreation.

Structure and management

Q-RAPID is a professionally managed incorporated association owned by members and strategically directed by a board of directors.

Operating under the Incorporations Act, Q-RAPID is also registered as a Deductible Gift Recipient and Charity by the Australian Taxation Office.

Q-RAPID delivers its services via a group of paid professionals and volunteer staff. The association's philosophy is to refer to all workers as staff (whether paid or unpaid). Approximately 86 per cent of Q-RAPID's current staff are unpaid.

The current board of directors consists of:

- high-profile business leaders
- experienced industry professionals
- specialist representatives (legal, accounting, etc.)
- parents.

The ideal number of directors is 10, with one of these positions being filled by the chief executive officer as the non-voting Secretary. Positions are filled at the annual general meeting, as per the *Associations Incorporations Act 1981*. However, the board may appoint individuals to fill vacancies as required.

Services

Q-RAPID programs provide opportunities for people with an intellectual disability to have fun in a safe environment, develop friendships, visit new areas and try new activities. These programs are comprehensive for all ages and include the following examples:

- day and weekend trips
- holidays
- art, cooking and fitness courses
- teenage camps
- sport development programs

- adult high-support weekend programs
- school holiday programs
- individualised recreation support services
- RAPID sports
- elite athlete support.

In a typical week, Q-RAPID provides services for more than 240 people and utilises 78 staff to deliver the programs. This number is increasing as programs are implemented in regional centres.

Teen camps and holiday programs are run during school holidays, and four high-support weekends involving 15 clients are conducted each year. These high-support weekends give participants a rare opportunity to enjoy sport and leisure pursuits. The high level of staff support required has meant limited opportunities to access this style of program. Additionally, the individuals accessing the high-support camps may not find other Q-RAPID services appropriate for their needs.

In addition to the direct services provided, Q-RAPID receives many calls for information related to people with a disability. Q-RAPID can often use its networks to refer clients to organisations that may be able to assist. On average, Q-RAPID receives approximately 1000 such approaches each year. It is expected that this number will increase as Q-RAPID's profile grows in regional areas of Queensland.

Q-RAPID increased its service delivery capabilities by approximately 600 per cent between 1995 and 2000.

Special events

In addition to the ongoing programs, Q-RAPID conducts the following special events:
1. RAPID Niteclub (to mark Disability Access Week)
2. Sport and recreation festival (to celebrate International Day for People with a Disability)
3. Christmas party
4. Staff/volunteer v. members sports day
5. Corporate golf day
6. Thiess/Q-RAPID fundraising dinner.

Competition

Competition needs to be considered from two points of view: service delivery and fundraising/sponsorship. Q-RAPID does not compete with any other agency delivering sport and recreation services. The association is about working with other groups to jointly meet the needs of people with an intellectual disability. Q-RAPID's growth is not about 'taking over' other suppliers, but about building networks and relationships to enhance and increase services. Consideration must be given to the type of industry Q-RAPID operates in and the need to minimise duplication.

Some small, regionally located groups provide recreation services. However, it is recognised that the demand for service provision is vastly greater than the current opportunities. Building the networks and creating solid partnerships with other service providers will be a real challenge in the coming years.

When seeking sponsorship and raising funds to deliver services, Q-RAPID is in competition with all other community groups, sporting bodies/teams and charities. The association must increase awareness within all sectors of the community, and continue to deliver quality professional services in order to attract and retain fundraising income.

Market profile

Individuals who access Q-RAPID's services are aged between eight and 80 and come from a range of backgrounds. Some are living independently, in supported accommodation or with their families; others are married and have children. Their financial situations vary widely — from individuals surviving on a pension to people in full-time employment.

Q-RAPID provides services for people with all ability levels, whether they are aiming for elite sport participation or simply the opportunity to have a picnic in the park. Some are very capable in most aspects of their lives; others require 24-hour-a-day support. Q-RAPID provides the service that meets each individual's needs and abilities.

Ability level and financial situation are the two most crucial issues when providing services for people with an intellectual disability. The wide variation in ability levels and financial resources among individuals requires a broad range of program types offered at various costs. This is one of the reasons why volunteers deliver 86 per cent of the association's services.

Q-RAPID has developed a network of more than 1000 agencies throughout Queensland. This network enables the association to reach a large number of clients in the most effective way. The agencies within the network assist with employment, accommodation, health and funding at a time when schools and other disability groups are continuing to reduce the services provided in sport, recreation and leisure.

Q-RAPID's services are currently focused on south-east Queensland. Over the next three years the focus will shift to major regional centres on the east coast of Queensland — specifically, Maryborough, Bundaberg, Rockhampton, Mackay, Townsville and Cairns. Once the major centres have been established, expansion will occur throughout each city's neighbouring towns.

Schools are a major area of growth for the association. This applies not just to 'special schools', since children with intellectual disabilities are mainstreamed into general primary and secondary educational facilities. However, Q-RAPID also needs to network with special schools, special education units, special education development units and private education facilities. Across these settings, pupils can range from eight to 18 years of age; in special circumstances, pupils may remain at school up to the age of 20.

Q-RAPID has relationships with approximately 23 state sporting organisations. These relationships help each sport to deliver programs for people with an intellectual disability. The programs, which also filter through to local clubs and groups, are owned by the individual sport and receive a variety of development assistance from Q-RAPID, ranging from program development to coach education courses. For example, the state basketball team is known not as the 'Q-RAPID Basketball Team', but as Queensland Basketball's state team for people with an intellectual disability.

The population of Queensland in 2002 was estimated at 3 690 000. Since approximately 2.4 per cent of the population have an intellectual disability, this indicates that 88 560 people with an intellectual disability live in Queensland. Table 9A shows the regional distribution of this population.

Table 9A	Projected population figures, 2002
Region	**Number of people with an intellectual disability**
South-east	56 324
Wide Bay–Burnett	6 642
Darling Downs	5 845
Far North	5 314
Townsville and surrounds	4 959
Rockhampton, Gladstone, Fitzroy	4 517
Mackay and surrounds	2 922
Central, North & South-west	2 037
TOTAL	**88 560**

Sources: Data from ABS 1996, *Census of Population and Housing*; *1993 and 1998, Survey of Disability, Ageing and Carers*; *Disability Services Qld Strategic Plan 2000*.

Funding

General revenue and expense

The grant income presented in figure 9A represents grants from the state government and other granting authorities, such as local councils, and philanthropic organisations specifically targeting individual projects or programs. For the 2001–2002 financial year, state government grants accounted for 47 per cent of the total revenue amount.

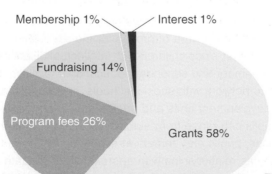

Membership 1% — Interest 1%
Fundraising 14%
Program fees 26%
Grants 58%

Figure 9A: 2001–2002 revenue budget

Fundraising income represents sponsorship and fundraising activities. The figure does not include contra donations, through which a company may provide equipment or services pro bono. For example, a printing company may print the quarterly newsletter at no cost to the association.

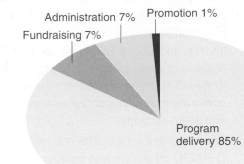

Figure 9B:
2001–2002 expense budget

The amount allocated to promotion is extremely low. However, most marketing activities are built into fundraising events (the Annual Thiess/Q-RAPID Fundraising Dinner, for example). Additionally, the association is able to secure contra arrangements to cover specific promotional or marketing initiatives.

State government grants

Q-RAPID currently receives funding through two Queensland Government departments:
1. Disability Services Queensland (recurrent)
2. Sport and Recreation Queensland (three-year agreement, 2002–2004).
Q-RAPID has to self-generate 53 per cent ($334 611 in 2001–2002) of its annual revenue to maintain service delivery. This amount will continue to grow as service delivery increases.

User pays

All Q-RAPID's services are delivered following the user-pays principle. Although programs are run under a user-pays system, the cost to the client is extremely low. A minimal surplus is built into service charges.

Thiess partnership

Q-RAPID and Thiess Pty Ltd have formed a cooperative, five-year (2001–2005) partnership committed to the growth and enhancement of Q-RAPID's vision to increase the accessibility to and involvement in community sport, recreation and leisure activities by people with an intellectual disability.

Benefits for Q-RAPID from this partnership are broad and encompass all business areas. They include:
- *Staff training opportunities.* Q-RAPID's staff are able to access all internal Thiess professional development activities at no cost. The 12-month training calendar is prepared by Thiess; Q-RAPID then nominates the courses and how many staff it wishes to send. The courses range from Stress Management to Project Management and Negotiation Skills.

- *Information technology assistance.* Thiess's information technology unit provides technical and servicing assistance to Q-RAPID. Every year Q-RAPID may be supplied with new computers along with ongoing advice on software and hardware issues, and some basic repair and maintenance assistance.

- *Fundraising opportunities.* Thiess staff and management create a number of small fundraising opportunities during the year. These initiatives range from internal auctions of tickets for upcoming sporting events (e.g. the Goodwill Games) to minor raffles. The major focus in the fundraising area is the annual Thiess/Q-RAPID Fundraising Dinner. This event attracts support from senior corporate executives of Queensland companies, and offers raffles, auctions and silent auctions.

- *Marketing assistance.* The marketing unit at Thiess provides advice to Q-RAPID on design and printing of promotional material and promotional strategies in general.

- *Voluntary service from Thiess staff.* Thiess staff volunteer their personal time to assist in delivering Q-RAPID programs. The partnership has established an annual target of 600 volunteer hours by Thiess staff.

- *Extensive business networking opportunities.* Q-RAPID can access a broad range of networks through Thiess's customer and supplier networks. By this means, Q-RAPID has been able to enhance the association's profile and increase the number of corporate sponsors supporting the association.

Corporate activities

Each year, Q-RAPID conducts a Golf Day and the Thiess/Q-RAPID Fundraising Dinner to raise funds and increase the awareness of Q-RAPID's role in the community and the corporate sector. Through events like these, and through the development of key networks, Q-RAPID has extended its corporate links to more than 60 companies. Currently, Q-RAPID is supported through financial contributions, in-kind donations and human resources.

Q-RAPID has a range of corporate relationships, from five-year partnerships with Thiess Pty Ltd to one-off, event-based contra support. The current focus is on event-by-event sponsorship (such as the Golf Day). There is now a need to develop and secure major association sponsorship over a multi-year period.

Fundraising

Q-RAPID conducts many low-level fundraising activities, ranging from mail-out donor appeals to minor raffles and specific fundraising drives. These activities are small in scope but give the broader community an opportunity to support the association.

Current promotional material

The following items are the basic tools used to promote the organisation through all stakeholder groups:
- quarterly newsletter (member)
- quarterly newsletter (staff)
- strategic plan (three-year plan)

- information flyer (annual)
- holiday brochure (annual)
- program guide (quarterly)
- video.

Almost all publications are developed and printed in-house by Q-RAPID's staff. The only publication to be printed professionally is the quarterly members' newsletter. This was a cost-based decision.

Ambassador

At the time of printing, a major ambassadorial role is being established for Loretta Harrop (Australian National Female Champion Triathlete 2002 and Goodwill Games Gold Medallist 2001). This long-term role will be used in a range of ways to benefit both Q-RAPID and Loretta.

Questions

1. How should Q-RAPID be positioned in the marketplace?
2. Develop recommendations for establishing initiatives with other organisations to make more efficient and effective use of marketing resources.
3. To what extent should the marketing strategy focus on the corporate versus the consumer base?
4. What initiatives might be taken to leverage smaller sponsors to a higher level of support?
5. How should the new Ambassador role be structured to obtain maximum benefits?

Freedom from fear

By Robert J. Donovan, Donna Paterson and Mark Francas

The Western Australian 'Freedom from Fear' campaign is a 10-year community education program complementing criminal justice and other community interventions. As far as we are aware, this campaign is a unique initiative, being the first non-punitive campaign focusing primarily on perpetrators of domestic violence, asking them to voluntarily seek help to change their violent ways. The logic is that if violent men voluntarily change their violent behaviour, this will not only reduce the incidence of violence, but also reduce the fear felt by their female partners (and children). Therefore, there will be substantial benefits to mental and physical health for all parties.

Campaign goals and strategy: the social marketing context

The overall goals of the campaign are the reduction of violence against women by male partners and, consequently, increased physical and mental health among victims. Consistent with Andreasens's (1995) definition of social marketing, the campaign aims to achieve the goal of reduced violence by voluntary behaviour change among male perpetrators, and the prevention of first and subsequent acts of violence among potential perpetrators.

Given the nature of the primary target audience, the first phase of the campaign essentially used a 'pull' strategy (Kotler et al. 1998). Mass media advertising (promotion) was used to create and maintain awareness among the primary target audience of a men's domestic violence helpline (product), and to encourage such men to call the helpline. The helpline was staffed by counsellors (people) who were specifically trained to deal with violent men and could assess the needs of callers and conduct lengthy telephone counselling (product) with members of the primary target audience. The primary aim of the helpline counsellors was to refer as many qualified callers as possible into no-fee, government-funded (price) counselling programs provided primarily by private sector organisations in 12 locations throughout the state (place). Although results vary, counselling programs have been found to be effective in reducing violence.

In the social marketing context, the following headings and descriptions indicate the four Ps of tangible product marketing and the fifth P — people for services marketing.

Product (and service)

The core product, that is, the end benefit being offered to violent men in relationships, was the opportunity to keep their relationship (family) intact by ending the violence toward their partner — and its impact on children. There were also 'actual' products and services:

- Government-subsidised counselling (batterer) programs, delivered by private sector providers, were the primary end product. Prior to the campaign launch, there were few such programs available and they were mostly attended by men under court order. Six new counselling programs for perpetrators and five new counselling programs for victims/children were funded by the state government. These new services were mostly located in rural centres.

- The Men's Domestic Violence Helpline was staffed by trained counsellors who offered counselling over the phone (many calls lasting 45–60 minutes) and who attempted to get violent callers into batterer programs (referrals). The helpline was a new product. Before this campaign, there was no helpline specifically for 'batterers' who voluntarily sought help, nor were counselling programs promoted. If the caller could not be encouraged to accept a referral — which required the caller to provide contact details for forwarding to the service provider — the telephone counsellors delivered counselling over the phone. Further aims were to engage the callers to the point where counsellors could obtain permission to send educational self-help materials (at no cost) to an address nominated by the caller, and to encourage callers to call again when in need if they were reluctant or not able to enrol in a counselling program.

- Self-help booklets provided tips on how to control violence and how to contact service providers. These were also provided on audiocassettes.

People

The telephone counsellors were men who had considerable training and experience in dealing with violent men. These counsellors were able to gain the trust of callers, listen to their stories, assess their level of denial and minimisation [of the seriousness of their actions], yet confront these men with aspects of their behaviour and then counsel and encourage them into programs. Anonymity was assured and there was no pressure on men to disclose their name. Helpline advertising was not 'branded' to the police department, as many campaigns are, and the content of the advertising was clearly nonpunitive. It communicated the simple, clear message that help was available to violent and potentially violent men. All of these factors served to assure anonymity and a non-threatening response to callers.

Promotion

The primary medium for reaching violent and potentially violent men was television advertising (especially during sporting programs), supported by radio advertising and posters. Extensive formative research was undertaken to ensure acceptance of the advertising messages by the target group without negatively affecting victims/children and relevant stakeholders. There was minor publicity of individual cases (willing to be photographed) who had undergone counselling.

Extensive public relations activities were undertaken with a number of relevant stakeholders, especially various women's groups, counselling professionals, police and other government departments. This involved repeated visits to these organisations to update them on campaign developments.

A number of publications were prepared for professionals, employers, victims and the primary target audience. Several of these were combined into campaign information packs for distribution to worksites (promotion channel) with the assistance of a number of trade unions. The campaign information packs were distributed by mail. Many worksites now offer various health and other counselling services to their workforce.

The main aim in phase one was to distribute posters advertising the helpline and to alert relevant worksite professionals (usually the occupational health and safety officer or human resource manager) about the campaign. The aim of this was to sensitise them to the phase two objective of including domestic violence counselling programs in the worksite. The campaign's advertising and publications avoided threats of imprisonment and other legal sanctions. Instead, focused on arousing feelings of guilt and remorse (already felt by the primary target audience) by emphasising the effects of domestic violence on children.

Price

Although domestic violence occurs across all income levels, investigations and service-provided experience suggested that fees for courses and materials could serve as a barrier (or be rationalised as such) for many members of the primary target audience. Hence, all materials and most counselling programs were to be provided at no cost to participants who were referred through the helpline. This pricing strategy was established to ensure that victims of low-income perpetrators would not be disadvantaged by their partner's limited income. Because there are legal implications for disclosing violence, as well as potential shame and embarrassment, the helpline assured anonymity, and counsellors were trained to deal with these issues and feelings. This need for anonymity guided the strategy of the helpline as the first point of contact for these men, with mass media advertising creating awareness and motivating contact.

Place

Service providers were located throughout the metropolitan area and in six regional areas throughout the state. Access to counselling programs was therefore limited in rural and remote areas. Programs were scheduled to allow employed males access in non-working hours. It is acknowledged that access to programs (but not to telephone counselling) was geographically limited outside major population centres. Later phases of the campaign will adopt distribution strategies designed to provide greater access to violence counselling service providers. The telephone counselling and self-help booklets were especially useful for those not able to access a Counselling Program. The helpline was staffed by counsellors during the night to provide maximum access.

Source: Donovan, Paterson & Francas 1999, 2000

Questions

1. What market research would you recommend for evaluating the Freedom from Fear campaign?
2. Why was the market segment of male perpetrators of violence chosen? How appropriate do you believe this segmentation to be and why?

3. Discuss the communications mix employed in this campaign. Are there any additional methods that could have been used?
4. What features of the people element of the marketing mix contributed to the success of the campaign?
5. Evaluate the consistency and effectiveness of the overall marketing mix of the campaign.

References

Andreasen, A. R. 1995, *Marketing Social Change: Changing Behaviour to Promote Health, Social Development and the Environment*, Jossey-Bass, San Francisco.

Donovan, R. J., Paterson, D. & Francas, M. 1999, 'Targeting male perpetrators of intimate partner violence — Western Australia's "Freedom from Fear" campaign', *Social Marketing Quarterly*, vol. 5, no. 3, pp. 127–44.

Donovan, R. J., Paterson, D. & Francas, M. 2000, 'Formative research for mass media based campaigns: Western Australia's "Freedom from Fear" campaign targeting male perpetrators of intimate partner violence', *Health Promotion Journal of Australia*, vol. 10, no. 2, pp. 78–83.

Kotler, P., Armstrong, G., Brown, L. & Adam, S. 1998, *Marketing*, fourth edn, Prentice Hall, Sydney.

The perfect holiday

By Tony Ward

Samantha, Betina and Prudence (Sam, Bet and Pru) were three months away from finishing uni. They had worked very hard over the previous three years, as all of them wanted to do their best but also had to work part-time to finance their studies. While hanging out at the beach one Sunday afternoon, they decided that they should reward their hard-earned efforts with a holiday to Singapore immediately after final exams. And so they started to plan their perfect holiday.

The first action they decided on was to talk to several travel agents in order to get an idea of what was being offered in the way of prices and general assistance. None of them had been overseas before and they had little idea of how to go about planning such a holiday. They decided, therefore, to visit three travel agents.

John was having a quiet day. He had no new customers and just some routine bookings — a typical Monday. Suddenly, in came three girls looking for a holiday in Singapore. While they were obviously very excited about their trip, he immediately sensed apprehension, so he asked them what they had done so far. They told him about their experiences with two previous agents they had just visited.

The first had been quite specific about what tours were on offer, but was vague about prices and left the three of them feeling uncomfortable. The second travel agent was also very informative but kept trying to push them to add on extras, and stay in the most expensive hotels. Thus, in coming to the third agent they were a bit despondent.

So John provided much information and lists of prices, plus advice on how to get passports and the best way of exchanging Australian dollars into Singapore dollars. He also recommended they consider upgrading to a better class of hotel, as that would provide a better location and safety. This approach was just what they wanted: someone who was prepared to provide basic assistance and spend extra time explaining what the product included and excluded. John took time to listen to their needs and concerns and to nurture a relationship with the three of them. So, after this initial selection process, they unanimously decided to book through John.

There were a number of tour operators they could go through providing many options, which John narrowed down to those shown in figure 11A.

Initially, Sam, Bet and Pru were confused, and even despondent. It was all so complicated and it seemed there was no end to the extras. However, John took them through it all and provided advice on how much they should budget for meals (breakfast was included) and other minor items. They went home to study the brochures and figures. Even though they had gained much information, they were still slightly confused.

	Basic cost (**) (7 nights in 3-star hotel)	Extra nights (per person)	Add. flight to Brisbane	Upgrade to 4-star hotel (7 nights)	Taxes	Insur.*	Booking fees
Tour operator A	$726	$65	$410	$356	$58	$125	$20
Tour operator B	$808***	$35	$278	$125	$56	$85	Nil
Tour operator C	$695	$75	$365	$256	$76	$107	$20

Note: All of the above prices apply only if pre-booked.

* — Recommended

** — Including airport transfers, breakfast and cocktails on arrival; a high-season charge of 15% applied at certain times

*** — After $100 discount for booking 10 weeks in advance.

Figure 11A: Tour options and prices

They decided to list a number of questions that they had to answer in order to help make their decision:

1. How long did they want to stay in Singapore — seven or ten days?
2. Did they want to pay extra for a four-star hotel (extra safety, bigger room, nicer location, etc.)?
3. Would it be worth taking the coach down to Brisbane ($50 with student discount) instead of flying?
4. Could they avoid the high-season time by delaying their holiday by two weeks?

They decided they wanted to stay for 10 days in Singapore; they would like the four-star hotel; they could delay two weeks; and would take the coach to Brisbane. These decisions clarified the situation, as they could now calculate the cost of the three options. They made their decision and eventually had a great holiday to celebrate graduating.

Questions

1. Identify the goals that Sam, Bet and Pru identified, and how this helped them make a purchase decision.
2. Identify and briefly describe the fundamental pricing factors encountered in this purchase process.
3. What market force factors did Sam, Bet and Pru encounter?
4. What pricing strategies are evident in this case?
5. What customer service techniques did John use to assist Sam, Bet and Pru?

Is it worth the wait?
Sizzler restaurants

By Carol Osborne, Zoe Zhao and Farrah Yusof

On a cold Friday night in August, Carol and Zoe joined the queue at the entrance of the Sizzler restaurant at Riverton, Perth. This is a scene that is repeated at any one of the 29 Sizzler restaurants across Australia on Friday, Saturday and Sunday nights. With 40-odd other patrons, the two friends faced a wait of at least 30 minutes or, at the worst, an hour.

Week after week, customers queue for the privilege of buying a meal that will cost them on average $18 per person, but why do they do it? Australians aren't as renowned for queuing as the English, and it isn't a football grand final or a concert. So what is the attraction and why are they prepared to queue for a Sizzler dine-in meal when they could purchase a similar meal at many other hotels, restaurants and fast food outlets?

Background

The first Sizzler restaurant was opened in California in 1958 by young restaurateurs Del and Helen Johnson. The initial concept of a self-service budget steakhouse featured a fairly simple menu, with just two types of steak plus small salads and bread rolls. By the early 1960s, a hamburger had been added to the menu and the restaurant had expanded to three locations in Los Angeles. Over the next decade, Sizzler continued to grow rapidly but changed from a totally self-serve restaurant into the current model, which combines self-service and table service.

In 1984, Collins Foods International, a privately owned company (who by now controlled the Sizzler franchise), moved Sizzler into the Australian market by acquiring existing restaurants in Brisbane and converting them into Sizzler restaurants. Collins Foods International's office in Brisbane is the Asia-Pacific head office for 89 Sizzler restaurants in 10 countries, including Indonesia, Japan, Korea, Taiwan, Thailand, Singapore and New Zealand.

The Sizzler concept

Although Sizzler prides itself on having 'invented casual dining' in Australia, the truth lies closer to its being the first restaurant chain to offer a soup, salad, pasta, fruit and dessert bar for the average Australian family. Its success hinges on appealing to this fairly broad market segment by offering a casual dining alternative that comfortably sits between fast food and fine dining. Sizzler provides the type of restaurant where customers don't need to put on their best clothes but still feel that they are 'dining out'. It is a dining experience for the whole family and a healthy alternative to fast food. The distinctively designed green, red and white restaurants offer a friendly atmosphere and quick service with a variety of high-quality, good value, freshly prepared meals.

The menu

Sizzler has gradually expanded its menu offering from the classic grilled steak to include seafood, chicken dishes, BBQ ribs, combination meals and burgers. Diners can order a main meal ranging from $15.25 to $22.95 and included in the price is the all-you-can-eat soup, salad, pasta and dessert bar selection (drinks are an additional cost). Alternatively they can order a 'complete meal', which is the all-you-can-eat selection for $15.95, including bottomless soft drink and coffee. The lunch menu is even cheaper, ranging from $6.75 to $16 for slightly smaller main meal serves and $9.95 for the complete meal. The all-you-can-eat meal choice accounts for approximately 50 per cent of all meals purchased at Sizzler restaurants in Perth.

Children are well catered for, with a choice of three main dishes at $8.50 for dinner and $5.50 for lunch (under the à-la-carte pricing system). The all-you-can-eat pricing for children is determined by age; for example, $4 for four- to seven-year-olds, and $8 for eight- to 12-year-olds. There is no charge for children under four years of age.

Promotions directed to the target markets

Sizzler has a very clear view of its target markets, and profiles of these can be identified in its promotional material, including its website. Although the family unit comprises the main target market for Sizzler, particularly during the peak dinner period (6 p.m. to 7.30 p.m.), they have also targeted young singles to fill the restaurants after 7.30 p.m. Retired couples and older singles have also been targeted for the weekday lunchtime trade and account for approximately 30 per cent of lunchtime diners. The website features images of the three target markets: a family, a senior/retiree, and a young single. Interestingly, they have associated each target with a menu item that is not the food you would normally consider as matching that particular stereotype.

Sizzler introduces key promotions on a six-week cycle directed at the specific market segments. To maintain interest in the menu selection, price specials are offered on the current menu items and new products are introduced for the promotional periods. Recent promotions have included 'Steak & chips just $2 extra when you buy a complete meal' and 'Premium steak and a whole lot more', which featured steak with crumbed mushrooms or steak with golden-fried seafood as new menu items.

Each new sales promotion is introduced by either television advertising or a letterbox leaflet drop. At the conclusion of the promotional period, there is a two-week gap before the next one starts. These promotions are directed at regular diners, particularly families, and provide a reason to revisit Sizzler. They also attract new customers who may be interested in the price special or the particular menu item. The retired or older singles market is targeted with Sizzler's own Seniors Card, which is offered to anyone over the age of 60, and entitles them to a 20 per cent discount on normal menu prices. Children are targeted with television advertising, which features a catchy jingle 'Don't be a tease Mum — can we go to Sizzler please?' This clever ploy almost gives children an excuse to pressure their parents into taking them to Sizzler. Through the use of sales promotions and television advertising, Sizzler begins the process of recruiting the right customers and training them for the dining experience.

Back at the queue

Carol and Zoe had approached the restaurant with similar expectations for a pleasant meal. They had both seen the explicit promise of sizzling steak featured against a flame grill background in the Sizzler television advertising, and Zoe had also been impressed when Carol said to her 'Sizzler! That's a great place. Let's go there for dinner. It's excellent value — I know you will enjoy it'. So, after a busy week and with a typical 'thank God it's Friday' feeling, they joined the queue. From this point on, their appreciation of the experience differed greatly.

Zoe, having recently arrived from China, had not eaten at Sizzler before and was visibly surprised by the crowded corridor. 'It's always like this on the weekend, but don't worry, it's worth the wait', Carol said reassuringly. Carol had been to the restaurant many times before with her family and was familiar with the menu and the ordering procedure but Zoe was already having doubts. She was tired and hungry and found the wait frustrating. In recognition of this, some Sizzler restaurants have televisions mounted so that the customers don't notice the length of time spent in the queue. Another way Sizzler attempts to pacify impatient customers is by serving complimentary snacks, and it wasn't long before a service attendant was moving along the queue with a platter of finger food. As Carol and Zoe were at the end of the queue, the platter was well picked over by the time it got to them, and all that remained was carrot and celery sticks, which Carol readily accepted. Despite her hunger, Zoe declined the peace offering and commented that she preferred the taste of cooked vegetables. Before long, another service attendant was moving through the queue checking the number of customers in each group and allocating table numbers in advance.

Strategically placed along the walls of the queuing area were large menu boards and, as they waited in line, Zoe scanned the selection and was a little disappointed with the limited choice. Carol, however, was delighted with the new promotion item of a steak and chips for only \$2.00 extra with a complete meal. Zoe decided on the garlic prawns but was looking for someone to ask about the size of the serve before deciding whether to order the salad bar as well. After a 40-minute wait Zoe was bored and even more hungry and her thoughts drifted to going home and reheating a pizza. She at last found herself at the front of the queue and was greeted by a smiling cashier to whom she handed over \$22.50 for her meal. Carol ordered the promotional meal but was oblivious to the amount she had just signed for on her visa card and was off eagerly following the waiter to their table.

Time to eat

The young waiter politely asked if they had been to Sizzler before, to which Carol replied 'Yes', but he then disappeared before Zoe could order a glass of iced water or a serve of complimentary nuts. Carol excused herself to take a call outside on her mobile phone while Zoe waited at the table, observing the crowded seating arrangements and the loud conversation at the adjoining table. A large family had pushed two tables together, a baby was crying and a little boy had spilt his ice-cream on the floor. Carol was soon back with a bowl of pumpkin soup and a glass of Coke. Her comment of 'I thought you would have got something to eat while I was out' was greeted with 'I didn't realise I had to get my own food' from Zoe. This wasn't going well, although Carol didn't seem to notice as she spun around and ordered cheese bread from another waiter as he sped past.

Guided by Carol, Zoe collected her plate from the table and a spare plate from the stack against the wall and proceeded to the salad bar, only to be confronted by another line. But this time it was different; customers were cruising around the salad bar in a clockwise direction and Zoe soon realised that the required etiquette was to dive in, a bit like driving into a traffic roundabout. Zoe returned to the table with two plates heaped with food. Maybe this was the great value Carol was talking about.

Having almost finished her mountains of food, Zoe went to the self-serve soft drink bar and returned to find her two plates still on the table. She was now feeling more confident with the all-you-can-eat concept, and had returned with two drinks but nowhere to put them. As she stood there commenting on the lack of service and small tables she glanced around to see many plates of half-eaten food on all the tables. Surprisingly, the other customers in the restaurant did not seem to notice the dirty plates as they talked and laughed, occasionally pulling a young child away from another table after she had wandered too far. As she sat down again, Zoe noticed that Carol had stacked her empty plates on the edge of the table and was lining up again to refill her single glass of Coke.

When, after about 20 minutes, Zoe's main course of garlic prawns arrived, it looked and smelt quite appetising but she wasn't hungry and began to wonder if she had filled up on too much salad and drink. As Carol cut her first slice of steak, she enthused that it was just the way she liked her steak to be cooked. Why wouldn't it be? thought Zoe. After all, Carol had even pointed to a coloured photograph at the cashier's station when asked 'How would you like your steak to look?'. What ever happened to rare, medium and well-done? Zoe thought. As Zoe slowly waded through the garlic prawns, Carol finished off a small chocolate mousse coated with crushed nuts. There are complimentary nuts, Zoe thought. But no, you have to serve yourself and they're crushed!

Did you enjoy the meal?

While the friends ate, people moved in and out of the restaurant at a fairly steady pace, and for most of the time the 200-seat restaurant was filled to capacity. The salad bar was tidied, freshened and restocked by efficient and almost invisible attendants. Waiting staff, or service attendants as they prefer to call them at Sizzler, were there but almost in the background. Dirty plates were eventually removed but mainly when the tables were being cleared to reseat another group of customers. And there was no shortage of customers. As the two friends left the restaurant, they glanced back at the queue and noted that it had reduced significantly. The queue now consisted of younger couples, as it was now past bedtime for the younger children who, with their parents, had filled the restaurant at six o'clock.

As they stepped out into the cold night air, the dazzling lights of the Sizzler facade beckoned yet another two carloads of customers into the carpark, but Zoe was glad to be heading home. Carol paused to comment on how delicious her steak was, but for Zoe the meal was not the 'excellent value' that her friend had promised and it certainly wasn't worth the wait. 'That was great, we must do it again' Carol called out as she opened her car.

Questions

1. Draw a blueprint for the service process at Sizzler.
   (a) Define the zone of visibility, that is, the processes that are visible to the customer.
   (b) Show the average timing of each principle task/function (you may need to make some guesses here).
   (c) Identify the relevant Sizzler personnel responsible for each task/function.
   (d) Show the acceptable tolerances in timing for each task/function for both Zoe and Carol. Where do they differ? Why?
   (e) In view of your blueprint, define the Sizzler process in terms of complexity and divergence.
   (f) Identify the bottlenecks in the Sizzler process. Suggest what could be done to alleviate these.
2. Identify the boundary spanning employees at Sizzler. What role stressors are they likely to experience and how can management ensure these are kept to a reasonable level?
3. Zoe is not familiar with Sizzler's service process and becomes frustrated when she cannot follow the process sequence. What strategies could Sizzler's management take to facilitate first-time customer participation?

E-complaining: the world of online complaint sites[1]

By Nichola Robertson

Company background

Kiwi Insurance Services' call centre is located in Auckland, New Zealand. Kiwi Insurance is one of New Zealand's leading insurance companies in the motor vehicle and home insurance markets. More than 50 per cent of all Kiwi Insurance's interactions with its customers are channeled through its Auckland call centre. Indeed, call centres are nowadays at the forefront of many New Zealand businesses (Yousef 2001).

Contrary to the public perception that call centres do not offer a high grade of customer service, Kiwi Insurance's centre does a great job in meeting and exceeding its customers' expectations. Generally, the first personal contact a customer has with Kiwi Insurance is with the customer service representative who answers the phone. Good customer service often starts and ends with a pleasant telephone manner. The call centre provides the crucial, and often lasting, first impression of Kiwi Insurance.

All customer service representatives undertake six weeks of intensive training before starting work at the centre. Training programs are designed to teach representatives about the variety of insurance products offered by the company, the ins and outs of the business, and, most importantly, a range of customer service related skills designed to ensure caller satisfaction. Kiwi Insurance sees its call centre as an increasingly important part of its differentiation strategy — not to mention a tool both to acquire new customers and to retain existing ones.

The quarterly customer service meeting

It is Monday morning at Kiwi Insurance Services, and Jillian Smith, who heads the Customer Service Division at the call centre, is about to report to her customer service representatives on the past month's customer satisfaction ratings, and how well they have addressed their customers' complaints. She begins: 'Welcome, everyone. Our quarterly customer satisfaction survey results are now in, and you'll be happy to know it's been another great quarter. Overall, our customer satisfaction ratings were up a little on last quarter.' (Figure 13A outlines the customer satisfaction ratings for the first quarter, 2002.)

Jillian distributes a handout detailing the ratings and congratulates her representatives on a job well done. Satisfaction ratings are based on many specific elements that together make up the caller's service experience, and

---

[1]This is a fictional case based on research regarding consumer complaint behaviour and independent complaint sites. The call centre referred to in this case is based on the experiences of a composite of firms.

therefore can 'make or break' a customer's satisfaction. This debriefing session is just one of the key steps taken by Kiwi Insurance to ensure that customer feedback is always acted on.

Customer service interaction element	Performance rating (5 = mean score)	Relationship to overall performance rating	Percentage of customers affected
Answered phone promptly	4.2	.66	100
Call closed on first contact	3.8	.82	50
Polite representative	4.6	.87	100
Knowledgeable representative	4.1	.75	100
Not on hold too long	3.6	.56	40
Representative followed up as promised	3.7	.66	40
Fulfilled needs promptly	3.9	.72	100

Figure 13A: Customer satisfaction ratings – first quarter, 2002

Jillian continues: 'However, despite these positive ratings, I am still a bit concerned, because although ratings are up, we are not resolving as many complaints as I would like. Now, I know you'll think I'm crazy for saying this, because you may assume that one of our goals is to receive fewer complaints. But you know what they say: one of the surest signs of a declining relationship with our customers is the absence of complaints. It seems to me that very few of our customers are complaining'.

As she pulls out a document from her briefcase, Jillian goes on: 'I have just finished reading this recently published nationwide survey, which reports that only a very small percentage of New Zealand customers actually take the time to complain. This research also shows that a large proportion of those customers who have a problem, and do not complain, stop doing business with that organisation'. Jillian flicks to the results section of the report and, with whiteboard marker in hand, begins to jot down some of the main reasons why their customers may not be complaining. Figure 13B lists some of the key findings of the report as outlined by Jillian to her customer service representatives.

The team briefly discusses these findings, and a number of the customer service representatives comment on the results, sharing past experiences of instances in which their own customers had been unwilling to complain. These examples seem to support the results Jillian has presented. Jillian thanks her representatives for sharing their experiences, and adds: 'There is something else I have just discovered that I want to discuss with you today. I was surfing

the Internet the other day when I came across a website called
Complaints.com. Apparently, this is just one of a number of independent online
complaint sites where our customers are now able to post their complaints.
Have any of you heard of these sites?'.

- Too much effort required to lodge the complaint — 'don't have the time'
  or 'too much trouble'
- The dollar value of the complaint does not warrant the time it takes to
  complain — the purchase was just too small to worry about.
- Fear of retribution
- Simply do not know where or how to complain. For example, some
  consumers do not feel comfortable writing a complaint letter, as they do
  not know what information to include, and they don't know where to send it.
- Doubt it will do any good — fearful that nothing will be done about their
  complaint
- Accept part of the blame for the service failure
- Wish to avoid confrontation, and don't want to kick up a fuss
- Annoying, but not a big enough issue to complain
- Find it easier simply to go to another supplier of the service

Figure 13B: Why don't customers complain?

David, a senior representative who has been with Kiwi Insurance for some
10 years, begins to reel off some of the other complaint sites. 'Yes', he says, 'I've
read about these sites. I know that eComplaints.com and PlanetFeedback.com
do the same thing.' Kato, another officer, then claims that she has a couple of
friends who swear by Complaints.com, but not for complaining. 'They do all their
product research on these sites. All they do is go online and read complaints and
comments about hundreds of organisations and their products', she says. 'After
all', she adds, 'I guess you can't go past the experiences of "real" customers as
a source of reliable information before purchasing!'.

Jillian listens attentively to the remarks made by her representatives. 'That's
great', she says, 'because what I would like you to do for the next hour, in
groups, is to discuss your thoughts on these sites. I would like you to consider
the following questions in your talks. What do you think about these sites? Do
you believe they offer any benefits to our organisation? Do you think our
customers would use the World Wide Web to make complaints? To what extent
do you think it would be worthwhile for us to monitor such complaint forums?'

The team notes Jillian's questions while she breaks them up into three small
groups. Then brainstorming begins. The groups work on this exercise for the next
hour, and Jillian asks them to write out the key points of their discussions on
some butcher's paper. Presented below are the key points made by each group.

Group 1

Discussion in Group 1 begins when Alex, one of the more vocal members of the
group, suggests that they look at the motivations of their customers and the
current processes they use to complain. Alex explains: 'If we look at why
customers use online complaint sites, as opposed to issuing their complaints

directly to us, we might uncover some of the advantages and disadvantages of becoming involved with these sites. What do you think?'. The group seems generally happy with Alex's suggested approach, and discussions commence.

The group begins by looking at some of the reasons why their customers might not complain directly to them, and why these sites might be seen as a preferred channel through which to complain. As indicated in the report Jillian had referred to, whether or not a customer complains about an unsatisfactory experience may depend on the expectation of effort required to lodge the complaint. The group talks about the fact that customers who find it difficult to voice their complaints are unlikely to express their problems directly to Kiwi Insurance. Group members conclude that the ease and convenience of complaining is a key reason for using these sites.

Another group member then raises the issue that many customers simply do not know where or how to complain. The group suggests that customer confidence to complain directly to Kiwi Insurance could be enhanced by making the process of lodging a complaint well defined, simple and acceptable.

Finally, various group members suggest that some customers could use these complaint sites to acquire power and control in the complaint process. As one group member puts it, 'If I'm going to bother making a complaint, I need to believe that it will lead to a resolution that will sufficiently compensate me'. The group notes that those customers who consider complaining to be worthwhile — that is, those who believe that the benefits of complaining exceed the costs — would be more likely to direct their complaints to Kiwi Insurance itself. Indeed, the need to complain to one of these sites is thought by the group to indicate that the offending organisation did not provide adequate complaint resolution.

Discussions have been going on for about 40 minutes when Alex, who seems to have assumed the role of group leader, jumps in: 'Well guys, I think we have thrashed out enough of the current processes and motivations for complaining, so do you think we should get involved with these sites? Is it worth monitoring them?' Surprisingly, the responses to Alex's questions are in the negative. Based on their discussions, the group feels that there are more compelling reasons to focus instead on facilitating customer complaining directly to Kiwi Insurance. Group members think that by creating an improved complaints management system that responds to customer dissatisfaction quickly and fairly, Kiwi Insurance could increase the number of complaints it receives.

In closing, the group notes that no matter how their customers decide to complain (whether by email, telephone, mail or face-to-face) it is vital that the complaint be handled immediately and professionally. If this can be achieved, why would Kiwi Insurance need to monitor these sites? Surely then their customers would not even contemplate using one of these external sites?

Group 2

A few members of the second group have no prior knowledge of complaint sites. So Kate, who previously mentioned that she had a couple of friends who used these sites, gives the group a brief run-down on their general purpose. Kate tells them: 'Sites such as Complaints.com are geared to provide customers with a place to get their frustrations off their chest, and share their stories with others. Complainers can read what others have said and issue a response. Many of these sites categorise complaints by product type — from restaurants to retailers — posting complaints for the world to see. So beyond their use as a complaint channel, the sites serve as a resource for customers researching products. These sites are prompting customers to spread negative word of mouth online.

'Complaint sites offer a credible source of information, as the complaints and comments of real-life customers, who have had direct experience with the product, carry far more weight than any ad on TV'. The group immediately recognises the benefits that Kate refers to.

She goes on to explain: 'So the way I see it, if we fail to monitor these sites, negative word of mouth may thrive, and if our customers are using these sites, then they remain unheard by us'. Another group member agrees, and asks Kate, 'So are these complaints accessible to us?'. 'Yes', says Kate, 'I'm fairly sure that Complaints.com do in fact inform the offending organisation that a customer complaint has been posted, and I know for certain that Complaints.com always posts both sides to complaints — that is, the customer side and the business side. So I guess that by acting as an independent third party, they can really help us to improve our service, and recover customer relationships'.

In summary, the group concludes that if customers who use these sites have the ability to tell the world whether they like or dislike Kiwi Insurance, it would seem crazy not to monitor them. Although customers who currently use independent complaint sites on the Internet make up a small group in the population as a whole, they are an increasingly vocal and powerful one.

Group 3

David, who has read a bit about these sites, sets the ball rolling. 'You know, in my readings I remember that a number of these sites are currently expanding their businesses into the compiling and selling of data in the form of detailed customer satisfaction reports. The aggregation of complaints would help us to identify common service problems as perceived by our customers, and this information could then be used to make the necessary strategic changes. This information would be especially useful for monitoring our customer service programs, and would also provide a good opportunity to develop new product ideas.'

The group consensus appears to be that, as well as doing a good job at listening to direct customer complaints, Kiwi Insurance should welcome complaint sites as another source of information. However, the group also expresses some concern about losing control of the process. Another problem is that some customers might not be willing to provide demographic details or contact information when making a complaint. If customers choose not to disclose their identity, Kiwi Insurance cannot contact them, and the customer might have less leverage as their claims would not be perceived as credible.

Finally, the group concludes that it would also be possible for customers to create a false identity and mislead others about the identity of the sender or the origin of the message, and this is noted as a matter of concern. Other ethical issues include the possible publishing of inappropriate, profane or defamatory information or material. The group suggests that the code of ethics under which these sites operate should therefore be immediately investigated.

Final thoughts

Each group presents its findings to the team and they discuss the issues raised. At the end of their discussion, they agree that the fundamental question exists: Will customer use of complaint sites increase over time as customers find these forums an effective way of getting an organisation's attention? Or, if customers perceive organisations to be responsive to their complaints, will they recognise that making direct contact with the offending organisation is the best method of complaining?

Questions

1. Based on the discussions of the three groups, to what extent do you think it would be worthwhile for Kiwi Insurance to monitor complaint sites?
2. Explain the courses of action open to a dissatisfied customer. Which of these actions represents a customer complaint made to an independent complaint site? What factors may deter a customer from complaining directly to an organisation?
3. What are the benefits to a service organisation of effective service recovery?
4. Explain the concept of online word of mouth. How might word of mouth differ in an online environment as opposed to face-to-face?
5. Visit a complaint site referred to in this case. Critique the site, outlining its pros and cons. Would you use this online complaint site if you had an unsatisfactory service encounter? Why, or why not?

References

Harrison-Walker, L. J. 2001, 'E-complaining: a content analysis of an Internet complaint forum', *Journal of Services Marketing*, vol. 15, no. 5, pp. 397–412.
Yousef, R. 2001, 'Managing customer relationships', *New Zealand Management*, vol. 48, no. 8, pp. 39–45.

Driving online legal services at Minters

By David Rymer, Director of KnowHow, Minter Ellison

From bricks to clicks

Minter Ellison is one of Australia's leading legal practices. Since 1995, Minter Ellison has doubled in size and now has over 2000 people working in seven countries with annual revenue of over $340 million. In a recent *Business Review Weekly* survey, it was ranked second in Australia in fees generated.

Initially, online legal services were seen as a threat to a profession that rejoiced in its traditional approach to client service. Now these products and services are very much part of the legal landscape.

Demand drivers behind online legal services

Minter Ellison's adoption of online legal services was driven by its appreciation of three compelling forces for change:
- client demand
- productivity/cost considerations and
- competitive pressures.

Client demand

Clients who have undergone an extensive organisational change process increasingly look for professional service organisations who mirror their own efficiency. Without IT investment and streamlined internal systems, it is difficult for clients to achieve the benefits offered by online legal services or to utilise the online products effectively.

Productivity cost considerations

Like other sectors of the economy, Australia's legal companies are rationalising in search of economies of scale. A large company can afford to invest in the IT infrastructure investment required to deploy cost-effective, sophisticated online legal technologies. Client extranets, portals and information systems are very cost-effective ways of delivering client contact details, legal information and administrative updates.

Similarly, dedicated online products such as SAFETRAC provide low-cost delivery systems in areas of the law where the ability to adapt standardised legal documents quickly and efficiently are major considerations in choosing a legal representative.

Competitive pressure

As legal companies grow larger and ever more international in their orientation, the provision of legal services through online technologies has come to be viewed as simply yet another pragmatic investment decision.

In seeking to compete locally with larger Australian-based companies and globally across Asia, the United Kingdom and the United States, Minter Ellison has sought to differentiate its brand from its competitors by being a technology-enabled and knowledge-management-rich company. By doing this, the company hopes to achieve the optimum blend of personal and online legal service.

Delivering this differentiation demands an understanding of the drivers behind client demand, sophisticated revenue and cost modelling and an insight into end-to-end value chain support.

Minter Ellison's online legal product and service portfolio

Over the past two years, Minter Ellison has deployed a portfolio of online legal services including:

- SAFETRAC: an award winning online risk management training and evaluation product designed to deliver best practice compliance
- LeaseKeeper: an online commercial leasing software and documentation package designed to standardise documents, sign-off procedures, matter management and compliance facilities
- virtual case rooms: designed to support litigation teams, facilitate the discovery process and enable online document sharing in a secure environment
- client extranets: facilitate clients' access to contact details, matter management documents, client bulletins and continuing legal education
- information services: online delivery of continuous updates on legal issues, judgements, trends and background briefings.

So why online legal services?

Firstly, Minter Ellison increasingly operates on a national and international basis. Online legal products are an essential tool in operating a global business effectively. Secondly, its focus on national clients requires innovation to deliver productivity and efficiencies. Thirdly, Minter Ellison operates in an increasingly complex information environment. Online legal services help to simplify this wall of information.

Most importantly, however, Minter Ellison's clients are changing. Clients are increasingly sophisticated in the way they source professional services. They are looking for advisers who have creative problem-solving skills that add value to their business as well as the traditional technical legal expertise. At the same time, they want to simultaneously reduce costs and accelerate turnaround times.

In developing its online legal services strategy, Minter Ellison has been highly conscious of the need to optimise the mix between its traditional approach to legal services and the new opportunities for delivering value to clients via web-based tools.

Moving forward

Effective online systems demand more than technology. They demand a clear business strategy and an economic model. In Minter Ellison, the development of online legal services is being driven by the desire to deliver economic value to our clients in the form of:

- ease of access
- convenience
- cost savings.

Online legal services involve cultural change that will facilitate the day-to-day operational support for these technologies within the company. To do this, Minter Ellison must develop innovative processes that will leverage the company's proprietary intellectual capital (IP) to deliver unique value to clients via online distribution channels.

Leveraging IP online with clients enables the company to:
- reduce costs and speed up response times on client matters
- create opportunities to value-bill
- identify new revenue streams
- compete effectively against our competitors.

Thus, online legal services in many ways complement our traditional approach to client service.

Three key questions

In commercialising its online legal services strategy, Minter Ellison asked three basic questions:
- How well positioned is the firm to learn from its experience?
- How readily can the firm convert its experience and expertise into proprietary intellectual property (IP)?
- How fast can the firm apply its IP to clients and prospects to deliver value online and differentiate its brand?

Finally, the success of any online legal services program rests with the company's culture and values. Firms that are able to learn and develop have a far greater chance of successfully using online legal services to grow the company's collective wealth.

Questions

1. Three main drivers influenced Minter Ellison's adoption of online legal services. Which one do you think would be the most important? Why?
2. Minter Ellison has deployed a portfolio of online legal services. Go to its website (www.minterellison.com.au) and find at least three of these services. Provide an evaluation of each in terms of ease of access, clarity and usefulness.
3. In what ways do changing client needs affect Minter Ellison's online strategy? How do you think it is able to track these changes?
4. What are the three key questions for Minter Ellison in commercialising its online legal services strategy? Can you think of any other questions it should ask?

Rejuvenating a mature tourist destination

By Carmen Tideswell, Beverley Sparks and Steve Noakes

Creating a new tourism vision for the Gold Coast

In 1999, a group of researchers and tourism industry leaders began to ponder the question 'How do we ensure that the Gold Coast continues to have a successful and viable tourism industry?'. Often described as Australia's foremost holiday playground, the Gold Coast region in Queensland had enjoyed a thriving tourism industry for several decades. Questions were beginning to be asked, however, about how long this success could continue. Was it time for changes to be made in the industry? What would the future for tourism on the Gold Coast hold? The Gold Coast Visioning Project was developed to address these questions and to ensure that the future of the industry was bright. This case study outlines some of the key marketing and strategic issues that arose from the program as it concluded in 2002.

Tourism on the Gold Coast

The Gold Coast has long been acknowledged as Australia's 'premier holiday destination'. This position had been established because of a fortunate combination of natural assets and a sequence of visionary entrepreneurs, whose initiatives had ensured the destination was always at the cutting edge of many innovations in Australian tourism development. The Gold Coast may not have been a conventional city, but it was efficient. The coastal strip had historically been the focus of the city, with activities and places on and off 'the beach strip' popular with residents and tourists alike.

The Gold Coast also had one of the fastest growing resident populations in Australia. With over 405 000 local residents and more than 4.3 million visitors to the region a year, the capacity of the city to cater for the needs of both locals and tourists had to be addressed. The challenge for industry stakeholders and urban planners was to jointly identify tourism development options that were both economically sustainable for the region and capable of enhancing the quality of life and opportunities of its residents.

By 1999, the Gold Coast was receiving over 4.3 million overnight visitors per annum (Bureau of Tourism Research 1999a,b). Domestic visitors accounted for approximately 70 per cent of visitors. The majority of tourism growth had occurred, however, from the international markets. The strength of the Gold Coast in the inbound market has been attributed particularly to its performance in Asian markets. Nevertheless, with two-thirds of all international visitors coming from Asian countries, the vulnerability of the Gold Coast to potentially crippling external shocks was highlighted during the Asian financial crisis.

The impact of the Asian crisis was clearly evident by 1999. The number of Korean visitors had declined by almost 43 per cent from 1997 (Bureau of Tourism Research 1999a). Likewise, the Japanese market, which accounted for almost 40 per cent of international visitors, had contracted by seven per cent (Bureau of Tourism Research 1999a) and other Asian markets had declined by 15 per cent. Overall, international visits had declined by two per cent per annum between 1997 and 1999. Some industry stakeholders were quick to suggest that this decline was typical of that experienced by other tourism regions in Australia, as the Asian crisis was a nationwide problem. The figures, however, suggested that the Gold Coast's performance in the international market was not typical of what was happening in Australia overall. While Australia continued to increase its volume of international visitor arrivals by 1.5 per cent per annum, despite the Asian crisis, the Gold Coast was experiencing a decline of over six per cent (Bureau of Tourism Research 1999a). Of even more concern was the fact that the domestic figures told the same story. The number of domestic visitors to the Gold Coast, while not yet declining, was not growing at the same rate of that experienced elsewhere in Australia.

The Gold Coast Visioning Project

It was soon apparent, through these and other indications, that the Gold Coast was losing ground to other destinations, particularly in regards to the holiday market. The Gold Coast was clearly facing many of the challenges confronting maturing destinations elsewhere in the world. The attractions and facilities available in the region were in danger of lagging behind changing patterns of market demand. A new vision was needed for the Gold Coast tourism industry. It was at this stage that the researchers who were focusing on the future of tourism on the Gold Coast spoke out about the need for a more strategic approach to tourism planning and marketing of the region:

> The Gold Coast is at a development crossroad and faces massive challenges in meeting the expectations of the next generation of visitors and residents. The past ad hoc attitude to tourism development will not work in the future as increased competition and more discerning markets require a more sophisticated approach.

> Professor Bill Faulkner, Project Leader for the Gold Coast Visioning Project

What the visioning project proposed was a series of 12 interrelated research projects. They would investigate issues relating to the Gold Coast tourism industry, ranging from how tourism affected the lives of local residents, to the economic impact of tourism in the region and the level of visitor satisfaction with tourism facilities. This research would identify key development issues that were crucial to ensuring the region did not reach the decline stage of the destination life cycle. However, research alone would not solve the Gold Coast's tourism industry dilemmas. Ensuring that industry and government stakeholders supported the visioning project was the linchpin needed to make the process viable.

Marketing the visioning project to tourism industry stakeholders

Capturing the attention and commitment of key industry stakeholders to the visioning project was no easy task. Before the visioning process could be of any use in addressing the needs of the Gold Coast tourism industry, a concerted internal marketing exercise was required to 'sell' the value of the process to industry and community stakeholder groups. No amount of market research was going to enable the local tourism industry to flourish if the research team could not demonstrate that the process would produce practical outcomes to help the industry remain competitive. Members of the tourism industry, in particular, had to share the vision that resulted from the research process. The essential ingredient for any industry vision is that it reflects the shared and valued aspirations of the relevant stakeholders.

One of the key strategies employed to market the visioning program to tourism industry members was to seek the endorsement of one of Queensland's most prominent and well-respected tourism leaders. Sir Frank Moore, the inaugural Chair of the Queensland Tourist and Travel Corporation for over 12 years, took on the lead role in selling the concept to an initially sceptical industry. He addressed the industry, capturing their attention in a way that no researcher could have done:

> I know some of you hard-headed industry leaders have expressed doubt about any further ongoing research projects. Give us action not words is the catchcry, and it is action coupled with research that this Gold Coast Revision- ing program is all about. With the help of the CRC for Sustainable Tourism established at Griffith University, we can translate a vision for the future into practical terms, knowing we have the correct foundation to make it work.

> Sir Frank Moore, Chairman, CRC for Sustainable Tourism

Another critical strategy used as an internal marketing tool was the establishment of an industry steering committee. The committee consisted of representatives from the CRC for Sustainable Tourism, Gold Coast Tourism Bureau, Gold Coast Airport Limited, Conrad Jupiters, the Gold Coast City Council, Queensland Police, Tourism Queensland, the Queensland Department of State Development and the Gold Coast Combined Chambers of Commerce. The Steering Committee set the direction and acted as a sounding board for the Gold Coast Visioning Project. Furthermore, each of the individual research reports within the Gold Coast Visioning Project had stakeholder reference groups that enabled two-way consultation and provided invaluable industry advice to the researchers.

The ups and downs of the visioning process

Having engaged the relevant stakeholders with the project, the visioning team commenced the three-year research agenda and consultation process. Through a series of meetings held between the research team and the stakeholder reference groups, an overall vision for the region's tourism industry was evident. Most stakeholders were unanimous in wanting a globally competitive destination image that provides a point of differentiation from other resort destinations.

Perhaps one of the most contentious issues that arose during the early stages of the process surrounded the original name given to the program. Originally, the project was dubbed 'Revisioning the Gold Coast'. Unfortunately, the connotations associated with 'revisioning' were not generally well received by some members of the industry, who believed that the term implied the current vision for tourism was simply 'wrong'. At the April meeting of the Steering Committee, therefore, it was decided to delete the prefix 're' and adjust the name of the project to the 'Gold Coast Visioning Project'. From this point on, the importance of marketing the program in a delicate manner to members of the industry was always at the front of the minds of those involved. After all, the process was never going to be of use if the industry did not fully support its efforts.

As specific research projects were concluded and their findings released, waves of enthusiam and dismay were reported by various sectors of the tourism industry. One of the delicate issues faced in trying to meet all the needs of stakeholders was how information should be disseminated. Sometimes the project leader found that releasing a report served to alienate industry, because harsh or critical evaluations of the destination were not well received. Furthermore, the local media seemed to always emphasise the negative aspects of a report.

As results continued to emerge from the research agenda, information was clearly and carefully disseminated to the industry, local government and the community at large. Prominent members of the tourism industry continued to be called upon to show support for the visioning process and to add their endorsement to its results. Ken Minnikin, Group Marketing Manager for Warner Village Theme Parks, highlighted the key role the visioning project would play in ensuring the Gold Coast was marketed effectively as a destination in future years to come:

> To remain a successful destination, the Gold Coast must understand and respond to the needs of future markets, while continuing to capitalise on its known strengths. That's no easy task, but the work of the Gold Coast Visioning Project will allow us to better address these issues and our position in our key markets.

Clearly the region would need to reposition itself in some markets to cater for the changing demands of future tourist markets. The Australian Tourist Commission also added its support to the Gold Coast initiative. ATC Research Manager Jane Mallam noted that 'for the Gold Coast to maximise the impact of its international tourism promotions, there must be a sound understanding of what market perceptions of Australia are held within specific international markets'.

Key outcomes of the Gold Coast Visioning Project

By the end of the visioning project in early 2002, several important outcomes had resulted from the research and consultation process. The visioning project had provided the tourism industry with a summary of key planning, development and marketing issues facing the Gold Coast as a leading Australian tourism destination.

Research had confirmed that the Gold Coast region was suffering from a major image and positioning problem in the domestic market in particular. The dominance of Surfers Paradise as a visual icon, and the perception of this precinct as 'glitzy' and deteriorating, compounded this problem. In order to address the apparent decline in the rate of domestic and international visitor growth to the region, a broader range of images would need to be showcased in future marketing activities. Tomorrow's potential tourists would clearly need to perceive that there was more to the Gold Coast than beaches and high-rise buildings.

From a strategic perspective, possibly one of the most positive outcomes for the region was a better understanding of the current policy void that existed in relation to tourism infrastructure, planning, investment, product development and service issues on the Gold Coast. Partly in recognition of this, the Gold Coast City Council established a new City Tourism Unit to provide both leadership and coordination for tourism issues within Council.

Finally, there was increased recognition by key tourism, government, general business, environmental, social, welfare and other agencies of the need for a more strategic approach to the long-term progress of sustainable tourism on the Gold Coast.

The future of the Gold Coast tourism industry was now a priority in the minds of numerous stakeholders. No longer were owners and operators of tourism facilities focused solely on the immediate, day-to-day management issues of their particular corners of the tourism sector. There was now a general feeling across the industry that a medium- to long-term tourism planning strategy was needed on the Gold Coast. The Gold Coast Visioning Project had been an exercise not only in providing a strong research platform for the tourism industry, but also in selling the need for a strategic vision to the industry itself.

Questions

1. Discuss why some members of the Gold Coast tourism industry may have reacted negatively to the initial idea of the visioning/revisioning project.
2. Why do you think the use of prominent tourism industry members was important to the visioning project?
3. What, in your opinion, would happen to a mature destination such as the Gold Coast if the research studies contained in the visioning project were not conducted?
4. Discuss the difficulties in keeping visitors 'loyal' to a mature destination such as the Gold Coast. What, if anything, should the tourism industry do to ensure visitors want to return to the Gold Coast?

References

Bureau of Tourism Research 1999a, *International Visitor Survey*, Bureau of Tourism Research, Canberra.

Bureau of Tourism Research 1999b, *Domestic Visitor Survey*, Bureau of Tourism Research, Canberra.

Just Cuts

By Lorelle Frazer

Introduction

It was December 2001, a busy time of year for the hairdressing profession. But instead of thinking of Christmas functions, Denis McFadden, founder of the Just Cuts hairdressing franchise, had his mind on other things. He had just received a report on his franchise system's performance conducted by an external consultant. Overall, the report was positive, indicating that the franchise network was strong and had the support of both management and franchise owners (franchisees). One of the findings was bothering him, however. The report noted that '70 per cent of Just Cuts franchisees believe that a franchise system should provide assistance to franchisees in local area marketing' and 'only 35 per cent of franchisees say that Just Cuts franchising does provide assistance with local area marketing.'

McFadden leaned back in his chair and stared out at the ocean from his Cronulla Beach office. 'Looks like we'll have to guide the owners more than we thought', he mused.

Background

During the 1970s and early 1980s Denis McFadden was a successful hairdresser who operated his own salon, 123 Hairdressing, in Sydney. His clients were generally middle class, and his salon provided high-quality, full-service hairdressing including permanent waves (perms), style cuts, blow waves and colours. As a promotion, he decided to advertise a 'No Appointment $6 Style Cut' for a specified period of time. The response was overwhelming and McFadden realised he had tapped into a new market — clients who wanted a convenient, quality haircut at an affordable price without having to make an appointment. Thus, the concept for Just Cuts was born, with the first salon opening in 1983. McFadden could barely keep up with the demand for this service, and several more company-owned outlets were opened in the Sydney region. As the brand name became known, enquiries from potential investors were common.

Franchising in Australia developed rapidly in the 1980s, and a lot of home-grown systems were opening and expanding. McFadden decided that franchising would enable him to expand the network more rapidly. In addition, he felt that local operators would be easier to manage than store managers whose wealth was not tied to the success of the outlet. In 1990 the first franchisee of Just Cuts opened a store, and expansion by other operators soon followed.

By April 2002 there were 124 outlets in the Just Cuts franchise across every state and territory in Australia and in New Zealand (table 16A). One outlet (the Just Cuts Academy) was retained by the company for training purposes and for trialling new products and services. Many of the franchisees owned more than one store, and multiple ownership of outlets was encouraged. For example, a family in New South Wales owned and managed 13 salons, one of which was located in New Zealand. McFadden felt that multiple outlet ownership provided benefits for both parties: 'Not only do multi-store owners enjoy cost savings in administration, but we also benefit by being surrounded by committed, proactive people. With fewer franchise owners we have better communication, greater economies of scale and we need fewer head office staff.'

Structure of the franchise system

Franchise owners

Whereas many franchisors require their franchisees to be hands-on operators working full time in the business, McFadden adopted a different philosophy. He views his franchisees as managers of their salons. Franchisees (or 'franchise owners' as he prefers to call them) do not need to have a hairdressing background, nor are they required to work full time in the salon. Instead, they manage the business operations, such as administration, marketing and finance, and employ staff for the salons. Encouraged to adopt a management role, many franchise owners have progressed towards owning multiple salons.

Franchise fees

Investment in a Just Cuts franchise costs between $100 000 and $200 000, depending on location and size of salon. A breakdown of the costs is provided in table 16B. Included in this start-up cost is an initial franchise fee of $25 000, which buys the rights to operate under the Just Cuts system for a period of 5 to 10 years.

The ongoing franchise service fee is structured as a fixed fee and is calculated on the basis of the price of 11 haircuts per week. Hence the fee always remains in line with price movements in the economy without the need to alter the franchise agreement. In April 2002 the price of a standard haircut was $17.50. In addition, an advertising fee equivalent to five haircuts per week covered corporate advertising of the brand and special promotions, such as at Easter and Christmas.

Positioning strategy

When Just Cuts was formed, McFadden positioned the product as an easy, no-fuss haircut for a standard up-front fee with no appointment necessary. The industry has always been competitive, with the well-known brands of Stefan and Price Attack the main competitors, along with independent hairdressers and the old-fashioned men's barber shops. McFadden now faced the challenge of warding off imitators of his concept:

> Until recently we had few direct competitors, but as we've grown and become more successful, so have the number of imitators. These people set up in similar locations to ours, offering a 'no frills' service with prices up to 50 per cent lower than ours.

Instead of entering a price-cutting war, Just Cuts decided to focus on attracting attention back to their salons through the use of promotional tools such as bonus cards and giveaways for children.

Thus, McFadden decided to reposition the Just Cuts image, with less emphasis on price and more on quality. Some 80 per cent of their clients are repeat visitors, so the promise of quality and consistency is important. Equal proportions of males and females make up the clientele, dispelling the myth that women necessarily require more hairdressing services, such as perming and colouring, than men.

In 2002, Just Cuts was servicing between 1.0 and 1.5 per cent of Australia's population, but McFadden's goal was to increase this figure to three per cent. International expansion began with salons in New Zealand, and plans are under way for investigating other South-East Asian regions such as Singapore and Malaysia, as well as parts of Europe such as England, Ireland and Germany. Until now, Just Cuts salons were traditionally located in large shopping centres. Future expansion will include locating smaller salons (Just Cuts 'Lites') in high street positions and country towns.

Promotion of Just Cuts — where to next?

The corporate office of Just Cuts conducts ongoing marketing and public relations activities to promote the brand image. A website (www.justcuts.com) is used to promote salon services and to provide information about the franchise to prospective franchise owners. A life-size costume character, 'Justine', is used for public appearances. In the past, major promotional activities have included sponsorship of the Just Cuts Outback Trek (a charity fundraising activity for the Flying Doctor Service), prize wheels on popular television programs, sponsorship of motor racing events, 'shave for a cure' campaigns to raise awareness of cancer, and promoting the role of official hairdresser to the 2000 Olympic and Paralympic Games in Sydney.

In addition to these corporate activities, franchise owners are expected to initiate their own local marketing activities. However, the consultant's review of the franchise indicated that franchise owners expect more assistance from the franchisor. McFadden pondered this issue. 'How can I encourage the franchise owners to be more proactive about promoting their salons?'

Table 16A   **Just Cuts outlets, April 2002**

State/territory/country	Number of outlets
New South Wales	58
Queensland	23
Victoria	15
New Zealand	13
ACT	4
South Australia	4
Western Australia	4
Tasmania	2
Northern Territory	1
Total	**124**

Table 16B Just Cuts franchise investment schedule

Cost item	Amount (range)
Initial franchise fee	$25 000
Equipment (e.g. shelving, chairs, lighting, basins, towels, cash register, signage)	$14 000–$22 000
Inventory (e.g. stationery, shampoo and conditioner, cleaning materials)	$2 000–$5 000
Leasehold improvements (e.g. building work, floor, electrical and plumbing, interior decoration, shopfront)	$50 000–$120 000
Opening promotion expenses (e.g, newspaper advertising, give-aways)	$2 000–$5 000
Opening capital (to cover utility expenses, local council charges, solicitor's fees, stamp duty etc.)	$12 000–$18 000
Total	**$105 000–$195 000**

Questions

1. What advice would you give to Denis McFadden regarding strategies to encourage more local marketing initiatives by franchise owners?
2. The Just Cuts franchise system is streamlined and simple. Its 'franchisability' makes it easy for competitors to copy. Several competitors have already imitated the concept and are offering cheaper haircuts than Just Cuts. Some franchise owners are concerned about their ability to compete with a lower priced product. What action should Just Cuts take in response to these imitators?
3. McFadden has chosen a fixed fee (equivalent to 11 haircuts per week) for the ongoing franchise fee structure. What are the incentives and drawbacks of such a structure for both parties (i.e. the franchisor and franchise owners)?
4. Traditionally, Just Cuts salons have been located in large shopping centres. McFadden is introducing a new concept, Just Cuts 'Lite', for smaller salons located in country towns and high streets. What has prompted his strategy to change locations?
5. McFadden is considering international expansion to areas as diverse as South-East Asia and Europe. What features of the Just Cuts franchise make it suitable for export to overseas locations?

Branding of sports stars

By Jane Summers

What do Ian Thorpe, Stacey Jones, Susie O'Neill, Anton Oliver, Greg Norman, Lleyton Hewitt and Barbara Kendall have in common? All are well-known sportspeople in Australia and New Zealand and all have the potential to be brands in their own right. But turning from a sporting celebrity into a brand is not as easy as it may first appear. Most of these sports stars have to rely on the expertise of managers to steer their careers and image in a direction that will hopefully last well after their playing careers are over. This result has been possible for only a few athletes so far, but many more are beginning to think seriously about their brand image.

In the last 12 months there has been a large increase in the amount of sport watched on television in both Australia and New Zealand. In a recent survey, 97 per cent of people indicated that they watched sport on television, and the number of sports being watched has also increased (Brian Sweeney & Associates 2001). The international success of a country's athletes appears to have a direct impact on the numbers of people turning on television sports programs. Both Australia and New Zealand have a large proportion of world champions per capita and the variety of sports in which we excel is enormous.

With this level of interest in sport generally, it is not hard to imagine why some athletes achieve almost superstar status in their chosen sport. People almost feel like they know sporting stars personally, having invested many hours in watching them perform and following all the media discussions about their lives on and off the field.

Every sport has its heroes and its villains, and it is obviously the heroes who have the potential to earn the highest return from their sporting endeavours. That is, of course, unless they fall from grace, as in the case of AFL superstar Wayne Carey. He earned $1.5 million in 2001, with approximately $1 million of this in salary and the remaining $500 000 in sponsorships. In March 2002, when he became the centre of media attention owing to an affair with a team mate's wife, he resigned his AFL position. His earning potential dropped to almost zero for a time, and he found it difficult to retain his sponsors and to re-sign with another club. He may now find it almost impossible to become a successful brand in his own right.

The fluctuation of success is one of the biggest problems potential sponsors face with sporting celebrities. When they are winning, everyone wants them and everyone knows them. However, when they are on a losing streak, they are suddenly non-marketing commodities. Unfortunately for most sport sponsors, their contracts with sporting stars are long term, which can leave them with real problems. Moreover, this poses problems for the sports stars themselves. Having to think of themselves as brands or commodities can interfere with the training and mental preparation required for high level competition. In addition, athletes have a limited shelf life. Most are near or in retirement by the time they hit 35, and few athletes manage to maintain their marketing appeal in retirement. Some find new careers as commentators or motivational speakers but most just fade from view. Planning for retirement is an important part of managing a sports person as a brand.

Finding the right match between endorsements and the personality attributed to the sporting celebrity is also important. There must also be a balance in the mix of products they are associated with. For most popular Australian and New Zealand athletes, approximately 85 per cent of their income will come from sponsorship and endorsements so this balancing act is critical.

In Australia at present, two of the most popular sporting celebrities are Lleyton Hewitt and Ian Thorpe. Both have a number of products that use them to leverage their brands. Likewise, Susie O'Neill's management is attempting to develop a range of branded O'Neill products that will build on Susie's personality and perceived credibility, and on perceptions that she is a great role model for young children. She will thus become a brand in her own right, and not just an endorsement for someone else's brand.

The key to the successful branding of sporting celebrities is in matching their sport and media image to the products they are supporting. Former Australian Wallaby David Campese has a line of Canterbury clothing, Greg Norman has golfing apparel and equipment, and Barbara Kendall, a New Zealand sailboarder, has sailboards. All of these associations relate either to the credibility of the sportsperson or to their personality.

The other issue that potential sponsors need to consider is the market they are attempting to attract. Those in the 12–20 age bracket love branded products and have high disposable incomes. However, this age group has moved away from more mainstream sports such as basketball and football and is moving to extreme sports such as downhill skateboarding. When targeting this group of consumers by means of sporting celebrities, the celebrities must be quite different from people such as Ian Thorpe, Alan Langer, Stacey Jones, John Eales and Anton Oliver. Members of the 12–20 age group are looking for non-traditional stars who match their ideas of street fashion, music and other interests.

Why do organisations want to associate with sports stars? Recent research suggests that most people are in favour of sport sponsorship (Brian Sweeney & Associates 2001), but it seems that people are very particular about what sorts of companies they feel should be associated with sport. There has been a swing away from the support of banks, insurance agencies and financial institutions as sport sponsors. Likewise, beer companies, cigarette companies and gaming and lotteries are also seen as inappropriate sport sponsors by many people (Furlong 1994). These figures are important indicators for organisations considering entering the sponsorship arena, particularly because nearly two-thirds of all people indicate that they are influenced by sponsorship in sport.

The key, it seems, to successful sport branding and the use of sporting stars as brands is to keep watching the market and the lifestyles of those who we are trying to attract and to match the endorsements or sponsorships carefully with the athletes. Changes can come quickly and you have to be alert.

Questions

1. What are the marketing issues involved in treating sporting celebrities as a brand?
2. Can you think of any examples of a mismatch between a sporting endorsement or sponsorship and a sporting celebrity? Why was the match not successful?
3. Are there any products that you feel would not benefit from being associated with sporting celebrities? Why or why not?
4. As with all branding questions, the real issue is the perception the consumer has about the brand. How would you test the brand image for a sporting celebrity? How do you think you should manage negative publicity and public opinion about a celebrity?

References

Brian Sweeney & Associates 2001, *Australians and Sport*, Brian Sweeney & Associates, Melbourne

Furlong, R. 1994, 'Tobacco advertising legislation and the sponsorship of sport', *Australian Business Law Review*, vol. 22, June, pp. 159–89

The Perc Tucker Regional Gallery

By Janet Campbell

Introduction

The Perc Tucker Regional Gallery in Townsville is one of more than 50 public galleries in Queensland. Regional public galleries differ from private galleries in that they are usually owned and operated by local government, although a few are associated with universities. Other differences include the following:

- They only occasionally sell art, although they may have a gallery shop with various gift and publication lines.
- In many cases, these galleries are repositories of gifts and bequests to the city such as paintings, sculpture and ceramics.
- They often have a strong education focus.
- Collections and exhibitions will often be influenced by the nature of the local region.
- They are regarded by the local community as valuable public assets.

The Perc Tucker Regional Gallery is highly regarded by the Townsville City Council and the local community. However, few public institutions are immune from financial pressures, and the gallery is being encouraged by the council to seek additional sources of funding. The director also wishes to identify ways to make more effective and efficient use of limited marketing resources and establish cooperative marketing initiatives with other organisations.

The region

Townsville is located about 1400 kilometres north of Brisbane on Queensland's north-east coast, and is widely regarded as the unofficial 'capital' and development hub of North Queensland. Local industries include raw sugar production, beef processing, grazing, manufacturing, copper and nickel processing, tourism, fishing, research and tertiary services. Key government initiatives include James Cook University and TAFE, extensive Commonwealth and state government offices, the upgrading and addition of new tourism facilities related to the Great Barrier Reef and Magnetic Island, and Lavarack Army Barracks, the largest strategic defence base in Australia with over 8000 military personnel.

The *Social Atlas* (Townsville City Council 2001) shows that between the 1991 and the 1996 Census, the population of the Townsville region grew from 124 981 to 132 667, indicating an annual growth rate of 1.2 per cent. This is lower than the average Queensland rate of 2.6 per cent but the same as the national growth rate. The current resident population of the twin cities of Townsville and Thuringowa is approaching 145 000, which is larger than Cairns,

Darwin or Mount Isa. Population projections for the Townsville region to 2005 estimate a steady rate of growth to approximately 150 498.

The Townsville region has a population that is younger than the Queensland average, owing largely to the presence of James Cook University and the Lavarack Army Barracks. Approximately 35 per cent of residents fall within the 15–34 age bracket.

The 1996 Census indicates that 4.5 per cent of the regional population are Aboriginals and Torres Strait Islanders. The proportion of Aboriginal and Torres Strait Islanders is higher in the Townsville regional population than in Queensland (2.8 per cent) or Australia as a whole (2.0 per cent).

Art and culture in Townsville

The Townsville City Council's *Bright Arts Guide* (1996) lists more than 200 arts and cultural organisations within the region, including over 40 music-related organisations, over 30 dance-related organisations and a range of museums, visual arts, education and other bodies. These organisations are engaged in about 400 activities each year, including dance, music, theatre, literature, arts and crafts, film and video, as well as cross-cultural and multicultural art forms. About 20 per cent of respondents to a council survey of local residents (Townsville City Council 1999) participate in organisations concerned with cultural activities. According to consultants Positive Solutions (1999), the quantity and spread of cultural activity is unusually high for a city with this population.

Local cultural organisations' views of the sector, sought by the council (Townsville City Council 1999), found that its strengths include cultural diversity and tolerance for this diversity, collaboration between arts groups, local talent and a climate conducive to outdoor events. Respondents identified the weaknesses as a lack of recognition for local and Aboriginal and Torres Strait Islander talent, a lack of promotional support from local media and a lack of support from local business.

Positive Solutions found that Townsville City Council has made a significant contribution to local cultural development through the ownership and funding of a range of cultural facilities and the development and/or financial contribution to a substantial number of special events and festivals. Council's overall 1999–2000 investment in cultural activity was a little under $7 million.

The gallery

A former mayor of Townsville (1976–1980), Alderman Perc Tucker would be proud to see the public gallery that bears his name. The Gallery was established by Townsville City Council in 1981, and continues to be owned and operated by the council.

Its central location in Townsville's Flinders Mall, near the Townsville Visitor Information Centre, is a major advantage in attracting visitors, both locals and tourists. Nearby attractions include shops, restaurants, nightclubs and hotels, the Museum of Tropical Queensland, Reef HQ and the Omnimax. Because of its location, parking is somewhat limited. The gallery is open seven days a week, Monday to Friday from 10 a.m. to 5 p.m., and Saturday to Sunday from 10 a.m. to 2 p.m.

Townsville has retained many lovely examples of colonial architecture and heritage buildings, including the one that houses the gallery (see figures 18A and 18B). The first level of the building was established by the Union Bank of Australia in 1885, with the second level built in 1922. Since it is a restored historic building, conservation guidelines must be observed. It has been air-conditioned but it is not a purpose built venue specifically designed to meet the needs of a gallery. This brings some difficulties, such as delivery access and limitations on collection and storage space. Art workshops have to be conducted in the main gallery's carpeted space, limiting access to resources such as water and sinks.

Figure 18A: Perc Tucker Regional Gallery

Figure 18B: Perc Tucker Regional Gallery — the main entrance on Flinders Mall

The Perc Tucker Regional Gallery actively promotes the art of North Queensland artists alongside the work of many other Australian artists. It has committed itself to a collection policy based on the theme of 'The Tropics'. The collection comprises 1450 works, focusing on contemporary Australian paintings and prints together with a small but significant collection of historical works. Also featured is a range of ceramics, drawings and photographs and an emerging collection of contemporary Melanesian art. The collection has been valued at more than $1.7 million.

The gallery is a dynamic visual arts centre and the premier gallery of the North Queensland region. It offers a diverse program of local, national and international exhibitions with a special focus on exhibitions of North Queensland art and artists. These displays are complemented by floor talks, lectures, education programs, and performances of music, theatre and dance in the gallery that target a range of audiences.

The gallery offers a busy exhibition program, as illustrated in table 18A. In 2001 this included *Federation: Australian Art and Society 1901–2001*, which attracted 12 402 visitors over a seven-week period. Townsville was the only Queensland city to host this National Gallery of Australia travelling exhibition. The gallery also organises a number of its own touring exhibitions, with three currently touring Queensland.

Table 18A	Perc Tucker Regional Gallery exhibitions, 1999–2001		
	Main exhibition area	Two project spaces	Display cabinet
1999	21	20	8
2000	20	13	10
2001	20	13	8

In 2001 the gallery also organised *Strand Ephemera*. The refurbishment of Townsville's waterfront area, the Strand, by the council has provided the city with a popular public recreation area. To celebrate, the Perc Tucker Regional Gallery initiated *Strand Ephemera* in September 2001. More than 30 artists produced 26 sculptures and installations on the Strand for an appreciative audience of more than 40 000 over the 10 days of the exhibition, which gained extensive media coverage. Cash prizes were awarded, including a people's choice award, and forum for artists, artworkers, architects, urban planners, designers, landscape artists and visual arts students was held by the gallery. It is now hoped that *Strand Ephemera* will become an annual or biennial event.

Funding

Public facilities are experiencing increasing pressures to generate income streams additional to their state or local government funding sources, and Perc Tucker Regional Gallery is no exception. Nor is total reliance on public funding desirable from the gallery's perspective. The local community's high regard for the gallery risks being eroded if it is perceived as a drain on the council coffers. Further, success breeds success: if a public facility has a track record of generating funds from a range of sources, this becomes an effective strategy for positioning it favourably when funds are sought for special projects.

In addition to the annual operating funds (excluding provision for capital expenditure) it receives from Townsville City Council of approximately $500 000 (FY 2001), which includes provision for building rental of $100 000, sources of income in 2001 included:

- membership fees $5 000
- gallery hire for other organisations' activities $5 000
- merchandise, including catalogues $8 300
- commissions on sales of art $2 000
- hire of art works from the gallery to local organisations $5 000
- admission and donations $2 500
- grants and sponsorship for specific projects $180 000
- workshop and art class fees $12 000

Membership

Currently, membership stands at approximately 500; however, only about 300 of these are paid memberships, with the balance held by media contacts, heads of other cultural organisations, council employees and key community representatives. Three types of membership are available: single, household and concession (table 18B). Membership benefits include personal invitations to gallery exhibition openings, artists' talks, lectures, workshops, artistic performances, public programs and gallery activities held throughout the year, as well as complimentary subscription to the quarterly membership newsletter.

Table 18B	Membership fees in 2001		
	Single	Household	Concession
One year	$27.50	$38.50	$16.50
Two years	$38.50	$44.00	$22.00
Three years	$49.50	$60.50	$27.50

A recent membership drive, which cost $16 000 including the production and distribution of a new membership brochure, appears to have generated only about nine new memberships per month, representing a disappointing return on investment.

A number of other cultural organisations, including local associations and interest groups, the Museum of Tropical Queensland and Dance North, also have membership programs. The gallery's director has flagged membership as an area for review in terms of community relationship development, income generation and return on investment. Gallery staff need to better understand the factors that make membership attractive, the motivations to join, how best to add value to memberships and to evaluate the priority that membership should take among the gallery's many other activities.

Gallery hire

Gallery hire is viewed by staff as having considerable scope for development. The gallery is available for functions and events such as cocktail parties, intimate dinners, wedding ceremonies and product/company launches.

Merchandising

Merchandising is usually linked directly to specific exhibitions. However, space and resource limitations inhibit growth opportunities. The gallery used to have its own shop, but it was poorly designed, had inadequate systems and required too much staff time in sourcing product, some of which had to come from outside the local community, which conflicted with council and gallery policy of local support. Some craft work featuring and promoting the work of local artists is sold from a display cabinet located on the ground floor.

Commission

On occasion, the public can purchase art works from community exhibitions held at the gallery. The director is careful to maintain a good relationship with local commercial galleries so they do not have grounds to complain about competition. To date, the gallery has made a claim on these groups only for the merchant fees applicable to credit card transactions. However, it is the gallery's resources that are facilitating these sales, and the director is considering levying a commission of perhaps 20 per cent in future.

Hire of art works

The gallery has provided the facility for local organisations to hire art works from the gallery's collection. However, the costs incurred in this activity, such as insurance and restoration, also have to be considered. There is some doubt as to whether this initiative is financially viable, although it is unlikely that it could be discontinued.

Admission and donations

Admission to the gallery is free. Separate entry fees for special exhibitions are very rarely levied, as this is seen by the local population to contradict the nature of a public gallery. A 'gold coin donation' applied to the Federation Exhibition raised about $2000. The gallery does not have a fundraising foundation.

Grants and sponsorship

The gallery has had considerable success in winning grants and sponsorship for specific projects such as *Strand Ephemera* and the Federation Exhibition. Financial assistance has been received from Townsville City Council, Arts Queensland, QNI Ltd and BHP Cannington.

Service delivery

The gallery employs four permanent staff, one casual and two trainees. Roles these staff fulfil include Director, Gallery Exhibition/Collection Officer, Gallery Programs Officer and Administrator. The high regard for the gallery in

Townsville and in the wider arts sector reflects the calibre and commitment of the professional staff. However, this is a very small team in view of the range of activities and initiatives with which they are engaged.

The gallery is supported by a small group of volunteers. They staff the reception desk during opening hours and can elect to assist with installation and demounting of exhibitions. More than 40 volunteers are registered and about 20 are actively involved. The volunteers make a very valuable contribution; however, the director believes that there is scope for better utilising their services and willingness to learn new skills.

Current marketing

One staff member, the Gallery Programs Officer, who also oversees the public education programs, is substantially responsible for the gallery's marketing activities.

Local media support is critical: the survey of local residents (Townsville City Council 1999) found the local media to be the most significant source of information for cultural events. Residents nominated their key sources as the *Townsville Bulletin* (65 per cent of respondents), television (60 per cent), local radio (53 per cent), free newspapers (50 per cent), word of mouth (50 per cent) and library (24 per cent).

Each gallery and touring exhibition has its own dedicated promotional plan. This may include a media kit, a catalogue, exhibition fliers/brochures, community service announcements, feature articles prepared for a range of arts and general publications, advertising and a weekly 'time out' listing in the *Townsville Bulletin*, local radio advertising and limited television advertising. A range of exhibition-related activities will usually be organised, and may include an official opening event, a sponsors' reception, forums, floor talks, related music and dance activities, workshops, children's activities and school tours. These activities generate strong local media coverage for the gallery, including an average of three to four press articles, two television features and three to four radio interviews each month.

A marketing plan providing a detailed promotional plan for gallery exhibitions and programs was prepared in 2000 and revised in 2001. The marketing budget includes $12 300 for advertising and $22 400 for other activities. Neither human nor financial resources have permitted strategic marketing initiatives such as the establishment of specific marketing objectives and key performance indicators, or market research to measure gallery visitor and local resident motivations and to provide more detailed analysis of market segments. As the director confirms, the staff are already 'doing all we can do'. They cannot take on any further activities without determining how their current commitments can be carried out, 'smarter, more effectively'.

Visitation

Townsville City Council's 1999 survey of local residents found that roughly 50 per cent had visited an art exhibition in the past year, a figure comparable to that for theatrical performances and significantly higher than those for other forms of performing arts. About 47 per cent of respondents had visited the Perc Tucker Regional Gallery during the previous year.

This level of visitation for art exhibitions is high compared with state and national attendance statistics. The Australian Bureau of Statistics (1999) found that in the 12 months ending April 1999, 19.3 per cent of Queenslanders and 18.5 per cent of residents in Queensland's north/north-west region visited an art gallery. This is slightly lower than the national figure of 21.2 per cent. Of those people, 43.4 per cent of North Queensland gallery visitors attended on just the one occasion, 42.2 per cent visited an art gallery two to four times, and 14.4 per cent visited five times or more. No distinction has been made in ABS figures between public and private galleries.

The gallery currently attracts approximately 50 000 visitors each year. Figures for recent years include 51 034 in 1998, 55 833 in 1999 and 47 933 in 2000. In addition, visitors are attracted to the gallery's off-site initiatives, such as touring exhibitions and *Strand Ephemera*.

The gallery's director sees the current level of visitation as both sustainable and desirable, and would prefer to aim for consolidation rather than further increases. She believes that one of the principles of relationship marketing — that it is more cost effective to retain existing clientele than to constantly seek new customers — is as relevant to public galleries as it is to commercial enterprises. Marketing a gallery requires the constant review of resource allocation in view of limited budgets and human resources.

Gallery staff classify visitors according to five main groups:

- *General visitors*, including local residents likely to visit exhibitions, attend openings, floor talks and other gallery events; tourists; representatives of a diverse range of cultural groups; and specific interest groups/individuals. Gallery staff believe that general visitors predominantly visit for specific events and activities. For example, the gallery organises exhibitions linked to local events such as the Australian Festival of Chamber Music and the Palmer Street Jazz Festival. General visitors are also thought to enjoy the quiet, cool, contemplative nature of the venue and the opportunity to make their own, self-paced discoveries.

  It is estimated that some 40 per cent of gallery visitors are tourists. Winter is a popular time to visit Townsville, with the Festival of Chamber Music in July and an influx of southern Australians keen to escape the cold weather.

  The gallery caters expressly for the needs and interests of groups with specific interests and cultural characteristics. For children aged 4 to 12 years, the gallery organises an annual children's exhibition and KIDZART, an art club for children offering workshops and activities and its own newsletter. Community arts groups such as Fibre & Fabrics, the Townsville Art Society, the Wood Turners Association and the North Queensland Potters Association are catered for by the provision of exhibition facilities. The gallery has considered local military personnel in organising war memorial exhibitions relevant to Townsville's military history. Activities are also organised for senior citizens and members of the local indigenous community (e.g. Elders' morning teas and the annual NAIDOC exhibition).
- *Gallery members and volunteers*
- *Local and emerging artists*. The gallery purchases art works and organises local artist exhibitions and an annual Young Artists Award. These artists are also invited to present talks and workshops.

- *Event clients.* The gallery has the potential to become a popular venue for conference and meeting groups wanting exhibition tours and facilities for product launches, cocktail parties, dinners and the like. Wedding celebrations present another opportunity.
- *Education groups*, including primary, secondary and tertiary students. Gallery initiatives include school programs, artist-in-school projects, weekend and holiday art classes, final-year exhibitions for James Cook University and TAFE visual arts students, young artists' awards and annual children's exhibitions. Community education programs are also organised for people enrolled in TAFE and the University of the Third Age.

The only gallery market research undertaken in the past few years is a small-sample (83 respondents) self-completion survey of visitors conducted in August 1999. Findings included:

- a breakdown on how visitors learned about the gallery and/or exhibition on display (29 per cent of visitors discovered the gallery while walking past; 18 per cent from the newspaper; and 14.5 per cent by word of mouth)
- data on visitor ages. Most visitors (43 per cent) were over 50 years of age, with the next most represented age group being 20 to 30 years (20 per cent). All age groups were represented in the sample.

Relationships

Research undertaken by NFO CM Research in 2001 for the Regional Galleries Association of Queensland found that Queensland's regional residents place a very high value on the contribution of their regional galleries to the local community, a view shared in Townsville. A gallery members survey (Perc Tucker Regional Gallery 2000–2001) generated such comments as:

'The gallery is getting a broader spectrum of the community involved.'

'Great to see community involvement, especially in the kids workshops.'

'It's a really nice space to be in, in terms of staff ... as well as the physical space.'

'I love the place and find it very relaxing.'

Similar comments can be found in the gallery's visitors' book:

'I am grateful and pleased that such a gallery exists in my neighbourhood.'

'Great for kids' — local family

'A great enjoyable learning time' — Annandale State School Year 2B/D

'I think it is very creative' — student, Marian School.

To extend the reach of their marketing resources, gallery staff are keen to form more mutually cooperative relationships with other organisations. However, their efforts are meeting with mixed success.

For example, exhibition fliers are regularly included in mail-outs of other cultural and community organisations such as Dance North, Umbrella Studios, the Townsville Art Society and the Museum of Tropical Queensland. The gallery also undertakes joint promotions with other cultural organisations, thereby providing greater promotional reach into the local population.

On the other hand, the gallery's director has approached her counterparts at other council facilities and a private sector operator of a popular market. Admittedly it is early days, but she is finding it a difficult concept to sell and is keen to discover how to make this strategy more attractive to prospective partners. The director is confident that a range of joint marketing opportunities may be identified once the necessary level of interest and cooperation is developed with key organisations with an interest in the same markets.

Sponsorship is another strategy to develop mutually cooperative relationships, and the gallery has had some success in attracting sponsorship partners for its major exhibitions. However, raising sponsorship support from the private sector outside the capital cities can be challenging, with too few prospective sponsors, too little time to prepare proposals and too little training in effective proposal preparation.

Relationships with the local community are also formed through the gallery's membership program.

Competition

Townsville offers many cultural and recreational venues and attractions, including access to nearby Magnetic Island, Billabong Sanctuary and the Great Barrier Reef.

Since the gallery does not charge an admission fee, it competes for visitors' time rather than the cultural/recreational dollar. Competitors to the gallery are identified as organisations and places that provide cultural, educational or recreational services. They include the nearby Museum of Tropical Queensland, which is a world-class gallery incorporating a central display of the shipwreck of HMS *Pandora*, Reef HQ, the Reef Education Centre for the Great Barrier Reef Marine Park Authority, which offers a 'walk-through' Coral Reef Aquarium; and an Omnimax (Townsville Enterprise Ltd 2001). However, their proximity may also be an advantage if the gallery can partner with them to attract visiting tour groups. Similar potential exists for a range of other attractions and cultural groups.

The gallery has found that evening events, such as exhibition openings, compete with basketball events, which have a strong local following. The gallery liaises through the Community Information Centre to avoid clashes with other cultural groups' openings.

Questions

1. Prepare a SWOT analysis (strengths, weaknesses, opportunities and threats) for the gallery as a service provider.
2. The gallery offers a number of services that generate income in addition to its council funding. If you were the director, how might you review and set the prices for this range of services? Use the characteristics of services to identify issues that the gallery might have to address when trying to generate additional revenue.
3. Given the gallery's limited resources, one of the director's key concerns is how to undertake marketing in a smarter, more effective manner. Develop recommendations for establishing cooperative marketing initiatives with other organisations to make more effective and efficient use of marketing resources.
4. Identify examples of gallery services that are produced and utilised simultaneously. What marketing challenges might this create for the gallery?
5. What cues might visitors use when evaluating their satisfaction with their visit to the Perc Tucker Regional Gallery?

References

Australian Bureau of Statistics April 1999, *Attendance at Selected Cultural Venues*, cat. no. 4114.0.

Townsville City Council 1999, *Resident Consultation Survey*.

NFO CM Research 2001, *Audience Development Project*, commissioned by Regional Galleries Association of Queensland.

Perc Tucker Regional Gallery 2000 (revised 2001), 'Marketing plan'.

Positive Solutions 1999, *Towards a Cultural Plan for Townsville*, report commissioned by Townsville City Council.

Townsville City Council 1996, accessed November 2001, 'Bright Arts Guide', www.townsville.qld.gov.au.

Consultancy Unit, Community and Cultural Services Department.

Townsville City Council 2001, accessed November 2001 'Social atlas', 4th edn, www.townsville.qld.gov.au.

Townsville Enterprise Ltd, accessed November 2001, www.townsvilleonline.com.au.

Glossary

Activity-based costing: a costing technique that focuses on the activities that an organisation has to undertake in order to produce a (service) product

Added value: offering benefits, beyond those offered by both the core service and essential facilitating services, that are valued by one or more customer segments

Ad hoc data collection: surveys or other research activities that are one-offs, usually directed at answering or responding to a particular problem

Advertising: any paid form of non-personal presentation of ideas, goods or services

Affect: feeling or emotion

Affective state: the emotions and mood of an individual at a particular time

Agents: online businesses that can represent either the seller or buyer and will represent the interests of whichever has hired them

Aggregators: online businesses that perform the task of bringing together products from multiple suppliers to provide consumers with a range of choices in one location

Assimilation: the effect through which performance evaluation tends towards what was expected

Assurance: the competence, courtesy and security a firm offers its consumers

Attribution: consumer allocation of responsibility for perceived positive or negative performance levels

Backstage activities: all those that are part of the production and/or delivery of a service but are not visible to the customer

Behavioural control: the individual's perception of their level of control of a situation, which is due to their own actions

Benchmark data: data that is used to compare one's performance with others

Boundary spanners: organisational members who interface with customers at the organisation's boundary

Brand value: an intangible amount that an organisation places on its brand name

Broadened domain of marketing: the use of marketing in non-commercial areas

Brokers: online businesses that do not represent either the buyer or the seller, but provide the services that make exchange and negotiation possible

Burnout: a stress syndrome that includes feelings of emotional exhaustion, depersonalisation and non-accomplishment

Business format franchising: a common form of franchising characterised by the adoption of unique business and marketing systems, ongoing support and training, and standardised outlets

Business/media publics: those publics that look at investing in or are involved in the sport product for a business purpose

Business purchasing: the process of deciding and specifying what to buy, from which source and how much, as well as implementing these decisions, paying, and monitoring performance

Business-to-business or **B2B services marketing:** services marketing that is concerned with the exchange of services between organisations, not between individual consumers

Buying centre: all those involved in a purchase decision

Buy-phase model: commonly followed steps in the purchasing process — identification of need, establishment of specification, identification and subsequent evaluation of alternatives, selection of suppliers, and performance feedback

Co-branding: the side-by-side positioning of two or more different franchises

Cognition: thinking or reasoning

Cognitive control: the individual's perception of their level of control of a situation, which is due to their knowledge, perception and beliefs

Cognitive dissonance: the discomfort buyers may feel after purchase, for example, 'Did I get value for money?'

Comfort zone: the collection of behaviours, experiences and knowledge with which the customer is wholly familiar

Communication: the creation of shared meaning between participants

Competition: the struggle and rivalry between opponents that is the central component of a sport product

Complaints: expressions of dissatisfaction or disapproval

Complex exchanges: situations in which the exchange between provider and user is part of a complex relationship and does not involve simply handing over money for goods and services

Complexity: the number and intricacy of steps required to perform a service

Consumer behaviour: the actions and mental processes that lead to and comprise the purchase and subsequent use of a product or service

Contractual relationships: relationships centred on a contract that focuses on shipments and on the resolution of disputes

Contrast: the effect through which we mentally emphasise positive or negative differences between what we expected and what we perceived we were given

Convergent validity: a characteristic of measures (such as items in a questionnaire) which allows us to determine whether a construct measured as being the same or similar to another is actually the same or similar to real world phenomena which are alike

Conversion franchising: the conversion of an independently owned outlet to a franchised outlet within the same industry

Co-producers: those who do the work of inputting data and undertaking transactions that would normally be carried out by an organisation

Core product: the core services offered by the franchisor to franchisees as part of the franchising agreement

Correlation matrix: a matrix that arrays all variables measured across and downwards, so that we can see at a glance the level of correlation between any two variables

Counterfactual thinking: thinking that is contrary to the facts

Credence qualities: service attributes that cannot be evaluated by consumers with any certainty, even after they have experienced the service process

Credence services: services that are difficult to evaluate even after use

Cross selling: trying to sell a second, or ancillary, product once the first purchase decision has been made by a customer

Culture: the sum total of learned beliefs, values and customs that serve to regulate the consumer behaviour of members of a particular society

Customer delight: 'a profoundly positive emotional state generally resulting from having one's expectations exceeded to a surprising degree' (Rust & Oliver 2000)

Customer loyalty: 'a deeply held commitment to rebuy a preferred service consistently in the future, despite situational influences and marketing efforts having the potential to cause switching' (Oliver 1997)

Customer mix: the optimum combination of customer types that will complement the service provision and provide the fewest negative effects on other customer groups

Customer needs: the customer's perception of the need that is satisfied by purchasing the product

Customer perception: the process by which customers select, organise and interpret information

Customer relationship management (CRM): a business strategy for selecting and managing the most valuable customer relationships. CRM requires a customer-centric business strategy and philosophy to support effective marketing, sales and service processes, which are supported, not driven, by CRM technology.

Customer satisfaction: 'the customer's fulfilment response; a judgement that a product or service feature, or the product or service itself, provided a pleasurable level of consumption-related fulfilment, including levels of under- or over-fulfilment' (Oliver 1997)

Customer service: service provided directly to customers to support or facilitate a company's core products

Database marketing: a method that uses information technology in an organisation-wide process of gathering and storing relational data about individual past, current and/or potential customers

Deep acting: attempts to actually experience or feel the emotions displayed

Deep ethnography: a methodology that systematically describes the culture of a group of people in terms of activities and patterns

Demand: the purchasing of goods and services from an industry, thereby influencing the form and structure of the product

Derived demand: demand that is derived from the demand for other products and services

Descriptive statistics: statistics that summarise response data in a descriptive way, summarising such characteristics as central tendency and spread

Direct mail: a promotional tool that uses the postal service to target particular customers

Direct marketing: a promotion or marketing communication tactic that involves cross selling; that is, offering an existing customer some other products from the organisation that he or she has not yet bought

Disconfirmation: state in which expectation levels are perceived to have been met, exceeded or not met in actual performance of the service

Discriminant validity: a characteristic of measures (such as items in a questionnaire) which allows us to determine whether constructs measured as being different do reflect differences in the actual phenomena measured

Disintermediation: the process whereby traditional intermediaries are eliminated

Distributive justice: what the customer receives as an outcome of the recovery process

Divergence: the degree of freedom or variability of steps required to perform a service

Double deviation: a situation in which the organisation fails again in service recovery after having failed in the first place

Dualistic: (in expectations, performance etc.) exhibiting dimensions of process and outcome

Dyadic: involving two parties (in an interaction)

E-banking: online banking; the provision of banking services through means other than traditional branch banking

E-complaining: voicing dissatisfaction through a website

Ego involvement: the extent to which a situation touches an individual's ego-identity, which involves self-esteem, social esteem, personal value, moral value, meanings, ego and ideas

Elasticity: the degree of price sensitivity, relating change in price to the effect on demand for a product

Electronic shopping agents: software tools that assist users to search the Internet for products and services by providing items matching the search criteria, as well as prices and direct links to the site

Emotional intelligence: 'the ability to perceive emotions, to access and generate emotions so as to assist thought, to understand emotions and emotional knowledge; and to reflectively regulate emotions so as to promote emotional and intellectual growth' (Mayer & Salovey 1997, p. 5)

Emotional labour: the degree to which felt emotions are controlled so that socially desirable emotions are expressed

Emotional tactics: strategies used by service organisations to reward customers for their loyalty, usually through non-financial rewards such as service upgrades or services especially tailored to the customers' needs

Emotions: feelings or affective responses

Empathy: the ability of a firm to provide individualised, caring service

End users: final consumers

Ephemeral: transient or fleeting, short lived

Equity: consumer perceptions of fairness, equality

E-services: services made available over the Internet in a user-friendly way

Exclusivity pricing: a pricing technique where the high price of the product indicates the degree of 'exclusivity' that the product may have in customers' minds

Expectations: standards for comparison, based on excellence, prediction or normative belief

Experience qualities: service attributes that can only be evaluated by consumers after the service production process

Experiential consumption: intense consumption experiences providing identifiable levels of emotion that are appealing to consumers

Experiential services: those that are easily evaluated after use

External information sources: sources other than one's own memory or past experiences (such as travel agents, tourist brochures and so on)

Federation: a system of government based on a group of states that form an alliance under a common national government

Franchise services or management fees: ongoing fees paid by franchisees to a franchisor over the term of an agreement in return for ongoing franchise support

Franchising: an agreement under which a franchisor grants exclusive rights to a franchisee for distribution and/or sale of a service or product, in return for payment and conformance to quality standards

Frequency distribution: a tabular or graphical summary of the frequency of all possible responses

Frontstage activities: those that are visible to the customer

Functional quality: the components of the process used to arrive at the service outcome

Gaps model: a diagnostic model that helps identify the gaps between expectations and perceptions of management, employees and customers

Generalisability: the ability to draw, from the research, conclusions that apply to other situations or contexts

Generic features: the largely tangible things that all sports have in common

Get components: what the customer perceives they have received when using a service

Give components: what the customer perceives they have given up when using a service

Goal incongruence: the extent to which an event does not meet the desires of the customer, or is judged to be inconsistent with the customer's wants

Goal relevance: the extent to which a problem is perceived to be relevant to the customer's well-being

Government departments: traditional public service departments under the control of a minister

Government-owned corporations: corporatised organisations, often former monopolies, in which the government is the major shareholder (for example, electricity authorities)

Government publics: government interests at local, state and national levels, including both funding bodies (supply function) and regulating bodies (demand function)

Greater than maximum supply: higher demand than maximum available supply

Heterogeneity: a difference or variability in a service

Hidden (support) services: services an organisation offers to support, promote and/or facilitate its physical goods

Hierarchy of effects: the order of responses a consumer has to a marketing communication

Home-based franchise: one in which the franchisee works from a home office instead of holding a separate fixed outlet

Imagery: a set of visual cues, such as pictures, colours, words and associated personalities or attractions, that are typical of a travel destination or service provider

Indirect revenue: the money realised from selling advertising and merchandising rights to sporting events

Information search: an expressed need to consult various sources of information prior to making the final purchase or destination selection decision

Initial franchise fee: a fee normally paid by the franchisee, granting entry to the franchise system

Intangible: describes something that cannot be seen, touched or tasted

Interactional justice: the manner in which the problem is dealt with and the interactions between the service provider and the customer

Intermediaries: those companies that play a role in transferring a product, service or information between the supplier and consumer within their distribution channel

Internal search: information retrieved from one's own memory based on past experiences with a product or service

Involvement: the amount of time, effort, interest and emotion invested by a consumer in the purchase of a service

Ladder of loyalty: the six ascending steps of a relationship from prospect, to first-time customer, to repeat customer, to client/member, to advocate and to partner

Less than optimum supply: lower demand than optimal supply levels

Lifetime value: what customers are worth over a lifetime of their custom

Market orientation: the pursuit of organisational activity reflective of market demand

Marketing of sport: the coordination and facilitation of the delivery of the sport 'product' and extensions in order to satisfy the goals of various stakeholders

Marketing or advertising levy: the ongoing levy collected by a franchisor from franchisees for promotional activities benefiting the whole franchise network

Marketing using sport: any strategy that aims to associate a product, service, idea or company with the emotive force of a sport, sports association or sporting event in order to appeal to target markets in a way that traditional promotion cannot achieve

Master franchisees: franchisees (or sub-franchisors) who provide the services of a franchisor in remote locations

Matchmaking services: services that match buyers' needs with products and services from sellers

Maximum supply: higher demand than optimal supply levels

Merchandising: the selling of goods related to the sport experience as a means of extending the product

Metamarkets: virtual trading spaces

Metamediaries: sites that connect customers with goods and services that fill their needs for life events or major asset purchases

M-marketing: the application of marketing to the mobile environment of mobile phones, smart phones and PDAs

Mobile franchise: one in which the franchisee drives to the customer to provide the service, instead of holding a fixed outlet

Mobilemediary: a new kind of intermediary that uses wireless technology and can break into the value chain at any point to provide information and transactional capabilities to customers at the time and place that they want to buy a product or service

Moment of truth: the time when the customer comes into contact with a service or service personnel and makes an evaluation

Multiple concepts: the technique used by a franchisor to offer several complementary franchise systems under one central administration

Multiple systems: diversification through ownership of several franchise systems

Multiple unit franchising: the practice whereby a single franchisee holds multiple units within a franchise system

Network: the group formed from relationships between organisations

Notification services: services that let customers know when a service becomes available, when it goes on sale or when it is cheaper

Operational outcomes: outcomes that can be clearly specified, clearly implemented and clearly measured

Opinion leaders: individuals or organisations whose opinions have a key influence on a consumer's purchasing process, products or services

Optimum supply: when demand and supply are well balanced

Organisational boundary: zone where the external customer and environment meet the internal operations of the organisation

Organisational consumers: those who take the product and then on-sell it or use it as a component in the production of another product

Outcome dimension: a dimension of constructs such as expectations, performance and disconfirmation that reflects the outcomes of service delivery

Outsourcing: an arrangement in which one company provides services for another company that could, or would normally, be provided by the client company

Overbooking: a technique used in temporal demand situations where more bookings for units of a product are taken than are available, to counter potential loss of business due to late cancellations

Partial customers: the portrayal of service employees as customers of the organisation

Partial employees: temporary participants in the service delivery process, who contribute resources to the service organisation in the form of information or effort

Participation: the extent of effort and involvement needed to produce and deliver a service

Partner relationship marketing (PRM): a CRM concept applied to business-to-business (B2B) relationships

Penetration pricing: a pricing technique for promoting a newly launched product at a heavily discounted price to boost initial sales

People: all those who play a part in the production and delivery of a service

Perceived value: 'the consumer's overall assessment of the utility of a service based upon perceptions of what is received and what is given' (Zeithaml 1988)

Perception: the overall impression gained by the consumer after the service encounter

Peripheral aspects: the non-core components of a service

Perishable: likely to decay or perish

Personal identification: a state of mind in which consumers feel that they 'know' the sports participants and the administration of sports sufficiently to express opinions about how things should be done

Personal selling: a two-way communication process in which a salesperson engages with a potential customer for the purpose of selling a good or service

Physical evidence: all physical representations of the service, such as business cards, reports, signage and equipment

Player or participant publics: the players or participants in a particular sport

Positioning: the process of influencing the consumer's perception of a good or service using the marketing mix

Post-purchase phase: the stage in which the consumer evaluates the outcome of the service and determines their level of satisfaction or dissatisfaction

Pre-purchase phase: the stages through which a consumer progresses before the purchase and consumption of a service

Price: the amount of money (or some other item that is exchanged or bartered) that a buyer exchanges for a service product provided by the seller

Price bundling: a practice in which several service products are combined and offered at one price (often at a discount compared to separate purchase)

Price fixing: a (generally) illegal activity where two or more organisations conspire to fix prices of competing products in an uncompetitive manner

Price leader: the organisation that leads or dominates price setting in a market segment (usually the organisation with highest market share)

Price segmentation: the use of different price brackets where different segments of the market are prepared to pay different prices

Pricing: the process by which an organisation decides on the price of a service product

Pricing goals: goals that are set to guide the pricing process in order to help the organisation achieve marketing objectives and overall goals

Pricing regulations: a set of laws that restrict the setting and movement of prices

Primary data: data that is collected, for a specific purpose, directly from informants

Problem recognition: the awareness by the consumer that there is a difference between their actual and desired states

Procedural justice: the process used to resolve the problem

Process: all activities involved in producing and delivering the service

Process dimension: a dimension of constructs such as expectations, performance and disconfirmation that reflects the processes of service delivery

Public relations: the process of managing communications with key stakeholders of an organisation for mutual benefit and a positive outcome

Public sector: a combination of government departments, government-owned corporations and statutory bodies

Public sector marketing: any marketing activity undertaken by government-owned or government-managed organisations

Raw data: unprocessed data that has not been organised or analysed

Real-time analysis: the analysis of data as it is being submitted or recorded

Relationship: a mutual orientation of two parties, with a sense that this will develop and persist over a period of time and that both parties need to invest in the relationship

Relationship marketing: occurs when an organisation is engaged in proactively creating, developing and maintaining committed, interactive and profitable exchanges with selected customers or partners over time

Reliability: 1. consistency and dependability in performing the service **2.** the ability of research results to be reproduced

Renewal fee: the administrative fee sometimes charged by a franchisor when granting a franchisee an additional term of operation

Response rate: the proportion of consumers who have responded to a survey in relation to the total number surveyed

Responsiveness: the timely manner in which a firm provides its services

Reverse auction: where the website serves as a purchasing agent for individual buyers who specify a price, and the sellers bid for the buyer's business

RevPAR: a term used in hotels to indicate revenue per available room

Risk: exposure of the consumer to the chance of injury, loss, damage or other negative consequences resulting from the purchase decision

Role: characterisations assumed by the buyer and seller that are based on the type of service encounter

Role ambiguity: the degree to which clear information is lacking about expectations associated with the role and/or consequences of role performance

Role conflict: the degree of incompatibility of expectations associated with a role

Role overload: the degree to which the expectations of a role are far greater than the individual's abilities and motivation to perform a task

Sales promotion: a promotion that directly stimulates a sale, usually offered at the point of sale

Script: a learned sequence of buyer and seller behaviours that are expected for that service encounter

Search: the collection of data on the service of interest, either from personal recollections or conscious activities

Search qualities: characteristics of the product or service that are physically evident rather than abstract

Second generation shopping agents: sites that are created exclusively by consumers as a way for new or potential buyers to find out what others think about products

Self-regulation: a practice whereby an industry relies on all organisations voluntarily adhering to a set of rules or a code of conduct, rather than on legislation, to regulate business practices that reflect customer rights

Service blueprinting: a visual, graphical approach that maps out the steps in service acquisition from a customer's perspective. All invisible processes (backstage) are included, as well as those that the customer sees (frontstage).

Service bundling: the practice of combining different services and charging a single price

Service delivery: the interaction between customer and firm necessary to deliver the service

Service delivery interface: the point of interaction between the service organisation and the customer

Service encounters: interactions between customers and service providers, involving exchange, and varying in complexity and duration

Service environment: the internal culture of the organisation and the external or physical surroundings of the organisation

Service experience: the time in which the customer is directly using or consuming the service

Service failure: a breakdown in the delivery of a service

Service management trinity: the mutual interdependence of human resources, operations and marketing — a combination that will successfully produce and deliver services

Service operations: the system of translating organisational resources into service outcomes

Service product: the consumer's overall perception of the service and any augmented services accompanying service delivery

Service quality: the result of an evaluation process in which the customer compares their perceptions of the service with their expectations

Service recovery: the actions a service provider takes in response to a service failure in order to 'put right' the service

Services: acts, performances and experiences

Services marketing mix: includes the elements of product service, price, place (distribution), promotion, people, process and physical evidence

Servicescape: the environment in which a service is produced and delivered

SERVPERF: an instrument used to measure customer perceptions of service quality

SERVQUAL: a 44-item instrument used to measure customer expectations and perceptions according to five service quality dimensions: responsiveness, tangible aspects, assurance, empathy and reliability

Simple economic exchanges: situations in which one person exchanges money for a product or service

Skimming: a practice whereby early adopters of new products are charged a high initial price for the opportunity to own the new product soon after release

Social bonds: investments of time and energy that produce positive interpersonal relationships between two parties, ranging from formal, organisational contacts to informal and personal ones

Social constructionist theory: contemporary communication theory that views communication as the dynamic creation of shared meaning between participants

Soft/non-contractual relationships: relationships that are normally developed from repeated transactions without the existence of contracts

Special event pricing: a pricing technique that is limited to the time span of a special event, during which very high demand is expected

Specific features: the unique aspects of a particular sport that differentiate it from other sports

Specifications: a detailed description of the requirements of the service

Spectator publics: those who watch sport in either a live or indirect form

Sponsorship: where an organisation provides funds for an event or another organisation in order to create a positive association

Sport: the management of people, activities, businesses and organisations involved with producing, facilitating, promoting, organising and maintaining sports activities and products

Sport industry: the market in which the products offered to buyers are related to sports, fitness, recreation or leisure, and these may be activities, goods, services, people, places or ideas

Sport marketing: all activities designed to meet the needs and wants of sport publics through the exchange process

Sport publics: those key groups of individuals who affect sporting organisations and who can include customers, shareholders, employees, suppliers and investors

Sport sponsorship: investment by companies in sport participants, sporting teams or sporting events in return for promotional media coverage; for access to particular client groups; and for special privileges such as celebrity endorsements, corporate entertainment and so on

Sports: a collection of separate man-made recreational and/or physical activities in which participation can be professional, observational, health-related or social

Sports management: the management of sports activities

Sports marketing: the individual marketing of individual sports activities

Staff empowerment: the latitude in decision making and support from management that gives staff the power to take whatever action is necessary to fix a problem

Stakeholder: any individual who feels they have a stake in the consequence of an organisation's decisions

Statutory authorities: organisations created by a government statute (for example, universities)

Structural bonds: bonds forged when two parties adapt to each other in some economic or technical way, as they do when making product or process adjustments

Supplementary facilitating services (and goods): services and goods that make it possible for the customers to use the core service

Supplementary product: the extra services provided by the franchisor to franchisees in addition to core services

Supplementary supporting services (and goods): additional services beyond the core and facilitating services

Supply: the supplying of goods and services to an organisation without influencing the form and structure of the product

Support goods and services publics: those organisations and individuals who provide essential support goods and services to those at the core of the sport product

Surface acting: display of emotions that are not actually felt

Systematised data collection: surveys or other research activities that are ongoing and programmed

Tangible: describes something that can be seen, touched or tasted

Tangibles: the tangible elements of a service that create a physical presence

Technical quality: the outcome of the service

Temporal fluctuations in demand: variations in demand over time, often within a time span of a few minutes

Three-component model: model that brings together the three service quality components: service product, service delivery and service environment

Transactional marketing: a transactional exchange involving a single, short exchange with a distinct beginning and ending

Transactional tactics: strategies used by service organisations to reward customers for their loyalty, usually through some form of frequent user rewards scheme

Transfer fee: an administrative fee sometimes charged by a franchisor when an existing franchisee sells an outlet and leaves the system

Transmission model: a model that views communication through a conduit metaphor as messages that are 'transmitted' from one party to another

Unitary system: a system of government with a single national government

Value: the customer's perception of whether or not the service product represents good value for money; that is, a trade-off between the attributes and benefits of the product against the price paid

Value package: all aspects that contribute to the perceived value of a service

Vicarious violence: experiencing violence second-hand, through another person

Webform: the electronic input that receives customer-entered online data

Westminster system: the system of government from Britain on which both the Australian and New Zealand systems are based

White collar franchising: franchising in the professional services industries

Word of mouth: conversations by consumers about a product or service

Yield management: the use of variable pricing techniques to obtain optimum return from a temporal event with limited capacity

Zone of invisibility: backstage processes that are hidden from the customer's view but are part of the production or delivery of the service

Zone of visibility: frontstage processes or activities that are visible to the customer and in which the customer is likely to participate

Index